Reinventing Bach

Reinventing

Bach

Paul Elie

Farrar, Straus and Giroux   New York

Farrar, Straus and Giroux
18 West 18th Street, New York 10011

Grateful acknowledgment is made for permission to reprint the following previously
published material: Excerpt from "Howl" from *Collected Poems 1947–1980* by Allen
Ginsberg, copyright © 1995 by Allen Ginsberg. Reprinted by permission of HarperCollins
Publishers. Excerpt from chapter 1 of *Homage to Catalonia* by George Orwell, copyright 1952
and renewed © 1980 by Sonia Brownell Orwell. Reprinted by permission of Houghton
Mifflin Harcourt Publishing Company. All rights reserved. Excerpt from "Time: 1976" from
The Vigil by C. K. Williams, copyright © 1997 by C. K. Williams. Reprinted by permission of
Farrar, Straus and Giroux, LLC.

Library of Congress Cataloging-in-Publication Data
Elie, Paul.
Reinventing Bach / Paul Elie. — 1st ed.
p.   cm.
Includes bibliographical references and index.
ISBN 978-0-374-28107-6 (alk. paper)
1. Bach, Johann Sebastian, 1685–1750—Criticism and interpretation.   I. Title.

ML410.B13 E46 2012
780.92—dc23

2012003801

Designed by Jonathan D. Lippincott

www.fsgbooks.com

1   2   3   4   5   6   7   8   9   10

For my parents, Robert and Ellen Elie,
who filled the house with music—and still do

Contents

Reinventing Bach

Prelude

>>1>> Three hundred years later, you can inspect his manuscripts under glass, see the Bible he marked up while composing the Passions and the Mass in B Minor, walk the aisles of the churches where he made music. Eisenach, Arnstadt, Weimar, Leipzig: Bach's greatness is total and inviolable, and the holy sites associated with him are well maintained, the artifacts set out as if to counter the fact that it is hard to know what he was really like.

"Look for a glass harmonica invented by Ben Franklin, a flute played by Frederick the Great, and Johann Sebastian Bach's cembalo. The mighty Wurlitzer is cranked up at noon on Saturdays." So says Lonely Planet's *Germany*, so I go straight from the train station to the Musikinstrumenten-Museum-Berlin, in the Kulturforum, near the space-age hall where the Berlin Philharmonic plays. The place is more showroom than museum. The floor is comprehensively carpeted. Men in dark suits stand at attention doing nothing with great intensity. There are instruments as far as the eye can see—pianos, electric organs, banjos small and large, a brass family, some bassoons racked like weapons, a tin drum.

I doubt there is another place on earth where so many assembled musical instruments are so quiet.

The harpsichords are upstairs. Most are obviously too recent to have been Bach's. But here is one tagged "Cembalo, Gottfried Silbermann, um 1740"—a cherrywood harpsichord by the instrument maker who worked with Bach to renovate pipe organs all over Saxony. And over there, against a wall in a proverbial corner, is the thing itself—the Bach cembalo.

I consider it the way an estate assessor would. It is a third smaller than a baby grand piano, low-slung, like a European compact car. The body is shellacked brown wood; there are knots in the curved sides, and the legs are stout and tapered, plain rather than carved. The lid is propped open, and if you look closely you can see that the instrument has no strings on it.

There are two manuals, or keyboards, one atop the other, each with five sets of twelve keys plus one more. Each is a negative of the piano keyboard: the big keys are black, the small ones white. There are scalloped pieces of wood at the two ends, like bookends made in shop class. Above the manuals, where *Steinway* or *Yamaha* usually goes, dark woods are inlaid in squares and diamonds, setting off an ivory inlay, a compass or cross.

I move in and marvel. The white keys are yellow. The black keys are worn down to a color akin to the skin of an eggplant. It is amazing to think that they were worn down by Bach himself—that his fingers ranged across those keys over and over, playing the minuets children learn, the *Well-Tempered Clavier*, the fifth Brandenburg concerto with its exuberant cadenza, the *Goldberg Variations*.

Amazing: and yet something is lacking. I don't know the reason, but this cembalo actually owned and played by Bach himself seems inadequate to him—disconnected from him. There is a gap between the instrument and the music he made, and not just because, unstrung, it is unplayable.

It takes a stranger calling out spontaneously from another corner to make me realize why. "Hey, look—they have the synthesizer Pink Floyd used on *Wish You Were Here* . . ." I follow his voice, and there it is: the EMS VCS3 Mark. II (London, 1972), a keyboard cased in walnut veneer and connected to a console with rows of brushed aluminum knobs.

This is the real thing: the actual instrument played on an album I have heard a hundred times.

The Bach cembalo is something else. Yes, Bach owned it, but its sound is conjectural. He played it, but we don't know what it sounded like when he played it, and we don't know him through its sound the way we know Pink Floyd through the sound of the gurgling synthesizer—this very one—on "Shine On You Crazy Diamond." Bach is thought to have been the greatest keyboardist who ever lived, but none of us has ever heard him play. Only through others—other musicians, on other instruments, in other times and places, by other means—can we know the music he made.

That's all right: and, if you ask me, it is true to the music of Bach. There's a portrait of him on the wall, but he is not here. He is in my pocket.

>>2>> This is a book about the music of Bach and the ways it has been reinvented in our time.

Sixty years ago Leonard Bernstein said that you had to go to certain churches or special little concerts if you wanted to hear Bach; and although he was stretching the point, he did have a point. Already things were changing, though. Already classical musicians were approaching the music of Bach with thrilling creativity and passion. At the same time, the music was making its way in society through film, television, and pop music. By the time Glenn Gould rerecorded the *Goldberg Variations* in 1981, his 1955 recording was a cultural touchstone, like *Lolita* or *Annie Hall*; and the *Goldberg Variations* themselves became touchstones, heard in the films *The Silence of the Lambs* and *The English Patient*, in an episode of *The Sopranos*, and in plenty of other places. On the first anniversary of the 9/11 attacks the music of Bach was at the World Trade Center site, played by Yo-Yo Ma; Yo-Yo's friend Steve Jobs introduced the iPad to members of the press by playing Bach on iTunes. A couple of years later Bach was declared the greatest composer ever in a reader-participation exercise conducted by *The New York Times*.

Some would say that the music of Bach is in revival; and to say that is to enter into a conversation about Bach that has gone on for two hundred years.

From Martin Luther onward, religious revival has been a distinctive Protestant practice, rooted in the conviction that something vital is passing out of this world and can be saved only through ardent personal devotion and a return to the original sources of inspiration. Bach is the greatest of Protestant artists: born in Eisenach, where Luther was schooled, a true believer himself, a public "servant of God" as organist and music director at Lutheran churches, the composer of sacred works beyond numbering.

For many years it was an article of faith that his music had been saved by revival. In a commanding book about Bach, published in 1908, Albert Schweitzer told the story of a Bach revival in the nineteenth century as the background to his own argument that only a further revival of Bach's music and the human values associated with it could save European civilization as it hurtled toward world war.

Over time, a rival view formed around the evidence that Bach's music has thrived all along—that it has been central to musical life in the West ever since he wrote it, taking different forms in different times and places.

Revival has a key role to play in the telling of Bach's story; but I think it is more precise and illuminating to say that the music of Bach has been reinvented in our time: by performers, and scholars, and scholar-performers, who have produced fresh truths about the music and how it was created. At the same time, the music has been reinvented through astonishing developments in recording technology, which have enabled musicians to approach the music in the inventive spirit of Bach himself.

>>3>> Bach was technologically the most advanced musician of his era—a technician of the sacred.

He served as organist, keyboardist, cantor, and music director, and his biographer Christoph Wolff sees these roles as stages in his life's way as a "learned musician"—the most learned of the age. He was especially learned about the pipe organ, the most complex mechanical apparatus of his time: he built, repaired, and renovated pipe organs, and put dozens of them to the test throughout Saxony and Thuringia.

But there are good reasons to see him, rather, as an inventor—an artist whose career was rooted in the Baroque conception of *inventio*, drawn from classical rhetoric. He invented a musical instrument, the *Lautenwerck* or lute-harpsichord, and composed the two-part masterwork the *Well-Tempered Clavier* in part as an investigation of the nature of tuning, or temperament. He wrote the *Two- and Three-part Inventions*—short, tight, sparkling keyboard pieces, fifteen to a set, each of which reaches a frontier of sublimity, then vanishes into thin air.

Together the two sets of *Inventions* take less than an hour to play. But the notion of music as invention applies to Bach's vast body of music: as one of those scholar-performers, Laurence Dreyfus, argued in a book a few years ago, invention is the essential pattern of Bach's creative life. For Bach an invention was an idea—a melody, a pattern, a contrapuntal motif—worth developing. *Invention* was also a term for the act of discovery, and for the mechanism—the application of rules, the habits of art—that made discovery come about. An invention was "a strong foretaste of composition," a "workable idea" developed just to the point where it could be most fruitful and suggestive and delightful to others.

The idea of invention is itself worth developing. It enables us to push past the preoccupations with fugue and counterpoint, theme and variations, sacred and secular, that characterize the writing about Bach's music. It allows us to see Bach not only as a technological adept but as an inventor in his own right, a Leonardo of sound.

>>4>> It also enables us to look to Bach to understand our own era and our experience of music.

The change in Bach's reputation has coincided with a profound change in the way we hear music, due to the spread of recording technology. In the years after the Great Depression, as record players dropped in price and radio broadcasts multiplied, it suddenly was as common to hear music via a piece of furniture as from a musician standing nearby; it became common to "play" music by twiddling a dial or flicking a switch. For the next half century, the story of new developments in music generally involved the corresponding story of a breakthrough in technology— the 78, the LP, stereo; the car radio, the hi-fi, headphones; the cassette, the compact disc, the iPod and smartphone—and a corresponding change in the role music plays in people's lives. The age from the 1930s to the present can be called the age of recordings, and our experience of recordings—audio, video, film—defines our age and sets us apart from our ancestors as distinctly as democratic capitalism, indoor plumbing, or air travel. In the age of recordings, the past isn't wholly past and the present isn't wholly present, and our suspension in time, our intimacy with the most sublime expressions of people distant and dead, is a central fact of our experience. This is at once a benefit and a quandary, and in it, I would venture, are the makings of a spirituality of technology.

More than any other classical composer, Bach anticipated this state of things. Along with invention, he made profound use of transcription—the "writing across" of music from one context to another: a cello suite for lute, for example. And he used parody—the recasting of cantatas written for civic occasions as sacred works, so that something like the same chorus was used for the investiture of a local potentate and in the *Christmas Oratorio*. All through his working life Bach was continually adapting his music for different formats and contexts, and the music's openness to transcription is one reason for its staying power.

The story of Bach's music in the age of recordings is in many ways the story of its encounter with new formats and contexts. Bach's music has been interpreted to suit new inventions from the 78-rpm record and the LP to headphones and the Walkman to the compact disc and the digital file. And these inventions, in turn, have situated the music in new contexts, taking it into the parlor and out on the highway, into the isolation chamber of the recording studio and to outer space—where the *Voyager* spacecraft carried a recording of the first prelude from book one of the *Well-Tempered Clavier*.

>>5>> This book, then, is a story of invention—a series of variations about inventions in different media, if you like. The musicians who figure into the story, all of them steeped in the music of Bach, deliberately or intuitively worked out patterns of invention through their encounter with the music of Bach by way of new technology.

Albert Schweitzer, Pablo Casals, Glenn Gould, and Yo-Yo Ma; Leopold Stokowski, Rosalyn Tureck, Ralph Vaughan Williams, and Dinu Lipatti; Wendy Carlos, Joshua Rifkin, Masaaki Suzuki, and Lorraine Hunt Lieberson: all in their different ways made music in the aural space that one of them, in a celebrated set of sleeve notes, called "the realm of technical transcendence." They were not technicians only. No, they were artists who were inventive in the way of Bach: leaving the invention itself intact, they developed it through technology, completing it by taking it to unexpected places. From invention they fashioned a particular kind of transcendence, at once faithful to Bach and distinctly contemporary.

>>6>>   Not revival *or* invention, then, but revival *through* invention, which is revival's counterpoint or flip side: this is how old art forms are made new through the encounter with technology.

So familiar is the language of revival that we can overlook how fully it pervades the discussion of the arts—classical music, opera, painting and sculpture, dance, literature, drama. The good thing is going out of the world, threatened by questionable forms of progress, and stands in need of revival. This is the story our society has told itself about the arts for a century or more—really, ever since the arts were firmly established in this country—and the arts themselves thrive on the notion that they are threatened with extinction.

There is a certain kind of listener for whom classical music is a lost paradise. Like Joseph Cornell consecrating shadow boxes to long-dead ballerinas, this listener measures greatness in terms of remoteness from the present. It makes sense, in a way. All recorded music represents a past event; music characteristically takes us out of ordinary time—and so all the better if the music was made in a time other than ours, and if the aural space created in the music overlaps with the thin air of history. Obviously, the effect is compounded by recordings—which, as often as not, are what elicited this listener's devotion to the music in the first place. Cornell never saw his muses dance, and so he imagined them spectacularly with his boxes. But the devotee of, say, the string trio of the interwar years called the Holy Trinity knows its music intimately through recordings, knows it better than the people who heard the musicians in performance—knows it through recordings made with equipment that was considered tradition-killing at the time.

The drumbeat of revival in classical music—often set up in opposition to the shriekback of a popular culture enchanted with technology—obscures the fact that, for most of a century now, technology has been the means of classical music's survival.

So this is a story of the revival of a traditional art through the technology that was supposed to be its undoing. A new electronic medium, invented half a century ago and in common use for a couple of decades, is suddenly ubiquitous—the usual and natural way of doing things. The presence of the new way does not mean that the old way will disappear in the near future. But the new way will have profound effects on the nature of the art and its place in our society. Past is prologue here. In literature, for example, the change now taking place is from an experience rooted in books printed and bound on folded paper to one rooted in texts shown on screens. What forms will literature take? The story of the reinvention of Bach in the age of recordings is as good a guide as any. In classical music, the sudden ubiquity of recordings —on phonographs and the radio—didn't stop people from playing music "live." They kept on making music on stringed instruments, playing and singing it in their homes and churches, performing it for audiences, teaching it to their children. It is possible to argue (and many have) that the spread of recorded music dealt a blow to amateur music making and to music in public life— and that it banished classical music to the margins. But it is impossible to deny the extraordinary quality of the music-making in those years—the sixty years between the time when Pablo Casals recorded Bach's cello suites in London and Paris and the introduction of the iPhone in California. That was a golden age, and we know that it was because we can hear the music for ourselves.

The reinvention of Bach in the age of recordings makes this clear. Again and again in the age of recordings the music of Bach has been used as a whetstone for new technology, a test of what a new medium can do.

And yet, for all that, the experience of Bach is still strikingly immediate and uncomplicated. Via wax cylinder, 78, sound track, LP, stereo box set, CD, or compressed digital file, Bach comes through. Bach is not simply the sum of what we make of him, a shape-shifter congenial to a postmodern age. The more various our encounters with Bach, the more objective his genius is. The many recent takes on Bach, rather than competing or canceling one another out, have deepened our sense of him in such a way as to make him seem more human and more complicated than he seemed in past ages.

In a sense, the power of the music to cut through the white noise of society is the key to its appeal. Bach is the great exception, a site of purity in our sullied lives.

In another sense, though, the music of Bach is a leading edge, an opening to an understanding of technology as a source of awe and wonder. The music of Bach, it seems to me, is the most persuasive rendering of transcendence there is; and its irreducible otherworldliness, its impress of eternity even in a ringtone or mix tape, suggests that these qualities have not, in fact, been mediated out of existence, but are there for us to encounter in our lives if we are open to them.

>>7>> Our lives are half-lives, our experience mediated, and so diminished, by technology. So we are told by our age's best and brightest; and the literature of the varieties of media experience has all the traits of the literature of religious experience, an account of the adept's valiant struggle with our fallen state—of the struggle to stay afloat in the sea of artifice, the polluted data-stream.

To this conviction, the recorded music of Bach is contrary testimony. It defies the argument that experience mediated by technology is a diminished thing.

That is my own experience, at any rate. Though it has come, in my case, almost completely through recordings, this experience of Bach is as rich an encounter as one could hope for in a lifetime. It is as direct, as real, as the experience of a young woman learning to play the piano in a mining town in the Rockies, or a dangling man going about the streets of the city with a song in his heart. It is the thing itself—and often the experience feels more real than the rest of life, not less so.

And what is the experience? It is an experience that the movement of the music into new formats calls forth and makes obvious. It is of music and art as life's counterpoint—a presence at the center of our lives, at once personal and objective, that enables us to make sense of the world and our place in it, enriching our lives and helping us to understand them.

With that experience in mind, I have sought to tell Bach's story, and the story of his music in the age of recordings, through a sequence of inventions—ideas developed to the point where they offer a foretaste of the music. The music itself, after all, can be encountered through recordings—encountered in ways I have sought to dramatize in the pages that follow.

PART I

Revival

>>1>> This, you say to yourself, is what the past sounded like: rougher, plainer, narrower than the present yet somehow more spacious, a place high-skied and open to life.

The pipes ring out once, twice, a third time. Then with a long, low swallow the organ fills with sound, which spreads toward the ends of the instrument and settles, pooling there. The sound is compounded of air and wood and leather and hammered metal, but how the sound is made is less striking than what it suggests: the past, with all its joists and struts and joinery, its sides fitted and pitched so as to last a lifetime.

The organ is a vessel on a voyage to the past, and that opening figure is a signal sent from ship to shore—a shout-out to the past, asking it to tell its story.

Now the sound spreads emphatically from the low pipes up to the high ones and down again, tracing a jagged line of peaks and spires—an outline of the lost city of the past, a message tapped out from the other side.

>>2>> Albert Schweitzer recorded Bach's Toccata and Fugue in D Minor on December 18, 1935, at the church of All Hallows by the Tower in London.

He was the world's best-known organist, although he lived many miles from an organ; he was far better known than Bach himself had ever been, and the fact weighed on him, for he thought of Bach's music as a refuge from his fame—as the music of an earlier, purer time.

He climbed the steps to the organ loft, took off his coat, and tried to concentrate. For two nights he had played Bach's preludes and fugues to the empty church. It was the oldest church in the City of London, already seven hundred years old when it was threatened by the Great Fire of 1666. Now the worn stone of its walls and the smoky glass of its windows seemed to echo his fear that European civilization was ending—"beginning to melt away in our hands," as he put it. The old City was overrun by motorcars. The organ was recent and mechanized, not the trim eighteenth-century type he favored. The windows rattled when he sounded the low pipes. He and his two apprentices took turns climbing a ladder to dampen the loose glass with towels.

Making a recording was complicated, too. The technicians spoke English, a language he had not mastered. He had to stop playing in odd places or repeat whole fugues three and four times. The wax cylinder process would never fully capture the sound of the organ in its surroundings—the essence of organ music, in his view—and he would never be a natural recording artist.

Yet as he settled behind the organ he felt at home. After two nights, he was familiar with the two keyboards and the hand-worn wooden stops. He sat upright, exhausted but invigorated, in vest and shirtsleeves, feet on the pedals, arms spread as if to echo the two wings of his white mustache, eyes on the pipes tapering up and out of sight.

Thirty years earlier he had renounced a life in music for one in medicine, training to run a clinic for poor people at the village of Lambaréné in the French Congo—to be a "jungle doctor in Africa," as the press put it. He had wanted to do "something small in the spirit of Jesus"—to make his life an argument for a way of being that was grounded in what he now called reverence for life. But his act of renunciation had turned into something else: a double life in which he spent half the year in bourgeois Europe describing the poverty of Africa. Was this really the way to be of service—to become a freak, an exhibit of human virtue at its most self-congratulatory? Might it not have been better to do something small the way Bach had done, hunkering down behind the organ in Leipzig and making music that shouted from the housetops about reverence for life?

It might have been. But it was too late. At age sixty, he felt old—"an old cart horse . . . running in the same old pair of shafts." He had written an autobiography as a kind of testament. He had made arrangements for the supervision of the clinic after his death. Germany was lost to Nazism. Europe was going to war again, and he was struggling, in a book, to set out the political and social dimensions of his philosophy as a corrective. For the first time in his life, the words would not come.

The recordings offered a way out. The hope of making them had sustained him on long nights in the tropics, as he played Bach on a piano fitted with organ pedals and lined with zinc to ward off moisture. The sale of them, in a press-board album of shellac discs, would raise money for the clinic—for medicines, lamps, an X-ray machine. More than that, they would do with a few nights' work what he had striven to do over several years in his book about Bach's music. They would express his life as a musician and spread it across long distances. They would set the past against the present, and would put forward the music of Bach as a counterpoint to the age, a sound of spiritual unity to counter "a period of spiritual decadence in mankind."

To his schedule of lectures and recitals, then, he had added these recording sessions at All Hallows. The technicians had brought equipment from the EMI compound in St. Johns Wood, crossing London in a specially outfitted truck, which was now parked in the lane outside. A microphone hung from the ribbed vault in the nave. Electrical cables threaded up the aisle and around the altar to the sacristy, where the wax cylinder console stood at the ready.

Now a handbell rang, a signal from the technicians that a fresh cylinder was turning. It was time to make a recording.

The Toccata and Fugue in D Minor: it was in this, the music of Bach, especially, that Schweitzer felt reverence for life—felt the "real experience of life" that had led him to medicine and Africa. Making these recordings, he was fully alive. He straightened his back and began to play, repeating the opening figure once, twice, a third time.

He played for about ten minutes, pausing once while the technicians replaced one wax cylinder with another. He played Bach's Toccata and Fugue the way he had played it in Paris in his student days: as a sermon in sound, an expression of the unity of creation that he feared lost forever.

>>3>> For those ten minutes Schweitzer's life overlaps with ours. In the music, he is present to us—more so, it seems to me, than he was to most of the people who were actually in his presence while he was alive.

At the peak of his renown *Life* magazine called him "the greatest man in the world." Since then he has faltered in the test of time; the adjectives once affixed to him have come unstuck, and the great man—doctor, musician, philosopher, humanitarian, and celebrity all in one—now appears a problematic, compromised figure: his project paternalistic, his methods condescending, his view of the people he worked with in Africa more akin to the crude racial stereotypes in Kipling and Conrad than to any ideal found in the gospels.

But his take on the Toccata and Fugue hasn't lost its power. The music he made in those ten minutes is still bright, brave, confident in its cause. It beams

Bach out into the night with an electric charge, which will outlast us the way it has outlasted him.

The question is: How does that happen? How does a snatch of recorded sound survive? How is it that a little night music made a long time ago can withstand the wear and tear of time?

The obvious explanation is that it is the music of Bach that survives, brought to life in Schweitzer's performance. That composer, that work, that church, that instrument, that organist, that night—all combined to produce an "inspired" performance, one that (fortunately for us) was recorded.

That is true, but it doesn't begin to tell the story. The performance is extraordinary, and yet so much of the power of this Toccata and Fugue in D Minor seems to be more than merely technical. The mysteries of that experience of music-making were cut into some pieces of soft wax that night, and now they are to be found between the lines of the recording—in the blurred edges, the high notes ground down to points, the surfaces that seem part of the structure, like the rattling windows of All Hallows.

Schweitzer characterized Bach as a technician of the sacred and a representative of a prior epoch in which spirit and technique went hand in hand. "In that epoch, every artist was still to some extent an instrument maker, and every instrument maker to some extent an artist," he declared, setting the mechanical present against a past in which knowledge and know-how were indistinguishable. But to read Schweitzer on Bach is to recognize Schweitzer too as an exemplar of such an epoch, in which to "play" music was to take up an instrument, and in which examples of the music perfectly played were not near at hand but existed mainly in the imagination.

The Toccata and Fugue recording registers the technique of that age. By professional audio standards, it isn't a "good" recording. It isn't clear or accurate; it isn't high fidelity, not even close. At times the great organ seems to wheeze, its sound as small and fragile as an accordion's; in range, the recording goes from black to gray, from muddy to soupy, from loud to a little less loud.

This lack of fidelity is the source of its power. Recordings usually become more transparent the more you listen to them, until you feel that the recording is the music itself. Not this one. This is a recording, and it sounds like one: the more you listen to it, the more audible its extramusical qualities become. It is an old recording, and it sounds its age: the dark corners and muddied entrances are pockets of mystery; the hiss of the tape transfer is the sound of the mists of time.

It sounds like the past, that is. It isn't timeless; it is full of time, dyed with it. Yet it isn't historical, an artifact of a certain time. It is full of the European past prior to 1935.

Across London T. S. Eliot—sharp nose, knotted tie, emphatic Adam's apple—was bent over a typewriter, pondering the afterlife of the past. "Time present and time past / are both perhaps present in time future": so goes the formulation that he came up with in the beginning of his *Four Quartets*, and so it is in Schweitzer's Toccata and Fugue in D Minor. The recording evokes the night a long time ago when the music of Bach ("in appentency, on its metalled ways") coursed through the pipes of a big organ at a church in London; it evokes the past of Bach himself, emerging from a tribe of musicians in the Black Forest; and it evokes the longer past that found late expression in Bach's music—the past of castles and cathedrals, of incense and stained glass and torchlight, of plague and pestilence and bloodletting, angels and devils, saints and martyrs.

"Age confers on all music a dignity that gives it a touch of religious elevation," Schweitzer remarked, and the phrase—"a touch of religious elevation"—characterizes this recording. The age of the recording, and the epoch it calls forth, suggest a grandeur that the present lacks. This is the past as a time more complicated than ours, one that sponsored an encounter with life more direct and dramatic than the ways we live now.

Even as the recording gives us access to that past, it reminds us that we will never hear the past whole. It sends two signals that blend into one: it brings the past close to us, and it makes clear how distant the past really is, makes decline and fall audible.

That is what it does to me, at any rate. To me, it is *the* Toccata and Fugue in D minor, the one that sets the expectations for all the others. And yet it is unsettled and unsettling. The sonic boxiness of it—the very quality that makes it sound historic—makes it hard to listen to for simple enjoyment. The qualities of awe and wonder that it suggests have an alienating affect. This is the past made real, the sound of an era done and gone; it leaves the listener on the wrong side of history, in life's postlude, a man in a room clamped into headphones.

Schweitzer entered the Toccata and Fugue in D Minor into the record in London on December 18, 1935. Now that performance, meant to evoke the past, is itself a piece of the past. The further we get in time from it, the more antique the recording sounds, the more awe it calls forth. A diminished thing, it points to the thing itself. It is a relic or fossil, a bony shard of sound; it is a relic of the true cross, light from a dead star.

For all that, it is a beginning, not an ending. "And time future contained in time past," Eliot in the poem went on, and the recording, even as it evokes the past, faces forward. Like Enrico Caruso's aria recordings (from the first decade of the twentieth century), or Louis Armstrong's Hot Fives sides (from 1925 and 1926), or the Carter Family's records of the twenties, it stands at the junction of the age of recordings and the ribbon road of time—call it pre-recorded—that had gone before. Like those recordings, it delivered on the promises of the new technology. Performed by Schweitzer, recorded and distributed around the world by EMI and its subsidiary Columbia, in the half century after 1935 this recording made Bach's Toccata and Fugue in D Minor one of the best-known pieces of classical music, as familiar as a church bell tolling the hour.

The Toccata and Fugue in D Minor is a beginning in another sense, too. It was composed when Johann Sebastian Bach was in his teens, some 230 years before Schweitzer etched it into wax at All Hallows: early in Bach's career and in the classical tradition. Now great in age, it was made when Bach, and Western music, and modern Europe, were still young; it is the sound of a much earlier beginning.

>>4>> "Music is one of the best arts; the notes give life to the text; it expels melancholy, as we see in King Saul. Kings and princes ought to maintain music, for kings and princes should protect good and liberal arts and laws; though private people have desire thereunto and love it, yet their ability is not adequate. We read in the Bible, that good and godly kings paid and maintained singers. Music is the best solace for a sad and sorrowful mind; by it the heart is refreshed and settled again in peace."

Martin Luther was a music lover: a natural singer who incanted his sermons from the pulpit, a player of the lute (his namesake instrument), the author of hymns so stirring that a foe of his claimed they had "killed more souls than his [prose] works and sermons."

Famous as a reformer, Luther was also a revivalist, and in him these two dispositions, these two ways of making the old world new, were fused. The reformer works to change the structures of things, striving to produce a glimpsed ideal. The revivalist calls for a change of heart, recalling a prior state of ardor. Luther did both: he evoked a purer past as the model for a purer future. After him, reform and revival would run in counterpoint through the Protestant experience, and so through the modern West—through religion, politics, culture, the arts.

Music was a key to Luther's approach. It was a "handmaid to theology" and a straight line to the human heart. A hymn such as "A Mighty Fortress Is Our God" combined aspects of the old church and the new: a tune familiar from the Latin missal, the fresh words of the German vernacular, and an image that at once gave shelter and sent the believer onto the ramparts.

This use of music fit in with a striking change in the lives of Christians in Europe: the change from image to text, from a church that communicated its truths through paintings and frescoes, tapestry and statuary, reserving the sacred language Latin for the clergy, to churches that cherished the Bible as the Word of God and proposed that God's ways could be known not through ritual but through the Word only. The effects of this change were dramatized best at the other end of the era it brought about—by Victor Hugo in *Nôtre Dame de Paris*, published in 1831. The novel is set 250 years earlier, in 1482, and the great French cathedral is seat and symbol of a civilization under threat—under threat from the newly invented printing press. From "the origin of things up to and including the Christian era," Hugo explained, the "great book of mankind" was its sacred architecture, which gave visual evidence of the past. Now the printing press had emerged as a rival. "This will kill that," Hugo had the arch-deacon Dom Claude darkly prophesy, meaning that "the book of stone, so solid and durable, would give way to the book of paper, which was more solid and durable still."

It is commonly said that the printing press stimulated Protestantism, as Luther's revival spread hand in hand with the new technology. And yet the taking of the Bible and other books to ordinary people had a surprising side effect: even as it enabled those people to read, it brought about a shift from a visual culture to an aural one—"prescribed a new precedence of ear over eye," as one historian put it, of sound over sight. "Faith cometh by hearing, and hearing by the word of God": this verse from the Letter to the Romans was one of Luther's cherished texts, and his reforms turned much of Europe away from paintings, sculpture, and architecture and toward argument, preachment, and song.

>>5>> Veit Bach, a baker, liked to strum a cittern at the mill while wheat was ground into flour. He went from Hungary to Thuringia in eastern Germany in 1600 in flight from religious strife. There, over the next hundred years, music-making Bachs descended from him like loaves multiplied. Veit Bach begat Hans Bach and Casper Bach; from Hans came Johann Bach and Christoph Bach and Heinrich Bach; from Christoph came Georg Christoph

Bach and Johann Ambrosius Bach and Johann Christoph Bach, and from Heinrich came Johann Christoph Bach and Johann Michael Bach and Johann Günther Bach.

Many of the male Bachs became church musicians. They tutored each other. They arranged for one another to get jobs as organists, mastering the instrument best suited to Luther's reforms. They married into other musical families, extending the Bach influence. They were a clan, even a dynasty, centered in Thuringia—Eisenach, Erfurt, Arnstadt—and there the surname Bach came to mean musician: when one of the family players died, a town councillor at Erfurt put out a request for "a new Bach."

Eisenach, a small town in the foothills of the Thuringian Forest, had a reputation exceeding its size, and was full of reminders that it was a place of consequence. Up a mountain in the forest outside of town was the Wartburg, as formidable a castle as any in Europe, with twin stone lookout towers rising over a walled village set on a huge, repelling slab of rock. There in the twelfth century the local landgrave had held a singing contest, which became part of the lore of the place. There a generation later Elisabeth, princess of Hungary, had married a local prince, then founded an almshouse and hospital for the poor, and her great piety and good works led the Catholic Church to canonize her. There in 1521 Martin Luther, apostate and in flight, found a hideout in the castle, which he had known since his years as a student at the Latinsschule in town. In a planked room in the castle he translated much of the Bible into German, creating a proof-text for reformation and for the spread of vernacular language in Germany and throughout Europe.

The castle and the forest surrounding it were a reminder of something else: that the town centered there had been carved out of the wild through human effort.

The Eisenach town hall has a tower with twin porticoes near the top. Twice a day, at ten and five, Johann Ambrosius Bach climbed to the balcony of the tower and played a tune through a trumpet; sometimes a folk tune, sometimes a chorale. He was the *Hausmann*, or town musician: he arranged music for religious services, council meetings, and wedding receptions, hiring others from the guild of town musicians, or freelancers—so-called "beer-hall fiddlers" and the like. He had come of age in Erfurt, thirty miles away. Arriving in Eisenach for an audition, he was recognized straight off as remarkable and was hired on the spot. He and his wife, Maria Elisabeth, had conceived a child, who died in infancy, and then conceived another; and in Eisenach they conceived five more. He earned enough to support the family and a gaggle of apprentices in an ample house on Lutherstrasse, just off the market square. An artist painted his portrait: a florid, bearded, robust man, made to appear the more so because the collar of his white shirt was open to the chest—the iconographic touch that indicated a horn player.

Three of Ambrosius Bach's cousins died, probably of the plague, in the winter of 1682. By the time Ambrosius and Elisabeth conceived another child in the summer of 1684, three of his brothers had died, and two others would die in the years to follow. He was thriving in Eisenach, but he faced death on all sides.

>>6>>   The child, a boy, was born on March 21, 1685, and was baptized Johann Sebastian in the stone font of the Georgenkirche two days later. Sebastian was not a family name; it was taken in recognition of a forester by that name who stood as a witness at the baptism.

The story of J. S. Bach's ancestry is usually told to affirm that he came into a great musical family whose expectations he was destined to fulfill. But the documents tell a different story, of ordinary elements wrought, as in a fugue or canon, into a pattern that is logical but not inevitable—that might have turned out otherwise.

As an adult Bach wrote an account of the "musical inclination" in his family, and this text became the basis for a hand-drawn family tree. The tree is a grotesquerie, a forest unto itself. From a narrow trunk, the branches are heavy with offspring. The descendants do not descend—they ascend aggressively, rising up shoulder to shoulder, out of the grip of their parents like snakes wriggling free of the underbrush toward the light.

That history of musical inclination also serves as the basis for scholarly grids of the Bach lineage: births, deaths, marriages, children. Complex as mazes, these give order to the Bach family ties, joining relatives at right angles and bracketing off fact from conjecture. But they also make clear, as a row of gravestones in a churchyard might, that the Bachs were not the stable, sustaining family of legend. They lost as many members to disease as they gained in childbirth. They increased and multiplied in defiance of death.

There were sixteen male Bachs in Johann Sebastian's generation. The question of talent arises: Why should Johann Sebastian be a genius and not one of the others?

He survived: that is one reason. Just before he was born, three other Bach children died in infancy. Two months after he was born, his brother Johannes

Jonas died, age ten. The year he turned six—1691—his older brother Balthasar died, age eighteen. The next year his cousin Jacob, who lived with the family after the deaths of his own parents, died in his early twenties. In the spring of 1694, when Bach was nine, his mother, Maria Elisabeth, died. His father, Ambrosius, remarried quickly to a woman twice widowed. Then, twelve weeks and a day later, Ambrosius died. At age ten Bach was an orphan.

His eldest brother, Johann Christoph, was already married and out of the house, working as a church organist in Ohrdruf, thirty miles away. Bach and a middle brother, Johann Jacob, went there to live with him.

Johann Sebastian had heard his father play the trumpet, had seen his uncle play the organ and take it apart; he had watched them make music their livelihood. In Ohrdruf, he became a musician. Through music, his brother Johann Christoph had gained a kind of independence. He would try to do likewise. The Bachs were numerous, well placed, and devoted to their kin, but these were not obvious advantages to an orphan of ten, surrounded by death. They were systems of dependence. This family was no dynasty; it was a forest that he had to find a path out of, a maze he had to master.

>>7>> The two most vivid stories of his childhood make the point emphatically; in them he is as independent as a member of a musical clan could hope to be.

In Eisenach he had been out of the Latinsschule for long stretches as his parents were dying. In Ohrdruf, he was enrolled in the local lyceum and established himself as the most brilliant student there, even though he was the youngest.

In Eisenach he had learned to play the violin from his father. In Ohrdruf, he learned to play the clavier, or keyboard. He studied the rules of composition, devising fugues in multiple voices until he was "a pure and strong fuguist." He mastered the works of prominent composers by copying their manuscripts in his own hand.

The emulation of the *exempla classica* was the key to the Baroque, but a well-known story suggests that Bach took the practice to an extreme. It goes like this. In the house in Ohrdruf where they all lived—husband, wife, infant, and younger brothers—Johann Christoph kept a collection of sheet music locked in a cabinet with latticed wood doors. Bach, now perhaps twelve, yearned to make music, not run through the exercises his brother assigned him, which he had already mastered. One night while the others were asleep he slipped a hand through the latticework, took hold of a sheet of music with thumb and forefinger, drew it out through the slats, and copied the notation onto a fresh sheet. Working by moonlight, he copied the manuscript the next night, and the next, until the moon entered a new phase. After six months of moonlit nights he had a complete work. Finally one morning he brought the fresh piece of sheet music to the clavier and played it—whereupon his brother took the music from him.

The story feels like a legend, but it originated with Bach himself. More than a legend, it is a parable of his dedication to music, and an account of the pattern of his education, in which he learned to write music (he explained) "largely through observation of the works of famed and skilled composers of the time and through earnest reflection of his own." It suggests his determination to push past the examples of his relatives—church and town musicians, not composers or virtuosi—and master a broader musical tradition for himself. It brings him close to us: a teenager in a small town, up late, alone in the dark, sitting rapt next to a piece of cabinetry with music coming out of it.

>>8>> "Poor boys with good voices" were sought for scholarships by a school in Lüneberg, near Hamburg in the north, the other end of the country from Thuringia.

Bach was fourteen when he finished school at Ohrdruf. He was the youngest in the class by several years. In the choir he was still a treble—a boy soprano. It would be a loss of opportunity for him—so obviously gifted—to end his schooling and go to work as a musician, as his elder brother Johann Jacob had done. But there was no money in the family for university, and it was a strain for him to stay with his brother: Johann Christoph's wife, Dorotea, had given birth to two children, and there would be nine in all.

Early in 1700 he went north to Lüneberg in the hope of getting a scholarship. It was a bold move. About this, Christoph Wolff, the most scrupulous of Bach's recent biographers, is emphatic: in setting out for Lüneberg "the boy demonstrated an astonishing degree of independence and confidence, for he was the only one of Ambrosius's children . . . to break out of the family's ancestral territory." Wolff is just as emphatic about the motive: Bach went north out of a strong "desire for emancipation and autonomy."

He got the scholarship. He moved north. Then his voice broke. He kept his scholarship, singing lower parts and playing violin in the orchestra. Already adept at the clavier, he turned to the pipe organ.

>>9>> The organ loft is where art and religion met, and where the forces of tradition and progress converged and went into new forms.

The pipe organ was in the service of a tradition of sacred music a thousand years old, going back beyond Luther's reforms to the Middle Ages, the monasteries, the end of Rome, the catacombs. Built into the back wall of the church, the organ was a bulwark of the mighty fortress; and yet the organist was unusually self-sufficient—facing the instrument, with his back to the minister and congregation, elevated and walled into a space all his own.

The Bach family's emergence as a musical dynasty coincided with the emergence of the pipe organ at the center of German musical life. Organs of one kind or another had existed since antiquity, and Gothic churches were equipped with organs, but with the Reformation came a surge of innovation: pedals were added, pipes were grouped in sections according to their sound, and a large bellows (pumped by a hired operator) kept air moving steadily through the instrument. Suppressed by Protestant rules against graven images, the German craftsman's skill in the fashioning of sacred space found expression in the organ as a piece of handiwork: the pipes were ever more elaborately shaped, the cabinet and pipe-mounts more intricately carved, until pipe organs adorned the otherwise spick-and-span churches the way the music they made adorned the service.

By 1700 the pipe organ was a mechanical wonder: a device that made use of wood and wire, air and fire, to produce a range of sounds as various as any chorus or orchestra.

That Bach turned to the organ does seem inevitable. Half a dozen of his uncles were organists, and a local congregation had had one Bach or another as its organist for more than a century. His uncle Johann Christoph was "a real wonder of an organist" and had renovated an old organ in Eisenach, making it the best of its kind in the region. At the age of fifteen, his brother Johann Christoph had studied the organ with Johann Pachelbel, the most admired organist in their part of Germany.

Johann Christoph had shown Bach how to play the organ. But the instrument at St. Michael's church in Ohrdruf, though not old, was so broken down (Johann Christoph complained) that "almost nothing good could be played on it." The organ in Lüneberg, by contrast, was a good-size instrument with three manuals, or keyboards, and a full array of pipes. Here at last was a pipe organ as a piece of advanced technology.

Lüneberg also had an exceptional music library, with works by 175 composers, Protestant and Catholic, German and French and Italian, living and dead. There were plenty of examples of the musical forms of the time: passacaglia, toccata, fugue, chorale prelude, fantasia, capriccio. Sheet music enabled these works to leap the bounds of family, church, nation, and guild. Movable-type printing—a relatively new technology—was accelerating the process, making music available to more people than ever before.

No one knows whether Bach was allowed to handle the music in the Lüneberg library. But even if he just listened while a teacher or master organist played, he gained the advantage of the format; through it he encountered the music of the wider world.

Meanwhile, he sought out other organists and other organs: his eagerness to hear and play the organs of the region, Wolff proposes, is a reason he went north. In Lüneburg there was George Böhm, who let Bach write out copies of pieces from his music library. At a church in Hamburg there was Johann Adam Reinken, and an "exceptional" organ; Bach and Böhm probably went to Hamburg together to hear Reinken play and to play this organ themselves. In Lübeck, far north, there was the Danish master Dietrich Buxtehude.

He spent two years in school in Lüneberg, mastering the organ. He accompanied singers, played preludes and postludes and the music for worship itself, and set a mood at weddings and funerals, as well as practicing, tinkering with the organ, and making music for his own pleasure only.

The development of the pipe organ allowed him to do so. The organ was engineered for solitude. With several keyboards, it enabled the musician to undertake complex counterpoint, setting one musical line, with a specific tone color, against another, different one. It let him use his feet to provide further accompaniment. It allowed him to change the character of the instrument while he played by pulling out some stops and putting others in. It required an apprentice to work the bellows—but more than most instruments, it freed the musician to play music all by himself.

>>10>> As an organist, Bach spent half his life in church. As a Lutheran, he came of age in a society permeated with Christian belief and the Protestant blend of reform and revival. Yet the record of his musical education—instruments played, texts mastered, and virtuosi sought out—has no corresponding account of his religious education. The strong evidence of his faith came later, in his music. What can be said with confidence about his religious upbringing is the same as can be said of his brothers and cousins: that he was baptized, studied scripture and doctrine in school, and observed

the seasons of the Christian year: Advent, Christmas, Epiphany; Lent, Palm
Sunday, Holy Week, Easter; Ascension, Pentecost, Holy Trinity, All Saints,
and the Feast of Christ the King.

>>11>> The churches went quiet for Lent, so as to purify the senses of
the congregation; then, in Holy Week, they exploded with music. From Christ's
arrival in Jerusalem to the discovery of the empty tomb on Easter Sunday, the
climactic episodes of the Christian faith were enacted in sound, in the forms,
taking shape one after another, that made up church music in Bach's time:
through chant, in Luther's chorales, in motets, and in the emerging form of the
oratorio Passion, in which all the forces of musical ardor—instrumental,
scriptural, choral—were drawn on to dramatize Christ's death on the cross.

Shortly after Easter Sunday, 1702, Bach finished school at Lüneberg. With
the clamor of death and resurrection still sharp in the spring air, he set out on
his own.

He was seventeen years old. Ever since his baptism his presence had been
entered into the records of family, school, and church. Now, with his schooling
finished, he disappeared, going outside the lines of the Bach family chronicle.

A couple of entries in local registries suggest what he did with himself. He
got a job as a church organist in the town of Sangerhausen, a town in northeastern Thuringia, and then was pushed aside when the local duke installed
his own candidate instead. He served as a "lackey"—apprentice musician—in
Weimar, about forty miles from Eisenach.

That is all. This gap in the record points up the ever-present gap between the plain facts of Bach's life and the profundity of his music. Even when
the facts are abundant, they don't open up the music as fully as they might be
expected to do. The life and the work are not of a piece; they are in intermittent
counterpoint.

Connecting the dots, his biographers conclude that he spent the year
looking for work and eventually returned closer to home in order to make the
most of the Bach family's influence there. That is probably true, but it passes
matter-of-factly over the mystery of his coming of age. Just when he was becoming a man, we don't know what he aspired to do with his life. Possibly
neither did he; possibly his time away on his own was a *Wanderjahr*, a search
for the self like the one Goethe would dramatize in the next century. What
kind of musician would he be? What kind of music would he make? He set
out to find out.

>>12>> When he emerged a year later, it was to play a new organ.

Arnstadt was a medieval town at the eastern edge of the Thuringian Forest. A fire had gutted the Bonifatiuskirche there: walls, roof, windows, organ. That was in 1581. Over the next century, as the Bachs became a local dynasty, the church was left unrestored. Bach's grand-uncle spent his life as the organist at the town's two other churches. His father was an organist in town for a dozen years. His uncle was a court musician for even longer. All the while, the church of St. Boniface and its bare ruined choirs were silent.

In 1676 a new church was erected on the site. Twenty-five years later, a new organ was commissioned. When, in the summer of 1703, the organ was completed, the church fathers sought out an expert to put it to the test. They chose Johann Sebastian Bach. A room was rented for him. A horse and carriage was sent to pick him up, wherever he was, and bring him to Arnstadt and the Neukirche.

Why was Bach, short on professional experience, invited to try out the Neuekirche organ, the best new organ in that part of Germany? The usual explanation is that his relatives got the job for him, but if that was the case, one of them might as well have kept the job for himself. It is more likely that he was chosen because he was already the best organist around.

So the man who had been playing the organ during its construction stood aside and the church fathers assembled to hear Bach play the new organ for the first time.

As new technology, it was state of the art. It had "twenty-three stops, pedal and two manuals," a recent biography reports, "and was displayed against the back wall of a light, galleried church." It was also a work of religious art, a cosmos in lead and wood. The pipes were arrayed in symmetric cabinetry so that they loomed overhead like a vast cloud formation. Gilt foliage stemmed from the lead pipes; chiseled wooden angels peered around the scrollwork. Bach came of age in the country of the Reformation but in the age of the Baroque; purity and ornament would be joined in his music, like the forces of tradition and progress, or reform and revival.

Compared with the organ, the organist's console was a humble thing: a wooden cupboard with a plank seat, facing two keyboards and a rack for sheet music flanked by a row of knobbed wooden stops on each side. Seen today, it suggests a loom or a printing press, not a musical instrument.

Bach took his seat and began the examination, which would last all day.

Nobody knows what music he played on that occasion, but an early biographer gave a precise description of the way he would test a pipe organ. "First of all he drew out all the stops, to hear the Full Organ. He used to say jokingly, that he wanted to find out whether the instrument had good lungs! Then he gave every part of it a searching test." He played tremendous low notes on the pedals—discovering "a bigger bass sound" than on the organs up north. He played high notes with his right hand. He sounded the great pipes and the small ones, playing chords and single lines. Then, "when the examination was over," he went on to "exhibit his splendid talent, both for his own pleasure and the gratification of those who were present." The church, so long silent, was filled with the music of Bach.

That was Wednesday, June 24, 1703. The following Sunday he played for the whole congregation. Whatever he played, the church fathers liked what they heard. They hired him as their organist.

A contract—it still exists, signed by Bach—spelled out the requirements of "the office, vocation and practice of the art and science that are assigned to you." He was to be a servant of God and a guardian of the instrument. He was urged to get to church services on time, "to keep a watchful eye" over the organ, and in his daily life "to cultivate the fear of God, sobriety, and the love of peace; altogether to avoid bad company and any distraction from your calling and in general to conduct yourself in all things toward God, High Authority, and your superiors, as befits an honor-loving servant and organist."

>>13>> Bach spent four years at the Neuekirche, and in a sense it was his university. The circumstances (Wolff suggests) "bordered on the ideal." The pay was good. The work was light, Sundays plus a service here and there. He played the organ and composed his first organ pieces, some improvised, others written out. He ate and drank freely. He met the woman he would marry. He grew up.

There was one drawback. The fixity of the pipe organ made the organist less free than a violinist or singer. His instrument, engineered for solitude, was also a piece of ecclesial architecture. It wasn't portable. It kept him in place when he wanted to roam.

This fixity is apparent in the chorale preludes he composed at Arnstadt. Based on Lutheran chorales—clear, strong melodies that carry the congregation's part of the liturgy—the preludes don't develop the chorale tunes so much as frame them, setting them off against a background of harmony and pedaled bass. The music, while often gorgeous, is symmetric, foursquare, self-enclosed. It seems to spread outward to the edges of an existing space—the

church, say; it is music meant to settle people in their places, call them to attention, and hold them there.

The fixity of the organ meant that the music, too, was something other
than portable. It was a solid melting into air, played on a particular organ on a
particular day in a particular room. It moved in place but didn't travel. If you
wanted to hear a certain organist, you generally had to go to him, making a
pilgrimage to his church and his instrument.

In the fall of 1705 word went out about an unusual musical event. To
mark the death of one Holy Roman Emperor and the coronation of another,
Dietrich Buxtehude would lead two performances with a chorus and an elaborate orchestra: violins, trumpets, trombones, French horns, oboes, and drums,
all accompanying the great organ, which had three keyboards and fifty-odd
pipes.

Buxtehude had spent thirty-seven years in Lübeck, which the Baltic Sea
separated from Denmark, his native country. He was renowned both as a performer and as a composer—as "the real creator of the German organ toccata"
and as "a kind of father figure who anticipated the ideal of the autonomous
composer, a category unheard of at the time."

Five years had passed since Bach copied out the works of living composers
by moonlight. He had begun putting together a manuscript library of his own,
copying the works of others onto fresh sheets in precise, lovely pen and ink. He
started with Reinken and Buxtehude, and the surviving sheets are things of
beauty: big grids of organ notation, lines linking blocks. And yet they are incomplete, and in this they suggest the limits of written music, then as now.
Notation was approximation. The true life of music was in performance, and
the music was only as good as the musician who was playing it.

Bach knew Buxtehude's music well but had never heard him play.

He got a month's leave of absence from his organ post, arranging for a
cousin to fill in at the Neuekirche. In late November he set out for Lübeck. In
ten days, alone and on foot, he traveled nearly three hundred miles to hear the
greatest living organist.

This is the other great story of Bach's early life. It, too, brings him close to
us: he is at once a believer on a pilgrimage to organ music's sacred site and a
young man going on a road trip to hear a concert.

How did he get there, and what did he do there? Possibly he took a carriage part of the way, instead of walking. Possibly he traveled with a friend,
not solo. Possibly he met the master right off; maybe he played for him, executing preludes or unfurling improvisations from behind the hallowed organ.

Possibly, with Buxtehude nearing seventy, Bach put himself forward as a successor; possibly he stood aside, deterred by the suggestion that he would be expected to marry Buxtehude's daughter.

Possibly: but it is known for sure that on Wednesday and Thursday, December 2 and 3, 1705, Bach listened from a pew below as Buxtehude played preludes, toccatas, fugues, and the like in the organ loft of the Marienkirche. It is enough to know that Bach was present. There, he met the musical past firsthand; there, the links between him, his family, and the long story of Protestant church music were established once and for all.

He stayed three months, then set out for Arnstadt. There was going to be trouble with the elders at the Neuekirche. It hardly mattered. His music was inside him now, the figures running free in his head like ink from a pen; the way was out ahead of him, a garden of forking paths that he strode through, first one foot and then the other.

Through his music we can follow the trail he took, and the Toccata and Fugue in D Minor is especially thick with the patterns of a musical coming of age.

The facts about it are as scanty and unyielding as the facts of his *Wanderjahr*. Even now nobody can say for sure when it was written or why, or how it came so completely to represent Bach the organist. But the fewer the facts, the greater the aura—the greater the power of the music to point to experience outside itself. This, you say, is what a story sounds like—and the sense of story is so strong, even when the story is undisclosed, that you want to know the story of how the music itself came about.

Possibly this is the piece Bach used to put the new organ to the test. With the opening blast, played three times, he made sure that the instrument worked and heard the sound of its voice. Next he examined it through some broken chords, which (Klaus Eidam explains) "draw from the organ as much air as a player can demand from it with hands and feet." Then he repeated a figure in octaves, hopscotching up the keyboard, lighting clusters of pipes with sound; as the musical line ran down the keyboard, the sound increased and multiplied.

The test of the organ was also a test of the organist. Bach declared himself with those opening blasts, then turned them upside down, inside out, so as to show—show off—what he could do. In its ambition and daring, the dips and swoops of sound across registers, the twists and turns of melody, the zeal with which it explores the organ's pipes and stops—in all these ways this toccata feels like a breakout piece, in which Bach threw off the role of organ music as accompaniment to the liturgy. With it, Bach ventured forth from the old world of other people's music into the new world of his own.

Its confidence obscures the fact that it was far from clear that Bach would be a composer at all. In this sense, it may be the sound track of his *Wanderjahr*— his search for the pattern of his life so far. With the dramatic opening riff he takes a giant step into his future, then two more. From a promontory he surveys the different routes, which loom up before him, spreading from low pipes to high. He follows one path, a jagged line upcountry. He follows another, like it but narrower, threading toward the mountaintop. Now he can see clearly, the landscape laid out; now he is over the peak and gamboling down the far side. Catching his breath, he stops to consider. What form should his life take: What is his vocation or calling? House musician, court musician, church organist; a Bach, a Lutheran, a Thuringian, a European? What should he do with his life? He cogitates, the music quickening and tightening its weave, as if the two hands are the two sides of the brain and the pedal point a gut feeling. The musical figures work toward a comprehensive insight, then settle on it; through them, he is figuring something out.

That is the toccata, which is the music of exploration and discovery. The fugue, by contrast, is resolute, a vow kept. It firms up, grows strong with supporting arguments, the hands echoing each other in their support for the resolution. Then the two lines become one, and, the quandary resolved, the organ begins to sing. He will be all of those things and none of them. He will be an organist but not just an organist. He will serve God and the music inside him. He will be a composer and an artist.

>>14>> Albert Schweitzer heard the Toccata and Fugue in D Minor as an annunciation, a triumphant organ blast with which Bach cleared the air for the music to follow. "In the D minor toccata and fugue, the strong and ardent spirit [of Bach] has finally realized the laws of form," he declared. "A single dramatic ground-thought unites the daring passage work of the toccata, which seems to pile up like wave on wave; and in the fugue the intercalated passages in broken chords only serve to make the climax all the more powerful."

For Schweitzer the Toccata and Fugue was one of a group of early works in which Bach rose to "independent mastery," transcending the influence of other composers for the first time. It was in these breakthrough works that Schweitzer felt closest to Bach: to hear them, he found, was always to be struck by their "spontaneous freshness of invention," and to play them "was always to experience something of what the master himself must have felt" when "he exploited the full possibilities of the organ" for the first time.

Yet for Schweitzer this beginning was the beginning of the end—the end of European sacred music and of Western civilization. Bach is "a terminal point. Nothing comes from him. Everything leads up to him." For a century before Bach, in Schweitzer's account, "the sacred concert struggles for a free and independent place in the church." In Bach it finds a place, and sacred music and concert music are gloriously united. But they are united in the music of Bach only. Bach is neglected, then forgotten. Reason and religion split, and then music and drama, with drastic consequences. Music turns Romantic. Europe falls prey to mass movements and mechanization. But all is not lost. The music of Bach is the evidence of a more perfect past. Through Bach, Europe can find its way again, recovering "the spiritual unity and fervour of which it so sorely stands in need."

That is how young man Schweitzer saw the situation. He was half right. In Europe, the events of the first half of the twentieth century would exceed his darkest imaginings. But the music of Bach would emerge not just as the music of the past but as the music of the shattered, anguished present.

>>15>> Schweitzer was born in 1875 in Gunsbach, Alsace, where both French and German were spoken, where Catholic churches and Lutheran ones stood out against the same sky. His father was a Lutheran pastor, as was one of his grandfathers. The other grandfather (like three of his uncles) was a church organist, "much interested in organs and organ building" and much admired for his improvisations.

Alsace was "annexed" territory—it had been cut off from the rest of France by the Franco-Prussian War of 1870, which placed it in German hands. But even before the war (as Graham Robb makes clear in *The Discovery of France*) the rural departments were cut off from Paris and from any notion of French unity. The Alsatian capital, Strasbourg, featured the world's tallest building—the hyper-Gothic Strasbourg Cathedral, with a spire that Victor Hugo called "a veritable tiara of stone with its crown and its cross"—yet the life expectancy in Alsace was several years shorter than in Paris. Many Alsatians spoke neither German nor French, only the local dialect. There was a railroad, but it was faster to go on foot—a fact made obvious by the many people who could be seen walking from place to place in the trackbed, the clearest road through the forest.

Looking back, Schweitzer characterized himself as a "donkey" from the provinces: a boy too big for his clothes, too "slack and dreamy" for his studies, too simple for bourgeois society. In truth, as his recitation of mentors and influences makes clear, he was a prodigy always. He first played the organ when he was eight ("my legs were hardly long enough to reach the pedals"), and filled in for the organist at the village church a year later. As a schoolboy he took organ lessons in addition to his coursework. He had a musical awakening during a concert by Marie-Joseph Erb, who was one of the best-known pianists in France. His first visit to the theater was for Wagner's *Tannhäuser*; by the age of twenty-three he had seen all of Wagner's operas performed and had made a pilgrimage to Bayreuth to see *Parsifal*, keeping to one meal a day to save money.

What set him apart from the other precocious French aesthetes of his generation was his complex religious faith. As a boy, he asked why Jesus and his family were not rich—they'd gotten gifts of gold, frankincense, and myrrh from the Magi, hadn't they? At the same time, he felt the sufferings of others so keenly, he recalled, and so keenly felt the duty to ease them in the name of Christ, that he never felt simply happy. He felt "captive" to Jesus, and as he grew older he sought to reconcile his disbelief in the literal truth of the New Testament with his conviction that the "ethic" of Jesus was the right way to live.

Inevitably, he went to Paris. But his experience there—in the last years of the nineteenth century—turned the sentimental education on its head. Schweitzer sought the past, not the future; it wasn't carnal experience he was after—it was religious insight.

Paris was being transformed by technology, as electricity and *la lumière* brought together the medieval Latin Quarter and the enlightened boulevards and arcades as the modern City of Light. The modernists rendered that transformation in art—through Symbolist poetry, Picasso's collages, Satie's *Parade*, and the like. But there are no moderns in Schweitzer's coming-of-age story. The Paris that drew his attention was one still gripped by the revival that Victor Hugo had dramatized: the Gothic capital of the world, a place of mystery and shadow, one still animated by the Christian faith, a faith for which its groined and spired and buttressed churches were especially grand stages.

Through his uncle Charles and aunt Louise, who lived in Paris, Schweitzer gained an introduction to Charles-Marie Widor, a prominent Bach interpreter and the organist at the church of St-Sulpice, which had a hundred-stop organ, one as fancy as any in France. Widor recalled: "A young Alsatian presented himself to me and asked if he could play something on the organ to me. 'Play what?' I asked. 'Bach, of course,' was his reply."

Schweitzer played some Bach on the big organ. Widor liked the way he played. He let Schweitzer enroll at the conservatory where he taught. (Charles Schweitzer paid the fee.) For five years, while studying theology at university in Strasbourg and completing a year of military service in Alsace, Schweitzer studied Bach with Widor in Paris, three hundred miles away. "He returned regularly for longer or shorter periods, in order to 'habilitate' himself—as they used to say in Bach's day—in organ playing under my guidance." He schooled himself in the workings of the organ as a piece of machinery, and grew convinced that Bach's music sounded right only on small Baroque organs, not the pipe-heavy behemoths that had replaced them in many of the churches of Europe: "We have lost the old organ sound that Bach requires." He gained admirers, who took to calling him "Bach born in Alsace." In his free time he took walks in the city with his uncle's young grandson, Jean-Paul Sartre, whom Uncle Charles had taken in after the death of the boy's father.

Schweitzer had been raised to think of Bach's music as inextricably bound up with Lutheran worship and liberal Protestant theology. Through Widor, he encountered a broader, Enlightenment-style religiosity. At a time when Germany and France were fierce rivals, Widor saw Bach as "the most universal of artists," not as a German artist. "What speaks through his work is pure religious emotion; and this is one and the same in all men, in spite of the national and religious partitions in which we are born and bred. It is the emotion of the infinite and exalted, for which words are always an inadequate expression, and that can find proper utterance only in art." A Bach revivalist, Widor characterized Bach as a revivalist too: for him, Bach was "the greatest of preachers" and the organ works were "sermons in sound"—the "manifestation of a will filled with a vision of eternity."

At university in Strasbourg, Schweitzer studied counterpoint and served as an organist at his college church, St. Wilhelm's. This church, he recalled (with his usual superlatives), was "one of the most important nurseries of the Bach cult which was coming into existence at the end of the last century," and its director, Ernest Münch, was one of the first interpreters to base his approach to the performance of Bach on the tempo and phrase markings found in Bach's manuscripts, rather than on "modernized" conventions and habits. He and Münch scrutinized the texts together in Münch's house, keeping Münch's family awake at night, and over a period of years Schweitzer accompanied the orchestra and choir in rehearsals, then in performance. "Thus while I was still a young student I became familiar with Bach's creations," he recalled, "and had an opportunity of dealing practically with the problems of the production to-day of the Master's Cantatas and Passion music."

When he was twenty-one he had had a religious experience, rooted in the gospel adage that anyone who wishes to save his life must lose it for Christ's sake. "One brilliant summer morning at Gunsbach, during the Whitsuntide holidays—it was in 1896—there came to me, as I awoke, the thought that I must not accept this happiness as a matter of course, but must give something in return for it. Proceeding to think the matter out at once with calm delibera-tion, while the birds were singing outside, I settled with myself before I got up, that I would consider myself justified in living till I was thirty for science and art, in order to devote myself from that time forward to the direct service of humanity."

Through his twenties Schweitzer asked himself what the best way to lose his life might be. He could act as a foster father to orphans; minister to "tramps and discharged prisoners"; act as a missionary. But all these seemed obvious and programmatic. "What I wanted was an absolutely personal and indepen-dent activity," he recalled. "Although I was resolved to put my services at the disposal of some organization, if it should be really necessary, I nevertheless never gave up the hope of finding a sphere of activity to which I could devote myself as an individual and as wholly free."

Meanwhile, he advanced as a biblical scholar. Fifty years after proponents of the German "higher criticism" began to appraise the Bible as a literary text, Schweitzer grew obsessed with "the problems of the life of Jesus." It was a paradoxical obsession, for the methods of the higher criticism—the breaking of the Gospels into parts and setting of the parts against one another so as to reveal the text as a historical hodgepodge—undermined the conviction about Jesus's importance that made the work worth undertaking. The paradox suited Schweitzer, who had trained as a curate in spite of his doubts about Jesus. In the early 1900s, during one summer spent struggling to learn Hebrew, a second reading Kant in the Bibliothèque Nationale in Paris, and a third studying phi-losophy at Goethe's old house in Strasbourg, he developed the set of ideas eventually published as *The Quest of the Historical Jesus*. There he argued that Jesus was not an ethical teacher so much as an eschatological prophet, urging people to repent and believe so as to prepare the way for the reign of God.

He saw Jesus as a revivalist, that is, and in this he went straight against the grain of liberal Protestantism. But the book was most striking for an insight into how Jesus is studied and written about. "There is no historical task which so reveals a person's true self as the writing of a life of Jesus," Schweitzer insisted. No one had ever managed to write about Jesus objectively. Rather, "each suc-cessive epoch found its own thoughts in Jesus, which was the only way they could make him live." For Schweitzer, this insight revealed the limits of scholarship, and so the necessity for action. The way to transcend one's age was through character and individual action, the way Jesus had done.

He sought a worthy cause, and he found one in a pamphlet for the French Missionary Society left for him by a neighbor. "We need humans! Are there none?"

Africa needed doctors. Schweitzer needed an ideal in which to lose himself, a chance to develop his idea of Christianity more freely than he could in Strasbourg. The juxtaposition of Europe and Africa, of scholarship and toil, was extreme and thus apt. He would turn thirty years old on January 14, 1905. He decided to enroll in medical school that fall. He would become a "jungle doctor," and would "make of my life my argument."

>>16>> His life would become his argument, but not yet. With his thirtieth birthday in view, he added another scholarly project: a book about Johann Sebastian Bach.

The way he later told it, he was prompted to write the book by Charles-Marie Widor, his organ teacher, and he undertook it against his better judgment. The Frenchman Widor had admitted that he could not understand the "musical logic" of Bach's chorale preludes, which seemed more convoluted than the preludes and fugues. "Why these sometimes almost excessively abrupt antitheses of feeling?" he asked Schweitzer, who, as a German-speaking Lutheran, knew the actual chorales better than he did. "Why does he add contrapuntal motives to a chorale melody that often have no relation to the mood of the melody?" Schweitzer told him why: the music was tracking the words of the individual chorales, as Bach created pictorial effects to match German expressions. Widor: "I showed him the movements that had puzzled me the most; he translated the poems into French for me from memory. The mysteries were all solved."

Schweitzer told him he would write an essay to explain the point. As he did so, one summer during his work on *The Quest of the Historical Jesus*, it became clear that "this would expand into a book on Bach. With good courage I resigned myself to my fate."

For the next two years, while teaching, pursuing his biblical research, and serving as a curate, Schweitzer "devoted all my spare time to Bach," he recalled. This was made possible by his habit of working to exhaustion ("My good health allowed me to be prodigal with night work. It happened sometimes that I played with Widor in the morning without having been to bed at all").

And it was driven by his conviction that soon his life would not be his own. In preparing to go to Africa he prepared himself "to make three sacrifices: to abandon the organ, to renounce the academic teaching activities to which I had given my heart, and to lose my financial independence . . ." The sense of an ending that he heard in Bach's music, then, corresponded to his sense that his encounter with Bach was ending. When he observes of Bach that "to give his true biography is to exhibit the nature and the unfolding of German art, that comes to completion in him and is exhausted in him,—to comprehend it in all its striving and its failures," the passage tracks his own mood precisely.

Beginning in 1850, the Paris Bach Society had published the scores of all Bach's works in an edition of 350, restoring the passages cut by Romantic-era interpreters. To meet printing costs the society sold subscriptions to the entire set, as if to an encyclopedia. There were dozens of volumes, so the cost was high, but the set sold out. Libraries subscribed. Productions of Bach's works spread from the big cities to smaller ones. "I happened to learn at a music shop in Strasbourg," Schweitzer recalled, "that a lady in Paris who had been a subscriber to the complete edition in order to support the enterprise of the Bach Society, now wanted to get rid of the long row of big gray volumes which took up so much space on her bookshelf. Pleased at being able to give somebody pleasure with them, she let me have them for the ridiculously small sum of £10." He arranged for the books to be brought to his rooms in college at Strasbourg.

"This piece of good fortune I took as an omen for the success of my work," he remarked.

It was more than a stroke of good fortune. It was an opportunity created by technology—the printing press—which transposed Bach's music into the new form of sheet music. For half a century the Bach revival had striven to publish Bach's works. Suddenly—unbelievably—the whole of Bach was in Schweitzer's study. Now, instead of working on Bach in the library, he could do so in his rooms through the night. Now he could meet Bach in the circumstances of his own life. Bach's music, so long confined to churches and town halls, palaces and libraries, was now personal and portable.

>>17>> *Bach: Le Musicièn-Poète* was published in Paris in 1905, not long after Schweitzer in Strasbourg "set out in a thick fog to attend the first of a course of lectures in anatomy." The next year, after trying to translate the book into German, his stronger written language, Schweitzer resolved to rewrite the book in German from beginning to end. He started one night in Bayreuth,

Wagner's sacred site, after attending a performance of *Tristan und Isolde*: "while the babel of voices surged up from the Bierhalle below into my stuffy room, I began to write, and it was long after sunrise that I laid down my pen."

Through the summer and then the fall, and into the next year he wrote, and the book, like a Bach fantasia, doubled in size, to two volumes and nine hundred pages thicketed with insight. "At the end of the eighteenth century it seemed, on the whole, as if Bach were for ever dead," Schweitzer declared. From an account of how Bach's music should be played, it became an account of the music of Bach as the music of revival—and as music that itself had been revived.

About Bach's "death and resurrection" Schweitzer had two stories to tell—two stories, contrapuntally joined, that suited his own life story, and that proposed distinctly different ways for the music of the past to be recovered.

One story, told by Schweitzer the philosopher of civilization, is of a treasure lost and found. During Bach's lifetime "it was the organist who was famous; the theoretician of the fugue was admired; but the composer of the Passions and cantatas was only incidentally mentioned." After his death, these Bachs were all forgotten. Bach's descendants didn't understand his work. The critics favored Handel, whose oratorios were popular in the concert halls of London. Conductors rejected his vocal music because it was grounded in chorales. Enlightenment thinkers dismissed it as too pious. "There has never been a movement so lacking in the historical sense as the rationalism of the eighteenth century," Schweitzer declared. "The art of the past, in every department, it regarded as mere affectation. Everything old was necessarily antiquated, at least in its form." The age's few, simple versions of Bach were "among the most barbarous things of their kind in the whole world."

Although "his greatness [was] not recognized," Bach's music found a few hearers anyhow. One critic placed Bach above Handel—"for his parts always move so independently, and yet work together with such marvellous unity as is hardly ever attained by other composers." Mozart heard a Bach motet and said, "That is indeed something from which we can learn!" Beethoven studied the *Well-Tempered Clavier* and came to think of the work as his "musical Bible." In time a German critic, who considered the music of Bach "a sign from God, clear, yet inexplicable," sought to convert Goethe to Bach. It worked: when Goethe heard some Bach preludes and fugues played on a pipe organ, he felt "as if the eternal harmony were communing with itself, as might have happened in God's bosom shortly before the creation of the world."

Goethe asked Felix Mendelssohn, a keyboard prodigy who was a guest in his house, to play "a good deal of Bach" for him. Mendelssohn did so, and his own feeling for Bach was deepened. Already his teacher, Carl Friedrich Zelter, the director of the Singakademie in Berlin, had sought to mount a *St. Matthew Passion*; and now Mendelssohn, who was eighteen, planned a performance to take place a hundred years after the first performance—taking hold of the irony that he, who was Jewish, should revive Bach's setting of the Passion of Christ.

The performance—March 11, 1829—was Mendelssohn's first time leading a full orchestra. There was a chorus of four hundred singers. He "conducted from the piano, his face turned sideways to the audience so that he had the first choir at his back." Schweitzer, seventy years later, described it as a sacred concert: " 'The crowded hall looked like a church,' " Mendelssohn's sister, Fanny, recalled. " 'Every one was filled with the most solemn devotion; one heard only the occasional involuntary ejaculation that sprang from deep emotion.' " Hegel was there—Mendelssohn had attended his lectures on aesthetics between rehearsals—and he went on to describe Bach as a composer "whose grand, truly Protestant, pithy yet learned genius we have only lately learned to value again properly."

With Mendelssohn's *St. Matthew Passion* the spirit of the age came to rest on Bach. The passions and the B-minor Mass went into production across Germany and became Romantic emblems of German identity. Bach was back.

It is a stirring story of the revival of Bach's music by an outsider much like Schweitzer himself. Even as Schweitzer the philosopher told it, though, Schweitzer the musician told a different story. This was the story of how Bach's music was passed on through the act of music-making, so that it was brought back every time it was played, rather than once and for all. In this story the music's survival was never in doubt. Its recovery was a simple matter of getting it played right. And getting it played right had nothing to do with the spirit of the age. It had to do with the reform of the processes whereby the music was reproduced, distributed, mastered, and presented to the public.

Because printed texts of Bach's music were scarce, most musicians had little firsthand knowledge of Bach. Schweitzer related another author's story about Mozart, who "knew Bach more by hearsay" than through the music itself. Mozart "was told that this school, at which Sebastian Bach had been cantor, possessed a complete collection of his motets, and treasured them as sacred relics. 'That's right! that's fine!' he said. 'Let me see them.' As there were no scores of these works, he got them to bring him the separate parts; and now it was a joy to the silent observers to see how eagerly Mozart distributed the parts around him, in both hands, on his knees, on the nearest chairs, and, forgetting everything else, did not rise until he had carefully read through everything that there was of Bach's. He begged and obtained a copy for himself, which he valued very highly."

By 1829 sheet music was widely available, but sheet-music editions of Bach lagged behind those of other composers, and as a result, Schweitzer proposed, an aura of mystery and obscurity still clung to Bach. The music critic who converted Goethe to Bach did so by sending him the sheet music of the *Well-Tempered Clavier.* Mendelssohn (Schweitzer said nothing of this) was able to undertake the *St. Matthew Passion* in Berlin because he received the giant conducting score as a gift; three choristers copied out all the parts for the orchestra and huge chorus.

In this story, Mendelssohn's *St. Matthew Passion* was decisive not because it was sensational but because it got Bach's work into print. The score was issued the next year, but the publisher did a bad job; as Schweitzer remarked, "If it were left to the publishers alone the complete Bach would never appear, but . . . the work would have to be taken in hand by the community of Bach-lovers." And so it was. In 1850 the Paris Bach Society began to print its complete edition, and the Bach-Gesellschaft was begun in Germany. Brahms (Schweitzer reported) "used to say that the two greatest events during his lifetime were the founding of the German Empire and the completion of the Bach edition."

>>18>> He was the complete composer: one distinctly German yet bold enough to make all the world his own; a master of vocal music, and of instrumental music and orchestration too; a genius committed to his vision of a total work of art—a sacred drama that enacted the life of his people and its roots in ritual, story, and song.

That is the image of Bach that emerged in the middle of the nineteenth century, as his music was played and studied across Europe. But it was also the image of Richard Wagner, the ruling musician of the age and the measure for composers living and dead.

This is the third story Schweitzer told in his Bach book: the story of the emergence of Bach as a counter-Wagner.

As men, Bach and Wagner could not have been less alike—one a husband and father of notable fidelity, the other a serial philanderer—and it was inevitable that they would be set against each other: present against past, innovation against tradition, pagan against Christian. But Schweitzer heard in them a crucial likeness, and for him the Bach revival was of a piece with the Wagnerian program, joining together poetic and pictorial elements that controversialists had put asunder.

Wagner in 1849 had set out his vision for "The Art-Work of the Future."

With *Die Meistersinger* he enacted it in music, making his slabs of sound and never-ending lines of vocal declamation a maximal musical ideal. *Die Meistersinger* revived the German musical past in national terms, styling the competition among the mastersingers in sixteenth-century Nürnberg as a pagan affair. The libretto de-emphasized the Christianity of the era when the Bachs became the master musicians of Thuringia; and yet in the music (Schweitzer declared) "the spirit of Bach is most evident."

Soon afterward Wagner in an essay put forward Bach as the ideal figure of German inner life, an expression of its spirit in one "incomparably eloquent image."

Wagner's Bach, as Schweitzer understood him, was not a pure ideal. No, Wagner found the greatness of Bach "almost inexplicably mysterious." This Bach had been a servile guildsman in a French wig, "a miserable cantor and organist in little Thuringian towns whose names we hardly know now, wearing himself out" in an effort to energize the "dry, stiff, pedantic" forms of the Baroque. And yet—Wagner exclaimed—"see now the world the incomprehensibly great Sebastian built up out of these elements!" In "their wealth, their grandeur, and their all-embracing significance," Bach found "the history of the inner life of the German mind during the awful century when the German people was utterly extinguished." There Wagner claimed Bach as a musical precursor.

Schweitzer saw the influence running in the other direction. Wagner had "prepared the way for Bach." Wagner, he explained, brought about "a revolution of the whole musical consciousness" in Europe. He rebelled against mere beauty in music, and fought hard for the "characteristic" and "dramatic" qualities of music instead. It worked, and led to a revaluation of the repertory that had developed between Bach and Wagner. "A whole mass of music sank slowly into the abyss of oblivion; and by the side of the music drama of Wagner the dramatic religious music of Bach came out in a clear light."

Furthermore, Wagner changed the audience's expectations for music. After Wagner, the hearer sought more than beauty—sought something more from music than listeners of the previous age had. Schweitzer (here his translator used a Latinate word for *demanding*) stated the case laconically: "The hearer became exigent."

The hearer was Schweitzer himself, who had come of age when Wagner was sovereign. What was it that this hearer demanded—this hearer whose passion for music was matched only by his distaste for the spirit of the age? He sought a sovereign greater than Wagner. He sought music with Wagnerian total effect but without Wagner's obtrusive personality. He sought music characteristic of Europe the way Wagner's music claimed to be characteristic of Germany—but music rooted in Christianity and right reason as he understood it. This music cleared a supernatural space where the hearer could leave the self behind without exchanging it for a Wagnerian superman. This music offered an account of life in its fullness, the past and the present contrapuntally present, each undiminished.

This was the music of Bach, and in this way Schweitzer interpreted Bach as a figure in counterpoint to the spirit embodied by Wagner. Schweitzer's portrait of Bach is a portrait of his own aspirations. Like him, his Bach is an outrider from the provinces, at once deeply spiritual and mulishly self-confident. Like him, his Bach is a man at the tail end of a tradition, fluent in the old ways and so out of step with his peers, who are bent on forgetting or defying them. Like him, his Bach is a person who succeeds through ceaseless effort and the conviction that his cause is larger than himself. Like him, his Bach is a musician and more than a musician—a witness against the age he lived in.

There are limits to the comparison, however, and they point up the limits of Schweitzer's enterprise, which were there from the beginning. What for Bach was hard work was heroic effort for Schweitzer. Where Bach's universality comes unbidden from within his music, Schweitzer's was overtly striven for. Where Bach sought to serve God and the church with his music, Schweitzer sought to serve humanity and a self-formulated ideal. "His immense strength functioned without self-consciousness," Schweitzer wrote of Bach. Himself, he was unshakably self-aware, the hero of his own drama. He would lose himself in service to others and tell the whole world about it.

>>19>> Schweitzer began work as a jungle doctor in 1913. He had survived "the terrible strain of the medical course." After years of courtship by correspondence he had married Hélène Bresslau, a woman born into a Jewish family, baptized a Christian, diagnosed with tuberculosis, who ran a home for unmarried women in Strasbourg and who had taken her own vow of service. He had written an essay on organ building and joined with Charles-Marie Widor to produce an edition of Bach's preludes and fugues for organ. He had begged for funding, had given benefit recitals, had defended himself against the charge that he was theologically too heterodox for medical missionary work. Finally, he steamed upriver in the French Congo and established a clinic in a corrugated-iron shed surrounded by straw huts.

For a parting gift the Paris Bach Society had presented him with an instrument that combined the features of a piano and an organ: two manuals, strings and hammers, pedals. The inside of it was lined with zinc to ward off moisture in the tropics. "I had accustomed myself to think that this activity in Africa meant the end of my life as an artist, and that the renunciation would be easier if I allowed fingers and feet to get rusty with disuse," he explained. "One evening, however, as, in melancholy mood, I was playing one of Bach's organ fugues, the idea came suddenly upon me that I might after all use my free hours in Africa for the very purpose of perfecting and deepening my technique." He resolved to learn all of Bach's organ works "by heart, even if I had to spend weeks or months on any particular piece."

As night fell, the music of Bach spilled out of the tin house. "How I enjoyed being able to practice at leisure and in quiet, without any slavery to time through being due to play at concerts," he recalled. For the first time since his childhood, he was playing Bach for himself, not for a church service, a recital, or a meeting of a learned society.

He played the Toccata and Fugue in D Minor. "It is not through knowledge, but through experience of the world that we are brought into relation with it," he wrote. Missionary medicine broadened his worldly experience, and experience deepened his encounter with Bach. The music in turn gave a pattern to the experience. Thus understood, his recording of the Toccata and Fugue in D Minor is a report from experience. Schweitzer saw Bach as akin to Wagner in his emphasis on "graphic characterization and realism" rather than personal emotion. So it is with the Toccata and Fugue in D Minor. The inked-in outlines of the playing and the heavy crosshatching of its counterpoint are the work of a maker of pictures in sound.

The pattern of the Toccata and Fugue suits the pattern of Schweitzer's search. He described the Brandenburg concertos as music of "the fundamental mystery of things—that self-unfolding of the idea in which it creates its own opposite in order to overcome it, creates another, which again it overcomes, and so on and on until it finally returns to itself, having meanwhile traversed the whole of existence." So is the Toccata and Fugue. The work is patterned on the interaction of two hands, the two keyboards and their sets of pipes— the lower and the higher, the majestic and the delicate. In Schweitzer's hands the pattern accords with the pattern of his inner life, in which he is called in two directions—between the past and the present, the aesthetic and the ethical, self and service, the study of philosophy and the call to action. The music suggests two voices in a strenuous argument, a debate or colloquy. The one declares, the other rebuts. The one insists, the other rejects. They echo and parry, qualify and deny. Schweitzer makes the Toccata and Fugue music of self-argument, turning counterpoint into autobiography.

>>20>> Schweitzer was right: he stood at the end of an era. But it was not the era of European civilization, which would survive the Great War. It was the pre-recorded era.

From the beginning of time till the beginning of the twentieth century, the making of music and the hearing of it were two aspects of a single experience. People sang or played musical instruments for themselves or for other people who were within earshot—in a cave or in a church, on a stage or a street corner, in a parlor in Vienna or an opera house in Milan—and the music, as they were making it, was already subsiding to silence. The sounds of music traveled as far in space as the air could carry them and lasted as long in time as the air could sustain them. Then they vanished. Between these instances of music-making the music itself did not exist except as a memory or an ideal. Musicians passed musical patterns one to one another in the act of music-making, and found other ways to indicate the sounds they had in mind, say, with black marks on white paper, so that the music could be made again, the ideal approximated. The surest way to have music in the home was to install an instrument there—and so the piano, at once a mechanical device and a piece of furniture, came into the middle-class parlor.

Audio recordings changed the situation profoundly. Through them, sound was unmoored from space and time. Music made at one time in one place could be "played"—played back—later somewhere else. It was possible to listen to music without the intervening presence of musicians. The encounter with recorded sound became a distinct experience. You weren't listening to musicians play, or even listening to music. You were listening to records.

In a sense, this change was just part of the greater change brought about by electricity, which was transforming everyday life. The streetcar now sluiced through the old city. The office building (equipped with an elevator) scraped the sky. But the change in music brought on by recorded sound was more elemental, for the workings of sound and those of electricity are, in some ways, two aspects of a single process: the contrapuntal movement of waves and particles through the air.

The pioneers of electricity recognized its kinship with sound, and they captured the public imagination with inventions that converted sound waves into electrical impulses and back to sound again. Alexander Graham Bell transformed the vibrations set off by the human voice into an electrical charge and sent the charge through a wire. This was the telephone. Thomas Edison devised "a cylinder wrapped in tinfoil" to take dictation in offices, and showed how it worked by singing "Mary Had a Little Lamb" and playing back the sound of his voice. This was the phonograph. Then Edison and his associates introduced an electrical charge to a wire and connected the wire to others. This was the power grid. Guglielmo Marconi sent a charge through the air, relying on the atmosphere's electromagnetic field to carry it in waves radiating outward. This was radio, or wireless.

As Albert Schweitzer turned thirty in 1905 the Victor Talking Machine Company perfected the gramophone, or Victrola. Like the piano, it was at once a mechanical device and a piece of furniture. It spun a flat, grooved disc set on a turntable atop a wooden cabinet, while a needle passing through the groove converted the movements to electrical impulses, which were processed inside the cabinet and transmitted, as sounds, through a brass horn. While the turntable was a mechanical device, and the cabinet a piece of furniture, the horn suggested that the gramophone was, in its way, a musical instrument.

The gramophone was not a new invention; it consolidated the break-throughs of several inventors. The most important was Emile Berliner, a German-born engineer who worked for Bell Laboratories in America before setting up his own laboratory. In 1887 Berliner perfected what he called the disc gramophone, and in the years that followed he and his coworkers set the parameters for the recording industry. They invented the shellac disc, introduced what would become the standard format—ten-inch-diameter discs spinning seventy-eight times per minute—and opened the first record shop.

Those advances changed the way people listened to music. Berliner also began to change the way music was made. In the first decades of audio recording, the musicians would crowd around a cabinet in a room to make a recording—just the way at the other end of the process people would crowd together to listen to it. The musicians would convene before a giant brass horn, like a tuba's, which took in the sounds they made and conveyed them to a stylus, which etched a pattern of the sound into a revolving disc or cylinder.

Berliner had formed Victor with two other inventors, one of whom held the rights to the slogan "His Master's Voice." The painting of a terrier listening to an Edison phonograph was already a well-known piece of advertising. Victor had the phonograph removed from the painting and had a gramophone painted in.

The recorded sound of the human voice would be the key to Victor's enterprise. The company began recording Enrico Caruso, the Italian tenor. He sang arias from beloved European operas, each three or four minutes long—just as much music as a shellac disc could hold. His voice, at once wooing and commanding, was recorded with striking clarity and intimacy. His records sold in the hundreds of thousands for Victor and its English counterpart, HMV. The phonograph—called the gramophone abroad—became standard equipment.

The process changed again twenty years later with two new inventions: the microphone and the vacuum tube. The microphone—developed by Bell Labs, the phone company—used a magnet to pull in sounds and transfer them to electrical impulses. Unlike the brass horn, the microphone could be positioned close to a particular instrument, such as a trumpet or banjo, and, especially, close to a singer's mouth; or it could be mounted above a large orchestra or chorus in a concert hall. This "electrical" recording process, introduced in 1925, was a striking advance on the so-called "acoustic" one.

The vacuum tube amplified the electrical impulses produced by the microphone. Developed during the Great War, tubes were first used in radio, which was introduced in the early twenties as a means of distributing sound, by transmitting electrical impulses radially through the air to magnetic receivers—radios. The tube was soon incorporated into the record player. Then the radio itself was incorporated. After Victor in 1926 introduced an all-electric unit that combined a Victrola and a Radiola, the home console—turntable, radio, magnetic speaker, wooden cabinet—took form.

HMV still used that famous painting as the company logo. The terrier attending to his master's voice became a figure for recorded music and a way of life associated with it: technically sophisticated yet tender and humane, faithful not only to the sound of music but to all the rituals and folkways associated with the past, which it promised not to displace but to carry forward into the present.

>>21>>   In 1926 a recording studio rolled out onto the streets of London. The "mobile unit" looked like a delivery truck, with a roomy cab, whitewall tires, high fenders, and brassy headlamps fronting a boxy main compartment with the attentive white dog painted on the side.

A photograph of the truck parked beside the Gothic arch of an old church suggests a comparison between medieval and modern, classical and commercial. In retrospect the mobile unit seems a piece of progressive audio equipment, a forerunner of all things compact and portable. But it was devised so that HMV could make use of the electrical recording process (the microphone especially) to record music made the old-fashioned way, in a church or a concert hall with a crowd of people listening. The new technology wasn't meant to displace live performance but to enshrine it—to overcome the constraints and artifices of the studio and record music made in the midst of life.

For a while, that is how it worked. After recording a revival meeting at the Temple Church in London, HMV's mobile technicians found that they had a few wax cylinders left over and invited a choirboy to sing something; the piece he sang—"O for Wings of a Dove," the solo section of Mendelssohn's anthem "Hear My Prayer"—sold a million 78s. Recording a Handel festival at the Crystal Palace, the mobile unit captured the sound of a five-hundred-piece orchestra and a three-thousand-voice chorus. The unit went to the opera festival at Glyndebourne, to La Scala in Milan, to the Wagner festival in Bayreuth. One poster for HMV's subsidiary Columbia advertised "Astounding Electric Recordings taken in the Bayreuth Wagner Theatre." Another showed Wagner's Siegfried approving "Authorized COLUMBIA RECORDS." Bayreuth was "the One Centre of the World Where Wagner is played . . . in Absolute Perfection and Regardless of Cost! If only such Performances Could Be Recorded for the Gramophone—What Perfection in Records could be assured!" The ad went on: "The Possibility has come true—Columbia has recorded the Bayreuth Festival!" Perfection in recording had been attained.

It is easy to mock the bright-eyed futurism of the old-time recording industry: the pretensions to perfection, the claims to be making the sound of things to come. But it is just as easy to overlook how profoundly the recordings of those years have shaped our sense of the recent past and have set that past off from prior ages. Through those recordings we can hear the music of 1929 in a way that we will never hear the music of 1829, when Mendelssohn led the *St. Matthew Passion* in Berlin. Those recordings really were the sound of things to come: the sound of an age in which the past would be present through technology. That truck with its brassy headlamps was a time machine, making a record of the past and delivering it to the future.

>>22>> In Africa, Albert Schweitzer liked to say, "there happened to me, what happened to Abraham when he prepared to sacrifice his son. I, like him, was spared the sacrifice."

He had prepared to sacrifice the pipe organ. Then the instrument had been spared and given back to him in the evenings on the riverbank with the zinc-lined portable. Then, unexpectedly, circumstances led him to play the organ in public more than ever. In Alsace at the end of the Great War, Schweitzer and Hélène Bresslau were detained as prisoners of war; and there, in a POW camp, both of them past forty, they conceived a child. After the child was born—a daughter, Rhena—mother and child all but settled in Strasbourg, while

Schweitzer returned to Lambaréné, making arrangements to see them in Europe from time to time. The clinic needed funds, so he turned to his two former sources of income: lectures and organ recitals. An archbishop he knew advised him to play and speak in Sweden, "to which country the war had brought considerable financial gains." Over two decades at the clinic the pattern of a double life took shape: periods in Africa spent working as a doctor alternating with periods giving lectures and recitals in Europe, where he burnished his reputation as a holy man, a philosopher, and a performer all in one.

Schweitzer was a revivalist, whether he recognized it or not. The revivalist is the Protestant performer par excellence. He looks to the past not to restore it whole but to call forth new life in the present. He begins with a sense that the golden age is past and the present is out of joint. But he stands back from the reform of society. That work the revivalist leaves to others—to the reformers. For himself, the revivalist strives to set things right through exhortation and example. The old home truths are sound. They need only to be kept alive. In revival they are made vivid so as to move a new audience. The aim is conversion, a collective change of heart.

Schweitzer's work as a revivalist was made possible by an organ revival. From Edison's invention of the phonograph it was feared that recorded or "canned" music would bring about the demise of live performance. But the emergence of recordings coincided with fresh interest in the pipe organ, and even brought it about. Expensive, fixed in place, wedded to an antique repertory, the organ came to symbolize the values of the age prior to recordings, when music was made with great effort on a certain instrument at a particular place and time.

As it happened, the organ revival was electric-powered. In Europe, the harnessing of electricity had stimulated a fresh round of renovations of existing pipe organs: some builders used electric power to move air through the pipes or make the keys easier to press. In the United States, where the oldest pipe organs had been around for only a century, organ builders had fresh territory for experiment. America was still a vast building site, and its churches needed pipe organs—ideally, instruments that would evoke the great organs of Europe and improve on them, usually by making them larger. Andrew Carnegie sponsored the installation of several thousand pipe organs in churches, schools, and town halls. He commissioned a pipe organ for his mansion on Fifth Avenue in New York and hired a full-time organist, who would play the instrument (a $15,800 alarm clock, in effect) as Carnegie awoke each morning. John

D. Rockefeller had pipe organs installed in his Manhattan town house and his estate at Sleepy Hollow up the Hudson River from the city. Henry Clay Frick had a pipe organ situated at the top of the stairs of *his* Fifth Avenue mansion for after-dinner recitals. "Such an instrument has become an almost necessary equipment of the great American mansion," an article in *The New York Times Magazine* declared.

The exploits of the very wealthy caught the attention of merchants and city fathers, who found that a pipe organ was an easy way to attract the public, which paid the costs with its nickels and dimes. Wanamaker's department store acquired an organ built for a world's fair in St. Louis, had it brought to Philadelphia by rail, installed it in the store, and added several thousand pipes to buttress its claim to be "the world's largest." When the organ was dedicated, twelve thousand people went to the store in the rain for a recital that began (after "The Star-Spangled Banner") with Bach's Passacaglia and Fugue in C Minor.

As it made recorded music intimate and domestic, then, electricity made organ music extramusical in its stress on spectacle and gigantism. Lacking sound, motion pictures—and the newsreels that preceded them—were shown to the accompaniment of an organ, and hundreds of music halls and movie palaces were equipped with pipe organs. Radio City Music Hall in New York, which opened in 1932, featured a "Mighty Wurlitzer" with pipes in eleven different rooms: the music hall of the future had no windows, no columns, no Latin maxims on the walls, but it had a giant pipe organ.

The mighty Wurlitzer was the last of its kind. The organ revival had subsided with the Great Depression. When the economy revived, the organ revival did not. Powered by technology, it was undone by technology. With the spread of the motion-picture "talkie" there was no need for organists to play under the movies. As if in acknowledgment of this, a number of early talkies included scenes featuring pipe organs—and so Bach's Toccata and Fugue in D Minor played by Bela Lugosi or Boris Karloff became a horror-movie trademark, the very sound of the city at nighttime as a lurid, ill-lit haunted house.

The newsreels had sound, too. Once sound-playback equipment was installed, the movie palace changed from an imaginative space to a realistic one, in which the events onscreen corresponded to those in the world outside.

"The only place the organ remained indispensable was the church," Craig R. Whitney observes in *All the Stops*, concluding a chapter about the organ revival. Yet if the organ was indispensable to the church, the church was not indispensable to the organ. Ever since the age of the Bach dynasty people had yearned to take organ music out of the church with them to have the sound of the church without the Sunday obligation. Now the gramophone made it possible.

>>23>> In 1934 the Columbia Gramophone Company, a subsidiary of EMI, invited Albert Schweitzer to make an "album" of Bach organ recordings: several discs packaged in a binder with thick cardboard sleeves, like a photo album.

It was an obvious request, even an inevitable one. The clinic and the organ together had brought Schweitzer renown as the saintly doctor who played Bach on the side. His book about Bach had given him authority among musicians; his book about Jesus had made him a sage among church people. His philosophy of civilization, set out in a series of volumes beginning in the twenties, had associated him with all things classic and timeless—the very qualities EMI sought to embody with the sets of 78s in its Society Series, a venture set up along the same lines that the Paris Bach Society had followed in publishing the scores of Bach, with members underwriting production costs by subscribing up front.

In other respects, the pairing of Schweitzer and the record business was paradoxical. In going to Africa, Schweitzer had set himself against modern technology and the ease and convenience that it promised. His time abroad had acted as a preservative, sealing off his approach to the organ from recent developments such as the electric-powered pipe organ. EMI's state-of-the-art recording process would register a way of playing Bach that he had developed three decades earlier—in the pre-recorded era, that is.

He was eager to make the recordings. He had spent much of 1934 in Europe, and that fall had settled in Edinburgh to give the first of two sets of Gifford lectures. He was due to return to Europe in the fall of 1935 and go to Scotland to give the second set of lectures. His schedule was thick with other talks and concerts. So he arranged with EMI to record in London in December 1935, after the Gifford lectures were done. He had taken part in a radio broadcast from a church in London and had made a recording in the city once before, at Queen's Small Hall, but the organ there was harsher than he liked. So he proposed that EMI record him playing at the church of All Hallows by the Tower, where the organ, though built only in 1909, had a warm, compact sound.

First came acknowledgments of his sixtieth birthday in January 1935. Universities competed for the privilege of awarding him honorary degrees.

The city of Strasbourg named a park in his honor. Schweitzer accepted; but for him Europe was now an alien place, a place of death, not life. The Great War had hardly ended and Europe was impelled toward war again; in Germany, great numbers of people were surrendering their individual wills to the mass "in deeds of violence and murders a thousandfold." Such "brutalized humanity" was sponsored by new technology. "Because he has power of the forces of nature, man built machines which took away work from man, and this makes social problems of such magnitude that no one would have dreamed of them forty years ago," he observed. "In some cities now air raid practices are held, with sirens shrieking and all lights out. People shove something over their heads which makes them look like beasts, and rush into cellars, while flying through the air appears the superman, possessing endless powers for destruction."

In Lambaréné he received a letter from Berlin inviting him to go to the country of Bach as the guest of the Nazis: it was signed, "with German greetings, Joseph Goebbels." He wrote a letter rejecting the invitation, and signed it "with Central African greetings, Albert Schweitzer."

He set out in August 1935, boarding a Europe-bound steamer on Africa's west coast. Mussolini's army was menacing Abyssinia, to the east, and the crisis of Europe was in the front of Schweitzer's mind. With the Gifford lectures he would address "the problem of natural theology and natural ethics," aiming to find a basis for a common ethics and spirituality in the experience of peoples outside the Christian tradition. With the Bach recordings he would attempt something similar.

The music of Bach represented the tradition that Europe seemed determined to do away with. "Bach, like every lofty religious mind, belongs not to the church but to religious humanity," he remarked, and "any room becomes a church in which his sacred works are performed and listened to with devotion." He would turn sitting rooms into churches. He would present Bach to a society in which the spirit of Bach was being violated. He would be a missionary to the Europeans, converting them to the civilization that had been their own once upon a time.

>>24>> The age of mechanical reproduction was at hand: as Schweitzer steamed northward, Walter Benjamin—German self-exile, freelance critic, book collector, author of radio scripts—sat writing, in pen and ink, an essay about the prospects of the work of art in the new era he called "the Age of Its Mechanical Reproducibility."

Benjamin was in a cabin in Denmark, far from Paris, the site of his encounters with movies, radio, phonograph records, and illustrated museum catalogs; but the cabin was that of Bertolt Brecht, playwright and evangelist of live art, and Benjamin felt the forces of new technology pressing in on him. "Just as water, gas, and electricity are brought into our houses from far off to satisfy our needs in response to a minimal effort, so we shall be supplied with visual and auditory images, which will appear and disappear at a simple movement of the hand, hardly more than a sign," Paul Valéry had predicted. As the Depression lifted, the cost of home appliances fell, and the phonograph, the camera, and the wireless were suddenly everywhere. This change made Benjamin anxious. Through mechanical reproduction, people of all classes were put on intimate terms with the great art of the past: "The cathedral leaves its locale to be received in the studio of a lover of art; the choral production, performed in an auditorium or in the open air, resounds in the drawing room." And yet mechanical reproduction uprooted the work of art from its place in time and space and in "the fabric of tradition." Reproduced, it was less distinctive and less awe-inspiring. There was a loss of its "presence" or "aura." Over time, the power of art was diminished, and the loss was akin to a loss of religious faith.

A young man upholding the old ways, entering into exile from European civilization so as to bear witness to its character through critique and example: Benjamin was Albert Schweitzer's secret sharer, a fellow diagnostician of decline.

Outwardly they were not akin, and not just in that one was Christian and the other Jewish. Whereas Schweitzer rose from rural provincial life, Benjamin, born in Berlin in 1892—as Schweitzer entered his final year as a scholarship boy at the Gymnasium in Alsace—belonged to the bourgeoisie of the capital. Where Schweitzer seized every opportunity, advancing in music, religion, and medicine all at once, Benjamin, slow and indecisive, struggled to find his way; where Schweitzer's book on Bach began at the prompting of an elder, Benjamin's early masterwork, a thesis on Goethe, challenged the top Goethe scholar in Berlin, and the conflict drew him into what Hannah Arendt called "the inextricable net woven of merit, great gifts, clumsiness, and misfortune into which his life was caught." Living simply but comfortably in Paris and Strasbourg, Schweitzer took as an ideal the hero striving to save humanity; Benjamin, living "without possessions, job, dwelling or resources," fancied himself a *flâneur* out of Baudelaire, aimlessly strolling the boulevards of Paris. Where Schweitzer had an iron constitution, Benjamin suffered from a cardiac condition that (as Arendt put it) made "even the shortest walk a great exertion," and came down with a bout of malaria that left him unable (he said) even to "climb the stairs of the cheap hotels among which I must select my place of residence."

Schweitzer seems the last premodern man, Benjamin the first postmodern one. But by his own account Benjamin was a nineteenth-century man measuring the change represented by the Great War, in which "a generation that had gone to school on a horse-drawn streetcar now stood under the open sky in a countryside in which nothing remained unchanged but the clouds, and beneath those clouds, in a field of force of destructive torrents, and explosions, was the tiny, fragile, human body." And in his account the change wrought by mechanical reproduction was just one aspect of a long process whereby the human person was alienated from his fellows, his environment, and his own experience.

He set out his position in "The Storyteller," an essay he wrote right after the one on mechanical reproduction. Once upon a time, he proposed, communication had been "mouth to mouth"—from one person directly to another. This was the age of storytelling. With the invention of the printing press, the telling of stories gave way to the writing, printing, and reading of them, bringing on "the rise of the novel." Whereas storytelling is social, the writing and reading of novels is solitary. Where a story points a moral, a novel has no instruction to give—other than "evidence of the profound perplexity of the living."

Just as the novel challenged storytelling, so the novel, in time, was itself challenged by a new form. This was information. Information, as Benjamin explained, describes the present in such a way that it is "understandable in itself." It is the story together with its explanation, and it has sufficient authority to do away with the need for an appeal to tradition, religious faith, magic, or any other source. The story is not so self-sufficient. Its compactness, its laconic lack of explanation, "commends the story to the memory." There "it preserves and concentrates its strength and is capable of releasing it even after a long time." But for its power to be released, the story must be told—again and again and again; and for the story to be told, it must be remembered, and the art of storytelling "is lost when stories are no longer retained." The decline from storytelling to information involved a loss of memory—involved the replacement of cultural memory with mechanical memory.

Benjamin (Susan Sontag later proposed) was an exemplar of the thinker "under the sign of Saturn"—solitary, deliberate, drawn by an "undertow of inwardness," prone to see the past as a ruin and the present as the shards of a lost unity. Instead of relating to other people, the saturnine person relates to objects, and finds in them that "the amount of meaning is exactly proportional to the presence of death and the power of decay."

Benjamin's feel for the "magic circle" of books and objects made him anxious about mechanical reproduction. And it set him apart from Schweitzer. Where Schweitzer the revivalist embraced recordings as a means to make himself heard, Benjamin the collector-writer (working in "freeze-frame baroque" style, Sontag called it) feared recordings as a threat to his sensibility.

Benjamin's anxiety was typical of devotees of the traditional arts in the face of new technology, who at once decried the power of technology and relished the intimacy with the past that it afforded. For Benjamin and his like, the past was not simply the past. The past—partial, fugitive, at once more substantial and more intangible than the present—was a figure for his inner life. It would spoil things if the past could be retrieved too easily or fully. It would do away with the imaginative space where he managed to stay alive.

>>25>> As night fell, the recording truck threaded through London traffic, bound for the City. The technicians sat in the cab up front, smoking and talking. A reporter from Fleet Street sat between them: not without adroit public relations had Albert Schweitzer come to be considered "the greatest interpreter of Bach," as the record company was billing him.

All Hallows by the Tower was a compound of period styles—a Roman floor, a Saxon doorway, medieval walls, collegiate Gothic windows with their flattened arches. The history of the place was recounted laconically in tags mounted near the door: built by monks in 675, claimed by the Church of England during the Reformation, topped in the next century with a spire of the Wren type. Like Christianity in Europe, it was an artful reconstruction, bearing within it the evidence of breakdowns and revivals.

Schweitzer was already there, his shadow thrown onto the back wall by the electric light in the organ loft. The rector would allow the making of recordings only in the evenings, outside the ordinary life of the church, and so for two nights they had worked from dusk to dawn. The schedule suited Schweitzer: he liked to spend half a day with an organ before a recital, trying out its pedals and stops. To those who said you couldn't burn the candle at both ends, he replied: "Oh yes you can, if the candle is long enough."

The organ loft looked out over the church, the size of a meeting hall, and to the broad stained-glass window behind the altar. The church had its back to the Tower. It had stood here six hundred years when the remains of Thomas

More, beheaded in the Tower, were brought there for burial. It had stood through the Great Fire, which Samuel Pepys, the diarist, who lived nearby, witnessed from a perch in the spire.

Against such a history Bach was a recent figure, and his music was not a thing of the past so much as the culmination of the past— a final expression from the religious treasure-house of Europe. And yet the hour for Europe, Schweitzer felt sure, was truly late. "Is religion a force in the spiritual life of our age? I answer, in your name and mine, 'No!' " he had written. "There is a longing for religion among many who no longer belong to the churches. And yet we must hold fast to the fact that religion is not a force." Musicians, not religious folk, were the custodians of these sacred places, dusting the corners of the past now that the spirit had vanished. It was to avoid such a fate that he had become a doctor and gone to Africa, making the music of Bach the motive force of a re-ligious adventure, a tailwind that pushed him against the spirit of the age.

In making his life his argument, what was he arguing for? What in the European past had been lost, and how should it be regained? What in Bach did he want to get back?

About this Schweitzer the Bach scholar had little to say. Bach for him was an end point, an artist in whose hands a civilization, rooted in Christianity but not limited to it, had reached its fullest expression. Bach was the exemplar of a stance toward life that Europe had nearly lost and needed desperately to re-cover. But how? What was to be done?

Schweitzer had sought to answer the question with his life. A holy man, he was also a showman, a performing artist in the role of the man living up-rightly. Acting holy, he would awaken his hearers and dramatize the ills of the present for them until they, too, were stirred to act.

He had made his life a revivalist's edifying discourse, a sermon on the text of cultural decline. In leaving music for medicine, he demonstrated his view that the thread of Bach's legacy had been lost. In leaving Europe for Africa, he declared that European civilization had come to an end too. His sojourn "on the edge of the primeval forest," as he put it, made the emotional truth a factual one, at least for him. Then the Great War lowered the curtain on the European past while he looked on from afar. From then on Europeans were remote peoples, two-legged killing machines, and Europe was a place he would visit the way a missionary or anthropologist would. Its people now spoke a for-eign language. Its past could be encountered only imaginatively, in performance.

As a revivalist, he stood apart from the modernists who were making it new in old Europe. Yet as the century deepened, his approach, more than theirs, was becoming the pattern of change for the arts and high culture generally: music, painting, poetry. Sometimes the change took place in a single person—T. S. Eliot turning his Symbolist sword into the plowshare of churchly upbuilding. Sometimes it took place across a society. The alarm would go up. The old ways were vanishing. The present was barren and indifferent. A crisis was at hand. It was up to the artist to make it new by making it old again—to set the past in counterpoint to the present lest the present go to ruin.

Schweitzer now sought to do likewise through Bach. A reformer of Bach, he would use his stronger language, that of revival. Thirty years earlier his book on the "musician-poet" had crowned the long Bach revival that culminated with the publication of the complete works. Now, sitting at the organ at All Hallows, he faced forward into another Bach revival, this one taking shape through the new technology of audio recordings.

After two nights, he knew this organ well. So he studied the works themselves, which he would never tire of examining. The Prelude and Fugue in C. The "Little" Fugue in G Minor. The Toccata and Fugue in D Minor. He tried to concentrate.

There were usually guests at these sessions—a reporter, a critic, a music-loving curate—and a stirring below the organ loft signaled that a guest had arrived.

"I have surprised him in the midst of his work, in shirt sleeves," the reporter wrote, invoking the characteristic image of Schweitzer, at once great man and craftsman, that Schweitzer himself had seen in Bach's life and sought in his own. "He has even taken off his vest here in the late autumn in the cold church. I see again the imposing head that reminds one of Nietzsche, the powerful form with broad shoulders which seems to me today even heavier and more crammed with energy than ever.

"Before the organ over the church pews hangs the microphone; it carries the tone of the organ to the receiving apparatus in the sacristy. Here the wax disc turns, and here the needle scratches the organ tones in the surface of what looks like a thick, deep yellow honey cake.

"'You are arriving just at one of the most difficult places,' said Albert Schweitzer to me, as he took me up to the choir loft with him."

The reporter watched carefully as Schweitzer returned to his position at the organ—and then turned his attention to the specifics of the recording process.

"He supports himself on the organ bench with both hands, and plays with assurance and energy the difficult foot pedals once or twice through. Then he telephones the sacristy that he is ready. The man in charge of the reception there puts on a new disc and lowers the needle. Now a muffled bell beside the console gives the signal . . .

"The organ begins."

The pipes ring out once, twice, a third time. The organ swells with sound.

The recording suggests what Schweitzer had seen and heard since he renounced music for medicine. It is an account of experience that is larger than his philosophy. It is full of the conflict that is never really present in his story of his life, in which all the conflicts are already resolved and the great man is always right. The exploratory lines of the toccata converge in a tightly organized fugue. Its theme is made up of a fourfold figure repeated at different points in the structure and different places on the organ. In later recordings, the effect is of a thickening weave, a brick wall of sound rising from the ground up. In Schweitzer's recording the low end is inaudible, and the lines subside to silence. The effect of that repeated figure is that of a long sermon—the revivalist in the pulpit making the same point over and over, voice going hoarse, finger stabbing the darkness.

What was to be done? Schweitzer sought to answer the question through the Toccata and Fugue in D Minor, setting Bach in counterpoint with the age one more time.

PART II

A Man in a Room

>>1>> "For the past eighty years I have started each day in the same manner," Pablo Casals, late in life, told an interviewer. "I go to the piano, and I play two preludes and fugues of Bach. I cannot think of doing otherwise. It is a sort of benediction on the house."

In 1935 Casals was living in a grand house on the sea near Barcelona. His cello had taken him to the ends of the earth, but after two decades of traveling and concertizing he had returned to the city in 1919 and founded the Orquestra Pau Casals, an ensemble made up mainly of Catalan musicians. Those years were "the most fruitful of my life," he said. He lived simply, playing tennis, riding horses, and passing time with his mother and brothers. The orchestra thrived, and when the people of Spain ousted King Alfonso XIII after free elections in 1931 it became, in effect, a national orchestra. To celebrate the new republic Casals led a performance of Beethoven's Ninth Symphony and then joined the musicians and the audience in singing the concluding "Ode to Joy." "For me, at that moment, there was a true joining of man and music . . . the coming into being of a government dedicated to the highest aspirations of man, to freedom and happiness and universal fraternity."

Civil war put an end to all that. Casals was on his way to a rehearsal at the Orfeó Català, a beloved blend of Gothic Revival and Catalan *modernisme*, when word of a coup rippled through the streets, stirring up "soldiers, Civil Guards, factory workers in overalls, and crowds of agitated men and women," he recalled. "Everybody's radio was on. Over loudspeakers set up in the streets, messages were being broadcast by the government: *Do not turn your radios off! Stay calm! Traitors are spreading wild rumors to sow fear and panic! Keep tuned in! The Republic is in control of the situation!*"

This concert, too, was set to end with Beethoven's Ninth. The rehearsal began, and the orchestra had just started to play the symphony when news came that a counterrevolutionary army was marching on Barcelona. Casals put the question to the musicians: Should they stop playing? They elected to go on. They played the symphony through and sang the "Ode to Joy," raising their voices to the ocher and aquamarine vaults of the hall. "Then they put their instruments in their cases, and we all left the hall and went out into the street, where the people were setting up barricades."

The story from there is a familiar one, made so by Orwell and Hemingway: the story of a citizens' army joined by a brigade of writers and artists from abroad in defense of a people's government. But for Casals there was no glory in it: "the splendid achievements of the Republic were drowned in blood." As they regained power, the Partisans sought reprisals against those involved in the coup. Francisco Franco and the Falangists rallied back. Abroad, the Allies did nothing, loath to break a nonintervention pact, even though Nazi Germany and Fascist Italy, which had signed it, were providing the Falangists with weapons. Civil war was subsumed by world war, and when it was over Franco was the strongest ruler in Europe.

Casals fled to France in 1939, joining a mass exodus of Catalans across the Pyrenees. But for him the Spanish Civil War never really ended. His experience of war would shape the efforts of his later life into an extramusical role: the artist of conscience, who gives voice to human ideals in the face of diabolical powers. A traditionalist in music, he was suddenly seen as a partisan of progressive movements worldwide. An ambassador for the cello and European classical music, he was now known for statements, not concerts. Past sixty, small, brown, bent, bald, permanently affixed to his pipe, to all appearances already old, he was the very image of moral independence—of the freedom of the individual to judge right from wrong and act accordingly.

"The only weapons I possess are the 'cello and the conductor's baton," he liked to say. "They are not very deadly, but I have no others, and do not wish to have any."

In fact, he had another: the recording studio. Beethoven, Brahms, Bruch, Dvořák: "The two and a half years of the Spanish Civil War coincide almost exactly with the most significant period in Casals' career as a recording artist," his biographer Robert Baldock observed. While the bombs fell, Casals recorded the cello repertoire "in one relatively concentrated burst."

The records he made were music and more than music. They were upraised fists and flags flown in a strong wind; they were acts of self-defense and messages of solidarity—eloquent statements of the power of music to overcome the worst extremes of human degradation. Or so they seem today.

His recordings of Bach's six suites for solo cello are still more remarkable.

They have been likened to Gaudí's distressed stone cathedral in Barcelona, called a Catalan cry of the heart. But they are closer to sculpture—sculpture like Giacometti's *The Palace at 4 a.m.*, a work in wood and wire whose common materials and simplicity of means convey a tragic sense of the human situation. Like so much modern art, they are human in their limits as well as their strivings. They are tender, vulnerable things, combines of wood and string and hair preserved, mounted in steel, and then etched into shellac one at a time.

Legend has it that Casals happened on the suites as a teenager, rescued them from neglect, and brought them into the classical repertoire. He was the first cellist to play a Bach suite whole in concert, rather than in part as an encore. He "created" the suites, the way a singer in a new opera is said to create a role, and invented them as modern concert music. But when he entered EMI's state-of-the-art recording studio in London in November 1936 he had not recorded them as a set, and neither had anybody else. There, and later at a studio in Paris, he sought to invent the cello suites again as music for the age of recordings.

He had taken refuge in Prades, a village on the French side of the Pyrenees. In a room in a hotel at the foot of a mountain, he played the Bach suites over and over the way he had as a teenager, striving to discover them again after half a century and to uncover what he knew he must express through them on record in a time of war. "My way of performing a work does not last longer than the actual playing of it," he liked to say. He meant that he sought to play it fresh each time, and that he recognized no absolutes: no change of tempo, no bit of phrasing, no expressive flourish was ruled out. When it came to recording the suites, it seems, this interpretive freedom weighed on him—made him feel the double burden of producing performances that were at once spontaneous and fit for posterity.

The suites were a benediction on his new home and his new life. In the years to follow he would refuse to perform in public in countries whose governments had accommodated General Franco; this meant most of the countries of the West, including Germany and the United States. But his Bach suites went in his stead. Made in small rooms, the recordings traveled the world; made in wartime, they became the sound of peace, of action in repose. They joined him to strangers he would never meet. They went where he would not go.

The suites were a benediction on the age of recordings, too. The studio where he recorded them would become a symbol for a new kind of music, made in a controlled environment, not as an echo of a live performance but as a sonic creation in its own right. And their voyage out from his hermitage is akin to the way recorded music acts in our own experience, crossing borders between life and art, public and private.

It is revealing to compare Casals's cello suites to the organ recordings Albert Schweitzer made at All Hallows. Schweitzer's Bach is a sound at the far end of a long, dark tunnel; Casals's cello is heard up close. Schweitzer takes us back to the remote place that is the past; Casals sets out from the past to come and find us where we are.

>>2>> "Cultivate a singing style in playing," Bach liked to say, and nobody has done it better than Casals did with the cello suites.

There are six of them, each with six parts: a prelude and five movements, the fourth repeated with a slight variation. Composed in six different keys, they have six different moods, six patterns, six shades of light and dark. Each is a set of three- and four-minute miniatures, about twenty minutes from beginning to end. All together, they are a couple of hours of music—the length of a recital.

You can hear their equipose in Casals's recordings: in the balance between fast and slow, delight and struggle, and in the serenity of his playing even in passages of outward agitation. But balance and serenity are not what you hear first of all. What you hear is a voice. At first, it is the voice of the cello itself: the sound of wood carved, glued, polished, strung, and tuned in ways so as to replicate the tubes and chambers of a creature's innards.

It is an animal sound, all furred and tendoned. In the slow passages it is elephantine, or older—a dinosaur's cry. In the fast ones it is equine, a steeplechase run in stop-motion. But before long, the sound of this music, played this way, is a human sound. The instrument sighs. It grunts. It swallows. It inhales and exhales. Sometimes the sound is dry and nasal. Sometimes it is a chesty honk, a double lungful of sound. Sometimes it is glottal, the tongue enunciating against the roof of the mouth. Sometimes, as the bow is pulled across the strings as across a row of teeth, it is a shout. But it is a voice, no question about it. Like a voice, it seems to come from a source at the center of the body. And like a voice, it seems an inherent trait, given to the performer, not striven for.

The vocal quality of the cello suites is well served by recordings. The replacement of the brass horn with the microphone in the 1920s improved recordings of all kinds of music, but especially those of the human voice and the string instruments, which emit sound at a volume such that the microphone can be placed close without distortion. The bare-walled, windowless recording studio, developed a few years later, focused and shaped the sound much the way a musical instrument does. The combination made the music startlingly intimate and lifelike.

This was especially true for the cello. The cello's sound—not too big and not too bright, coming from an instrument held steady between the performer's legs rather than one wrestled back and forth beneath the chin, as a violin is—suited the microphone very well.

The suites are patterned on dances known at court in Bach's time. In Casals's hands the cello is a partner, a shapely body loosely embraced with his arms and legs. And yet for Casals the suites are not dances but songs—from the first prelude, like a lullaby in its upwardly rocking movement, to the last, a monks' chant made exultant. Bach sings. The sheet music sings. The cello sings. The room sings. The phonograph sings. Casals sings, finding his voice in the voice of Bach, and making us feel that he is singing to us.

It is this that sets him apart from Schweitzer, so sharply that they seem to inhabit different epochs in the same span of time.

They were contemporaries, paragons of virtue, devotees of Bach, and each lived long enough to represent in his person the enduring human qualities he had sought to embody in Bach's music. But there the resemblances run out. In going to Africa, Schweitzer turned his back on Europe, and from there he evangelized Europe without considering it squarely, the way a church organist, an anticleric, edified the congregation from behind. When Schweitzer climbed up to the organ loft of an old church he entered the lost world of Bach. Not so Casals. His discovery of the Bach suites suggested a way forward for the cello. His embrace of the Spanish Republic augured a better future for his country. His instrument traveled with him by railroad and steamship and motor car. When he entered the recording studio he took a giant step into modernity. He faced forward, bow in hand, pipe in mouth, and saw his future listener in his mind's eye.

>>3>> Casals's cello suites are records of life during wartime, anchored in the exploits of a man who discovered the suites and then, blood-soaked, discovered them again. But how did he do it? How, exactly, does the sound of people killing one another in the plain air get behind closed doors, into the cello, in between the lines of Bach's music, and onto the steel-cut disc that is the master recording? Did he play the suites the way he did in the late

thirties because of the state of the world, or in spite of it? And is it right to suppose that music is somehow more human when it is made while there is a war on?

Those are the questions running through his recordings of them, in cogitational counterpoint to their armature of wood and wire.

Casals maintained that his music was a response to experience. He thought that a musician's "attitude to life" was even more important than his or her technique, and he insisted on the "human" qualities as those most vital to his own music and the music he admired. "Music must serve a purpose," he said, "it must be something larger than itself, a part of humanity, and that, indeed, is at the core of my argument with music of today—its lack of humanity."

It is a noble conviction. But it doesn't tell us very much. It is one thing to say that Casals in the Bach cello suites has a distinctly human voice. It is another to explain what this means. Because Casals's recordings of the suites were the first available, his versions are literally incomparable: there are no earlier ones to turn to, and the later recordings—there are dozens of them—all bear traces of his influence. It is doubtful that there is a cellist of any stature who has not heard Casals's recordings. So there is no sure way to know what in his playing is characteristically his and what is a discourse on an emergent occasion, a response to what he had seen and heard in the Europe of 1936–39.

And yet war, or the rumor of war, is there in the music, as surely as the light dusting of surface noise, a glaze of historical context. The question is: How is it there?

The answer is in the story of Casals and the suites, which suggests that the influence runs in the opposite direction. Casals's experience of Bach prepared him for war, not the other way around. As a young man Casals found in the cello suites both a model for independence and a pattern for its attainment. When, forty years later, he was thrust back on his own resources as a refugee, he turned to the suites again. New technology invited him to self-examination. As he played the suites into the record, he strove to be a person worthy of them, renewing his independence in the independence of Bach himself.

>>4>> He turned in his keys to the organ and left Arnstadt for good. Fifteen months had passed since his trip to Lübeck to hear Buxtehude, and

his ideal of a "well-regulated church music" was still only an ideal. He was not appreciated at the Neuekirche, and if the spat with one of his students and the clash with the elders over his free style of playing had not made it obvious, a fresh conflict did. This time the elders accused him of neglecting the student choir, even of being "ashamed" of it; and they accused him of "making music" with a young temptress in the organ loft, where women were not allowed.

So he loaded a wagon and set out for Mühlhausen, a day's journey north, where the Blasiuskirche, or church of St. Blaise, one of the largest churches in Thuringia, needed a new organist. He had auditioned in the vast medieval church over Easter. There was no time to waste: it was 1708, and he was twenty-three years old.

Maria Barbara Bach followed him. She was a distant cousin of his, five months older than he, and they were engaged to be married. It may be that she was the woman with whom he had made music in the organ loft.

A year later he loaded a wagon again. He explained why in an open letter to the congregation: sure, the people of Mühlhausen wanted good church music, but "the harmony that is fashioned here" couldn't match that of neighboring towns in Thuringia, and there was no sign that things would get better. The Blasiuskirche had a good-size organ, but it was 150 years old and in need of repair. The pay was too low for him to live well—especially, he might have added, now that his wife was expecting a child.

The main reason he was leaving was simple. He had gotten an offer he couldn't turn down: "the gracious admission of His Serene Highness of Saxe-Weimar into his Court-Capelle and Chamber Music."

Saxe-Weimar was a self-governing principality with its capital at Weimar, twenty miles northeast of Arnstadt. Wilhelm Ernst, a man in his forties, was the duke there. He lived in a palace known as the Weg zur Himmelsburg, or the Road to the Heavenly City: a brick enclosure with dozens of windows facing on a central courtyard, a whitewashed tower and cupola overlooking the town of Weimar, and a chapel with a pipe organ. A corridor connected the palace to a second, the Red Castle, home of the duke's nephew, Ernst August, whose father, also a duke, had recently died. An engraving from the period shows the two of them: Wilhelm Ernst in a wig curled and flowing, Ernst August in a wig combed straight and knotted tight. In the one palace, Wilhelm Ernst maintained a court orchestra and a *Hoforganist*; in the other, Ernst August played music and nursed a grudge against his domineering uncle.

Johann Sebastian and Maria Barbara Bach rented an apartment on the market square in Weimar, which put them at the heart of daily life in town. When their first child was born—a daughter, Dorothea—Maria Barbara's unmarried sister joined them there.

They would stay nine years at Weimar, and five children would follow: three boys and then twins (a boy and a girl) who died shortly after birth. Bach played the organ in Lutheran services in the palace chapel and played the clavier to entertain Wilhelm Ernst. He taught other organists, played the organ during services at the church of Sts. Peter and Paul in town, gave recitals there on Sunday afternoons, and examined old organs at surrounding churches to explain how they could be restored. He had gotten a harpsichord as a wedding gift, and it enabled him to make the apartment on the market square a place of music-making.

All at once the familiar image of Bach as professional musician and paterfamilias is substantially complete. With a salary, a patron, an audience, and an instrument of his own, he became a composer, and he began to write the music for which he is known: organ works, cantatas, and instrumental music—suites, concertos, sonatas, partitas, inventions, and minuets simple enough for a child to play.

It is true that he settled down at Weimar. But he would not be defined by his work there or anywhere else.

The scholarly practice is to divide his career into periods that correspond to the jobs he held. Working from church contracts, court account books, records of births and deaths, baptisms and burials, scholars play up the minutiae so as to bring out the texture of his life. An order for a large quantity of beer is taken as a sign that he was a man of hearty appetites. A dispute over money reveals him as proud, even headstrong. A tag like "at Weimar" comes to suggest a distinct stage on his life's way—and one with a distinct sound, a scheme akin to Michelangelo's periods working in sculpture, fresco, and architecture.

Certainly his positions were important, but the recitation of them obscures his independence, which is the character trait that his movements make obvious. Church musician, court musician, member of the guild—Bach was all these things, but mainly he was an artist committed to creating work that was his own, regardless of the circumstances. His jobs were way stations more than stages on life's way. He fit his music-making into the position he had, but he assumed that there was no perfect situation for him, no church or court where his musical ideal would be satisfied.

Recent scholarship bears this out, for it establishes that Bach's habits of composition didn't depend on the places he lived and the positions he held nearly as much as was commonly thought. It shows that he would work on some pieces or groups of pieces for several years before preparing the "autograph" manuscripts or arranging for a first performance. And it confirms that he worked on so-called secular and sacred works simultaneously. By revealing individual works as parts of larger wholes and showing wholes to be made up of parts written at different times and places, it helps to explain the remarkable unity of his music, and to suggest that its source was not in his social location but in the depths of his character, where he stood alone.

>>5>> Two early cantatas make the point dramatically: they mark off the breadth of Bach's vocal music like a voltage meter with a red needle swinging between the extremes of divertissement and sacred song.

"Christ lag in Todesbanden" is one of the first cantatas Bach wrote. Because its theme figures into Easter services, many scholars think that he wrote it as an audition piece for the job at Mühlhausen (where he played on Easter Sunday). It's possible that it was written as an audition piece in reverse—that Bach, frustrated with the choir at Arnstadt, decided to test the one at Mühlhausen by making the choirboys sing this cantata on sight so he could hear what they could and couldn't sing before he took the job.

The cantata dramatizes a chorale Luther wrote on the episode known as the Harrowing of Hell, in which Christ, while "in the thrall of death" on the cross, descends to the underworld to consider the souls damned there. "What a war it was, when Death and Life fought," the chorus declaims, and the shape of the work, a sinfonia and a series of vocal parts symmetrically set, evokes a descent and ascent. Christ passes through the strata of the underworld, touches bottom, speaks to the human predicament, and returns to the world above.

The lines of melody descend in giant steps, rappelling down the octaves. The choir, splitting in two, seems to increase and multiply, like the damned taking roost in the rookery of the underworld and mocking the Lord of the living—saying ha-ha-ha to him as each section, each verse of Luther's chorale, winds its way to the closing *Hallelujah*. That word, so shopworn today, is given a different mood each time, itself making a passage from foreboding to mocking to wicked irony and diabolical death-relish before, in the bass aria, as the soloist begins heroically to climb the scale, it becomes a word of thanks and praise once more.

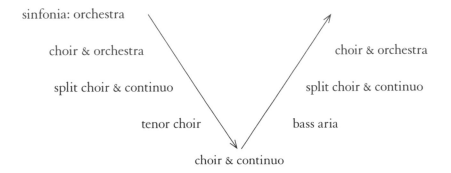

sinfonia: orchestra

choir & orchestra   choir & orchestra

split choir & continuo   split choir & continuo

tenor choir   bass aria

choir & continuo

This is the underworld as Bach imagined it in sound. In the sinfonia the sacred skyscape is inked in. The choruses take us down to the place where no light shines—where, as a consequence, the music is all the starker. Then the bass voice at once reports from the place of death and does away with death once and for all.

"As an early work, it is astonishing," the author of one set of liner notes remarks. Astonishing—if you assume that an artist always progresses from glib virtuosity to the wizened contemplation of last things. But that's not the way it was with Bach. There is no passage from simplicity to complexity in his music, no pilgrim's progress from innocence to experience. All that he knew, he knew all along.

In this cantata he is not, in the main, expressing himself with his music. He is trying to devise a structure that will make Hell seem truly hellish and the Harrowing of Hell really harrowing. His kin are Mercator, with his drafting tools, Hooke with his springs and gears, and Leeuwenhoek with his microscopes—men in small rooms trying to see the world whole and steady, mastering phenomena with precision instruments by the pale northern light.

The other cherished early cantata is the "Hunt" cantata, which Bach wrote to entertain guests after a hunt held on the duke's birthday in 1713. The title ("Wass mir behagt, ist nur die muntre Jagd") means "the cheerful hunt is all that pleases me," and pleasure is what this is about. It is a midwinter night's dream in which the music clads the singers in comic-opera costume and sends them romping pastorally over the hillsides to the sounds of twittering oboes and bouncy continuo, while horns at once announce the chase and urge it along.

This is Bach's first secular cantata and maybe his first secular work of any kind, and the first, it is said, to reveal an Italian influence. It doesn't sound so pathbreaking at first, though. The source text, written in Bach's hand, has no opening sinfonia, and the opening sections sound slack and undramatic. But just when it seems worth dismissing as a piece of courtly work product cobbled together for the duke, there comes a song as sweet and rich as any ever written by anybody. This is "Sheep may safely graze," an aria for soprano. It comes halfway through the cantata, and it is a turning point: in the winding staircase of its melody, and the shoals of choral writing in the sections to follow, there is the sound of Bach in full at last. Here, he has distributed his genius across the orchestra; here, he has found his voice in the voice of another.

>>6>>   "Here, he also wrote most of his organ works," the Obituary that informs all subsequent writing about Bach says laconically of his time at Weimar.

If it is true, it is a feat of creativity unlike any in the history of music: nearly three hundred works, every one sublime, composed in ten years—years when Bach had a choir to conduct, a band of instrumentalists to harmonize, and young children to teach the laws of music and the gospel according to Martin Luther.

It is probably not true. He probably wrote about half of his organ works at Weimar, shuttling back and forth between the organ in town and the one at Wilhelm Ernst's palace. Still, it is enough. *The New Grove Bach Family* lists page after page of work categorized as "Weimar," "?Weimar," "pre-Weimar," or "?pre-Weimar": several dozen chorale preludes, as many "free" preludes and fugues, and plenty of works that sit beyond category, such as the Passacaglia in C Minor, a vast tapestry of theme and variation stitched from a single sad thread of melody, and the "Pedalexercisen," which sounds at once sprightly and authoritative, like a tap dance on the vault of heaven. The instrument in the castle chapel was hardly worthy of Bach, but the duke's "delight in his playing fired him to attempt everything possible in the art of how to treat the organ."

How are we supposed to listen to so much music, all of it so good? One way is to hear it over a lifetime, the way churchgoers since Bach's time have done, encountering the pieces in many months of Sundays. Another way is to swallow it whole through recordings. Ever since Schweitzer played for the wax-cylinder machine at All Hallows, recordings of the organ works have come in box sets, the pieces listed by German catalog number, and to play the music in bulk is an experience without parallel in live music or in our usual encounter with recordings.

It seems irreverent to listen to the organ works this way. The music begins, the mote-filled sunbeams of the canon "Ach Gott und Herr" flooding the
room—and then vanishes as swiftly as it arrived as another piece is put in
place by the conveyor belt. The music pours out, chorales, preludes, fugues,
fughettas, fantasias, passacaglias, concertos, sonatas, partitas, variations, and
an imitatio or two. There is no way to give each piece the attention it deserves,
and the impossibility of doing so seems to confirm Benjamin's fears about mechanical reproduction—seems to violate the music in the act of honoring it.

But it doesn't. In fact, it does the opposite. The effect of hearing all this
music all together is not one of loss or diminishment, of thinning out or dumb-
ing down. No, on the contrary, it is the experience of boundless abundance—an
experience that is very close to the experience, the distinctive soul-swelling
delight, that characterizes the encounter with Bach's music generally.

Why, in the case of the organ music, does the marathon listening session
seem right? One reason is that the organ in Bach's day was seen as a comprehensive instrument, with which a musician could play any work, make any
sound, all by himself. It was a performance-enhancing device; it played in its
day the role played by the record player three centuries later.

Bach composed so much organ work that even he, a systematizer without
equal, didn't devise a scheme for it. The efforts that came closest—the various
books for students—are provisional and incomplete. At Weimar, for example,
he designated a small blank book, the *Orgel-büchlein*, to hold his chorale preludes for the church year, from Advent to Pentecost, along with preludes on
themes like the Judgment, each based on a chorale he had grown up singing
from the thick hymnal in Eisenach. He began to write them in, a prelude per
page, envisioning 164 chorales in all. It was to be an otherwordly anthology, a
box set of the music of his childhood—but he never finished it.

On top of all the Bach organ music we have, something like a quarter
more is lost, and lies submerged offshore, a buried treasure challenging our
ideas of quantity and completeness. It just doesn't matter how many pieces
there are or how much time you take to listen to them. What matters—what
you feel, listening to it—is that you will never get to the bottom of it. Its
abundance is not an abstraction, like infinity. A recondite theological term
catches the sense of it: *supererogatory*, which means "more than is necessary for
salvation."

As you listen, perfectly formed works pop out of their surroundings. There
is the exacting demonstration of BWV 574, each line of melody added to the
previous one like beads on an abacus, and the reedy whirling-carousel sounds

that open BWV 564, which follows it. There is BWV 540, which over eighteen minutes extends a set of variations akin to a ladder to heaven in Orthodox iconography. And there is BWV 697, a tiny fughetta that sparkles prayerfully for a few moments and then is gone.

Set apart in the organ loft, the church organist is the Protestant individual par excellence, independent of priest and congregation, able to attain transcendence without the aid of other people. Bach's organ work is the music of Protestant mysticism. The Reformation emphasized the primacy of the word over the image, and the individual's ability to grasp the word directly—that is, immediately. It replaced stained glass with clear glass, the chanted Latin with the printed vernacular, the sacred drama with personal experience. Every believer could hope for a direct encounter with the thing itself.

Recordings heighten the effect, completing the transition from eye to ear, from seeing to hearing, that the Reformation had brought about. The organist is done away with. So is the church building. So are the limits of space and time, of stamina and attention. The music of Bach is all that is left. The recordings pour out perfection: they enable the listener to import transcendence into an ordinary room, to "play" the music without making it.

>>7>> The city had never been grander, and now it was the center of everything. The high windows of the churches and festal halls overlooked the canals, which ran through the historic center to the harbor and beyond. All Europe passed below those windows—priests and princes, inventors and discoverers, traders and artists—and the confluence of art and commerce, canalized by the merchant class, gave rise to high culture as we know it, a blend of religious memory, civic patronage, private wealth, and the open market.

This was Venice in the early eighteenth century. This was Amsterdam, too. The two cities, one Catholic and one Protestant, one symbol-soaked and one resolutely matter-of-fact, were the centers of musical invention. While Bach was working out the possibilities of the organ at Weimar, musicians in Venice and Amsterdam were creating the new, fresh, international *musica della camera*—chamber music.

Bach never traveled to either place, but he put himself in the stream of the two cities at a crucial moment, and transformed their transformation of classical music into something distinctly his own.

In June 1712 Wilhelm Ernst, in the foursquare brick castle overlooking

Weimar, decided to renovate the chapel, including the pipe organ. Soon the instrument was in pieces; it would remain so for eighteen months, and although Bach oversaw the work, "for half a year he could not play the organ at all."

The next summer Ernst August's nephew Johann Ernst returned to Weimar from a year spent in Amsterdam and Utrecht. He was a student of the clavier; Amsterdam was a center of printing. He brought home a cache of sheet music by composers from all over Europe, and engaged Bach to help him master it. Already Bach had time on his hands. Now he had an eager student and all the latest releases, too. As he taught Johann Ernst, he steeped himself in the new chamber music.

It included *L'estro armonico*, a set of twelve concertos for violin and orchestra by Antonio Vivaldi. The composer, a Catholic priest in Venice—the youngest son of a violinist at the great church of San Marco—had arranged for them to be published first in Amsterdam. They were brand-new, and Bach turned to them as if Vivaldi were his personal discovery. Here was a gifted composer outside the ambit of the Bach dynasty. Here was a religious man whose music was obviously worldly, giving glory to God through its heated harmonies. Bach read Vivaldi's orchestral scores and transcribed them for organ or harpsichord: he distilled the ensemble into lines for keyboards and pedals and firmed up the counterpoint, giving the pieces a clarity and rigor the originals lacked.

The Bach-Vivaldi pairing has launched a thousand chamber concerts, but another Italian chamber work prompted Bach just as emphatically. It was the *Invenzioni da camera*, by F. A. Bonporti. These inventions are pieces for violin and continuo. Musically, they are nothing special—long Baroque rolls of aural wallpaper. Formally, they followed a long line of works that made use of the inventions conceit. But Bach noted the term *invenzioni* (there and elsewhere), took it over, and made it his own. It echoed the classical rhetoric he had studied as a schoolboy, which identified three stages in the working-up of an idea: invention, elaboration, and realization, or invention, development, and performance.

Like *L'estro armonico*, with its hints of passion and ardor, *inventio* was a term that served Bach as a figure for the creative process. The scholar and gambist Laurence Dreyfus sees the invention as the secret of Bach's music. The invention is "the essential thematic idea underlying a composition." It is not complete in itself: it is "the idea behind a piece, a musical subject whose discovery precedes full-scale composition." And it is the discipline that gives rise to the idea. It is not static but dynamic, not an object but "a mechanism that triggers further elaborative thought from which a whole piece of music is shaped."

Bach himself referred to the invention primarily as a teaching tool. By 1712 his two eldest children, ages three and five, were ready to learn to play music. He would teach them himself, using music he had written for the purpose, such as the book of keyboard exercises, assembled later, that included a set of inventions—pieces meant to give the student "a strong foretaste of composition."

Invention would come to characterize his music, both as a habit of art and as a pattern of the art itself. His music develops ideas in ways that dramatize the act of invention. His use of "structured repetition" highlights the process. And while scholars stress his thoroughness in working out his ideas, his music doesn't sound exhaustive; it sounds inventive—it doesn't finish the musical thought so much as keep it aloft.

Bach was a "discoverer and tinkerer standing behind his inventions," Dreyfus writes. That is appealing but understates the point. Bach was more than a tinkerer, improving other people's creations. He was not quite a discoverer in the usual sense, a figure venturing into terra incognita. He was an inventor, making new things, at once ingenious and practical, which could be put to use by everybody.

At Weimar he applied the process of invention to chamber music. Nobody knows which chamber pieces he composed during his years there. The first English suite, for clavier, is probably one—and the opening figure, which breaks a big chord into demonstrative arpeggios, suggests the role of the suites as exercises, meant to help the player build technique. The violin sonatas, which were probably started at Weimar, go in the opposite direction: they were written for a violinist who played in the court orchestra, and it takes a virtuoso to play them. The cello suites, which he may have started at Weimar, are inventive in the extreme—a work that remakes the cello as a solo instrument.

Only the suite for lute in E minor is Weimar-era music for sure, and the story of how it was written suggests how literally inventive the chamber works are.

Bach had a cousin in Jena, a university town a dozen miles southeast, who made musical instruments, and together they conceived of one called the *Lautenwerck*. It would be a cross between a harpsichord and a lute: a keyboard and long strings like the former, strings made of gut and plucked by quills as on the latter. It would have an ovoid body, like a giant turtle or oyster. It would be unlike any instrument ever seen in that part of Europe.

Months passed, the cousin busy in his workshop. Then the *Lautenwerck* was brought to the Red Castle, where Johann Ernst was studying the clavier with Bach.

Because the suite *aufs Lautenwerck* is usually arranged for lute or guitar, to hear it played on the instrument it was written for is an arresting experience. The music clanks into being, the notes pinging off the sides of the instrument as if there is a musician inside it plucking each string. It sounds like nothing anybody had ever heard before. It opens a passage to an age when the physical properties of music were still being worked out, and when the composer *had* to be an inventor, conducting experiments in sound.

>>8>> Many years later, as he faced the bright lights of fame, Pablo Casals was to remember that distant afternoon when he discovered the cello.

A traveling folk-music ensemble had come to his village. They called themselves Los Tres Bemoles: the Three Flats. They played instruments they'd made themselves—hammered together from pots and pans, drinking glasses, a kettle—as well as guitar, mandolin, and bells. "One man played on a broom handle that was strung something like a cello—though I had never seen or even heard of a cello at that time . . ." Casals said. "I couldn't take my eyes off it."

He went home and told his father what he had seen and heard. His father, Carlos, was the organist at a church in the village, El Vendrell, near Barcelona. He was unhappy in his work but bent on giving his son an exceptional musical education. He had shown him the organ, but Pablo, who was eight and small for his age, couldn't reach the pedals. Now, while Pablo looked on, he affixed a plank of wood to a dried pumpkin shell and stretched a string tight from end to end. "I suppose you might say that this instrument was my first cello," Casals recalled. One night he took it to the cloister of a monastery nearby: "I played in the moonlight and the music echoed among the shadows and against the crumbling white monastery walls . . ."

Later that year they went to the church hall in their Sunday best. A chamber trio—violin, piano, cello—was playing there. Casals was drawn to the cellist, "a handsome man with a high forehead and a handlebar mustache." The instrument fit the man's body exactly—so much so that it seemed to Casals that his body was fitted to *it*. The sound astonished him in its beauty and tenderness, its sinewy humanity. He turned to his father when the piece ended: "That is the most wonderful instrument I have ever heard. That is what I want to play."

There in a few strokes is how Pablo Casals was converted to the cello: through a sudden, life-changing experience. It was characteristic of him—or rather, it was characteristic of his sense of his own story. His memoirs, taken down sixty years later, record one conversion experience after another. Whereas Albert Schweitzer told his story in superlatives—the best teacher, the most renowned organist—Casals spoke with undiminished awe of once-in-a-lifetime encounters that shook him up and set him apart.

The central figure in the stories is as much holy man as musician. Like Mohandas Gandhi, born seven years before him, he is a person who has known great suffering and is happier as well as wiser on account of it. His tale is as smooth and polished as his bald head in the photographs, his humility as absolute as his small stature. The telling lacks the complexity of his performances, which show the shadow side of all that brightness. It is not that he is lying. It is that his interlocutors bask in his eminence instead of examining it. They see the great man in the armchair, sipping an iced tea, and miss the awful, death-drenched ground of his story, which made him a prodigy just for surviving.

Carlos, his father, was from Barcelona; Pilar, his mother, was from a Catalan family that had moved to Puerto Rico and then returned. In their early twenties they married and conceived a child, the first of eleven in all. That baby died in childbirth, and the next one, in 1876, was born with the umbilical cord wrapped around his neck, nearly strangling him. That was Pablo, and he survived as three more children, all boys, died in childbirth or shortly afterward.

Carlos had worked as an apprentice in a piano factory in Barcelona and had first come to El Vendrell to repair the church's organ. He taught music by combining enchantment and indoctrination. "To hear my father play the piano was an ecstasy for me," Casals recalled. "When I was two or three, I would sit on the floor beside him as he played, and I would press my head against the piano in order to absorb the sound more completely. I could sing in tune before I could speak clearly; notes were as familiar to me as words.

"My father used to have my little brother Artur and I stand behind the piano—we were too small to see over the top of it—and he would stand in front of the piano with his back to it. Reaching behind him and spreading out the fingers of both hands, he would strike chords at random on the piano. 'Now what notes did I play?' he would say. And we would have to name all the notes in the dissonant chords he had played. Then he would do it again and again."

Casals wanted to be an organist. "I kept on trying, sitting at the stool alone in the church and stretching out my feet," he recalled, but he could not reach the pedals. His father taught him to play the piano, introducing him to Beethoven and Chopin, and Bach's preludes and fugues from the *Well-Tempered Clavier*. He trained him on the violin. He drafted him to help write music for a Nativity pageant, showing no surprise as Pablo sat "diligently writing notes and musical signs on the stave." He took him to hear the trio at the church hall, then promised to get him a three-quarter-size cello, even though it would be both expensive and hard to find. And yet his father held back from raising him to be a musician, afraid that he, too, would wind up poor and thwarted.

His mother saw it differently, especially as her own life turned grim. Artur, age five, died of meningitis. A baby girl survived six days, then choked to death. A third son, Carlos, age three, died of diphtheria. Then Pablo was bitten by a rabid dog and nearly died. As he recovered, his mother made up her mind that he was going to study the cello in Barcelona.

His father was against it. They argued. She prevailed. Once it was decided, he was as bold about it as she. He wrote to the Municipal School of Music, asking if they would admit their son and help them procure a three-quarter-size cello. Word came: yes, and yes.

His mother took him to Barcelona, enrolled him at the Municipal School, and made arrangements. He would live with relatives. She would go back and forth between the village and the city, dressed in black, overshadowed by the deaths of seven children. Somehow, she would bear three more, but she would never let up in her devotion to Pablo, the survivor and, in time, the provider in the family. He was twelve years old.

Barcelona just then was "a bourgeois paradise," Robert Hughes remarked in his history of the city. A World's Exposition was winding down. Broad new avenues stretched away from the pillar raised in honor of Christopher Columbus, who was claimed as a native of Catalonia, not Genoa. The life of the cafés and music halls reflected the influence of Catalan modernism—surrealist in literature, closer to Art Nouveau in the visual arts, and consecrated in opera to Richard Wagner. "The special strength and glory of Catalan *modernisme* was architecture and its assorted handicrafts: ceramics, iron forging, stained glass, fine woodwork, and the virtuoso use of brick," Hughes observed. Pablo Picasso would make Barcelona notorious, but Pablo Casals was more representative of the city: modern, powerfully sure of himself, yet classical in his fidelity to the ideal of the work of art as a harmonious whole and of the artist as a craftsman, not a demiurge.

He had never held a real cello before, yet he was enrolled in a conservatory of music. He caught up immediately, and the story of his time there is one in which he was invariably recognized and singled out. He studied with Josep Garcia—the cellist with the handlebar mustache whom he had heard play at the church hall. He trained in harmony and counterpoint. After a few months he took a nightly job with a string trio, playing "marches, waltzes, and well-known operatic airs" at a place called the Café Tost. A choral society met above the café, and one member began to tutor him in Wagner, working from the scores. The proprietor took him to concerts at the Teatro Lirico, from Richard Strauss to local composers. After he introduced a weekly night of classical music—Bach, Brahms, Mendelssohn, Beethoven—he gained a reputation as *el nen*, the kid, the little virtuoso.

One night at the café the Catalan composer Isaac Albéniz, hearing him, offered to take him back to London with him to further his career. When his mother stepped in and declined on his behalf—"My child is still a child," she said—Albéniz drafted a letter of introduction instead. It was to Count Guillermo de Morphy, a counsellor to the queen of Spain, and he told her to use it when the time was right.

His mother now lived in Barcelona, having lodged the other children with neighbors in the village. His father visited them there once a week. Father and son would take long walks, popping into music shops, where Casals would look for sheet music to play at the café. It was during one such walk on a Sunday afternoon in 1890 that what he called "the great event of my life" took place.

Sixty years later, he told the story: "First, my father bought me my first full-sized cello"—which might have been a life-changing event in itself. Then they stopped at an old music shop near the harbor. "I began browsing through a bundle of musical scores. Suddenly I came upon a sheaf of pages, crumbled and discolored with age. They were unaccompanied suites by Johann Sebastian Bach—for the cello only!

"I looked at them with wonder: *Six Suites for Violoncello Solo*. What magic and mystery, I thought, were hidden in those words? I had never heard of the existence of the suites; nobody—not even my teachers—had ever mentioned them to me. I forgot our reason for being in the shop. All I could do was stare at the pages and caress them."

From there, he jumbled the story from one telling to another, but the point is clear. It is this: in his experience, the discovery of the cello and the discovery of Bach's cello suites were essentially a single discovery. They were the first moments of his adult life—his life apart from his parents and his native village. He would gain his independence through the cello, and he would find independence dramatized in all its agonized complexity in Bach's cello suites.

"I hurried home, clutching my treasure as if it were the crown jewels," he recalled. But he didn't play the music right away—even though, as the story goes, he had a new full-size cello to try out. Instead, he opened the bundle of pages and considered them silently. The sheet music, faded and battered, belonged to another era. The music itself, the notes and rests, dwelled in some place of imagined expectation, as a line of Baroque melody unfurling in his head. This was music he had never heard before. This was music he hadn't known existed. Now it was spread out on a table in his room, awaiting him.

He began to play. Right away, he recalled, he recognized the music as "something of exceptional importance." It was like nothing he had heard for the cello. And it didn't sound the way he had expected. Bach was supposed to be objective and impersonal, a gray eminence a long way away. But the music of the suites was "immediate and real," and full of "vitality and radiance." He explained: "In those days these compositions were thought of as cold and academic works. How could anyone think of Bach as 'cold,' when these Suites seemed to shine with the most glittering kind of poetry?"

He played the suites every day. He would end each of his practice sessions by going through a suite, the way he would begin the day by playing from the *Well-Tempered Clavier* on the piano. Simple as it sounds, this approach was unusual at the time. Most cellists extracted individual movements from larger works and made them into expressive showpieces. But Casals played each suite from beginning to end, trying to uncover the "pacing and structure of every movement" and "the full architecture and artistry" of the suites as a whole.

It worked. Bach changed him, working on him from one day to the next. Playing the suites invariably reminded him of discovering them: "That scene has never grown dim. Even today, when I look at the cover of that music, I am back again in the old musty shop with its faint smell of the sea." At the same time, they evoked society: in Bach's "infinite gradations of musical allusion" he heard "the simple joy of the people, the popular dances, the elegance, the perfume, the loving contemplation of nature and the rest." They were life in abundance. They closed the gap between Bach and himself, between the canon of Western music and the instrument, more or less his own size, that he cradled in his hands.

>>9>> "I studied and worked at them every day for the next twelve years," Casals said. "Yes, twelve years would elapse and I would be twenty-five before I had the courage to play one of the suites in public at a concert."

It is an astonishing revelation, even by the monkish standards of Casals's contemporaries. Joyce spent eight years re-creating a single day in Dublin; Proust spent half his life in search of lost time. But they were making something out of nothing. Casals was learning to play music already composed and printed—music that, when he finally played it straight through, would last only a couple of hours.

What was he doing all that time? The span of years suggests a prophet struck dumb by an encounter with the holy of holies, a saint of art called to take a vow of silence. But Casals's own remarks describe a practical experience, in which he allowed his conversion to the cello and to Bach to shape him as a person as well as an artist.

He was learning how to play the suites, first of all. They are hard to play correctly, and—cellists say this—even harder to play musically. They were all the more challenging for Casals because he was teaching himself. From his boyhood, when he sat against the soundboard of the piano, he had learned about music from his father and other virtuosi. But his father had not told him about the Bach suites. Neither had his tutor at the conservatory. There was no recording of them, no exemplary version to serve as a comparison and show how things should be done. Casals was on his own.

Having discovered the suites whole in the shop near the harbor, he discovered them in his room, measure by measure, line by line. He could "see from day to day the growing of Bach's greatness," and the experience shaped his approach to the suites, so that he came to see himself as allied with Bach against the academicians of the time. The view of the suites as mere technical exercises confused things. So did instructions such as the one insisting the bowing arm should be held stiff against the body. He was "groping" for the depths in the music, and he wanted to move his arm freely. He decided that he would have to "discard deliberately the old prejudices"—decided that "my duty was to reject strongly the examples and the traditions around me, and to persevere in search of my own way of feeling these works." In time, he came to feel that he was not only entitled but called to do things his own way, and that that is what it means to be an artist in the first place:

"An artist must be strong enough to feel independent of everything that has been done, and of everything he has learned, and he must convince himself that to 'feel' independent of any routine or tradition is his main duty or purpose. He goes the wrong way who does not question himself or listen to the 'voice' of his artistic nature . . . What *does* matter is what we feel, and that is what we have to express."

What *did* he feel? What *was* his artistic nature? Alone in a room, he was trying to understand himself. He had already seen more, felt more, than most of us can imagine: the deaths of six brothers and sisters, the grief of his parents, the pressure to support the family and to ennoble it through his talent. The suites were a means of escape: playing them, he found he could enter "a state of mind we call, in turn, feeling, passion, dreams."

At age sixteen he had a crisis. He felt himself "at loggerheads with a world where there was no justice, selfishness was rampant and charity non-existent. When I saw people walking peacefully in the streets, or going to their occupations, I thought: 'How stupid they are to enjoy this miserable life!' I was desperately searching for a door through which I could find peace of mind." He roamed the streets of Barcelona like a character in a novel. He dreaded the day and yearned for night. He began to haunt a church near the conservatory: "I would sit there in the shadows, trying to lose myself in prayer, trying desperately to find consolation and an answer to my questions, searching for calm and some easement of the torment afflicting me."

For the first time in his life he couldn't concentrate on music. Even Bach was no way out. He decided to kill himself.

It was then that his mother took out the letter Isaac Albéniz had written and sent it to Madrid, hoping for a miracle. The letter was answered, and they went to the palace for an audition: Casals, his mother, and her two youngest children. While she nursed a baby at the breast he played for Count de Morphy, who acted as tutor to the Infanta Isabel, younger sister of the king. The count liked what he heard. Casals was given a scholarship. For the next three years he lived a double life, spending half his time at court—learning foreign languages, roaming the library and the Prado, and playing chamber music for the royal family—and the other half in a garret with his mother and brothers.

The time came when there was no more for him to learn in Madrid. The count recommended study in Brussels. Casals went there and sailed through an audition, but took offense when the instructor called him "little Spaniard." So he turned down a scholarship and went, with family, to Paris, where he took a job playing the cancan in a Montmartre revue. "I earned four francs a day," he recalled. "I walked to and from the Folies-Marigny carrying my cello—it was far from where we lived but I did not have a sou to spare." At one point his mother cut off her her long hair and sold it "for a few francs." That winter he decided that they should return to Barcelona, where at least the weather was warmer. His father wept when they arrived: he had seen them only once in three years.

There Casals took over the role held by Josep Garcia, the cellist who had first excited him about the cello. All of a sudden he was the first cellist in the city orchestra, the cello instructor at the conservatory, and a private tutor. Together with a job playing to Portuguese royalty on holiday at the shore in the summer, he was set up well for a career in Catalonia. It was 1897. He was twenty years old.

Through all this he played the Bach suites every day. Why did he cleave to them? What role did they play? One biographer suggests that they challenged him to reveal his inner life in his playing, which he was loath to do. But Casals himself declared that they did something more. They "opened up a new world," he recalled. "As I got on with the Suites, I discovered a whole new world of space and beauty— and I can say now that the feelings I experienced were among the purest and most intense of my artistic life." The suites didn't just force him to express his feelings. They shaped his feelings, sharpened them. They sounded the way he felt. They opened up his inner life as if for the first time.

And yet he didn't play them in public. The story of his life so far suggests why. Alone in a room, he had gotten to the heart of the suites, which, it seems to me, is this: they are music of solitude. Solitude is their theme, their mood, their means of approach. Complete in themselves, they are diminished by an audience.

The suites were music Casals had discovered himself, and his encounter with them was the most immediate experience of music that he would ever have. So he held them back, keeping them for himself rather than revealing them to others.

For four thousand days he played them. The sheet music, historic when he discovered it, receded further into the past. But the notation didn't change, and he found, as he would find for the rest of his life, that the printed notes "every day reveal new things to the sensitive performer. The more he studies them, the more marvels he discovers."

Alone in a room, he was becoming a man, and the cello suites became for him what the Toccata and Fugue in D Minor became for Albert Schweitzer: the music of his coming of age. In them he found a quality of Bach's music that was just coming into view: its solitude or independence, its radiant self-sufficiency. From them he fashioned an *ars poetica*, a declaration of his independence as an artist.

As it happened, his coming of age coincided with the coming of age of audio recordings, through the invention of the gramophone, the shellac disc, the microphone, the Victrola, and the radio, or wireless.

The change was not felt immediately. Most musicians went about making music in traditional ways. Schweitzer studied the organ at Widor's side in Paris. Casals in the palace in Madrid gave concerts not so different from those Bach had given at Weimar two centuries earlier. Artists trained in the age prior to recordings were slow to adapt to them, and some even suffered from "gramo-fright," the sudden inability to perform when faced with the big brass acoustic horn.

Listeners, too, were loath to change: they gathered around the gramophone as they would around the piano; they played records rarely, lest the grooves get worn out and the music be left unplayable. Record buffs felt the need to defend their habit of solitary listening to the less obsessed, who saw it as idle and anti-social, like drinking alone or snorting cocaine.

In time, recordings stimulated a new way of listening. Call it the invention of solitude. They enabled the ordinary person to be alone in a room with the music as never before. They made it possible for that person to play the music over and over and so to enter into the experience of the musician. Through recordings, the solitude of the virtuoso could be mass-produced. The act of sitting alone in a room and playing music was available to all.

Casals, playing the Bach cello suites in garret, palace, rehearsal studio, and rail station, recognized this change. "The development of the 'cello as a solo instrument is fairly recent," he later remarked. "Bach is an exception, in that he foresaw, two hundred years ago, the future development of the instrument." Now Casals foresaw the ways new technology could develop the cello further. He grasped the solitude of the modern listener and the immediacy of the listening experience the way he had grasped the solitude and immediacy of the Bach suites, and he saw how each could enhance the other. The strain and exultation of performance, the player's absorption in the music, the effort put into expressing its ease and grace: he would magnify these qualities, knowing that they would be magnified further by the recording process. He would close the gap between the performer and the listener, each alone in a room. As he plunged into a life of recitals and recordings, he cordoned off the suites as virgin territory, untouched by the crowd. Instead of playing them in recital, he would play them as if for an audience of one, making them the music of the new electric solitude.

>>10>> A house on a quiet street in London served as the epicenter for this change, the recording artist's labyrinth of solitude.

To call it a recording studio is to get ahead of the story. At first, any room where musicians and recording gear could fit together for a few hours would do. The producer Fred Gaisberg, roaming Europe on the trail of musicians, would woo the ones he liked to a hotel room he had converted into a makeshift recording booth. Mobile units were used to record performances in venues such as the Crystal Palace or All Hallows by the Tower. Then, as the gramophone became standard equipment in sitting rooms and parlors, the rooms where records were made were outfitted more and more elaborately. The Gramophone Company repurposed the "smoking room" behind its Maiden Lane offices as a recording room, with the piano and bench placed on stilts near the fireplace to get the instrument to the height of the acoustic horn. By the thirties, with the swift advance of the electrical recording process, the room used to make audio recordings was becoming a distinct and specialized place, meant not to capture the sound of a concert but to produce a sound all its own.

This development can be heard through the music of Bach. There are dozens of Bach recordings from the early days of recorded sound, and when you listen to them today what you hear, even as you hear the music—bright or dark, grand or intimate, fleet or flat of foot—is the sound of the room. Over time, the sound changes: as the technology improves, the surroundings recede, and the musician, in fact the music itself, seems to leave the place where it was made and move closer, to come into your room.

Among the early Bach recordings are a couple of violin pieces played by the Viennese virtuoso Fritz Kreisler: a prelude in E, and the "Air on the G String," from 1904. Though they were made in Berlin, they sound like field recordings, sugar in the raw; though they were made in the year of the Model A Ford, they might have been made during the Civil War, such are the hints of old stuff in them, of burlap, straw, and tallow. Kreisler sprints through the two pieces in three minutes each (so each could fit onto one side of a 78), and the most pronounced sonic effect is the heavy sledding of the needle across the wax cylinder.

In the teens, the first full-length recording of a classical work (Beethoven's Fifth) was made, and on January 4, 1915, Kreisler recorded the complete Bach concerto for two violins with the Russian-born violinist Efrem Zimbalist. This was itself (the notes to a reissue say) "a landmark in the history of recording. Not only was it the first complete recording of a major Bach work, but it was the first time that two leading violinists were brought together in a recorded performance." A photograph taken at the time shows them flanking a phonograph console: two men in vested suits and ties, one mustached, the other clean shaven, one holding a violin tucked under his arm, the other clutching it against his chest. Leave out the violins and they might be a couple of funeral directors in the quiet moment before the mourners show up.

Early recordings promised ordinary people a close encounter with virtuosity. But the effect of this recording is to make the virtuosi seem ordinary people. The performance is sweaty and unbuttoned. The orchestral music has been scaled down for a quartet—a Bach combo—and the two violinists might be peasants or rustics, such is the rough passion of the fiddling and the grainy, scumbled quality of the recording. They are two farmers on the way to a dance, having a heart-to-heart as they go.

The early orchestra recordings offered a different attraction: a full orchestra in your sitting room. Alas, it really wasn't possible. The acoustical process collapsed the armature of Bach's orchestral music, turning the ice palace to slush. The electrical process worked better, but with a pronounced side effect: while the sound of the music was reproduced more accurately, so was the sound of the room. The recordings, even as they amplified the music, called attention to the concert hall that the gramophone was reconstituting in the home.

They still do. With their grand string sections, swooning tempos, vast changes in volume, and passionate vibrato, the performances enshrined in the Bach recordings of the late twenties and early thirties represent the style now genially put down as Big Bach. But those records reproduce the old days, not the old ways. The record of the Air from the third orchestral suite made at Carnegie Hall in 1929 is as plush as a plutocrat's pockets: you can hear the heavy curtains, the gilded ceiling, the cherubim and putti; you can hear, in the slow breaking-through of the strings, the cigar-stale air under the chandeliers. The third Brandenburg concerto as recorded by the Berlin Philharmonic in 1930 pours out into the hall—the Hochschule für Musik—which seems to expand and contract, accordion-like, with the music inside it; the second orchestral suite led by Wilhelm Mengelberg in Amsterdam the next year gives us the Concertgebouw, Big Bach spreading slowly outward to fill the vast old space like gravy staining a tablecloth.

Listening to those records today is like taking an aural tour of the Old World. But the people making the records, who lived in that world, devised ways to bring the music into the foreground. Microphones once slung over the rafters were now placed at points on the stage floor. Baffles were wheeled in, making the room a giant instrument. In the Berlin Philharmonic's 1933 recording of the first Brandenburg concerto you can hear the plain rectangles of modernity closing in. A passage for solo oboe is an isolated specimen of virtuosity. The site of the recording—Lutzowstrasse 111, Room VIII—suggests the movement away from the concert hall and toward the clinic, the cell block, the office tower.

And, inevitably, the movement toward the full-on recording studio.

The Gramophone Company made its recordings at halls around London: Queen's Hall, near Oxford Circus, and Kingsway Hall, a Methodist mission site in Holborn whose records are said to feature the "Kingsway Rumble," the sound of Underground trains running along the Piccadilly Line below.

A company executive named Osmund Williams tried to buy a concert hall in west London to convert to a studio. The deal fell through. In the meantime another property in the neighborhood had come onto the market: "a Detached Residence containing: Nine Bed Rooms, Bath Room, Five Reception Rooms, Kitchen, Two Servants' Rooms, &c." Williams bought the place—3 Abbey Road, St. John's Wood—and the company spent the next two years overhauling it for use as a recording studio. The façade and steps of the house were kept. So was the kitchen. Some buildings next door were bought, too, and converted into three studios in all, with the largest big enough for 250 musicians and an audience of a thousand people.

"London's Latest Wonder" opened on November 12, 1931, with Sir Edward Elgar conducting the London Symphony Orchestra. Pathé made a newsreel of the occasion, and to see the old bear Elgar climbing the steps to the podium and leading the musicians in "Land of Hope and Glory," you would think it took place in an Art Deco concert hall. But Abbey Road was not a public place. It was private, a repository of rare air. The walls were "specially designed to give correct resonance to any sounds and to avoid any echo. A special system of air cleaning and ventilation" kept the air "continually washed and purified." Six million feet of cable connected the studios to the "central control room." In the newreel the camera cuts from Elgar to a technician in a lab coat in the control room, positioning a stylus on a metal disc cutter and then muttering into a telephone handset: "Are we all ready?"

Oddly, the photo-laden commemorative histories of Abbey Road Studios and EMI pass over the question of why the company installed a studio on a residential street rather than in an office building or a warehouse or a new building designed for the purpose. Why a house, and why this house, with its stuccoed walls and o'ershadowing oak tree? Why here, on a street where a banker in a bowler hat might live, with the nearby entrance to the tube station the only evidence of its location in a great city? Why is Abbey Road in Abbey Road?

Whatever the reason, the domestic setting was apt: there, recorded music became the new chamber music. The big house in London at once harked back to a time before concert halls and paying customers when music was made in the great houses of Europe, and faced forward into an era in which music would be passed from house to house without the middle term of the public recital. Abbey Road was at once a hearth for communal music-making and a laboratory of pure sound. Like the lost monastery that was its namesake, it was a place apart, where the musicians, like a family, or some people touched by the spirit, could be alone together.

>>11>> Pablo Casals would reinvent Bach, and himself, at Abbey Road—but not yet. As Bach's music was entered into the historical record in the first third of the century, he was working different territory. Although he counted himself one of the first musicians to make a commercial recording—and felt his early wax cylinder recordings "helped dispel the prejudice among musicians against the gramophone"—he made his name as a touring recitalist, a real live virtuoso come to town. And although he played the Bach cello suites onstage to acclamation, he played them one at a time: each was the centerpiece of a large and miscellaneous program, neither a freestanding work of art nor a part of a larger whole.

In Paris, his luck had changed: Charles Lamoureux, a French conductor and tastemaker, had heard him play and taken him on as a soloist with his orchestra. Then, when Lamoureux died, Casals began a solo career. He set out from Paris in 1899, and although he kept an apartment in the city, and then a house—20 Villa Molitor, in Auteuil—he was on the road for most of the next twenty-five years. "I lost track of the number of concerts I gave," he said. "I do know that it was around two hundred and fifty a year." He traveled by rail, coach, steamship, and automobile, accompanied by his cello, and his itinerary belies the notion that today's musicians are global figures as never before. He played all over Europe; Mexico, Cuba, Buenos Aires, and Spanish-speaking South America; Russia, where he went every year until the revolution broke out. He toured the United States a dozen times, often traveling with a singer, playing concerts and having adventures. "We wanted to see everything we could of this strange, exciting land," he recalled. "No sooner had we arrived in a new town and unpacked our things than we'd be off exploring." They went down into a mine in Pennsylvania coal country and ventured out into a western desert. At a saloon in Texas, Casals got into a dice game with some cowboys, who reached for their revolvers as he had a run of good luck. While hiking Mount Tamalpais near San Francisco he was struck on one hand by a falling rock. He stayed in the city for several months, recuperating.

No one knows for sure when he first played a Bach cello suite onstage. It was probably in 1901 in Barcelona, where he had come upon them twelve years earlier. A book about Casals and the cello suites furnishes references to a Bach suite in reviews of three Casals recitals that fall in Barcelona and in Madrid—where "a Bach suite earned Señor Casals a prolonged ovation"—and in recitals in London, New York, Rio, and elsewhere in the years to follow.

Casals, who made so much of his encounter with the suites, didn't say what prompted him to start playing them in public. All of a sudden the suites are his signature pieces: in a command performance for the queen of England and at the Mayflower Hotel in Washington, at a friend's deathbed, and at Princeton, where a student, asked what he would like to hear after showing Casals the campus, said "Bach" and was given an impromptu recital.

Casals tutored younger cellists in the suites, and the year he turned thirty he entered into a relationship with one: Guilhermina Suggia, a seventeen-year-old Portuguese prodigy whose career he had followed since she was ten. She came to Paris to study with him, then took a room in his house, and when he was there, which was not often, he would introduce her to guests as his lover or his wife. They had an arrangement about the Bach suites: she played the first and third suites and left the others for him "until the angels took over." But when he proposed marriage she turned him down: it would interfere with her career.

A year later he proposed marriage again, this time to a singer: Susan Scott Metcalfe, an American, raised in Italy, who was making a career as a mezzo-soprano in New York. They had met in 1904 during a recital at Mendelssohn Hall on West Fortieth Street, where Casals played Bach's third cello suite and Metcalf sang a sequence of art songs. They had seen each other again in Europe, notably in 1913, when she visited him backstage in Berlin after a recital and he arranged some Spanish songs for her to perform. Now, after two weeks together in New York, they were married by a judge in New Rochelle, north of the city, on April 4, 1914. They went to Europe, where they made a Casals recital tour a kind of honeymoon, then spent time at an estate Casals had acquired on the sea outside Barcelona. They were in Paris when the Great War broke out; they returned to New York, unhappy together, and then remained there because of the danger of a wartime ocean crossing.

Two of the most advanced audio recording facilities were nearby: the Columbia Graphophone Company's facility in Manhattan, and the Victor Talking Machine Company's headquarters in Camden, New Jersey. Confined to America, Casals made some recordings. In eight sessions for Columbia, he recorded seventeen short pieces, mainly excerpts and transcriptions he used as encore.

On April 23, 1915, he faced the brass horn and ran a scale down the neck of the cello from C to C—the beginning of Bach's third suite.

This acoustic recording is the closest we will ever get to the Bach suites as the young Casals played them. Yet it is underwhelming. The Casals tone is there—a burred roar—but something is lacking. The prelude is steady and well-regulated in the extreme, without strong contrasts or drama. The second and third parts are missing. The fourth part, the sarabande, is a patchwork, and the bourée is so rapid as to seem a run-through. All the music is heard through a wintry mix of surface noise.

Hearing it, you would not say that this is some of the greatest music ever played. So much is absent: a sense of occasion, a quality of inwardness, and the shape of space, the effect of the sound in its immediate surroundings, that suggests a man in a room.

"Of course the [gramophone] was then in its infancy, and it left much to be desired," Casals later said, and he was probably dissatisfied with the session. Although he recorded the last part of the suite (the gigue) a year later, he stopped there: one suite, and that one incomplete.

A decade later Casals made his first electrical recordings in a series of sessions at Victor's vast headquarters in Camden: Chopin, Debussy, and Fauré; Schubert, Schumann, and Wagner; Vivaldi, Handel, and an adagio and a musette by Bach. They are miniatures, like those he had played in the cafés of Barcelona: short, rich, swiftly expressive works, each a quick take on a strong emotion. The musette, bright and forthright, is adapted from the sixth English suite, and the splitting of the keyboard music into parts for two instruments brings out the dance qualities of the piece: the cello and piano might be partners taking a turn around the ballroom. The adagio is different. It is the middle section of an organ piece that Bach wrote at Weimar, and the microphone comes up on a performance already in progress. The pianist is playing a somber, spacious figure; Casals lets out the line of the melody with great deliberation. When after a minute and a half or so the melody winds upward from the dark minor key to the sunny major, the piece seems to be ending—but no. Casals turns it outward and holds it up to the light. The pianist draws a line with the left hand, putting down a cluster of notes on every beat of every bar. The cello is bold, gorgeous, heartbreaking, but it is the piano that is remarkable. It is, literally, marking time, like a church bell in a tower, and to hear it is to eavesdrop on a past era in which the musicians themselves, not the recording equipment, measured out the duration of a performance.

This adagio is a bridge, written to join a toccata and a fugue, and, even excerpted and played on the cello rather than the organ, it has the character of a bridge. This is the first of Casals's Bach recordings to sound like part of a whole.

On February 26, 1928, Casals gave a Sunday-afternoon solo recital at Town Hall on West Forty-third Street in New York. His marriage to Susan Metcalfe had ended, and he returned to Spain alone. Exhausted, he spent a few months recuperating at his estate. He brooded and sulked in the Hall of Remembrance, a personal museum he had created there, featuring mementoes from his tours and travels as well as his gourd-cello and the piano his father had played in El Vendrell. He replaced the estate's tennis court with a neoclassical sculpture garden. Then he rallied and set out on tour again. He went to Paris and London; Vienna, Geneva, Stockholm; Prague, Budapest, Bucharest, Copenhagen. But he did not go to the United States. At first, he kept clear to avoid Metcalfe and her lawyers. Later he would keep clear for other reasons. From this point forward he would be represented in America by his recordings.

>>12>> The HMV recording truck left London, was borne over the Channel, rolled across France, and crossed the border to Barcelona to record the Orquestra Pau Casals.

Electrical recording was now commonplace, and a twelve-inch record had been developed: it held ten minutes of music, not three, on each side, enabling the record companies to release longer works in multidisc albums. Prodded by HMV's Fred Gaisberg, Casals took advantage. Though he was impatient with the recording process, he set down versions of the cello music of Brahms, Haydn, and Boccherini, as well as some works with the trio dubbed the Holy Trinity: Casals on cello, Alfred Cortot on piano, and Jacques Thibaud on violin.

The nickname conceals the intimacy that is the key quality of their most famous recordings: piano trios of Schubert and Beethoven made in London in 1926 and 1928. The records were made with the mobile unit in concert halls— Kingsway and the Queen's Small Hall, a room upstairs from Queen's Hall— and the instruments sound spatially arranged the way they probably were on stage: violin in the center, cello down and a bit to the left, piano thrumming the floorboards. A photograph shows Casals and Thibaud, in suits and starched collars, seated just behind Cortot at the piano, each of them near enough to reach out and touch the others, and their physical closeness suggests an emotional one. They are friends, and more than friends; they are a band of brothers, a secret society; they are Picasso's cubist musicians, restored to three dimensions.

Now they played Brahms with Casals's orchestra in Barcelona, with Casals in charge, Cortot conducting, and Gaisberg at the controls. The Orquestra Pau Casals was its namesake's own creation. "If I have been so happy scratching a violoncello," Casals had said, "how shall I feel when I can possess the greatest of all instruments—the orchestra?" It had emerged alongside the Republican movement. Supported at first with fees from his recitals, by the late twenties (he claimed) it was financially self-supporting. The Orquestra embodied the Republican ideal: collective, but with a strong leader; at once distinctly Catalan and international in its aspirations. The recording of the Brahms Double Concerto suggests these qualities. It is public-spirited in the extreme, an open-armed embrace of the audience and the city given through the sound of many bows thrust in unison.

With the truck set up, Casals also set down a number of short pieces, including two by Bach. They are strong, grave, profound, but small—and are made smaller by the recording, which gives only a partial view, as if through a half-opened window. Of "Komm, süsser Tod" Casals said, "I cannot hear this without being moved in the deepest regions of my soul." With this piece he invited sweet death to come, and with the andante for violin, adapted for cello and piano, he welcomed it.

Two decades earlier Casals, taking part in a performance of Bach's *St. John Passion* in Switzerland, had had a premonition and rushed back to Catalonia, but too late: his father had died—at the very moment, as he told it, when he had felt the premonition through the music. Now, on March 13, 1931, death came for his mother in Barcelona. She was seventy-seven years old, a miracle of fortitude. In a sense, she had always been by his side; in a sense, now he was alone for the first time in his life.

Two weeks later the people of Spain elected a representative government: the aspiration of forward-thinking Spaniards ever since Casals's boyhood, when his father had indoctrinated him in the rights of man and the ills of monarchy.

Casals was offered a position as a minister in the government. He turned it down. But his role as a modern Spanish representative man could not be turned aside. He was fifty-five years old, and he was eminent as well as rich, famous, and accomplished. When he mounted the podium to lead the Orquestra Pau Casals in its commemorative performance of Beethoven's Ninth, he was the best-known person in Catalonia, and the one best positioned to carry forth its culture to the wider world.

The president of the new republic gave him a medal and arranged the loan of a state-owned Stradivarius cello. The fathers of El Vendrell renamed the main square there for him; the city of Barcelona created an Avinguda de Pau Casals. Awards and honors came from abroad.

One was an honorary degree from the University of Edinburgh. He accepted, postponed a trip, and then, in November 1934, went to Scotland. He would receive the degree; he would renew his friendship with Donald Tovey, a composer and Bach expert in Edinburgh; he would give the premiere performance of a concerto Tovey had written for him.

There was one other reason for his visit. Albert Schweitzer was in Edinburgh to give the Gifford lectures, and was staying with Tovey. "I had looked forward to meeting Schweitzer," Casals recalled. "Not only was I familiar with his writings on Bach, but I had of course an intense admiration for him as a man."

Born a year apart, the two of them had lived in Paris at the turn of the century, each a pilgrim from the provinces, and each had carved out an approach to Bach that was rigorous, fiercely personal, and cagey about modernity. As Bach interpreters, they complemented each other: Schweitzer, even as he revived the Bach of ages past, was a man alone in a room, set apart by his medical mission; Casals, even as he invented the sound of solitude, was a missionary for Bach, taking the music to crowds at the ends of the earth. They were two of the most famous Bach performers alive. But they had never met, and, notably, they didn't know each other's approach to Bach well through recordings.

Already the next generation of Bach interpreters were making records of breakthrough clarity and intimacy, in which you can hear the sound-world narrowing down on the individual through improved technology. Andrés

Segovia, Casals's Spanish opposite—Andalusian, self-taught, royalist in politics—was rehabilitating the guitar the way Casals had done the cello, and his transcriptions of work for lute and violin are prim, icy things. Wanda Landowska, born in Warsaw, played a harpsichord custom-built for her to use at the school she ran outside Paris, and her *Goldberg Variations* is an edifice of hammered-out sound: it is as if Bach's bookmatched, cross-hatched patterns are passing on a conveyor belt through the instrument and its keys and levers and pedals are breaking down the music into the raw materials of the Baroque. The Swiss pianist Edwin Fischer's *Well-Tempered Clavier* recordings are something overheard, his playing exact and clangorous under the whetstone of the 78; between each prelude and fugue there is a band of silence where the recorded sound drops out, and it is as if a keyhole to the past has been closed—as if Fischer caught us eavesdropping and has stood up and shut the door.

Yehudi Menuhin had already had a hit with a recording of the Bach double concerto when he recorded Bach's sonatas and partitas for violin in 1934. He was eighteen. He idolized Charles Lindbergh, and his recording of the D-minor partita (to take one example) is a solo flight, a high-wire act done for the eyes of the crowd. "From the very first note of the *Allemande*—to the *Courante*, the *Sarabande*, the *Gigue*, and finally the *Chaconne*—a massive structure is being built," he later explained. The structure is "dependent on a single builder." He is alone in this, holding it up all by himself, and that he is doing it alone is a great achievement, a challenge met, a personal test, rather than a quality of being. We are watching him in his struggle as he strains against the work, now taking hold of it, now nearly faltering, now getting it upright once and for all. But we are not with him, and the recording makes sure of it: there is no headroom in it, no space for us to join the solo artist in his solitude.

Those records were all Society issues, promoted as the first full-length recordings of the classical canon. Albert Schweitzer would begin his own Society recordings of Bach in London before returning to Africa, and he probably played the organ for Casals in Edinburgh. A photograph shows the two of them with Donald Tovey in academic gowns in front of an organ console: Schweitzer, who is sitting, seems twice the size of Casals, who is standing.

Casals played the piece that Tovey had written for him. With Schweitzer looking on, he played some Bach. Then he made to go: he had to catch a train to a recital. Schweitzer was disappointed. "He urged me to stay on," Casals recalled. "He wanted to hear more Bach."

From there the story is a parable of the power of talent and fame to make friends out of strangers. "I had gotten my things together and was hurrying down a corridor when I heard the sound of running footsteps," Casals recalled. "It was Schweitzer. He was all out of breath. He looked at me with that wonderful expression of his which mirrored the great compassion of the man. 'If you must leave,' he said, 'then at least let us say goodbye with intimacy.' He was speaking in French. 'Let us *tutoyer* one another before we separate.' We embraced and parted." It was an affecting goodbye, but the point was clear: Casals had left the saint of self-denial begging for more.

>>13>> "The revolutionary posters were everywhere, flaming from the walls in clean reds and blues that made the few remaining advertisements look like daubs of mud. Down the Ramblas, the wide central artery of the town where crowds of people streamed constantly to and fro, the loud-speakers were bellowing revolutionary songs all day and far into the night. And it was the aspect of the crowds"—George Orwell reported—"that was the queerest thing of all. In outward appearance it was a town in which the wealthy classes had practically ceased to exist. Except for a small number of women and foreigners there were no 'well-dressed' people at all. Practically everyone wore rough working-class clothes, or blue overalls or some variant of the militia uniform. All this was queer and moving. There was much in it that I did not understand, in some ways I did not even like it, but I recognized it immediately as a state of affairs worth fighting for."

For Orwell Spain was a cause, the modern European tug-of-war staged on the "arid square" of Iberia that Auden described. But for Pablo Casals, Spain was a country, his country, and the Spanish Civil War was something personal and painful—an electric shock to the senses, and one from which he would never fully recover.

The Republican victory of 1931 had been shaky, and power passed spasmodically from one side to the other. The fascists—church, army, monarchists—took back the government in 1933. The left formed a so-called Popular Front, uniting democrats, anarchists, and a "fifth column" of international comrades, and sought to regain control. When the new movement won elections in 1934, the fascists sought to spoil its legitimacy. "There were acts of provocation, violence, killings—plots and intrigues. Sometimes one felt the country was a seething volcano," Casals recalled, and went on: "In the summer of 1936, the volcano erupted." The fascists staged a *pronunciamento*: a coup.

The months to follow were "a nightmare of unrelieved horror." The left fought back, supported by the Soviet Union. The right got help—guns—from Italy and Germany. The anarchists stirred up unrest on all sides. It was "neighbor against neighbor, brother against brother, son against father," Casals recalled. The civil war had begun, and it would claim 75,000 lives by the end of the summer.

Casals later spoke of the "ruin" of Barcelona and the "courage and dignity" with which ordinary Catalans had stood against the fascists and cared for the stricken on all sides. He had stood as an artist in support of the Republic—playing benefit concerts, appealing to the anarchists (for peace) and to the government (for order), and chairing an international committee of artists and writers. But music was not enough, and he had joined the humanitarian effort, too: "When I see innocent blood spilled and the tears of innocent victims of injustice, it becomes more important to me than my music and all my 'cello recitals!"

He was entering into the role of his seniority: wise elder, witness, person of conscience, man of unshakable moral authority. But he also responded to events in a more characteristic way. For hours at a stretch he sat in recording studios in foreign countries and played the major works in the cello repertory into the microphone, trying to transform the shock of war into art.

He left Barcelona for London in October 1936, as Orwell was making plans to leave London for Barcelona. He had been abroad once already that fall, visiting friends in Paris. There were plenty of reasons for him to get out of Spain. Anarchists had menaced him at his estate, whose splendor allied him with the ruling class in the eyes of the populace no matter where his heart lay. His younger brother Lluís had clashed with a new Communist mayor in town, and there was a chance that the Casals estate, with its beach and sculpture gardens, its stone lions and hand-chiseled Apollo, would be impounded by the Party. Before leaving he burned his correspondence, which was thick with letters from deposed royals—proof (to those who sought such proof) that he was an enemy of the people.

"I did not go abroad with an easy heart—I felt my place was at home with my countrymen in their dreadful ordeal," he recalled. And yet he went. Away, he would be safe; home, he might be murdered. Besides, he had made concert and recording commitments and he wanted to honor them. The fees he would earn could be applied to good causes.

Once gone, he was distraught over Barcelona. The accounts he gave in his memoirs suggest that he was having a nervous breakdown, akin to the one that had led him to try to kill himself in his boyhood. He had trouble playing in public, such was "the choking pain inside me. I would read in the newspapers about the battles ravaging my land, the burning towns, the hungry children in cities under siege. While I was playing, I knew bombs were falling. I could not sleep at night. Often when I spoke with people, I felt as if someone else were talking and I was not there. After concerts I would walk the streets, alone in torment . . ."

What was he doing in London, fiddling while Barcelona burned?

The answer is in the fine print of his records: *Recorded in London, 1936*; <*rec. 1936*>; **rec. 1936*; *Enregistré/recorded/aufgonnomen: London, 23.XI.1936.* Consumed by events, busy with his orchestra, he had not entered a recording studio in six years, and in those years there had finally emerged a studio which yielded recordings worthy of the music: EMI Studios in Abbey Road, St. John's Wood. In one week in London that fall he recorded more music than he had ever recorded at once. A Boccherini concerto; a fresh, expansive arrangement of Bruch's *Kol Nidre*, long compressed to fit onto 78s; a sonata by Beethoven, and the second sonata of Brahms—which, in its subtlety, its lightness, its micro-fibered Mitteleuropean emotion, is a last bastion of old-world chamber music at the edge of the wild sea of modernity.

All that—and two Bach cello suites, which Casals entered into the record once and for all. Why, after nearly forty years, did he decide to record them?

Possibly in Edinburgh he heard Albert Schweitzer speak of recording the organ works and was emboldened to make his own Society Series recording.

The story usually told is that Fred Gaisberg got him to do it. For years Gaisberg had been asking Casals to record Bach. The merger of HMV and Columbia as EMI made it possible: with the Society Series, EMI could pay Casals a high fee. The merger also made it necessary: it brought the company another standout cellist, Emanuel Feuermann, who was eager to record the suites if Casals didn't want to do so. So Gaisberg booked a session for Casals to play the Boccherini B-flat concerto with the London Symphony Orchestra, then persuaded him to play Bach, too.

Even if the idea came from Gaisberg, surely Casals finally decided for himself that the occasion was right to record the suites. The Bach suites are the first of the works he recorded in London, not works squeezed in during the time between other sessions, as is often said. And he had definite personal reasons for doing so. He was nearly sixty years old. His mother was dead. The

Republic was foundering. The blood of his fellow Catalans ran in the streets. His own life was at risk. Once, bandits had broken in as he played the cello at his estate outside Barcelona and demanded that he inform on a neighbor.

EMI's new studio complex was an alternative to all this: state-of-the-art, forward-looking, hermetic, a shelter from the storm. The "steel monster" of the microphone could make a recording that approximated the sound of the music; the steel disc cutter could inscribe it and store it for better days, entering it into the historical record.

"An artist must be strong enough to feel independent of everything that has been done, and of everything he has learned, and he must convince himself that to 'feel independent' of any routine or tradition is his main duty and purpose." Casals had felt that way since he first came upon the Bach cello suites in his boyhood. Now, in 1936, he had something fresh to express in Bach, a stance toward life that could find expression in the suites as nowhere else. And he had, in EMI Studios, the possibility of producing recordings that could convey his conception of the suites as solo music par excellence.

That week's *Illustrated London News* carried a photo spread of war-torn Spain—big brown-and-white pictures of "Madrid as Seen by Franco's Men," a bomber's-eye view of the city, and a column of smoke rising from the land in "the Most Important Onslaught of the Civil War that has Brought Devastation to Spain." It was a feature crafted to make the British reader feel that the Spanish Civil War was very grave and very far away.

Heartsick, homesick, Casals would make a record of the cello suites for the reason he had always played them: to encounter life in its fullness. He would play them for himself, in consolation; he would play them for Barcelona, so as to evoke a world and time now past in the strict sense but still existing in memory and art. Once he had looked to the suites as models for independence. Now he would play them as spiritual exercises—lessons, learned from Bach, in how to stand alone.

>>14>>   He climbed the steps, rang the bell, and was shown in. Outside, the house looked like several others on Abbey Road, except that the windows were blacked out. Inside, it smelled of burning coal.

There were three studios warrening the house: Studio One, the one big enough for an orchestra, with a late-model electric pipe organ screwed into one wall; Studio Two, designed for chamber music; and Studio Three, the site of choice for piano recordings, and, this day—Monday, November 23, 1936—for the cello music of Bach.

The studio in effect was a concert hall turned inside out. The technician in lab coat might have been a ticket taker, peering through a small window and speaking to Casals via intercom. A pair of microphones faced him like metallic hands about to clap. There was no audience, no curtains or chandeliers, no gold leaf, no extramusical life leaking in through the sealed door. Really, he was alone here.

"Are we all ready?"

After nearly fifty years, he was ready: so he began, running a scale down the neck of the cello from C to lowest C, moving to the middle, then away and back.

The Suite in C Major is the third one in the set, and if you are used to hearing them in order, and thinking of them as a whole, the third suite feels like the vital center: it is here, you say to yourself, that the suites gain assurance, claim territory, take flight, start to sing. Plenty of experts have thought so: one standard account sees the six suites as a *Gradus ad Parnassum*—an ascent from simple to complex in which the cello steps out of an accompanying role and becomes a solo instrument, as "increasingly individual formal elements are combined with a gradual increase in technical difficulty."

It makes sense. The interpretive schemes applied to Bach usually do. But for Pablo Casals the Suite in C Major was a beginning. It was the Bach suite he played when he first played a whole suite in public in Barcelona in 1901. It was the suite he played into the brass horn in New York in 1915 and 1916 but left unfinished. Now it was the first suite that he played at EMI Studios in London. To hear it as a beginning, and as *the* beginning in the experience of this musician with whom the recorded history of the cello suites begins, is to hear it all over again—and to hear, and feel, and grasp it anew the way Casals tried to do when he decided to make a recording of it.

In what sense is it a beginning? It is in C, the middle of the keyboard and of Bach's well-tempered world: both books of the *Well-Tempered Clavier* begin with preludes and fugues in C major. It is in the key of the cello (Cello), whose strings, low to high, are C, G, D, and A. And it begins with a figure that could be a finger exercise or warm-up riff, running down the neck from C to lowest C—the very scale to which the suite returns at the end, the cello chasing its tail.

But it sounds like a beginning for other reasons. More than the other suites, it is a group of independent parts—six short pieces that stand on their own rather than developing one another. It is a suite that is a series of beginnings, or, to put it differently, inventions—melodies conceived and nurtured and then let go.

Allemande, courante, sarabande, minuet, gavotte, bourée, gigue: Scholars call attention to the names of the dances the suites are based on, they savor them, so as to dress the music in britches and clogs—to place the suites in the social history of music that was codified in the Baroque and made high art by Bach. But the piquant old-world terms can be distracting. They can obscure the obvious quality of these three-minute solo pieces. These are not folk dances uprooted from court or square. They no longer are, at any rate. They are songs, and the cellist is singing them.

Casals liked to point out that the maid at his house outside Barcelona could hum the preludes and fugues from the *Well-Tempered Clavier*, so accustomed was she to hearing them played on the piano in the morning. So it is with the parts of the third suite. They have the things that make a song a song: they are short, memorable, hummable, and somehow independent of the singer. They can survive on their own.

They are not songs in the forms we know. There is no ballad here, no hymn, no anthem, no lover's prayer. They are songs as songs must have sounded when music began, straying from a keynote and then finding a way home. In each one the cellist goes pleasurably away—the central C—and just as pleasurably returns. He scampers off (the allemande). He goes and comes back again and again (the courante). He goes with fear and trembling (the sarabande); he goes stridently off into the gloaming (the gigue), bent on staying away as long as he can. In all of them, he goes away joyfully, as he did when a young man—not in exile, not in flight, but on a great adventure.

With the Suite in C Major, Casals is heard in full voice for the first time. Undertaken late in his sixth decade, this session is the true beginning of his career as a recording artist. The legend says that his voice was there all along. It is there, robust and brawny, in the acoustic recordings he made in the teens. But it is there in contrast to the murky backing music, the boxed air of the hall, and the glaze of surface noise from wax cylinder and spinning disc. At Abbey Road all of a sudden his voice is all there on the recording, complete and immediate, wholly itself. The space of the hall is gone. So is the gap between cello and microphone. So (mostly) is the surface noise. This is the sound of the music of Bach; this is the sound of the cello and the person playing it.

It is not perfect sound, but it is good enough, even most of a century later.

As with Schweitzer's Toccata and Fugue in D Minor, there is no reason to wish it any different. Schweitzer's recording is an evocative sound at the far end of a dark tunnel, gaining power from its occlusions and hidden spaces. Casals's recording actually sounds clearer for its age; the austerity of the studio—a small room, a single channel—lends the music character and purpose, as if all but the voice has been left out.

>>15>> EMI Studios made recordings on a schedule of three sessions a day: "10 am to 1 pm, 2 pm until 5 pm and 7 pm through to 10 pm, with no exceptions." With the Suite in C Major complete, Casals, recorded another suite—the second, in D minor—the same day. So most sources say. Whatever the case, the second suite, in his hands, stands in frank counterpoint to the first. That one was all beginnings; this one is a series of second thoughts, reconsiderations. There is no through-line or leitmotif. But this time the whole is the thing. The parts do not stand alone: they exist only in relation.

"Nothing is more difficult than to rediscover the marvellous simplicity of live shapes," Casals said, and explained: "First they must find an echo in our minds, after which we must pursue the work of investigation and elucidation of different problems." In the second suite he uses the live shapes of the different parts to approach a problem from different angles. With the prelude—angular, unsettling—he states the problem. With the second part he restates it, defining the terms of debate with several harsh strokes of the bow: you can see the orator at the rostrum, the preacher in the pulpit, discoursing on affairs of the day. In the third he takes a run at it, climbing up to the top of the instrument and slaloming toward the bottom with jagged shards of eighth notes, as if to consider the full range of possible responses. With the fourth, the slow movement, or sarabande, he considers: Well, all right, what should I do? In the fifth, all stately rigor, he comes to a conclusion, which he then repeats: This is right; this is what I should do. The sixth and final movement seals the point, ending on the emphatic note—a big, round low D—that was missing at the beginning.

And what is the problem? It is the old problem of the anxious searcher—the mystic in the interior castle, the poet-pilgrim in a dark wood not sure how to proceed. Which way is the right way? Where will the truth be found? Those three opening notes might be *"Je sais pas,"* or "I don't know." The way is unclear, but the music has the clarity and sobriety whose absence it seems to describe.

Casals liked to say that in music "the work of preparation ruled by discipline should finally disappear, so that the elegance and freshness of the form should strike us as being spontaneous." There is no record of his preparations for the Abbey Road sessions, but whatever he did to prepare, it worked. In its elegance and freshness, his second suite sounds spontaneous. And its spontaneity, or seeming spontaneity, suggests why he was reluctant to make a recording of it. This second suite is not an argument so much as an exploration, a minor-key adventure. It moves so slowly at first that it might not be moving at all. The cellist is no recitalist, no missionary or crowd-pleaser. He is a spelunker, cave-crawling in the dark. In mystical terms, we'd say he is following the *via negativa*; in musical terms, we'd say he is going off the charts—improvising. He clambers onto a rope bridge—not a melody, really, but a somber, focused sound—and wriggles forward into the gorge so that it is hard to tell exactly when he has left solid rock for thin air. The rope bridge toggles from side to side: a bit farther this way or that and it will flip him over into the streambed below. But it doesn't: the farther out he goes, the steadier he gets, until he is putting one foot ahead of the other. High above the rocks he spreads his arms. His movement is beautiful to behold, but there is no spectacle in it. We feel now how recorded music is not like live music. This is not a performance. We are not watching him. We are with him. We are holding on to him. He is carrying us.

Monday, November 23, 1936, was a good day for recorded music. While Pablo Casals was playing Bach at Abbey Road, Robert Johnson was playing his blues in an ad hoc recording studio in a hotel room in San Antonio, Texas, making the records that are for the modern blues what the Bach suites are for the cello: at once their high point and their point of origin.

On the surface, Johnson is the anti-Casals—a composer rather than an interpreter, a virtuoso recognized only posthumously. But the two are alike in what Greil Marcus, in *Mystery Train*, called the "emotional commitment" to the music.

Today the legend derived from Johnson's "Cross Road Blues"—that he sold his soul to the devil at a small-town crossroads in exchange for other-worldly abilities as a singer and guitarist—is as vivid a legend as any in modern music. But the aura attached to Johnson derives as much from the intensity of the recordings he made as from his songs per se, the facts of his life, or the story of his death at age twenty-seven when a rival for a woman's affections put poison in his whiskey.

The notion that Johnson sold his soul to the devil arose because he left the

Mississippi Delta an indifferent musician and returned a few months later making blues fiercer than any before or since. Since then, he has been seen as the boldest of the Delta blues singers—a restless, haunted man who sang the blues out of urgent necessity, untainted by electricity, the profit motive, or the hunger for fame.

Maybe he did meet the devil at a crossroads and make an exchange of gifts. What he certainly did is acquire a phonograph—say, in the business district at the crossroads of Desoto Street and the present Highway 61 in Clarksdale— and the phonograph is probably the source of his sudden virtuosity. In the late 1920s documentarists arrived in Mississippi, lugging huge "field units" from one plantation to the next to record the music they found being played there, and by 1930, 78-rpm records by Charley Patton, Bukka White, Son House, and Crying Sam Collins were for sale in shops and juke joints across the South. Those singers had assimilated influences over time, learning from local players or from musicians passing through. Robert Johnson was able to learn from them all at once by sitting beside the phonograph with his guitar and playing their records over and over. Recording technology was the devil that sponsored his virtuosity.

Other musicians heard those records too, but Johnson was the first blues singer formed primarily by recordings. His own blues (as Robert Palmer made clear in *Deep Blues* and Elijah Wald developed further in *Escaping the Delta*) worked variations on songs recorded by Kokomo Arnold, Peetie Wheatstraw, and Skip James. The days he spent recording his music—in the San Antonio hotel room on November 23 and 27, 1936, and in a warehouse in Dallas seven months later—weren't efforts to document the situation on the ground so much as to outdo his rivals and make their sounds his own.

Because the best accounts of Johnson stress the darkness of his outlook, the actual sound of the recordings can come as a surprise, akin to the surprise of seeing the famous photograph of this prince of darkness wearing a pin-striped suit, fedora, and carefully knotted tie. He is not supposed to look like that; he is not supposed to sound like this. The guitar playing is bright and chimey, like a banjo as the open strings ring out. Likewise Johnson's voice. This man who would have possession over Judgment Day sings in a high tenor, more like Caruso than Blind Willie Johnson. Where the clarity of Casals's Abbey Road recordings makes him our contemporary, the limits of Johnson's hotel-room sides make him seem earlier and so more advanced than he was. The moment in "Me and the Devil Blues" in which Johnson wishes for his dead body to be buried at the side of the road "so my old evil spirit can catch a Greyhound bus and ride" seems anachronistically modern. So even more does the "Phonograph Blues," in which the phonograph with its pointed tonearm is an image of the power of a man to get and hold a woman's attention through music, with a little help from technology.

>>16>> In December 1936, Casals went to the Catalan south of France in a preview of exile. He visited a friend in Prades and was beguiled by the place: small, within shouting distance of Spain, unravaged by modernity, oriented toward the Catalan holy mountain Le Canigou and the Benedictine abbey of Saint-Michel-de-Cuxa. The landscape, he found, "acted as a sedative"; the language made him feel at home.

He rented a room in the hotel on the main street and stayed into February 1937, then made plans to return as soon as possible. Already Prades was becoming his "Pyrennean retreat," a place where he, so public-minded for so long, could be alone.

In Prades he played the Bach cello suites over and over. After recording the second and third suites, he was committed to recording the whole set, a serious undertaking. "It took me over a year to prepare" the cello suites for recording, he later said. He was trying to discover them again, and he was adjusting his approach to suit the recording process. He feared that "once the playing has gone through a machine, it loses the vitality the artist has put into it." He found his tone alien and unrecognizable when a recording was played back to him. And he felt that the recording process, with its emphasis on "external perfection," could be "conducive to mechanical performance" rather than a musical one.

"The fact is that when making a gramophone record where every little detail is registered, the imposition on the artist is a real servitude," he declared. So he fought it. Just as he was determined not to be a slave to the score, he was determined not to become a slave to the machine. In Prades he sought, through Bach, to stay free.

On April 26, with Casals at his estate outside Barcelona, the Luftwaffe, in support of Franco, carpet-bombed the Basque town of Guernica. Fifteen hundred people were killed, most of them civilians. The Spanish Civil War entered a new and terrifying phase.

That day Casals traveled to Prague for a performance of Dvořák's cello concerto with the Czech Philharmonic and the conductor George Szell. Fred Gaisberg of EMI had arranged for cellist and orchestra to make a recording of the concerto the day after the concert, for release as a set of 78s. In his memoirs he recalled the session: "Casals flew from Barcelona, looking more dead than alive"—whether from the strain of travel from France, to Spain, to Czechoslovakia, or out of horror over the bombing of Guernica, Gaisberg didn't say. "The dress rehearsal and concert before packed houses were a huge success. Casals's *élan* and stamina kept him going for the whole of the next day when over twelve unsurpassed (78 rpm) records were made . . ." with cellist and orchestra pausing repeatedly to accommodate the breaks between sides.

It was Gaisberg's role to make big claims about the records he produced, but in this case the superlative is apt. The opening passage of the Dvořák concerto may be the most exciting thing Casals ever recorded. A photograph captures the drama of it. Casals is seated at the lip of the stage with orchestra and pillared gallery behind him. His head is that of an emeritus professor, with rimless glasses and big-bowled pipe, but his body is that of a gladiator, bearing the cello like a shield and the bow like a lance pointed outward, holding back the world's thugs and marauders.

The concerto begins with a giant step of an orchestral figure, a kick of the jackboot in B minor, which makes clear that something awful is afoot. A pastoral in the major sketches the scene that is about to be despoiled. Then with the orchestra already at a climax the cello breaks in. With a roundhouse of a B, Casals punches through the string accompaniment; then he moves down the instrument, playing the low notes so loudly that they rattle the microphones. As he shimmies back up the neck, tailed by the strings, and begins to bend and sway with the force of the music, fiddling this way and that, his voice in the cello, familiar from so many other recordings, seems to swell and fill his body. He stands upright now, the human animal in full cry, wounded but able to say what ails him and how he might be made whole again.

"As the last record was made," Gaisberg recalled, Casals "collapsed completely and allowed us to take him to his hotel, where we saw that he was carefully looked after. We waited until he lit up his pipe and got it going and then left, knowing the little man was all right."

Gaisberg called the Dvořák "something rare and precious snatched from the cauldron of Europe before the storm." It is a recording as a piece of the historical record; it is history heard loud and clear.

For a year Casals toured the world. He had ceased to play in Germany when Hitler took power, and had crossed off Italy when Mussolini fell into the Nazi line. Now he went to several dozen cities, racing to set foot in each once more before war broke out. He played in Paris, Boulogne, and Barcelona;

made a two-month tour of South America; played London, Amsterdam, Prague, Vienna, Budapest, Bucharest, Zurich; went to North Africa—Rabat, Casablanca, Oran, Algiers, and Tunis; and nearly went to Tokyo, too. Many of the concerts raised money for refugees of the civil war, but surely Casals had a deeper motive. He had been an emissary for classical music, a circuit rider for the cello. Now he was a target for fascists, a man on the run, a displaced person before the fact, and he was giving voice to the experience through the cello.

"Periodically I returned to Spain," he recalled, "and each time I saw more frightful evidence of the havoc and agony of the war. Great areas of Barcelona were in ruin. Skeletons of buildings on every side. The city overflowed with refugees. Food was desperately short . . . Thousands were homeless and orphaned; thousands had been wounded and killed in the endless air raids."

He played benefit concerts in Barcelona all along, and on October 17, 1938, he played a concert at the Liceu—site of so many grand evenings with his orchestra—to benefit children uprooted by the war. The government broadcast the concert on the radio and arranged a two-hour pause in the workday so anybody who wanted to listen could do so. During the intermission, Casals, standing before the audience, which included government ministers and wounded civilians on stretchers, gave a speech in English and French, meant as a message for people listening on the radio abroad. "If you allow Hitler to win in Spain," he declared, "you will be the next victims of his madness. The war will spread to Europe, to the whole world. Come to the aid of our people!"

For Casals the concert was itself a message: a demonstration of "how men and women, fighting for their very lives, at a moment of gravest crisis, found time to express their love of art and beauty."

He had delivered the same message a different way at a rehearsal the day before. As he conducted the orchestra, bombs fell nearby. "The whole building shook, and the musicians scattered in the hall—as was not unnatural," he recalled. "I picked up a cello on the stage and began to play a Bach suite. The musicians returned to their places . . ."

He had delivered the message through recordings, too. His life was so thick with events just then that his biographers pass over the sessions, but in the whirlwind of performing and pontificating he took two days in Paris—June 2 and 3, 1938—to record the first and sixth Bach cello suites at Pathé's studio in the rue Pelouze.

Heard together, they are a matched pair: serenity and exaltation set in counterpoint as two sides of the same world-embracing emotion. They are so untouched by events, or so it seems, that the notion of Casals bringing history to bear on Bach comes into question—unless you consider that Casals was trying to bring Bach to bear on history, turning to the music to show him the way and carry him through.

The first suite, in G major, was presumably the first Bach cello music Casals heard the day he discovered the sheet music of the suites in Barcelona and brought it home, and it is the first encounter with the cello suites for most people. In the opening arpeggio we hear Bach booting up, kick-starting the mechanism of the suites as a whole.

Now Casals turned to the first suite in a state of in-betweenness. He was sixty-one, still in the middle of his life. He was suspended between Spain and France, between citizenship and exile, between political action and witness. He was midway through the recordings of the cello suites, and the project placed him at a midpoint between his careers as a recitalist and as a recording artist.

The challenge was to make the first suite sound like a beginning—to step out of wartime and into the peaceable kingdom of Bach's music. For Casals this—how to begin again—was *the* challenge for the musician. "Every spring the leaves of the trees re-appear with the spring, but they are different every time," he observed: "How can we expect to produce a vital performance if we don't re-create the work every time?"

With the first suite he shows how. There is so much to single out in the recording: the slow unfurling of the prelude, as the melody is let out like a kite on a string; the way Casals makes the cello at once sing and growl in the Allemande; the range of inflections he gives to the semicolon of paired notes that ends each figure in the Courante; the bagpiper's rasp of chords in the sarabande, as the skein of sound is threaded through the loom of art. But it is all there from the very first note, in which Casals declares his commitment to new sounds. In the Dvořák concerto he entered aggressively; in this Bach suite he slips in quietly, almost accidentally, pulling the first note out of nowhere with the bow, so that the note, a low G, goes from soft to loud from the beginning of the stroke to the end. It is a sexual entry, a lover's deft approach. All of a sudden we are in: the melody is moving on its own, the music leading the musician.

Casals played the Suite in G Major hundreds of times; recording it, he could play that first note only one way, but for the listener it is always surprising. This is what he was doing in Prades: working against technology's tendency to rob the music of vitality through repetition. Though not fond of recordings, he found a way to make his experience of the suites correspond to the listener's, so that we, like he, hear them invented anew every time.

In this, Casals showed the kind of foresight that he admired in Bach. "The development of the 'cello as a solo instrument is relatively recent," he said. "Bach is an exception, in that he foresaw, two hundred years ago, the development of the instrument."

The sixth suite shows what he means. The last in the set, it is a beginning even so, in that Bach wrote it for an instrument then not in common use. This was either the five-string cello or the smaller *violoncello piccolo*, an instrument custom-made for Bach by a local luthier. For Casals, informed by scholarship proposing that Bach had written it for a third and even smaller five-string instrument (the *viola pomposa*), the sixth suite showed Bach's exceptional powers of invention. "We constantly notice Bach's preoccupation to go beyond the technical limitations of the instruments of the period," Casals said, and it was just like Bach that after writing five suites he "foresaw new ways of using the upper register of the violoncello which, so far, were unknown." In any case, Casals plays the suite in a way that brings out its kinship with the works for solo violin. The prelude anticipates Appalachian music, as terraces of harmony and counterpoint are chiseled out from beneath the sawn-off high D that opens it, and then, below a D in a lower register, the unpacking commences all over again. Casals brings out the folk character of the suite, droning on the strings. He is not building a structure or developing an argument. He is making music.

>>17>> "An affront to human dignity is an affront to me; and to protest injustice is a matter of conscience. Are human rights of less importance to an artist than to other men? Does being an artist exempt one from his obligations as a man? If anything, the artist has a particular responsibility, because he has been granted special sensitivities and perceptions, and because his voice may be heard when other voices are not. Who, indeed, should be more concerned than the artist with the defense of liberty and free inquiry, which are essential to his very creativity?"

He was in an apartment in Paris, bent double in torment. "I shut myself up in a room with all the blinds drawn and sat staring into the dark. Perhaps in the darkness I hoped to find forgetfulness, relief from the pain. But an endless panorama passed before my eyes—horrors I had witnessed in the war, scenes from my childhood, faces of dear ones, cities in ruin and weeping women and children. I remained in that room for days, unable to move. I could not bear to see or speak with anyone. I was perhaps near to madness or death. I did not really want to live."

He had left Spain in January 1939, taking a handwritten honorary degree from the city university and facing a death threat from a Falangist commandant, who told him his arms would be cut off at the elbows if he returned to Spain. In despair, he went to Prades. Once a figurehead of the crafty new Catalan *modernisme*, now he was one of several hundred thousand Catalans— men, women, and children, refugees and soldiers, the wounded and the bereaved, the lame and the halt—going over the mountains in heavy weather as the fascists seized Barcelona.

The proprietor of the Grand Hotel passed along complaints from the other guests: Casals's cello, keening through the walls, was too much for them to bear.

From his room, then, he acted directly. He helped organize a relief effort, renting a truck to bring bread and water to the refugees, who had been herded into camps just over the border and left to fend for themselves behind the barbed wire. Many people had written him letters, asking him for help, and he sought to answer each one, enclosing some coins or franc notes.

He played a concert in London in March and one in Cannes in April. In June he went to Paris, and there, at the Pathé studio, he recorded the fourth and fifth suites: Tuesday, June 13, 1939.

To the question of whether history can resound in music, this session is the answer. With it Casals brought to fruition a fifty-year encounter with the music of Bach, and with it he completed his anxious counterpoint to life during wartime.

He was staying in the apartment near the Place de la Porte de Champerret where he had spent two weeks in a darkened room earlier in the year. He was better now, but just barely. He was committed to expressing what he felt through music, and the feelings of torment were still fresh. Already in London and Paris he had made the recording studio a safe house, a hall of remembrance. Now he made the arduous fifth cello suite itself a site for his anguish— not just a darkened room but a camera obscura, where images from the outside world, concentrated by a pinhole, show through with great clarity and power.

The circumstances suggest that Casals may have hurried through the fourth suite in order to get to the fifth. The fourth, in E flat, is the least distinctly his. It is not introspective like the second suite, or faced outward like the first, third, and sixth. In its exact arpeggios, its sequenced sixteenth notes, his performance is strikingly literal. It is not a spiderweb, a staircase, a suspension bridge: it is a Bach suite, straightforwardly played. And it is rushed at times, or so it seems: Casals hastens through the downward passages of the allemande, thwacks a string and makes an off note in the Gigue.

Even so, it is as beautiful a recording, in its ways, as any there is. Cool, severe, relatively uninflected, it is an introduction to the strenuous life and an early example of the austere approach to recorded Bach. Heard today, the sarabande, for example, resembles one of the arias—now cherished set-pieces for soprano and harpsichord—that Bach wrote into a notebook to be sung in the house. On the cello, the music is passed back and forth between the melody on the thin strings and the counterpoint on the thick ones, and in Casals's hands this song without words is medieval in its delicacy, a sacred drama carved in ivory.

The fifth suite, in C minor, comes as a counterblast of expressionism. The Picasso comparison is inescapable; the recording is Casals's *Guernica*—an agonized response to the horrors of war on a grand scale and in his own distinctive idiom.

The resemblances are real, but in this instance the music of Bach is best compared with the music of Bach. If the legend is to be believed, Casals was the first musician since Bach himself to be confident of the cello's power to sketch a whole world in sound. The fifth suite is Casals's Harrowing of Hell, his "Christ lag in Todesbanden"—a descent to the underworld where no light shines, to a sunken Barcelona where the pillared monument to Cristofo Colombo and the church of the Sagrada Familia are covered in darkness.

Scordatura is a technique whereby one string of an instrument is tuned up or down from standard pitch—a cello's A string down to G, for example. Tuned that way, the cello's tone becomes darker, thicker with overtones, more ponderous—so much so that some Baroque musicians called it *discordatura*. Bach wrote the fifth suite for this tuning, and Casals took full advantage. The first note is a tremendous low blow, like his forced entry in the Dvořák concerto but without any preliminaries from the orchestra. One man is playing one instrument, but the sound is symphonic: you can practically see a conductor thrust his arms downward and hear the massed sound swell out to the walls of the concert hall—except there is no concert hall, just the four walls of the recording studio and a pair of steel-tipped microphones.

With those first long strokes of the bow, a line is being drawn, a series of ultimatums issued. I will not. Here I stand. Get back. Do no more.

There is a long pause; then the music starts moving again, the bow going back and forth, as if setting out alternatives or delivering messages at a checkpoint. They come in paired sets of three, extracted from the depths of the cello. This is wrong. You will pay. The world knows. Enough is enough. A risk is being taken with each one. each stroke of the bow pushes past some unstated limit, rattling the recording equipment.

Casals has touched bottom, pushed low notes past their natural limits with the microphone. In the next section he finds his way back to a middle ground. He might be singing a dirge on the battleground as the smoke clears; the music stays in place as he surveys the damage—the collapsed towers, the skeletal buildings with women and children huddled within, the bodies of the dead blocking traffic.

He liked to say the cello was his only weapon, and with the Courante he goes on the attack. A dance movement couldn't be any less like a dance than this. He strikes out. He strikes back. He takes huge bow-strokes, like a samurai slashing the air, or a lumberjack chopping the wood that will go to make the cello. Even the abrupt ending has a physical effect, a blow with the blunt end.

Then in the sarabande he considers the dead. This section has the fewest notes of any section in the suites, and the drama is one of skips and gaps. It is more a Kandinsky than a Picasso: a series of points connected in empty space, spasms of color against the darkness.

With the fifth suite the world, as Casals sees it, is fully, darkly rendered. It is a world whose borders are at once the borders of modern Europe and the sides of his head.

There is one more section, the Gavotte. In it an odd thing happens. Casals comes back in. For some technical reason, the room is more audible than before, and so is the man sitting in it. Now we can see him and hear him, in the recording studio, sleeves rolled up, pipe tucked between his lips, breaking away, a minute or so in, to play the flattened jig Bach slyly inserted between the upright solemnities of the piece. It is surprising, fitting, even charming. It is the artist at the finish, giving the work his signature.

PART III

Playing Together

>>1>> Bach was in jail: and there, in compulsory solitude, it is said, he began to compose the cat's cradle of prelude and fugue that is the *Well-Tempered Clavier*, because jail was "a place where boredom, ennui, and the absence of any kind of musical instrument forced him to resort to this pastime."

It is a good story, but there is no telling whether it is true. In 1717 Bach was offered a position as chief musician to a prince in Köthen, at double the money he was making in the ducal court at Weimar. He took it, and received a signing bonus of a month's salary or more. When the duke of Weimar heard the news he refused to let Bach go—especially because the deal had been brokered by his cousin and rival. The duke told Bach not to go. Bach, insisting on his independence, lost his temper. The duke had him jailed, and kept him there thirty days, then set him free to his new assignment.

Bach's biographers suggest that time spent in jail for insubordination was commonplace, just one of the quasi-feudal terms of a musician's employment. But for Bach it was more than a career setback and an annoyance. It was a challenge to his sense of his calling. In jail, he was no servant of God in music. He was away from organ, clavier, and choir; he was away from his wife and children for as long as he had ever been. He was out of the public eye just when he was finally gaining renown.

He was eager to take up the new appointment. He had sought to leave Weimar for several years—auditioning for an organist's job in one town, playing at Good Friday services in another. A pay raise and a new title, *Konzertmeister,* had kept him in the duke's employ (and kept him writing church cantatas, a condition of the role), but he found it hard to compose there. The death of Johann Ernst—the clavier student who had brought the cache of sheet music from Holland—led to four months of ritual silence at the palace, a dry season of mourning. A quarrel between the duke, Wilhelm Ernst, and his cousin Ernst August led the one to forbid musicians to play at the other's court. Then, when the duke's Kapellmeister died, the duke refused to promote Bach to take his place.

In the midst of these conflicts Bach provided music for Ernst August's wedding. The bride, Eleonore Wilhelmine, was a sister of Leopold, the prince of Saxe-Köthen, and the wedding was held at a palace on the Saale River, with Bach leading an ensemble from behind the clavier. It was after hearing him play that day (and twice more) that Leopold, a young man who had just acceded to the throne, offered him a job as court keyboardist and concertmaster. Not only a doubling of his salary made the offer attractive. The prince was a musician himself. The prince was a Calvinist, not a Lutheran, and Calvin's strictures on liturgy—no concertizing, only sung psalms—meant that there would be no great demand for church music. The prince would be more patron than overseer. Bach would be free to make music for house and family, not chiefly for the church, a freedom he had never had before.

He took the position; then suddenly he was in jail, executing preludes and fugues mentally as the hours passed. As a boy he had reached through the slats of a cabinet to draw music out; now he was trapped inside, and the bar lines of the music in his mind corresponded to the bars of his confinement.

It seems unlikely that the *Well-Tempered Clavier* could have been written in confinement. The work is two sets of twelve preludes and fugues, forty-eight in all, a many-sided figure of wholeness, harmony, and radiance. But it is possible that the work was begun in jail. The title is inadvertently suggestive; it may be a hint of Bach's predicament in the title, a suggestion that the music's wholeness, harmony, and radiance is compensatory—that Bach wrote these "well-tempered" pieces in response to his loss of temper. Heard that way, the pairs of prelude and fugue suggest moral qualities—passion and discipline, freedom and obedience, emotion expressed and emotion held in check.

Once out of jail, Bach hastened to Köthen, seventy miles northeast of Weimar. The story is that he went there right away in order to play music for the prince's birthday. He had more obvious reasons to want to get there quickly. He had not played music in a month. He had not seen his family. In jail he had had occasion to consider what it meant for him to be away—what form his music would take if he were no longer around to play it, and how his children would be trained in music if he were not there to teach them.

The music he made in Köthen in the years that followed is his answer. With his wife, a daughter, three sons, and his wife's sister, who helped with the child care, he settled in a spacious apartment just outside the palace gates. The place had a music room, and there in the next few years he devised works that, while spectacularly artful, were also tools for the musical and moral instruction of his children.

In jail more than ever he had had to conceive his musical inventions as works existing apart from his role as the performer and teacher of them. The *Well-Tempered Clavier* is a demonstration of a way of tuning the instrument so that it sounds more or less harmonious in any key. More than that, it is a demonstration of the extraordinary order and clarity of Bach's approach to composition: a prelude and a fugue in each major and minor key, the pieces harmonizing with one another like strings on a well-tuned instrument. The musicians' term for it—the "48"—captures its suprapersonal qualities. It is Bach's periodic table of the elements. The preludes and fugues are his theorems and formulae; all together they are a correspondence course in melody, harmony, and counterpoint. They are the lessons he would give, the classes he would teach.

>>2>> The prince liked to travel, and he liked to take musicians with him. He liked music in the midst of life, all about him, and his pursuit of this pleasure, one so commonplace today, was intense and involving enough to shape Bach's life in the next few years—to shape it, as things turned out, more than Bach might have liked.

Leopold had become prince at the age of ten, and while the principality was ruled by his mother he studied in Berlin and then spent two years on a tour of Europe, going to The Hague and Amsterdam; Venice, Rome, and Florence; Vienna, Prague, Dresden, and Leipzig, meeting musicians and taking on provisions of printed music all the way. When he returned to Germany he learned that Friedrich Wilhelm I, the "Soldier King" of Prussia, had dissolved the chamber group assembled by his father in Berlin, and Leopold hired the musicians for Köthen. Once Bach joined him, Leopold had one of the best court orchestras in Europe—and Bach, for the first time in his life, was in the company of other musicians who could play his music as well as he could.

For much of his first year with Leopold, Bach was on the road. He went to Dresden and Leipzig. He went to Carlsbad, a town built near a natural spring, where the prince, on a doctor's orders, took the putatively healing waters. He went to Halle in the hope of meeting Georg Friedrich Handel, a native son whose music had gained him fame in London, but got there too late: Handel, there to visit his mother, had left earlier that day.

With his wife, Maria Barbara, pregnant with their fifth child, he went to Berlin to arrange the purchase of a new harpsichord for the prince's household. This trip was as consequential as any encounter with Handel could have been.

For one thing, the harpsichord that he purchased in Berlin probably became his touring instrument, conveyed from one town to the next by three men in the prince's entourage. For another, one day in Berlin he performed for a nobleman on harpsichord, and the new instrument, back in Köthen, was well suited for the six concertos, written "for several instruments" but emphasizing the harpsichord, that will always be associated with the nobleman he played for: Christian Ludwig, the margrave of Brandenburg.

The child, born in November 1718, was a boy, and Bach and Maria Barbara named him for Prince Leopold, who stood as the child's godfather at the baptism in the palace church—a festive occasion, and one that Bach celebrated with music.

The child died ten months later, and Bach was plunged into mourning. Of course, he had a large family; he had seen twins die in infancy; infant mortality was common—but there is no reason to suppose that he felt the death of one of his children as anything less than a total loss.

Bach's eldest son, Wilhelm Friedemann, turned nine that November, and early the next year—January 1720—Bach presented him with a musical instruction book. He had filled some of the pages with his own music: the two-part Inventions and the Sinfonias (three-part inventions), along with some of the preludes he had been writing and a few simple works by other composers. He left the rest of the pages blank, to be filled with pieces that father and son, teacher and student, would compose together.

One Bach scholar has called the book—the *Clavier-büchlein vor Wilhelm Friedemann Bach*—"perhaps the most precious gift any child has ever received." It is precious because of the music that it contains; beyond that, it is precious because the book, and its presentation as a gift, and the occasion on which it was given, give an extraordinary glimpse of how Bach understood life and music's place in it.

The pieces are instructive: on the piano, even an amateur's brief encounter with the first few two-part inventions reveals the inner logic of the piano, and of Western music generally, in the way the two parts, right and left, point and counterpoint, fall in ways sympathetic to the hands and the ears alike. At the same time, they are more than instructive. They are chamber music, music of the household. And they are music simple enough for a child to play for pleasure.

The invention is where all these qualities meet. Bach saw the musical invention as a foretaste of composition, rather than a composition that he had finished himself. He sought to construct his inventions to the point where they would suggest further developments to other musicians, who would bring them to fruition.

This is why Bach's inventions are so apt as music for children. They are like children themselves: each has a distinct character, and yet one that is still in formation.

And this is why they were so apt a gift. At nine, Wilhelm Friedemann had reached the age of reason, the beginning of independence. With the book of inventions Bach expressed his love for his eldest son, an emotion that the recent death of his youngest son made especially palpable. With it, too, he affirmed his role in his son's life going forward. The blank pages awaited father-son compositions; at the same time, they left possibilities open—allowing that the son, like the music in the book, would develop in ways that his father could foresee but could not single-handedly bring about.

>>3>> In May 1720, Bach left Köthen for Carlsbad in the prince's entourage. The journey, 130 miles south, took several days; they traveled in horse-drawn coaches, and possibly one coach contained the prince's new harpsichord.

Carlsbad was as unlike Köthen as any town in Germany. Around the healing waters there had emerged a spa and resort, and with them (Christoph Wolff catalogs) "a seasonal atmosphere in which the villas, watering places, hotels, casino, and pavilions of Carlsbad formed an exquisite backdrop to what may have been the earliest summer festival of the performing arts."

The prince planned to stay a couple of months, taking the waters and showing off the crack chamber ensemble he had assembled.

It was an ideal setting for Bach to mix with other musicians. But it kept him away from his wife and their children longer than ever before, and at a time when, for once, his circumstances were wholly to his liking. In its thirteenth year, his marriage to Maria Barbara was happy, even (a son said) "blissful." As their mourning ebbed, his family was thriving. The music he was composing was abundant, inventive, inspired. The prince had become a friend and then, as godfather, a relative of a kind. The members of the chamber ensemble were committed musicians, rehearsing freely every week outside the hours they spent at court. The rehearsals were held in Bach's apartment, and he had persuaded the prince to pay him rent for the arrangement. It was ideal. He could play chamber music, and be paid twice over for doing so, while his wife and family looked on.

Then a strange thing happened. Maria Barbara died. She was thirty-five, the same age as Bach. The cause of her death was obscure. One biographer suggests that she died in childbirth—and if she and Bach had conceived a child shortly after the death of their infant son Leopold, the pregnancy would have been coming to term.

She was buried in Köthen on July 7, 1720; music for the funeral was provided by the full schoolboy choir, paid for by the prince, rather than the usual small choir.

Bach was still at Carlsbad, unaware. Their son Carl Philipp Emanuel, who was six at the time, later explained that Bach had the experience of arriving home and "finding her dead and buried, although he had left her hale and hearty on his departure. The news that she had been ill and died reached him only when he entered his own house."

Not only was his wife dead, just like that; the rite that marked her passing had taken place without him—he who had played the organ at numberless funerals and had written cantatas and motets on the deaths of people he hardly knew.

Once an orphan, he was now a widower, a single father of four. He reconsidered his situation in Köthen, where the school his children attended was not as good as the one they had left in Weimar. He began to look for another position. And he composed music that dramatized the aloneness death had forced on him.

He was already well along in the writing of solo works for the keyboard: the Inventions and Sinfonias, the suites, and the preludes and fugues of the *Well-Tempered Clavier*. The cello suites, which he had begun in Weimar, were completed in Köthen, and if he needed an existential prompt for the anguished, bottom-trawling solitude of the fifth suite, the sudden death of a beloved spouse might have provided it.

Bach from "Christ lag in Todesbanden" onward seems to have been able to dramatize any emotion or theme at will. But there is evidence that one set of solo works bears the marks of his bereavement—the works for solo violin—and even that he incorporated within them a musical epitaph for Maria Barbara, drawing on the liturgical music of death so as to mark her death in music the way he was unable to do in person.

Sei solo a Violino senza Basso accompagnato, Bach wrote on the title page. Like the cello suites, the solo violin works are a set of six. There are three sonatas and three partitas. They are usually characterized in superlatives: "the very pinnacle of his musical achievement," "the culmination of his polyphonic writing for a string instrument," "the Everest of the violin repertoire." This is because they are hard to play, but also because they are hard to listen to. Transcribed for guitar they sound serene, but on violin they take place in rare air, far up the neck of the violin, and as one scholar delicately puts it, their "conspicuous sense of 'struggle' in the sensitive part of the aural spectrum . . . can be distancing."

They are also hard to listen to because there is no bass accompaniment—no ground to their figure, no net to catch the wire-walker if he slips and falls. That scholar, Peter Williams, insists that it is wrong to call them unaccompanied "because the instrument makes its own accompaniment." But it is one thing to be accompanied—to have a companion—and something very different to accompany oneself. The solo aspect of this music, in which the violinist is not solitary so much as going it alone, contributes to the notion that Bach wrote it while mourning Maria Barbara.

The first sonata begins abruptly, the strings scratched into the semblance of a grim minor chord; and in the way that the cello suites are defined by the bodily scale and sound of the cello, the solo violin works are characterized by this sound—plain, parched, resistant to human effort, like driftwood carved and strung with wire. Already, as the parts of a fugue are layered one atop another, the music is at a sonic extreme, and it will stay there for a while. There is great formal variety in the parts to follow—the kinds of fugues, the combinations of dance movements—but to the listener the effect is one of fixity, even monotony. Though the music ascends by force, things are not looking up, and there is a reason: in this set, alone among the solo sets, the first four pieces are in minor keys, one after another.

From the fugue of the first sonata, Bach makes the violin accompany itself, but the adding of a second part creates an effect of division, not expansion. The two lines clench together, untangle, then clench again. An allegro that could be joyful is not; a sarabande is not a dance but a dervish's expiatory whirl; a fugue, in dialogue form, is an exchange in which each partner keeps interrupting the other. Only in the slow movement of the second sonata, fifty minutes in, does the pressure drop: the piece, at first akin to a sad aria, comes to sound like a lullaby, and to suggest the music the Bachs made at home, music that, like mother and child, has gone to its rest, to be heard no more.

Then with the Partita in D Minor this solo music changes. It opens in the middle range of the instrument, a single line of melody without chords or double-stopping. For the first time since the early bars, that is, the violinist is fully alone, no longer trying to provide self-accompaniment or make up for the absence of another. And yet the music sounds richer and rounder than the nominally more complex parts that preceded it. Two middle parts are spacious and gorgeous, the accompaniment folded back in, and by the time the allegro winds around to an emphatic thrust of the bow, we have come out on the far side. Once, the violin was keening; now it is singing.

If the partita ended there, a case could be made for it as the music of grief: denial, anger, acceptance; first chill, then stupor, then the letting go. But it doesn't end there. To this second partita Bach added a chaconne—a long, convolute, quasi-independent violin solo—and this, now the piece for which the set is best known, is also, it appears, the piece in which Bach makes a monument of his grief for Maria Barbara.

A chaconne is a piece developed from the creative repetition of a simple four-bar figure. The musicologist Helga Thoene proposes that this chaconne is a musical headstone or *tombeau*, and that it contains a coded epitaph for Maria Barbara. The argument, combining insights from music theory, theology, numerology, and chemical analysis of paper and ink, is as follows. Bach had long since written the three violin sonatas, completing them by 1718. In 1720, writing on paper he brought home from Carlsbad, Bach in the grip of grief augmented these with three violin partitas, making them, like the sonatas, follow a scheme representing life, death, and resurrection. The middle partita, representing death, he devoted to the memory of Maria Barbara, especially the lengthy Chaconne, whose melody everywhere echoes church chorales by Bach and others that have death as their theme—notably "Christ lag in Todesbanden." As if to seal the point (Thoene proposes), he used *gematria*—a Baroque system that gave numerical values to letters, words, and musical notes and combines them—to inscribe his name, his late wife's name, and the literary motifs for the feast days of Christ's death and resurrection into the work itself.

This kind of thinking is inventive, provocative. It is broad enough to make it possible for any aspect of any work to be read allegorically: say, could the Chaconne, with its four parts, be a reference to the Bachs' four surviving children, and could its descending form be meant to dramatize the act of burial, so as to put Bach imaginatively at the graveside?

The case for the Chaconne as a musical tombeau (Martin Geck allows) is "speculative at best." Speculative or not, it brings us strikingly close to Bach in a time of trial. *Morimur*, a recording that juxtaposes sung snatches of the chorales with skeins of the Chaconne, is aurally persuasive; it makes clear (if there was any doubt) how deeply rooted in church chorales Bach was and how apt he was to aver to their melodies and forms, whether instinctively or deliberately. More than that, it underscores the presence of religious motifs in Bach's instrumental works as well as in his church music. It enables us to hear that his gift for transcription had a religious dimension—that he created so-called secular works out of sacred ones, not just vice versa. In Köthen, working formally outside the church for the first time in his life, he made, in chamber music, what Geck calls an "inner emigration" away from the expectations of his job and toward the imperatives of his calling.

For all the sickness and death in his family, Bach was lucky in love. A few months after Maria Barbara's death he fell in love again. He knew of a soprano singer back in Weissenfels who was coming of age, and at various points in 1721 (it is hard to tell what happened when) he passed through her hometown, recruited and hired her for the Köthen choir, stood with her as godparents of another musician's child, and proposed marriage. This was Anna Magdalena Wülcken, age twenty, and it is possible to consider the cadenza (Williams calls it the "final solo episode") of the fifth Brandenburg concerto, completed in March 1721, as counterpoint to the Chaconne for solo violin—its confident, exultant, many-voiced gamboling across the keyboard the sound of new love dispelling sorrow. In the way of great bandleaders down the ages, Bach would marry a singer in his ensemble.

The wedding was held at his house in Köthen on December 3, 1721—a Wednesday, enabling church musicians from all over to travel to Köthen and then return home to play at Sunday services.

In their first months of marriage Bach gave Anna Magdalena a *Clavier-büchlein* as a present. It was the size and shape of the one he had given his eldest son, but all the music in it was his own. It was music for husband and wife to play together.

>>4>> "I can remember so clearly, when I was about eight years old, playing for hours every day the music of Bach, Beethoven, Mozart, Schubert, Brahms, Chopin, Debussy," Leopold Stokowski said. "I was not forced to do this, but did it of my own free will. Nor did it prevent me from enjoying such games as football with my friends. This daily communion with music gave me a vision of an ideal world of beauty with which I gradually became familiar, just as surely as I learned to know the material world of school and play."

Stokowski considered children the best audience for classical music. As the conductor of the Philadelphia Orchestra, he instituted Young People's Concerts, and he sought to make these concerts more than field trips to the Academy of Music on Broad Street. He kept adults out, and he sought to delight the children as well as edify them. During a performance of Saint-Saëns's *Carnival of the Animals*, he told the children in the audience that there was an elephant backstage. They groaned incredulously. "You do not believe me? Or perhaps you do not want to see an elephant?" He went backstage and returned leading an elephant by the ear. They whooped it up. He went back again and returned with two more elephants. A musician rose from his chair and spoke into Stokowski's ear: there was a whole herd of elephants on the street outside, trying to get in. Conductor and musician went to the stage door and shouldered it shut, holding back the thundering herd—and then Stokowski regained the podium and led the orchestra in part five of the *Carnival*, "The Elephant," for a transfixed audience of children and elephants.

Walt Disney didn't know about Stokowski's enthusiasm for children the night he saw him eating supper by himself in Los Angeles. Disney was alone himself at Chasen's, which was a new place in Beverly Hills, when he spotted Stokowski, whose appearance—pastel suit, strong nose, thick white hair pulled straight back—made him stand out even among movie people. In Hollywood circles, Stoki (as he was called) was a cartoon figure: a libertine and vegetarian who liked to sunbathe in the nude, who had played himself in a couple of pictures and was fanatical about the new recording technology.

Disney knew Stokowski better than that. They had met and corresponded, and Disney had given him a tour of Walt Disney Studios.

"Why don't we sit together?"

They sat together, ate supper, and, somehow, conceived *Fantasia*. Either Disney pitched Stokowski an animated "short" of a piece called "The Sorcerer's Apprentice" and Stokowski offered to conduct it without a fee; or Stokowski pitched Disney—"I've been hoping for years for you to do a full-length animated musical picture in which the dramatic and dynamic range of great music would be coordinated with the unlimited freedom of your cartoon imagery. What a magical *fanta-zee-ah* that could be!"

They were ready to work together. Disney had bet his company on *Snow White*, his first feature-length animated work, and now he bore down on the picture, which was running over budget and behind schedule for a Christmas release, forcing the Disney crew to work around the clock, including weekends. But he found time to secure the rights to "The Sorcerer's Apprentice," a piece of program music by the fin-de-siècle Paris composer Paul Dukas, and told a story man to write an outline with Mickey Mouse as the apprentice, who uses his master's magic to get his broom to do his work for him.

"I am greatly enthused over the idea," Disney told a colleague, "and believe that the union of Stokowski and his music, together with the best of our medium . . . should lead to a new style of motion picture presentation." He was glad to have a new vehicle for Mickey Mouse, his most cherished creation. He was eager to get started "immediately."

Stokowski, returning east by cross-country rail—he hated airplanes—was equally enthusiastic. A Londoner of Polish extraction, he had always been the most progressive of the émigré conductors. While the others toured America, he took U.S. citizenship. In twenty years in Philadelphia he had made the orchestra there the conductor's personal instrument by rethinking standard practices—the seating chart for musicians on stage, the conductor's use of a baton to hold their attention—in the effort to produce the plush, ample, embroidered sound he thought proper to a modern orchestra. While other maestros submitted passively to the recording process, he had sought to master it—to shape, caress, and perfect the sounds produced by his musicians. He had gone to Hollywood to exploit its technical opportunities as much as its money and celebrity. Well before he met Walt Disney he envisioned a movie devoted to music, and as the vision developed in his mind, he focused on his own most cherished creation: his transcription of Bach's Toccata and Fugue in D Minor for symphony orchestra.

Stokowski had trained as an organist, and his orchestral transcriptions of Bach organ works were his signature pieces: outsize, high-test post-Wagnerian workouts that elicited aspects of Bach no one else had heard. Now with Disney's help he would transcribe Bach again—refashioning the music for America and for Hollywood, for children and curious adults, by transcribing it for the movies.

Stokowski's venture outside the classical music culture would produce the one work of his that is unquestionably a classic. *Fantasia*, with its long, sportive opening sequence set to the Toccata and Fugue, has introduced many thousands of children to classical music. By presenting the music in Disney's distinctly American animation, it made clear that the music had taken root in this country at last. And it pioneered the use of the "sound track"—a long piece of music that synched with the action, replacing the "occasional music" of early pictures with a solid sonic ground from beginning to end.

Each of these developments had consequences. They were themselves consequences of the change in the listener's relationship to music that this book is about. Stokowski and Disney with *Fantasia* made explicit what was implicit in Albert Schweitzer's sessions at All Hallows and Pablo Casals's at Abbey Road. Those two musicians were emboldened by the recording process. Schweitzer's grasp for the past in an empty church had a proto-existential pathos; Casals's one-to-one encounter with Bach in a small room concentrated sixty years of ardor and anguish. At the same time, their music was made vital by its eventual arrival in bedsit and parlor. Their recordings of Bach's music owed much of their power to the fact that they were recordings.

So it would be with Leopold Stokowski. His collaboration with Disney would produce a new thing altogether, not an approximation; the story of *Fantasia* is the third part of a three-part invention in which old-school European musicians, each already renowned and in midlife, made the music of Bach new through technology.

>>5>> The timing was right. Classical music was changing in America, and Disney and Stokowski had prospered by working changes on a traditional repertory.

For a hundred years classical music had been (as Joseph Horowitz put it) a "mutant transplant" from Europe. It was at once a holdover from the old country—a tradition whose grand complexity made clear just how small and rough America was—and a means of escape from that smallness for an evening, a lifetime.

Generally it was a German transplant. We forget "how large Germany loomed in American culture during the late nineteenth century," John Rockwell has observed. " 'The land of poets and thinkers' shaped our educational system, our philosophical and scientific ideas, and not least our music. Germans, Jewish and non-Jewish, conducted our orchestras and played in them, and young American composers went to Leipzig and Berlin to complete their studies. Just as he dominated Europe itself, Richard Wagner was the preeminent influence on younger composers in this country."

"There was a touch of Europe in Nebraska everywhere during her girlhood," Alfred Kazin remarked of Willa Cather, and Cather's novel *The Song of the Lark*, set in "a world full of memories of Grieg and Liszt," presents the spirit of an American musician as the spirit of the pioneers. It is the story of Thea Kroger, whose talent for music sets her apart from her family in Moonstone, Colorado, where women go to church just to hear her sing. Through music, represented by the dissolute music teacher Fritz Wunsch—who "played in the dance orchestra, tuned pianos, and gave lessons" but had to offer "a trunkful of music" in lieu of unpaid board—Thea learns to nurture the creative desire in herself and follow it where it takes her. Through *lieder* she learns German, and through giving piano lessons she fills the long hours of summer. She arrives in Chicago as a young woman who is ready to consecrate herself to music but who has "never heard a work by Beethoven or a composition by Chopin" or a symphony orchestra, either.

Published in 1915 in Boston—then still the center of classical music enterprise in America—*The Song of the Lark* made clear through tender retrospect that the United States was musically provincial no more. And yet very little distinctly American music had emerged. The big-city orchestras were still led by European maestros. Mostly they played the music of nineteenth-century European composers. The two most ambitious American composers, Edward MacDowell and Charles Ives, rooted their work in the rustic and provincial aspects of U.S. society that Thea Kroger sought to escape, as the titles of their signature pieces—MacDowell's *Woodland Sketches* of 1896 and Ives's *The Circus Band* of a year later—made obvious. When people went to hear classical music they went to hear a touring virtuoso, ideally a pedigreed European who had been educated in a palace and who when in England played for the queen, the way Pablo Casals did.

American music found its voice as war broke out. The best writers on the subject give distinctly different accounts of how it happened. Rockwell thinks American music was changed by the force of pop music and by a flood of political émigrés, whose twelve-tone theories and atonal adventures brought about a restoration of supposed European superiority. Horowitz sees a Great Schism —a double schism—in which the Great War prompted American classical music figures to favor the music of France over that of Germany and the exploits of performers and conductors over those of composers.

Powerful as they are, those explanations scant the obvious: the sudden ubiquity of records and radio in the early twenties. The phonograph made classical music available and relatively affordable; the radio made it free. The technology was American-made even when the music was not. Scores of records were "cut" in studios in Manhattan or Camden, pressed nearby, and played on devices that (with an assist from Britain) had been invented in the United States, whose size made it a crucial market for recorded music even to musicians who would never cross the Atlantic.

Recording technology would not catalyze classical music in the United States only. But recordings and the record-business apparatus surrounding them would be America's contribution to the art, speeding changes in the classical music canon that were under way in Great Britain and Europe. When John Cage, an engineer's son from Los Angeles, composed a piece called *Imaginary Landscape No. 1*—"for muted piano, Chinese cymbal, and variable-speed turntables"—he was not just suggesting a way forward for composers; he was acknowledging a new place where listeners had already arrived. In a lecture called "The Future of Music (Credo)" in 1940, he envisioned a music, composed partly of noise, "produced through the aid of electrical instruments which will make available for musical purposes any and all sounds that can be heard."*

>>6>> Stokowski was thinking along the same lines. "Soon we shall have entirely new means of tone production," he had written. "Thus will begin a new era in music."

That is characteristic Stokowski: oracular, a little bombastic, said in perfectly clear English that sounds translated anyway. It is characteristic of his reputation, too. "A nineteenth-century man and a twentieth-century musician with a twenty-first-century outlook," one devotee called him, and it was his rhetorical embrace of the future, as much as his recordings, that gained him the reputation he still enjoys: as the most forward-looking of the old transcontinental maestros and the first to grasp the possibilities of recordings. But he was no Cage or Stockhausen, making "music" that sounded like radio-shack outtakes, reports from the chilly electronic frontier. He was a musician of the old school whose gift for transcription led him to embrace the microphone—"the electric ear," he called it—as the pipe organ of his time, that is, as the most advanced instrument available to him.

In a sense, his whole career was an act of transcription—and a transcription Stokowski-style, in which the particulars of his early life were brilliantly orchestrated and broadcast for the delight of American audiences.

All the facts of his life were amplified. He was born (in 1882) on Upper Marylebone Street in London, but claimed Kraków or Pomerania when the mood struck him. His given name was Leopold Anthony Stokowski, but he dubbed himself Leopold Boleslawowicz Stanislaw Antoni Stokowski. (His younger brother, Percy John Stokowski, reduced himself to Percy Stock.) He

---

*Cage's teacher, Arnold Schoenberg, a Viennese serialist transplanted to Los Angeles, remarked: "Of course he's not a composer, but he's an inventor—of genius."

liked to say he was named for a great-grandfather who was a general in Napoleon's army, but his namesake was a grandfather who was a cabinetmaker in Surrey. Raised in central London by his mother, a Londoner of Irish descent named Anne Marion Moore, he spoke with a Mitteleuropean accent. He shone early—entering the Royal College of Music near his home at age thirteen—but later exaggerated his precocity even so, claiming that he was twenty-five years old when he was twenty-nine. He studied piano and organ, not violin, yet liked to reminisce about a stint playing first violin in the Berlin Philharmonic. He said his career began with an appointment as organist of the grand Wren-designed church of St. James, Piccadilly, a church associated with Purcell and Handel, but in fact he first spent a year as the organist at a humbler church on Charing Cross Road. He claimed that he didn't master the organ until middle age, but he must have played well when he was young: he was a fellow of the Royal Society of Organists at sixteen, and when he was hired as organist by the Church of St. Bartholomew on Madison Avenue in New York in 1905 the organ there, paid for by the shipping heir Cornelius Vanderbilt, was the most complicated in New York, if not the United States—an electrified rig that had three banks of pipes which could be played from a single keyboard console, and which could be turned on or off with the flick of a switch. Emboldened by the instrument, Stokowski would play it deep into the night, in time, he made it his own, using stickers to give obscene, scatological names to the stops.

His transformation to conductor was his greatest makeover of all. When after four years at St. Bart's he came up for consideration as the next music director of the Cincinnati Symphony, he had never conducted an orchestra. A girlfriend fixed the problem for him. She had transformed herself from Lucy Hickenlooper, Texas pianist, to Olga Samaroff, graduate of the Conservatoire de Paris. In New York she had gone to St. Bart's to cast an eye on the new organist, who (a friend told her) "looks like a poetic Viking." Seeing him, she resolved to marry him. Now she used her social connections in Cincinnati (one cousin was a judge; another ran Cincinnati Gas and Electric) to book the city's orchestra for a concert in Paris, slot in Stokowski as a fill-in for the regular conductor, and arrange for Cincinnati's top donor and top critic to attend. He got the job. She got him: they were married in 1911. His scant conducting experience made him a bargain for the orchestra, but a series of newspaper write-ups on his arrival made getting a dynamic young English conductor seem a coup. It was a coup. In a year he made the orchestra his own—replacing musicians, booking a national tour, instituting stage risers and an intermission (both firsts for an American orchestra), and planning future repertory well in advance, so he could master the scores, which, after all, he had never conducted before. The musicians, who had played for Wagner, Strauss, and Toscanini, warmed to "the inmost pleasure of association with Mr. Stokowski, who we feel is divinely gifted, who by the turn of a finger sweeps us all before him."

He did it all over again three years later in Philadelphia, a city stolid like Cincinnati but closer to New York. The orchestra was in poor shape when he arrived in 1912. But the city had an advantage in its concert hall. The musicians he could change. The donors he could charm. The audience he could rouse. But the hall he had to use as it was, and the Academy of Music was "acoustically unsurpassed." There he could develop the Stokowski sound—as he would do over the next twenty years in dozens of recordings for Victor, most of them made at the Academy of Music, even though the best recording facility in the country was the Victor studio in Camden, New Jersey, across the Delaware River. The Stokowski sound would begin with the sound of a room, not a studio.

How did Stokowski do it—create a sound so enchanting that it is known even to people who have never heard it?

In part he did so through spectacle, such as his breakthrough performances of Mahler's *Symphony for a Thousand* in Philadelphia and New York. He had felt like "the first white man to behold Niagara Falls" when he heard Mahler lead a performance of it in Munich in 1910. The audiences for the American premiere in 1916—nine sold-out concerts at the Academy of Music and one at the Metropolitan Opera House in New York—were, in a sense, the last. The phenomenon of a symphony in performance had been taken to an extreme; the spectacle of a-thousand-plus musicians assembled on stage (a 110-piece orchestra, 950 choristers, and 9 soloists) would not be seen often in the age of recordings, which would minimize both the sound and the impact of such large forces. The electric ear couldn't hear such spectacle. The drive to miniaturization had begun.

Grasping this, Stokowski decided to stake his and the orchestra's reputation on recordings.

In 1917 he made the pilgrimage across the Delaware from Philadelphia to Camden and assembled a chamber-size reduction of his orchestra in front of the big brass horn for an "acoustical" recording of two of Brahms's *Hungarian Dances*. The next year he signed a contract with Victor which made him the first stateside conductor to become a recording artist. There was only one problem. He hated the boxy, inexact sound of such recordings. He would make them infrequently and always against his better judgment.

When the electrical process was devised, Victor asked him to introduce it, and he obliged. He led the Philadelphia Orchestra in the first symphonic "electrical" recording (of Saint-Saëns's *Danse macabre*), and the first full symphony (of Dvořák's *New World Symphony*). Suddenly musical space is divided into foreground and background. The horns are bright and upfront, the strings sinuous behind. Hearing the Dvořák, you might be sitting in the living room while a brass quintet plays a fanfare on the front porch.

With those recordings the orchestra crawled out of the mud and stood upright. But Stokowski was not taken in by the claim that the process approximated the sounds of music in a concert hall. Even as he made one recording after another—four hundred in the early years of electrical recordings—he rejected most of them for commercial release out of the conviction that the sound on the phonograph was unworthy of the Stokowski sound.

The other great prewar conductors faced the same limitations. But "for some mysterious reason," as one musician raised on Stokowski put it, "his innumerable recordings tended to sound better than those of his colleagues." Why is this? Partly it is the care he took in making them and then in suppressing those he considered subpar. Partly it is the fact that the orchestra's qualities—smooth, controlled, thriving on carefully calibrated contrasts of mood and timbre—were easily picked up by microphones he had placed strategically around the hall. But those recordings probably sound so good now because the music sounded so good then. Seventy-five years on, they make clear that there really was a "Stokowski sound": elegant, confident, bent on subduing both the symphonic warhorses and the ornery new works of modernism to the Philadelphians' strings-and-brass omnicompetence. Stokowski's Wagner is grand, his Scriabin intimate. The orchestra is tightly wound in Tchaikovsky, operatic in Mussorgsky. There are Arabic touches in the oboes, notes of gratuitous elegance in the harp. But all of these qualities, these distinctions between different works or composers, are overcome by the smooth-running, fine-tuned, fuel-injected, high-horsepower engine of the Stokowski sound.

The sound has its drawbacks. Stokowski's *New World Symphony* of 1935 is a good example. It is a sleek, dashing piece of music-making, an aural projectile aimed at the heavens. But when you compare it with the Czech Philharmonic recording made at Abbey Road two years later with Pablo Casals, it seems to lack a sense of occasion. In the Czech musicians' playing—crisp and exacting, with real pauses to set off the long lush bits or direct the listener's attention to a particular instrument—the music seems at once to capture and to alter the moment in which it was made. The Philadelphia Orchestra recording, for its part, could have been made on any day between Black Friday and Pearl Harbor: it is as if the era has been smoothed out by the orchestra's free bowing.

This points up a crucial difference between Casals and Stokowski, between the upright man and the "sonic sybarite" (as Joseph Horowitz calls him). If Casals's recordings now sound historic but not dated, Stokowski's sound dated but not historical. Made long ago, they move outside historic time in a sonic epoch of the conductor's own making.

>>7>> Stokowski's Bach is the exception to all this. Aurally, it is showing its age, a scriptural threescore and ten. But it doesn't sound outdated. Like an artfully fashioned tapestry, it is expressive of its epoch but is built to outlast the occasion of its making.

It partakes of the timelessness of Bach's music, that is. It is Bach increased and multiplied by mid-century technology, but Bach all the same: noble, independent, needing nothing from the musicians but faithful ardor and yet able to receive the impress of their personalities while remaining what it essentially is.

Stokowski called Bach "my favorite composer always." At the Royal College of Music he studied with an organist who was said to be able to play all of Bach's organ preludes and fugues from memory; at St. James's Piccadilly, he made a signature piece of the Toccata and Fugue in D Minor. At St. Bart's, the first organ voluntary he played was Bach's "Little" Fugue in G Minor, and the last was Bach's Fugue in A Minor; in his years there he led performances of the *St. Matthew Passion* at a time when these were still uncommon. At Christmas in Philadelphia one year, he presented Mr. and Mrs. Edward W. Bok—chief patrons of the orchestra—with an "Aeolian Duo-Art player pipe organ roll recording of Bach's *Passacaglia*, BWV 582"—the Passacaglia in C Minor—in a velvet-lined rosewood box. But as a conductor he was relatively slow to embrace Bach and even slower to transcribe Bach for orchestra. In Germanic Cincinnati he might have stuffed the schedule with Bach, but in three seasons there he programmed only the "Air on the G String" from the third orchestral suite. And in his first decade in Philadelphia he programmed familiar works written expressly for orchestra: two orchestral suites, two Brandenburg concertos, a concerto for solo violin, some Christmas music, and a harpsichord concerto with Wanda Landowska (still based in London) as the soloist.

Stokowski's revival of his passion for Bach coincided with the advance of recordings. As the process improved, he recognized that the music of Bach especially gains something in the recording process—or that he could adapt Bach's music to suit the demands of the new medium. So he doubled down on Bach, making him new at once through recordings and through transcriptions.

Stokowski's first Bach transcription (played at two concerts in Philadelphia in March 1915) was an apt beginning, a piece of music that threw open the doors of the palace. It was from Cantata 140, the cantata known as "Wachet auf," or "Sleepers, Wake." The text (in English translation: "Zion hears the watchmen singing; her heart leaps with joy") suggests both the stirring of a lover for her beloved and the waking of the dead at the final resurrection; the music, gently but inexorably climbing, makes it a song of ascents. Extracted from the cantata, it was one of the first Bach vocal works to find a popular audience, and by 1900 it had become music for all manner of beginnings, from weddings to the first Sunday of Advent.

Bach had transcribed this solo song for organ. Stokowski made it anthemic, a blast of gilt-edged grandeur. It begins as if in the middle- -the aria is the second of three chorale movements—and the opening chords roll in rather than announcing themselves, a sweet soft tide lapping the shore of the auditorium. And yet the mood is climactic: each surge of brass and swell of timpani suggests the music of royal procession—suggests the circumstantial pomp of Edward Elgar, whose *Falstaff* had opened a few months earlier.

The cantata begins: "Awake, the voice calls to us." In transcribing Bach, Stokowski was hearing the call of his own voice- -that of an organist whose instrument was now the hundred-headed creature of the symphony orchestra.

"Wachet auf" stirred an audience that knew Bach's concertos but little else. "Nobody played [Bach] except maybe in church," recalled a woman who was there. "He revived Bach; believe it or not. Now people stood up and cheered."

Seven years passed before Stokowski undertook another Bach transcription: a phenomenal repurposing of that great and grave work for organ, the Passacaglia in C Minor. His hair—still long and thick and worn combed back in a curve like the one on the head of a violin—had turned gray. He had become an American citizen and divorced Olga Samaroff. At forty, he was better known than any of the musicians he played with or the composers whose works he premiered at the Academy of Music.

His transcription of this passacaglia and the companion fugue was an act of radical simplicity and severity. And yet it, more than "Sleepers, Wake," opened a new way for him. It was a way back, for it took him to a point prior to the orchestral tradition he had done so much to advance and rerooted him in Bach's organ music. And it was a way forward, a reduction of means that cleared space for further splendors.

A passacaglia is a continuous set of variations on a short theme, which is repeated in the variations. It is a term that Bach had never used before and would never use again, which suggests that he considered the piece exceptional.

The theme itself is a severe, brooding melody: sixteen notes, sounded in eight pairs—short-*long*, short-*long*, short-*long*, short-*long*, eight times in all, loping laconically up the C-minor scale and down again. On the organ, the work is as unyielding as a test pattern: the organist transfers those eight pairs of notes to different points on the keyboard, plays them using various stops on the console, and divides and subdivides them into fourths, eighths, sixteenths, and so on, playing the whole figure twenty times more in all. It is a work of otherworldly regularity: it is long division, a natural law, an electrical circuit sonically diagrammed.

"Stokowski was remarkably faithful to the texts of Bach's organ music in his transcriptions," one expert has observed, and so he was with the Passacaglia and Fugue in C Minor. The power of his transcription lies not in invention per se but in the contrast between the cool exactitude of the theme and the sumptuousness of the variations.

From St. James's Piccadilly onward he had programmed Bach's organ music as a luxury item. St. Bart's was the wealthiest congregation in New York, and of its forty-three millionaires, half a dozen had installed pipe organs in their homes. The sound of the tripartite electric-powered organ in the church itself reminded Stokowski of an orchestra, "where, on the conductor's left are certain instruments, on his right, certain instruments, and on the center at the back, still a third group of instruments." Then, he had studied the organ and sought to combine its different sounds symphonically. Now he reversed the process, scoring the Passacaglia and Fugue in C Minor so as to reproduce in a natural acoustic the tripartite sound he had heard electrified through technology.

The result is Protestant church music de luxe. Bach used twenty variations in about thirteen minutes. Stokowski efficiently assigned them to different factions of the orchestra like a project manager breaking his team into workgroups. And yet each variation has a distinct attitude. The strings are ascending, developing, complicating, multiplying the melody; the brass counters the strings, now decorating the whole, now undergirding it; the woodwinds are holding the whole steady, as in chamber music; the strings are affirming, sustaining, culminating, triumphing. Every fifth variation is a lean, chamberish reduction for woodwinds, and these, evenly spaced along the extent of it, serve as milestones on the thoroughfare of the whole.

The mechanical regularity of it makes this transcription modern and American. The girders and cables and bolts and turnbuckles are functional but beautiful, too, and their symmetry, their confabbings of mass and wire, are akin to that of a musical instrument. It is a work of precision engineering—a suspension bridge, a skyscraper in sound.

The years to follow were frenzied ones. After his divorce, Stokowski's affairs with the women of Philadelphia—debutantes, socialites, students at the Curtis Institute of Music—had become local news. He moved from posh Chestnut Hill to a simpler flat and then to a refurbished carriage house next to a parking lot near the Academy of Music- –luridly painted, patchily furnished, centered on a fireplace of his own design—and the image of the place as a freethinking artist's lair was completed by reports that the patrons of a hotel across the street couldn't fail to notice Stoki sunning himself in the nude on the terrace. He married again, to Evangeline Johnson, the Johnson & Johnson pharmaceutical heiress, and fathered a daughter with her, while maintaining an open marriage.

Musically, too, he was continually seeking new partners and new positions. He conducted Stravinsky, Schoenberg, and Varèse, three paragons of modern difficulty. After accidentally striking his left hand while emphasizing a downbeat with the baton in his right, over time he stopped using the baton; henceforth his music would be "handmade music." For the 1926–27 season at the Academy of Music he had the house lights dimmed nearly to darkness, with the aim of approximating an "invisible orchestra," as he called it. "The great conviction in me has been growing in me," he explained, "that the orchestra and conductor should be unseen, so that on the part of the listener more attention will go to the ear and less to the eyes." His shadow on the ceiling was produced by a spotlight at his feet. All attention was on him, and his spidery hands and bobbing head seemed at once to conduct the music for the orchestra and dramatize it for the audience.

He opened the first such concert (the first in New York: Carnegie Hall, October 19, 1926) with "Sleepers, Wake," setting its gently ascending opening in counterpoint to the plunge into darkness. But he had already devised a new Bach transcription that incorporated his growing conviction that the orchestra should be a distinctly modern instrument, at once invisible and more dramatic than the usual city symphony.

This was the Toccata and Fugue in D Minor. It had been the centerpiece of his career as a church organist. Now Stokowski, who generally wrote in his transcriptions with pen and ink over the printed organ music, tattooed the work with his imprint.

"This work is one of Bach's supreme inspirations," he remarked, and the transcription of it is one of Stokowski's. In it the sharp contrasts of the Passacaglia and Fugue in C Minor are brought forward and fashioned into full opposition. It is a thrilling move, as if the bold young organist who wrote the piece has met his match for the first time. With the opening figure the orchestra takes a deep breath and then dives off a cliff, from the strings through the brass and woodwinds down to the subbasement of basses and timpani. Suddenly the different sections of the ensemble are not blending together so much as running alongside one another. The sculpted, polished Stokowski sound is set against the sharp angles of Bach's counterpoint. When a downward run of arpeggios in the strings is paired with the same run plucked on a harp, all of a sudden you can hear the room—can feel the gale force of the orchestra battering the windows. This is the orchestra as a force of nature, held in check by the integrity of Bach's architecture.

He introduced the new transcription at the Academy of Music on a Monday evening in 1925, led several performances of it that year and the next, and purveyed it to the carriage trade during a concert at Wanamaker's department store. Then—Wednesday, April 6, 1927—he made a recording of it at the Academy of Music. He was considering leaving the orchestra to freelance, and he, the Philly management, and Victor, thinking alike about the implications of a move, booked plenty of recording sessions, hoping to amass enough releases to sustain them all for a few seasons if he moved on.

The Toccata and Fugue recording was symbolic as well as practical. It was the first piece of Bach's music, and the first of his own transcriptions, that Stokowski submitted to the electrical recording process. Heard alongside other recordings of the same year—the Dvořák, say—it is another thing altogether. To the foreground and background accessed by the recording process, this transcription adds space above. There, in the place a few feet above ground where the ears and the brain are situated, the music rushes past—and the space opened up in the process, heard as if for the first time here, is the headroom where, in the age of recordings, much of our experience of music takes place.

The transcription of the Toccata and Fugue in D Minor is the beginning of Stokowski's career as it is known today, in which his powers as a conductor and orchestrator were at once amplified and archived by technology. More than ever, the symphony orchestra was his instrument. Finally he had found ways to make recordings that could approximate the sound of the orchestra of his experience. At last his concern for the production of sound and the reproduction of it was being rewarded. As he approached fifty, his talents as artist, showman, and sonic pioneer were sounding together.

>>8>> *This will kill that.* While Stokowski made records grander than anybody else's, the public was captivated by a simple, cheap communications network that promised to bind the population together as never before.

This was radio, or wireless. Three people, working independently, had figured out how to use electricity to transmit sound radially across long distances: the inventors Major E. H. Armstrong and Lee de Forest, through slightly different versions of the process called "regeneration," and David Sarnoff, the president of the Radio Corporation of America, which amassed several thousand patents that applied to the new technology.

With wireless technology growing at once more complex and less expensive, Sarnoff and several rivals competed to make sound transmission available to everybody. Broadcasts of public events—such as the Jack Dempsey–Georges Carpentier prizefight of 1921, heard at several thousand shops and saloons that rented radio gear for the occasion——made radio the next big thing. Sears and Montgomery Ward offered a one-way home wireless receiver for sale in their catalogs. Sarnoff established the National Broadcasting Company in 1926 as a branch of RCA. There was a run on radio sets following NBC's broadcast of the tumultuous daylong reception given Charles Lindbergh in Washington after his solo airplane flight across the Atlantic the next year. In 1928 William S. Paley, an immigrant's son from Chicago with scant experience in radio, founded the Columbia Broadcasting System. He grasped that news and entertainment could travel long distances through the air unaided just as Lindbergh had done, and just as miraculously.

The business model for radio is strikingly familiar. It would be essentially free to use, once you bought the device. Programs would be transmitted via a network. The costs of transmission would be incorporated into the cost of the device (NBC) or supported through advertisements mixed in with the programming (CBS). The broadcast network would blend commerce and public service. The process would create a new figure—the listener—and put this listener in a fresh relationship to society. The point was not profits alone. The goal was social change through greater connectivity.

The captains of radio needed programs to broadcast. That is where Stokowski came in. Sarnoff had bought a chain of theaters (soon to be called RKO) and had made a deal with General Motors to develop radios for the dashboards of automobiles. Then Sarnoff bought Victor: its record distribution channels, its foundrylike Camden recording-and-pressing facility, its contracts with famous musicians, and its claim to the image of the dog listening to "His Master's Voice."

On Sunday, October 6, 1929, Stokowski led the Philadelphia Orchestra in an afternoon concert. The "electric ear" was present, as was often the case for recordings in Philadelphia, but this time it was for the radio—the first nationwide, sponsored live broadcast of a symphony orchestra. Air time was 5:30 p.m.; Stokowski, who for once was conducting for an audience that could not see him, wore "a loose sport jacket and golf knickers" rather than a bespoke suit. Once again he was making a new beginning, and once again he began with Bach—a transcription to signal his transcription of orchestral music from one format to another.

More Sunday broadcasts followed, but Stokowski was unhappy with them. He disliked the sound of the radio signal, which was compressed (tamped in at its low and high ends) so as to travel through the air without grave loss of fidelity. He loathed the surrender of aural control that the process called for. Before conducting the musicians, he conducted the technicians—supervising the placement of the microphones, scrutinizing the recording equipment, and quarreling with his new rival behind a mixing console. "He was at the conductor's stand, and off to the side in the wings there was a man sitting at a sort of keyboard with dials," Evangeline Johnson recalled. "He was called the mixer. Stokowski stopped the orchestra and asked what the man was doing." When the need to compress the sound for broadcast was explained, he retorted: "Then you're paying the wrong man. He's the conductor and I'm not. I don't want this to be broadcast under my name if I'm not controlling the pianissimo, the mezzo forte, and the fortissimo."

As the story goes, for the next broadcast Stokowski made the technicians place a portable mixing board near the conductor's podium; as the story goes, the technicians disconnected the wires at their end, placating the maestro with the illusion of control. Eventually Stokowski had a simple mixing board permanently installed on the podium of the Academy of Music. Engaged or not, it sent a clear signal. The mixing board had replaced the baton. The recording process was now central, even in the concert hall.

Stokowski would never embrace radio. For one thing, David Sarnoff favored a different conductor: Arturo Toscanini, a transplanted Italian who programmed crowd-pleasing works from the previous century and didn't give a whit about the sound of the broadcast. For another, radio was already a rear-guard enterprise, left behind by a new technology. This was motion-picture sound. For most of the century, people as forward-looking as Stokowski—Edison, De Forest, an upstate New York inventor named Theodore W. Case—had tried to incorporate recorded sound into motion pictures. For most of the century the Hollywood studios had resisted, disliking the results and the prospect of sharing their medium with tinkerers from the east. Then in 1926 a film version of *Don Juan*, with the title role played by John Barrymore and with music played by the New York Philharmonic, proved that a "sound picture" could work artistically. The next October *The Jazz Singer*, with Al Jolson, proved that it could succeed commercially.

Sound made movies the leading edge of new technology. Then, with the stock-market crash of 1929 and the Great Depression, the "talkie" became, for many in the seats, a momentary respite from poverty and anxiety; and the orchestra concert by contrast was suddenly both a luxury and a diminished thing.

Stokowski responded by venturing out to the far frontier of conductorial experiment. He led the American premieres of Berg's *Wozzeck* and Schoenberg's *Die glückiche Hand*, and programmed dozens of new works by lesser-known composers. He made the Saturday concerts for young people a bargain, capping ticket prices at seventy-five cents. At the behest of Bell Laboratories, whose technicians were experimenting with two-channel "binaural" sound, he made advanced recordings of Wagner and Beethoven, recordings whose power and clarity are said to confirm Sergei Rachmaninov's reckoning that Stokowski's ensemble was not only "the finest orchestra I have ever heard at any time or any place" but "the finest orchestra the world has ever heard."

The recordings languished in a warehouse in New Jersey. Meanwhile Stoki exercised his social conscience outside the Academy of Music. One day in 1931 he led a ragged ensemble of out-of-work musicians in a concert in Rittenhouse Square—and "as their wives and children passed the hat," recalled Abram Chasins, who happened upon the performance, "the strains of band repertory such as operetta potpourris, Strauss waltzes and Sousa marches loosened the pockets of entranced passersby."

Stokowski then led the Philadelphians in a benefit concert for the jobless musicians. The first half of the program was all Bach; the "Little" Fugue and the Passacaglia and Fugue flanked a new transcription. This was of a tenor aria from "Christ lag in Todesbanden," the dramatic setting of Christ's descent to hell that Bach had composed in his teens.

If ever a Stokowski transcription had a sense of occasion, this was it. His orchestrated aria (heard on a recording from that year) is all *about* descent. Beginning at full power, the orchestra goes down, down, down, sounding the depths of the material again and again before touching bottom, settling there, and surveying the underworld with a series of minor-chord minesweeps of the territory. This, you say to yourself, is what depression sounds like.

Philadelphia had become a kind of hell for him. His experiments with large-scale atonality had gotten him onto the cover of *Time*, the first conductor featured there ("Magnificently gaunt last week was Stokowski's translation of Stravinsky's primitive, pornographic music—music which in its finale is tremendous enough truly to suggest an upheaval of the brutal earth"). But some trustees found the music repulsive, and the orchestra's manager, Arthur Judson, was unhappy. Stokowski would threaten to resign, then allow himself to be wooed back after the press and public made their affection for him known. But he would never be bound to Philadelphia in the same way again.

He dreamed of taking the orchestra on a cross-country tour, but Judson was resistant. So he went west on his own. California was already an outpost for a *Klatsch* of European moderns: Arnold Schoenberg, Ernst Lubich, Greta Garbo. Stokowski liked to sunbathe, but there was more than good weather in California. There was the opportunity for serious play, too. In California he would be free to experiment not only with the music but with the means of production, making a chain of movie palaces his concert hall.

>>9>> "This is the place for you—a real country to work and play in," Walt Disney declared in a letter to Ub Iwerks, his collaborator back in Kansas City. Disney himself had left Kansas City on the Santa Fe California Limited ten months earlier. His journey west in 1923 had hit every note in the legend of the small-town rube going to the coast to find his fortune: borrowed suit, battered cardboard suitcase, home-cooked meals wrapped for the journey, a berth on an uncle's spare bed at the end. He was only twenty-two, but in Kansas City he had struck out with several lines of filmed, animated cartoons: Laugh-O-Grams, Song-O-Reels, Lafflets. He was determined to make

a go of it in Los Angeles, which styled itself the capital of the modern American imagination. His suitcase held animation equipment. His ticket was first class.

Improbably, it worked. By 1930 Disney—with Iwerks as his chief animator—had established himself as the most successful producer of animated motion pictures in America. His reversal of fortune is usually credited to a cartoon mouse, which he named Mortimer, then renamed Mickey (his wife's idea) so as to make the little patrician seem a plucky outsider. But Mickey Mouse's success—and Disney's—was due emphatically to the introduction of sound to motion pictures. After two silent Mickey Mouse cartoons drew no special attention, Disney, shortly after *The Jazz Singer*, made a third with sound, then a fourth in which the mating of sound and pictures was the point of the story. He had new business cards printed (SOUND CARTOONS), devised a method of synchronizing pictures and sound, and introduced the Silly Symphonies— eight-minute cartoons in which the action was accented by music from beginning to end. Overnight, Mickey Mouse, the biographer Neil Gabler has observed, became "a wholly musical creature—as much Fred Astaire as Charlie Chaplin. Hearing notes, Mickey cannot help but dance, sing, and make music himself, turning everything he spots into an instrument and converting reality into happiness."

No musician, nor even a lover of music, Disney knew that music had turned his business around. He opened a recording studio in Los Angeles; and when, a few years later, he sought to change his career again, establishing himself as an innovator rather than a purveyor of novelty and silliness, he looked to music.

Disney was a small-town Midwesterner, lightly educated, with no musical training or heritage. He was a man of the market, one made nervous by art, especially the art of old Europe, which he had missed altogether while in military service in France at the tail end of World War I. He was devoted to his wife, his brother Roy, his dog, and his cat, not always in that order; he lived in a standard-issue house on a street named Lyric Avenue in a subdivision of Los Angeles called Silver Lake, with Roy living in an identical house next door. He dressed like a golf caddy, in a sweater and knickers and a soft cap; he drove a Packard and then a Plymouth rather than a Cadillac, and claimed his favorite supper was canned beans. His chief concession to the world of businessmen and money was a pencil mustache, which he grew to make himself look more mature. His idea of a full day was to work, work some more, go home for supper, then return to the studio with his wife and work late while she snoozed on the office couch. He was outsized only in his passion for the work, which consisted of thousands of tiny drawings of a dog, a mouse, or a dancing flower made so that, filmed in order, they produced his ideal dramatic combination of "motion and emotion."

Disney was the very embodiment of the shallow and self-satisfied culture from which Leopold Stokowski hoped to convert America. Yet Disney and Stoki were kin in many ways, especially in their relationship to new technology. Disney was to animation what Stokowski was to the recording of orchestras—the visible, irrepressible, demanding figure whose high standards elevated everybody else's.* As he saw it, only through a mastery of the new technology of animation could his studio claim the top of the heap, and his obsession with animation inspired the artists who worked for him to try harder and harder to be the best. He took the risks associated with excellence. He paid extra to use positive film stock instead of negative, because positive stock produced a sharper image. He refused to slash salaries after the Depression set in. He arranged a loan from his father (who took on a second mortgage) in order to build a sound studio and music room to experiment in, because he knew that his sound pictures weren't distinguished by music per se but by the new ways sound allowed his characters to interact with music.

His signature character—Mickey Mouse—dramatized the change for animator and viewer alike. In the early Mickeys (as Disney called them) and the Silly Symphonies, the background music set a limit on the action. A Disney animator disdainfully recalled "that bouncing, dancing, musical age of Disney shorts, where all of our characters with big smiles on their faces kept time with the music or played an instrument." One way around this limit was to have the story be about music, as in *The Band Concert*, in which Mickey is a hapless conductor. But Disney sought a fundamental change, urging the writers and artists to move away from the music. He hired a life-drawing coach, so that the animation would be more realistic, and in script meetings he began to insist that the characters—mice, dogs, cats—have clear motives for their actions.

This turn toward realism (Neil Gabler proposes) set Disney apart from his competitors. But the turn to realism had consequences, and what truly set Disney apart was his determination to do something about them. The stress

---

*Disney "was seeing something new and more things that he could do with animation, and the layout men would give him new drawings, and everybody was coming up with new ideas and so Walt was going, 'What have I got here?'" one animator recalled. "He was like an organist playing all the stops."

on character rather than incident abruptly made the cartoons less silly: instead of just putting a character in a situation and having things happen to him—pulling gags on him—the artists had to give him a motive and a consistent way of going about things. The commitment to dialogue reversed the flow of the production process: now the animators had to match their drawings to the characters' voices, which were recorded beforehand. Speech made the music seem arbitrary: now that Disney characters spoke in the human way, the musical interludes stuck out as awkward and unsophisticated. The gain in realism led to a loss of play.

Mickey Mouse lost the most in the process. Disney had always seen him as a charming innocent. Now he was a simpleton. People complained that Mickey had become a pure merchandising character. The studio needed to find something else.

Disney's reckoning was postponed by a Silly Symphony called *The Three Little Pigs*. In the old tale of three pigs besieged by a nasty wolf he saw an opening for a cartoon short that emphasized "personality." He assigned a small group of animators to adapt the story, making the pigs cute and the wolf dastardly. Seeing a gap in the story, he called for a song, and his crew, improvising in the studio's music room, came up with "Who's Afraid of the Big Bad Wolf?" for the pigs to squeak in unison. *The Three Little Pigs* is so soaked with Disney effects—the bouncy protagonists, the taffy-pull pratfalls, the flummoxed villain, the zany and uproarious background music coercing you to find the whole thing zany and uproarious—that it is hard to recognize it as a breakthrough. But on its release in May 1933, during the run of Roosevelt-led New Deal legislation known as the Hundred Days, *The Three Little Pigs* was an immediate hit throughout the country—and, more surprising, was seen as a parable of the Depression, in which two feckless little pigs are led out of adversity by their unflappable brother, who is not afraid to take on the Big Bad Wolf of the economy. "Historians of the future," one movie figure declared, "will not ignore the interesting and significant fact that the movies literally laughed the big bad wolf of depression out of the public mind through the protagonism of *Three Little Pigs*."

The film was a parable for the life of its maker, too. Disney recalled that it brought him "recognition from the industry and the public that these things could be more than just a mouse hopping around or something." Making shorts, he felt he was building a house of straw—was, like the two feckless pigs, playing music with a flute and a fiddle. He yearned to produce something permanent, like the pig who taunted the Big Bad Wolf from behind brick walls by playing a brick-framed piano. The Silly Symphonies were never going to transcend silliness. It was time for him to build with brick. He didn't know what picture he would make next, but he knew what qualities it would possess. It would be artful, elaborate, elevating, technically advanced, and full-length.

>>10>> "The limitations of music are becoming less and less," Stokowski said in his convoluted English. "I believe the composer of the future will create his harmonies directly in tone by means of electrical-musical instruments which will record his idea exactly. Over sound films of the future I believe we will be able to convey emotions higher than ever thought—things subtle and intangible—almost *psychic* in their being. Radio and television will project them *all over the world*."

He spent the early thirties showing what he had in mind. He let technicians from Bell Labs set up a recording studio in the basement of the Academy of Music. He asked audiences to assess recordings of sounds ranging from an "addled contralto" to "a bull in pain." He led a concert in which the sound of the live orchestra was piped in from the basement while the audience, sitting in the dark, attended to an empty stage; then he upped the ante, leading a concert, sponsored by the National Academy of Sciences, in which the sound of the orchestra was sent by telephone lines from Philadelphia to Washington, D.C., where Stokowski, sitting in the back of Constitution Hall, used a mixing board to "conduct" Bach's Toccata and Fugue in D Minor.

He spoke more like an inventor than a musician. But he never lost touch with the nature of a concert as a gathering in which some people played music together while other people listened. "Aren't you sad it's all over?" he asked the audience after one performance, then invited them to consider what the music meant "to our civilization, to our culture." He went on: "I think it means, first of all, delight—delight in sound, in the beauty of this thrilling sound—just the delight of it—the essential delight. And what else? Well, that's something still higher—inspiration . . . That's what all this stands for."

He liked to perform for young people because they were still alive to such pleasure. "Children are much more elastic and receptive," he declared. "It is easier for them to take in all the new phases of life that are developing today." He arranged to broadcast concerts of new music into Philadelphia's public schools on Friday afternoons. But as it turned out, the Youth Concerts—an outgrowth of the Saturday concerts—were not for children but for people age thirteen to twenty-five, and the first concert featured his transcriptions of Bach's

"Little" Fugue in G minor and "Sleepers, Wake." He would get to Stravinsky and Schoenberg, but the shock of the new would begin with Bach.

"He walked off with the hearts of young Philadelphia in his pocket," a critic observed after the second Youth Concert. But old Philadelphia was not beguiled. He held a series of concerts incorporating national anthems: the "Marseillaise," for France; the "Internationale," for the Soviet Union. The press smelled communism: one paper's headline read, RED ANTHEM WILL BE SUNG TONIGHT. The trustees were displeased. Stoki was annoyed. When, in 1934, the trustees backed a new opera series for the next fall and asked him to serve as musical director, he turned them down. He had conceived of a way to use technology to invigorate opera: actors would dramatize the music—lip-sync it—while the tenors and sopranos sang into microphones offstage. But he thought that it was too complex for the trustees to grasp. After their opera series flopped, he wrote them a long letter of resignation—and sent it to the press first. "You asked me to conduct opera also, but I declined because I wished to have us produce certain operas in new ways, and there was not then time to prepare the new methods . . ."

The conflict played out in the newspapers; children sent letters in support of him. "For Philadelphia to lose Stokowski is unthinkable," one admirer declared. But it was thinkable. As Joseph Horowitz points out, it is remarkable that Philadelphia kept Stokowski as long as it did: twenty-eight years. Stokowski had sought ways to advance the cause of classical music through new technology. To put it differently, he had sought to break the association between the music he made and the fact that it was made in Philadelphia. He wanted his music to be played everywhere.

The movies were the logical next step. After another trip to the West Coast, he bought a house in Santa Barbara. He turned over leadership of the Philadelphia Orchestra to a protégé, agreeing to serve as guest conductor for one more season. Before stepping down, he led the orchestra in Christmas performances of Bach's Mass in B Minor.

>>11>> For their tenth wedding anniversaries Walt and Roy Disney and their wives went to Europe. They took the Grand Tour, 1935 edition: they saw London, Scotland, and the Lake District, Paris and the rural eastern part of France (where Walt had had his walk-on in the Great War), Munich and Baden-Baden, the Swiss Alps, and Venice and Rome, then boarded a liner in Genoa and returned home.

Disney was welcomed as a celebrity and an emissary for America. He had audiences with Pope Pius XI and Benito Mussolini and sketched Mickey Mouse on a napkin for the president of France. He was a guest of honor at the League of Nations. He was followed by a pack of reporters and photographers wherever he went. Police officers were detailed to protect him. His wife, Lillian, started calling him Big Shot.

Taken for pleasure, the trip had an immediate effect on his work. For one thing, it made him realize that the use of spoken English could limit the audience for his pictures. Five years earlier he had wondered whether audiences would believe an animal that spoke. Now animals that spoke were so effective that he felt hemmed in by them. "I found that all over the world people want to laugh," he said, "but you cannot translate American slang and American humor into any other language, so I will try to keep my comedy, so far as possible, in pantomine." He had already authorized work on a full-length feature based on the life cycle of a deer. This was *Bambi*, and a photograph shows several dozen Disney animators, their pencils and sketch pads at the ready, all seated around a live deer scampering in a bed of hay. *Bambi* would promote animation as a form of realism. Bambi would not speak: her silent wonder would be a universal language.

Before leaving California, Disney had arranged for the studio's employees to divide their time equally between shorts and a full-length feature. On his return he set the shorts aside and focused all the studio's attention on the feature. This was *Snow White*, and just as its length would serve as a statement of his seriousness of purpose, so would its subject matter: a Germanic folktale, made notorious by the Brothers Grimm, with a castle, a nasty queen, a beautiful princess, and a pack of dwarves. From the world of steamboats in Missouri, Disney had moved into the chthonic territory of myth.

He put the entire staff to work on the film. After traveling to Europe he had dismissed the furor over Nazism as an overreaction. In February 1936, as Mussolini relished his conquest of Ethiopia and Hitler planned an occupation of the Rhineland, Disney marshaled his platoons of animators, story men, colorists, and technicians, five hundred people in all, to tell a story of innocence threatened in the Bavarian forest.

>>12>>   The city of Los Angeles had no real concert hall. When the Philadelphia Orchestra came to town, a promoter rented the Pan Pacific Auditorium, a former skating rink on Beverly Boulevard, and set several thousand folding chairs on a temporary wooden floor.

Los Angeles was the farthest point west on the orchestra's six-week transcontinental tour, the first of its kind. The musicians traveled by train to two dozen cities, playing a concert nearly every night. The tour would bring Stokowski's everyday association with the Philadelphians to an end. Before the concerts in Los Angeles—April 27 and 29, 1936—he gave a valedictory speech of sorts. "The position that this orchestra holds in the esteem of this great country has been shown to you night after night from the Atlantic to the Pacific," he told the musicians. "We have no soloists. None is needed, for each of you is incomparable, supreme on your instrument. These concerts must be our best, for our programs are a synthesis of a monumental era of music."

He led the orchestra in the music of Bach: the Toccata and Fugue in D Minor, followed by four more Bach pieces done Stokowski-style, the strings moving like warm air masses in the clear California night. After the intermission they played Wagner. Hugely ambitious himself, Stokowski recognized the breadth of Hollywood's ambition, its taste for the old, the grandiose, the outsize, the monumental.

When the tour ended, the musicians returned to Philadelphia. Stokowski returned to Los Angeles. The concerts there had made clear to him and the Hollywood brass alike that he was ready for the movies. He had a house built in Beverly Hills, parked a Rolls-Royce in the garage, and sifted the many offers that now came to him.

He appeared in two movies in the next year. In *The Big Broadcast of 1937*, a film contrived to feature celebrity walk-ons, he conducted an orchestra (billed as "His Orchestra") in his transcriptions of Bach's *Ein Feste Burg* and the "Little" Fugue in G Minor. In *100 Men and a Girl*, he reprised an episode from his own life. Set in the Depression, the movie tells the story of a young woman who tries to persuade Stokowski to lead a benefit concert with an orchestra of jobless musicians, who can turn their lives around if only they can play together. It opens with a five full minutes of Stokowski conducting Wagner's *Lohengrin*; the "girl" finally convinces him to take part in her scheme by springing in on him while he sits alone in a room playing the Toccata and Fugue in D Minor on a piano.

In movies as in music, Stokowski liked his own ideas best. Somebody had suggested that he play Richard Wagner. What he really wanted to do, though, was don a wig over his mane of whitening hair and play the title role in a big-screen life of Bach.

>>13>>   Walt Disney was in the audience at the Pan Pacific Auditorium. He sat in a folding chair and tried to keep his attention on the music, not *Snow White*.

He had a new musical piece of his own in mind: a dramatization of "The Sorcerer's Apprentice," in the version by Paul Dukas. It is the story of a lackey who dons his master's hat and gains magical powers but not the ability to control them. Dukas had adapted it from Goethe, who got it from the ancients; Disney had heard it in a recording made in 1929 by Arturo Toscanini and the New York Philharmonic. At twenty minutes, the piece was apt for a Silly Symphony, and Disney's people had all but reached out to Toscanini's people, hoping to arrange a collaboration.

Then Disney spotted Stokowski by himself at Chasen's restaurant, and they ate supper together.

"I am all steamed up over the idea of Stokowski working with us on *The Sorcerer's Apprentice*," Disney wrote to his New York agent in October 1937. "I feel that the possibilities of such a combination are so great that . . . I have already gone ahead and now have the story in work with this crew, on the possibility that we will be able to get together . . ." He had assigned teams of scriptwriters and animators to the new project. Now he sent a series of memos to the whole staff. One, thick with superlatives even for a Hollywood document, announced "a special short subject in collaboration with Leopold Stokowski . . . in his own interpretation of the world-famous descriptive score of *The Sorcerer's Apprentice*." Another urged a smaller group to respond creatively to a typed list of twenty questions about the "special." It would be "a musical fantasy offering an opportunity for a new type of entertainment," without dialogue or story, gags or slapstick. "It offers a challenge to the best imaginations on the lot," Disney declared. "Please *give*."

The biggest idea, credited to Disney himself, was that the "special" should feature Mickey Mouse as the sorcerer's apprentice. The implication of this bit of casting, as John Culhane has written, is that Mickey represented Disney, who, on the threshold of success with *Snow White*, was at once thrilled and daunted by his new powers. A dream sequence featuring Mickey, roughed out in mid-November 1937, supports the point:

> He struts to the brink of a cliff overlooking a calm sea; he whips it up to a rhythmic frenzy, waves dashing on the rocks as the music builds toward its climax. With a wave of his hand, Mickey causes huge storm clouds to gather over the ocean. His actions are those of a conductor

leading a symphony orchestra of the elements. He points a finger to the left—a bolt of lightning flashes. He points in the other direction—another bolt of lightning explodes. He repeats the action with both hands and a terrific crash is heard overhead—each outburst to be synchronized with a dramatic spot in the music. Mickey is enjoying himself immensely. When he has whipped up a terrific storm, he calms everything down.

The maker of animated films is a maestro of images, but he derives his powers from technology, specifically recorded sound. If *Snow White* would be the culmination of Disney's work since sound was introduced, "The Sorcerer's Apprentice" would be the story of his career so far. With it Mickey Mouse would be made new and the Silly Symphonies would be left behind.

"I have never been more enthused over anything in my life," he wrote to Stokowski, who was in Philadelphia, leading the orchestra in one last series of concerts at the Academy of Music. In reply Stokowski said he was "thrilled at the idea of recording *The Sorcerer's Apprentice* with you, because you have no more enthusiastic admirer in the world than I am." He had only one suggestion: What would Disney think of dropping Mickey Mouse and "creating an entirely new personality . . . a personality that could represent *you and me* . . . ?"

Disney ignored the suggestion. He saw Mickey as perfectly representative the way he was: a mouse who was auteur, maestro, and ordinary man all in one.

Snow White had its debut in California on December 21, 1937, then at Radio City Music Hall in Manhattan in January 1938. It brought Disney the acclamation he craved. Clark Gable and Carole Lombard, who attended the California screening, were heard crying at the end. Charlie Chaplin and Cecil B. DeMille wired congratulations. The *New Republic* critic Otis Ferguson called the movie "among the genuine artistic achievements of this country." The news from the business side was just as validating. *Snow White* brought in nearly seven million dollars in its first six months, making it the highest-grossing American film to that point. Suddenly, Disney said, "we became aware that the days of the animated cartoon, as we had known it, were over."

Stokowski held two "final" concerts in December, and in each he set new American music against the "antique" music (said one reviewer) of Palestrina, Frescobaldi, and Bach. The Bach program, all in a minor key, was a long denouement: the somber Prelude and Fugue in E minor, the latter shaking off the torpor of the former; the chorale "Mein Jesu, was für Seelenweh," in which the whole orchestra seems to hold its breath; and the Passacaglia and Fugue in C Minor, a cavalry charge of thrumming timpani and surging brass, with Stokowski out in front flying the flag of his ardor one last time. He let the music speak for him, ending at the Academy of Music where he had begun at St. Bartholomew's.

He arranged to go to Europe with Garbo. Their trip would be a spontaneous getaway after his three decades of marriage to an orchestra. As it turned out, it would be as demanding as conducting. Actress and maestro would be dogged by paparazzi. A photograph taken in Rome shows them with eyes averted, faces shielded by big hats. Stokowski would leave America as a famous conductor and return as a famous person, period.

First he had to consummate his affair with Disney. On January 9 and 10, 1938, he led a freelance orchestra in a recording of "The Sorcerer's Apprentice" at a soundstage in Los Angeles. The session began at midnight: that way the musicians, primed with coffee, would be more alert than in the daytime. They played for three hours. A mechanical click track, indicating a preferred tempo for the animators to work with, was set against Stokowski's tempestuous variations. He ignored it, removing the headphones.

Once the music was done, the animators could begin in earnest. Right away Disney's team, working at twenty-four frames per second, set images to the music, beginning with the scene in which Mickey Mouse rises after his dream, a sleeper awaking to his new powers of invention and persuasion.

>>14>>   A fantasia is a piece of music freely constructed—created through a process somewhere between composition and improvisation, so as to suggest freedom. Bach used the term freely in characterizing his music. He used *fantasia* to denote pieces in which he worked through a set of melodies (such as those in a chorale) one by one, enfolding each in a fugue. He gave the name *fantasia* to the instructive, beguiling three-part keyboard works that he later renamed the *sinfonias*, which would then be paired with the two-part *prelaudia* to form the inventions, calling attention to the act of invention at the center of his music. He applied *fantasia* to preludes paired with fugues—the *Chromatic Fantasia and Fugue*, for example—and to freestanding organ pieces that he left complete in themselves, preludes to nothing except the experience and imagination of the listener.

A fantasia is always playful, but not always delightful. In November 1720, the autumn after Maria Barbara's death, Bach had gone from Köthen to

Hamburg in pursuit of an open position. There, at the giant organ of the Catherinenkirche, he played his Fantasia in G Minor: a sonic dust storm, free of strict tempo, clear melody, sharp contrast—a work whose extreme freedom suggests, in his choice of it, that he was at a loss. Then he took up a blocky chorale fantasia perfected by the great Hamburg organist J. A. Reincken and elaborated on it for half an hour or more, like a surveyor dividing the land into freeholdings extending from the town square all the way to the horizon. Reincken, age ninety-seven, was there that day, and he was touched and awed: "I thought this art had died," he told Bach, "but I see it still lives in you." The critic Johann Mattheson was there too, and he gave Bach's free way of playing the name *stylus fantasticus*.

Even in grief, Bach was a fantasist extraordinaire. This quality was at the root of Stokowski's identification with him, and it was the basis of Stokowski's transcriptions, which, at their most adventurous, are symphonic fantasies on the themes of Bach.

It was at the root of Stokowski's interest in Walt Disney, too. Of the many ideas that Stokowski brought to Disney, two were crucial: that the movie they were making together should be called *Fantasia*, and that it should begin with the music of Bach. These ideas were frankly oppositional; with them Stokowski brought in Bach as a bulwark against the sentimentality of "The Sorcerer's Apprentice" and the cloying charm of Mickey Mouse. These ideas would change the "concert feature" (as Disney was calling it) from a presentation to a transcription, a refashioning of classical music for the instrument of the cartoon. And they would make it possible for everyone involved, from Disney and Stokowski to the animators and "continuity men" to the gardener who contributed a story idea now and then, to recognize that the animation process was a fantastic new invention: disciplined to the point of ritual, Baroque in its creation of movement through repetition, yet childlike in that it began with some people in a room, playing together.

>>15>>

DISNEY: What does the Toccata and Fugue represent?

STOKOWSKI: It is a motif or decorative pattern which gradually develops more and more . . . Finally, it becomes perfectly free. The theme which comes at the beginning develops more and more, with more and more voices and instruments. It is a growth like a tree growing from a seed.

The setting was Room 232 at the Disney studios on Hyperion Avenue in Los Angeles. Disney typically spent part of each day in the "sweatbox"—the small, dark room where animators screened their work for him, often sequences of several hundred drawings that produced only a few moments of action. In the fall of 1938 he had spent as much time in Room 232, listening to records with Stokowski as his tutor. Stokowski would play a selection on the phonograph, and Disney would tell him what he saw in his mind's eye ("the ends of a bunch of violin bows going up and down," for example). Now the two together were explaining Bach's Toccata and Fugue in D Minor to a team of animators and story men, proposing that the best follow-up to *Snow White* would be a "concert feature" involving classical music and that the best way to open it would be with a semiabstract rendering of the music of Bach.

> STOKOWSKI: The Toccata is "A," the Fugue is "B," and we return to "A" at the end. The Toccata starts off with three phrases, which are like the playing of immense trumpets to call you to attention. For that reason, this composition is a wonderful selection with which to begin your picture. It is very arresting. After that, the music goes down low and swells up to a tremendous climax at the end of the Toccata. The Toccata is really all in one mass, very much alike. Then follows the immense contrast—the Fugue.
>
> DISNEY: We don't want to follow what anyone else has done in the abstract. We have never dealt in the abstract; we have given things a reason for existing, and tried to convince the audience that it could happen, or was possible. I think, even in this, if we take the sound track and use that and build through on that, it furnishes a reason for whatever we are doing on screen.
>
> STOKOWSKI: How will we represent the silence on the screen?
>
> DISNEY: At first, it will all be dark. Then the light comes up . . .

Fantasia was "an experimental thing," but its creators had definite aims. They hoped to "change the history of motion pictures" (Disney told the animators) and to change people's minds about classical music. "There are things in that music that the general public will not understand until they see the things on the screen representing that music," he said of the Toccata and Fugue in D Minor. "Then they will feel the depth in that music. Our object is to reach the very people who have walked out on this Toccata and Fugue because they didn't understand it. I am one of those people; but when I understand it, I like it."

Five months passed before the animators began their work, and Disney and Stokowski kept brainstorming. Disney proposed that the Toccata and Fugue be animated using 3D effects, which audience members would see through glasses given to them with their tickets. Stokowski suggested injecting bursts of evocative perfume into the theater at key moments. They went back and forth as to whether the Bach piece should open the feature. They worried about the title—"Fant-a-*zee*-ah," as Stokowski said it—out of concern that it would be mangled by the speakers of American English.

Disney brought in Oskar Fischinger, a German maker of abstract films, to oversee the animation, and engaged the music critic Deems Taylor to tell viewers what they were hearing. Stokowski decided to record the sound track with the Philadelphia Orchestra, but first was filmed conducting a freelance orchestra in Los Angeles—the symphonic equivalent of lip-synching. He postponed the session for a week while waiting for a specially fitted tailcoat to arrive from the east.

In March and April 1939, Stokowski led a series of concerts at the Academy of Music in Philadelphia, opening with his transcription of the Toccata and Fugue in D Minor, now more than ever his signature piece. Over three days in April the orchestra played the music for the movie. Baffles were set up to separate the woodwinds from the brass, the brass from the strings; these made the recorded sound clearer but made it harder for the musicians to play together. Stokowski remonstrated with the technicians. A recording crew huddled in the basement, watching the wooden stage floor flex overhead like the soundboard of a musical instrument. Disney, in from Los Angeles, sat listening in the empty hall, seeing moving pictures in his mind's eye.

The title stuck. So did the opening sequence. And so Bach, not Beethoven or Stravinsky, became the muse of *Fantasia* and of the Stokowski-Disney collaboration, one as unusual as any in the history of the arts in America.

>>16>> The colors are faded now, even after a digital restoration. The special effects are not so special. The dinosaurs and fauns and fairies and other creatures from the age of enchantment now seem to belong to the age of the movie, like the gilt heroes on the ceiling of the old music hall downtown.

Fantasia is a cave painting from cinema's golden age, an artifact of the days when giants walked Hollywood Boulevard. And yet it has never been matched. No movie producer has treated high culture as imaginatively as

Disney did, and no musician—not Sinatra or Elvis or the Beatles, not Madonna or Prince or Beyoncé—has stormed Hollywood with Stokowski's pluck and dash. Like Bach's cello suites, *Fantasia* is a first of its kind that is also the best; like *Citizen Kane* (made a year later) it seems at once to have opened up new creative possibilities and to have fulfilled, even exhausted, them.

The Toccata and Fugue in D Minor is the most antique-looking episode in the movie, and yet, seven decades on, it is the one that has the greatest power. There are a number of reasons for this. A crucial one is that the episode dramatizes the process of invention that inheres in Bach's music—the process of invention that Disney and Stokowski, responding to the music, called forth in each other as never before.

From the moment the curtains part on a field of blue and we glimpse the assembling musicians, each a moving silhouette, it is clear that this work is something different. For one thing, it is filmed, not drawn: it is closer to cinematic realism than to animation. For another, it is in color, and the musicians, set against the field of blue, are larger, realer than life: they are cartoons of themselves. There's the sound of a horn playing a few bars, a violin fiddled as if in a Carpathian village. There's the clomp of footsteps as some musicians—violin, bassoon, flute, bass fiddle—climb the risers and take their positions. Two harpists in tight-waisted dresses go to their instruments, which await all aglint like a pair of steeds. This is the symphony personified by the shapes of its instruments; this is the orchestra as a little society, like the little society of Snow White and her seven underlings, where every member has a character type and a role to play.

Deems Taylor comes into the scene as an interloper from the everyday. He stands between the harps, ill-lit and ill at ease; he reads from notecards, slope-shouldered and casual even in evening dress. He tells us that it is his pleasure to welcome us—"on behalf of Walt Disney, Leopold Stokowski, and all the other artists and musicians whose combined talents went into the creation of this new form of entertainment, *Fantasia*."

A music critic, he explains the piece in terms that can be grasped by a child. "What you're going to see," he says, "is the designs and pictures and stories of what music inspired in the minds and imaginations of a group of artists." The opening number will be absolute music—music that exists for its own sake—and the movie will try to depict what might go on in the mind of the person listening to it. "At first you are more or less conscious of the orchestra," he explains, "so our picture opens with a series of impressions of the conductor and the players. Then the music begins to suggest other things to your imagination—oh, just masses of color, or cloud forms, or vague shadows, or geometrical objects floating in space."

The shadow of the conductor ascends in front of him as he finishes and yields to the music at last: "the Toccata and Fugue in D Minor, by Johann Sebastian Bach, interpreted in pictures by Walt Disney and his associates, and in music by the Philadelphia Orchestra and its conductor, Leopold Stokowski."

That shadow says more than Taylor's whole commentary. It says that the Bach sequence, the most abstract in the film, will also be the most realistic, held together by the silhouette of Stokowski, who at once will act as the conductor and represent the composer.

He is everything the critic is not: statuesque, imperious, a mystery. He mounts the podium with his back to us; he spreads his hands, turns eaglishly to the orchestra; turns left, throws down his hands together, calling forth music; repeats the gesture to the right, and then straight ahead, until the music spreads through the orchestra and surges up, lighting him with sound, a circle pink at the center.

You know immediately that Disney and Stokowski were right to fret about the opening, and right to settle on Bach. With those three giant bolts of sound the Toccata and Fugue in D Minor ignites the film, positions it as forever forward-looking.

Stokowski described the toccata's theme to the animators as akin to a seed growing into a tree, and now we see that seed distributed through the orchestra: blue in the oboes, green in the clarinets, pink and gold in the strings, and then again, purple this time, in the hands of the conductor, arms upraised, extended, outspread. Then the whole thing takes flight. The musicians are in the air, silhouettes flitting against the scrim, the horn players on their feet, the tympanist at the kettledrums like a blacksmith at his anvil.

There is suspense, or the music of suspense, as the orchestra ascends, the strings racing across the sky, the horns trailing. As they peak, all together, the camera—this is a film, after all—returns to the conductor. He is a hieratic figure, soaked in red. But as he turns we see his profile, pink and shadowed, the face of a human being after all.

So much of Stokowski's sense of Bach is dramatized in the toccata sequence: the variety of colors; the strict, almost canonical rotation of the theme from one voice to another; the sense that all this order and splendor proceeds, phrase for phrase, from the hands of genius—that it is a man's outsize passion formally expressed. The sequence features the musicians, but it belongs to Stokowski, who is as much a performer as they.

In the seam between the toccata and the fugue, the movie changes. The blood-red sky gives way to a gray-blue cloudscape. Colorized live action gives way to animation. The creative impetus is passed from Stokowski's orchestra to Disney's crew of a dozen animators. The change corresponds to the change in Bach's music. Repetition, a general motif in the toccata, is an obsessive one in the fugue, and the repetition of key images in the orchestra—violinists pulling their bows two or four times per second—gives way to the twenty-four-per-second repetition of images in the animation process, which produces movement by subjecting a theme to ever-so-slight variations.

Some streaks of color dot the sky. They look like kites—no, like violin bows, which dance like fireflies, then give way to a violin bridge turning in space, like the Golden Gate Bridge. The animators are working in the boss's idea as early as possible.

Animation is collective work in the extreme, occupying a space between collaboration and the assembly line. The key to Disney's process was that he suppressed or disguised the collaboration, so that the final product was a Walt Disney Production. Disney told the animators that there should be a single strong image on the screen at any time, rather than the multiple images Oskar Fischinger favored. It sounds restrictive, even authoritarian. But the presentation of images in sequence makes each one seem to come from the hand of an artist. The animators are taking turns, like square dancers, or jazz musicians jamming on a riff, or runners in relay, or performers on parade. As the images follow one another—lines rippling over a landscape, an ideal Midwest seen from the air; strings rolling solo, the superhighway a decade before the fact; light sparkling on the ripples running across a still lake; those violin bows again, plunging beneath the surface—you can feel the artists collaborating, like actors stepping out for curtain calls before the company bow at the end.

The total effect is not of a group effort, though. It is of the individual imagination. This is why the Toccata and Fugue sequence of *Fantasia* has such power. It is Hollywood's most vivid representation of the interior life.

Stokowski was a showman, and his Bach transcriptions are known as showpieces, exuberant demonstrations of the prowess of the symphony orchestra and its conductor. It is true: he revealed the organ works as polychrome, spacious, worldly creations; he took them out of the church, installed them in the concert hall, and faced them out toward the high skies and wide-open spaces of America. But the real change he brought about was a subtler one. His transcriptions open up the inner life of the organ works, and of Bach's music, and of classical music generally, for the modern listener, the ordinary person who has been made ready for transcendence by recordings.

With *Fantasia* Disney's animators did it all over again, transcribing his transcriptions for the big screen and the large audience. They recognized the spaciousness of the music and saw that space as inner space, as music of the mind. By the time a boulder, a stumbling block, tumbles down a passage, we realize where we are. We are in the place, the human center—the soul, let's say—where the human person lives his or her true life. There is plenty of headroom here; there is space for patterns and images, for fantasy. If it is lacking in conflict, prepsychological in its sense of things, well, that is a lack but not a liability, not yet. *Fantasia* is not an end: it is a beginning. It opens up the layers of the imagination, its hidden passages, its still pools and hot springs; it shines a light on Bach's colossal interior life, extends a hand, and beckons us to come in.

>>17>> "What war?" Walt Disney said. While he was in the sweatbox, working on rough cuts of *Fantasia*, *Pinocchio*, and *Bambi* all at once, world war came again to Europe. Nazi Germany, Fascist Italy, Soviet Russia: the countries most invested culturally in music were the most belligerent, as if to prove Albert Schweitzer's proposition that musical discord from Bach onward augured political strife.

Schweitzer had just arrived in Bordeaux by ship when the rumors of war became facts. He booked a fresh passage on the same ship and returned to Lambaréné, trailed by Hélène and Rhena, the better to be prepared when war came to central Africa and the better to keep Hélène, with her Jewish ancestry, out of reach of the SS. As doctors and nurses returned to Europe, he struggled to maintain a staff, and soon all but the neediest patients were turned away. "Many of the homeward bound were able to travel by steamer or motorboat, but others had to make their way to distant villages by long and difficult jungle trails," he wrote. "At last they had all gone and the heart-rending scenes were at an end."

Pablo Casals was in the Grand Hotel in Prades. The Nazis sought to occupy France, and General Franco's troops were expected to come over the border with Spain at Hitler's behest. Casals's friends insisted that he must leave the country, and he agreed that they were right. But after a planned escape by sea from Bordeaux fell through—the ship struck a mine on the approach to the harbor, caught fire, and sank—he returned to Prades.

Stokowski was touring South America with a new orchestra. His work for Disney done, his attention claimed neither by Philadelphia nor by Hollywood, he had acted on a long-standing desire and formed an ensemble of musicians in their teens and twenties. *Fantasia* would appeal to young people imaginatively; the All-American Youth Orchestra would involve them directly, in the time-honored way. At the same time, it would represent U.S. interests in countries whose governments were being courted by the Nazis. So he and a hundred musicians had set sail for Rio de Janeiro, with his copyist, Lucien Cailliet, working up a transcription of Bach's third violin partita during rehearsals aboard ship.

Myra Hess was at the National Gallery in Trafalgar Square. With London theaters and concert halls observing a nightly blackout so as to avoid detection by the Luftwaffe, the city's musical life was diminished. Hess, a Londoner, had become a household name with "Jesu, Joy of Man's Desiring," her transcription of a Bach chorale: sheet music parts for solo piano and for four hands were on the racks of tens of thousands of pianos. She wrote to Kenneth Clark, director of the gallery, proposing daytime concerts, and they were arranged: a concert at 1:00 p.m. each weekday, and Tuesdays and Thursdays at 5:00 p.m. More than a thousand people showed up for the first concert, where Hess played two Bach preludes and fugues, along with Scarlatti, Beethoven, Schubert, Chopin, and Brahms. She concluded with "Jesu, Joy of Man's Desiring."

Walt Disney was in the sweatbox, now focused on *Fantasia* alone. With *Pinocchio* released to acclaim (the "happiest event since the war," *The New York Times*'s critic said), the studio's sales reps called on theater owners across the country, urging them to install a sound system specially designed for the new film. Disney saw *Fantasia* as akin to a theatrical "road show" more than a motion picture. He envisioned a system that would "create the illusion that the actual Symphony Orchestra is playing in the theater." So it was that as the remaining Jews in Germany went into hiding, as Paris fell and was occupied by German and Italian troops, as the people of London rigged blackout curtains and perfected air-raid procedures, technicians in New York, Boston, Chicago, and San Francisco climbed stepladders with screwdrivers to equip theaters with Fantasound.

The film was done except for the final sequence, a slow-motion tableau set to Schubert's "Ave Maria." This called for a long shot using a new "multiplane" camera, which gave two-dimensional animation the illusion of depth. All through the summer of 1940 a crew shot and reshot the "Ave Maria" on a soundstage at the Disney studios. One take was ruined by the use of the wrong lens. Another was shaken up by an earthquake. Another had "jitters" that

Disney found intolerable. The day before the premiere the crew got it right. The print was taken by motorcycle to the airport and put on a plane to New York, where it was matched to the sound track Stokowski had recorded long before.

"Ave Maria" is set in counterpoint to the sequence before it, "Night on Bald Mountain," in which Mussorgsky's tone poem calls forth a story of the worship of a devil modeled on the Dracula of Bela Lugosi. "The forces of good on one side and evil on the other is what I'm trying to see in this thing," Disney said. Deems Taylor introduces the two sequences together as "a picture of a struggle between the profane and the sacred," in which the devotees of darkness on Bald Mountain (he wrote) are overcome by "a vast host of worshippers" of the God of Light.

The more telling counterpoint is between the "Ave Maria" that ends the film and the Toccata and Fugue in D Minor that began it. The pilgrims processing slowly in dim light recall the silhouetted musicians taking their places onstage. Here again the ensuing action takes place in the sky, and the spectacularly varied skyscape of the Fugue has become the serene one of the "Ave Maria," a canopied forest meant to suggest a vast open-air cathedral, one consecrated, in effect, by a Gothic arch, or ruin of an arch, set mysteriously in the middle of it— so that you have "the feeling that you are inside a cathedral," Disney told the animators, "without showing anything that is actually recognizable as a cathedral." The spiritual character of Bach's music, implicit in the orchestrated organ work of the Toccata and Fugue, is made explicit in Schubert's choral "Ave Maria." Disney had set out to establish film animation as more than mere cartooning. But Stokowski, urging him to begin with Bach, had set him on a higher path, and they made the transcription of classical music for a new audience into a sacred calling.

>>18>> "Let us begin by noting that motion-picture history was made at the Broadway Theatre last night with the spectacular world premiere of Walt Disney's long-awaited *Fantasia* . . ." the *Times*'s movie man declared. "Let us temperately admit that *Fantasia* is simply terrific—as terrific as anything that has ever happened on a screen. And then let's get on from there."

Fantasia had its premiere on November 13, 1940, in a posh theater on West Fifty-third Street. London had been blitzed by the Luftwaffe almost every night since August. "Paris," Janet Flanner reported, "is now the capital of limbo. It is a beautiful city on the banks of the Seine which only Berlin, the capital of Germany, knows all about." In Manhattan, it was raining.

The event suggests how little has changed in the sacred rites of publicity. Disney was profiled in *The Atlantic* ("Walt is the spark plug of production. No story starts toward a picture until Walt has bought or invented it . . ."). Stokowski was on the cover of *Time* ("Before it was finished, white-haired Maestro Stokowski had come out with so many other bright ideas for symphonic animovies that . . . Stoky and Disney decided to build around Mickey Mouse's sorcery act a whole program of cinesymphonies"). The screening was a benefit for a new charity, British War Relief. Philanthropists outnumbered starlets. They were given printed programs, as at the opera or the legitimate theater. When the music began, they felt it surge through their seats.

"The beginning of the picture is an absolute stroke of genius," Stokowski told Disney. "It begins so imperceptibly. The public's attention is gradually attracted and before they know it they are in the picture." He went on: "The audience's interest in the Bach and its applause after the Bach was very great. I saw clearly that we did not misjudge the interest that this number can have for its audience and its value as an Overture to the picture."

Fantasia clearly changed the way we see movies. That it changed the way people think about classical music is less clear. For one thing, the people who saw it, then as now, were people who were drawn to classical music anyway. For another, the movie's innovations challenged the classical music culture rather than fostering it. Fantasound and later sound systems made movie theaters competitive with concert halls, setting up a contest the concert halls would lose. The sound track, fusing the music with the image, ushered in an era in which orchestral music was heard most often as the accompaniment in movies. And the notion that classical music stands in need of popularization, and that the public will be educated—elevated—in the process, has brought forth works that are not worthy of the music, and at the same time has instilled the idea that the music itself cannot be appreciated without assistance. *Fantasia* deserves acclaim not for what it did, but for what it is—an ecstatic one-off, a transcription unlike any before or since.

As Disney read the reviews the next day, Stokowski went into a recording studio with the All-American Youth Orchestra. The session included Bach's "Little" Fugue in G Minor, which he had tried to persuade Disney to use in *Fantasia*. The Stokowski sound is there: robust, confident, spatially grand. But there is no serenity in it, even in the light woodwind passages. The orchestra surges at the music. The playing is brisk, even frantic. Soon Stokowski would replace Bach's Toccata and Fugue in D Minor with "The Star-Spangled Banner" as a concert opener. He would contact the army and volunteer to help raise the standard of U.S. military bands. He would sign a contract for a book—to be called *Music for All of Us*—in which he would present music as "an inspirational force in all our lives . . . one element to help us build a new conception of life in which the madness and cruelty of wars will be replaced by a simple understanding of the brotherhood of man." Even for Stokowski, sonic sybarite, the hour was getting late.

One night a month later the Luftwaffe massed over London once and for all. December 29, 1940, was a quiet Sunday in the city. The BBC Home Service had scheduled an evening broadcast of Bach. "Tonight is the *Christmas Oratorio*," one Londoner wrote to a friend, "and we have records of two Brandenburgs—could life be better?"

The alert sounded just after six. "The sound goes from a low to a high pitch, up and down every few seconds," Ernie Pyle reported. Next was the sound of air-raid sirens, placed every fifteen blocks, "like a series of great sound waves crashing over the city."

Tens of thousands of bombs and incendiaries whistled through the air that night. A skirt of fire encircled the City of London, curtaining it off from past and future alike. Several hundred buildings were struck. One was the church of All Hallows by the Tower. Bombs punctured the roof. Explosives tumbled end over end and sprang alight. Flames licked at the stone foundations and tendriled skyward, joining other flames like a chorus of applause. With a snowfall of shattered glass, the Gothic windows were lit up from the inside. The bells, long tied up for the nightly blackouts, were set loose as the ropes burned through, and rang wildly before falling to the ground. The tower stood reverent amid the horror as the great organ, all its lead pipes swelling at once with hot air, screamed with the pain of war and then, the cabinet burning, the pipes melting into air, went silent.

>>**19**>> "We wander in darkness now, but with one another we all have the conviction that we are advancing toward the light; that again a time will come when religion and ethical thinking will be united," Albert Schweitzer had written when Hitler took power. "This we believe, and hope and work for, maintaining the belief that if we make ethical ideals active in our lives, then the time will come when peoples will do the same."

Schweitzer had hoped to scale back his work at the clinic when he turned sixty-five; he had expected to spend more time in Europe, to give more recitals, to write more books. "I even dreamed of some time taking several weeks' vacation," he wrote. "And here comes the war to supervene and change every-thing." His daughter, Rhena, who had grown up in France, had come to see the clinic for the first time, but was forced to return home in haste; his wife, Hélène, returned to Lambaréné from France on a voyage shot through with the fear that she would be seized by the Nazis. Schweitzer himself was forced to redouble his efforts to support the clinic, because the war made it hard to buy supplies and even harder to get them shipped to Africa. He spent money intended for an X-ray machine on stocks of medicine. He obtained supplies of minerals scarce in the local diet: calcium, phosphorus, iron. He supervised the clearing of land and the building of retaining walls to prevent erosion. He got a good price on a vast supply of rice, which would feed the village for three years.

He had never been to the United States, but some American devotees of his work organized an Albert Schweitzer Fellowship, named for his notion of "a fellowship of those who bear the mark of pain" and who "are united by a secret bond" in consequence. Philanthropists raised money for medicine and supplies (including extra-large surgical gloves for his big hands); the American Guild of Organists held a series of benefit recitals.

Schweitzer himself, fixed in Lambaréné for the duration, played for the community that was the clinic—patients, doctors, nurses, staff, and neighbors. "We are all awfully tired, but the Doctor is the most courageous of all," one nurse reported in a letter to the Fellowship. "After the day's duties he plays on the piano with organ pedals and from our room, in the silence of the night and in the midst of the big forest, we enjoy the most perfect recitals." The village also had a small radio station, and one day Schweitzer, listening to a BBC broadcast, heard one of his own recordings.

>>20>> Pablo Casals played the cello, taught, read, followed the news on the radio, and answered his mail, which was full of requests for him to come and play.

He had bought a house with a view of Le Canigou, to which he tipped his hat when he passed. In the house he kept a framed photograph of the late vio-linist Eugène Ysaÿe, with whom he had spent many evenings making music in Paris. "Our group would come together, like homing pigeons, from all parts of the globe," he recalled. "Ysaÿe would have just returned from a tour of Russia, Kreisler from the United States, Bauer from the Orient, I perhaps from South America. How we all longed for that moment! Then we would play together for the sheer love of playing, without thought of concert programs or time schedules, of impresarios, box-office sales, audiences, music critics. Just ourselves and the music!"

The photograph showed Ysaÿe, a Belgian, playing the violin atop a sand dune in La Panne, where the Belgian army had joined the Allies in trench warfare against the German army. It had been taken in 1916 by Elisabeth, who was now the queen of the Belgians. It was an image of the artist as hero: there was the great violinist and national treasure, stout and dignified in concert dress, making music in the contested space.

Casals played benefit concerts for the Red Cross in Switzerland and free France. But he declined most of the invitations that came to him. It was a simple yes or no for him. If the invitation came from a country that had recognized Franco as the head of Spain—and several dozen countries had— he refused it. His refusal was meant as a statement about the nature of art, which celebrated freedom and depended on it. And it was a statement about the conditions suitable for an artist in exile from Spain. The terms of his participation were that Franco's illegitimate dictatorship be called by its name.

He was as engaged politically as any musician who had gone before him. But the terms of engagement had changed. During the Great War, to make music in wartime had been a form of resistance. Now it could be seen as a form of collaboration.

How had this happened? Through recordings. The ubiquity of recordings had altered the power of music. When music was dependent on the musician, the musician gained power through the ability to make music. With recorded music widely available, the musician gained power through the ability to withhold the music—to shape the conditions of a performance, even through a refusal to participate, the way the recording studio shaped the aural surroundings.

One day some SS officers called on Casals at his house in Prades. They introduced themselves as admirers, men who had grown up knowing his name. They asked him to come to Germany to play for the Führer. He declined, saying he was old and loath to travel. One officer asked a favor: "'Would you play some Brahms or Bach for us?' I had the strange feeling that this officer actually wanted to hear me play.

"I told him that the rheumatism in my shoulder wouldn't permit my playing.

"He walked to the piano, sat down, and played a passage from a Bach aria."

Then he asked to see Casals's cello. Casals took it out and showed it to them. The officers touched the cello, picked it up.

" 'We cannot go away without a souvenir from you.' I understood their chief would ask them for proof of their visit; I signed a photograph on which I wrote: 'In remembrance of your visit to Prades.' As they went, and I looked out of the window, they asked me if they could take a photograph (another proof). I did not see them again. But I had not played for them."

Casals would withhold his music liberally in the years to come. But he couldn't withhold it altogether. During the war EMI released his recordings of the cello suites—first suites two and three, then suites one and six. With them he had made a new beginning through Bach. He had turned the recording studio into an ideal space governed by the laws of art. Now he found fault with them; he wished they could be sped up slightly "in order to recover the liveliness that was lost during mechanical recording." He thought of doing them over again. But he left them alone. In the circumstances, they were good enough.

PART IV

Technical

Transcendence

>>1>> "Afterwards, in the cold, almost unheated train compartment," the still-young genius recalled, "I sketched on the blank edge of my newspaper what I remembered of the B pattern. Then as the train jerked toward Cambridge, I tried to decide between two- and three-chain models. As far as I could tell, the reason the Kings group did not like two chains was not foolproof. It depended on the water content of the DNA samples, a value they admitted might be in great error. Thus by the time I had cycled back to college and climbed over the back gate, I had decided to build two-chain models. Francis would have to agree. Even though he was a physicist, he knew that important biological objects come in pairs."

That is James Watson, describing how he and his scientific partner, Francis Crick, discovered the structure of DNA in 1953. The discovery would characterize the second half of the century the way the discovery of the structure of the atom had characterized the first half. It revealed the underlying pattern of organic matter, a sequence paired and stranded. It proposed that many of the qualities we most prize in humanity and society are biological rather than cultural. It suggested that our existence is at once more orderly and more mysterious than we can grasp. It invited us to imitate the pattern of life, and to alter it; it inspired awe and fear alike.

The discovery won Watson and Crick a Nobel Prize. But in retrospect it is their process, as much as their discovery, that reveals the spirit of the age. They went about things more like private detectives than research scientists. Is it any wonder why? Half a century of collective scientific inquiry had wound up producing an atomic killing machine, and that grim outcome suggested that the ardor of vast research projects was akin to the mass manias of communism, fascism, and Nazism. So Watson and Crick set up as outriders. They worked in a small laboratory in a backwater of Cambridge. They sketched chemical models on newspapers in train cars, on napkins in pubs, in conversation during long coffee breaks at the lab. They improvised with slide rules and chalk. They crossed the scientific method with the spirit of Rube Goldberg in order to uncover hidden structures and bring them to light.

The great Bach recordings of the postwar years were made in that spirit. Yes, plenty of musicians played Bach in traditional ways, producing a sumptuous, Western Civ–saturated sound for recitals, festivals, anniversaries, and the like, and the upholding of this approach was a brave act of cultural reclamation. But many others scraped away the accretions of history and culture, of tradition and performance practice, in order to uncover the structure of the music, its inviolable inner architecture. They sought to transcend history and society so as to make Bach's music a music of the mind.

Is it any wonder why? History had dead-ended. The war had shattered ancient social structures and left them open to the burning sky. Now the place was being "rehabilitated." Europeans (Britons, too) were rebuilding their cities, restoring their landmarks, raising walls and bridges to replace the ones the bombs had brought down. They asked themselves which structures from their past should be kept and which should be let go. They asked what a rehabilitated Europe should look and sound like.

Meanwhile in North America the people who ran things were devising a society unlike any in Europe: skyscrapers and suspension bridges and power plants, planned communities and state colleges and office parks. They proceeded as if there were no underlying structures, and much of what Greil Marcus calls "the old, weird America" was razed in the process.

In a sense, the new Bach interpreters were in line with all these developments. For the first time North American musicians were devising approaches to Bach that were not dependent on European examples. At the same time, they were discovering in Bach a counterlife—finding structures and working methods defiant of the emerging American society, which was defined by the mass market. Their musical austerity was rich in social purpose. It was set against European ruin and American abundance alike.

Albert Einstein was the ideal. Now a U.S. citizen, ensconced at the Institute for Advanced Study in Princeton, Einstein had become the cynosure for the postwar civilized person, and if the substance of his civilization was his concern about the perils of nuclear war, the image of it was the *Life* photograph of him playing the violin near a laboratory blackboard in a baggy suit and a loosened tie. His love of music began and ended with Bach. Mozart he cherished; Wagner he abhorred; Beethoven he declared too "naked" and personal, explaining, "Give me Bach, Bach, and more Bach." In Berlin he had relaxed after work by playing the violin, first improvising, next turning to Mozart, and then moving to the "clear constructions of Bach in order to follow through." In Princeton, he mainly played the piano. "This is what I have to say about Bach's life and work," he had said. "Listen, play, love, revere—and keep your mouth shut."

Pianists led the way. In the twenties the Bach interpreter Donald Tovey (Albert Schweitzer's host in Edinburgh) had distinguished between the "architectural" music of the Baroque era and the "dramatic" music of the Classical period. Now pianists brought the distinction to life, taking an approach to Bach that blended art and engineering. The score became a blueprint, the music a scale model constructed at the worktable of the instrument. Preludes were topped by fugues, variations set upon one another like dominoes. The two hands, at the keyboard, moved like elevators in their shafts, only intermittently coinciding. Decorative elements were employed within a formal economy, easing the rigor of the straight lines. The parts of the music were set at angles and screwed together like an Erector set, then straightened and tightened. The new Bach would be an alternative to the old one, a musico-cultural counterpoint.

The pianists took full advantage of technology, beginning with the piano itself. Unlike the human voice, the violin, the cello, and the organ, the piano was not common in Bach's lifetime, which means that to play Bach's music on the piano was to commit a transhistorical act. At the same time, the piano's bulk (a grand piano, a thousand pounds) wound up making it distinctive to America. Year after year, many European pianos were shipped across the Atlantic, from the Vienna-made Bösendorfer on down. But by midcentury the pianos favored in American concert halls and recording studios were those made by Steinway & Sons in a factory in Astoria, Queens, across the river from Carnegie Hall. The new Bach would be played on New World instruments.

Recordings compounded the act of abstraction, making the music itself a cultural artifact twice removed. Before the war, recording technology had taken the music of Bach out of churches and concert halls and conservatories and into flats and houses, bedsits and country estates, and movie theaters, too, with effects as profound as they were various. Albert Schweitzer had used recordings to revive Bach for the modern age, Pablo Casals to situate him in private life, Leopold Stokowski to transcribe him for the movies. Owing to them, and their counterparts, by 1945 there existed a vast body of recorded music alongside the canon of sheet music, the life of the churches, and the schedules of touring virtuosi. Now these recordings enabled the music of Bach to transcend the making of it. They uprooted it from the society where it had originated. They offered access to it outside the standard programs of European and American cultural education. They empowered and emboldened the individual listener. Now it was possible to know the music of Bach well without knowing how to play the music of Bach at all.

Recorded music made the musician, too, less a player and more a listener, whose knowledge of the music was gained at the record player and the radio as well as at the piano or in the auditorium—not painstakingly and sequentially, from minuet to fugue to partita to suite, but through the immediate apprehension of a great performance registered by a recording. And it rendered classical music not so much a tradition, a canon, or a discipline so much as an ever-expanding collection of peak experiences.

>>2>> Rosalyn Tureck wagged her hands in a magnetic field, making sounds that approximated a Bach concerto for clavier. Then and there, onstage at Carnegie Hall, she knew what she must do with her life.

She was a piano prodigy from Chicago. While a student at Juilliard, she sought to win a scholarship by mastering a new electrified instrument called the theremin, whose inventor had wowed her in Chicago. To play the theremin you moved your hands between two steel poles, creating sound from the resulting fluctuations in their magnetic field. In this way, in the fall of 1932, Tureck, age eighteen, female and vivacious when such qualities were rare in a concert artist, made her New York recital debut.

Already a "sudden blinding insight" had prompted her to devote herself to the music of Bach. She had been playing a Bach fugue on the piano when suddenly (she recalled) she "went into a trance. How long it lasted I don't know, but when I came to I knew I'd seen both the multi-levelled structure of the concept and the technique required to fulfill it. Like Alice, I'd gone through a small door into an infinite green universe and I wanted to stay in that universe forever."

She pledged to commit her talent to Bach, and enlisted her teacher at Juilliard, who knew Bach's power. This was Olga Samaroff-Stokowski. Following a pattern established by Leopold Stokowski, her long-ago ex-husband, Samaroff-Stokowski trained Tureck in the Romantic repertoire and in new music while reserving special attention for Bach. Special attention became vocation, then obsession, then a career strategy. In the fall of 1937, Tureck played six all-Bach concerts at Town Hall, as well as a diverse recital showcasing the complete *Goldberg Variations*. The concerts sold out. Her commitment had met its match in an audience that felt the magnetic pull of Bach. But the critics wrote as if she were playing an adding machine, not a piano: they derided her as cold, brittle, aloof, inhuman. "With increasing frequency, as the 'mechanical age' engulfs us in its iron maw, we may expect to encounter the kind of artistry displayed by Rosalyn Tureck, a true child of her generation," the *Times*'s reviewer remarked of her debut piano recital two years earlier (Brahms, Chopin, Ravel, Debussy, Albeniz, Stravinsky, and Bach's Concerto in D Minor—his own transcription of a sonata for unaccompanied violin). "We may anticipate the day when the growing tendency to allow the intellect to usurp the place of the emotions will have blotted out all human feeling in music and the other arts and reduced them to nothing more than static design."

Tureck kept her eye on the prize of Bach. In a competition she played only Bach, and actually was not given the prize because the judges were sure (as she put it) "that nobody could make a career in Bach." She was sure that she could. She repeated the all-Bach recitals at Town Hall in 1943. The next year she devoted the middle of three recitals to the *Goldberg Variations*, and "gave each variation with so distinctive a character and with such verve and vitality that the listener had the illusion of hearing Bach himself playing them on the harpsichord" (the *Times*, now converted). She played three all-Bach recitals in 1946 and was fêted at Samaroff's apartment near the Museum of Modern Art. A photograph from that time shows her seated at a gleaming black piano in an all-white room, surrounded by rectangular shelves and boxy glass cabinets: she is the human figure in a geometrical ensemble.

She joined the Juilliard faculty and made attention to Bach's structures imperative. "There will always be more than one possibility in details of phrasing, dynamics, tempi, etc.," she later explained, "and sometimes marked differences in conception, all of them good. But they must adhere to the frame and idiom of the work itself." She sounded like a European finance minister making the case for an austerity plan, but her way with Bach was culturally au courant, akin to the stylized severities of Beckett and Giacometti, a reduction of the work to skeletal essences.

>>3>> By 1948 Tureck's all-Bach recitals had become a rite of autumn in New York. A dozen years into her career, her stress on Bach alongside the "composers of today" seemed new and forward-looking, a postwar variation on virtuosity.

The time for new approaches was at hand. George Orwell, finishing a novel that year, called it *1984*, and with the Bachlike transposition of the 4 and the 8 of the current year he made the point (darkly) that "the future is here." A thousand days after the war, a new era was taking shape. As postwar geopolitics were shaped by the Marshall Plan and the peacetime assertiveness of the United States, so postwar culture was brought into being through new technology.

In retrospect, television is seen to define the age, and 1948 was a crucial year for television: sales of TVs increased nearly ninefold, from 44,000 to 350,000, and ABC and CBS began network operations. But the changes in music were just as dramatic. In 1948, in Fullerton, California, Leo Fender sold his radio-repair business so as to focus a new company on the production of pedal steels, amplifiers, and a new product: the solid-body electric guitar. Meanwhile, recording technology was advancing swiftly. In audio research, as in biology, new developments came in pairs, and there were two dramatic advances in the way recordings were made: magnetic tape, which made it possible to record long performances or splice several performances together, and the microgroove "long-playing" record, which made it possible to release those performances to the public.

Commercially, there was no need for new advances in recording technology. The record business was booming. Four hundred million records—78-rpm records—were sold in the United States in 1947, a third more than the year before, three times as many as in 1941, and twelve times as many as in 1938 (all of them strong years as reckoned at the time). The increase in sales was partly the result of a relaxing of the privations of wartime, when the government had rationed the use of shellac, the basis of most 78s. It reflected the penetration of the 78-rpm format, which was so deep that EMI, in Britain, resisted developing a new format to compete with it. And it reflected a triumph over the music business's fear of technology. During the war James Petrillo, the bellicose president of the American Federation of Musicians, was in a standoff with the record companies: arguing that recordings served as a substitute for live music and so threatened musicians' livelihoods, he disassociated the union from the record business, declaring that any musician who played on a recording would be ousted from the union. "The edict," Roland Gelatt remarked in *The Fabulous Phonograph*, ". . . applied equally to Leopold Stokowski and Benny Goodman, to the drummer in Tommy Dorsey's band and the tuba player in the Boston Symphony." Petrillo's goal was to force the record companies out of business. But the record companies had a counterstrategy. They stopped making new recordings, and reissued old ones instead. Union musicians were now hurting twice over: due to recordings, they had less live work than in the past, and they had no recording session work at all.

After two years, Petrillo and the label heads hammered out a compromise: the record companies would pay a small royalty on each sale to the AFM, which would distribute the funds to unemployed musicians. The record companies raced to make new records; and when the war ended and the ban on shellac was lifted several hundred records were released in a matter of months.

There were many new Bach recordings among them. Columbia had a hit with two versions of "Ave Maria"—Schubert's setting on one side, backed with Gounod's setting of the prayer over the first prelude from the *Well-Tempered Clavier* on the other. Early in 1946, RCA brought out Wanda Landowska's new recording of the *Goldberg Variations*, done in New York on the jumbo harpsichord built for her in Paris in 1912. It was clearer and fuller than her 1933 recording; it was also squarer and statelier. Forty thousand sets were sold, ten times the number anticipated. The next year, Rosalyn Tureck made a recording of the *Goldberg Variations* on piano for the Allegro label, striving to bring out the "vertical and diagonal" connections in Bach; and Helmut Walcha, a Leipziger who had been blinded in his late teens, began recording all of Bach's surviving organ music in a program of purification that he called the "new objectivity."

The market was robust when tape and the LP were introduced. The two innovations, developing at the same time, stimulated each other.

Tape recording had been around since the turn of the century. Thin metallic strips coated with magnetized particles were passed under a metal "head" as sound was sent to the head through a microphone, which converted the sound to electrical impulses. The head transferred the impulses to the magnetic tape. To hear the sound, you reversed the procedure. Miraculously, it worked: but the tapes were short, the sound poor, the signal weak. During World War II, Nazi engineers figured out that tape in large reels, run rapidly past the tape head and amplified, could play back recorded sound with much greater fidelity for half an hour or more. Then, after the war, Minnesota Mining and Manufacturing—3M, maker of Scotch tape—developed a long, thin plastic tape coated with silver oxide. This "quarter-inch tape" became the industry standard. Reel-to-reel tape machines replaced metal disc cutters at recording studios and soundstages, such as the one at Abbey Road, as big and plain as the gas cooker in a Surrey kitchen. Variety shows were "taped" for later broadcast over the radio. Recording engineers figured out that tapes of different performances could be spliced together, producing recordings that were aurally clear and musically spotless.

The long-playing record brought these advances to the marketplace. Peter Goldmark, a Hungarian émigré who was on staff at Columbia Records in New York, spent several years trying to improve on the 78-rpm disc. He came up with a new disc, the 33⅓-rpm "microgroove" disc. It was made of vinyl, a new synthetic material, rather than shellac; it was light, durable, and fairly cheap to produce. It was twelve inches in diameter, like the largest 78s; but instead of a deep groove spiraling around 100 times, it could hold 220 circuits of a narrow one, cut in a V, with two surfaces that could be read at once by the stylus. Together, the two grooved sides of the disc could carry the full *Nutcracker* suite—CBS chairman William S. Paley's criterion for a long player.

In a meeting in April 1948, Goldmark, Paley, and the Columbia brass revealed the microgroove record to their rivals at RCA, who were developing a new format, the 45-rpm, 7-inch disc. In June—the twenty-first, the longest day of the year—Columbia introduced the long player to the public with a press conference at the Waldorf-Astoria Hotel on Park Avenue.

Tape and the LP changed the way music was made, not just the way it was recorded. Previous developments in recording technology had relocated music in space, bringing it out of the church and the concert hall and into the home and the movie theater, where the listener could encounter it intimately or while doing something else. Tape and the LP advanced on this in ways that affected the performer as much as the listener—altering the nature of music itself for each. The LP allowed orchestral works to be heard complete with just a few flips of the discs. More than that, the LP invited musicians and listeners alike to conceive of all music at a larger scale. Works of small units that usually were broken up for practice, for recital, or for release on 78s—Chopin's études, say—could now be heard as wholes extending outward in time, unspooling at a leisurely thirty-three and a third turns per minute. Meanwhile, magnetic tape had the opposite effect: it made recorded time plastic, so to speak. Large sets of pieces did not have to be performed consecutively, in one go. Works that would have wearied the musician in live performance could be played in shorter sessions and then spliced together—composed after the fact in the recording studio.

The outpouring of new recordings prompted by tape and the LP (and, in pop music, the 45) makes it easy to overlook the fact that, in many ways, the new formats were limiting forces. They gave control of the market to big companies, which licensed the formats to smaller companies. They crowded out "amateur" performers and raised the bar for "professional" ones. They placed the responsibility for choosing which music would be recorded and made public with record-company executives, many of whom had extramusical motives in the front of their minds. And they proved so attractive that they drove the existing format—the 78—into oblivion, and, with it, the thousands of recordings that existed only as 78s. This would be the pattern of progress for recordings in the postwar period. The new formats were advanced forms of mechanical memory, and they entered experience into the record with ever greater fidelity. Yet they were not means of revival so much as of forgetting. Like modern architecture, they left the old forms behind.

>>4>>   "I think . . . you are going to Washington Wednesday the 17th," Elizabeth Bishop wrote to Robert Lowell, one poet to another. "—if not I was going to ask you if you'd like to go to a Bach concert Wed. night—a pianist friend of mine who is just about the best Bach player there is."

Rosalyn Tureck's all-Bach recital at Town Hall that night—November 17, 1948—featured the "little" preludes, the third English suite, three sets of preludes and fugues from the *Well-Tempered Clavier,* and an encore sonata. The recital—recorded but not released at the time—marks a turning point both in the performance of Bach's music and the transmission of it. Tureck, now thirty-four, is serenely confident of her approach to the music, which she meets and sponsors instead of trying to have her way with. After a thumping first prelude, she plays with gathering interiority, so that by the time she reaches the paired preludes and fugues from the *Well-Tempered Clavier* she sounds alone and obsessive (the applause comes as a surprise). You can hear her making Bach architectural for the postwar years, replacing the upholstered surfaces of prewar Bach with straight lines.

At the same time, the crispness of the playing means that you can hear technology lagging behind. The recording was probably made onto acetates by a pair of disc cutters and then transferred to 78s. They are (the reissue producer says) "clean, well-recorded sides." Still, they are 78s made by a microphone hung from the fly space over the stage. In passages played with anything but the lightest touch, the echoes and overtones smudge the pointed bricks of Tureck's counterpoint. The right hand dances; the left hand clumps prosthetically along. When the two hands come together, it sounds like a player piano, the perpetual-motion machine that actual musicians set themselves against as something other than music.

Six weeks later Tureck went north to give a pair of recitals in Canada, again presenting Bach in a diverse program. She played two of the Inventions and the Italian Concerto as parts of a longer program at the Technical Hall in Ottawa. On Monday, January 24, 1949, she appeared at the auditorium connected with Eaton's, an elegant department store in downtown Toronto, playing Beethoven, Chopin, Scriabin, and Bach: the third English suite, "Jesu, meine Freude" from the *Little Organ Book*, and transcriptions, possibly her own, of two chorales.

Glenn Gould was there. He was sixteen years old and in training for a career as a concert pianist. He had finished the standard course at the local conservatory, surpassing students ten years older. He had played at Eaton Auditorium himself beginning when he was twelve. Now he was studying daily with a private teacher, a specialist in the music of the Baroque.

Tureck's playing was a "revelation" to him, he later said. But it was not a revelation vouchsafed to him all at once in the concert hall that night. He had Tureck's records; he played them over and over, and heard in them not just piano-playing but an approach to music, especially the music of Bach. "She was the first person who played Bach in what seemed to me a sensible way," he recalled. "It was playing of such uprightness, to put it into the moral sphere. There was such a sense of repose that had nothing to do with languor, but rather with moral rectitude in the liturgical sense."

Through technology he was joined to her. "I was fighting a battle in which I was never going to get a surrender flag from my teacher on the way Bach should go, but her records were the first evidence that one did not fight alone."

>>5>> Gould was a prodigy, raised at the piano, which was his fortress, his log cabin, his schoolhouse, his playground. Looking back, he had relatively little to say about his boyhood, but what he did say had a Baroque order and clarity. In half a dozen recollections, deployed in different essays and interviews but stylistically of a piece, he developed the theme of his early years: a passion for music consummated through a romance with technology. These expressive miniatures stand in his story like the canons in a set of diverse variations, at once subdividing the structure and holding it upright.

> I was definitely homophonically inclined until the age of about ten, and then I suddenly got the message. Bach began to emerge into my world then and has never altogether left it. It was one of the great moments of my life.

The Goulds lived in Toronto. Bert was a furrier, running a business he had inherited from his father. Florence, a distant relative of Edvard Grieg, had hoped to have a career as a singer; now she taught voice, and she resolved that she would have a son, name him Glenn, and see to it that he was musical. After two miscarriages, at age forty—September 25, 1932—she gave birth to a boy and named him Glenn. They lived with a dog and a maid in a plain house on a quiet street near Lake Ontario. The family name was Gold, but they changed it to Gould. They went to services at the United Church of Christ, where an organ was played. They kept a cottage on a lake ninety miles north, and drove there on weekends.

> I remember, when I was a kid, I always associated the New York Philharmonic broadcasts, which we used to hear on Sunday afternoons, with great, vast fields of snow— white and grey. We used to go up north to the country for weekends and, about four o'clock in the afternoon, the Philharmonic would be on when we were on our way back to Toronto. And, in wintertime, it was usually grey—a sort of endless vista of snow, frozen lake, horizon, this sort of thing—and Beethoven never sounded so good.

He liked to press the keys of the piano one at a time and listen to the sound of each note as it faded out. He was found to have perfect pitch at age three; he began lessons at the age of four and could play songs at five—hymns, folk songs, and tunes of his own devising. His mother taught him to sing each note as he played it. She would play chords and ask him to identify each note and call it out from the other end of the house.

When he was six his parents took him to a recital by Josef Hofmann, a Romantic piano virtuoso who had toured North America ever since his own days as a child prodigy in the nineteenth century.

> It was, I think, his last performance in Toronto, and it was a staggering impression. The only thing I can really remember is that, when I was being brought home in the car, I was in that wonderful state of half-awakeness in which you hear all sorts of incredible sounds going through your mind. They were all *orchestral* sounds, but I was playing them all, and suddenly I was Hofmann. I was enchanted.

He had already played in public, backing his parents on piano as they sang a duet. He played in church during an anniversary gala the next year, and a reviewer called him "something of a musical genius in the making." After that, he played piano and organ at churches around Toronto, sometimes wearing a white Fauntleroy suit with short pants, and at the elementary school he attended after a year of homeschooling. He played in a recital program called "Today's Children," which was broadcast on the radio. He took music theory and organ lessons. His father bought him one new piano after another but refused to install a pipe organ in the parlor.

I was eight when *Fantasia* hit Toronto and I hated every minute of it.

It showed at a downtown theater called the Hippodrome, preceded by a twenty-minute demonstration of the "Mighty Wurlitzer"—

> an electronic mammoth which was disgorged from beneath the stage and lit so that each manual and row of couplers appeared to be a different color . . . In any event, my parents informed me that I was going to see *Fantasia*, that it was in color, all about music, and that I would get to hear one of the world's greatest conductors. At the time, I had only seen one movie in color—*Snow White*—and I hadn't been too thrilled with that; besides, everybody knew that the really good movies—the ones with plots, and enemy agents, and German battlecruisers—were in black and white. I did not, however, figure on pink hippos, or green dinosaurs, or scarlet volcanoes, and it began to seem less and less likely that Jack Hawkins or John Clements or Clive Brook or any other self-respecting destroyer captain would ever agree to turn up in a movie like that. I went home depressed, feeling faintly nauseous, and with the first headache I can remember; the images of the Mighty Wurlitzer and of the Disney creations had all run together in my head.

His mother worried about his health, and so did he. He stayed home from school whenever he didn't feel well. He slouched and squirmed and didn't comb his hair. He dressed for winter in the Northern Territories even in summer in Toronto. He carried a bottle of pills in a pants pocket and took them often. He dreaded germs and refused to wear old clothes, shake hands, or catch a ball. He steered a boat on the lake near the family cottage but would not fish, and compelled his father, a fly fisherman, to give up the sport.

As Bach came into his life, he learned to play the preludes and fugues of the *Well-Tempered Clavier*. He was enrolled at the local conservatory, where he took piano, organ, and theory. The youngest student at the conservatory, he aced all the tests and won all the prizes, year after year.

He studied with Alberto Guerrero, a pianist from Chile. Guerrero trained him in the Romantic repertoire and in new music while giving special attention to Bach, notably the Inventions, which Guerrero himself played in a recital. Guerrero urged Gould to adopt aspects of his own approach: to sit as low as possible, to tap the keys with the tips of the fingers, to memorize a new score away from the piano before playing it the first time. He taught Gould that music "must be architecturally conceived." He guided him toward live performance, which Gould resented:

> When I was a lad of thirteen a misguided pedagogue at my alma mater, the then Toronto (now Royal) Conservatory of Music, suggested that I might prepare for my debut with orchestra, which was to coincide with the annual year-end blowout of the school band, and play Beethoven's Fourth Concerto. The suggestion, of course, was enthusiastically adopted, but, as I saw it, very little preparation was required: for two years I had been in possession of an RCA album—acquired with funds painstakingly set aside from my allowance—featuring Artur Schnabel, Frederick Stock, the Chicago Symphony, and, on the cover, the earliest example of pop-album art extant . . . Almost every day during the two years I owned it prior to the above mentioned invitation, some or all eight 78-rpm sides served as accompaniment for practice sessions in which I faithfully traced every inflective nuance of the Schnabelian rhetoric, surged dramatically ahead whenever he thought it wise—that is to say, in most reiteratively inclined and/or motivically awkward situations—and glided to a graceful cadential halt every four minutes and twenty-five seconds or so while the automatic changer went to work on the turntable. These changeover points proved an especially significant formative influence; . . . to this day I am unable to tolerate any performance of this mellow opus that ignores these obvious points of demarcation, that does not pay at least token homage to that phenomenon of flip-side overlap—which those of us reared in the 78 era came to cherish and anticipate—but strides blithely, uncaringly, onward to the finish.

Gould played the piece exactly the way Schnabel played it on the record. Guerrero took the record away. Gould struck back. In a rehearsal with the orchestra he played the concerto differently—played it the way Rudolf Serkin did, instead of the way Schnabel did. The night of the performance came. "This," Gould recalled, "was a time for personal statement—a moment to grasp and to make one's own"—that is, to make it sound like Schnabel's much-interrupted recording. So he played it à la Schnabel. He got the result he wanted: the orchestra was confused, the teacher "shattered," the press "quite kind," and Gould pleased with himself.

He gave his first solo recital six months later in the Eaton Auditorium. He had played Bach's "Little" Fugue on the pipe organ there as a twelve-year-old curiosity. Now, at age fourteen, already a local celebrity, he played Scarlatti, Chopin, Beethoven, Lizst, Mendelssohn, and a Couperin piece (his biographer Kevin Bazzana explains) "arranged by Guerrero in imitation of Landowska's 1934 recording."

He began performing regularly, in Toronto and throughout Ontario, at schools and art galleries and Massey Hall. A chronology of his teens consists of one outstanding achievement after another. *Competed victoriously in the First Kiwanis Music Festival . . . Orchestral debut . . . Awarded diploma, associate of the Royal Conservatory of Music in Toronto . . . First public solo piano recital as a professional artist . . . Composed his first major work, a piano sonata . . .* A photograph of Gould (probably arranged by his mother) shows a strikingly clean-cut young man in jacket and tie sitting upright at the piano in the parlor, with his setter, Nicky, poised at the keyboard alongside him.

Meanwhile he developed a parallel life of musical solitude. His father had a music room added to the back of the house, and bought a portable tape recorder soon after they came onto the market. Gould took to the machine immediately. He recorded himself playing at home, and made recordings of some of his recitals, but there was more to it than that. He was (he later recalled) "indulging in experiments at home with primitive tape recorders—strapping the mikes to the sounding board of my piano, the better to emasculate Scarlatti sonatas, for example, and generally subjecting both instruments to whichever imaginative indignities came to mind." Gangly, with a big Adam's apple, he might have been a member of the Mad Scientists' Club, set apart by technical know-how as much as by precocity; the music room was his clubhouse, a sanctum stocked with gadgets, where he could play the piano, the phonograph, and the tape recorder into the night.

In his teens Gould became the subject of a sonic "experiment," one that became "a determining moment" in his approach to music.

I happened to be practicing at the piano one day—I clearly recall, not
that it matters, that it was a fugue by Mozart, K. 394, for those of you
who play it too—and suddenly a vacuum cleaner started up just beside the instrument. Well, the result was that in the louder passages,
this luminously diatonic music in which Mozart deliberately imitates
the technique of Johann Sebastian Bach became surrounded with a
halo of vibrato, rather the effect that you might get if you sang in the
bathtub with both ears full of water and shook your head from side to
side all at once. And in the softer passages I couldn't hear any sound
that I was making at all. I could feel, of course—I could sense the
tactile relation with the keyboard, which is replete with its own kind
of acoustical associations, and I could imagine what I was doing, but
I couldn't actually hear it. But the strange thing was that all of it suddenly sounded better than it had without the vacuum cleaner, and
those parts which I couldn't actually hear sounded best of all.

The vacuum-cleaner moment is the primal scene in Gould's encounter
with music in the age of recordings. Already he anticipated a state of things in
which music is not set against silence but is one element in a sonic mix, with
sounds brought forth acoustically from wood, felt, and wire mingling with the
sounds made by electric appliances and machinery.

Gould himself presented the incident as the story of his imaginative awakening, engendered by technology. "What I managed to learn through the acci-
dental coming together of Mozart and the vacuum cleaner was that the inner ear
of the imagination is very much more powerful a stimulant than is any amount of
outward observation." At the piano, with the vacuum cleaner running, he saw
the imagination as if for the first time—saw it as "a sort of no man's land between
that foreground of system and dogma, of positive action, for which you have been
trained, and that vast background of immense possibility, of negation, which you
must constantly examine, and to which you must never forget to pay homage as
the source from which all creative ideas come." And he saw that technology, no
threat to his imagination, stimulated it—multiplied its possibilities.

>>6>> "My soul magnifies the Lord / my spirit rejoices in God my Sav-
ior, / for he has regarded the low estate of his handmaiden. / For behold,
henceforth all generations shall call me blessed; for he who is holy has done
great things for me / and holy is his name."

So begins the Magnificat, which Bach set to music for presentation on Christmas Day 1723 in the church of St. Nicholas, Leipzig. The string orchestra surges. The brass flashes and blares. The singers chant, exult, declaim, purl, mourn, lament, and give glory, alone, severally, all together.

The Magnificat had been set to music a thousand times. The text, from Luke's gospel, is the virgin Mary's response to her cousin Elizabeth's recognition that she has been specially blessed—and the news that she shall bear the Christ child, the Messiah the Jews have looked for. Her song is a *yes* to new life, a *yes* variously expressed: through the fresh invocation of an older biblical text; through a promise of service, a taking-on of new responsibilities; through the delight and confidence in the challenge ahead.

Bach's Magnificat is a coat of many colors. It is a buoyant setting of the scripture, and a compact anthology of sacred music: joyful choir, tender aria, double-barrel duet, strident crowd chorus, children's nursery song. It is a piece of theological wit, a German Lutheran's demonstration of his Latin prowess. On top of that, it is an announcement of Bach's aims, a musical declaration of intent. In Leipzig, he would devote himself to sacred song: music sonically varied, semidramatic, edifying, magnificent, corresponding at once to the seasons of the Christian year and the voices in his head.

His working arrangement with the prince in Köthen was hard to improve on. Why did he leave? Because the prince's bride was an *amusa*, a woman with no ear for music: that is one explanation Bach himself gave. There were other reasons. A key violinist went missing from the ensemble. Disputes between Lutherans and Calvinists poisoned the environment at the school his children attended. But there was more to his departure than that, and the Magnificat makes clear why he had to move on. He had musical needs that the prince couldn't satisfy. He needed a chorus, a first-rate string orchestra, a passel of brass players to draw on in a pinch. Now as ever, he needed the life of the church, its rhythms as natural to him as those of the dances he adapted for his suites. He needed a public—a metropolitan audience, made up of people he would not meet otherwise.

Leipzig offered all these things. It was a city, first of all: the second-largest in Saxony after Dresden, and one of the larger in Germany. It was the seat of a university, and so an apt place for the education of Bach's children. It was the site of trade fairs that drew merchants from all points to do business: Poles, Czechs, and Austrians come west, Belgians, Swiss, and Frankfurters stopping on the way to Mitteleuropa. It had four city churches, the two larger of them each drawing a congregation of 2,500 people every Sunday; these, the churches of St. Nicholas and St. Thomas—the Nikolaikirche and the Thomaskirche—were open, resonant spaces, alive to artful sound. There was a committed orchestra and choir, two dozen or more musicians in all. There were good pipe organs in the four churches and in the university church, too.

Bach was thirty-eight, aflame with invention. A move to the city of Leipzig would be more than a career change. It would be a technical advance—a new format for his music.

For the historian Jaroslav Pelikan, Bach was a genius who was called to be a church musician, and the church year was "the basic framework in which the vocation of this genius was to express itself." There were various ways for Bach to take his music out into the world: by performing it, by teaching it to others, by printing sheet music, by touring on its behalf. The most emphatic way—the most elaborate, and the most efficient—was to lead an ensemble in the music of the liturgy in a good-size city. No less than a pipe organ, the church ensemble of orchestra and choir was a sound-making machine. It was a musical means of production, and the church calendar was a means of distribution. So was the city. The demand for sacred music in Leipzig—four churches; sixty Sundays and feast days needing music—would maximize Bach's opportunities to compose new work and have it performed in public. They would let him make himself heard.

The Magnificat (Wolff declares) "represented the fullest and most elaborate compositional effort" of Bach's career so far. Like "Christ lag in Todesbanden"—the dramatic anthology of musical effects written for the audition in Mühlhausen sixteen years earlier—it showed what Bach could do in a new position. A new position in Leipzig would enable him to magnify his work by distributing it more broadly—broadcasting it.

>>7>> "This past Saturday at noon, four wagons loaded with household goods arrived here from Cöthen; they belonged to the former Princely Capellmeister there, now called to Leipzig as *Cantor Figuralis*. He himself arrived with his family on 2 carriages at 2 o'clock and moved into the newly renovated apartment in the St. Thomas School." Bach's arrival in Leipzig was reported as far away as Hamburg—reported there a dozen times. Compared with Georg Philipp Telemann, the pride of Hamburg, Bach was a musicians' musician, but among them he enjoyed a kind of fame.

The cantor in the Thomasschule, the conservatory and choir school in

Leipzig, had died after twenty years in the job. The city councillors sought to replace him with a "famous man, in order to inspire the students." Amazingly, there are detailed records of the selection process. Six musicians were named as candidates. Bach was not among them. Telemann was. He was working in Hamburg, but he had worked in Leipzig. They appointed him. He accepted the job. But his employers refused to let him go: they gave him a raise and more freedom to compose as he liked. Two more candidates were named. Neither was Bach. Then two more candidates "presented themselves." One was Christoph Graupner; one was Johann Sebastian Bach. Graupner led a chorus in two "test" cantatas and was offered the job, but his employers gave him a raise rather than let him go. That left Bach. He went to Leipzig, probably at the eager invitation of the town council, and at the Thomaskirche led an ensemble in a pair of cantatas, complex showpieces for the last Sunday of the season before the beginning of Lent, when the churches went quiet. The committee, evidently delighted, was concerned that he was not prepared to teach some courses in Latin. He was tested in theology, partly in Latin, and then was offered the job.

In Köthen, meanwhile, the tone-deaf new princess had died, clearing the way for fresh music-making there. The role of cantor and music director would be a step down socially, and would involve more teaching and administration than Bach liked. But he took the job in Leipzig, promising that he would hire a Latin instructor to team-teach with him at his own expense. Recalling the move later, he remarked simply that "it pleased God that I should be called hither to be Director Musices and Cantor at the St. Thomas School." So a casting call became a calling.

The Thomaskirche and the Nikolaikirche are a short walk apart, a few steps in opposite directions from the main square, the Markt, with the vast and gorgeous town hall, or Rathaus, occupying one long side. The Thomaskirche had been erected beginning in 1355, a gray stone Gothic church with a steep roof, a Baroque bell tower, and a baroquely remodeled interior: whitewashed walls, hexagonal columns, and a raised gallery running around the church to an ample choir and organ loft. The Nikolaikirche, built of brown stone, was older, larger, and darker, its Romanesque design highlighted by ribbed arches throughout; though plain on the outside, it was at the center of things—the intersection of two trade routes, adjoined by a square with a stone fountain.

In his new role Bach wore a path between the two churches. He composed for one or the other church each Sunday; on feast days he led music for services at both. As the role of cantor and music director magnified his talent, so did city life, enabling him to conduct his affairs wih great efficiency in the shops, taverns, market square, and town hall.

His daily life centered on the Thomasschule, a plain, blocky building next to the Thomaskirche where his sons were enrolled. His family now numbered a dozen or more people, including a newborn daughter. He settled them in a rambling apartment in the schoolhouse, three stories plus a basement, backed by a garden, and equipped with a composing room, or *Komponirstube*, which contained a large music library. There, in the family apartment, Anna Magdalena soon was carrying another child. There, in the *Komponirstube*, Bach soon was writing music. In the next nine months he composed a whole cycle of cantatas and other sacred works—probably fifty pieces, each twenty minutes or more.

He began by leading orchestra and chorus in another pair of cantatas, this time for the first and second Sundays after Trinity—first at one church, then the other. These are the first Sundays after the feasts of Easter and Pentecost, a liturgical downtime. Bach could have used the music for those Sundays to bring the musicians up to speed. This he would not do. Instead, he wrote cantatas that are extraordinary, and extraordinarily apt, for they give voice to the relationship of poverty and splendor that is at the heart of his music in Leipzig.

The first is based in one of the best-known stories in all the gospels: "There was a rich man, who was clothed in purple and fine linen and feasted sumptuously every day. And at his gate lay a poor man named Lazarus, full of sores . . ." The second opens with the famous declaration (from Psalm 19) that "The heavens are telling the glory of God," then presents a parable about a banquet: the invited guests all make excuses so as not to go, and the host invites the poor and outcast instead, "that my house may be filled."

Each is a story of want and abundance. They were apt for mercantile Leipzig, and their themes suited Bach's own circumstances too. What should he do with the musical abundance inside him? That was the question, arising again with each new position, and the music he made suggests his answer. He would give, more than was necessary. He made each cantata a "double" cantata, to precede the sermon and follow it. He set them with splendor: featuring a trumpet, the instrument of a feast. He incorporated music from Leipzig feasts of years past, extravagantly updated. Music, these cantatas suggest, is a kind of finery, and should be given away—shared with others and offered in service of the holy.

Twenty-five cantatas followed; then a cantata for the first Sunday of Advent that he had written at Weimar; then, on Christmas Day, the Magnificat; then another fifteen cantatas. The churches of Leipzig were suddenly filled with Bach's music. Those cantatas were not all wholly new, but as music mainly composed serially, week by week, in the slack season of the Christian year, they are astonishing. In the last two of them, Christoph Wolff declares, Bach reaches "a new plateau of artistic accomplishment in the church cantata genre, both in the intricacy of their compositional design and in the vigorous musical expression and rhetorical power of their opening choruses." This is the music of life in abundance: poverty overcome by splendor, rote by invention, solitude amplified by orchestra and chorus.

It was enough—more than enough. "The singers or instrumentalists or the composer, or indeed everyone involved including clergy," Peter Williams proposes, "had found the cantor's initial efforts too taxing." Even Bach, he implies, was relieved to reach the *tempus clausum*: the forty days of Lent, when full choral music was set aside in favor of chant and silence.

Lent opened up time for Bach to compose, and he bore down on a new work. In those forty days he completed the *St. John Passion* for presentation on Good Friday at the Nikolaikirche—at once taking up a form relatively new to him, composing a work more intricate than any he had done, and dramatizing the central event of Christianity for the first time.

It is amazing that he composed the Passion at all, working in his few free hours while settling into a new job. But it may be that the Passion was part of his plan, and that it was a key reason for his move to Leipzig.

The form, built on a cappella renditions of the crucifixion narratives given in the gospels, was pioneered in Germany early in the century, as one church after another opened its Holy Week services to "figural" or "concerted" music of the kind heard the rest of the year. Telemann had composed a so-called "oratorio" Passion a few years earlier. So had several others. Possibly Bach wrote one while serving in the ducal palace at Weimar. The late Leipzig music director had introduced a Passion in 1721; the practice was repeated the next two years, alternating between the Thomaskirche and the Nikolaikirche, and Bach probably knew the precedent when he took the job. "Now he was faced with the fact that a Passion setting in the style of a cantata was expected of him for performance on Good Friday of the next year," one commentator remarks, presenting it as a burden Bach had to bear. That doesn't seem right. The oratorio passion had emerged as a rich and fresh form of sacred music, one that would allow Bach to employ his musical strengths all at once, and to enter fully into the life of sacred music in the city of Leipzig. The chance to write such a Passion was a chance he couldn't let pass.

The words of the opening chorus of the *St. John Passion* make his ambitions clear. As one English translation has it, they go: "O Lord, our Sovereign, Whose Glory / Is magnified in all lands, / Testify to us by Thy passion . . ." The sentiment echoes that of the Magnificat, and so does the piece as a whole: as Holy Week follows on and fulfills Christmas, so with the Passion Bach will fulfill the Magnificat, following the story of Jesus's time on earth through to its climax. As another version has it, the chorus stresses that through the Passion the Lord will be made more lordly—will be glorified. Both senses suit Bach's efforts. Through the Passion, Bach will see his own work magnified, all his talents concentrated on a setting of the story of God put to the test—all his music glorified.

Although other Passions preceded it, the *St. John Passion* is so foundational, and has been taken to be for so long, that it seems, like the cello suites, to be the first work of its kind. The grand, doleful opening chorus; the evangelist's plainspoken recitation; the sonorous voices of Jesus, Pilate, Peter, and the others; the crowd, wide-eyed and sharp-tongued, exultant, fierce, righteous, astonished; the rueful piety of the individual believer as expressed in sacred aria; the chorales, softened by five centuries of Sundays; and all this over the polished stones on the streambed of the orchestra—this musical plan, this set of patterns in satisfying alternation, is so right as to seem permanent, and makes it seem as if the *St. John Passion* is a sacred work that existed "in the beginning."

And yet the *St. John Passion*, considered at this point in Bach's career, can be seen as achieving a technical transcendence that was new even to him. His music is so strong always that it is odd to speak of him making progress. The breakthrough, the great leap forward: these expressions don't fit his career. Such breakthroughs as he did make involved changes in his circumstances. So it is with this Passion. The occasion (the Good Friday reading of the Passion text) prompts Bach to enter narrative time—to tell a story, that is; and this change leads him to magnify his work at both ends, making it at once profoundly social and heartbreakingly individual and intimate.

After the opening chorus (ten minutes or so in most renditions), the evangelist begins, declaiming the gospel text in German in a plangent tenor. In English, the text reads: "Jesus went forth with his disciples over the brook Kedron, where there was a garden, into which he entered, and his disciples." This is significant. Crossing the brook, they enter narrative time, leaving the typologically patterned world of the cantatas for the one of human events. "Bertolt Brecht, the master of epic theater, was fascinated two hundred years later by the 'model of dramatic music' shown in the Evangelist's first words . . ." Geck reports, and he explains that Bach "gives the music, in its unadorned directness, a vividness and availability to the senses that lets us see the events in their historical facticity and yet also having a significance that goes beyond it. These are not opera recitatives, condensations to advance the plot and give the singers their cue for the next aria. He is setting the doctrine of salvation in the actual words in which it was spoken."

The Passion is a work of realism—biblical realism—and to present it, Bach creates a dramatic architecture, extending the patterns of his music into space and time. Where the cantatas are slices of the Christian story, the Passion is the thing itself. Where the cantatas follow the seasons of the year, the Passion (it seems) happens once and for all. Where the cantatas can be joined in, the Passion can be entered into. Where, in the motet "Jesus meine Freude," Bach built a broad arch, here he raises a sacred canopy (in the Romanesque interior of the Nikolaikirche) under which the action takes place, a scaffolding surrounding the cross.

The *St. John Passion*, one scholar says, sums up the music of Bach's first year in Leipzig. But when you listen to it after listening to those cantatas, the difference is loud and clear. Something new is happening here—really two things, two musical effects that are bound up with each other.

One is the voice of Jesus, which rings out as if for the first time. It is as if Jesus, the center of attention in the cantatas—commended, called on, proposed as a model for imitation—has shown his face at last. The baritone voice, heard only in recitative, is the voice of his authority, and also of his solitude. The Jesus of the *St. John Passion*, this servant of humanity, is even so a solo practitioner, going about his work alone, right up to the episode in which he carries his own cross.

The other effect is the crowd. In its choruses—turba choruses, they are called—the voices are sharp as spear points, now objecting, now condemning, now insisting on their rights. That these voices are controversial—that they too vividly and insistently follow the gospel text in representing the Jewish people as the accusers of Christ—is bound up with how convincing they are. These voices are menacing in their solidarity, unified and sure of themselves as they send a man to his death.

Controversy would come later. Heard in connection with Bach's first year in Leipzig, these effects, even as they magnify the Christian story, concentrate attention on Bach's own state in life. In the city, in his most public role to date, he identified with the lonely man of faith; as his music reached a large audience, he dramatized the shortcomings of the crowd.

>>8>> Pablo Casals, in Prades, received hundreds of pieces of mail. Most of them were letters from displaced Catalans, simple requests for help that he answered each in his own hand. So when a bulky set of parcels came from America marked CADEAU- -DOMMAGE, it stood out. Opening it, Casals knew what it was. It was, truly, a gift and an honor. It was the *Bach Gesellschaft*: the sheet music for all the music of Bach, complete in forty-odd volumes photo-offset from the Paris edition by a company in Ann Arbor, Michigan. Alexander Schneider, the violinist, had arranged the gift, asking musicians in New York to chip in ten dollars each. Opening it, Casals felt pure joy—"one of the purest joys of my life."

Fifty years earlier the *Bach-Gesellschaft* had changed Albert Schweitzer's life, enabling him to pore over the music into the night at his student rooms in Strasbourg after a day spent studying anatomy or the interpretation of Scripture. Now the Bach set, and the gesture of concerted friendship behind it, would change Casals's life, turning the soloist into a concertmaster and the village of Prades, a remote "Pyrennean retreat" as he styled it, into a place incomparably rich in the music of Bach.

Casals had become famous for his withdrawal from the world. He had gone to London and Paris after the war and had played for huge audiences, who greeted him as a virtuoso and a hero of resistance. But when it became clear that the Allies, having defeated Germany and Japan, would leave the fascist regime in Spain alone, he was incensed. He turned down honorary degrees from Oxford and Cambridge and canceled a plan to record Bach's Brandenburg concertos in London. He vowed not to accept any invitation to perform in a country that recognized the Franco government. This vow turned into a vow not to give any concerts at all.

So he lived simply in Prades. He rose, dressed, took a walk, tipped his hat to Le Canigou, and played a prelude and fugue on a battered upright piano, "renewing contact with Bach's immortal message." He had founded an agency for the care of Catalan refugees, and he met with them, learning of their needs and hearing their stories. He kept company with Franchisca Vidal de Capdevila, a woman he had helped escape from Barcelona, who had developed Parkinson's disease. He composed. And he played the cello, working through the Bach suites he had played since his boyhood. He was seventy years old.

Inevitably, the world found him in Prades—and found, in Casals the hermit and exile, a figure for its postwar crisis of conscience.

José María Corredor came on Sunday afternoons, one of a group of Catalans resolved to help Casals deal with the mail. "Our illustrious fellow-countryman would welcome us with unvarying warmth and friendliness," he recalled, "sitting in his patriarchal armchair in front of a table covered with books and papers—and, of course, pipes and tobacco. More and more papers, on the table, on an old piano, sometimes on chairs and sometimes on the bed, which is occupied at night by the Master and in the daytime by his 'cello." They talked and talked, and Corredor began taking notes of their conversations, a virtuoso's inadvertent autobiography.

Other musicians sought him out. First a cellist came to Prades, asking for a chance to study with him. Casals agreed, and Bernard Greenhouse, who was thirty years old and from Newark, stayed a year, living in a rented room, where in the winter he put a toaster under a chair to warm himself as he practiced. Casals gave him a lesson several times a week. They devoted most of a month to the Suite in D Minor, with Casals giving precise instructions about bowing, fingering, phrasing, vibrato. One day Casals picked up his cello and played along, using the same techniques he had taught. "It was as if that room had stereophonic sound—two cellos producing at once," Greenhouse recalled. Then Casals played the suite again, and beautifully, but utterly differently. Concluding, he told his student: "Now you've learned how to improvise in Bach."

Other cellists came. One stayed seven weeks, playing morning, noon, and night. Another gave ten months to the Dvořák concerto and a Bach suite. Many were allowed to audition, then turned away. A young woman, an American, showed up without a cello or a wish to study. "'I came to Europe to see you,' she said to Casals. 'After, I shall go to Africa to see Dr. Schweitzer. Then I shall return to the United States.'"

Alexander Schneider came. At age forty-one he was a top chamber musician who was determined to master Bach's music for solo violin. A Lithuanian Jew, he had managed to flee the Nazis and settle in America, but his mother and sister had not, and it was on a trip to Europe to determine their whereabouts—they had died in Auschwitz—that he called on Casals in Prades. He and Casals became friends right away, and Schneider returned the next summer to prepare the violin suites for performance. He arranged the gift of the *Bach-Gesellschaft*, then had a grand piano sent from Paris. For the summer of 1949 he arrived with two peers, a violinist and a violist. With Casals they made a string quartet, and Casals had the experience of playing with musicians of his caliber for the first time since the war.

Invitations to perform came too, Casals's vow notwithstanding. Albert Einstein wrote from Princeton urging him to come to America. Leopold Stokowski asked him to play with his new orchestra, the Symphony of the Air; Eugene Ormandy proposed the Philadelphia Orchestra. Casals said no to all of them. Then, in 1948, invitations of a different kind came. The two-hundredth anniversary of Bach's death would occur in 1950, and Casals was importuned to take the occasion to break his silence: at Harvard; at the Library of Congress; at the Thomaskirche in Leipzig; in Strasbourg, where Albert Schweitzer would give an organ recital. No, no, no, no. Learning of this, Alexander Schneider and the pianist Mieczysław Horszowski, at dinner in New York, came up with a plan for an event that they thought Casals would be willing to attend, and sent him a letter, proposing it: "a Bach festival, in June or July, in Prades or Perpignan, under your direction." He could choose the musicians and donate the proceeds to the cause of Catalan refugees. Maybe he could persuade Dr. Schweitzer to take part.

Casals said no. But by the next summer he relented, and as Schneider and a counterpart made the arrangements, Casals readied himself musically, he later recalled, "with the fervor of a youngster about to make his professional debut." The Bach Commemorative Festival would be a bicentennial tribute as apt as it was unusual: thirty-five world-class musicians would travel from the United States and Europe and converge on Casals's adoptive village to play the music of Bach in the local churches and schools, staying in private homes or in the single, simple hotel in order to take part in what Casals's biographer Robert Baldock calls "a gigantic Bach masterclass by his supreme interpreter." There would be six evening orchestra concerts, with Casals conducting, and six evening recitals for soloists or small groups, all held in the small, Gothic-style Cathédrale de St.-Pierre in Prades. A month of rehearsals preceded the festival, and these became performances in themselves. "Thank you for coming. I love you. And now let's begin," Casals told the musicians assembled in the refectory of the local Collège Moderne des Jeunes Filles. Then he led them through the first Brandenburg concerto, and musicians, devotees, and villagers saw how Casals put a Bach piece together.

Tape and the long-playing record made it all possible. When the Fulbright Foundation declined a request for funding, Columbia Records stepped in. The record company would advance Schneider the money needed for expenses ($25,000) and recoup it by tape-recording the festival and issuing the performances in a deluxe box set of long-playing records—"an estimated twenty-seven platters," said one report. The box set would call attention to the vital qualities of the new LP format: its length and its sonic fidelity. It would affix the prestige of Bach and Casals to the LP.

On Friday, June 2, 1950, a town crier rode through Prades on a bicycle, announcing the first concert. It was already old news on the other side of the Atlantic. *Life* had run a photo essay: "Pablo Casals: At Last He Is Preparing to Play in Public Again." The *New Yorker* correspondent Janet Flanner was there. "By nine o'clock," she wrote, "what looked like the village's entire population (about five thousand) was massed in two watchful lines, between which eight hundred concertgoers, more than half of them American, self-consciously marched up to the church door," which was lit up by floodlights, the better to show in the apertures of cameras.

The local Catholic bishop gave a benediction, at once welcoming the audience and asking them to respect the sacred character of the church by not applauding. So it was that when Casals entered from the sacristy, cello in hand, the concertgoers rose from their seats without a sound. He sat in a chair on a makeshift wooden platform in front of the gilded and bejeweled altar, beneath the cherubim and seraphim, the wood and stone saints. He set the cello on its end pin. Then, with the sinuous opening G of the first suite, he broke their silence, and his own.

He opened each of the recital evenings with a Bach cello suite. The morning after each concert, the musicians would play the program again in the refectory, which had been rigged as a recording studio. But Casals did not play the cello suites over again. None of the reports from Prades says why. It may be that Columbia did not want a new recording to compete with the studio recordings from the thirties. It may be that Casals felt that the studio recordings could not be matched, that his technique had declined, or that he hadn't had time to prepare the suites. It may be that he sought to maintain his resistance. A *Life* photograph shows him with a grin on his face as he made "wisecracks about a wire recording of his playing which his friends made unbeknownst to him with the recorder hidden in the parlor." But his silence was serious. When the commemorative LPs went on sale in Britain and the United States—countries that legitimized Franco, lionized him—the cello suites, the model for his moral independence, would not be there.

>>9>> The Bach bicentenary was being celebrated at points across Europe, but musical unity was compromised by political division. Thuringia and Saxony were parts of the new "East Germany," not eastern outposts of a German culture that expressed itself at points across Europe, but as regions in a new Soviet state claimed as the spoils of war. The Thomaskirche and Nikolaikirche were still places of worship, but in a parody of the stages on the life's way of the most religious of great artists, they were controlled by a state that was officially godless.

In the circumstances, a grand Bach festival was held in Vienna. The Allies had divided the city into American, Soviet, British, and French quadrants, each run by military police. "Vienna's landmarks—St. Stephan's Cathedral, the State Opera House and the Burgtheater—were still in ruins," a later critic explained. "Yet Vienna's cultural life was reawakening, especially with music." At the Musikverein, Herbert von Karajan, seated at the harpsichord, led the Vienna Philharmonic and Singverein in the *St. Matthew Passion* and the Mass in B Minor, performances recorded for broadcast on state radio. They are era-opening recordings, intimate, sonically rich, and balanced between the voices and strings in the way prewar recordings were not. The Passion is a Last Supper of old-world singers, who are meeting one more time in a world all but lost; the Mass opens gravely, with the choir begging the Lord for mercy, but by the fourth part, a fist-pumping, chest-thumping Gloria, the fog over Europe has lifted and the continent is coming back to life.

Over two nights in Vienna, Yehudi Menuhin played Bach's six works for solo violin. This stroke of programming was as consequential as the music itself, for it made the festival a model of postwar cultural amity, in which Menuhin, a London-based Russo-American Jewish émigré of conspicuous virtue (yoga, health food, and the like) could take part along with Karajan, who as the young director of the Berlin State Opera a decade earlier had been a Nazi and a prized product of the Third Reich's cultural program. Germany had been ruined, and Austria with it, but about Bach, performer and conductor, Jew and German, could agree.

In Geneva, Dinu Lipatti made a recording of Bach's first partita. A Romanian prodigy, Lipatti had studied with Alfred Cortot, the pianist in Casals's "Holy Trinity," after dazzling Cortot during a competition in Vienna when he was seventeen. He had remained in Bucharest until 1943, then left for neutral Switzerland. Soon after he got there he was diagnosed with leukemia. Undeterred, in the next six years he played, taught, composed, made recordings, wrote criticism, gave recitals, and took experimental treatments with cortisone, a new (and thus expensive) drug paid for by donations from Menuhin, Igor Stravinsky, and other prosperous musicians.

Lipatti's first partita is clear, strong, unified, tight of carriage. In press photographs he looks like the Italian American singers who ruled the radio in the United States at the time, and there is something of their committed elegance or *sprezzatura* in his approach, which is lean but not severe, like a slim-cut suit. But it is with his recordings of four shorter works in the same sessions—three chorales and a transcription of part of a sonata for flute and harpsichord—that he opened up new postwar territory. They are frankly contemplative—reverent approaches to a composer whom Lipatti saw as one of the "chosen instruments of God Himself." Like Casals, Lipatti was wedded to no single interpretation: he was said to play a piece a dozen or more different ways before discarding the various pianistic effects involved so as to play the piece "straight" once and for all. This leaving-out is apparent in the chorales, from which Lipatti subtracted the musical weight. The chorale prelude "Ich ruf du zir, Herr Jesu Christ" suggests a music box in a minor key, or the slow turning of a sublime carousel. The chorale from Cantata 147—"Jesu, Joy of Man's Desiring"—is a performance of impossible simplicity; the plain notes in the middle range of the instrument, played lightly to sound out and then decay rather than sustain, give the feeling of a perfect melody heard in something like its original state, somewhere between God's hour and the children's hour.

In Eisenach, the Bachhaus was being renovated. It was not the house where he had first lived, but it was around the corner; his later relatives had lived there, and since the turn of the century it had housed memorabilia from his early life. Now it would be a museum, a reminder of East Germany's previous life.

In Los Angeles, Theodor Adorno rose to Bach's defense. With the essay "Bach Defended Against His Devotees" he telescoped the energy of the bicentenary into a dozen pages of dialectic. He was a philosopher and an émigré, having left Hitler's Germany to settle in Southern California. Music (as a later devotee put it) was his "cognitive workspace," the social matter on which he tried out his ideas. He had denounced Sibelius as retrograde; set the atonal Schoenberg against the neoclassical Stravinsky, calling the latter a fascist for his regard for the authority of older forms; mocked the New Objectivity as kitsch; and declared that the destiny of all "mechanical music" was "oblivion." Inevitably he turned his argumentative energy to Bach. He adored Bach as the first modern composer, a thinking man who set rationality against inherited forms, an early Enlightenment figure whose workshop was "equipped with all the technical discoveries of the epoch." In the postwar embrace of Bach, however, he saw Bach "degraded" as an "antique"—craftsman, cantor, church musician—and saw Bach's extraordinary individual achievement reduced to the expression of a late-medieval tradition. Against that view he characterized Bach as "an anachronism" who stuck out in his own age and every later one through the form-transcending freedom his use of rationality gained for him. When this is not recognized, Adorno proposed, Bach "suffers the very fate which his fervent protectors are least willing to admit: he is changed into a neutralized cultural monument, in which aesthetic success mingles obscurely with a truth that has lost its intrinsic substance. They have made him into a composer for organ festivals in well-preserved Baroque towns, into ideology."

All together, the Bach bicentenary events were the public side of a fresh interest in Bach represented in scholarly terms by the *Neue Bach-Ausgabe*. This New Bach Edition was a mighty undertaking: a complete set of Bach's works, edited according to state-of-the-art practices in musicology, philology, textual editing, and the like. As scholarly editions of composers' works went, it was the first of its kind; and it had a biographical counterpart in *The Bach Reader*, a compendium of documents relating to Bach's life.

But it was the Prades festival, produced out of a violinist's back pocket, that captivated the press. The Bach festival in Prades was "one of the most copiously documented musical events in history," Robert Baldock has written. "Prades was full of photographers, reporters, music critics, and sound engineers . . . After each concert critics cabled reviews to papers around the globe. Music-lovers knew exactly what Casals had played and how he had played it." *Life* ran a second feature: "Casals Breaks His Silence." In *The New Yorker*, Janet Flanner, while duly recording the reverence paid to Casals and his performances of the cello suites, singled out his leadership of the orchestra. "He made Bach sound popular, in a new, noble, fast way, instead of traditional, boring, and dull . . . being Latin, he gave the Second 'Brandenburg' an un-Germanized, southern, joyful rhythm that made it sound like the most well-tempered dance music of the ages."

Once Prades had emptied of outsiders, Casals wrote a long letter, addressed to the White House in Washington, D.C., urging Harry Truman to veto a bill that would allot Marshall Plan aid to fascist Spain. "In . . . despondency I settled down in this peaceful town where I have been living in silence for many years," he explained. "This silence was broken for the first time just a few weeks ago when the time came to commemorate the bi-centennial of

Johann Sebastian Bach in a fitting manner . . . Mr. President, I address you now without any political credentials. A life devoted to the service of art and a faith in the dignity of man are my only credentials. It is with these that I appeal to you and hope and believe that my appeal will not go unheard." It went unheard: the bill passed, Truman signed it into law, and later in the year Spain was welcomed back into the United Nations.

Dinu Lipatti was overcome by leukemia. He died on December 2, 1950, in Geneva. Some said his death was hastened by the effort he expended in a recital in September in Besançon, France, just over the border with Switzerland. He staggered to the piano and faltered halfway up a major scale while testing the instrument. Then he performed heroically. He played Bach's first partita, a pair of Schubert Impromptus, and Chopin's waltzes. The waltzes, meant as a finale, were too much for him, or else they were not enough. He played thirteen of fourteen, then left off, let go, and played a Bach chorale.

>>10>> On the morning of December 24—Christmas Eve—Glenn Gould performed on CBC radio for the first time. As he mock-grandiloquently put it, "I wandered into a living-room-sized radio studio, placed my services at the disposal of a single microphone belonging to the Canadian Broadcasting Corporation, and proceeded to broadcast 'live' sonatas by Mozart and Hindemith." For him the significance of the debut had nothing to do with the prestige of a coast-to-coast broadcast. It was memorable "not simply because it enabled me to communicate without the immediate presence of a gallery of witnesses . . . but rather, because later the same day I was presented with a soft-cut 'acetate,' a disk which dimly reproduced the felicities of the broadcast in question and which, even today, a quarter-century after the fact, I still take down from the shelf on occasion in order to celebrate the moment in my life when I realized that the collective wisdom of my peers and elders to the effect that technology represented a compromising, dehumanizing intrusion into art was nonsense, when my love affair with the microphone began."

That passage is often misread, so seductive is it as a theme awaiting variations. So it is important to see what it actually says. It does not describe the beginning of a love affair with the recording studio, but an affair with the microphone. ("The fact that in most forms of broadcasting a microphone six feet away serves as a surrogate for an audience has always been, for me, prominent among the attractions of the medium," he said.) The recording studio was not a secret hideout but a space in a government broadcasting company headquarters in downtown Toronto. There, Gould did not splice each piece together from different takes, but played the music straight through, for "in those days radio broadcasting still observed the first-note-to-last-and-damn-the-consequences syndrome of the concert hall." The session was of great significance to him, he explained, not because of the way he felt in the studio or the way he played there, but for what he got out of it: a recording, in high quality, of the music he had just made.

Gould was eighteen, and had decided that "it was time to set out on my own snowshoes," as he put it. He dropped out of high school, which he had been attending part-time. He stayed home when his parents went to church on Sunday mornings. Eventually, he cut off his piano studies with Alberto Guerrero, in circumstances that remain mysterious.

Freshly independent, he spent time at the family cottage, on Lake Simcoe, north of Toronto. It was a small, square house, with a sloping roof, white siding, and windows all around, which looked out on a stand of trees and the lake beyond. There was an upright piano there. He would drive north with books, records, sheet music, dog, and tape recorder, and settle into the cottage for weeks at a time, playing music, taking long walks in the woods with the dog, and piloting the family's motorboat on the lake. "He was practicing, and preparing himself," Bert Gould said laconically.

Gould himself saw his time at the cottage as his higher education. "The greatest of all teachers is the tape recorder," he later said. "I would be lost without it." At the cottage, he used it to study his playing. He would set the tape running, play a piece on the piano, rewind and play it back on the tape recorder, assessing the music he had just made. Then he would roll tape and play the piece again—differently, in light of what he had heard.

The tape recorder shaped his approach in a double sense. By enabling him to assess his own playing, it empowered his perfectionism. And it prompted him to alter his approach—tempo, attack, sustain, and the like—so as to produce those effects that sounded best on tape.

A photograph shows him working a tape recorder at the cottage. It is the Ampex 600, a valise-size model with two open reels, a row of dials, and a VU meter. His eyes are on the spinning reels, his right hand on the rewind dial. Probably he is about to listen to a piece of music he had just played on the piano. He looks ordinary and at ease, an electronics enthusiast operating a choice piece of gear. But he was a pioneer in shirtsleeves, akin to Watson and Crick in Cambridge, a theoretical pianist performing sonic experiments with piano and magnetic tape. At the cottage, he was incorporating the experience of recorded sound into his approach to the piano. There, day after day, he would "play" music as a pianist and then take the role of the listener, "playing" a recording, in a form of technological counterpoint.

At the cottage, Gould consummated his affair with Bach. His biographers report that he played Bach at the cottage and leave it at that—which is bewildering, because Gould cited a particular piece of Bach's music as the theme of his independence. This was the *Goldberg Variations*, the aria and thirty "diverse variations" for keyboard. Landowska, Tureck, and Hess had recorded them, but Alberto Guerrero, in five years as Gould's teacher, had kept clear of them. So Gould was free to master the *Goldberg*s in his own way, with the aid of the tape recorder and the microphone. "This was a work which I learned entirely on my own," he later said. "I never really had a lesson with anyone on it, and in fact it was one of the first works that I did learn entirely without my teacher. It was a work which I made up my mind about relatively [early], much more so and much more decidedly than was the case with most works in my repertoire at that time."

In his approach, the *Goldberg*s were a series of meditations on independence. What's surprising about them, he explained a few years later, is that there is no direct relationship between the variations and the "singularly self-sufficient little air" that precedes them—a "richly embellished soprano line" that "is totally forgotten during the 30 variations." He admitted that, in making such an insight, he might be playing a "dangerous game, ascribing to musical composition attributes that reflect only the analytical approach of the performer." That is, he emphasized that this approach to the *Goldberg*s was his own singular interpretation.

At the cottage, Glenn Gould was coming of age. As the cello suites were for Pablo Casals, the *Goldberg Variations* were for him: at once the means of his independence and the model for it, a structure that suggested a way of life. He played them over and over, to uncover their true nature; he played them, and then played them back, devising variations on the variations.

>>11>> Albert Schweitzer had spent the Bach bicentenary in Lambaréné and Strasbourg, but in important respects his key missionary territory was now America. He was a paragon of virtue in an age anxious for paragons, and nowhere so much as in the United States. "The Greatest Man in the World—That Is What Some People Call Albert Schweitzer, Jungle Philoso-

pher": so *Life* introduced an adulatory photo-profile of him in 1947. When he went to America for the first time two years later, he was welcomed as "Philosopher—Musician—Doctor—Theologian—Writer—Man of God." A passenger on the transcontinental train Zephyr asked him for his autograph, thinking he was Albert Einstein. "I am an old friend of Dr. Einstein's," he replied. "Would you like me to give you his autograph?" A poll in Europe placed him with Goethe and Leonardo as the renaissance men of the continent. A *Saturday Review* poll ranked him first, above Einstein, in a list of the greatest living people outside of politics. *Time* put him on its cover: in the Luce empire, a good Christian generally made good copy. The Swedish Academy gave him the Nobel Peace Prize.

Since the turn of the century Schweitzer had urged Western civilization to cultivate reverence for life, lest it bring about its own destruction. Two world wars bore him out, but only partially. Not until the invention of the atomic bomb, and then the hydrogen bomb, was the end of the human race a practical possibility rather than a pulpit conceit. Suddenly Schweitzer's end-times dread was au courant; suddenly reverence for life was a strategy for survival.

It was a philosophy that suited the progressive international community, from Einstein and Robert Oppenheimer to Thomas Mann and Dag Hammarskjöld. In an epilogue to a scholar's study of his theology, Schweitzer rephrased it for the atomic age. "We are no longer content like the generations before us, to believe in the Kingdom that comes of itself at the end of time. Mankind today must either realize the Kingdom of God or perish," he declared. ". . . The last petition of the Lord's Prayer has again its original meaning for us as a prayer for deliverance from the dominion of the evil powers of the world. These are no less real to us as working in men's minds, instead of being embodied in angelic beings opposed to God. The first believers set their hope wholly on the Kingdom of God in expectation of the end of the world; we do it in expectation of the end of the human race." He became a signatory to petitions against hydrogen-bomb testing and nuclear proliferation, and made his Nobel acceptance speech an anguished statement of conscience—declaring that the only hope of avoiding nuclear war lay in personal ethics, not international organizations.

His "life and thought," the basis of his reputation, was in decline. He had been a jungle doctor for half his life. The more time he spent in Europe (five long stays, about three years in all, in the decade after the war ended), the more vivid grew the legend of the little hospital at Lambaréné. And yet as medicine advanced and Schweitzer's fame gave him the means to obtain modern equipment, the simplicity of the clinic—more a camp than a hospital, with sheds open to the elements, chickens and antelopes roaming in and out, and heaps of dung in the corners—came to strike outsiders as something other than practical. It was a leftover from colonialism. It was a symbol of the holy man's renunciation of the fallen world. It was a form of condescension to the local people, who, in his view, it appeared, deserved less than the best. It was less about reverence for life than contempt for modernity.

His writing was stunted too. Like the clinic, the concluding third volume of his *Philosophy of Civilization* was often described but rarely encountered firsthand. "The Philosophy I carry with me constantly," he wrote to Einstein, who had invited him to join the Institute of Advanced Study in Princeton, where he could think and write in peace. "Many chapters . . . are finished and others are so far completed in thought that they can be put on paper right away." A visitor to Lambaréné was shown the manuscript: "stacks of sheets of paper, yellowing and brown with age," piled a foot high. "Looking at the oil lamp on the desk and thinking of the inflammability of this single copy of the precious manuscript, the visitor suggested microfilming. The doctor laughed: Microfilming? Too modern! His manuscript was durable. 'Look—see how these chapters have survived the teeth of the antelopes!'" He would not use a typewriter "because of the noise it makes." "The third volume is conceived as a symphony of thoughts—a symphonic performance of themes," he reported to Einstein, but it languished in draft, an aspect of his inwardness.

"Never before in my life have I thought and felt so musically as in these last years," he told Einstein. "One thing to which I rigidly adhere is practicing the piano with the organ pedal, even if it is only for three-quarters of an hour, to keep in form and also to improve." He gave the bicentenary recital in Strasbourg. Schirmer, a music publisher in New York, renewed its interest in publishing an edition of Bach organ chorales with Schweitzer's annotations, a project it had signed up before the war—the Great War. During a trip to Europe, Schweitzer met with a collaborator who would help finish the work. But he wrote nothing new on Bach, gave no attention to fresh approaches to organ-building, and made no new recordings.

It took two American filmmakers to change the situation. One, Erica Anderson, was determined to make a documentary about Schweitzer's life at the clinic. "I would rather burn in hell than have a film made of my life," he wrote in reply to a request from her. She showed up with camera gear and a production assistant. In time Schweitzer, like Pablo Casals, relented; and like Casals he did so only on certain conditions—in his case, that the film not be shown during his lifetime and that it not be publicized.

Anderson filmed him around the clinic. When he went to Europe, she was invited to film him playing a recital in Strasbourg and then to follow him to Gunsbach, where he would perform on the organ on which he had learned to play in his boyhood. She went, and her partner, a wealthy businessman named James Jerome Hill, joined her, arriving in a recording truck.

Their film opens with Schweitzer's mustached visage set against footage of shirtless Gabonese doing physical labor around the clinic. Then the camera follows Schweitzer "4000 miles north as the crow flies" to Gunsbach, where, as white peasants labor in the fields, the good doctor, having ridden third class (there is no fourth class anymore) steps off the train in heroic solitude. Soon he is at the village church, whose organ is one of many he "has rescued from destruction." The camera pans over the pipes, then draws back to show Schweitzer as he pulls out a few stops and starts to play the Bach Prelude in G Major, the printed text of which is open on the organ. He is right: the organ is just right for the size of the church and the scale of the prelude, which in this setting is guileless and emotive, country music. But the question arises: Why is he playing all alone in an empty, darkened church, and not for an audience? For this famous man, this exponent of organ music, the music of Bach is an aspect of his solitude, a refuge from the world—from Africa, from Europe, from fame, from ideas and ideology.

Now Schweitzer was eager to make recordings. He asked Anderson to arrange a session for his next trip to Europe. She did, and the Columbia LP that came out of it is a true record of Schweitzer's Bach at mid-century. The sleeve featured a hand-lettered title and a line drawing of a hirsute angel at the organ, making Schweitzer's Bach look as ancient and inviolable as the cave drawings of Lascaux. The recording is epochs nearer the present than the recording of 1935—due to a new way of positioning the microphones that Schweitzer, that detester of the telephone and other gadgetry, had devised himself.

After Schweitzer had returned to Lambaréné and Anderson and Hill to the United States, they sent him an eightieth-birthday present: a record player.

>>12>> Pablo Casals, too, had discovered the power of visual images of his iconoclasm.

Columbia's box set from the Bach Commemorative Festival had been released in December: ten LPs cased in red leatherette, like the sheet-music trea-suries of the Great Music of the Western World sold earlier in the century. (The Brandenburgs praised in *The New Yorker* sound, today, like an orchestra recorded in a small village—like a village orchestra, that is, sawing away at Bach.) The set was a fitting end to the Bach bicentenary (and "the platters," *Billboard* reported, "have emerged as solid longhair merchandise"), but it made a monument of informal music-making, and sales did not meet Columbia's expectations.

The next summer the festival was held again. This time it was in Perpig-nan, a larger town twenty-five miles from Prades, and this time it was broad-ened from Bach to feature classical music generally. This time, Casals allowed Robert Snyder, an American who had won an Oscar for a documentary about Michelangelo, to make "a visit to Pablo Casals" and even to film him playing Bach's first cello suite in the Benedictine abbey outside town. It is a crucial piece of footage, more suggestive of the spell Casals cast in Prades than the box set. Even front and center in the thousand-year-old church, Casals is emphati-cally prosaic, in dark suit and spectacles, straight of back in a straight-backed chair. But Bob Snyder of Brooklyn will not settle for prosaic. He goes at Casals from all angles; the camera lingers on his hands, his eyes, the stone walls behind him, the leaded glass above. The filmmaker is frankly striving for the iconic—for a vision of Casals as a man who brings down the fire from heaven to earth.

When the festival ended Casals left southern France for the first time in ages. He went to Zurich (neutral Switzerland had received tens of thousands of exiles from Franco's Spain) to conduct a series of performances of his own compositions. Albert Schweitzer, then also in Switzerland, "was kind enough to come to see me in Zurich," Casals recalled, and so the Hermit of Lambaréné (as the press styled him) attended a concert led by the Hermit of Prades.

Afterward they had an intense discussion about the nature of art. Was art a form of protest, sufficient unto itself, or must it be accompanied by protest of the worldly, explicit kind? On Sundays in Prades, José María Corredor had read out passages from Schweitzer's writings about Bach and let Casals re-spond to them. Now Casals picked up the conversation with Schweitzer him-self. A photograph shows them, seated, facing each other, nearly touching, Schweitzer's eyes (over his enormous mustache) straight on Casals's (behind rimless glasses). Confounding their public roles, the virtuoso made a case for protest and the sage proposed that great art was protest enough. "My great friend said, 'It is better to create than to protest!'" Casals recalled. "'And why not do both,' I answered. 'The Prades festivals have the double character of cre-ation and protest, and further, protest can be the most arduous creation and the most exacting.' 'In any case,' said Schweitzer, 'I accept everything you do since I know the moral motives which inspire you.' I explained to him the real reasons of my protest, and then we both remained silent, deep in thought, and without our noticing it someone must have taken this photograph of us which I treasure particularly." He had it framed and hung it on a wall of his house in Prades.

The Armenian Canadian photographer Yousuf Karsh was roaming Europe "in search of greatness" that summer, and his black-and-white portraits of Casals and Schweitzer consolidated the public image of each. Like the filmmaker Snyder, Karsh photographed Casals against a stone wall in a dark corner of the abbey church—seated in a chair, back to the camera, cello over his shoulder, stonewalling modernity. Karsh's portrait of Schweitzer is a close-up of the good man lost in thought, the thick hair, full eyebrows, and mustache suggesting the vigor behind the virtue.

W. Eugene Smith went to Lambaréné for *Life* to photograph the "man of mercy" in situ. Smith's portrait of Schweitzer at his desk is akin to Karsh's portrait: Schweitzer is hunched over the page, pen in hand, while a lamp in the foreground suggests the midnight oil of his labors. Smith's photograph of Schweitzer playing the piano is documentary work by comparison: Schweitzer is an ordinary man, in khakis and work shirt, picking out a melody on the keyboard with his hands and another with his feet on the specially rigged pedals. The latter photograph was published in *The Atlantic Monthly*, alongside photographs of Albert Einstein, Jacob Epstein, Martha Graham, and Ernest Hemingway. Schweitzer was in the company of people who had sought greatness, whether he liked it or not.

Casals visited Schweitzer the next summer in Alsace. It is possible that they played music together there; it is certain that they discussed the state of the world. A photograph shows them striding through Gunsbach, in vested suits and dark hats—figures from the pre-recorded era, media icons reinstalled in village life as it had existed when they left it for concert tours, lectures, broadcasts, albums, photographs, and magazine covers.

What was the nature of their friendship, exactly? It was a transcontinental collaboration in a moral key, like a Bach sonata for cello and keyboard. They supported each other as musicians, as exemplars, as refuseniks, as famous people, as devotees of the human spirit. Today, learning about them through laudatory press clips, it is easy to forget how unpopular their positions were. That is why they needed each other. Each affirmed for the other that he hadn't wasted his life in high-minded refusal. Together, they felt understood; together, they were a little less lonely.

>>13>> "I was raised on Bach," Daniel Barenboim said. Born in Buenos Aires in 1942, he was already recognized as a piano prodigy when he moved to Tel Aviv with his family at age ten. The next year, at Edwin Fischer's urging, Barenboim was "summoned to the old Festspielhaus [in Salzburg] to play and audition" for Wilhelm Furtwängler, whose recordings he admired. "I remember playing the Bach Italian Concerto," he recalled, as well as Beethoven and Prokofiev and "a couple of Chopin Études." Furtwängler tested his pitch the way Casals had tested his son Pablo's—asking the boy to turn his back to the piano and identify notes played on it. Barenboim's pitch was spot on; his natural gifts thus confirmed, Furtwängler invited him to play with the Berlin Philharmonic. But Barenboim's father said no. "My father told him that it was the greatest honor that he could have bestowed on me, but we were a Jewish family living in Israel—this was just nine years after the war and the Holocaust—and he didn't feel it was the right time. And he hoped that Furtwängler would understand."

Already Barenboim approached music philosophically, as an aural space where the great questions of life are posed; and already he felt in the music he played something like the drama of his own life and that of his people, centered on the question of what constitutes a home. "If you have a sense of belonging," he later said, "a feeling of home, harmonically speaking—and if you're able to establish that as a composer, and establish it as a musician—then you will always get this feeling of being in no-man's land, of being displaced yet always finding a way home."

Furtwängler did understand: he furnished Barenboim with a letter of introduction, which brought the boy invitations to play in other, less objectionable lands. Three years later Barenboim made his Carnegie Hall debut, playing a Prokofiev concerto; the conductor was Leopold Stokowski.

>>14>> At twenty, Glenn Gould was making a life for himself as a concert pianist, and his father, Bert, did what he could to advance his career. He hired a manager: Walter Homburger, a Berliner expatriated to Toronto. And he fashioned a chair that enabled his son to sit at the piano just the way he liked, whether in an auditorium in Ottawa or a meeting hall in Saskatoon. He began with a folding chair, wood-framed, slender-legged, with a floral pattern cut into the back. "I had to saw about four inches off each leg," he recalled, "and I made a brass bracket to go around each leg and screw into it, and then welded the half of a turnbuckle to the brass bracket so the legs

could be adjusted individually." Gould took to it right away. In the chair, he could extend his arms straight out and rock back and forth toward the far reaches of the keyboard. It was an ingenious adaptation of the fixed instrument; it was a technical solution to the human problem of his antipathy to the stage.

The CBC's Toronto radio studio was a solution too. Gould took part in several dozen broadcasts after his CBC debut, and the studio was a halfway house, a middle place between live performance and music assembled on tape. It was a place where he played alone but for the public, at once courting fame and guarding himself from it.

His career was launched through those broadcasts, but the CBC did not consider them worth archiving. The archivist was Gould himself, who kept the acetates, fully aware of their importance. Today, they make it possible for us to hear his approach to Bach develop the way he heard it himself: by playing the recordings, with the microphone as our surrogate.

The Christmas Eve broadcast from 1950 is now lost. So is a broadcast of some months later in which he played Bach's Partita No. 5 in G major. The earliest surviving broadcast acetate is from Tuesday, October 21, 1952, when Gould played a Sweelinck organ fantasia transcribed for piano, followed by the music of Bach: the prelude and fugue in E major from book two of the *Well-Tempered Clavier*, and the *Italian Concerto*.

The acetate was cut at 78 rpm. Heard today, it places Gould before his time, back in the thick and brittle 78 era. In the prelude and fugue, the lines made by the left hand and the right hand melt together; in the concerto, the piano is even more high-strung than the harpsichord Gould was approximating; clinking and chiming, it sounds like a vaudeville prop. His sprint through the third movement doesn't sound exhilarating: it sounds mad. In its primitivism, the recording makes clear, to us as it doubtless did to him, that his approach to Bach would require better-quality recorded sound.

He played all the cities of Canada: Saint John, Montreal, Ottawa, Winnipeg, Calgary. He played at the Canadian National Exposition, and ran long, so that the final bars of Prokofiev's Seventh Sonata were drowned out by fighter planes performing aerial stunts overhead. He performed at the Stratford Shakespeare Festival. With his childhood friend Robert Fulford he started an enterprise called New Music Associates, and they put on a pair of concerts for audiences of a few dozen. He went to the cottage. He read Tolstoy, Nietzsche, Thomas Mann. He composed. He took long walks with the dog, a collie he had named Banquo. He played Bach.

On Sunday, February 28, 1954, he played three pairs of preludes and fugues from the *Well-Tempered Clavier* for a CBC broadcast. The acetate tells the story. The sound is better than before: clearer, more spacious. The pieces are bright, but lacking in variety. The first and third are in minor keys. The preludes are as implacable as the fugues. They might be mallet pieces played with icicles. They point up the drawback of Gould's approach to Bach: it can become repetitive, even monotonous. These pieces sound like music made by a person who has been spending too much time alone.

Gould had plenty of Bach in his repertoire, but it was a thin vein of Bach's work, a severe reduction of the composer. Kevin Bazzana deftly summarizes: "For Gould . . . Bach was a paragon of order, logic, and structural integrity, and he conveniently ignored those aspects of Bach's music that did not support this view. He had little to say about Bach as a rhetorician, a Lutheran, a tone-painter, a man of the theatre, a keyboard performer; his Bach was an architect, a 'contrapuntal craftsman,' an idealist whose music stood apart from mundane matters like instrumental realization, and his preferences among Bach's works (fugues rather than toccatas, suites rather than fantasias) were of a piece with this view."

In the circumstances, the *Goldberg Variations* enter the record as an answer to a question. How to vary one's solitude? How to be alone?

He arranged to play them on a CBC broadcast. The network extended its usual classical performance program from thirty to forty-five minutes. "The 45-minute period," the *CBC Times* reported, "will make it possible to present in a single program by Glenn Gould on June 21st (1954) the complete *Goldberg Variations* by Bach." The "aria with diverse variations," which Bach wrote in part to divert a nobleman who could not sleep, would air on the summer solstice, the longest day of the year.

There is no piece of music whose history is so divided into "before" and "after" by one performer as the history of the *Goldberg Variations* is divided into before and after by Glenn Gould. To hear that acetate is to hear Gould's *Goldberg*s as they were before Gould, with the benefit of the insight we gain by coming "after" him. It is like seeing a photograph of your spouse from just before the two of you met. You know each other well, but not yet.

What does it sound like? In many ways, it sounds like what we know: bright, fleet, gallant, generous. But it is awfully well-behaved, the sound of Gould playing Bach with his shirt tucked in and his hair combed.

Does it sound like Glenn Gould? Absolutely. A recording of the young Dutch harpsichordist Gustav Leonhardt from the Konzerthaus in Vienna the previous June makes clear that the bright, fleet approach was not distinct to the piano, to North America, or to Glenn Gould. What makes Gould's approach already his own is how various it is, as he goes at the *Goldbergs* from different angles and in different moods. The first variation is a romp. The second is a dance done on tiptoe. The third is a trip taken in parallel tracks. The fourth is exultant, the fifth a race to the top; the twentieth is a roll in a barrel, the thirtieth a hymn. They are superabundant; the music is not developed, it is multiplied, so there is more than enough to go around. Conceived in solitude, in the company of a tape recorder, they are sociable, gregarious. Gould was taken with Ralph Kirkpatrick's image of the work as a classical palace or temple with "the variations grouped like the members of an elaborate colonnade"—in ten groups of three, with each group "composed of a canon and an elaborate two-manual arabesque, enclosing in each case another variation of independent character." But even as he cherished this "architectural analogy," he saw the variations as a family tree, with the aria as the parent and the variations as progeny. In his hands, the figures in Kirkpatrick's colonnade—a pair, or couple, enclosing a third figure of "independent character"—form a family unit, which is apt in a work that bears a family name, one akin to that of Gould's own family.

The broadcast left Gould feeling sociable. Through New Music Associates, he arranged a recital for himself: an all-Bach concert, centered on the *Goldberg Variations*. He invited Harvey Olnick, a critic new to Toronto and with connections in New York, offering him free tickets in exchange for a review. He wrote program notes, setting out his ideas about the *Aria mit verschiedenen Veränderungen*—"aria with diverse variations."

In early October he went to Montreal to give a recital for broadcast by the CBC's international service, and played Bach's fifth partita, the Bach work he played most often in public. This broadcast was recorded on magnetic tape rather than acetates. The difference is profound. To the variety and sociability of the *Goldberg Variations* is added the clarity of tape, which brings out the contrasts and counterpoint—low notes and high, left hand and right, deliberate and quicksilver—so crucial to his approach. The low notes are august in their precision; the right-hand ornaments sparkle and chime. The recording makes clear what he was doing in his private taping sessions at the cottage. He wasn't just using the tape recorder as a tool to help him develop his style. He was using it to develop a style of playing that was suited to the attributes of recording technology.

The all-Bach concert was held on Saturday, October 16, 1954. A hurricane

had struck the day before. Fifteen people showed up for the concert. One was
Harvey Olnick. A soprano sang arias; Gould and a violinist played a pair of
sonatas; and Gould played the *Goldbergs*. "I was just dazzled," Olnick recalled. "It was the only kind of playing I'd ever heard that was like this, particularly in this wonderful rhythmic pulse that he got, without accent and
everything just going lickety-split." Afterward he asked Gould: "Where did
you come from?"

>>15>> Gould went to the United States at the end of the year, accom-
panied by his father, his manager, and his adjustable folding chair. He brought
a reputation, too. An unsigned review in the *Musical Courier* (by Harvey
Olnick) had declared him the equal of Wanda Landowska, and of Rudolf
Serkin, who had played at the first Festival of Bach in Prades and had gone
on to develop a summer music festival in Marlboro, Vermont, along similar
lines.

Pianist, father, and manager had plotted a strategy for a U.S. debut. As
Leopold Stokowski had grasped twenty years earlier, New York had displaced
Boston and Philadelphia as the center of classical music in America. It was the
hearth of the cult of virtuosity, centered on Carnegie Hall, Philharmonic Hall,
and the Metropolitan Opera House. It was also the headquarters of the big
broadcasting networks and of record companies from Columbia to Vanguard.
Paradoxically, New York's cultural dominance had been compounded, not
vitiated, by tape and LP.

Homburger rented Town Hall, made hotel reservations, invited the press.
Gould put together a program—one not far from the Bach and "composers of
today" approach Tureck had made her own at the same hall. And he tried it
out with a recital at the Phillips Gallery in Washington, D.C.

The story of what happened next is one of the great foundation stories of
the arts: a recital and a rave review, followed by a recital and a record deal. But
a couple of faulty ideas distort it. One is that the concerts were a pair of tri-
umphs, a provincial's conquest of the dominant culture. The other is that the
concerts were boldly unorthodox, two shots across the bow.

Gould settled on the same program for both recitals: Sweelinck, Gibbons,
Bach, Webern, Beethoven, and Berg. His biographers all say how daring a
program it was, a bucking of Romantic convention and the cult of virtuosity.
But by Gould's own standards it was cautious. He had played the Sweelinck
on the CBC two years earlier; he had played the Bach partita more times than

he could count.* The Orlando Gibbons piece was a musical knuckleball, harder for the listener than the performer. He had ignored the piano-virtuoso-recital folkways for years in Canada—why should he suddenly put himself in thrall to them just because he was south of the border?

The two concerts were nonevents by the publicity standards of the time. In the previous few years Town Hall had hosted concerts by Tureck, Yehudi Menuhin, Andrés Segovia, and Myra Hess—and that's just to name performers virtuosic in Bach. It was a common venue for debuts and premieres by out-of-towners. How did you get to Carnegie Hall? Practice, practice, practice. How did you get to Town Hall? By renting the place.

For all his iconoclasm, Gould always wanted to make music for a wide public. In Canada, he was a "national treasure" who never missed a chance to perform on the CBC. He liked critics more than he liked other pianists, and had enticed Harvey Olnick to come to his all-Bach concert in Toronto. He expected rave reviews, got them, and saved them in a scrapbook.

His performances of the *Goldberg Variations* in the fall had changed his sense of himself and his sense of Bach. Why, then, didn't he make his recital debut with them? Why did he set aside the *Goldbergs* and introduce himself with a program that he had played many times before?

In one sense, the decision was simple. The recitals were means to an end. He was giving them so as to leave the United States with a record contract.

In another, it was complicated. He had developed an approach to the *Goldbergs* that was bound up intimately with the act of recording them. Only in a recording studio could he render them in all their variety. Once the reviews were in and the deal was done he would get on with his true aim: the making of a *Goldberg Variations* for the age of recordings.

He gave the recital in Washington: Sweelinck, Gibbons, Bach, et al. Paul Hume of *The Washington Post* was there. Hours later, Hume filed a piece for the next day's paper. "January 2 is early for predictions," he allowed, "but it is unlikely that the year 1955 will bring us a finer piano recital than that played yesterday afternoon at the Phillips Gallery. We shall be lucky if it brings us others of equal beauty and significance." Unstintingly, he concluded: "Gould is a pianist with rare gifts for the world. It must not long delay hearing and according him the honor and audience he deserves. We know of no pianist anything like him of any age."

Alexander Schneider, in New York, got word of the *Post* review. He had

---

*By the time he recorded it two and a half years later, he had played it (he reckoned) five hundred times.

played with Gould at the Stratford Festival and had found him brilliant but temperamental. On January 10 or thereabouts, David Oppenheim, a producer with the Masterworks division of Columbia Records, paid a visit to Schneider at his apartment on East Twentieth Street, bringing a Columbia LP of Dinu Lipatti playing Bach and Scarlatti. They listened to it together, and Oppenheim wondered aloud where the next Lipatti was. Schneider told him that such a one would be playing at Town Hall the next night and urged him to attend. "Go and take a contract with you right away, and sign him up," Schneider said, "because if you like Lipatti, you may like him."

Gould played Town Hall: Sweelinck, Gibbons, Bach, and the rest. Town Hall seats about fifteen hundred people. Two hundred people were there. Afterward a hundred of them sought out the pianist backstage.

David Oppenheim was one of them. He was taken with Gould's performance, all the more so because (he noticed) he was the only record company executive in the audience.

The New York Times ran a brief review of the recital. "The challenging program Mr. Gould prepared was a test the young man met successfully, and in doing so left no doubt of his powers as a technician," the paper's critic, John Briggs, declared, and went on: "The most rewarding aspect of Mr. Gould's playing, however, is that technique as such is in the background. The impression that is uppermost is not one of virtuosity but of expressiveness. One is able to hear the music."

David Oppenheim got in touch with Walter Homburger and offered Gould a contract with Columbia Masterworks. Gould bent and put his name to the document. The oddest of pianists was signed to the classiest of record companies, the label of Vladimir Horowitz, Dinu Lipatti, Albert Schweitzer, and Pablo Casals.

>>**16**>> "One Sunday morning in the summer of 1955, when I was fifteen years old, I was mooning around our back garden in the suburbs of Cape Town, wondering what to do, boredom being the main problem of existence in those days, when from the house next door I heard music. As long as the music lasted I was frozen, I dared not breathe. I was being spoken to by music as music had never spoken to me before."

The storyteller is J. M. Coetzee, the South African novelist, and the story is of the event he came to call his "revelation in the garden." He went on:

"What I was listening to was a recording of Bach's *Well-Tempered Clavier*, played on the harpsichord. I learned this title only some time later, when I had become familiar with what, at the age of fifteen, I knew only—in a somewhat suspicious and even hostile teenage manner—as 'classical music.'" His was not a musical family; there was no music instruction in the schools he attended, and in the colonies, by which he means South Africa, classical music was deemed "sissy" enough for him to be scared off. "At home we had no musical instrument," he explained, "no record player."

"The house next door had a transient student population; the student who was playing the Bach record must have moved out soon afterward, or lost his/her taste for Bach, for I heard no more, though I listened intently."

The encounter with the music of Bach, for Coetzee, was "a moment of revelation . . . of the greatest significance in my life"—a moment when "everything changed." Through Bach he felt "the impact of the classic."

In telling the story some years later, Coetzee sought to "interrogate" the experience in order to define the term *classic*. The music of Bach, he proposed, is classic in two common senses: it is work "which is not time bound, which retains meaning for succeeding ages"; and though it predates the classical period—the period of Haydn and Mozart—it belongs to the body of European music "loosely called 'the classics.'" He offered a third sense of the term—the movement for the revival of classical values—and placed Bach outside it. Then he turned to the sense that truly concerned him: the classic as a source of aesthetic transcendence. Could he say, he asked himself, that in that moment in the garden "the spirit of Bach was speaking to me across the ages, across the seas, putting before me certain ideals; or was what was really going on at that moment that I was symbolically electing high European culture" as a means of escape from provincial life? Are some works of art truly transcendent, he asked, or is every work, and our interest in it, expressive of the values of the society of a particular time and place? "Is being spoken to across the ages a notion that we can entertain today only in bad faith?" To answer his question he returned to the first sense of the term. The classic is "what survives"—and the classic survives by facing interrogations such as the one he is performing; the classic is work that withstands the scrutiny of subsequent ages, its phases of ardor and neglect, and so transcends them, so that listeners in other times and places can feel the "stunned overwhelmedness" he felt when he heard the music of Bach on his neighbor's record player.

In the summer of 1955 the record business was consolidating the classic for the public. Tape and the LP represented a new way to record music and a new way to distribute it—to sell it—and the record companies took full advantage, by ordering up fresh "high fidelity" or "full frequency" recordings of the entire classical music canon. Together the new technology and the Bach bicentenary had called forth dozens of new Bach LPs. Wanda Landowska had installed recording gear alongside the massive harpsichord at her house in Connecticut and made recordings of the *Well-Tempered Clavier*, released in a pair of multi-LP sets by RCA Victor. Rosalyn Tureck, playing piano, recorded the *Well-Tempered Clavier* for Decca. Ralph Kirkpatrick recorded two batches of the *Clavier-Übung*, including the *Goldberg Variations*, the partitas, and the Italian concerto. Vanguard brought out Gustav Leonhardt's *Goldberg*s: light, bright, chiming, jangling, it made an emphatic contrast with Landowska's two *Goldberg*s recordings, replacing her steel-framed drawbridge with a geodesic dome. In the same way, the Brandenburg concertos as recorded by August Wenzinger's Basel-based ensemble stood apart from the prewar versions in the use of harpsichord and gamba, rather than piano and cello; it made the regard for antiquity sound modern.

Tape and the LP, as they extended the length of recorded works, also extended the music forward in time. Once recorded in high fidelity, a piece of music could stick around; the recording took on a life of its own, and the recording, as much as the music itself, became, in Coetzee's terms, "what survives"—became a classic recording.

No one fully understood just how durable certain recordings would be; but 1955 was an unprecedented year of classic recordings, as the great performers of so-called popular music made records that aspired to the classic, and others made records that became classics in spite of themselves.

Frank Sinatra was recording in Hollywood with the Nelson Riddle Orchestra, whose elegant string settings now seem the aptest counterpoint to his voice; for his third Capitol LP, *In the Wee Small Hours*, released earlier in the year, he had recorded a group of songs meant to be heard consecutively, as a novel thing—a "concept album." Duke Ellington had signed a new contract with Columbia, entering a phase that would complete his passage in the public estimation from a Negro dance band leader into an American maestro. Louis Amstrong had finished recording frankly revivalist new interpretations of the music of W. C. Handy and Fats Waller, bringing the music of those early jazzmen into the age of high fidelity. Elvis Presley, already a star in the South, returned to Memphis and did a session (his last, it turned out) at Sun Studio. Sun released the first single by Johnny Cash, and recorded a second, with "Folsom Prison Blues" as the B side. Four Star Music Sales, in Pasadena, California, put out the first single by Patsy Cline. Chess Records, in Chicago, issued "Maybellene," Chuck Berry's first single, and Muddy Waters's "Mannish Boy." Atlantic, in New York, had a number-one R&B hit with Ray Charles's "A Fool for You," backed with "This Little Girl of Mine." In New Orleans, Imperial had a hit with Fats Domino's "Ain't It a Shame," and Specialty brought out Little Richard's "Tutti Frutti." *Blackboard Jungle*, a movie about rebellious high schoolers, featured "Rock Around the Clock," which Bill Haley & His Comets had recorded at the Pythian Temple on West Seventieth Street in Manhattan—the studio where Rosalyn Tureck had recorded book one of Bach's *Well-Tempered Clavier*.

In the summer of 1955, in a deconsecrated church downtown, Glenn Gould carried on a profound encounter with Bach, interrogating the idea of the classic with the piano, the score, and the recording studio.

The church was a Romanesque hulk on East Thirtieth Street, between Second and Third, in the vast ambit of the Empire State Building. Built in 1875, the church had a broad nave with a sloped roof, a rose window, and two rows of smaller round-topped windows, and was flanked by a pair of battlements flattened and filled in to suit the lines of a Manhattan apartment block. German Lutherans had worshipped there, then Armenian Evangelicals; then the church fell into disuse, and a radio station, WLIB, converted the front room into a broadcast studio. In 1949, with the introduction of tape and the LP, Columbia Records needed a new recording facility; it bought the church and repurposed the vast interior, creating what the company called 30th Street Studio, and the people who worked there—musicians, producers, engineers, technicians—called the Church.

In June 1955, Gould made the studio his own—a cross between stage and cottage, between chapel and radio shack, between laboratory and Baroque composing room. The studio was congenial to him: a vast, windowless space, a hundred feet deep and as many high beneath a circuit of arches, outfitted with a nestling pair of grand pianos, a thicket of microphones, some tape decks and mixing consoles.

There, he took a run at the *Goldberg Variations*; and through the *Goldberg*s, he approached the challenge of his career, which was the effort to combine the artist's craving for creative solitude with the artist's attraction to the ideal society that is his audience. It was a challenge akin to the one the people of North America faced in the immediate postwar years, as they sought to devise structures that would at once further their independence and firm up their bonds to Europe. And it was a challenge framed by new technology, which—as Gould was discovering—enabled the artist to multiply his audience without encountering it directly. With the piano and the recording studio, he could make the *Goldberg Variations* he heard in his head: the music of the mind of Bach.

>>17>>   He had returned to Canada in a crisis. It may be that the commitment of a record deal, and the prospect of a life in public, weighed on him. He made two CBC broadcasts in March, going through the Sinfonias (the three-part inventions) and the D-minor concerto without a hitch. He gave a recital in Winnipeg, and afterward (a friend recalled) he "was surrounded by so many admirers there was hardly room to breathe." Health concerns bedeviled him. He could not eat without worrying that he would swallow something toxic. He could not shake hands or touch other people without fear. He could not sleep without taking a sedative, or a handful of them: Drembutal, Luminal, Bevutal. He fretted over his circulation, and felt symptoms of fibrositis—a stiffness in his hands, arms, shoulders, and back. A cough, congestion, or trouble swallowing made him worry that he was going to catch pneumonia and die. His chiropractor, an older man, did die; the chiropractor's son, taking over the practice, treated Gould roughly. Gould sought out other doctors and was urged to see a psychiatrist. In May, after concerts in Ottawa and Toronto, he went to the emergency room in Toronto. Anxiety, trouble eating, and a fear of other people were getting the better of him. "Where it used to be just a fear of eating in public," he said a few months later, "now it's a fear of being trapped anywhere with people, even having any kinds of dealings with people."

In those circumstances he went to New York, where he was booked into 30th Street Studio for the two middle weeks of June. The weather in New York was sunny, the temperature in the sixties. He arrived at the studio by taxi from a hotel near Central Park, wearing an overcoat, beret, scarf, and gloves, and carrying a leather valise and his folding chair. He stripped down to a dress shirt and a sleeveless V-neck sweater. Opening the valise, he set out pills, bottled water, and towels. Rolling up his sleeves, he ran hot water in a sink, the sort of deep-basin porcelain sink that mops are wrung out in, and soaked his hands and forearms until they were red.

Early in the year he had paid a visit to the Steinway & Sons showroom on Fifty-seventh Street: in the basement, several dozen grand pianos stood side by side, and he had played them in succession, finally identifying one he liked.

Now the piano, known as number 174, was in the studio, with microphones arrayed around it. He set up his chair and settled himself before the keyboard. He took off his shoes, so he could move his feet without making noises that would be picked up by the microphones.

Over the next few days he fussed over the precise atmospheric conditions of the space around the piano. He complained of a draft. He insisted that a space heater be set up near the piano. He asked for a piece of carpeting to put under his feet. He jousted with a technician about the tuning of the instrument: "Listen, who the heck tuned this piano this morning? Listen to this," he griped, plonking an ever so slightly awry key. During breaks, he ate only crackers ("arrowroot biscuits"), instead of the sandwiches the label had brought in, and drank only water or skim milk.

He is often characterized as a perfectionist, and the recording process is said to have been a tool in the service of his perfectionism, enabling him to choose between takes based on microdistinctions of color and emphasis. But outtakes from the sessions, since made available, suggest that in 1955 he used the recording studio in the opposite way: to maximize risk-taking, to push each short piece to its furthest physical, musical, spiritual extreme.

In the same way, the outtakes complicate the received idea of the session. It is generally identified wholly with the *Goldberg Variations*, but the outtakes suggest that he began the session with a different work: the Sinfonias, a.k.a. the three-part inventions. Three of those inventions exist in complete takes, plus outtakes and the recorded patter of Gould and the producer, Howard H. Scott—seen in photographs as a bald man in his forties, in shirtsleeves, tie, and dark slacks—over the studio microphones.

Why the three-part inventions? It may be that Gould hadn't yet convinced Columbia that it made sense for him to record the *Goldberg Variations*. It may be that he was appeasing David Oppenheim, the label head, who had voiced a preference for the inventions. It may be that *he* was not yet convinced, and took a run at them to see what was there. It may be that he used the inventions, technically less challenging than the *Goldbergs*, to acclimate himself to the studio and the demands of his first major-label recording session—used them as a soft opening to ease the pressure he felt. It may be that he used them to sharpen his blade, so as to save the *Goldberg Variations* for an act of discovery once the session was under way.

In any case, the inventions stand as a headnote to the 1955 session, an invocation of the muse, and of the process of invention, through the intercession of magnetic tape. With them, Gould's use of the piano and the recording studio was joined to Bach's sense of the invention as at once the idea behind a piece and the "structured repetition" of its development—as the "mechanism that triggers further elaborative thought from which a whole piece of music is shaped." With the inventions, through invention, Gould would shape the music of Bach, reinventing it for postwar America.

The eighth three-part invention, in F major, is a bright, high flourish—a French curve, say—introduced three times, beginning high up the keyboard and moving farther down each time. Gould plays it at top speed, taking less than a minute with it, a quarter faster (eighteen seconds) than he had played it on a CBC broadcast in March. "I was cheated by one note," he mutters, as if the piece has a will of its own. "I almost got that; I was cheated by one note." He plays a bar slowly, then hurls himself at the piece and plays it through again. This take is very much like the one that Columbia calls the "complete performance." The difference is in the mix: the complete performance is cleaner and drier, with less of the sound of the room in it.

"OK, we'll call this B minor sinfonia, remake, take one," Scott says of number 15—"remake" suggesting that it had been played, and recorded, earlier in the session. It begins with a figure in the middle of the keyboard; Gould rattles it off telegraphically, then again and again, playing the piece as fast as you can imagine it being played. The trick, it seems, is to make the notes in that opening figure cluster like grapes on a vine without clumping or mushing together. They mush together, and Gould stops. "Take two," he and Scott say in unison. This take is even faster, more tightly wound. "I think there was a fadeout on one note," Gould says. "Take three," Scott says. Gould plays a few notes and falters. "Take four," he says, and straightaway plays it again, fleeter still, like a slalom skier pushing the course for all it can bear. "It faded out again," he complains, after reaching the end. "Take five," Scott says. Gould begins again, then muffs a note: "Oh, aw—" he says. "Take six," Scott says. This time, Gould plays the piece through to the end. "Let me hear that one," he says when he has finished. Scott has it played back, and they listen to it together. "OK, we've got it now," Scott says, but records Gould playing a seventh take for good measure. There are a few sticky notes, but this one ends beautifully: the intricate final figure is now upright and firm of gait. "Listen, we've got lots of endings," Gould tells Scott, which suggests that he is thinking of splicing parts of two takes together, and so suggests that this session is not a warm-up or an exercise: he is playing these inventions for keeps.

The third outtake is of number 9, in F minor. It is slow, perhaps fifty beats per minute (twice as slow as he had played it in the CBC broadcast), and spacious: each note, once struck, subsides to icy silence. Gould spoke of his approach as involving taking things out, and you can hear him doing it here. The outtake and the "complete performance," each just over five minutes, are nearly identical. The main difference is that the latter is stricter, more impersonal or superpersonal: the very slow, very slight crescendo of the last minute is absolutely regular, a calibrated increase in volume and pressure. Gould the pianist is also the engineer, mixing the piece from the keyboard.

That was Wednesday, June 8, 1955. The night before, Dwight Eisenhower had appeared on color TV (the first U.S. president to do so) to explain the Supreme Court's recent ruling that the nation's public schools had to desegregate "with all deliberate speed." *The Seven Year Itch*, with Marilyn Monroe, was in wide release. In a laboratory in Philadelphia, Dr. Thomas Stoltz Harvey was sectioning the brain of Albert Einstein, which he had removed while performing an autopsy on the scientist after his death in Princeton in April. Saul Bellow, on Riverside Drive in New York, was mourning his father: "Not that I was ever prompt at anything," he told Leslie Fiedler, "but life is particularly difficult in all departments just now." Flannery O'Connor had just returned to Georgia from New York, where she had seen *Cat on a Hot Tin Roof* on Broadway and appeared on television to watch a playhouse acting-out of "The Life You Save May Be Your Own." Dorothy Day and several dozen Catholic Workers and other peace activists were preparing to demonstrate at City Hall during a civil-defense drill—to voice their opposition to war, physical and psychological, and "as an act of public penance for having been the first people in the world to drop the atomic bomb, to make the hydrogen bomb." After years of struggle, Alberto Giacometti saw his work presented in three retrospectives at once: in West Germany, in London, and at the Guggenheim Museum on Fifth Avenue. An editor at the Viking Press was considering a novel by Jack Kerouac: "So here are these characters—in search of their identity—and the way they must do it—is by driving all over the U.S.—and the way they are really doing it is by 'feeling' life down to its very roots." On Montgomery Street in San Francisco, Allen Ginsberg was writing a long poem in a room kitted out with a Cézanne print, a woven basket, "Bollingen series books shelved, letters and essays Ezra Pound under bed-table clock, black-painted bureau with victrola-case & Bach on top"—a three-LP mono set of the Mass in B Minor recorded by Hermann Scherchen and the Vienna Philharmonic. There Ginsberg wrote of "angelheaded hipsters burning for the ancient heavenly connection to the starry dynamo in the machinery of night"—"who wept at the romance of the streets with their pushcarts full of onions and bad music / who sat in boxes breathing in the darkness under the bridge, and rose up to build harpsichords in their lofts . . ."

>>18>>   On Friday, June 10, Gould went back into the studio, this time
to make a recording of the *Goldberg Variations*.

Through tape and the LP, the record player had become for the second
half of the century what the piano had been for the first half: the instrument
of instruments, and the furniture of middle-class cultural aspirations. Gould,
more than most musicians, understood the implications of this change. He
grasped that this transformation of the listener's experience called for a transformation of the player's experience, too; he saw that tape and the LP opened
up what he envisioned as "the prospects of recording."

Gould's insight was owing to the fact that he was the first classical musician to come of age in the age of recordings. He idolized Stokowski the technician, the architect of orchestral sound. He strove to play Beethoven the way
Artur Schnabel played him on record, cueing up a 78 and matching it note for
note. He fell in love with the microphone, repurposed a weekend cottage as a
recording studio, and saw the CBC's studio in downtown Toronto as a home
away from home.

With his approach to recording, which produced a whole work from the
aggregation of different takes, he tapped the essence of the long-playing record, which set different pieces of music alongside one another in the bands of a
single disc, rather than giving each piece or section its own side as the 78 had
done. And with the repetition of each piece he approximated the listener's experience of music in the age of recordings, which was that of hearing the same
piece over and over again, becoming intimate with it through mechanized
repetition. It was as if through the playing of each piece over and over Gould
was pressing it into the microgroove of the LP.

At the same time, Gould had come to know the power of recordings in
an age when the music of Bach in particular was being revived through recordings. As he put it, he grew up in an age which "above all . . . paid homage
to the spirit of Sebastian Bach"—an age in which "virtually every major musician was determined to follow *his* example, to work as it was deemed *he* had
worked—as an artisan, a sober, conscientious craftsman in whom diligence
and inspiration were inextricably intertwined." This was Gould's ideal. For
him, Bach was "first and last, an architect, a constructor of sound, and what
makes him so inestimably valuable to us is that he was beyond a doubt the
greatest architect of sound who ever lived."

To transcend means to climb over, and that is what he was doing in the act
of recording. The *Goldberg Variations* is a piece of architecture. Gould is climbing over Bach's construction, clambering over the whole.

He used the studio, first of all, to give full expression to the variety of the parts. By recording the variations one at a time, in multiple takes, as he had at the cottage, he set them apart from one another, exaggerating their individuality. The aria is played swiftly in a kind of triple time, so that it is over before it is through. The seventh variation is a country dance, with Gould's hands hee-hawing over the keys. The ninth, full of overtones, is akin to a minimalist anthem. The twelfth is a holler: it sounds a little like a crazy person with his mouth up to your ear, giving you a piece of his mind. The thirteenth is a limpid modern chamber work, such as one of Milton Babbitt's graduate students might have played.

Each of them can be considered with wonder. But something is lost when the variations are taken apart—sold separately, as it were. Gould recognized this, and even as he used technology to isolate the parts, he used his technique as a pianist to make them whole. Through the fast tempos he took, and the sheer speed of his playing, he ran the variations together so that they can be heard in one go. He made them a musical aggregation, thirty voices exulting in a crowded room; he made them portable, so as to suit the phonograph on the bureau in Allen Ginsberg's rented room.

He liked to learn pieces of music away from the piano, and for him the charm of the *Goldberg Variations* lay in their incorporeality. His *Goldberg Variations* proceed at the speed of thought, and dramatize the semi-spontaneous working-out of a single complicated idea.

>>19>> "There's something *happening* at the studio on Thirtieth Street. We're doing these recording sessions, the *Goldberg Variations*, and we've got this nut, and everybody's talking about how absolutely marvelous he is, you've never heard anything like this."

By the second week the session had become an event, the studio a venue. Columbia's publicist, Debbie Ishton, phoned a music columnist for *Esquire* and a Columbia staff photographer and urged them to come over.

The columnist, Martin Mayer, went to the studio, and watched and listened to Gould play. He had lunch with him; when he commented on Gould's low stance, Gould explained that that was the way he had been taught, adding: "My teacher's the biggest hunchback in Canada." He went with Gould to his hotel and watched him take pills for his poor circulation. All this was fodder for a column. What is strongest now, though, is Mayer's recollection of Gould during playback, clear and commanding. "Gould was listening to tapes when I came, and he didn't like some of what he heard. The producer would say, 'That's good,' and he would say, 'We'll see.'"

The photographer's black-and-white images of Gould show a genius untouched by fame—still boyish, handsome, light on his feet, clearly at home and in command in the studio. At the same time, they show Gould and Scott working together, two men in shirtsleeves, one balding, one dashing. Scott peers at the sheet music on the piano as Gould "conducts" it. He considers the music over Gould's shoulder. He listens while Gould makes a point. He faces Gould squarely, as if to say, "So what do you want to do?" He appears avuncular, but Gould's hands, expressively superintending in midair, tell the story. Now Gould is running the session; Scott is sounding board and straight man.

The outtakes suggest the procedural tedium of the session: ninety sparkling seconds of Bach, ringing out from the piano—and then an exchange between a nasal-voiced, petulant young Canadian and a gruff New York studio pro over what number the next take will be. At the same time, they suggest how sure of himself Gould was and how aware of what was at stake. He calls out the take numbers as often as Scott does. "Once more for luck—take seven." He judges the results on the spot: "That was good—let me try one more." "I think that's it—but we might try another," he says, and Scott replies, "Glenn, that was *beautiful*," loath to let him do away with the beautiful thing he has just played. He suggests a splice: "Can we use the first half of that one and the second half of that other one?" He sings his way through a variation at half the usual tempo, then initiates a take: "And then I'll come back to five," he tells Scott. He explains that a variation is rooted in a bawdy German song (Scott looks it up); he tells him that he can blend "The Star-Spangled Banner" and "God Save the King" to "most marvelous effect," then does so with big, rolling chromatic chords, the very synthesis of public-square patriotism. "That was terrific," Scott says.

The outtakes include an early run at the aria. Beautiful and powerful as this take is, it is loaded with casual inflections—a sudden stress on the keys, a little swing in the tempo. It is almost jazzy, the aria as Bill Evans or Bud Powell might have played it. It sounds like music circa 1955, that is.

Gould later told the story of how he recorded the aria, and it is the clearest statement he ever gave about the approach he took to Bach in the studio. "I by-passed the theme—the very simple aria upon which the variations are constructed—and left it for recording until all the variations had been satisfactorily put down on tape. I then turned to the ingenious little sarabande [the aria], and found that it took me twenty takes in order to locate a character for it which would be sufficiently neutral as not to prejudge the depth of involvement that comes later in the work. It was a question of utilizing the first twenty takes to erase all superfluous expression from my reading of it, and there is nothing more difficult to do. The natural instinct of the performer is to add, not to subtract. In any case, the theme, as represented on my recording of the *Goldberg Variations*, is Take 21."

>>20>> What did Gould seek in Bach? Some say he was after ecstasy, for he made a film called *The Age of Ecstasy* and used the term there; but it is hard to say what *ecstasy* meant for him, except that (as he put it) "solitude is the prerequisite for ecstatic experience," especially the heroic solitude of the artist set apart from society. Some say he was after "a state of wonder," following on his remark, made about live performance, that "The purpose of art is not the release of a momentary ejaculation of adrenaline but is, rather, the gradual, lifelong construction of a state of wonder and serenity."

The photographs of the session show ecstasy taking hold of a twenty-three-year-old. They show a musician in constant motion, inhabited by the music he will transmit from his body into the world through the piano. He draws his arms in to his waist like a bullfighter; he raises himself up from the legs like a dancer en pointe; he declaims with a raised forefinger over the piano, sweeps an arm through the air to dramatize the sound he is about to make; singing, he spreads his arms from his chest, as if holding the sound like a plank of wood; he arrests the piano with his forearms, a musical laying-on of hands. He is dreamy, and ungainly; he is feminine and boyish at once; he is— this is what ecstasy is—commanding and yet unguarded, self-abandoned. He is a collegian aflame, the ecstatic next door, and the power of the photographs derives from the way they bring out his essential likeness with the listener— the ways they suggest that "This can happen to you."

The recording itself suggests ecstasy, too: it is ecstatic, with the wayward, otherworldly energy the word suggests. But Gould himself—in the sleeve notes he wrote for the recording—used terms that are at once more precise than *ecstasy* and more potent in their associations, and get to the root of why his *Goldberg*s were such a breakthrough.

One is invention. As Gould tells it, an aria and variations is a "challenge to the composer's inventive power"—a challenge to realize the melodic possibilities suggested by the aria and the harmonic possibilities that lurk beneath it when it is "stripped to its fundamentals, pregnant with promise and capacity for exhaustive exploitation." But he thinks the *Goldberg Variations* is different. The harmony is so complete that it does not breed variations so much as bear them architecturally. The melody is so "singularly self-sufficient" that the melodies that follow it must make their own way—more as inventions than variations, he might have said.

The other is transcendence. Gould is leading us toward his notion of what the *Goldberg Variations* is. Sure, it offers the "accumulative experience of depth, delicacy and display" typical in a theme and variations. But it doesn't take on weight as it goes. It ends where it begins, flaunting its "incorporeality" and "its disdain of the organic relevance of the part to the whole." It defies general criteria. "Thus," Gould sums up, "we are forced to revise our criteria, which were scarcely designed to arbitrate that union of music and metaphysics—the realm of technical transcendence."

The *Goldberg Variations* is a work of technical transcendence. Strong as an insight about the work, this is all the stronger when seen as Gould's insight into his own recording of it. Through technique he attains transcendence. He faces down the technical demands of the work—the complex passagework, the extreme independence of the two hands—and makes them matter-of-fact. He bears down on the technical aspects of the grand piano—shaking loose its levers, stirring up its hammers, rattling its frame—until the instrument can be heard as a percussion instrument and a piece of modern machinery. He takes advantage of the technical advantages of the recording studio: the blackout-level solitude Pablo Casals had discovered, the freedom to play a variation repeatedly until it came out sounding the way he liked, and the ability to spread out variations, rather than playing them one right after another, and so create some imaginative space around them.

Gould concluded his liner notes with the notion of the *Goldberg Variations* as an intentional community—a "community of sentiment," with the variations as members arrayed radially around the founding principle of the aria. It is not entirely "fanciful" (as Gould, defending his move to "supramusical considerations," put it) to suppose that the thought, or sentiment, is love.

That is what we hear in the recording. The swift finger runs, the fistfuls of arpeggiation, the skeleton dances of knuckles up the keyboard, those notes knotted and braided and tied semaphorically together: it is the sound of technique transcended, and transfigured by feeling.

This, I think, is what technical transcendence meant to him. The stress felt in his recording of the *Goldberg Variations*, and the conflict in the story, is the stress between the solitude of the artist and the sociability of the music he made—between his imminent fame and the intensely private way he would achieve it. The *Goldberg Variations*, in counterpoint to his solitude, faced him outward. Through them he transcended himself: his isolation and awkwardness, his phobias and idiosyncrasies. There at the piano in 30th Street Studio, with the old church ceiling arching over him, he felt himself a member of a community of sentiment for the first time.

>>21>> He shook hands with the studio staff (all phobias set aside) and left New York, returning to Canada.

That summer he spent time at the cottage on Lake Simcoe. He took part in the Stratford Festival, playing twentieth-century works. He gave recitals in Toronto, Montreal, Victoria, and elsewhere. He sat for a Toronto photographer, who made a formal portrait of him: dark jacket buttoned, hands clasped, hair parted. He hung around the CBC studios. He was fond of a young woman who worked there, and he went with her on a date, probably the first of his life. He proudly showed her a proof of the *Goldberg Variations* sleeve, which came in the mail. A designer had ingeniously laid out the photographs of him in five rows of six, like a contact sheet of the session: thirty images in all, thirty variations on a theme.

After he left town, Columbia's publicist put out a press release, her own variation on the experience. "Columbia Masterworks' recording director and his engineering colleagues are sympathetic veterans who accept as perfectly natural all artists' studio rituals, foibles or fancies. But even these hardy souls were surprised by the arrival of young Canadian pianist Glenn Gould and his 'recording equipment' for his first Columbia sessions."

His reputation would precede him, like an aria awaiting variations.

>>22>> The record was released on January 3, 1956, a year and a day after the recital in Washington. Half a century later, it is justly celebrated as an all-time great debut. The freshness of Gould's approach—thirty-eight and a half minutes; no repeats; no pedal, no rubato; no fidelity to older models—was obvious to people who knew something about classical music. But its power was also apparent to people who were coming to the music for the first time: bright, swift, sprung forward, urgent even in the slow variations, it is a record that opens up the music of Bach and the classical tradition through its arresting clarity and directness.

What qualities, precisely, account for the power of the record?

One is the shift in emphases it brought about. In it an old tradition is made new, and an old-world practice is planted on the North American continent. After a century of Romantic melody, rhythm is given its due.

Another is its fit with the long-playing format. A work of about forty minutes that splits in two right down the middle and circles back to its beginning at the end of part two: there could have been no better demonstration piece for the qualities of the LP. The LP, which needed flipping, legislated a pause between the first fifteen variations and the second fifteen—a pause so physically audible that today, in other formats, which allow the music to run straight through, the transition seems rushed. And the LP registered Gould's youth and vitality in its grooves: unlike the characteristic classical music recital debuts—each the stuff of legend and awed report—this one, made for the first time in a recording studio, can be heard as if for the first time now and forevermore.

The power of the record also has to do with an urge for "technical transcendence" that was being felt throughout the arts, and whose effects we still feel today. In *The Voices of Silence*, published in English translation eighteen months earlier, André Malraux had integrated technology into a grand view of art and its role in society. Malraux, a novelist and "adventurer" (styled such by himself and the French press), had developed a conception of art rooted in the idea of "metamorphosis," as artists, or whole groups of artists across time, transformed artistic forms—painting, statuary, fresco—into distinctive styles. In a postwar refashioning of his big idea, Malraux moved technology into the foreground. Another anti-Benjamin (worldly, prolific, self-confident, soon to be France's minister of culture), Malraux saw mechanical reproduction enabling a "museum without walls," in which artworks of different epochs and societies were brought together through photography. As he saw it, the representation of fine art through the new format of photography had transformed the public's sense of what art was and how to look at it. It brought lesser works front and center, altered the scale of different works (making ivory figures large and tapestries small), and sponsored comparisons of the kind that once were possible only if you traveled tirelessly and remembered every work you saw. In this way photographs were doing in the twentieth century what museums had done in the nineteenth: uprooting artworks from their contexts, so that they were "estranged . . . from their original functions," and placing them in dialogue with works made across the world a millennium earlier. Malraux was in favor of this development, because it was akin to the creative process as he understood it. Photographs of art brought style, rather than form or function, into the foreground; through photography, artworks "have lost their properties as objects; but, by the same token, they have gained something: the utmost significance as to style that they can possibly acquire."

Gould came to know Malraux's book, and through it to work out his approach to technical transcendence, in which for him, as for Malraux, technology enabled the art to transcend its form on the one hand and the individual artist on the other, creating a monument of pure style.

Gould's *Goldberg Variations* is so fully charged because his imperatives—for solitude and community, for technology and for a personal style—are matched by the themes of the piece and of the music of Bach broadly. The music of Bach became, for Gould, a pattern of invention, and the pattern for a way of life; again and again he entered into it imaginatively, and found there "that replenishment of invention upon which creative ideas depend."

Few artists have been so good at presenting a self-image and making it central to their art. But Gould went further: he imprinted his image of himself onto Bach. This is a good measure of Gould's achievement—that he made an unlikeness seem a likeness. From the *Goldberg Variations* on, he identified Bach with himself, and proposed that Bach heard things the way he did, and eventually the interpenetration of composer and interpreter became so complete in the public mind that each took on qualities of the other. Bach, like Gould, became a genius who found in provincial life the solitude he needed in order to conduct his researches into fugue and sacred song. Gould, like Bach, became a religious artist, giving the worldly music for keyboard a mystic charge—making the recording studio a sanctum, a concert hall with an unseen audience, and turning the recording-studio experiment into a sacred rite.

With Gould's *Goldberg Variations*, Bach became modern. The music of Bach was fully joined to the inventions of audio recording, and the music was thrust into the space where it exists today. If the Toccata and Fugue in D Minor that Albert Schweitzer made at All Hallows in 1935 is the beginning of our recorded past, the recording Gould made at Thirtieth and Third in 1955 is the beginning of our recorded present, in which to play music means to engage a piece of equipment to transmit music for us to hear while we go about our lives. The long war is over; the blackout curtains are lifted, the power is switched on, and a candlelit room is flooded with electric light.

>>23>> "I don't enjoy the business of being a concert performer," Gould said in 1955. And yet the record, the substitute for the living, breathing recitalist, sparked interest in Gould as (to quote *Maclean's*) "The Genius Who Doesn't Want to Play." *Time* ran a featurette about the recording session, saying that "his 'Goldberg' Variations are Bach as the old master himself must have played—with delight in speeding like the wind, joy in squeezing beauty out of every phrase, and all the freshness of the spring water which Hypochondriac Gould uses to wet his pipes." Edward Tatnall Canby, in *Harper's Magazine*, declared: "I think there is an older, more mature depth in this wonderful music that is not yet realized—but whatdya expect at twenty-two?"

The acclaim for the *Goldberg Variations* "meant a great deal to me," Gould later recalled. "But it also launched me into the most difficult year I have ever faced." Now he was a concert performer whether he liked it or not. He faced fame, heightened expectations, disdain for his eccentricities, strains on his physical and mental health, and the need for the performer to travel, which compounded the other effects and made them harder to bear.

On top of it all, the success of the *Goldberg Variations* took him away from the image of Bach he had identified with and made his own—Bach as "an artisan, a sober, conscientious craftsman in whom diligence and inspiration were inextricably intertwined." In the sleeve notes for a second LP, written that year, he characterized Bach as "a nomadic organist" and "the most forthright of itinerant chapel-masters," and the emphasis he gave to Bach's movements shows him framing a fresh image of Bach to suit his new life. He did it consciously; also that year, in an essay about the twelve-tone composers, he remarked: "To adopt Albert Schweitzer's penetrating observation of eighteenth-century German theological scholarship, 'Like every period when human thought has been strong and vigorous, it is wholly unhistorical. What it is looking for is not the past, but itself in the past.'"

The press, at Columbia's prompting, sought their own ideas of Gould. *Glamour* pitched him to readers as one of the "Men We'd Like You to Meet." *Vogue* featured him in a spread of "Young Men in the Arts." *Life* featured him as the "Music World's Young Wonder," and showed the wonder up close: the mittens, the beat-up chair, the stockinged feet, the hands (insured for $100,000 with Lloyd's of London) soaking in hot water. *Weekend* sent him and a photographer on a weekend trip to the Bahamas, where Gould, avoiding the sun, drove a sports car and a motorboat at top speeds, composed a few bars of his string quartet in his room, and vented to the photographer about his maladies—anxiety, "a spastic stomach, diarrhea, and a tightening of the throat."

The music world was suspicious of him. "The kind of selling campaign Columbia has waged on behalf of this artist can be exceedingly dangerous," Roland Gelatt wrote in *High Fidelity*, "for it is apt to irritate serious listeners to the point where they can be very hard to please. But it so happens that Gould seems to be every bit as remarkable a musician as the ads proclaim." And so it was around the country, as curiosity gave way to rapt admiration. He played nine recitals and a dozen concerts with orchestras, from Montreal to St. Louis, from Winnipeg, Manitoba, to Dallas, Texas. In Detroit, he filled in for a sick soloist, and a crowd of five thousand bid him come out for eight curtain calls. After a "homecoming" concert in Toronto, the mayor gave him a fancy wristwatch and *The Globe and Mail* put its review on the front page.

The wider world fixed on him for reasons having nothing to do with music. Today, the Gould seen in photographs is dashingly unbuttoned, a graduate student who has pulled an all-nighter cramming for his qualifying exams. But at the time he was seen as wayward and uncouth. A rival Toronto pianist sent him a thousand-word letter urging him to change his ways. A concertgoer wrote telling him to cut his hair, which made him look "Sissie." In Sarasota, two beat cops spotted him on a park bench, wearing overcoat and gloves in the heat, and told him to move on.

His manager had booked the 1956–57 season long in advance: forty concerts in North America, West Germany, Austria, and Israel. As fall 1956 came, he had to keep forty appointments with fame—forty too many. The more he performed, the more he hated performing. He canceled dates due to illness—illness brought on or aggravated by the dread of performing. He began to loath the press, and refused to be photographed taking pills or wearing gloves. Anxious already, he grew more so with the scrutiny of his stage manner. "I had not regarded any of the things attendant upon my playing—my eccentricities, if you like—as being of any particular note at all . . . I had never given any thought of the importance, to some people, of visual image. When I suddenly was made aware of this in about 1956, I became extremely self-conscious about everything I did. The whole secret of what I had been doing was to concentrate exclusively on realizing a conception of the music, regardless of how it was physically achieved. This new self-consciousness was very difficult."

There were bright spots in the grind of concertizing. One was a collaboration with Leonard Bernstein, whose fame put him at ease. At age twenty-five in 1943, Bernstein had stepped in to conduct the New York Philharmonic as a last-minute substitute in a concert broadcast by NBC, and had become

American classical music's best-known prodigy. Now he was a "crossover artist," the composer of *On the Town* and *West Side Story*. He had listened to Gould's *Goldberg Variations* LP endlessly in the summer of 1956: his wife, Felicia, was pregnant, and in the torpid last month of her pregnancy, she recalled, the *Goldberg*s "became 'our song.'" With the baby born and *West Side Story* in previews, he resumed conducting the New York Philharmonic, and he was on the podium when Gould made his debut with the orchestra: Saturday, January 26, 1957. "Mr. Gould strolled on stage," the *Times*'s critic reported, "sat at the piano, crossed his legs during the opening tutti, gazed calmly upon audience and orchestra, and then untangled his legs and got to work"—playing Beethoven's second concerto brilliantly. Bernstein was thrilled. To the press he said: "There is nobody quite like him, and I just love playing with him." To Gould, at a party afterward he said: "You played so beautifully in the cadenza that I almost came in my pants." He spread out a Mozart sonata for four hands on the piano and insisted that Gould sit on the bench and play with him. Gould did, until he began to feel sick from a cocktail he'd sipped earlier (feeling "this jelly-like feeling in my fingers") and excused himself. Never a drinker, he resolved on the spot never to drink anything alcoholic ever again.

Gould and Bernstein went into 30th Street Studio and made a record: a Beethoven concerto and Bach's Concerto No. 1, backed by Columbia's orchestra. As collaborations go, it was less than fully consummated. Gould air-conducted during the tutti and left the piano during other orchestral passages; he had to be called back from the men's room, where he was soaking his hands and conducting in the mirror.

One night after the session Bernstein invited Gould to his apartment, near Carnegie Hall. Felicia Bernstein, who was there, insisted that Gould take his hat off, and he did, revealing thick, clumped, matted hair. "And while I was fixing a drink or something," Leonard Bernstein recalled, "she lured him into the bathroom, sat him down on a stool, and cut his hair. And washed it, and combed it. And he came out looking like some kind of archangel . . ."

>>24>> Albert Schweitzer had discovered radio, like a man discovering ice in an age of fire.

The prospect of nuclear winter got him to the microphone. After Schweitzer was awarded the Nobel Peace Prize, the United Nations secretary general, Dag Hammarskjöld, a Swede, wrote to him in Lambaréné and invited him to set out "fresh and solid bases to the principle of 'coexistence'" in a "message to the world." Schweitzer said no. Hammarskjöld sent a group of emissaries to Lambaréné. Thus appeased, Schweitzer agreed to produce a message in the form of a press release. Then he arranged to give a broadcast on Radio Oslo. On Wednesday, April 24, 1957, Schweitzer made a statement in four languages (English, French, German, Russian), a message as sanguine about human nature as any politician's. "America and Soviet Russia and Britain are telling one another again and again that they want nothing more than to reach an agreement to end the testing of atomic weapons," he intoned. ". . . Why do they not come to an agreement? The real reason is that in their own countries there is no public opinion asking for it." Like his Bach recordings at All Hallows, the broadcast took the concentrated effort of a few minutes and delivered it to all times and places, magnifying it for modernity.

Pablo Casals heard the message. He and Schweitzer had exchanged letters in anticipation of their eightieth birthdays. Then, in his eightieth year, he had changed his life again. He fell in love with one of his students, twenty-year-old Marta Montañez; traveled with her to her native Puerto Rico; married her; and moved with her to San Juan, settling in the island country where his mother had grown up a century earlier. On April 16, 1957, he had a heart attack; as Marta nursed him back to health, he got word of Schweitzer's broadcast, and pondered the effects of his own silence—a silence whose moral authority, it seemed at once, was no match for the worldwide atomic crisis.

Schweitzer's message worked. President Eisenhower suspended atomic tests, and the man who had challenged him for the presidency, Adlai Stevenson, made the pilgrimage to Lambaréné, seeking a postpolitical blessing for his beliefs. Pablo Casals, for his part, arranged the relocation of the Bach festival from France to Puerto Rico, the better to bear witness through the music of Bach to the power of universal conscience only a thousand miles from Washington, which had replaced London and Paris as the center of world power.

>>25>> Glenn Gould went on a tour of the USSR in May—and there, of all places, he truly enjoyed life as a concert performer. A lover of northern climes and "battleship grey," he found the country aesthetically congenial, and Moscow and Leningrad were sufficiently exotic to compel him to stroll the streets like a tourist. He found the Russian people ravenous for music, especially the music of Bach—who, "while still the subject of academic study and conservatory practice," he later explained, "was considered dangerous to the

proletariat because of his pronounced ecclesiastical leanings." His reputation
for eccentricity did not precede him, and the role of cultural ambassador made
the concerts something more than the competitive exercises in virtuosity he
had come to dread in the West. He gave eight concerts in all in the Soviet
Union, and played the *Goldberg Variations*, the *Three-Part Inventions*, and
fugues from the *Art of the Fugue*. A photograph taken there suggests the
transformation that the tour momentarily brought about: it shows him in ani-
mate silhouette, rapt at the piano, all his idiosyncracies hidden in the archetype
of a virtuoso making music.

He went to West Germany, where he played three concerts in Berlin with
Herbert von Karajan and the Berlin Philharmonic and then traveled by train
through the lands where so much music had been made. "The most wonderful pastorale imaginable," he told his parents in a letter home. "I stayed up till
11:30 specially to sing *Die Meistersinger* as we went through Nurnberg." But he
did not go to Leipzig; it was deep in East German territory, and he was dis-
inclined to walk in Bach's footsteps in any case. "Bach, with all his burgherish
simplicity as a person," Gould held, "is music's supreme example of the genius
wholly out of touch with his time," and he disdained the "trail down which,
two centuries hence, casual tourists review the carefully calibrated columns of
his accomplishment."

En route to Vienna, Gould had to change trains in Frankfurt, and there
on the platform when he disembarked was "the century's most celebrated
podium profile"—Leopold Stokowski.

Gould recalled the sighting later in "Stokowski in Six Scenes," a
piece of portraiture, carefully worked over, that captures the great conductor
whole, and conveys Gould, too—his brilliance, his tenderness, his humor,
his capacity for awe, and his humility about his own gift and his debts to
others.

"We had both been touring in Europe—though neither of us had been
working in Frankfurt—and were both waiting for the call to board the sleeper
on the Amsterdam–Vienna express," Gould recalled.

He found it incredible that Stokowski was there—and no wonder. Since
leaving the Philadelphia Orchestra, Stokowski had been known to listeners
through broadcasts, recordings, and the movies as much as through live performances. For a listener in Toronto it had always been so. He wasn't a figure
whom you expected to see toting his own bags on a railway platform, whose
hand you hoped someday to shake. Like his orchestra, like music itself, he lived
in, and on, the air. Yet there he was.

In "Stokowski in Six Scenes" the meeting begins as a scene in a stage comedy. Gould sees Stokowski "pacing back and forth over a course that at its closest point put him within about eight feet of the post I had staked out just beyond the sleeper's steps. I watched while he marked off the same short, triangular circuit three or four times." Gould rehearses an interruption but knows that it isn't right, for "there was something about his slow, firm tread, with its relentless pursuit of the same patch of concrete—rather like a priest at exercise in the courtyard of a seminary, scriptures in hand—that made any move of mine seem an intolerable intrusion on his person." He creates an opening by dropping his ticket and recognizing Stokowski as he picks it up. It works. Not only does Stokowski stop. He recognizes Gould.

> STOKOWSKI: I have read that you were recently in Leningrad.
> GOULD: Yes, indeed, Maestro. Just two weeks ago, in fact.
> STOKOWSKI: Perhaps, then, later in the evening I will visit with you.

Gould found it "incredible" that Stokowski "knew who I was; he knew what I'd been doing." Incredible that "the knock came within half an hour." Incredible that Stokowski, there in the sleeper compartment on the overnight express to Vienna, spoke matter-of-factly about Leningrad and about Beethoven's Third, which Gould had played with Karajan in Berlin. And incredible that Stokowski wanted to carry on the conversation "at Vienna station" in the morning. He recalled: "I am not, and was not, starstruck—as I have already twice protested—but nonetheless a dream had come true."

In the essay, Gould (a fuguist even in prose) depicts their meeting as the intersection of two lines, an instance of biographical counterpoint. And Stokowski's career really was an apt counterpoint to his own. Thirty years earlier Stoki, already renowned, had found a new phase in his career by making recordings. He had used his fame to gain the conditions he wanted: the best studios, the Bell Lab engineers, the freedom to mix and nix. Through recordings he had made the music new, found fresh autonomy and solitude, and gained a new kind of renown. But he had no wish for recordings to replace concerts. As a showman, he required a crowd; as a conductor, he needed an orchestra, the instrument he had made his own. Officially, he was the music director of the Houston Symphony and the founding director of the Symphony of the Air, which he financed himself. In fact, he was an itinerant. His second marriage (to Gloria Vanderbilt, an heiress in her twenties) had broken up, leaving him the part-time father of two sons. His commitment to new music had brought him to 30th Street Studio in the spring to record a neo-Persian piece by the young California experimentalist Henry Cowell with a freelance orchestra. ("I'm convinced that he never laid eyes on the score before," a composer who was in the booth for the session recalled, but "he got that orchestra to sound like the Philadelphia Orchestra in about the first half-hour.") A new contract with Capitol Records called for him to record the great works of Western music with different orchestras in the great cities of Europe. So there he was at the Frankfurt Hauptbahnhof, pacing triangles into the platform. He was seventy-five years old.

"Music per se was discussed only once," Gould reports, but that one instance—an exchange that called forth Stoki's lofty condescension toward his young rival Karajan—sent Gould a message. "He had let me know that he was not in awe of the 'Generalmusikdirektor of Europe,' that soloists, as a breed, were to be shunned on principle, and that concertos, as a symphonic subspecies, were quite beneath his notice." He had let Gould know that he, too, despised the recital racket, and he had communicated to him that the only way to rise above the things you despised was to refuse to do them.

The European tour made clear to Gould what he already knew. In his experience, the usual terms of the virtuoso's life were reversed. The recording studio—that site of artifice and self-consciousness—was in fact a place of self-forgetfulness. The recording—that diminished thing—was the musical ideal, and the live performance was a pale approximation of it. "I thought of it as something that had to be got through," he later said of touring. "I thought of it as something that one must do while endeavoring to establish, I suppose, some sort of a reputation which would stand you perhaps in good stead later on. And it didn't seem to me that there was anything very productive [about it], even at the time . . ." He recalled a bout with the flu, caught in drafty Salzburg, that dogged him for nearly a month: "And I became not only thoroughly sick but I began to feel that it *was* very unproductive, that I was at best competing with myself once I'd begun to make recordings. The most that I could hope would be that my public statement would be as good as the equivalent recording of that work, if I had in fact recorded it."

Stokowski was the genius whose path Gould had to follow to get out of the fix he was in. Stoki had changed course drastically at the peak of his fame—by leaving the Philadelphia Orchestra for Hollywood, and by making recordings on his own terms and up to his own standards. Gould—the idea had seized him—would change course just as dramatically. Where Stoki had quit Philadelphia, he would quit performing altogether. Where Stoki had devoted himself to recordings, he would consecrate himself to them wholly. Where Stoki had made an instrument of the orchestra, he would make an instrument of the recording studio.

>>26>> Leonard Bernstein was making an instrument of television. Through the Young People's Concerts for the New York Philharmonic, Bernstein had become a past master of what Virgil Thomson called the "Music Appreciation Racket." For *Omnibus*, a public-spirited series that aired in the broadcasting dead zone of Sunday afternoon, he hosted a series of television programs about music. After programs titled "Beethoven's Fifth," "The World of Jazz," and "American Musical Comedy," the series brought Bernstein to the music of Johann Sebastian Bach.

"BACH! A colossal syllable, one which makes composers tremble, brings performers to their knees, beatifies the Bach-lover, and apparently bores the daylights out of everyone else," he began, and then argued that this fear, this devotion, this boredom had their source in the obscurity of Bach. "It's not very easy music to know, and you must know it to love it," he proposed, and went on: "Maybe the trouble is that you don't get a chance to know it; you don't hear much Bach. After all, to hear Bach you have to go to certain churches faithfully, or to certain very special little concerts." The program went on to show the reader exactly what Bernstein meant. In his discussion of the *St. Matthew Passion*—the work that had converted him to Bach at age nineteen—Bernstein, in formal wear, led a studio orchestra and a choir of female singers in gowns and ruffle collars, who stood on a checkerboard floor and sang beneath a pair of chandeliers and in front of a vaguely palatial façade. In this way, on the last Sunday in March 1957, the music of Bach was presented to a national television audience.

Either Bernstein was talking down to his audience or he didn't know what he was talking about. On top of the Bach bicentenary, the inventions of magnetic tape and the LP, and the strong sales of the *Goldberg Variations*, Bach's music was in the air, and the LP was largely responsible. The occasions passed, but the new records just kept coming.

James Friskin, a Scot who taught piano at Juilliard, had already recorded a batch of Bach works for Vanguard when he sat down at a piano in March 1956 to record the *Goldberg Variations*. Gould's recording, out two months, was drawing acclaim. Friskin went out to Brooklyn and into the Masonic

Temple, a neoclassical pile that saw less Masonic activity than in the past, and played his own interpretation, dropping some of the repeats so the work would fit onto one LP. Sonically, the record splits the difference between tutelage and romance. It is the first *Goldberg*s that isn't strictly necessary, but its reason for being seems clear enough. "Performances of this great composition, both on the harpsichord and on the piano, have increased in number so considerably that the work itself may even be said to have gained a certain popularity," he remarked in his sleeve notes. Everybody else was doing it; why shouldn't he?

Rosalyn Tureck recorded the *Goldberg*s over again. She was working out of London, touring in Europe, and preparing a teaching edition of excerpts from Bach's piano music. With her sets of the *Well-Tempered Clavier* out since 1953, she recorded the Bach partitas and the *Goldberg Variations* for EMI at Abbey Road. "He took a *very* great deal from me," she later said of Gould, and her *Goldberg*s recording, from 1957, is an elder's well-tempered rebuttal to a younger rival.* Like his, her *Goldberg*s is gleaming, angular, architectural; but hers is tidily proportioned where his is jagged, exaggerated. "A valid, living, and communicative performance is the result not of licence but of information, experience, and insight," she would say in the preface to the teaching edition. Gould could play it his way, but she played it Bach's way: of that she was sure.

Grete Sultan recorded the *Goldberg*s straight through. A Jewish Berliner, a student of Edwin Fischer's, she had escaped Germany only in 1940, settling near Vassar College in upstate New York, a penniless émigré steeped in the structurally ambitious music of Schoenberg and Henry Cowell. After the war she found a place in a loft on East Seventeenth Street; Merce Cunningham, the choreographer, lived downstairs, and became a friend, as did his collaborator John Cage. They probably all threw the *I Ching* together, and Cage began to compose with her in mind. Sultan had played the *Goldberg*s in recital in downtown Manhattan, and the title of Cage's crucial piano work of 1951—*Music for Changes*—could just as well be applied to Bach's "aria with diverse variations." (The work Cage composed for Sultan, *Études Australes*, prompted a critic in Germany to liken it to the *Well-Tempered Clavier*.) After playing the *Goldberg*s complete to a full house at Carnegie Hall in May 1958, Sultan recorded them, playing the whole, with repeats, in a single take: seventy-eight minutes, twice

---

*She began the recording on June 19, 1957 (two weeks after Gould met Stokowski in Frankfurt), devoted parts of four weeks to it that month and in August, and did two more sessions in November and December.

the length of Gould's recording. They are straightforwardly beautiful, not obviously the work of an experimentalist; the interest in them is in hearing them as counterpoint to her Cage and Schoenberg, which are clanking and defiant of tempo. In her hands, Bach is the original process artist, devising systems for artistic creation; recording the *Goldberg*s straight through, she affirmed live performance as a radical experiment, a means to the music of chance.

Mstislav Rostropovich went to Washington, bringing the cello suites as a form of cultural exchange. He was from Azerbaijan and had trained in Moscow; the same government program that took Gould to the USSR in 1957 took him to America, and Vanguard put out an LP of Bach recordings he had made in Europe the year before. Not yet thirty, he suggested, in his blend of precocity and maturity, what the young Casals must have sounded like: at once young and wise, his worldliness unspoiled, his sound a strong, lean line, like a flat stomach or a firm thigh. It is a sound that defies the pomp and circumstance of cultural exchange. Against the amity-inducing command performances forced on Gould, the solitude of the cello suites, in Rostropovich's hands, is outside politics. It is as if he had heard Casals's cry of conscience and made it his own; what Casals had to find, plunging into the suites, Rostropovich came of age knowing was there all along.

Jascha Heifetz went to Hollywood. In the half century since he and his parents had fled revolution-wracked Vilnius for the United States (so that he would not miss the chance to play Carnegie Hall), his name had come to mean prodigy the way Einstein's meant genius ("the kid's a regular Jascha Heifetz"). He had recorded most of the violin repertory, but not much Bach. This he rectified in two sessions at RCA's studios. RCA used a process called "direct-to-disk," which skipped the tape stage. It didn't work well: the playing is remarkable, but the recording is parched and airless, and in the high passages Heifetz, known for his round tone, might be scraping an arrowhead on a slate. In its failure, it called attention to the paradox of the age of recordings: in the name of fidelity, the music is stripped of surrounding life, but the recording winds up having a sound of its own. Stripped bare by technology, Heifetz's take on the violin works is the music of a rugged survivalist, in which the fiddler risks his life to bring Bach across the steppes to the town of tinseled brightness.

E. Power Biggs went to Westminster Abbey, bringing his own tape recorder to capture his first recital there. Biggs was Harvard's unofficial house organist, favoring instruments akin to the ones used in Bach's time—a Skinner organ at Harvard's Busch-Reisinger Museum and then the trimmer Baroque one that replaced it. His records, at once sumptuous and sparkling, are as effortlessly gorgeous as any Bach records ever made. But they are powered by pedagogy. The music is not so much played as presented; the mystique of the organist, so strong in Schweitzer, is replaced with the elevation of the organist as a transmitter of Great Sounds.

Biggs hosted a Sunday-morning show for CBS radio and recorded for Columbia. Through the fifties he carried forth, in steady state, the Bach revival that had Gould's *Goldberg Variations* as its high point: the great works in good recordings, played intimately and idiosyncratically but for a large audience. Gould couldn't fail to notice. In the midst of all this intense recorded activity, his own Bach releases were slight: a concerto here, a concerto there, a pair of partitas rounded out with a couple of fugues meant to fill up the LP and give him a fresh challenge. Fame had not only deprived him of privacy; it had postponed the encounter with Bach that the *Goldbergs* had gotten started.

Gould—nothing if not self-determined as an artist—did something about it. He entered into a new contract with Columbia, one that paid him better advances and higher royalties. He considered changing managers. He invested in the stock market. After years of frustration with the pianos provided for him at recitals, he settled on one he liked—a Steinway grand known as CD 318—and arranged for it to be sent from city to city when he was touring so it would await him when he arrived. He tried to set Donne's *Holy Sonnets* ("Batter my heart, three-person'd God" was one) for piano and mezzo-soprano. He struggled to complete a string quartet.

He wrote his first piece of journalism, a review for *Saturday Review* of a book about Bach by Erwin Bodky, a German Jewish expatriate who had resettled in the Harvard community. The magazine had run favorable reviews of Gould's records. Bodky, who had studied piano with Ferruccio Busoni in Berlin, had rebelled against Busoni and Romanticism—the way Gould did; but he had rebelled into the strict interpretation of texts and their limitations, rather than through the free interpretation Gould practiced. Gould's review, then, forced him to take a position, and he did so with relish. Author and reviewer alike were pro-piano, pro-structure, pro-architecture, pro-counterpoint. But Gould argued for the view of Bach's music as a harmonic landscape, one defined by its "inner architecture," against the "Schweitzer-induced" emphasis on the main line of melody.

He worked up an article on the modest proposal "Let's Ban Applause!" He lectured on Schoenberg, producing an essay of several thousand words. He struggled against paranoia, which led him to dread, especially, performing in Philadelphia; he befriended Peter Ostwald, a psychiatrist specializing in mental illness, who concluded that he was a "superhypochondriac." He led an orchestra in one of Bach's Brandenburg concertos from behind a strategically altered Steinway he called a "harpsipiano." Taking the stage for a recital in South Bend, Indiana, he asked himself: "Glenn Gould, what in God's name are you doing? Another platform, another place."

He read José María Corredor's *Conversations with Casals*, which had recently been published in English. The book opened with a prefatory letter by Thomas Mann, who commended Casals in terms that—coming from Mann, Gould's literary idol—spoke to Gould's own predicament. "A fantastic talent, sought after and assured of overwhelming success all over the world, offered fortunes to harness itself to business arrangements, but laying down its own conditions, which have nothing to do with either money or success"—through this refusal, Mann affirmed, Casals "ennobles and broadens our understanding of the artist." In the conversations, Casals made an argument for technical progress in music strikingly akin to the one Gould had been making. Casals noted "Bach's preoccupation to go beyond the technical limitations of the instruments of his period," from organ to violin. He spoke critically about his recordings of the cello suites, "which have been adapted to long-playing records," wishing he could hear them again. And he argued for the musician's right to refuse to perform—argued for the all-trumping independence of the true artist.

Glenn Gloud, what in God's name are you doing? That was Gould's question. Now he began to answer it. Casals had refused to perform so as to protest worldly injustice; Gould would refuse out of protest against the injustice he felt inhered in the act of performing.

As his thirtieth birthday approached, Gould began to reorder his life, arranging to withdraw from the world the way Casals had done so as to make music on his own terms. He would recast his relationship to live performance in ways that would become notorious even before the fact. And he would undertake a new run of recordings of the music of Bach—the *Inventions*, the *Well-Tempered Clavier*, and the *Art of the Fugue*—in order to renew his commitment to Bach and return to the source of his life as an artist. With them he would explore, in depth, the "harmonic architecture" of Bach's music, so congenial to him and—it was now clear—to the age. For Bach, as Gould set it out in an essay written at the far end of this run of recordings, the fugue was not a musical form so much as "an invitation to invent a form relevant to the idiosyncratic demands of the composition." As the fugue had been for Bach, so the recording studio would be for Gould—an invitation to invent a way of music-making relevant to the idiosyncratic demands of his career. He would try to attain, in these recordings, the "aura of withdrawal" he heard in the *Art of the Fugue*. In this, he would be following the example of Bach himself—"withdrawing from the pragmatic concern of music-making into an idealized world of uncompromised invention."

PART V

Both Sides Now

>>1>> From Puerto Rico, Pablo Casals rediscovered America, and made the United States a place for him to advance the cause of creative silence.

The move to Puerto Rico, which the press characterized as a return to his mother's homeland and an attempt to recapture his lost life in Barcelona, turned out to be a giant step in Casals's return to his life as a performing artist. So effective was the island as a base for dealings with the United States that it seemed Casals, like Fidel Castro, who returned to Cuba from jail in Mexico seven months after Casals's visit, had planned to situate himself just offshore so as to maximize his influence.

What about his vow not to perform in countries (such as the United States) where Franco's dictatorship was recognized and legitimized? It kept changing, as he sought to stay faithful to the spirit of it even as he varied the conditions.

Like his decision to record the cello suites, his decision finally to go to the mainland and play there was shaped by circumstances. His heart attack had made clear that he wouldn't live forever. Marriage made him wish to venture out into the world with his new bride. The tide of posterity pulled him northward, much as it had drawn him to a recording studio in London in the thirties. But the reason he gave for his change of heart—the real reason, it is fair to say— had emerged from his conversation with Albert Schweitzer about the need for the artist to place his art in the service of a cause. Spain was stuck under Franco; world peace, by contrast, was a going concern, and he could make something happen. "I have dedicated many years of my life to the cause of a free Spain," Casals explained, "and still wish to silence my instrument for that cause. But . . . I also feel now that I have the duty to do something (through music) for the cause of peace—an essential for a human being."

In his view, the need for peace had never been greater. The world was divided politically between the Western democracies and the Eastern bloc, between American-style freedom and Soviet-style communism. The two "superpowers" had nuclear weapons, ready to be deployed in a crisis. The symbolism of the Cold War had enshrined the division, producing the image of a world with two sides.

He would send a mixed signal: he would play for peace, but he would play no ordinary recitals, so as to keep silence for the sake of freedom. In retrospect, it seems a jesuitical distinction. It had real consequences (he passed up hundreds of thousands of dollars in fees), but it enabled him to play, teach, lead, and offer wise counsel through music in the way that he, more than anyone else a consecrant of musical wisdom, believed in.

While Casals was recuperating from heart surgery, Dag Hammarskjöld sent a delegation to San Juan to recruit him to play at the United Nations in a concert marking the UN's eighteenth anniversary. Casals said no. Then he said yes. He had already agreed to give a pair of "private recitals" at the Beethovenhaus in Bonn. For this occasion, too, he could make an exception. There was a technicality: UN headquarters, while geographically in New York City, was politically extraterritorial, a world unto itself. He wouldn't be playing in the United States.

The concert was one of a number of UN anniversary concerts held worldwide. After the Boston Symphony Orchestra performed a symphony by Arthur Honegger, a composer adept at blending classical and modern styles, Casals and Mieczyslaw Horszowski played Bach's second sonata for cello and keyboard. A photograph of the two musicians rehearsing the Bach sonata in the General Assembly Hall makes clear how fully the place—a stage, microphones, rows of seats—was a place of political theater. Casals prepared a statement to read out during the performance, in which he would explain to the delegates that he was there because of "the great and perhaps mortal danger threatening all humanity," which could be countered only by the human desire for peace—a desire "manifested . . . above all by that great citizen of the world, Dr. Albert Schweitzer." But the UN had its own technicalities. A rule forbade ordinary civilians from making political statements in the hall. So Casals delivered his statement into a microphone in a recording studio.

The performance (and the statement) aired on radio to seventy-five countries and was televised on CBS in the United States. Casals's biographers have nothing to say about the music, but about the event they are full of superlatives. It was the most widely aired classical performance in history. It drew five thousand pieces of mail. It turned Casals into a "geriatric superstar."

Having made an exception for the UN, Casals worked variations on it. He went to Marlboro, Vermont, to take part in the summer music festival that Rudolf Serkin ran there. Geographically, Marlboro was to Vermont as Prades was to France: an unsung village just north of the border with another state (Massachusetts, in its case), but one spiritually set apart. The festival (Alex Ross wrote years later) "functioned variously as a chamber-music festival, a sort of finishing school for gifted young performers, and a summit for the musical intelligentsia." Casals was drawn to the dairy-farm surroundings and to the spirit of the place, where a roadside sign advised CAUTION: MUSICIANS AT PLAY. Once he formed the habit of going there in summer, Marlboro served him as a northerly San Juan—a small, irreproachable place where a musician at play could have maximum impact.

He went to Berkeley to give a master class. Mixed signals abounded. Fifty years after he injured a hand while hiking on Mount Tamalpais and yearned to quit playing, he sat on a stage and showed students how to play; fifteen years after atomic bombs were dropped on Hiroshima and Nagasaki, he sat in the shadow of the Lawrence Livermore Laboratory—nesting place for the hydrogen bomb—and played in defiance of the prospect of nuclear annihilation; more than twenty years after his last official performance, he led some Cal students in the art of performance.

Cameras were rolling, and Casals's master class has been broadcast ever since, extending his influence in spite of his silence. There he is, a sumo miniature in a V-neck sweater and slacks, straddling a steel-pipe chair. A female student in a print dress and flats plays a bit of Brahms. After a minute or so Casals waves his bow conclusively: "Very good, very good." Now we see him from the front, wearing a crisp white shirt and dark tie under the sweater. He plays the same passage more expressively, swelling the volume, leaning into the neck, groaning here and there. When he stops, the audience erupts with pleasure. The old man will show the young lady how it is done. "Ta—ta—tata," Casals says. "Die—ya da da": He stands over her and points to the sheet music: "You see, you see?"

>>2>> Albert Schweitzer, master of dramatic renunciation, had come to the ultimate sacrifice: he was going to give up Bach.

He had returned to Lambaréné in September 1959 after a sojourn in Europe. The last stop was Gunsbach. He had arranged for the restoration of the organ at his boyhood church, and he gave a recital on it. It was enough. Once back in Lambaréné, he arranged for the zinc-lined piano in the compound there to be boxed up and shipped to Gunsbach. The wife of his age would join the mistress of his youth in the village where his reverence for life had been formed. Henceforth the music of Bach would be a pure ideal, not something to be played but something to be heard playing from the phonograph.

As Africa slouched toward self-determination, a dozen countries were at war internally, including the Belgian Congo, renamed the Democratic Republic of the Congo. The newly elected U.S. president, John F. Kennedy, appointed Adlai Stevenson ambassador to the United Nations, giving him special responsibility for U.S. relations in Africa. Dag Hammarskjöld felt a similar responsibility, arranging a trip to Katanga in the new Congo to mediate the secessionist war there. His plane was shot down, and he was killed. Schweitzer, loath to make political statements, broke his silence to denounce the policy of trying to unite warring peoples—the very policy Hammerskjöld had gone to his death to support.

Pablo Casals, in San Juan, sent a letter to the Kennedy White House stating his opposition to the U.S. accommodation of Franco's Spain. The letter found its way to Abe Fortas, counsel to the president, who took a special interest in Puerto Rico. Soon Casals received an invitation to be honored with a state dinner at the White House, followed by a performance. Casals said no: a yes, in his view, would mean a yes to U.S. policy toward Spain. Fortas rejigged the invitation, inviting Casals to give a recital at a state dinner in honor of the governor of Puerto Rico. Casals said no again. Fortas lawyerishly redid the invitation once more, insisting that the recital would be essentially a private event—a little night music, following the state dinner but not in support of it. This time Casals said yes. The German Democratic Republic had just built a wall through Berlin. The totalitarians were gaining ground. It was a time to speak out, to take a side.

The recital—Monday, November 13, 1961—crystallized the idea of Kennedy's Camelot as an earthly paradise for the arts. Jacqueline Kennedy invited the grandees of the classical music scene in America to attend, from Bernstein and Copland to Stravinsky and Virgil Thomson. Private or public, it was televised and recorded for release by Columbia Masterworks. No Bach was played that night; Casals, with Alexander Schneider and Mieczyslaw Horszowski accompanying him, played Mendelssohn, Couperin, Schumann, and his own "Song of the Birds." There was a supper afterward. The president stepped out partway through. Casals had had a chance to speak with him one-to-one for forty-five minutes earlier in the day; when he turned the conversation to Spain and the U.S. military presence there, Kennedy told him that unfortunately a chief of state had to do many things he didn't want to do. Thus ended the dialogue with the U.S. president that Casals had sought since the Spanish Civil War.

In San Juan a few days later the mail brought a letter from an honored guest, typed on Art Deco stationery. "Dear Master and Friend," the letter began:

> I shall always remember and treasure hearing you play again, so superbly, with such beauty of tone and phrasing, and such deep expression. Thank you for this unforgettable experience. How wonderful is the music of Couperin. I am hoping to go to Puerto Rico at Christmas time. May I have the pleasure of visiting you and your beautiful bride? I shall bring my two sons, and, of course, we shall not take too much of your time.
>
> Sincerely, your admirer and friend
>
> Leopold Stokowski

There came a letter from another admirer. This was Hiao-Tsiun Ma, who had fled the Communist revolution in China and established a new life as a music teacher in Paris. Earlier that year Ma and his wife had brought their six-year-old son, Yo-Yo, to the hotel where Casals stayed when in Paris. Yo-Yo Ma had a reputation already. When he was two, his father had declared that he would never amount to anything musically, so poor were his memory and discipline. At four he was taken to the Conservatoire de Paris: drawn to the double bass, he got a scaled-down cello and learned the second Bach suite. At five, knowing three Bach suites, he gave his first recital, sitting on a stack of telephone books. When he was six a luthier in Paris recommended him to Isaac Stern, who put him in touch with Alexander Schneider, who made an introduction to Pablo Casals. He played powerfully for Casals. "Would you like to play some more?" Casals asked, taking the boy onto his lap. He said yes, climbed down, and played some more. His mother looked on, intent on the scratches the end pin of Casals's cello had made in the wood floor—signs of how much the old virtuoso still practiced. Casals, for his part, told the parents to make sure that the boy had some free time to run and play in the street with his friends.

Now H. T. Ma was moving his family from Paris to New York, and was especially dependent on the kindness of strangers. In his letter to Casals, he declared that Yo-Yo Ma "thinks of you every day."

>>3>> Leopold Stokowski was a household name but one without a home. Separation and then a divorce from Gloria Vanderbilt (whom *Look* had likened to "an Arab wife: obedient, almost slavish" to Stoki) left him a dangling man, meeting their two sons for dinner and then returning alone to his own apartment. So he left New York as often as possible. He dug in as music director of the Houston Symphony, arranging premieres of many new works. He stepped in as a last-minute replacement for the Chicago Symphony after Fritz Reiner had a heart attack. He led the London Symphony, which was wracked by dissension, and soon was "miraculously transforming" it, one reviewer wrote, "into as brilliant a virtuoso body as anyone could ever want to hear." He led the handpicked aggregation of freelancers known as "the Orchestra" at City Center on West Fifty-fifth Street, often following a concert with a recording session the next morning. There were triumphs in all this concertizing. He played for Dag Hammarskjöld at the UN; he played in Soviet-run Leipzig. A tour of the Soviet Union (the first by an American conductor) enabled him to conduct a Shostakovich symphony with the composer present in the hall. A premiere of Carl Orff's neomedieval *Carmina Burana* introduced a work that soon caught on with the college crowd. A City Center Opera production of Monteverdi's *Orfeo* (perhaps influenced by Stoki's 1954 stint at San Marco, where Monteverdi had been *maestro di cappella*) broke new ground as Stokowski, usually indifferent to the fine points of past musical practice, used antique recorder, viola da gamba, and trunk organ to suit the Baroque-revival production—and to underscore the connection between himself and the first composer to conceive an opera as a total, all-encompassing work of art.

Past his threescore and ten years, he was classical music's oldest journeyman. At the same time, he was a recording artist in great demand. The reason was new technology. He had made dozens of recordings with the Philadelphians, then had done it all over again as a freelance maestro. He had brought the Stokowski sound to Bach and Wagner, Tchaikovsky and Shostakovich several times over. Now he did it in stereo, making records for several labels—Angel, Capitol, Everest, United Artists—so as to enter the Stokowski sound into the long-playing record. Of one new Stoki release, a reviewer remarked: "His mastery of these works has not changed in the slightest, but the art of recording has changed enormously for the better . . ."

The changes were significant. The new recording studios were better designed, better insulated, better equipped for sound and comfort alike. Tape decks with third and fourth tracks made it possible to record several tracks, then "bounce" those tracks to a single track and "overdub" new sounds.

TOP An eighteenth-century Bach family tree; ABOVE LEFT The organ console at Arnstadt (Photo: akg-images); ABOVE RIGHT The *Clavier-büchlein vor Wilhelm Friedemann Bach* (Image care of the Irving S. Gilmour Music Library, Yale University)

TOP The HMV mobile unit outside Hereford Cathedral; MIDDLE AND ABOVE EMI's
Abbey Road Studio, outside and in (All images courtesy of EMI Group Archive Trust)

TOP LEFT Albert Schweitzer at his piano with organ pedals (© 1954, 2012 The Heirs of W. Eugene Smith); TOP RIGHT Pablo Casals, who made the cello a weapon of peaceful resistance (Courtesy of EMI Group Archive Trust); ABOVE Leopold Stokowski near the micro-phone—"the electric ear," he called it (Collection of Gene Gaudette)

TOP Rosalyn Tureck, architect in Bach (© Tureck Bach Research Institute [http://tureckbach.com], with thanks to VAI Music [www.vaimusic.com]); ABOVE LEFT AND RIGHT Glenn Gould playing back tape recordings of himself at the cottage on Lake Simcoe (Courtesy of Fed News and the Glenn Gould Estate), and considering pianos at 30th Street Studio (Photo by Don Hunstein, courtesy of Sony Music Entertainment)

TOP Casals and Schweitzer ponder war and peace (Albert Schweitzer Papers, Special Collections Research Center, Syracuse University Library. Courtesy of The Albert Schweitzer Fellowship); ABOVE Stokowski and Gould compare notes (CBC Still Photo Collection)

TOP LEFT Gould's *The Art of the Fugue* (Courtesy of Sony Music Entertainment); TOP RIGHT *Switched-on Bach*; ABOVE LEFT Perlman, Zukerman, and Barenboim—the Israeli Beatles (Courtesy of EMI Classics); ABOVE RIGHT A canon from the *Musical Offering* depicted as a "strange loop" in Douglas R. Hofstadter's *Gödel, Escher, Bach* (Copyright © 1999 Douglas R. Hofstadter. Reprinted by permission of Basic Books, a member of the Perseus Book Group)

TOP LEFT Yo-Yo Ma circa 1979, out of college and into the recording studio (Waring Abbot/Premium Archive/Getty Images); TOP RIGHT Yo-Yo Ma playing at the World Trade Center site on the first anniversary of the 9/11 attacks (David L. Pokress/AFP/Getty Images); ABOVE LEFT Mstislav Rostropovich plays Bach at the Berlin Wall (Reuters); ABOVE RIGHT Masaaki Suzuki, whose Christian faith and training in historically informed performance have shaped a Bach cycle recorded in his native Japan (Marco Borggreve)

TOP Leipzig circa J. S. Bach: Thomaskirche at left, Nikolaikirche at right, and the Markt square at center, with Zimmermann's coffeehouse up the Catherinenstrasse running from the right corner of the Markt (Photo: akg-images); ABOVE Bach circa 1746, by Elias Gottlob Haussmann, with canon for six voices in hand (Courtesy of William H. Scheide, Princeton, N.J.)

Stereo was the greatest change of all. This aspect of audio recording is now as familiar as electricity, but in the late fifties it was explained in terms of wonder usually reserved for scientific discoveries. During the recording session the "stereophonic" process separated the sound into two channels, left and right, corresponding to the listener's left and right ears. When the recording was played back, the listener's ears and brain blended the two channels together. In this way stereo equipment maintained fidelity to the listener's natural equipment. Stereo headphones—a corresponding innovation—dramatized the effect. Stereo arrayed sound in two sides so as to make it more lifelike; it divided sound so as to unite it again.

Stereo first gained a presence in recording studios through magnetic tape—through a reel-to-reel machine that could make recordings in multiple channels. After Ampex, a reel to reel pioneer, sent out demonstration models of the new machine, record-company executives began to commission stereo recordings. But transferring a stereo recording to an LP was complicated and costly. A solution was sought. An inventor named Emory Cook devised a double stylus; a company called Westrex devised an LP with one channel carried by each side of the V-shaped groove. Decca and Columbia followed, and brought in a company called Audio-Fidelity to produce a stereo stylus. The race was on: from Christmas 1958 the big record companies produced stereo versions of their major classical releases, along with records demonstrating the magic of stereo—say, the sound of bongo drums moving from left to right and back again. In time they ordered up fresh stereo recordings of great classical works from Bach to Stravinsky. They did so because classical recordings, more than jazz or pop, stood to benefit from the sonic improvements that stereo offered, but also because many high-fidelity audio enthusiasts were classical music enthusiasts: paradoxically, classical music devotees, pledged to the music of the past, were early adopters of the new technology.

Stokowski had been stereo's original early adopter. He had recorded the Philadelphia Orchestra in stereo during the Bell Labs experiments in the thirties; he had made sure that *Fantasia* was recorded in stereo ("Fantasound") and shown in theaters with stereo sound systems. Now, as record companies began to make classical recordings in stereo, the techniques he had developed to get the "Stokowski sound"—close miking, baffling, strategic seating arrangements—became standard practices. So did readjusting the recorded sound of the orchestra at the mixing board.

The mix was bound to the limitations of the original recording: the sound of the hall, the skill of the engineer—and the quality of the performance. Technical standards varied widely from session to session, leading Stokowski to reject some recordings. Because most people still had mono record players, the record companies released many LPs in two formats, mono and stereo. In Stokowski's case, four record companies could not keep up with his productivity, and some records were not released—and he was not paid—until two years after he made them. Capitol Records wound up accounting him $81,000 in arrears for the production costs of records made but not yet issued—costs that could not be earned back as long as the records remained unreleased. "I am no worshipper of the golden calf," he declared in a letter to the company, "but . . . it seems to me that to be $81,000 in debt is a serious matter. Never in my life have I been nearly so deeply in debt."

Stokowski approached eighty overworked, underpaid, and ill-appreciated. Yet the drive for high fidelity was a vindication for him, and he relished the adoption of his fussy, gear-centered approach. A memo he wrote to a producer about a recording made with the French National Radio Orchestra at the Théâtre des Champs-Élysées in 1958 shows how he tinkered with the mix, in effect conducting the piece over again:

MOVEMENT #1

No. 3 the violins sound metallic. I suggest reducing highs so as to
    make the tone more velvety.
One bar before No. 8 much more dim.[inuendo] like an echo of the
    previous bar.
2 bars before No. 14 less forte and then cres[cendo].
1 bar before No. 27 start softer and then utmost cres. possible.
No. 27 violins more velvety.
2nd bar after No. 30 sf. stronger

And so it went, for the whole piece—and two other pieces recorded in the same session.

Not all approved of Stoki's ministrations. Reviewing the record, one critic observed that "everything is polished till it glitters," while another acidly remarked: "The orchestra sounds as if it had been recorded in a subway."

In some respects, stereo was not so much an innovation as a restoration. It sought to restore to recordings the space and proportion—foreground and background; high and low; loud and soft—that had been lost through the limitations of microphones and the narrow range of the wax cylinder and the 78, through the relocating of music-making from church, salon, and gazebo to concert hall and recording studio. Stereo was meant to make recorded music sound the way music sounded when it was heard in the place where it was made—to make it sound "live" again.

In other respects, stereo made recordings sonic worlds unto themselves. The wax cylinder had entered music into the historical record. The phonograph had brought music into the home and up close. The film sound track had joined music to images. Tape and the LP had allowed music to play long, going on and on. Now stereo divided the space opened up by recordings, adapting recorded sound at once for the human body and the postwar living room. As LPs and 45s had two sides, the A side and the B or 1 and 2, so stereo recordings would have two sides, left and right. Music in stereo would be made more real by way of artifice, through a great divide.

You can hear the change in the early stereo recordings of Bach transcriptions that Stokowski made at City Center: they are at once the fulfillment of his sound and a diminishment of it. Here is the orchestra fully empowered: the Passacaglia in C Minor begins on a spectrally extreme low note; "Komm, süsser Tod" rises and spreads outward as if to demonstrate the height and breadth of the recording process—the brass glints and sparkles; the long-bowed basses oakenly underlie the whole. The high opening string figures of the Toccata and Fugue in D Minor are not velvety; they suggest squadrons of jet fighters doing maneuvers. Possibly they sounded like that in all of Stoki's various orchestras, but they were first captured fully in these recordings.

With the gain in technical power there is a loss of emotion. Take the Passacaglia in C Minor. Two earlier mono recordings are almost identically pioneering. Beginning with that lowest of low Cs, played as softly as a hundred-piece orchestra can play it, the piece, in thirteen-plus minutes, rises and expands, slowly but inexorably, the figures increasing and multiplying, doubling, quadrupling, peregrinating across the orchestra. This is a piece that is all of a piece, as Stoki, like some pagan divinity, hefts sound from the primordial goo and shapes it into an artifact, a work of Bach. You can hear conductor and orchestra pushing against the aural limits of the recording. The sound they make is larger than the sound you hear, and this sense of a surpassing vastness seems to pose a philosophical question: Starting from silence, how loud, how grand, how complex can a sound be?

There is much of the same drama in the stereo recording: the same work, the same conductor—but in high fidelity, made to be pressed into the double-sided microgrooves of a long-playing record. The sound is richer, smoother, more various, more articulate. The strings are here, the brass over there. The woodwinds drift across the middle like cigar smoke in a boxing arena. There is plenty of headroom; but here the clarity of the recording produces a lack of resistance. The recording no longer sets a limit, an opposing force that the orchestra must strain against.

Through high fidelity, the way of music-making suggested by the opening sequence of *Fantasia* has been reversed. There, the musicians enter the scene singly, banally, taking their seats, unpacking their horns and tuning up, and over a few minutes they are shaped into a single entity by the Maestro. Here, the recording moves the parts to the foreground. The orchestra, which in mono sounded like the many-headed expression of the musical will of one man, can now be heard as an aggregation of individuals; the recording breaks down the Stokowski sound into its component parts.

In Marshall McLuhan's terms, the Stokowski sound was no longer cool. McLuhan was a Canadian who taught communications at universities in the United States and Canada. Having coined the aphorism "the medium is the message," he distinguished between a "hot" medium and a "cool" one. "A hot medium," he explained, "is one that extends one single sense in 'high definition.'" A cool medium is one of low definition. "Telephone is a cool medium . . . because the ear is given a meager amount of information." Once applied, his terminology became baffling (movies were hot, television cool); so was his conclusion—that a "hot" medium rendered the recipient passive, while a "cool" one engendered participation. And it was strangely at odds with the meanings the words were actually acquiring in social life, where "cool" bohemians in San Francisco liked "hot" jazz from New York, and the practitioners of West Coast "cool jazz"—the Dave Brubeck Quartet especially—owed less to John Coltrane's "sheets of sound" than to the disciplined swing of J. S. Bach.

For all that, the hot/cool distinction is apt for the appraisal of audio recordings. With magnetic tape and the LP, capped by stereo, audio recording became a hot medium, one that provided abundant sonic detail for the listener. Now older mono recordings, in McLuhan's terms, could be heard as cool by contrast: in their very lack of fidelity, their arbitrary emphasizing of some instruments over others, they left spaces for the listener to fill in imaginatively.

McLuhan's terms suggest the role of stereo in the age of high fidelity. The underlying principle of stereo—the doubling of a signal with slight but distinct differences between one side and the other—was analogous to that of current affairs in a world characterized by people living different lives side by side, and not just in wall-divided Berlin: Catholics and Protestants in Northern Ireland,

Jews and Palestinians in the Holy Land, blacks and whites in the still-segregated American South. At the very moment when the cool medium of early recordings was replaced by the hot one of the stereo LP, a hot war (one all too vivid and granular in its detail) was supplanted by a cool war—a Cold War, bold in outline but lacking in concrete particulars.

These distinctions make it possible to understand the lack of drama in Stokowski's stereo Bach recordings. "Exaggeration," McLuhan declared, ". . . is a major artistic device in all modes of art. No painter, no musician ever did anything without extreme exaggeration of a form or a mode, until he had exaggerated those qualities that interested him." Working in the cool medium of radio and 78s, Stokowski—like Louis Armstrong and Duke Ellington—made his music hot, filling in the details through stylized emphasis and exaggeration. Once recordings reached a state of high fidelity, Stoki could play it cool. In an age of steel and glass, Stoki was making tapestries: heavy, luxurious, embroidered works. Either the conductor had cooled, or his Bach had been lowered to room temperature by technology.

>>4>>   The penitents made their way through the square, past the school, and into the church through the doors at the foot of the bell tower. It was Good Friday, early morning, and they would be there till midafternoon.

The name Thomas means "twin," and Bach, in composing a Passion oratorio for the Thomaskirche, patterned it on the architecture of the church and the habits of his music-making in Leipzig. The church had two organs, two choir lofts, and, in effect, two choirs—the *chorus primus* and the *chorus secundus*, which served both the Thomaskirche and the Nikolaikirche. On Sundays the two churches held their own services, with Bach leading the first choir in a cantata at one church and a deputy leading the second choir at the other. On Good Friday there was a single Passion liturgy, which alternated churches from one year to the next. The Thomaskirche was Bach's home church, where his children were baptized. There, for this Passion, he would bring the two choirs together, and there he would crown the body of sacred music he was creating in Leipzig.

This was the *St. Matthew Passion*, and it would be the *St. John Passion*'s fraternal twin, at once a development and a variant on the earlier work (a kinship suggested by the fact that they share the same first chorale). The prospect of composing Passions had led Bach to Leipzig, a religious artist seizing the opportunity to sanctify the form. With the *St. John Passion* it had been new to him; with this one, he could master it, make it wholly his own. The text of that Passion had been cobbled together from the Passions of other musicians. For this one, he ordered up a fresh text written according to his own design. Christian Friedrich Henrici, nom de plume Picander, had provided him with texts for some cantatas and had published a Passion libretto of his own. Bach brought Picander in to help realize his design, and probably gave him a book of Passion homilies as a point of reference. This Passion, emphatically his own, would have a co-author.

The first performance—*enactment* or *presentation* would be better—was on Friday, April 11, 1727. Entering the church, the penitents saw a groined vault supported by hexagonal pillars with a crow's nest for the preacher halfway in. Above them was the choir loft, and above it the organ loft, flanked by "town piper" galleries for musicians. At the far end of the church was another choir loft, and above it a small "swallow's nest" organ, out of use but in plain sight above the altar.

Prayers were offered, scriptures read; and then the *St. Matthew Passion* was executed in two parts, each lasting an hour or more, with a preacher giving a sermon in between them. For once, Bach had been able to write the music fresh, composing by design rather than repurposing earlier work or trying out new work on emergent occasions. In the church that morning, Bach, seated in the organ loft, heard this, his most complex work, for the first time—the split choir below him, the musicians off to the sides, the congregants joining in the chorales, and then the whole subsiding to silence, the sublime yielding to the blunt pieties of the homily.

What *was* his design? "Much ink has flowed about the *St. Matthew Passion*," one biographer tartly remarks, "and anyone who writes about Bach feels obliged to worship at its altar." Bach's recent biographers, writing about the *Passion*, focus on its design. Boyd singles out the four levels of action, which it shares with the *St. John Passion*: "the narrative (or thematic), the lyrical, the devotional, and the monumental." Karol Berger stresses its circularity; Wolff celebrates its unity (owing to the fact that Bach was able to "compose it in a single sweep") and its inclusive use of "the widest possible range of musical expression." Geck celebrates its classicism, which he sees in the symmetries of its outline and hears in the Italianate sensuality of its arias.

All this is said in elucidation of what the listener hears: that the *St. Matthew Passion*, more than the *St. John Passion*, is a theater of voices, a vocal work of an extreme kind. The doubling of the choir, the contrapuntal arrangement of choruses and arias, the care the poet took in scripting them—all these serve to make them, more than Christ or the Evangelist, the center of the work and the locus of Bach's acts of vocal invention.

Partly it is due to the dramatic placement of the choruses. Often interstitial in the cantatas, often lachrymose, here they bracket the action from two sides, making it "monumental," in Boyd's term. The big vocal works frame the smaller ones; it is as if the musical action moves to the double choir while stagehands are changing the set for the action involving Jesus, Pilate, Judas, and the Evangelist.

Just about any episode in the *St. Matthew Passion* could be considered as evidence of this. Take the episode two-thirds of the way through where Judas, seeing Jesus bound and led off, confesses that he has done evil in betraying him. The action that follows is a complex, multipart drama, the heart of the matter even though Jesus is pointedly all but silent.

The Evangelist, stricken, relates the taking of Jesus. What follows is itself a small miracle of vocal dramaturgy. Judas—a bass—intones that he has done evil, he has betrayed innocent blood. A small chorus—chief priests, elders—answers him: "What has that got to do with us? You see to it, then!" The Evangelist reports that Judas then cast down the silver pieces and went and hanged himself. The chorus—chief priests this time—sings, in several parts, canonically, that it is blood money.

There follows a bass aria—the penitent, imploring "Gebt mir meinen Jesus wieder," or "Give me back my Jesus." It goes on for three minutes or so, the low voice backed by a dancing solo violin, with the vocal line expressing anger, betrayal, and self-interest—directed at the chief priests and elders, at Judas, and at the Evangelist himself, too, who has betrayed Jesus and would like to take the act back and have another chance.

The Evangelist carries forward the story: the elders used the silver pieces to buy a potter's field; Jesus stood before Pilate—a bass-baritone—who asked him, *"Bist du der Juden König?"*: "Art thou the King of the Jews?"

In two words, the answer comes: *Du sagest's*. This reply—"You are saying so"—divides the section; it is the center, like the spindle of a stereo turntable, around which the episode moves. It is a key to the method of this Passion: the story of Jesus is carried forward by the voices of others.

The gospel text, given in recitative by the Evangelist, has Pilate asking him if he has heard how harshly he has been accused, and Jesus answering him "not to one word."

The chorale, on the chorale melody (written by Martin Luther) that is stranded through the work, this time carries the words *Befiehl du deine Wege*:

"Commend your ways"—commend your ways to the care of God who controls the heavens and makes paths for the believer on earth. The believer who
asked "Give me back my Jesus" is urged to give God greater faith, and so get
Jesus back that way; the way to settle up (here following the English version) is
to "commit thy way to Jesus," to give him "thy burdens and thy cares"—a gift
that also receives. So this episode, involving Judas's exchange of the knowledge
of Jesus's whereabouts for thirty pieces of silver—and the exchange in turn of
the silver for a potter's field—ties into the grand theme of exchange between
two sides that organizes the work: the theological idea that Christ died to satisfy, to meet the debt incurred through human sinfulness, to even up the accounts once and for all.

The power of the passage owes something to the way the voices call out
across time. In some sense, all vocal music composed prior to the moment
when it is sung stands outside present time, but the effect is more complicated
in a work centered on a word-for-word narrative of events that took place long,
long ago. Boyd explains: "The Passions bring into conjunction two distinct
timescales: that of the biblical events and that of the present (whether Bach's or
our own). The actions are historical, but the reactions are contemporary, and it
is this interaction of past and present that lends the Passions their powerful
irony and layers of reference." The sense of that insight is right, but it depends
on a giant *whether* ("whether Bach's or our own"). It would be more precise to
say that the Passion brings together the present of the biblical events, the present
of Bach's day, and the present day of the listener. The effect is of a complex
simultaneity that (Berger suggests) points to eternity, which Bach understood
as "God's time." And the effect, it seems to me, is compounded in the age of
recordings. In a recording, the double timescale (biblical time, and Bach's
time) is doubled again by the listener's sense of the present in which he or
she is listening—and the listener's sense of the time when the recording
was made.

There is a further level of significance, involving Bach's own point of view
and character as they are expressed in the vocal passages. Only a literalist
would deny that the first-person pronoun in an aria such as "Give, O give me
back my Jesus" might take in Bach's own devotional stance—might express
his attitude directly. So it does all through the cantatas and the *St. John Passion*,
but the effect is especially strong in the *St. Matthew Passion*. Where in the
St. John Passion Bach seems to identify with Jesus against the choir—the
crowd—in this Passion he seems to identify with the choir, whether in the chorus
that goads Pilate to put him to death, the aria full of remorse over what was

done to him, or the chorale that urges the penitent to restore the balance by committing to Jesus afresh.

This is Bach at his least righteous, making us see, hear, and feel both sides. It is an effect that squares with his theology. Following a line of Lutheran commentary, Bach understood the crucifixion as an act of "satisfaction," whereby Jesus paid back the debt that humankind had incurred through its sins against God. As the Passion episode following on Judas's suicide suggests, the crucifixion then places latter-day humanity in Jesus's debt, and the believer progressively "satisfies" the debt by committing himself to Jesus more and more fully.

The *St. Matthew Passion* was Bach's own act of satisfaction, his great giving-back. Hearing it, in the choir loft of the Thomaskirche, he hoped that it was enough. Already he had in mind revisions for the next performance, at the Thomaskirche two years hence. He would further divide the two choirs, giving each its own continuo. He would make use of the small choir loft and the swallow's-nest organ to separate the two choirs physically, so that they would sing out from two sides. And he would write out a fancy display copy of the text. On the page, as in the church, the choral texts would predominate; but on the page the Gospel text would be in red, the blood of Christ restoring the balance.

>>5>> Since the war, the *St. Matthew Passion* had become a modern pilgrim's progress, and new technology called for new recordings. The length of the work (two hours plus) lent itself to the long-playing format. The architecture of it (orchestra, evangelist, players, orchestra, and not one but two choirs) was ideal for spacious recording studios and multitracking. The themes of it—human sin and divine justification; the execution of a paragon of the human race—spoke to the tragic reuse of postwar high culture, bewailing the fate of man in a world that had surpassed his ability to manage it.

Leopold Stokowski had a long and complex history with the Passion. He had sung it as a choirboy at the Temple Church in London; had led an early American performance at St. Bart's in New York in 1907; had performed it with the New York Philharmonic at the Metropolitan Opera House in 1917; and, during World War II, had organized a benefit performance at the Met for Quaker war resisters—a semistaged version in which Lillian Gish represented Christ, undulating onstage under a vertical beam of yellow light. Strangely, he had not made a recording of it. Rehearsing for the benefit, he grew frustrated. He thought the choir should sing "wild like a man who has lost control," but the choir—the Collegiate Chorale, led by Robert Shaw—made it come out like "tame church singing." He explained: "The cruel sound of those vocal phrases 'Let him be crucified' and that example where Pilate says 'Whom shall I release?' and they shout 'Barabbas' and the effect that Bach made with three notes shows that he meant for it to be dramatic. Like so much today, it has been leveled down."

Stokowski did not record it, and it seems clear why he did not. His was a religion of sound. For him, the medium was the message: the music was the sound the musicians made, full stop. The conductors who recorded the *St. Matthew Passion* made a spiritual pattern of it—made it music that pointed to a world and time outside of itself.

Ralph Vaughan Williams made the Passion the ur-text for his anti-Wagner, antiprogressive recovery of English traditional music. Vaughan Williams was as English as they come, born in a country village in 1872, descended from Darwin and Wedgwood, trained at Cambridge and the Royal Academy, a founder and principal conductor of the Leith Hill Festival, an enterprise dedicated to exalting English tradition each year in the Surrey village of Leith. With Gustav Holst, he sought to bring about a recovery and affirmation of the English musical tradition. He revised the Anglican hymnal, repurposed dozens of folk songs, wrote a pair of works of program music—a "Fantasia on a Theme of Thomas Tallis" and an opera treatment of Bunyan's *Pilgrim's Progress*—and edited *The Penguin Book of English Folk Songs* as a secular hymnal for the paperback era; and that became pieces of musical Britannia in their own right.

Vaughan Williams and Holst (Rob Young has written in *Electric Eden*) sought touchstones in "the previous golden ages of English music: sixteenth-century Tudor polyphony; the style of English language-setting which they admired in Henry Purcell; a love of Metaphysical poetry and Romantic visionaries like William Blake and Walt Whitman." But they had another touchstone in Bach. Williams's peer Hubert Parry—who orchestrated Blake's poem "Jerusalem" into the greatest of all English anthems—wrote a biography of Bach. His Chelsea neighbor Percy Grainger, besotted with Bach, played the organ works transcribed for piano. Williams himself led the Bach Choir and Handel Society after the Great War and conducted works of Bach at the Leith Hill Festival year after year. For the 1957 festival he organized a performance of the *St. Matthew Passion*, which he had conducted thirty times since 1931 in an English version edited by Edward Elgar. When he took the podium, tape was rolling. When the next spring's festival came around, he declined to take part. One reason he gave was that his wife, Ursula, whom he had just married, needed a vacation. Another reason was that he thought the 1957 *St. Matthew Passion* recording a definitive expression of all his efforts at Leith Hill.

More than definitive, it was valedictory, from the early recitative "When Jesus had finished speaking . . . ," sung in English, to the final chorus, "In Tears of Grief." Vaughan Williams died the next August, on the day of a recording session of his Symphony no. 9 with the London Philharmonic at the Walthamstow Hall in northeast London. Sir Adrian Boult, the conductor, recalled: "I was going down to breakfast that morning when the telephone rang. It was Ursula—'I'm sorry,' she said, 'we're not coming to the recording; Ralph died at 3 o'clock this morning.' "

Vaughan Williams's *Pilgrim's Progress* was likened to an "aftermath"—a second mowing—and that is an apt characterization of his *St. Matthew Passion*, too. Memories of the Blitz were fresh in Surrey, across the Thames from London, where many Londoners had fled as German warplanes carpet-bombed the city, mowing its great buildings down. The Leath Hall performance has patches of grandeur, but it is an emphatically local production, made so by the effortful communal uplift of the vocals and the rehearsal-quality piano accompaniment.

Karl Richter made a recording of the *St. Matthew Passion* with the Munich Bach Choir and Orchestra for Deutsche Grammophon's Archiv label. Taking advantage of the recording process, Richter brought in a Berlin-born baritone, Dietrich Fischer-Dieskau, to record the four bass arias in a separate session with the orchestra after the rest of the work had been committed to tape. "With forced cheerfulness I tried to break through the somewhat stultifying atmosphere," Fischer-Dieskau recalled. "The quiet, shy man on the podium and the new, not exactly quick-witted recording team all seemed determined to maintain a mute hauteur. Although I did hear criticism on details, which were immediately remedied, there was not a single encouraging or helpful word. I felt that my pleasure in the work was arousing suspicion."

Those Passions were run-ups to a Passion designed to outdo them all. In 1961, Otto Klemperer, recording for EMI, made the *St. Matthew Passion* a summation of a half century of grim history involving Germany and Great Britain. Beneath the crumbling plaster of an old revival hall, a world war in two parts was played out one more time.

A protégé of Gustav Mahler's, Klemperer, who was Jewish, had identified himself so fully with modernism that he was suspect in Germany, then so fully with the Weimar musical culture that he felt the anti-German blowback farther west: during the Great War, and during the thirties, when, in Los Angeles, he was passed over for positions in New York and Philadelphia because anti-German currents were running strong. Underestimated, he struggled personally. He contracted a brain tumor, and its removal left him partly paralyzed on the right side from the face down. "A period of extreme psychological disturbance followed," Joseph Horowitz recounts in a masterly piece of portraiture. "He took to hiring taxis (for which he could not pay) for entire evenings. His clothes were dirty, he ate irregularly, he walked unsteadily and with a stick. He wore an eyepatch. His mood careened from hilarity to rage." He checked into a hospital outside New York, not realizing it was a mental hospital; he left, and his "escape" made the front page of *The New York Times*. In later years he slipped and fell in a hotel in Montreal, and could not conduct standing thereafter; a heavy smoker, he set a fire while smoking in bed, tried to douse it with spirits, and was badly burned. When the U.S. government, detecting leftist sympathies, declined to renew his passport, he went to London at the urging of the EMI producer Walter Legge; and there, officially a West German citizen, suddenly the pride of EMI's studio orchestra, the Philharmonia, he made a series of recordings—Beethoven symphonies, Mozart operas—that established him, in his seventies, as an old German lion. "I am the last of the classical school—when Bruno Walter died, I put my fees up," he said, a wizened survivor.

Kingsway Hall had served as a refuge in wartime: a bomb shelter, a dormitory for displaced persons, and a canteen where vegetables from Covent Garden market were distributed and hot breakfasts and cups of tea were served by the tens of thousands. It survived the war but was grimy and in need of repair. Even so, as EMI sought a dominant position in the classical record market, it used Kingsway for dozens of stereo recordings, arranging sessions around services on Sunday mornings and holidays such as Christmas, Ash Wednesday, and Good Friday.

At Kingsway over five days in January 1961, Klemperer recorded a *St. Matthew Passion* with what music writers call "considerable musical forces": the tenor Peter Pears, Benjamin Britten's companion, as the Evangelist; Dietrich Fischer-Dieskau as Jesus; Elisabeth Schwarzkopf, the voice of choice in Wagner, singing the soprano arias; the Philharmonia, its choir, and a boy's choir from Hampstead. The performers were arranged on the wooden Kingsway stage by Klemperer and the producer, Walter Legge—a "division of musical forces" meant to bring out the doubled construction of the Passion itself:

ORGAN

CHORUS I   CHORUS II

SOLOISTS   SOLOISTS

JESUS   EVANGELIST

CONTINUO
(cello, double bass, harpsichord)

ORCHESTRA I   ORCHESTRA II

CONDUCTOR

A photograph of Klemperer suggests the gravity of the proceedings. The score is spread out before him. He is in black suit and black tie, thick white hair set off by boxy Bakelite eyeglasses; he sits erect atop a stool before the assembled multitude of the Philharmonia, smoking a pipe. Thus situated, he might be a sea captain at the wheel of a ship under full sail, piloting the vessel over the waves of the gospel text, propelled by the power of the great wind that Bach has provided and harnessed. This Passion, the image suggests, is an ordeal, an endurance test. Best to light one's pipe and settle in: it will go on for a while.

Immovable, commanding, Klemperer is the opposite of Vaughan Williams, who led a *St. Matthew Passion* by the people, of the people, for the people; and he is the opposite or inverse of Leopold Stokowski, whose transcriptions were a stylized form of self-expression, a modern magic act. Where Stoki was a performer, Klemperer was an executioner, ready to administer the grim business at hand.

His *St. Matthew Passion* did go on for a while: three hours and forty-three minutes. It has been described as "slow to the point of stateliness," but the tempos are not that much slower, chorus for chorus, aria for aria, than those in the *Passion* that Vaughan Williams led at Leith Hill.

What it is is long. There are no cuts. Everything is drawn out: the singing, the bowing of strings, the pressure of foot on pedal of pipe organ. By the end of the opening chorus, nearly twelve minutes (as opposed to nine minutes in the Leith Hill *Passion*), you feel that you have heard the whole work. From the first recitative by the Evangelist—the passage about Jesus finishing speaking, sung in German—the phrasing is squared off in a way that suggests medieval notation, blocks and bars extended across the page. Arias are tightropes stretched between the pillared edifices of the choruses. The chorales, long draughts of breath in the action, suggest a reproach to a restive child in a church pew: Yes, dear, we are going to sing every verse; yes, we are going to stay until it is over. "Klemperer ended each measure with a ritardando," a slackening of the tempo, Fischer-Dieskau recalled; and the words of Jesus, in Fischer-Dieskau's baritone, seem to issue from him in defiance of the lengthening of the music—to suggest that his very steadiness, his level-headedness in the event, is what makes him divine.

What effect does all this elongation achieve? It extends the Christian drama of Bach into the epic territory of Wagner. It makes the *St. Matthew Passion* a world unto itself, like the Sistine Chapel or the monastic isle of Patmos. It makes Jesus's final hours seem to pass in real time, so that the event one believer styled "death on a Friday afternoon" really does take an afternoon to transpire.

Musically, the length of the work fulfills the possibilities of tape and the LP and applies them to Bach. Heard now, the Kingsway *Passion* is long. In 1961, it was unprecedentedly long. Finally it was possible to make a *Passion* like this, and so Klemperer went to extraordinary lengths to do so.

Stereo, correspondingly, offered unprecedented clarity. Klemperer and Walter Legge were following the time-honored practice of arranging the musicians for the *Passion* so as to bring out the two-sided, doubling effects of the score; but they were among the first to capture the effect in a stereo recording. This *Passion* is long, but spacious, too. By the standards of live performances of the day, the two choirs used at Kingsway were relatively small, and the sound of them—set against each other in the dramatic choral passages, brought together in the chorales—is one of clarity, of choirs emerging distinct from the massed voices of the mono era. Where Stokowski, working in mono, exaggerated vertically, upping the highs and scooping the lows, Klemperer, in stereo, exaggerated horizontally, stretching the work until its parts stood out from one another.

It is hard to listen to Klemperer's *Passion* straight through, and the endurance it requires is part of its effect. This work which seems to be ending from the start refuses to end—so that when it does, with a giant chorus that moves like a caravan across a continent, you feel that you and the musical forces of London have been through a war together.

At Kingsway two months later, Klemperer recorded Brahms's *A German Requiem* with the same forces, the same producer, and the same equipment. The liner notes for the *Requiem* suggests that Klemperer's recording "places Brahms on the continuum of German sacred music going back through Beethoven to Handel, Bach, and Schütz." In fact, it does the opposite. At the far end of war-torn modernity, the *Requiem* places the *Passion* in the line of modern works that ask, in Western civilization's behalf, *My God—what have we done?* This *German Requiem* is the double to Klemperer's *Passion* the way his *Passion* is the flip side of Vaughan Williams's *Passion*: it completes the earlier work, bringing out the virtues native to each of them. The *Requiem*, major chords abloom from the beginning, makes clear how darkly minor the *Passion* is. The *Requiem* stirs but it does not move; the *Passion* is nimble and agitated in comparison, a work on the way. Where the *Requiem* is all of a piece, a stationary panegyric, the *Passion* begins in one place and ends someplace else.

>>6>> The title page read: "Keyboard practice, consisting of preludes, allemandes, courantes, sarabandes, gigues, minuets, and other galanteries, composed for music lovers, to refresh their spirits, by Johann Sebastian Bach, Actual Capellmeister to His Highness the Prince of Anhalt-Cöthen and Director Chori Musici Lipiensis. Partita I. Published by the Author. 1726."

This was the *Clavier-Übung*, the first of Bach's keyboard music to be published, and the title page, no less than a Passion text, tells a story about the pattern of Bach's music-making. It is handwritten in a mix of German and Latin, in curvaceous script. It says that he saw his keyboard music as music for practice first of all; that he had written it for ordinary people ("music lovers"), not virtuosi, for a clear and straightforward effect ("to refresh their spirits"); that even as he was producing a vast body of sacred music (choral music—"Chori Musici") in Leipzig, he kept the title of capellmeister to the prince; and that this first partita was his own publication, a work of his own hands and an expression of his musical independence.

He sent a set of the printed music to Köthen, where Prince Leopold's wife had given birth to their first child, a son. Partita no. 1 was Bach's gift to the newborn prince, and a poem he sent with it drew on the likeness between the infant in his cradle and the "playful page" of music:

It is the first fruit of my strings in music sounding;
Thou the first son round whom the Princess's arms have curled.
It shall for thee and for thy honor be resounding;
Since thou art, like this page, a firstling in the world.

Generous as a rule, Bach gave unstintingly in those years. He wrote letters on behalf of his students, spreading his influence around. He identified candidates for cantors' posts, sent letters of introduction, and offered recommendations—coolly assessing one candidate as someone who "no doubt . . . will, with further work at the organ, show his ability to new advantage," and requesting an audition for another, whom he then described with faint praise as essentially well-behaved and helpful around the church.

He sent one music lover a "puzzle" canon, or *canone enimmatico*—a canon in four voices, with no clear beginning or ending. When it arrived, "Every member of the company that was present had to set himself at it, and seek to find the solution," one of them recalled. Which voice should enter first, last? Where should the canon begin and end? "One hit upon this solution; another upon that; until at length" two of them reached the same solution. They never found out whether they were right.

When he agreed to make music of mourning for Christiane Eberhardine, late electress of Saxony, he met with resistance. She was a saintly Lutheran; when her husband, Augustus the Strong, became a Catholic in order to claim the throne of predominantly Catholic Poland, she remained a Lutheran, separating from the king and setting up a reformed royal nunnery outside Leipzig. On her death—September 6, 1727—the Lutherans of Saxony commenced mourning. A nobleman enrolled at the university arranged a memorial service, commissioning music from Bach and verse from Johann Christoph Gottsched, a poet of renown. The university's head of music objected, insisting that the music was his to compose. Bach refused to yield. The head of music insisted that Bach sign a waiver calling the event a one-off, no precedent for future performances. Bach refused. The other man backed down. The performance went on, two days after Bach finished writing the music.

The "Trauer-Ode," or ode of mourning, is an apt comparison piece to the *St. Matthew Passion*, for it suggests how the expectations of our own time invert those of Bach's. The stacked choruses and darting string figures of the *St. Matthew Passion* are there, but not the soaring arias or the pitched conflict. The melodies are subdued, and the words are now courtly formulaic, now blandly matter-of-fact in their obsequies, describing the queen's bravery in death, the country's need, the bells that carry the sound of the people's distress all over Europe. Compared with this, the *Passion*, with its scene of Jesus stripped, robed in scarlet, crowned with thorns, spat upon, and struck on the head with a reed, is documentary work in its vividness. The queen is dead—enough said; the death of Christ is an event.

And yet the occasion called forth a vivid write-up of Bach in performance. "In solemn procession, while the bells were rung," a newspaper reviewer reported, school and town officials entered the university chapel, where nobles and their ladies were seated. "When, then, everyone had taken his place, there had been an improvisation on the organ," followed by "the Music of Mourning, which this time Capellmeister Johann Sebastian Bach had composed in the Italian style, with *Clave di Cembalo* [harpsichord], which Mr. Bach himself played, organ, violas da gamba, lutes, violins, recorders, transverse flutes, &c. half being heard before and half after the oration of praise and mourning."

He led the music at another funeral a year and a half later. Prince Leopold had died, thirty-four years old. Bach traveled to Köthen for the service with his son Wilhelm Friedemann, now eighteen years of age, and played music adapted from the "Trauer-Ode" and also from the *St. Matthew Passion*—adapting a great work for a great patron (and for a fee of 230 thalers, a third of a year's income). He returned to Leipzig for Holy Week and led a second enactment of the *St. Matthew Passion*, making use of four new string instruments acquired by the Thomaskirche. He followed this, six weeks later, with a cantata whose opening was rooted in the third Brandenburg concerto: "Ich liebe den Höchsten von ganzem Gemüte" ("I love the highest with my whole heart"), as lushly exultant a piece of sacred music as any he had written.

The two *Passion* presentations prompted Bach to envision his ideal church music ensemble. This he did by writing a memorandum to the Leipzig town council in 1730, much as he had set out his ideal for keyboard music by publishing the text of his first partita. In the memo he made a case for an ensemble of thirty-six musicians, and lamented that Leipzig lacked such an ensemble: some members had no talent, others had talent but lacked training, and few had shown the ability to "satisfy the present musical taste, master the new kinds of music, and thus be in a position to do justice to the composer and his work." He argued that music in Leipzig would falter unless the town council gave it greater support.

His closest counterpart, Georg Friedrich Handel, had had an English hit with his opera *Giulio Cesare in Egitto*. When Handel, a north German who had traveled to Florence before making his career in London, returned to visit his mother in Halle, not far from Leipzig, Bach sent Wilhelm Friedemann to Halle as a messenger, proposing that they meet; but Handel had left for England the day before.

Bach went to Kassel, 125 miles west, to examine a new organ and give the first recital on it. He played a toccata and fugue in D minor. It was the one dubbed the "Dorian," not the one he had played at a tryout years earlier. It is gloriously methodical, a four-note figure passed insistently through the instrument like thread through a loom. To hear it after the omnidirectional splendor of the cantatas and Passions, after the missed encounter with Handel, is to realize how internally consistent Bach's music was from year to year. Even at its most communal, dramatizing the religious lives of his fellow Lutherans, his music developed along its own lines, without parallel.

>>7>> What we see of the organ is the console: the two manuals, or keyboards; the switches, in a horizontal line above the upper keyboard, crème-colored and stamped with their functions; to the right, the stops, their knobs protruding in diagonal rows, like racked wine bottles. Sheet music is spread out on a plate-glass stand at the top of the photograph; at the console, hands flat on the lower keyboard, androidal in appearance—short hair, strong jaw, dark eyes, heavy brows, full lips, blank look—is the organist.

The organist is Glenn Gould, the organ an instrument built in the Baroque Revival style—old-school with some mod cons—and installed in 1960 at All Saints Anglican Church in Toronto.

The photograph was printed in sepia tint on the sleeve of Gould's *Art of the Fugue* LP. The record—the photograph suggested this—represented Gould's own rejection of his career to that point, whether or not Columbia Masterworks recognized it.

It was recorded in Toronto, not Manhattan. This was significant in several senses. It served as a statement of independence. Other artists moved from polestar cities to New York to gain their independence; Gould, nearing thirty, had shunned New York and settled emphatically in his hometown, buying an apartment in a building called the Inn on the Park. Recording in Toronto also allowed him to maintain his routine of sleeping by day and reading, writing, playing, and recording through the night.

It was cut in a church—All Saints, Kingsway—not a recording studio. Gould, who had done more than anyone to extricate Bach from "very special little concerts" in "certain churches" (as Leonard Bernstein had put it), now restored him there. At home in the studio, he ventured forth and went native, situating his project of technical transcendence in a place set up for transcendence through the cross.

It was played on the pipe organ, not the piano. Gould, who had made Bach sing on the modern piano, reverted to the earlier instrument. Why? He wanted to try the All Saints organ, which had become known among organists in Toronto for its brightness. But there was more to it than that. Made on the organ, this record especially would refuse to approximate his sold-out recitals. It would refuse to be "cool," a counterpart to records by Dave Brubeck and Bill Evans. And it would withhold the virtuosity he was known for. He hadn't played organ since he was a teenager; he did his prep work for the session on a piano, and did not follow the organist's ritual of working out different combinations of pipes beforehand: "I set up the registrations only at the last minute," he confessed. Like his CBC performance on the harpsipiano, this record would be an experiment, a sonic adventure.

In other respects, the hermetic quality of the record (and its packaging) concealed just how busy he was.

"As of two months ago," he told a BBC commentator in a letter in April, "I decided that when next season is over, I shall give no more public concerts. Mind you, this is a plan I have been announcing every year since I was 18 . . . but this time I think I really mean it." When he went with his friend John Roberts to a Chinese restaurant, the proprietress turned off the radio playing in the background and put on Gould's *Goldbergs* record. Over supper Gould told Roberts that he was quitting performance. People at Columbia were telling him it would be the end of his career, but he was not convinced. "Well, we'll see," he said. "It will be a terrific challenge."

He was not withdrawing; he was broadening the range of his activities. In the year after the release of the *Art of the Fugue* record that June he kept a schedule that rivaled Stokowski's. He gave nine recitals in the United States. He recorded two Bach partitas, a toccata, and a batch of preludes and fugues from the *Well-Tempered Clavier*. He wrote and narrated CBC-TV programs about music in the Soviet Union, about Richard Strauss, and about *The Anatomy of Fugue* in which (as Kevin Bazzana described it) "the music is there to illuminate the commentary." For this last he composed a jingly vocal fugue in four parts, complete with rhymed, Cole Porter–ish lyrics. He drafted three talks on Strauss—robust essays, really—and completed a two-hour radio program about Strauss for the CBC. He gave the Macmillan lectures over three evenings in Toronto and a long talk on Schoenberg at the University of Cincinnati, and began revising the latter for publication as a small book. He wrote program notes for a concert in Baltimore, explaining his oh-so-slow approach to Brahms, which had sparked controversy when he played a Brahms concerto with Leonard Bernstein and the New York Philharmonic earlier in the year. He served as the music director for the Stratford Festival in Ontario and took part in two concerts there. He composed a few bars of a sonata on hotel stationery, and told one reporter that the sonata was "95 percent complete." He sat for an interview in Ottawa with Leonard Cohen, poet and songwriter, who abandoned his questions to listen to Gould talk.

Is it any wonder he dreaded plane flights, left hotel rooms messy, and had to take sedatives to get to sleep? Is it any wonder he had to struggle to maintain his sanity?

There are two sides to the appraisal of Glenn Gould. It is easy to see him as a freak, doubly set apart by genius and eccentricity. In the video footage from those years, he seems anything but artistic: overdressed and balding, shoulders hunched, arms atwitch, speaking voice orotund. Yet he was an artist so fully as to define the type. He was an artist phenomenal in both his output and his concentration. He was an artist who found ways to work with others, often total strangers. He was an artist attuned to the worldly currents of the age, and the *Art of the Fugue* is a form of engagement with them.

He had played four of the fugues (called *contrapuncti*) on piano in a program with the *Three-Part Inventions* in New York in 1957, and then played a similar program in Moscow. He later praised their "intense, self-entrenched concentration" and called them "my favorite Bach work." It is no surprise that he recorded them. Nor is it especially surprising that he did so on the organ, for Bach was thought to have composed them for no particular instrument—and in Gould's view, "this magnificent indifference to specific sonority is not least among those attractions that emphasize the universality of Bach."

As it happened, he recorded them on the organ shortly after two organists, each with a record label's support, began the vast project of recording all of Bach's organ music. Beginning in 1961, Walter Kraft set out to play the organ works on instruments from Bach's time in churches in Europe—Germany, France, Switzerland, the Netherlands, Denmark—for release as triple-LP sets by Vox. The same year, Lionel Rogg began recording a set on a new organ in Zurich, and a small Swiss label found distribution in Britain for the records, each in a textured cardboard sleeve with a grand foldout insert (program notes, registrations, pictures of the organ) like a menu in a posh restaurant. These were musical moon shots, made possible by the market for the LP, which could support projects that would take years to complete. And they were the yield of Germany's postwar reconstituting of itself, which prompted scholars on both sides of the Berlin Wall to restore shattered archives, recatalog surviving cultural treasures, and consolidate German culture for a new era.

Those records stand in stark opposition to Gould's organ record. They are parts of a whole; his is fragmentary. They are vibrant with history, the wood and stone and lead pipes and stained glass of the Christian past; his is chilly and abstract. He plays the fugues like demonstrations rather than pieces of music, quarantining the two lines from each other and hardly playing the third line on the pedals. Like the man in the photograph, they seem cryogenically preserved, hardly human.

That is the way Gould wanted it. Just as he preferred pianos with light action, so he favored a church with hardly any echo or ambient sound. Finding this "dry" quality at All Saints, he accentuated it by telling the Columbia engineers to put the microphones right up against the organ pipes—"so that the pipes could speak, as they say, and perhaps even wheeze occasionally as well." The idea was to create the sound of an organ for the living room, not the sound of the organ in the church. "The central strands of the music are each allowed to have a life of their own—they're not embalmed in reverberation as organ recitals in churches tend to be," he later explained. "There was no attempt to glamorize the sound, to surround it with a halo for relevance, or to 'mike' it so distantly as to suggest that one was listening to it from far back in the congregation. There was, in fact, no attempt to capitalize on a sense of 'occasion' . . ."

It was an original approach but a perverse one, for the sameness of the sound suppressed his gifts for variety, movement, and surprise. His *Art of the Fugue* is like a Romanesque monastery weighed down by Brutalist renovations. It made Bach tedious, and Gould not Gould-like.

A few days after Gould experimented with close-miking at All Saints, the composer Terry Riley, passing through New York after a tour of U.S. military bases in Europe, heard a new work by his "spiritual brother" La Monte Young. This was *The Well-Tuned Piano*, an epic piece played on a piano tuned in "just intonation," a harmonically rich undoing of the "equal" and "well-tempered" approaches. Riley had hit on his own key compositional idea: "the use of repetition as the primary organizing principle in music." Returning to San Francisco, he worked out a piece of loosely principled repetition called *In C*; and he combined tape loops and improvised keyboard figures into a new style, involving natural sound pressure-treated with technology.

Riley's approach—called minimalism, derided by Gould as "monotonously monochromatic"—was defined by a deliberate poverty of means; but it was characterized by his chosen instrument, the electronic organ, on which he would improvise on repeated figures for hours and hours. Where Riley went on the organ, Steve Reich and Philip Glass followed. Gould's organ music opened a door that others walked through; his *Art of the Fugue* is a piece of electronic music.

>>8>> What *was* he doing with his career? That was his question; and now, with his agent turning down requests for future bookings, Gould had to answer it for himself instead of denouncing a classical-music culture he considered hostile to transcendence sought in solitude.

As he worked through the last few recitals, he sought to answer the question by way of a fresh encounter with Bach in the recording studio. He would record the *Two and Three Part Inventions*, a.k.a. the *Inventions and Sinfonias*. Where the *Art of the Fugue* was made up of endings, the *Inventions* were beginnings; a decade after he had used the *Inventions* to acclimate himself to 30th Street Studio, and to a career as a recording artist, he would use the *Inventions* to begin his career as an artist working only in recordings.

He went to New York in the fall and got started on the recordings, and then broke off the sessions and returned to Toronto. There, he subjected his best piano, CD 318, to an overhaul—and undertook some self-examination, looking to his musical heroes for wisdom and counsel.

He had played Steinways since his teens, but had never found one that approximated the small, ringing Chickering piano in his apartment. A favorite Steinway, number 174—the piano he had played for the *Goldberg Variations* LP—had been damaged in transit. CD 205 seemed too stiff after a while; CD 90 seemed too loose. When he played CD 318 in a corner of Eaton Auditorium in June 1960, he was enchanted—by the lightness of its action in particular; and when he learned that it had been the property of Eaton's since 1945, and had been used for concerts at halls in Toronto since then, he hypothesized that he had played this very piano in his first recitals. It was battered and in need of servicing. Gould—asserting his prerogative as a famous Steinway artist— arranged for it to be sent to the factory in Queens. "I don't have to enumerate for you the many admirable qualities of this klavier," he told a Steinway agent in a letter, "suffice it to say that it was the piano which assisted in many of the memorable moments of my career as a child prodigy."

After an overhaul, for three years it was sent back and forth between Toronto, the Steinway factory, 30th Street Studio, and concert halls in North America. Gould evidently used it to record the preludes and fugues of the first book of the *Well-Tempered Clavier* in 1962 and 1963. Now he arranged for it to be overhauled again and sent to the studio once more. "Prior to each of the Bach sessions of the last few years, CD 318 has undergone major surgery," he later explained. "The alignment of such essential mechanical matters as the distance of the hammer from the strings, the 'aftertouch' mechanism, etc., has been earnestly reconsidered in accordance with my sober conviction that no piano need feel duty-bound to always sound like a piano. Old 318, if released from its natural tendency in that direction, could probably be prevailed upon to give us a sound of such immediacy and clarity that those qualities of non-legato so essential to Bach would be gleefully realized."

While it was gone, he sought to answer his question in writing. He considered "the dilemma of the contemporary musical situation" in the text of his short book on Schoenberg, and recast his remarks on Strauss into an article for the *Saturday Review* called "Strauss and the Electronic Future." For him the two composers represented the two sides of the dilemma—a dilemma about the nature of creativity or invention. "All art is really variation upon some other art," he observed. How, then, should the artist who stood apart from his own time work variations on other art? Schoenberg's ideas were more consequential than his compositions, which led the music itself to be overlooked; Strauss was a great composer whose consistency—his refusal to change significantly over half a century—was held against him. One had too many ideas (a problem afflicting Gould the theorist), the other too few (a problem for Gould the aspiring composer).

There was an artist who had gotten the balance right: Johann Sebastian Bach. In a long prelude to the Strauss piece, Gould invoked Bach in a way that put his own situation plainly in mind. "If we think for a moment about the way in which our concept of history has influenced our use of words such as 'originality,' some conventional judgments about artistic figures are placed in a very curious light indeed," he declared. "For instance, we are forever being told that although Bach was a great man, he was decidedly retrogressive in his own musical tastes—the implication being that had he been a little less of a genius, his remoteness from contemporary fashion would have quite done in his inspiration." That Gould identified with Bach was already obvious: in defending Bach's "retrogressive" taste, he was defending his own taste for Baroque music over Mozart and the Romantics.

In March 1964 he went to New York and 30th Street Studio. There he found CD 318 in a sublime state of readiness, and responded accordingly. "The operation performed just before the sessions . . ." he recalled, "was so successful that we plunged joyfully into the recording without allowing old 318 its usual post-operative recuperation." Ever since the *Goldberg Variations* Gould had typically recorded each part of a piece in a complete take and, if necessary, one or more alternate takes or "inserts" used to correct finger slips in the playing. This time, he went straight at the whole group. He treated the inventions as inventions—each a foretaste of a more fully executed composition; he searched them for a way out of the contemporary musical situation and into the electronic future.

He played a recital in Chicago: four *contrapuncti* from the *Art of the Fugue*, all the *Three-Part Inventions*, the fourth partita, a Beethoven sonata, and work by the twentieth-century composers Hindemith and Krenek. He played a similar program at the Wilshire Ebell Theatre in Los Angeles two weeks later—Friday, April 10, 1964.

At a reception after the recital he met Lukas and Cornelia Foss. Lukas was a conductor and composer in residence at UCLA, darkly handsome, known for modern music indebted to the music of Bach. Cornelia was a painter and sculptor: blond, trim, in her early thirties, working fitfully at her art while raising their two children in Los Angeles, a city she detested. They had encountered Gould through his recording of the *Goldberg Variations*. When she encountered him in person, Cornelia Foss was taken with him, and she let him know.

He returned to Toronto and started calling her, disguising his voice in case Lukas Foss picked up the phone. He had been involved with a few women over the years, always in connection with his career—young assistants and publicists who mothered him, took his calls, hung on his every word, and kept their relationship a secret from their bosses. This was different. Cornelia was married. He was one point in a love triangle involving a woman and two men each devoted to her and to Bach.

CD 318 arrived a few days afterward. It had appeared in its last recital. From this point forward it would travel between Toronto and New York, between the auditorium of Gould's boyhood and the studio he had made his own.

Gould's "retirement," usually represented as a dramatic act, was fugitive, gradual, and partial. Usually represented as singularly bold—the act of the pianist of the future—it took place in counterpoint with the return of Vladimir Horowitz, the Russian-born prodigy. Horowitz had gained fame after a debut at Carnegie Hall in 1928, which he opened with Busoni's showpiece transcription of the Bach Toccata, Adagio, and Fugue in C—Bach reconfigured as late Romantic roots music. Horowitz stopped performing due to nervous exhaustion in 1953, just when Gould's recital career was getting going. A decade later he signed with Columbia Records, began attending concerts regularly, and told his wife—Wanda Toscanini, the conductor's daughter—that he wanted to play for an audience again. Carnegie Hall was the natural venue; the Toccata, Adagio and Fugue, in Busoni's transcription, was a natural opener: "a good-luck piece for me," he explained, ". . . the first piece on my debut program after I left Russia forty years ago." The line for tickets stretched along Fifty-seventh Street. Wanda Toscanini arranged for a hundred cups of coffee to be brought to the people waiting in line—and got a telegram of thanks FROM ALL OF US UNSIGNED. It was just the type of theatrics that Gould was tired of trying to match.

Two weeks after the Los Angeles recital, Gould recorded a set of pieces for later broadcast in a CBC television studio with giant slabs of ersatz marble arrayed Stonehenge-style around the piano. One was Sweelinck's *Fantasia in D*, which he had played in recitals in Canada in the early fifties and then in his U.S. debuts. Now it served as a hinge between two phases of his career. Heard in narrow mono, as if from a remote location, it begins akin to the slow, brooding twenty-fifth variation of the *Goldbergs*, then turns into a boxy, major-key mechanical anthem; on the far side of tone rows and organ registrations, it has a wind-up, chain-and-gear simplicity.

The *Two and Three Part Inventions* LP was released that August. The sleeve featured an airbrushed photograph of a fresh-faced Gould: the artist of the *Art of the Fugue* has been dragged out of the church into daylight and given a makeover. But this record, too, has an air of invention about it. In "A Word About the Piano," Gould, in mad scientist mode, explained an unfortunate unintended consequence of the surgery on CD 318. "Our enthusiasm for the rather extraordinary sound it now possessed allowed us to minimize the one minor after-effect which it had sustained—a slight nervous tic in the middle register which in slower passages can be heard emitting a sort of hiccup—and to carry on with the sessions without stopping to remedy this minor defect." He declared his fondness for the hiccup, as for the piano itself, and asked the listener to indulge it, likening the recording to an interrupted telecast: "STAY TUNED IN—WE'RE FIXING IT."

As the *Art of the Fugue* and the *Inventions* had been featured together on Gould's Soviet tour, so the records of those works together show Gould in crisis, trying to set things right in his career through controlled experiment. That the *Inventions* record is an experiment is the best thing that can be said about it. The swift inventions are often brilliant, but the many slow ones are strained and ponderous, off center. They have the monotony of the *contrapuncti* from the *Art of the Fugue* but without their oddness. As recorded in 1955, during the ecstatic run-up to the *Goldberg Variations*, no. 15 in B Minor was a trail into inner space; this time, its lack of aural openness (just the effect Gould sought through close miking) makes it a musical migraine. These pieces are not the music of struggle; they are the sound of a musician searching for something.

>>9>> Hiao-Tsiun Ma brought home a new gadget and presented it to his children. It was made of chrome and molded plastic, the size of a cigar box, and slipped into a leatherette satchel with a shoulder strap. It looked like a toy, but it was a tool. It was manufactured by Norelco, known for electric razors, but it was something else altogether. It was a tape recorder—but the tape wasn't wide-gauge stuff spooling around open reels; it was narrow and moved on spools within a self-contained plastic body, or cassette, which clicked into the tape heads without human hands touching it. It was called the Carry-Corder, and Hiao-Tsiun Ma's idea is that it would enable Yo-Yo and his sister, Yeou-Cheng, to hear how they played right after they played. "That was a big thing, a portable device that actually might be able to record things in live situations," Yo-Yo Ma later recalled. "One of the hardest things to do is to be in one place and somewhere else at the same time . . . to be empathetic to a space other than your own." The cassette recorder gave him a new perspective on his playing. "It makes the tempo sound different . . . what you think may have been the right speed to do something—it may be wrong by the time you go sixty feet away. You can only really know that when there's evidence. And a tape recorder actually gives you that evidence."

>>10>> "What do you think of Beethoven?"
    "I love him," said Ringo Starr. "Especially his poems."
    Outside 30th Street Studio the 1960s were becoming The Sixties. Kennedy was dead, Martin Luther King a Nobel laureate, much of Africa fully independent. Columbia Records was the label that put out the records of Bob Dylan and Barbra Streisand, and a spoken-word LP featuring the poems of Cassius Clay, read by the author; in 1963, EMI had had fifteen of nineteen UK

number-one singles, led by its Parlophone subsidiary, which had signed the Beatles. "The outstanding English composers of 1963," a London *Times* writer soberly declared, "must seem to have been John Lennon and Paul McCartney, the talented young musicians from Liverpool whose songs have been sweeping the country since last Christmas . . ."

The Beatles, playing their first North American concerts at the Coliseum in Washington, D.C., and Carnegie Hall in New York, opened with "Roll Over Beethoven"—and a line was drawn. Roll over, Beethoven, and tell Tchaikovsky the news: magnetic tape, the LP, the electric guitar, and the modern recording studio together had bred a new invention—pop music—that put them all to use. Never again would classical music lord over rock and roll, rhythm and blues, soul, surf, and the maximum R&B of the Who. In pop music, classical music had a full rival, an equal and opposite force; from now on, the two sides would contest for dominance.

That is how the story was told at the time (and for a decade or more afterward). The 33⅓ long player vs. the pop 45; the hi-fi vs. the jukebox and the car radio; the musicians who could read music vs. the ones who played the guitar by ear and sang straight from the heart into the microphone: there was truth to the story, at least in outline.

The other side to the story is that, in the Beatles' case, the new music came from the same place as the music it supposedly pushed aside. This was EMI's recording studios in Abbey Road. The Beatles had recorded there since late 1962, using Studio Two, where, the next year, those fifteen number-one singles (by the Beatles and four other groups) were recorded. One photograph taken at Abbey Road shows the four Beatles playing to the left of a grand piano, which has a topcoat thrown over it (and a glass of milk near the propped-open lid); another shows John Lennon and Ringo Starr at opposite sides of a two-manual electric organ. As they became more adept with the studio gear, they started experimenting with it. As they became popular beyond imagining, they treated the studio as a clubhouse and hideout from the young women who streamed up and down the streets of St. John's Wood hoping to glimpse, greet, or grope an idle Beatle. "Coming to the studio was a refuge for them," their producer, George Martin, later explained. "It was the time and place when nobody could get at them."

Glenn Gould hated the Beatles; he dismissed their music as "a happy, cocky, belligerently resourceless brand of harmonic primitivism." He was only eight years older than John Lennon, but it might as well have been half a century. And yet the Beatles and other pop musicians would make things easier for him. No longer would his hair be considered too long (not after the Beatles stirred the sale of "moptop" wigs) or his manner too insolent (not after Bob Dylan flipped off a hostile audience by tuning his electric guitar for an hour between songs). In this sense, Gould didn't retire just in time; he retired a moment too soon.

The Beatles didn't hate Bach. That is the flip side to the story. Beethoven was rolled over, but Bach was left standing. The counterculture had no wish to counter Bach; the most forward-looking figures of the sixties put the music of Bach in play here, there, and everywhere.

There it was in the movie houses of the Village, Harvard Square, Dinkytown, and North Beach—in the Rome of Fellini's *La Dolce Vita*. Fellini, with Marcello Mastroianni as his double, saw to it that this figure's crisis of life's meaning, his struggle between realism and absurdity, was split down the middle by Bach. An hour in, he encounters an old teacher, Steiner, in an empty church—a new, spartan church to go along with the apartment blocks seen from the sky in the film's famous opening shot. Steiner, a serious man, shows Marcello a big Sanskrit grammar a priest friend has given to him and heaps praise on a piece Marcello has written: it is vivid, passionate, distinctly his. He invites him to drop by his apartment sometime. Then (in Italian) he asks: Can you stay five more minutes? Marcello says he can. Steiner calls out to a priest: Can he bring a friend up? The answer comes. "You see, these priests don't fear the devil," Steiner says. "They even let me play the organ." Upstairs, he takes a seat at the console and plays a few bars of hot jazz. Then, as if the organ is a spliff, or a sexual position, he asks: "You want to try, Marcello?"

Marcello presses a note here, a note there.

"We're not used to hearing these sounds anymore. Such a mysterious voice. It seems to come from inside the Earth. What would you like to hear?

"You choose. I trust you."

Steiner plays the opening figure of the Toccata and Fugue in D Minor. The organ is notably modern-sounding. Marcello is unmoved. He averts his eyes, then lowers them—whether contemplatively or dismissively, it is hard to tell. As Steiner, stirred by Bach, goes into the rapidly ascending part, Marcello walks to the open doorway, then turns back. He lowers his eyes, and the camera pulls back to show the nave of the church, where a woman has just come in, young and slim but dressed demurely in churchgoing black. There in church, Marcello ogles her. Fellini's modern man has been called back to the traditional life he was raised in, but he isn't listening.

Twice as many guitars were sold in 1964 as the year before, and the music of Bach had a role to play in the guitar revival. The Beatles and Dylan got the sales going. The Beatles turned it toward classical music with "And I Love Her," which featured a figure finger-picked by George Harrison on a Spanish classical guitar. ("Segovia is a person that I admire very much," Harrison said. "He gets more feeling out of his guitar than anyone else I've ever heard.") In May Columbia brought out *Columbia Records Presents John Williams*, its first release by the classical guitarist, born in Melbourne in 1941 but raised in London, where his father established a school of classical guitar. The record, produced by Paul Myers (who was producing Glenn Gould's records), opened with Williams's transcription of Bach's fourth lute suite in E major for guitar; the sleeve showed a man who might have been a folksinger or Merseybeat musician, with wire-rim glasses and a shirt with a white tab collar. The next year RCA released an LP of Bach's lute suites played on guitar by Julian Bream, who had brought out *A Bach Recital for the Guitar* in 1957 and then founded an ensemble devoted to the revival of Elizabethan music. Bream and Williams were as English as Lennon and McCartney; they cut Bach loose from the "Spanish guitar" cult and joined him to the British invasion and the tradition of English music.

If you walked along Page Street in Haight-Ashbury one night in the summer of 1965 you could hear the music of Bach played on recorders wafting through a high bay window of an old Victorian house. The players were Peter Albin, a bluegrass musician who had dropped out of San Francisco State, and a friend of his, a Hindu jack-of-all-eccentric trades who "also juggled and practiced acrobatics." The Victorian was a boardinghouse, with six bedrooms, twenty-five tenants: Irish laborers, students and ex-students, musicians, wanderers, and miscreants. It had a skylight cut into the roof and a ballroom in the basement, complete with arched and planked wooden stage. The owner, Albin's uncle, was letting Albin and his brother run the place, and in time they moved the performances from the bay window to the basement, followed up Bach with some LSD-infused bluegrass jams, and began to charge fifty cents' admission to the people, several dozen per night, who came to the house on Page Street to hear the sounds.

You could hear Bach at Abbey Road. Through dozens of sessions the Beatles had become masters of the recording studio, devising new techniques and applying them on the spot. They were also using more diverse instruments—sitar on "Norwegian Wood," and keyboards, from the studio's Steinway grand piano to Vox and Hammond organs to the harmonium, the German-made Pianet, and the Mellotron. They had the help of George

Martin, who had trained at the Guildhall School of Music. Martin would sit on a high stool as John and Paul (and sometimes George and Ringo) would play a new song, singing and strumming guitars. He would listen and then suggest a "head arrangement": instruments, harmonies, tempo, effects. "He would translate," John Lennon recalled. "If Paul wanted to use violins he would translate it for him. Like [in] 'In My Life' there is an Elizabethan piano solo in it, so he would put things like that in. We would say, 'Play like Bach,' or something, so he would put twelve bars in there." Recording "In My Life," for *Rubber Soul*, they left a gap for a solo; during a break Martin worked up a Bach-like melody and counterpoint. "I did it with what I call a 'wound-up' piano," Martin recalled, "which was at double-speed—partly because you get a harpsichord sound by shortening the attack of everything, but also because I couldn't play it at real speed anyway. So I played it on piano at exactly half normal speed, and down an octave. When you bring the tape back up to normal speed again, it sounds pretty brilliant. It's a means of tricking everybody into thinking you can do something really well."

Rubber Soul went straight to number one. So did *Revolver*, which featured "Eleanor Rigby," played by string quartet, with no guitars at all.

>>11>> In a perfect world, Albert Schweitzer would have played the organ one more time, gliding through a Bach postlude as the doors of the church were flung open to let in the light.

As it was, the world was imperfect, and so was the way of his dying. He grew weak, let go of his obligations at the hospital, and named his daughter as his successor. He ordered a coffin made and took a walk through an orchard on the hospital grounds, identifying the fruits one by one. One day in August he got up, had breakfast, tried to walk, faltered, and went back to bed. There, he had a stroke; he passed in and out of consciousness for several days, asking for beer at one point (he got it), and died shortly before midnight on September 4, 1965. In the morning his passing was recognized with the ringing of church bells and the beating of tom-toms; in the afternoon his body, in the coffin, was buried beneath some palm trees on a bank of the river. Hymns and a chorale were sung. A wooden cross he had made himself was put up as a grave marker.

"Only at quite rare moments have I felt really glad to be alive," Schweitzer had concluded his autobiography. "I could not but feel with a sympathy full of regret all the pain that I saw around me, not only that of men but that of the whole creation." His reverence for life was rooted in the vow not to be the willing cause of another creature's death, and at the same time in the recognition that the life of every creature was sustained through the deaths of others. With reverence for life, he had extended the idea of satisfaction found in Bach's Passions—the belief that Christ gave his life to cancel out the debts of sinful humanity—into the natural world, where the role of the individual, as he saw it, was to reduce the sum total of suffering in creation.

Schweitzer conceived of death in terms of the music of Bach, finding in Bach a pattern that he sought to make a pattern for his own death. "This robust and healthy man," he had written, "who lived surrounded by the affection of a great family, this man who embodied energy and activity, who even had a pronounced taste for the frankly burlesque, felt at the bottom of his soul an intense desire, a *Sehnsucht*, for eternal rest. He knew, if any mortal ever did, what nostalgia for death was. Never elsewhere had this nostalgia for death been translated into music in a more impressive way." Schweitzer heard this "nostalgia for death" most strongly in the so-called mystic cantatas—somber works that feature a bass soloist, among them "Christ lag in Todesbanden" and "Ich habe genug," or "It is enough." "They begin with the idea of weariness of life; then, little by little, the expectation of death quiets and illumines; in death Bach celebrates the supreme liberation; and describes in lovely spiritual lullabies the peace that at this thought invades his soul; or again, his happiness is translated into joyous and exuberant themes of a supernatural gaiety. We feel that his whole soul sings in this music, and that the believer has written it in a sort of exultation."

"So desired, so awaited, death did not surprise him." The recital in Gunsbach had been his last: a return to the beginning, a da capo aria.

Embassies sent cables of condolence to Lambaréné. Radio stations played Schweitzer's recordings. Set against 1965, the reedy sound of his Toccata and Fugue in D Minor from All Hallows can be heard as the ancestor of the spindly Farfisa organ and the tubular Vox Continental—as the sound of the city of London made portable for transport to the colonies.

"Schweitzer's reputation outran his accomplishments, but his accomplishments were real enough." So he was eulogized in *Time*, which, with *Life*, had canonized him in postwar America. The results of his hospital, his biblical scholarship, and his philosophy were mixed, in the magazine's account, but his work on Bach was all good: "Schweitzer's two-volume biography of the composer, analyzing his mystical genius, is generally acknowledged as the starting point of the modern Bach revival."

Two years earlier *Time* had called him "an anachronism"—as a compliment. For so long the model of entropy-defying vigor, by the end he was the image of old age. Pledged to the revival of earlier ways, he wound up an ambassador from the past, left behind when the flag came down.

In some respects the way of life he had been born into, and which he had tried to save from decline—a life of hard work and gratuitous learning, piety and personal philosophy, well-intentioned service at once to the less fortunate and "the whole of humanity"—had passed out of being, replaced with ideals of equality and efficiency: with independence and economic development in Africa, with biblical criticism based on quasi-scientific redaction of the source materials, with simple hymns and folksinging in place of traditional liturgical music.

In others, his way was being adopted: in the Peace Corps; in the nuclear test ban treaty signed by the United States and the USSR; in the emerging concern for the natural world; in the doggedness of organists who traveled from old church to old church to make records of the music of Bach played on historically appropriate organs.

The "sense of an ending"—an idea that a literary critic, Frank Kermode, was developing for a series of lectures that fall—had shaped Schweitzer's life. Coming of age at the end of the nineteenth century, Schweitzer had felt the sense of an ending that Arnold and Hardy and Henry Adams had characterized, and he had carried it forward into the middle of the twentieth century, where the end was seen through the grim futurism of Orwell and Huxley. In his life the sense of an ending was the basis for a one-man revival, rooted in religion but set apart from it. In his Bach the spirit of revival, for so long faced outward toward a recalcitrant society, was turned inward and made the engine of elegiac art—art that backlit the culture bent on leaving it behind. The role he perfected—the last man—was central to high art in an age of advancing technology. From this point forward the story of high art would always be almost over; in concert halls and recital rooms, in libraries and salons, the end would be ever nigh.

The musicians who had entered Bach into the record were passing on like the 78-rpm discs to which their efforts had been applied. Wanda Landowska had died in Connecticut in 1959, with her two sets of the *Well-Tempered Clavier* in wide circulation, along with a commentary, which she had described as "simply the story of my experiences as a worker in music, a worker who jots down her impressions, prelude after prelude, fugue after fugue." Edwin Fischer had died in London the following year, his recordings already the casualties not only of the late-Romantic flourishes in his playing but of their brittle sound.

Dame Myra Hess died in London in 1965. After suffering a stroke, she went into the studio once more, and tried to record a Haydn sonata, but she could not play it through; the recording, a niece lamented, was "spliced together and patched up like a jigsaw puzzle."

Pablo Casals had become an honorary citizen of the world. His vow quietly set aside, he traveled widely: to London, where his oratorio *El Pessebre* was performed at the Royal Festival Hall; to Jerusalem and Tel Aviv, where he anointed a teenage violinist, Pinchas Zukerman, as the next humanist virtuoso; to Budapest for a staging of the *Oratorio*. When he was living in Prades the world had come to him: now he ventured forth into the world for residencies at San Juan, Prades, and Marlboro. Marta was making plans for his ninetieth birthday in 1966. Meanwhile, he lived a day at a time. Each morning he played two Bach preludes and fugues on the piano, then did cello exercises: "I practice as if I am going to live a thousand years."

Leopold Stokowski did likewise. "Work until you die because if you stop working, you are already dead," he said, and he seemed bent on guest-conducting as many orchestras as possible. He led the Boston Symphony Orchestra, which he had admired for half a century. He led the BBC Orchestra in London, with Charlie Chaplin in attendance. On a trip to Asia with his sons, he led the Japan Philharmonic in Bach and the Honolulu Symphony in "The Stars and Stripes Forever," joined by four hundred high-school musicians. He led his own American Symphony Orchestra in a world premiere, at Carnegie Hall, of Charles Ives's Fourth Symphony, which had not been played in public since Ives composed it fifty years earlier.

Glenn Gould was there, and he wrote a review of the premiere for *High Fidelity* and its partner magazine, *Musical America*. No Ivesian, Gould was a devotee of Stokowski. The premiere, he allowed, was "an extraordinarily moving experience, but I am not sure that it is appropriate to describe it as, in the ordinary sense, a musical experience." It was a mental exercise, a "proof of invention, not of greatness." Yet it showed Stoki's greatness. "Leopold Stokowski's performance was a marvel of identification with the score," Gould wrote, and went on: "He is surely made for such music, or it for him, as the case may be, and we can only recall again the debt which we owe to this superb artist, who has so often led us into an encounter with the great and/or problematic works of our age."

Stokowski appreciated the "brilliant, penetrating, and witty article," and he wrote a note to Gould to say so. In reply Gould asked Stokowski if he would be willing to sit for an interview for his next article for *High Fidelity*, a piece about what Gould was calling the prospects of recording.

>>12>> "The Maestro met us at the door, invited us to settle in before the fireplace, offered a drink, made a waspish comment in response to my profession of teetotalism, and shuffled off to the kitchen to attend to our orders in person," Gould recalled. The scene was Stokowski's apartment on Fifth Avenue, with a fireplace, a piano, a hi-fi rig, and a view of Central Park. With Gould was Leonard Marcus, *High Fidelity*'s editor of "special projects," such as interviews conducted by prickly recording artists.

"Special projects" was an apt description of Gould's own musical activities in late 1964 and 1965. He had given a graduation address at the conservatory in Toronto from which he himself had graduated. He had sat for a long, rangy interview with the CBC. He had made several records. These projects were different approaches to the same question: the question of the role of the artist in the age of recordings.

The graduation address was Gould at his most solitary and obscurantist. He began by rejecting the role of advice-giver on the grounds that "the separateness of our experience limits the usefulness of any practical advice that I could offer you." He then went on, in effect, to advise himself. He took as his theme invention, and "that replenishment of invention upon which creative ideas depend." As he offered the students insights about the world of music "you are about to enter"—the world he had, in some respects, just left—he refreshed his own insights so as to replenish himself for a world of music not defined by live performance.

Music, he proposed, is a system "hewn from negation" and set against "the voice of negation which surrounds it"; and musical invention is "a cautious dipping into the negation that lies outside system from a position firmly esconsced in system." He then developed the point in terms that fit his circumstances uncannily. Free from the stage, emboldened by the recording studio, he faced the challenge of limitless possibility. Suddenly he was free to do anything, and this led him to consider how little his training and experience had prepared him for such a challenge. It forced him to recall (as he told the students) "that the systems by which we organize our thinking, and in which we attempt to pass on that thinking to the generations that follow, represent what you might think of as a foreground of activity—of positive, convinced, self-reliant action—and that this foreground can have validity only insofar as it attempts to impose credibility on that vast background acreage of human possibility that has not yet been organized."

Against this background, he sought the replenishment of invention in the "no-man's-land" between system and negation, between positive thinking and

negative thinking. As if addressing himself, he went on: "You must try to discover how high your tolerance is for the questions you ask of yourself," and to
recognize that some creative exploration "extends beyond the point of tolerance and paralyzes the imagination by confronting it with too much possibility, too much speculative opportunity.

"To keep the practical issues of systematized thought and the speculative
opportunities of creative instinct in balance will be the most difficult and most
important undertaking of your lives in music," he concluded; and, lest there be
any doubt that the "speculative opportunities" he had in mind involved technology, he told the story of the day in his childhood when he played Mozart
against the roar of a vacuum cleaner.

He created a radio documentary about "the recording industry and its effect upon the lives of modern man." His friend and neighbor John Roberts
had taken a job as a producer with the CBC. Aware of Gould's love of the
microphone, Roberts invited him to make programs for the company, and created a workspace for him at CBC headquarters, putting a desk and telephone
in an unused corner and setting up baffles for walls—something like a studio
within a studio.

For his first program, Gould worked up his ideas about performance,
recording, brass bands, movie music, and background music, or Muzak. He
interviewed producers, scholars, and other musicians. He inserted passages from
his favorite records. He called it a "Dialogue on the Prospects of Recordings"—
"one hour and twenty-five minutes of fervent conviction and furious debate
provoked, written, and narrated by Glenn Gould—taped, spliced, tweetered
and woofered" by the production team. A photograph shows him in a CBC
studio: sleepless, haggard, rumpled, balding, he looks like a cousin of Lee
Harvey Oswald, but there, surrounded by reel-to-reel tape decks and turntables, he is in his natural environment, with his feet up on the mixing
board.

The program led off with Beethoven's Eighth Symphony in a tinny
recording—the one by Felix Weingartner, which had caught Gould's ear when
he was a teenager. "Recordings do that: they insinuate themselves into our
judgments, and into our lives," he declared. "They are capable of giving the
people who make them . . . an awesome power over the people who listen to
them . . . and this is an awesome power that was simply not available to any
earlier generation. It's a power uniquely responsive to the technology of our
day." Through recordings, he went on, music surrounds us, it sells us things, it
distracts and compliments—it provides "an emotional backdrop against which

we can play out our lives." Music, once separate from ordinary experience and so religious in nature, was now pervasive through recordings, and "as our dependence upon it has increased, our reverence for it has declined." The insight was straight out of Walter Benjamin's essay on the work of art in the age of mechanical reproduction; but Gould, taking the other side, presented the spread of mechanical reproduction as a good thing, a humanizing development. Where our ancestors, he proposed, liked recordings to have an "aural halo" of reverberation, present-day listeners valued "clarity, immediacy, an almost tactile proximity." Mechanical reproduction was a means of intimacy.

As an example he played his own recording of Bach's first partita. "It was recorded in a large studio which is, as a matter of fact, a converted church . . . ," he explained. "The microphone was placed very close to the instrument . . . every effort was made with that recording to cultivate an acoustic of extreme intimacy, so that the frame of sound which would accompany the piano onto disk would very much resemble the acoustic in which it would most likely be replayed by the person who would buy the recording: the acoustic of the living room."

Now here he was in Leopold Stokowski's living room in search of wisdom about recordings. In Stoki he sought an elder and a conversation partner, whose ideas could be set in counterpoint to his own.

Looking back, he deprecated himself, the visit, and the project with a knight-errant's comic humility. It was "my first 'professional' contact with the Maestro." He didn't know how to conduct an interview. He had brought handwritten notes, but he thought it might not be right to work from them. Instead he did the interview freestyle, asking questions "appropriate for a deejay or an A&R man." Did recordings led by the composer make those by others obsolete? (No.) Did Stoki shape the sound of the orchestra to fit the recording? (Yes.) What did he think of Muzak? (He thought it "deadened" our response to music.)

Stoki's answers (as Gould told it in the pages of *High Fidelity*) were not memorable, but his way of answering a question was. A Stoki reply was like a Stokowski transcription, sculpted to an expressive impersonality. Near the end of each answer, Stoki—a conductor even in his living room—signaled that he would soon stop talking by signalling a cutoff with his right hand. "I found this mannerism exceedingly unnerving . . ." Gould recalled. "As a consequence, after about thirty minutes of ill-conceived questions, truncated answers, and disconcerting cutoffs, I gave my own signal . . ."

Their interview was over. Their encounter was not. At the door, Stokowski asked: "May I ask why we have never been asked to make records together?" On the spot Gould proposed that they record Beethoven's *Emperor* concerto; on the spot Stokowski said yes, as long as he could use his own orchestra. It was a surprise: the last soloist Stoki had accompanied with orchestra was Sergei Rachmaninov sixty years earlier.

The session was held in March 1966, and Gould later described it in detail, from the struggle to achieve a decent sound to the surprise visit from Barbra Streisand, who was working in the studio next door and popped in to declare herself a fan: Gould, though a fan of hers, didn't recognize her, and Stokowski drummed his fingers at the interruption. Gould captured the mechanical efficiency that Stokowski—in his sixth decade of making recordings—brought to the session. Gould had already made recordings of Beethoven's other concerti, and he was used to having to explain his preference for slow tempi to the conductor. But Stokowski accepted his tempi immediately and without objection, and let him air-conduct with one hand from the piano while he, Stoki, conducted from the podium.

"'Okay so far?' I ventured.

"'Please proceed,' Stokowski replied.

"'There's one thing about this tempo,' I added, getting carried away. 'It makes all these themes work within the same perspective.'

"'Yes, that is true,' the Maestro conceded. 'But do you not think that there are a few moments which should perhaps go a little faster and a few which might go a little slower?'"

Gould commented on the oddness of his interpretation, but the odd thing, for listeners steeped in their Bach recordings, is that Gould and Stokowski made the record at all, so far is its theatricality from the awesome self-sufficiency of their Bach recordings. It leaves you asking, "Is is really them?"

In the months after the interview with Stokowski, Gould made a record of Schoenberg pieces, recorded twenty-four Strauss songs with Elisabeth Schwarzkopf, and recorded four Beethoven sonatas, a Mozart sonata, and the *Fantasy in D* of the Canadian composer Oskar Morawetz. He also took part in half a dozen CBC programs, including a series of conversations about his own work and *Duo*, a joint appearance with Yehudi Menuhin. Watching *Duo*—the slow movement of Bach's fourth sonata for violin and harpsichord— you can see the qualities in Gould the performer that put people off: while Menuhin, devotee of the higher health, stands serenely upright, Gould moves his lips wordlessly and corkscrews his upper body over the battered folding chair, going around and around like an LP on a turntable. For all that, his hands are precisely disciplined; they seem to operate independent of the rest of him. After the broadcast, Gould wrote an essay celebrating Menuhin as his opposite: as a musician who seemed to thrive on public life, whether performing Bach chamber music with "an ungainsayable conviction" or founding a soup kitchen in London—as "one of those rare individuals who could in time succeed to that unique place in the affections of mankind left vacant by the death of Albert Schweitzer."

Gould's major work that year was the essay he had described to Stokowski. At age thirty-three, released from the rituals of live performance but still attuned to them, Gould was an instrument perfectly calibrated to register the changes that new technology was bringing to music and society. From the small rooms where he lived his life—apartment, cottage, makeshift office, recording studio—Gould surveyed "The Prospects of Recording," envisioning a future in which his own approach to music-making would be perfectly ordinary.

Gould's starting point is his notion that concerts will be extinct in the next century. He dismisses resistance to this as evidence of "an endearing, if sometimes frustrating, human characteristic—a reluctance to accept the consequences of a new technology." Then he moves on. Structurally, the essay is not terminal but radial, a set of insights arrayed around the theme of "music and its recorded future." The insights are bipartite, paradoxical, exaggerated to the point of provocation; though he name-checks McLuhan and Malraux, they are eccentrically his own. Records made in concert-friendly Europe, he says, are more reverberant than those made in North America, where the public "to a considerable extent has discovered music through records" and "split-level suburbia" is equipped with "twelve-tone doorbells, nursery intercom, and steam room stereo." The record business is at once "preservative and translative," enshrining the great works of the past but doing away with the notion of music as a thing made at a particular time and place. The recording process allows the contemporary composer to leave behind an exact account of how he wanted a work to sound, and lets the performer approach the music the way a composer does: "It permits him to encounter a particular piece of music and to analyze it and dissect it in a most thorough way, to make it a vital part of his life for a relatively brief period, and then to pass on to some other challenge and to the satisfaction of some other curiosity." Recordings will bring about nothing less than "a new perspective on the history of music," moving music off the grid of the Western canon, away from the personalities of the musicians, and toward a musical equivalent of Malraux's imaginary museum—an "editorial mix" characterized by "its unselfconscious juxtaposition of a miscellany of idioms." This new perspective will at once open up the past and shape the musical future. The musicologist, who can document past performance practices, will become a key figure alongside the musician. And the musician will play a new role—that of the "technician-cum-performer" whose mastery of the craft of recording will replace the "devotion of the itinerant virtuoso," and whose devotion is to "that elusive time-transcending objective which is always within the realization of recorded music."

What, exactly, was a "technician-cum-performer"? The example in the essay is Gould himself, a pianist executing a "tape splice." "A year or so ago, while recording the concluding fugues from volume 1 of *The Well-Tempered Clavier,* I arrived at one of Bach's celebrated contrapuntal obstacle courses, the fugue in A minor," he recalled. "This is a structure even more difficult to realize on the piano than are most of Bach's fugues, because it consists of four intense voices that determinedly occupy a register in the center octaves of the keyboard— the area of the instrument in which a truly independent voice leading is most difficult to establish." He recorded eight takes, found two satisfactory but both "monotonous." By splicing together the two takes in an "editing cubicle," he joined the "Teutonic severity" of take 6 and the "unwarranted jubilation of take 8"—and produced "a performance of this particular fugue far superior to anything that we could at the time have done in the studio."

It was apt that he brought Bach into the argument. Not only was Bach the composer whose music he had first subjected to his studio process in 1955; Bach in his account was also the composer who gained the most from the prospects of recording. Because records were produced "for an audience which does most of its listening at home," Gould explained, "it is not surprising that the creation of a recording archive has emphasized those areas which historically relate to a *Hausmusik* tradition and has been responsible for the triumphant restoration of Baroque forms since World War II. This repertoire—with its contrapuntal extravaganzas, its antiphonal balances, its espousal of instruments that chuff and wheeze and speak directly to a microphone—was made for stereo. That prodigious catalogue of cantatas and concerto grossos, fugues and partitas, has endowed the neobaroque enthusiasm of our day with a hard core of musical experience."

Recorded music, he was saying, had become the new house music. The new house music had called forth a figure he called the New Listener, a technician-cum-enthusiast who participated in the music by twiddling the dials of the home stereo, adjusting the mix. And this new house music favored the old *Hausmusik,* the music of Bach in particular.

As if to prove the point, he made a new Bach recording at 30th Street Studio, some preludes and fugues from book 2 of the *Well-Tempered Clavier*— singing himself back home with a little *Hausmusik.*

>>13>>   The musicians met on Friday evenings from eight to ten at Zim-
mermann's coffeehouse. It was a place just off the market square, with an
entrance under an awning over the sidewalk and an alley running alongside
it. Zimmermann kept a collection of instruments on site: strings, horns, a
harpsichord. The patrons would order coffee or hot chocolate and sit at tables,
ready for music, food and drink, and conversation all at once. The players,
working musicians from around the city, would tune their instruments, take
their places, and sight-read the music the director put before them, in most
cases playing it for the first and last time.

     Zimmermann's coffeehouse, in the Catherinenstrasse, Leipzig, is the most
attractive setting in Bach's life story. It was a coffeehouse, akin to those of our
day, where music was made and heard for the simple pleasure of it. It was a
musician's place, run to suit Zimmermann, a musician himself. It was a mov-
able feast: in the warmer months, the music program was relocated to a coffee
garden he operated. There, the musicians played outdoors on Wednesdays
from four to six, and twice a week when Leipzig was hosting a trade fair; during a fair the place filled up with businessmen who, away from their homes
and their wives, with money in their pockets, came to be entertained before
going to rented rooms for the night.

     The very familiarity of the place obscures how original it was. Martin
Geck, who writes with authority about the everyday circumstances of Bach's
music, makes a case for the scene at Zimmermann's as "a wonderful early
example of cultivation of music by the middle class, with connoisseurs and
dilettantes equally represented among both performers and audience, and
both groups talking about music in a more relaxed atmosphere than the later
'symphonic concerts,' with their strict rituals, would allow." The music made
there—freshly written and run through by professional musicians while the
public listened in—was a new kind of house music.

     Bach played a key role at Zimmermann's after becoming the director of
the Collegium Musicum. It was a working group founded by Telemann early
in the century. Bach took over the directorship in 1729 and renamed it the
"Bachische" Collegium Musicum, while staying on as music director for the
churches of St. Thomas and St. Nicholas. He had plenty of reasons to take on
another role. He was frustrated by the limits of the student music-making in
the churches and the lack of respect the headmaster showed him. He hoped to
woo crack city players from the collegium to round out his church ensembles,
and sought access to Zimmermann's instruments for his own use. He yearned
to compose instrumental music as well as cantatas and Passions. He was a

proud father, and he wanted to make music in public with his eldest sons—Wilhelm Friedemann and Carl Philipp Emanuel—before they left the city to further their own careers.

All these were important, but so was the chance to make something new. His work with the churches had enabled Bach to put his stamp on the Passion narrative. Now the working group at Zimmermann's coffeehouse gave him an opportunity to shape the new house music. With the Collegium Musicum, Bach introduced much of the instrumental music he is best known for today: the concertos for one and two violins, the harpsichord concertos, the orchestral suites, the flute sonatas. Hearing these pieces, you can see the musicians at the coffeehouse or the garden: two violinists fiddling neck and neck in the double concerto, two brothers rattling away on the house harpsichords with their father joining in on a third. It is sportive stuff, music of brotherly rivalry, as Bach, who was always outdoing himself with his music, invited the musicians to outdo one another.

The coffeehouse also gave Bach a venue from which to press his case for the title of chief composer to the elector of Saxony, the ruling nobleman of the region. This was Friedrich Augustus I, a.k.a. Augustus the Strong, who was the king of Catholic Poland as well as elector of Lutheran Saxony. Augustus's court, at Dresden, a day's journey from Leipzig, was rich in music of all kinds: sacred works, chamber music, oratorios, opera. Bach was known there: an organ recital he gave in Dresden prompted a poet to compare him with Orpheus, who, "whene'er he plays, does each and all astound."

When Augustus died in February 1733 the region went quiet for a six-month period of mourning. In June the new elector, Augustus's son, lifted the silence. Music-making could begin again. A notice went out: "Tomorrow, Wednesday, June 17, the beginning will be made by Bach's Collegium Musicum at Zimmermann's Garden on the Grimmische Steinweg, at 4 o'clock in the afternoon, with a fine concert. It will be maintained week by week, with a new harpsichord, such as had not been heard here before, and lovers of music as well as virtuosos are expected to be present." The new instrument that broke the silence was probably a fortepiano.

Six weeks later Bach sent Augustus a gift: a beautifully inked composition, together with a cover letter at once obsequious and confiding. "For some years and up to the present moment," Bach told him, "I have had the *Directorium* of the two principal churches in Leipzig, but have innocently had to suffer one injury or another, and on occasion also a diminution of the fees accruing to me in this office; but these injuries would disappear altogether if

Your Royal Highness would grant me the favor of conferring upon me a title of Your Highness's Court Capelle . . ."

The composition he sent—"the present small work of that science which I have achieved in *musique*"—consisted of two parts of a Mass. Bach had used the mourning period to push into a new area with a magnificent work, one that, like a three-part invention, combined his piety, his genius for Christian patterning, and his wish to suit the prerogatives of the new court. It was the Kyrie and Gloria of the Mass in B Minor.

The new elector, Friedrich Augustus II, was married to a Hapsburg, Maria Josepha. She was a lover of music, a collector of music manuscripts, and a Roman Catholic. This made Augustus a Lutheran with a Catholic wife and, in his role as the king of Poland, a Catholic court.

Bach honored this arrangement with the Mass in B Minor. The Kyrie and the Gloria were the two parts of the Catholic Mass that had been retained in the Lutheran service, the two parts where the Roman church and the evangelical Lutheran church were still joined. The Mass, then, was a figure for Augustus's mixed marriage to Maria Josepha, and for the mixed character of his rule of Catholic and Lutheran territories at once. This act of religious joinery is reinforced through the structure of the work, a pair of pieces (Kyrie and Gloria) that feature pairs (paired solos, paired choruses) through which all the different groups of voices and instruments are introduced. Extending the pattern, Bach paired the emerging Mass in B Minor with his other Latin Mass setting, the Magnificat, which he had revised intermittently since 1723.

It was enough, you would think—but it wasn't enough for Bach. Christoph Wolff speculates that Bach wrote the Kyrie and Gloria to be sung during Augustus's first visit to Leipzig, as a sudden flare-up of music during the period of mourning. On April 20, 1733, the people of Leipzig (several thousand of them) lined a main street to witness the elector's arrival in the city. The next day, Wolff reports, "His Royal Highness was carried in a sedan chair from the church to the bourse" for a service that, he proposes, featured Bach's Kyrie and Gloria. Three months later (says Wolff) the Mass, now substantially complete, was sung at the Sophienkirche in Dresden, with Anna Magdalena Bach and Bach's sons Wilhelm Friedemann and Carl Philipp Emanuel as members of the ensemble, for Wilhelm had just gained a position as the organist at the Sophienkirche.

As the *Inventions* had been Bach's gift to Wilhelm Friedemann, so the Mass was a gift to the elector of Saxony. It was the first of many. Already Bach had written music for four civic occasions involving Augustus; now he wrote a dozen more, for birthdays, name days, election days, coronation days, and other occasions "extraordinaire."

A report tells of the royal couple's visit to Leipzig in October 1734. Bach had written a cantata for Friedrich Augustus's birthday, which would fall two days later. Now, for fifty thalers (a month's income) he freshened up an earlier cantata for a procession in honor of the anniversary of Friedrich Augustus's election. "At seven in the evening a cannon was fired as a signal, and then the whole town was illuminated," so brightly that lit up the towers of the Thomaskirche and the Nikolaikirche could be seen for miles. At nine, Bach and the players of the Collegium Musicum took their instruments out into the torchlit streets, and a vast crowd moved through the city to the sound of music. "Six hundred students carried wax tapers, and four Counts acted as marshals in presenting the music. The procession made its way up to the king's residence. When the musicians had reached the *Wage* [weigh house], the trumpets and drums went up on it, while others took their place in another choir at the Rathhaus." The elector stood at a window and heard his praises sung to music as sublimely joyful as ever honored any ruler.

Bach's congratulatory cantatas, as they are called, suggest a ridiculous excess of talent: here is music for the Saxon nobility worthy of a heavenly choir. But they are more than court and spark, for he probably wrote them with a double purpose in mind. He refashioned the processional music heard in the street that night—trilling trumpets, pummeled drums—as the hosannah from the Mass in B Minor. The music that had welcomed the elector would welcome the King of Kings; as the people had gone in procession to the king's house, so would they line the streets of a liturgical Jerusalem with palms in their hands.

This process of adaptation—a transcription from a worldly context to a sacred one—is called parody, and it was Bach's connection between church and coffeehouse in those years. The Christmas oratorio was followed by an Easter oratorio, then an oratorio for Ascension Day, each built from parodies of certain parts of "secular" cantatas. With great musical thrift—with an unrivaled grasp of how the things of the world can be consecrated by the religious artist—Bach made his music serve two masters. In the contest between church and world he took both sides.

The urge to sanctify the secular was more than pious. It was the urge of an artist in midlife. While a visit from an elector of Saxony was a one-time affair, Christmas, Easter, and Ascension Day would be celebrated every year. As Bach in his first years in Leipzig had used the demands of the liturgical calendar to call forth a vast new body of work, now he used it as a form to preserve music he had already written. By using parody to transform secular cantatas into liturgical works, Bach was making music for listeners of the future.

The composing room at the Thomasschule was his redoubt, a book-lined place in counterpoint to the performance space of Zimmermann's coffeehouse. There Bach produced the inked-in Kyrie and Gloria for the new elector of Saxony. He thoroughly revised the *St. Matthew Passion*—splitting the vocal sections emphatically into two choruses that could sing from two sides of the church—and prepared the sumptuously red-inked copy of the text. And he arranged some of his keyboard works into sets for publication as the *Clavier-Übung* ("keyboard practice"). The first part, published already, consisted of the six partitas. Part two, published in 1735, was two ensemble works scored for solo harpsichord, one an Italian concerto and the other a suite or overture in the French style.

In 1736 Augustus granted Bach the title he sought: *Hofcompositeur*, or Court Composer. In recognition of this honor, Bach went to Dresden to play for him. The master organ builder Gottfried Silbermann, whose instruments were in use all over Saxony, had just finished an organ for the Frauenkirche, and at 2:00 p.m. on Saturday, December 1, 1736, Bach gave a recital on it. Among other dignitaries, Count Hermann Carl von Keyserlingk—ambassador from Russia and president of the Academy of Sciences in St. Petersburg—was in the audience, and he acted as a signatory to the certificate that made Bach's new title official.

Bach resigned the directorship of the Collegium Musicum in Leipzig and bore down on keyboard music. He wrote preludes and fugues for a second book of the *Well-Tempered Clavier*. He composed the third part of the *Clavier-Übung*: "consisting of various preludes on the catechism and other hymns, for the organ." And he considered his options for part four, which would be a work unlike any he had written before.

He had spotted a familiar bass figure in a sheet-music collection of Handel's works. It was a figure common to Baroque music of all kinds. Seeing it, hearing it, Bach heard the stuff of further variety—harmonies, inversions, counterpoint and the like. He would move the figure out of the bass and make it a melody, and would foreground it in an *aria with diverse variations*. Having missed the chance to meet Handel in 1729, Bach would collaborate with him through the common property of melody.

>>14>> "Both Sides Now" blended folk and the Baroque, marrying the music of the college-town coffeehouse to the music of Bach.

Judy Collins had found a calling as an interpreter of songs by denizens of the folk-music scenes in Greenwich Village, Harvard Square, the Sunset Strip, and Montreal, singing their rough-hewn songs in her unadorned voice over folkish arrangements executed by New York session musicians. "Both Sides Now" was different. The song was by Joni Mitchell, who in her early twenties had followed the path of Bob Dylan from the north country to New York to descant her own earnestly unusual material; the string arrangement was by Joshua Rifkin, a recent graduate of Juilliard and a pianist and harpsichordist specializing in the music of the Baroque; the recording session, for Elektra, was held at 30th Street Studio. The harpsichord enters first, with Rifkin playing bright major-chord arpeggios (just like the twelve-string-electric arpeggios Roger McGuinn was playing with the Byrds) over a long pedal point sustained on an electric organ. Bass and drums come in behind the vocal, and musical styles merge—Baroque in the left ear and folk-pop in the right, joined together by Collins's voice, the voice of a singer who could just as well have appeared on stage with a lute as with a flattop guitar.

Collins's records were released by a small New York record company that was really two companies in one: Elektra, for folk and pop, and Nonesuch, for classical music. Rifkin was a new employee on the Nonesuch side when the head of Elektra, Jac Holzman, hit on the idea of a Beatles-meets-Baroque novelty record and called on him to put it together—and to get it done in a month so that the record could go on sale for Christmas 1965. "I embarked on a schedule of writing ten to eighteen hours a day," Rifkin recalled, with a Broadway copy agency duplicating parts as soon as he wrote them. "One of the things I learned from this was a kind of hands-on sense of what it was like for Bach, Handel, or people like that to turn out music at the incredible pace at which they worked . . ."

The novelty treatment of Bach was already something other than novel. An eight-voice French ensemble—the Swingle Singers—had gotten noticed since 1963 with ingenious scat versions of Bach instrumental pieces: easy listening for the same people who bought Bach LPs. In April 1965 Peter Schickele, a young Juilliard graduate posing as a Baroque music scholar, presided at Town Hall over the first full recital devoted to the works of P.D.Q. Bach—"the last, and certainly the least," of J. S. Bach's musical offspring. Vanguard released a live LP of the recital later in the year. P.D.Q.'s unacknowledged musical influence was the pun-filled music used under cartoons; Schickele's banter was derived from the Smothers Brothers and Woody Allen ("Cantata for Iphegenia in Brooklyn," "Concerto for Horn and Hardart"). P.D.Q. Bach was an inside joke strong enough to sustain a career—in fact, two careers, those of the composer and his mock-exegete.

The Baroque Beatles Book followed Schickele's approach closely, from the liner notes, written in the manner of Bach's importuning letters, to the puns and in-jokes (the "Epstein Variations," named for the Beatles' manager, or the "Cantata for the Third Sunday After the [concert at] Shea Stadium"). The sleeve showed a bewigged Bach in eighteenth-century dress save for a T-shirt that read I LOVE BEATLES. But the music itself was played straight, not for laughs. It sounded less like Bach than like the theme for an English drawing-room drama played twelve times in a row, and its regularity inadvertently highlighted Bach's (and the Beatles') variety. The record was a hit: it went into the pop Top 100, and Holzman tapped Rifkin to work with Judy Collins on *In My Life*, which featured her neomedieval take on the Lennon-McCartney song, and then *Wildflowers*.

From those first arpeggiated flourishes of the harpsichord, "Both Sides Now" nailed the points in common between the folk revival that had taken shape in the coffeehouses and the emerging Baroque revival: an emphasis on simplicity, a concern for origins, a sense of the present age as inferior to a past age that was at once purer and more glorious. The record made clear that from then on most serious musicians would see and hear from both sides—classical music and popular music—whether they wanted to or not.

The Beatles themselves got back to Bach more than once after *Rubber Soul*. One night in January 1967 Paul McCartney found himself at home in London watching a BBC telecast of the English Chamber Orchestra. When the orchestra played Bach's second Brandenburg concerto, with its percolating opening line played on the small, bright horn called the piccolo trumpet, McCartney heard how the sound could fit into a song that he had written. George Martin placed a call, and the orchestra's trumpeter, Pete Mason, came to Abbey Road. He was surprised to meet the Beatles freshly mustached and dressed in "candy-striped trousers and loud ties," and he was surprised that there was no written part. "Paul sang some notes and George Martin sat at the piano writing them down for me. This took some time to do." The rest was easy: in two takes Mason put down the hop-skip-and-a-jump solo and fanfar-ing obbligatos—a perky high-street variation on the Bach trumpet part Paul had heard on the telly at home.

That June the Beatles took part in a satellite TV broadcast, a rare thing at the time. The number they had put together, "All You Need Is Love," called for the four of them, in full pop-psychedelic regalia, to sing the forward-and-backward chorus live over two string quartets, a brass section, McCartney's thumping bass, and a reel-to-reel tape machine (shown in the foreground), which played a musique-concrète backing track that blended "Greensleeves," "In the Mood," and a Brandenburg concerto. A few months later, McCartney wrote a fanciful ballad around a Bach-like pavanne he had worked up for acoustic guitar: "Blackbird," with the name of the composer echoed with every line about a blackbird singing in the dead of night.

From *Sgt. Pepper* onward pop music would always be open to the classical touch. The week that album was released the number-one single in Great Britain was Procol Harum's "A Whiter Shade of Pale," whose languid organ opening drew on Bach unmistakably. ("It does a bar or two of Bach's 'Air on a G String' before it veers off," Gary Brooker, who wrote it, recalled. "That spark was all it took. I wasn't consciously combining Rock with Classical, it's just that Bach's music was in me.") Iggy and the Stooges, out of Detroit, would take the stage to the sound of a Brandenburg concerto blasting through the PA system, then plug in their guitars and pound out brutal, lusty rock. Jimmy Page from the Yardbirds would complicate the blues with his new group, Led Zeppelin, bringing in modal English folk picking, Indian ragas, electronic effects, and, in the long, stretchy stage version of "Heartbreaker," a thickly distorted bit of the bourée from Bach's lute suite in E minor. The Pentangle would play a Bach sarabande arranged for handbells and amplified guitar, making it the missing link between English folk traditions, Tudor church music, and folk rock. The Move updated their "operetta" "Cherry Blossom Clinic" by appending a coda featuring an amphetamine-powered race through "Jesu, Joy of Man's Desiring" and other Bach melodies on spiky electric twelve string guitar.

Then came *Switched-on Bach*. As a student at Cornell, Robert Moog made pocket money as a maker of the theremin, which he assembled and sold one at a time. After graduating, he developed his own instruments: the Clavivox, the Electronium, and then, in 1963, the "synthesizer" he gave his own name. The Moog was a console the size of a refrigerator, with knobs, dials, meters, and patch cords, all connected by cables to a set of speakers and to a keyboard in traditional black and white. When pressed, each key, instead of activating a hammer, sent an electronic signal to the console, which processed it—"synthesized" it—so as to produce a particular sound.

The Moog was monophonic: it could make only one sound, from one key, at a time. Chords were impossible. So was harmony. So was counterpoint. To play Bach on the Moog, then, would be to transcend the nature of the instrument, to make it something other than it was.

That is what Walter Carlos did. Carlos was a Rhode Islander who had studied electronic music at Columbia University and had made two records on an early version of Moog's synthesizer. His versions of Bach were a personal project, recorded on an Ampex tape deck customized to work with the Moog. He sent the recordings, along with a version of Paul Anderson's schlock classic "The Waltzing Cat," to Paul Myers of Columbia Masterworks in 1968—around the same time that he began to live "as a woman" in anticipation of a sex change. "Tell me what you think," Myers said to Peter Mumves, who, as the Masterworks director of marketing, was developing a line of "crossover" LPs with sleeve art by Milton Glaser. Mumves loved the recordings and thought they could sell well, as long as the LP was devoted exclusively to Bach. "For a title I suggested *Turned-on Bach*," Mumves recalled. "Somebody looked over and said, 'No, too drug related' because it was turned on, tuned out, drop out, turned off. So Bill King said, 'What about *Switched-on Bach*?' and I said, 'Perfect.'" Mumves had the counterculture audience in mind: "I said, 'Look what's going on! The synthesizer is a popular instrument in rock bands. This is an audience that doesn't know diddlysquat about Bach so we'll do Bach on the synthesizer and we'll get 'em by the balls!'"

Mumves's sales pitch was inside out. The synthesizer was not yet a popular instrument in rock bands. It was hardly in use at all in rock music. *Switched-on Bach*, as it turned out, would be a switch on the typical crossover album. It would not use the popularity of the synthesizer to advance the cause of Bach. It would use the popularity of Bach to advance the cause of the synthesizer, a pioneering new technology.

Masterworks launched *Switched-on Bach* with a party in New York also devoted to the LP of *In C*. "There was a nice big bowl of joints on top of the mixing console, and Terry Riley was there in his white Jesus suit, up on a pedestal, playing live on a Farfisa organ against a backup of tape delays," said Robert Moog, who demonstrated the Moog synthesizer.

Myers sent the two LPs to his prize artist, Glenn Gould, who commented insightfully on both of them. *In C* Gould dismissed as a trendy, jokey, "participatory" work, right in line with the mood of the sixties—but took as evidence that "a great deal of the liveliest music today, when not in fact at sea, is, more or less, in C." *Switched-on Bach* he praised unreservedly in a piece for the Canadian magazine *Saturday Night*. He began by explaining that he despised anthologies and thought the genre exhausted. "It's a bit surprising, then," he declared, "that the record of the year (no, let's go all the way—the decade!) is an unembarrassed compote of Bach's greatest hits"—"Air on the G String,"

"Sleepers, Wake," "Jesu, Joy of Man's Desiring," F-major and B-flat-major *Two-Part Inventions*, and so on: "an assemblage that not even the *Reader's Digest* . . . could have topped." And it was a bit surprising that the performer was not a crack recitalist but "a young American physicist and audio engineer named Walter Carlos, who has no recording contract, whose most esoteric musical endeavor heretofore was the supervision of sound track material for a Schaefer beer commercial on TV, and who, over a period of many months, produced, performed, and, with the aid of a friend and musicologist, Benjamin Folkman, conceived the extraordinary revelations afforded by this disk in his living room."

Walter Carlos was the type of musician Gould had envisioned in "The Prospects of Recording": more a technician than a performer, one whose site was the recording studio and whose chosen instrument was emphatically a piece of technology.

Switched-on Bach was itself in line with Gould's sonic ideals. Because the individual lines of notes had been recorded one at a time, the space between them is absolute, the counterpoint distinct and emphatic. This makes the music "inhuman" or "otherworldly," but it achieves the structural exactitude Gould strived for. In the same way, the Moog keyboard's lack of touch response produced an uninflected, vibrato-free stream of notes, much as Gould sought to do with his high-strung, screw-tightened pianos. And yet Carlos—like Gould—managed to infuse the music with character even so. The warmth of the synthesizer tones—the plump bass notes in the "Air on the G String," the clear, lean high notes, like the sound of dolphins singing—makes the music personal, not mechanical.

Robert Moog complained that Masterworks underestimated *Switched-on Bach*, but the label's marketing people clearly did something right. In the next six months, after Carlos played the Moog on the *Today Show*, the record sold several hundred thousand copies (many times the sales of Gould's *Goldberg Variations*); it was recognized as a symbol of the moment and a crossover album extraordinaire. If proof were needed that a Bach revival had come about, and that Bach's music was strong enough to become wildly popular without being violated, the proof was there on the half a million record players—woody flip-down consoles, brass-buckled portables, rubberized radio-station platter-players, crushed-felt turntables with diamond-tipped tonearms—all burbling early electronic Bach.

The record was symbolic in a deeper sense. The method of its making was akin to the method of the Bach revival. In it single lines were brought together and made into a complex whole through technology. In it the inventive powers of Bach were the spur to musical and technical invention, which brought out qualities in the music that were there all along. In it some music made in small rooms went out into the world and then was brought back home by technology, there to roost in the small rooms—living room, bedroom, dorm room, finished basement—that were the sites of the modern person's imaginative life. In it the promise of technical transcendence lurking just below the surface in the age of recordings was brought to light and made a goal to be yearned for openly, the goal to which the person in the age of recordings aspired.

>>15>> Pier Paolo Pasolini had brought out *Il vangelo secondo Matteo* (*The Gospel According to Matthew*), filmed in Calabria in a stark, rustic, unguarded style—a style made to seem all the starker through contrast with the film's sound track, centered on the controlled excess of Klemperer's *St. Matthew Passion*. Jean-Marie Straub brought out one of the most straightforwardly literal art films ever made: the ninety-minute biopic *Chronik der Anna Magdalena Bach*, built around long sequences of Bach and family making music together, wigged and costumed, in Baroquely anachronistic black and white. Walt Disney Productions released a new print of *Fantasia*, promoting the film as a piece of psychedelia with a swirly pink-and-green poster (the name BACH was squished into the upper-right-hand corner). The organ showman Virgil Fox gave an amped-up run-through of Bach called "Heavy Organ" at the Fillmore East and elsewhere, playing an electric-powered Royal V touring organ.

Meanwhile, transcendence through Bach was sought in the time-honored way. High and low, classical and popular; stage or studio, acoustic or electric, performed or recorded, plucked or struck or synthesized—these were vital distinctions, but a world war had not been fought over them. Twenty years on, World War II was being fought all over again, as Germans and Jews sought to understand what had happened back there; and German musicians and Israeli ones sought reconciliation in Bach, making his music speak to both sides.

Dietrich Fischer-Dieskau had come of age through Bach during wartime. He sang from the *St. Matthew Passion* in a bunker on Good Friday, was consoled by the piano works in a military hospital, and sang Bach arias along with Schubert lieder before returning to the front; as a prisoner of war held captive in a mansion in Pisa furnished with a collection of two thousand records, he felt called to carry German music out of the ruins: "How can we creatively continue to keep up the tradition of what has gone before our own?" His first professional engagements were the Bach Passions, and in 1947 he was invited to join the state radio choir in the American sector of occupied Berlin just as it programmed a long sequence of Bach cantatas—so that "I was allowed to take the bass part in almost all of them." A few years later he took part in the Casals festival at Prades, singing Brahms.

In July 1968 he went into a studio in Munich to record a pair of Bach cantatas with Karl Richter and the Munich Bach Orchestra and Choir. That spring, the Europe patched together after the war had started to come apart again. French students were in the streets of Paris, staging *évènements*; Italian students were in the streets of Rome, seeking places at a university suddenly too small for all of them. In Germany, artists and writers were collectively pondering the national condition that two of them—Alexander and Margarete Mitscherlich, in a groundbreaking book—called "the inability to mourn." After the "political murder" of a demonstrator by German police, students massed in West German cities, too, and the philosopher Jurgen Habermas warned them that "Left Fascism is as lethal as the right-wing kind." When a student leader was shot by a neo-Nazi, order broke down in Berlin. The government declared a state of emergency. The events, Tony Judt later observed in *Postwar*, aroused "fear that the Bonn Republic was on the verge of collapse, like Weimar just thirty-five years earlier."

Fischer-Dieskau sang "Christ lag in Todesbanden" and "Ich habe genug." The two cantatas, doleful in any circumstances, suggest a two-sided sonic analogue to the mood of the day, the 1968 mix of apocalypse and strong-backed, stiff-necked resignation.

"What a war it was, when Death and Life fought." The drama of "Christ lag in Todesbanden" begins near the end: prepare for descent, it seems to say, for the hour is getting late. The chorus is desperate, full of haste. The soloist is the very voice of steadfastness—singing of the "ardent love" of the Passover Lamb—but his own ardor is shaky. The string players wield batons and truncheons, which they pull across the necks of their instruments; they have turned their plowshares back into swords again, and are striking them against the paving stones, squeezing forth sparks. For Bach—who was the age of a student agitator when he composed it—the descent into Hell was an act of empathy as a feat of engineering, a measuring of human crimes; for Fischer-Dieskau, it is documentary work, a cultivated man's account of what he saw and heard during the war and its aftermath. Thank God we are saved, his singing suggests; otherwise we should be truly lost. His voice is oaken, the last tree standing in a city of steel and glass; the final choral "alleluia" is a sigh of relief. Finally it is over. Finally we can begin to mourn together.

After all that, "Ich habe genug" is more than enough. In Fischer-Dieskau's interpretation, it is twenty-four and a half minutes, two and a half minutes longer than "Christ lag in Todesbanden"—but it is essentially a postlude. It ends, it ends again, it ponders its end, it accepts its end, and it ends once more. The orchestra, so strenuous in the earlier cantata, is now subdued; the strongest instrument, played over a bamboo weave of strings, is the thin-reeded oboe (and so the last shall be first). As for the soloist—well, never has a heavy voice been so lightly deployed. Roland Barthes in "The Grain of the Voice" chided Fischer-Dieskau as the very type of the singer whose voice lacks "grain"— whose singing is expressive of the "tissue of cultural values" surrounding a song rather than the significances lurking in its language. His singing "never exceeds culture: here it is the soul that accompanies the song, not the body." So it is in "Ich habe genug." Here it is not Dietrich Fischer-Dieskau but a postwar German representative man who is singing. With death in the offing, glimpsed and grasped, this man would like to be pure spirit—an ethereal soprano, not a chesty bass-baritone; backed by a string ensemble, not a state-supported orchestra; representative of himself, not the coil of body and history and culture that binds him. Likewise the orchestra, which signs off in a stroke the moment the vocal is over: it would like to accompany the singer, not haul the whole German symphonic past into the studio—but no. This "Ich habe genug" is more than more than enough; as the Velvet Underground put it in a song at the time, it's just too much.

In Tallinn, Estonia, Arvo Pärt made the first prelude from the *Well-Tempered Clavier* into a protest and a profession of faith at once. Pärt, born in 1935, had come of age under communism, composing twelve-tone works. Now he overlaid the chords of Bach's first prelude with a chorus of many dozens, who sang the *Credo* from the Latin Mass ("I believe in Jesus Christ . . .") as a prelude to cacophony. The music came apart serially, in slashing orchestral strokes; then it came back together around the piano, drawn together by the prelude's familiar C major arpeggios. *Credo* was defiant of the Soviet authorities, official atheists all. It was performed only once, with the conductor withholding the text from the censors. Pärt's government commissions were withdrawn, and he went silent. But for *Credo* once was enough.

In Tel Aviv and London, Bach was binding three prodigies together. In the sleeve photograph they are young men in black suits, collared shirts, and crisp ties. Itzhak is the cute one, his curly hair and round cheeks set off by a paisley tie. Pinchas is the quiet one, courteously attentive to the camera but eager to get back to his violin. Daniel is the intellectual and the revolutionary; there is vision and judgment in his deep-set dark eyes.

They are the Israeli Beatles—musicians whose sound, clean and bold and rich with brotherly togetherness, suggested the sound of their country.

They had grown up with the state of Israel. Itzhak Perlman was born in 1945 in Tel Aviv, but trained at Juilliard in New York and made his Carnegie Hall debut in 1963. By the middle sixties, he was renowned in New York, London, and Tel Aviv. Pinchas Zukerman was born in Tel Aviv in 1948, and he, too, enrolled at Juilliard (he and Perlman were classmates of Joshua Rifkin) after Pablo Casals and Isaac Stern heard him play. Out of Tel Aviv, Daniel Barenboim was developing a dual career as pianist and conductor, and had signed a recording contract with EMI.

The violin—and the violin concerto—had come to play a signal role in Israeli culture. From its founding in 1948 Israel had taken shape as a communal society, where citizens were kin and the social model was the kibbutz, an extended family organized around shared work. In such a society, the Israeli social scientist Yaron Ezrahi has argued, the opportunities for individual expression were few. The most cherished—and the most admired—was virtuosity on the violin. The violin was the missing link between the old country of the shtetl, the shattered world of modern Europe, and the new life of the state of Israel. The violin soloist emerged as the expressive individual par excellence, at once standing apart from and collaborating with the communal society of the orchestra.

Perlman signed with EMI, where Barenboim had already made several dozen recordings. His first LP would be a collaboration with Barenboim: Bach's violin concertos, recorded with the English Chamber Orchestra. So it was that in 1971, with Isaac Stern's fiddling gracing the film of *Fiddler on the Roof*, two kids from Tel Aviv went to Abbey Road Studios to put the music of Bach to their own lofty purposes.

It is a thrilling recording, a bridge between the muscular fiddling of the 78 era and the shrinkwrapped high fidelity of the stereo LP. It was made in the vast Studio One, not the pocket-size Studio Three Pablo Casals had made the wartime approximation of a small room or the Studio Two the Beatles had made their redbrick submarine. The violin is miked close, but the orchestra is given plenty of room, and the effect is to suggest a live recording but one of unusual focus and intimacy.

The difference from Yehudi Menuhin's 78-rpm records is subtle but crucial.

The strong emotions of the playing—which there suggested the lost world of old Europe—now suggest postwar directness and daring. Barenboim later cited Hans von Bülow's remark that the *Well-Tempered Clavier* is "the Old Testament" of classical music and these Bach concertos are a return to home truths and first principles: succinct, direct, played with the swagger of young virtuosi who have mastered the canon and can do whatever they like with it.

It is not a personal record, though; it is a slice of public life. For Barenboim the orchestral is not yet a political instrument, but it is akin to a community with a political dimension. There is symbolism in two Israeli musicians fronting an orchestra native to a country long tone-deaf to Jewish culture. There is a cooperative aspect to the playing—as in the first concerto, where the orchestra pounces on the big opening A-minor chord and succumbs it, clearing space for the soloist. And there is, in the relationship of soloist to orchestra, the relationship of the individual to society: "the accompaniment can support or complement the main or subsidiary voices," as Barenboim later put it, "but it can also act in a subversive way, characterizing the music in such a way that it forces the main voices to be permanently aware of the accompanying figure." Unlike the Bach of Glenn Gould's recordings, which grew hermetic and self-enclosed as if in defiance of Gould's popularity, this Bach is social music, played by large ensembles expressly for large audiences: the promise of the stereo equipment of the period to "turn your living into a concert hall" suits its civic aspect exactly—it makes the living room into a small community.

And yet this postwar Bach is more akin to Gould's northern European anchorite than is apparent at first. Like Gould's Bach, the Bach of the German orchestras and the Jewish violinists is something like religious, an index of the postwar spirit, and in their music-making the distinction between Bach's secular music and his sacred music breaks down once and for all.

Three years later Perlman and Barenboim returned to Abbey Road to take a run at Bach again. This time Pinchas Zukerman was with them; this time they recorded the double violin concerto. "In music, different voices meet and are linked to each other, either in joint expression or in counterpoint, which means exactly that—one point, or note, working against another," Barenboim later wrote. "But in the act of challenging each other, the two voices fit together perfectly, even complementing one another." Here the violin is the instrument of fellow feeling. Perlman and Zukerman twine their lines together so that you can't tell which player is which. You imagine them dipping and swaying at the edge of the stage, and realize that the record was made at the moment of the great electric guitar duos: Duane Allman and Dickey Betts of the Allman Brothers, Allman and Eric Clapton of Derek and the Dominos, Jerry Garcia and Bob Weir of the Grateful Dead. Here is stereo, fulfilled; here, after the violent upendings of the war years, after the communal groanings of the 1960s, is a new model for how people can make music together.

>>16>> "At present, all over the world is war—so much destruction and so little, compared with that destruction, that is creative," Leopold Stokowski told Glenn Gould. "Many minds who are in what we call 'war'—those minds might have enormous creative power. But they are killed, smashed by the destruction."

Stokowski and Gould met for a second time in December 1969—when "Vietnam was at its height," Gould recalled. "The scene was once again his New York apartment, but this time, for the benefit of a camera crew, I sat next to the window that looked out toward Central Park and Stokowski sat opposite, across a desk, and with a score of one of Haydn's 'Paris' symphonies opened before him." A photograph shows them: two men in suits, fifty-four years apart in age, one white-haired and one dark-haired, but bent identically over the score from two sides of the desk.

Cameras notwithstanding, Gould was making a radio documentary, a "montage" of Stoki's voice and excerpts from his recordings. He planned to ask Stoki about the late Romantics, about fidelity to the score, and for "your recollections of early experiences in the recording studio and for your predictions about future contacts between music and technology." But his first question—about how Stoki would explain art to space aliens—called forth an eight-minute monologue in which Stoki gave an artist's history of the planet, setting "creative power" as the power capable of opposing that of war. Creativity was a source of progress, in which "there is no limit to further improvement, further reaching upward." As an example, he gave his own interest in ambient sound—"street noises. Taxicabs are blowing their horns and all kinds of sounds are going on—they have a rhythm, they have a blending of life in the streets, and it is a kind of music."

It was just the answer Gould sought, for it could be understood as an endorsement of his efforts in what he was calling "contrapuntal radio."

By the end of the sixties Gould was committed to radio the way he had been committed to recordings and then to essays. "During the years since our chat for *High Fidelity*, I had become a pro," he explained. He had interviewed "politicians, academics, theologians, artists, psychiatrists, bureaucrats," and figures from the prime minister of Canada to Marshall McLuhan to Milton Babbitt to Arnold Schoenberg's widow. He had produced a trilogy of documentaries on solitude: one on Canada's upper regions, *The Idea of North*; one on the Mennonites, throwback Christians known as "the quiet in the land"; and one on Newfoundland called *The Latecomers*.

About the documentaries, Gould's biographers tell a story of a boy wonder in midlife, who has cut out the middleman—the piano—so as to work with electronic gadgets directly. Following his cue, they show him as a radio artist, single-mindedly following a new calling. Owing to the title of the "Solitude Trilogy," they see all his radio work as a plunge into aloneness; picking up on his attempts to produce contrapuntal effects in editing, the scripts are seen as a new form of counterpoint. But this line of storytelling obscures the true nature of Gould's life and work in those years.

For one thing, Gould's documentary work was the very opposite of solitary. It was about other people and it involved other people in the production—a dozen people or more, whose schedules, talents, and expectations Gould had to keep in mind.

For another, Gould's solitude, such as it was, involved Cornelia Foss. Lukas Foss had gotten a position as conductor of the symphony orchestra in Buffalo, New York, across Lake Ontario from Toronto. Traveling alone, Cornelia visited Gould in Toronto and spent time at the CBC offices and his apartment. She told Lukas Foss that she and Gould were involved; then, surprising all of them, she abruptly left Foss and moved to Toronto with their children—"to be with Glenn," she announced. She bought a house a few minutes' walk from Gould's apartment, with a backyard opening onto woods. She and Gould were together there several times a week. They would talk, read, play with the children, stroll in the neighborhood and the woods. They would kiss, snuggle, make love. On weekends she would take the children to Buffalo to be with their father. Now and then she and Gould would go to a party, and people who knew him would be surprised to see him with a grown-up woman, and treating her so kindly. But he told everyone he knew to keep the romance a secret—an aspect of the wish for control, verging on paranoia, as she saw it, that always sent him back to his apartment, and always stood between them.

One other thing stood between them. She didn't like the way he played Bach. "Bach has a religious theme . . ." she said later. "You can't treat Bach like a clock, take it apart and put it back together. But Glenn liked to play around with it, rather than to stay with the intention of the composer. Bach would have been horrified."

In Buffalo, Lukas Foss, mentally on edge, was taking Bach apart. Leonard Bernstein, a friend of his, was concerned; he thought that Foss was "going through a period right now of what seems to be publicly destroying the music he's always loved most—Bach. In some compositions he takes a piece by Bach and breaks Coca-Cola bottles over it and makes it fragmented and distorted. It's like watching him publicly claw the stuff out of his brains to make room for something new."

Gould, for his part, kept up a phenomenally active life as a pianist—making recordings in profusion and writing, talking, and broadcasting about music, especially the music of Bach.

"The company had always been unified on one subject: Let Glenn record anything he wanted," the Masterworks producer Andrew Kazdin later recalled. At the same time, the company kept in mind that Bach sold best and made sure that Gould delivered a steady stream of Bach releases, working his way through the keyboard music. In the years characterized as his radio period—1969 through 1972—he recorded two concerti; sixteen of the twenty-four preludes and fugues from the second book of the *Well-Tempered Clavier*; the *Overture in the French Style*, the Italian variations; two French suites; then an English suite; and then the remainder of the French suites; as well as incidental Bach recordings for the sound track of the film of *Slaughterhouse-Five.**
Shortly after those recordings were done, he turned to the sonatas for harpsichord and viola da gamba, recorded the six English suites, and tossed off three organ toccatas for good measure. If the *Goldbergs* are the cornerstone of his recorded work, these records are the dwelling itself, the point to which his essays, scripts, and radio work are counterpoint.

Gould put finishing touches on *Stokowski: A Portrait for Radio*, then did something most un-Stoki-like: he stopped making records in New York. For years he had traveled to the city from Toronto once a month, taking a night train and arriving energized for sessions at 30th Street Studio that could run several days and nights. When the night train was discontinued, he figured out how to make records in Toronto instead. "Glenn did some calculations," Andrew Kazdin recalled, "and came up with the following astounding proposal": he would buy recording equipment, rent Eaton Auditorium, set up the gear there, and then rent his rig to Columbia Masterworks for his own recording

---

*The film's title sequence—the war-addled GI Billy Pilgrim striding through a snowed-in forest to the slow movement of Bach's keyboard concerto in F Minor—is a gorgeous Hollywood-style evocation of what Gould called "the idea of north."

sessions. The plan was approved, the equipment bought, and the microphones set up around Gould's piano in Eaton Auditorium in an arrangement that was maintained without variation. "There were even little crayon marks on the recording console that indicated the level setting of each of the three microphones," Kazdin recalled, and "a careful three-dimensional plot that pinpointed the location of each microphone in space was drawn so that the setup could always be reconstructed." It was "adhered to so strictly that it was possible to record a new insert to fix a blemish heard in a tape made years earlier and have the splice match perfectly." This was technical transcendence, Toronto-style.

You can hear the difference from New York, subtle but distinct, in the recordings of the second book of the *Well-Tempered Clavier*. Preludes and fugues one through sixteen (recorded at 30th Street Studio) are a triumph of Gould's dry style, gotten through close miking: some of them, such as the eleventh, sound positively rapped out on the keyboard. Then with the seventeenth (recorded in Toronto), the sound of the room, and the world, returns, if only slightly. The keyboard is lighter, brighter, more reverberant, even chimey.

Gould recorded the *Overture in the French Style* at Eaton's in April 1971, three months after the last group from the *Well-Tempered Clavier*, but its kinship is not with the music of Bach so much as that of the composer Gould called "my favorite composer—always has been." This was Orlando Gibbons, the seventeenth-century English virginalist. "There is a spiritual attachment that I began to feel for his music when I was about fourteen or fifteen and first heard some of the Anthems." He had played Gibbons's *Lord Salisbury's Pavan and Galliard* in recital beginning in 1952, and he played it at his 1955 recitals in Washington and New York. He recorded it in 1968 and played it for the CBC. "I can't think of anybody who represents the end of an era better than Orlando Gibbons does," Gould remarked, and the piece, slightly shorter than six minutes, has the mood of a recessional, as if the music—quarter-note-spaced figures, set in the middle of the keyboard—is being matched to the strides of pallbearers. It has the severity of Bach's minor-key fugues without their complexity. It is (Michael Stegemann observed) "music of a supreme beauty that somehow lacks its ideal means of reproduction."

With the French overture Gould keeps the solemnity, the spaciousness, and the sense of occasion he found in Gibbons, but with the complexity of Bach. The opening processional, in two voices, is Bach at his least adorned, and the right-hand trills suggest brass figures being played off in the distance— suggest the pianist as a Baroque portraitist, sketching a scene at court.

With the French overture the removal of Gould the recording artist to Toronto is complete. This overture is music for indoor fireworks, a prelude to solitude. And yet, paradoxically, the recording process has doubled back on him. The sound of the room, painstakingly squeezed out through years of work at the studio in New York, has come back in, and the musician at the piano is again a recitalist in an auditorium—a recitalist without an audience.

Later that year Gould's favorite piano, Steinway CD 318, was destroyed. He had had it sent by truck from Eaton's to Cleveland, where he planned to make a record of Beethoven concerti with the city orchestra. Reconsidering, he canceled the date and arranged for the piano to be crated and returned. It was dropped en route, probably in the loading dock of Eaton's: its soundboard was split, its 350-pound iron plate cracked in four places. Although he subjected it to endless repairs, never again would it work to his satisfaction. With the piano in the shop, Gould—who more than anyone else had made Bach's music sit well on the piano and had made the piano seem a piece of modern technology—made a record of Handel's first four suites for harpsichord, playing a harpsichord.

Gould probably recorded the French suites on a reconstructed CD 318 equipped with the action mechanism swapped in from a different Steinway. Whatever piano he played, it is the most likable of his Bach records from those years. Working out of order, he tapped into the charm of the suites. Suites one and two are as different emotionally as minor-key suites can be: the one tightly wound and hectoring, a speech made with a pounded fist; the other delicate and exploratory, like a name sketched with a forefinger on a dusty window. When, with the fourth suite, the set moves into E-flat major, it is as if a minor-key mechanism has been replaced with a major one.

In August 1972, Gould spent a week at the Marlboro Festival, getting material for a radio documentary about Pablo Casals.

Yo-Yo Ma was there, the cello prodigy from Paris via New York who had appeared with Leonard Bernstein on the *Tonight Show*; he spent the summer "working with Casals and Serkin and Sascha Schneider and Izzy Cohen. On details, always details. You could *see* their commitment. That's when I knew for sure that music was what I wanted to do."

Casals, now ninety-six, spent an entire rehearsal session perfecting the details of a four-measure figure with a student orchestra—and the students testified into Gould's microphone about how dedicated the old master was. Once again Gould's approach was doubling back on itself. Just as he had shaped his sound in opposition to Casals's rubato-heavy sound (which he called "the Romantic sensibility . . . welded onto the Baroque"), so he had arranged his career to avoid an outcome like the one he saw for Casals at Marlboro: the roomful of reverent supplicants, the virtuoso working through the same piece for the umpteenth time. But there he was, celebrating it in a documentary. It is not surprising that he found it "far more instructive to talk with Pablo Casals . . . about the concept of the zeitgeist, which, of course, is not unrelated to music," than to talk about music directly.

Their conversation is hardly heard in *Casals: A Portrait for Radio*. Casals could still play the cello, but his voice was too weak for the microphone.

>>17>> "I was in Basel, Switzerland, taking part in a performance of Bach's *St. Matthew Passion*," Casals recalled. "The great Dutch singer, Johannes Messchaert, was singing one of the most magnificent arias in the work, and I was playing the cello part, when suddenly I was overwhelmed by a terrible feeling. At that moment I knew with dreadful certainty that my father was dying. As soon as the performance was over, I canceled all other engagements of my concert tour, and I left directly for Vendrell. When I arrived, I learned that my beloved father had died on the day I had been playing in Basel. He was buried not far from the church where he had been organist and where, as I child, I had sung while he played."

Pablo Casals died in San Juan on October 22, 1973. Marta was with him. He had been weak ever since suffering a heart attack after a trip to Israel, where he had hoped to celebrate his centenary in 1976.

He had nearly died as a boy, and since the 1950s people had asked him the big questions as if for the last time: What did the cello mean to him? What did death mean to him?

"My cello is my oldest friend . . ." he said. "My cello is my companion. I love him and he loves me. And he sounds well to make me happy."

His last Bach studio recording was a perfect piece of schmaltz: orchestrally sweetened versions of "Jesu, Joy of Man's Desiring" and "Sheep May Safely Graze" ordered up by Columbia for a Christmas record sponsored by Goodyear, the tire company. They were akin to the short, sweet Bach excerpts Casals had played as encores in the teens and recorded for 78s, before his recording of the cello suites—a man in a room, in wartime, in anguish—changed the conception of Bach's music for strings.

What did Bach mean to him? From the beginning, Bach represented life itself and Bach's cello suites were a model for his independence. This was music worthy of a man in a room. Over time, it gained other significances. It was universal music, which crossed borders. It was music in which all the possibilities of the instrument were explored and fulfilled. It was an ideal to be approached asymptotically, to be shaded as the mood and the occasion suggested, but never to be locked into permanence. It was music of transcendence, in which the human story was told by a single person and a human-size piece of wood.

In the end, the cello suites represented a force of life against death, a work of circulatory energy. Dietrich Fischer-Dieskau recalled seeing Casals prepare for a concert in church in Prades: "Lacking other space, he sat in the sacristy in the midst of all the other soloists. While violin, viola, and clarinet doodled scales, he steadfastly played one Bach suite after another, as if he were the only person in the world."

His body was placed in a casket strong enough to withstand eventual shipment to Spain, and he was buried in San Juan, after a requiem Mass. Music was played: Beethoven, Mozart, and excerpts from his own compositions. Concerts were held: New York, San Juan, Marlboro. The CBC aired *Casals: A Portrait for Radio.*

Leopold Stokowski moved to England, bought a country house, and signed a new recording contract with Columbia. The house, a brick Tudor in Hampshire, was called Nether Wallop; Stoki and Natasha Bender, latterly his partner, found it through an ad in *Country Life.* The contract was for six years, a year longer than Columbia's standard contract, so that it would be in force when Stoki, who was ninety-four, turned one hundred. After half a century on the frontiers in America he was an old-world figure again: elfin, vested, neomedieval, the famous profile topped with a thatch of white hair.

Stokowski was a Londoner, after all, and the city became the center of his music-making, beginning with a concert for the sixtieth anniversary of his first concert with the London Symphony Orchestra. As he returned to London, he returned to Bach. He planned a record of Bach transcriptions which would be made at the church of St. Giles, Cripplegate. After spending several days recording Mahler in north London, he filled extra studio time by recording the Toccata and Fugue in D Minor. "Stokowski knew the Mahler well, but he knew that Toccata and Fugue like crazy," the producer recalled; and yet "he had a fainting spell and slumped forward on the podium. They had to give him smelling salts."

A year later—July 22, 1975—Stokowski led an orchestra in a concert for the Festival of Vence, in the South of France. He arrived "bent, leaning on a stick, supported by two people," a reporter wrote, but when he reached the town square, where a stage and podium had been set up, "he became another man. He sighted the music as a navigator in distress sights land on the horizon." He led a chamber orchestra from Rouen (lacking brass) in five Bach transcriptions: the "Air on the G String," the "Little" Fugue in G Minor, and some others. With the smaller forces, the effect is diminished, even austere. Maybe Stoki knew that this was the orchestral sound of things to come.

In the spring of 1977 the Recording Academy of Arts and Sciences (marking fifty years of the Grammy Awards) presented a "golden anniversary" Grammy to Stokowski's 1927 recording of the Toccata and Fugue in D Minor. So Stokowski, who more than anyone had advanced the "arts and sciences" of recording, had a gold-plated miniature gramophone for Nether Wallop; so Bach had a Grammy for the Toccata and Fugue in D Minor.

What did Bach mean to Stokowski? In this Stokowski is Casals's obverse, the Bach revival's other side. Stoki had plenty to say about the human significance of music: *Music for All of Us* is not so much a book about music as a great man's perennial philosophy. Others had plenty to say about the liberties he took with Bach. But the evidence of fifty years of Stoki's Bach recordings is of constancy. Stoki found a sound in Bach and stuck with it. For him, as for Casals, the music of Bach was a life force. The approach Casals took abashedly and in private with the cello suites—to play them, to plumb them, over and over again—Stokowski took from the get-go and in public. He would play this music endlessly. Bach's music was an aural space where, moment to moment, he could create anew. Early recordings were too small for him. Those of the thirties were just right: spacious but intimate. With stereo recordings, anything was possible, and a firm grasp of those possibilities was the essence of the Stokowski sound.

He died at Nether Wallop on September 13, 1977, having postponed a recording session at Abbey Road Studio.

He was buried, after cremation, at Marylebone Cemetery in London. An organist played "Jesu, Joy of Man's Desiring" and "When I Am Laid in Earth," the searing lament from Purcell's *Dido and Aeneas*, on the crematory organ. After excerpts from his writing were read by Edward Heath, once the prime minister, the rite concluded with Bach's "A Mighty Fortress Is Our God." Although death cannot have been sweet for him—it was the end, a double line and no dots; it was silence after superabundant sound—the New York Philharmonic and the Philadelphia Orchestra honored him by opening their scheduled concerts with Bach's "Komm, süsser Tod."

Glenn Gould, in tribute (and on assignment for *The New York Times*), wrote "Stokowski in Six Scenes." The piece ended with Gould expressing admiration for all Stokowski did. "In his lifetime he had witnessed the triumph, and confirmed the essential humanity, of those technological ideas which had inspired his activity as a musician; for him, technology had indeed become a 'higher calling.' He had understood that through its mediation one could transcend the frailty of nature and concentrate on a vision of the ideal. His life and work had testified to our ability to remove ourselves from ourselves and achieve a state of ecstasy."

An inadvertent tribute had taken place the previous September at St. Mary's Cathedral in San Francisco. There, Virgil Fox ("in sequined jacket and diamond-studded shoes") played Bach organ works while a kaleidoscopic light show was projected onto the walls of the cathedral.

The invocation of Bach by the vox populi had extended without letup into the seventies. The Band, playing a New Year's Eve show at the Academy of Music in New York, moved from 1971 to 1972 with an instrumental bridge in which Garth Hudson, on Hammond organ, slid from the Toccata and Fugue in D Minor to "Auld Lang Syne" to "Chest Fever." Joshua Rifkin had a hit in 1973 with an LP of Scott Joplin rags played on piano in light-fingered Baroque style. In Seattle, Mark Morris, age sixteen, already a dancer and a maker of dances, learned to whistle the *Two-Part Inventions* as an oral pas de deux with a friend. In Southern California, two classically trained sons of a Dutch clarinetist formed a rock band: Alex Van Halen, a drummer, and Eddie Van Halen, a guitarist whose playing would prompt a producer to marvel that "Eddie can play thirty-second-note melodic lines with a complexity that rivals Bach."

With the "Festival of Organ Virtuosos & Illumination," Virgil Fox sought to bring the popular enthusiasm for Bach back into the church. The shows drew audiences of several thousand people, and they carried forth the promise of *Fantasia* to make Bach's music the inspiration for exuberant visual imagery called forth by the musician as conjurer. But videotapes of the shows suggest that you had to be there: by comparison with the hand-drawn skyscapes of *Fantasia*, the swirling lights and symmetrical tableaux look mechanical. They lack the quality that Stokowski's "transcription travesties" had in glorious abundance: the complexity of Bach.

PART VI

Strange Loops

>>01>> Bach was in a carriage on the road to Dresden, sixty miles from Leipzig. The *Aria with diverse variations*, newly printed and published, was in his baggage. Even for him this was a work of extraordinary symmetry: thirty-two pages, thirty-two pieces, each one of sixteen or thirty-two measures. The aria, set at the beginning and the end, bracketed the variations, thirty in all. Every third variation was a canon, each one a greater step up the scale. The variations were the most demanding music he had written for clavier; at the same time, they were dances, thirty dances.

Already he had ideas for further variations on the aria and variations. Would the count, Keyserlingk, like the variations? Would Goldberg—a top student but just thirteen years of age—be able to play them? In an important sense, it didn't matter. He had written them for Wilhelm Friedemann, who surely would be able to play them, as much as for anybody else. A quarter century after he gave Friedemann the *Clavier-büchlein* to set the boy on his way, he gave him the *Aria with diverse variations* to mark that the man had arrived.

>>02>> One evening 235 years later two harpsichords were wheeled onto the stage of an auditorium in Berkeley. Programs were distributed, seats taken, lights dimmed. The musicians—teacher and student at the university—strode in from the wings; and there in Northern California, a few weeks before the nation's bicentennial, they gave the first public performance of a newly discovered piece of music by Bach. First they played it: fourteen canons, each one a variation on a familiar progression in the ground bass. Then for about an hour the teacher played the *Goldberg Variations*, and there running through the work was the same progression. Then teacher and student played the fourteen canons again.

The canons had been found written on the inside back cover of Bach's own printed text of the *Goldberg*s: fourteen sequences of notes, each a few measures at most, placed one right after another on the staff lines in fluent, even buoyant notation, and carrying explanations—*Canon simplex*; *Canon duplex*; *Canon uniform* . . . —in elegant script.

A *Handexemplar* is the composer's own printed text of one of his pieces, marked with his further revisions in his own hand. For much of the twentieth century the *Handexemplar* of the *Goldberg Variations* was in the possession of the director of the conservatory of music in Strasbourg and then of a professor there, but neither one understood what it was. In 1974, an organist from Italy, seeing the text, suggested that it was Bach's own printed text and that a handwritten series of "puzzle" canons on the back had been written there by Bach himself. Experts were called in. In 1975, Olivier Alain—a composer and organist who held the French government post of inspector of music—confirmed the handwriting as Bach's. The next year Christoph Wolff—a musicologist, native to Germany, who was preparing a new edition of the *Goldberg Variations* at Columbia University—seconded him. Working independently, they "solved" the puzzle canons, figuring out how each sequence of notes could be doubled, inverted, stacked, and so forth to produce a sonorous piece of music. Alain arranged performances of the canons at academic conferences in Strasbourg and Paris, Wolff at conferences in Freiburg, Leipzig, and Los Angeles. In Berkeley, the canons were "played for the first time at a public recital," as Andrew Porter, the music writer for *The New Yorker*, remarked in a long piece, set in the magazine amid ads for the Klipschorn bass loudspeaker ("delivers goose pimple-inducing dynamic peaks. With virtually no distortion") and for a "stereo 'scrapbook,' " *200 Years of America in Sound*.

The *Handexemplar* was Bach's way of improving on the technology of his age. In the printing process a piece of music written by hand was taken over by mechanical means. Published, distributed, and sold, the piece went into worldly circulation in a standard, semipermanent form. By revising the printed text in his own hand, then, Bach made it personal and provisional again. And by composing a set of canons on the aria from the *Goldberg Variations*, he moved the *Goldberg*s into the territory of invention. For him an invention was a piece of music realized fully enough that it could be developed further by others; through the *Handexemplar*, we can see him developing one of his own inventions after it had gone out into the world.

"The Handexemplar of the Goldberg Variations must be considered the most important Bach source that has come to light in a generation," Wolff declared. Its importance was obvious from the beginning. Its implications were not. Presented with this "new" work of Bach's, scholars tried to figure out how it fit with the works related to it. Alain saw the set of canons as preliminary to the *Goldberg Variations*; Wolff, working from "well-known characteristics of Bach's late handwriting style" in the text—in particular, his way of writing a C clef—saw it as a bridge out of the *Goldbergs* to an astonishing run of works that followed. Other scholars dated it even later, as Bach's return to a subject he especially liked.

The works that followed would be works written for no occasion, in some cases for no particular instrument, and characterized by the intense development of a single theme. With them Bach would push past invention to explore the frontier. But he had not given up on the eventful and the encyclopedic. Since the Kyrie and Gloria of 1733 he had written four more *missae*, each consisting of a Kyrie and a Gloria. He would compose a full Mass, refashioning pieces he had written over the years and fitting them like puzzle pieces into a liturgical frame, a pattern of supra-ecclesial sacred music.

>>03>>   A young man in the suburbs south of San Francisco had an acid trip that centered on the music of Bach and a wheat field.

This was Steve Jobs: adopted child, college dropout, computer enthusiast, fanatic for pattern and design. He had been devoted to Bach since he was a teenager in Cupertino. "I was listening to a lot of Bach," he later said, recalling the episode. He was tripping on LSD with his girlfriend in a wheat field near Sunnyvale, California, and heard the music in his mind. The music and their surroundings merged in a way he found extraordinary. "All of a sudden the wheat field was playing Bach. It was the most wonderful experience of my life up to that point. I felt like the conductor of this symphony with Bach coming through the wheat."

A few years later, with the Apple computer in development, Jobs was photographed in the empty living room of his home in Cupertino, clad in black silk pajamas, sitting contemplatively cross-legged, drinking a cup of tea, and holding a magazine; the only furnishings were a high-end stereo and a stack of LPs. The symbolism was obvious: the home computer would be the stereo's successor, technology you could love and call your own.

>>04>>   A few miles away, another Bach-addled genius was "on fire with ideas about mind, brain, and humanity"—a sane counterpart to the Richard

Dreyfuss character in *Close Encounters of the Third Kind*, who kept muttering "if everything is operational here on the dark side of the moon, play the Bach tones" as a giant mound rose in his backyard.

This was Douglas R. Hofstadter, postdoctoral polymath. He had finished a Ph.D. thesis in solid-state physics and had moved back in with his parents, not far from Stanford University, with the idea that he would "'retool myself' as an artificial intelligence researcher." As it turned out, he spent most of his time at a Stanford computer center, using a freshly invented word-processing program called TV-Edit to create an intricately patterned text about "strange, twisty patterns," which he called "strange loops." It was, he later explained, "a long proposal for strange loops as a metaphor for how selfhood originates, a metaphor by which to begin to grab a hold of just what it is that makes an 'I' seem, at one and the same time, so terribly real and tangible to its own possessor, and yet also so vague, so impenetrable, so deeply elusive." He found his strange loops in several places. He found them in the pictures of M. C. Escher: spine-bending Möbius strips, waterfalls that seem to rise, staircases that lead to the place of infinite regress. He found them in the number theories of the logician Kurt Gödel, who devised a theorem of incompleteness often paraphrased this way: "For each record player there is a record which it cannot play."

He found them in the fugues and canons of Bach, whose music he had loved since childhood. The Yale literature professor Harold Bloom was developing a theory of creativity he called "the anxiety of influence," and a view of the major writer as distinguished by "strength and strangeness." Hofstadter rendered Bach strong and strange. As he wrote, the music of Bach looped back on him, for not only was it a subject of the text he was writing; it also suggested the form of the text, prompting him to think that he could create a giant "metaphorical fugue" by setting discursive passages in counterpoint with neo-Platonic dialogues, which would frame the main text or nest within it:

> ACHILLES: Well, in the mathematics of acoustico retrieval, there arise many questions which have to do with the number of solutions of certain Diophantine equations. Now Mr. T has been for years trying to find a way of reconstructing the sounds of Bach playing his harpsichord, which took place over two hundred years ago, from calculations involving the motions of all the molecules in the atmosphere at the present time.

ANTEATER: Surely that is impossible! They are irretrievably gone, gone forever!

ACHILLES: Thus think the naïve . . .

"This off-the-wall idea of marrying Bach-like contrapuntal forms to lively dialogues with intellectually rich content grabbed me with a passion," Hofstadter told it later. "Over the next few weeks, as I tossed the idea around in my head, I realized how much room for play there was along these lines . . ." Now, two years later, as he rewrote the giant text from start to finish on TV-Edit, he found that "the new version just flowed out, and ever so smoothly." He typeset it himself, and called it *Gödel, Escher, Bach*.

>>05>> Onstage in Nashville eight modern dancers in short dresses and bell-bottoms were performing a new piece for public television.

This was *Esplanade*, by Paul Taylor. The dancers were lithe, adult, a symmetrical ensemble. The music was Bach's—the giant, scooped opening arpeggio of the second violin concerto. The piece is in E major; the footage is in a mellow tone, the pastel colors softened and smudged by time. The dancers circle; cross; form a line and loop it, twist it, licorice it; figure-eight it; wriggle it to the ground and, one after another, hopscotch through it, write tic-tac-toe on the Etch A Sketch of the stage floor. The contrast between the elasticity of their bodies and the geometry of their movement is total but not paradoxical. Geometry and elasticity lie down with each other, nestle side to side. This is the body electric—electrified by Bach. The violin roams away from the orchestral setting and then rejoins it; the dancers scatter and regroup. The music moves with their bodies, not the other way around. And then the piece is over and the nature of it is obvious. They were dancing in the street, and the music of Bach was dancing with them.

>>06>> An engineering professor in Salt Lake City was figuring out how recorded sounds could be represented with numbers rather than waves.

This was Thomas Stockham, founder of Soundstream. Trained in the practice of "waveform processing," Stockham had begun analyzing audio recordings after joining the MIT faculty in the late fifties. During the Watergate controversy, Stockham was one of a panel of experts who testified that the tapes made by President Nixon's aides in the Oval Office had been altered:

using a computer program he had written, Stockham (as Greg Milner told the story) demonstrated "the frequency response caused by the desk drawer that had contained the hidden microphone" and then showed that these frequencies were missing from the notorious eighteen-and-a-half-minute gap in the tape, proving that the gap was a deliberate erasure, not "a mistake made by Nixon's secretary while she transcribed the tape."

With Soundstream, Stockham sought to remove the sound of the desk drawer, so to speak, from commercial audio recordings. A century after Edison invented the gramophone, Stockham sought to revise some of the basic assumptions that had governed audio recording since then. An audio recording, it was understood, was a document of a past event. All audio recordings carried the sound of the recording device in addition to the sound of the event itself. For the listener, the sounds of commercial recordings were further shaped by the formats in which they were issued and played back. The sounds of countless great recordings were the result of the interaction of these elements: a bright organ, a soft wax cylinder, a steel master, and a 78-rpm disc; a tightly strung piano, a closely placed microphone, magnetic tape, and an LP. For fifty years, musicians and recording engineers had worked toward two contradictory objectives. On the one hand, they hoped to minimize the intervention of the recording device, so as to produce records with "fidelity" to the original performance; on the other, they sought to manipulate the sound through mixing, mastering, stereo processing, and the like, so as to produce a result that, faithful or not, was interesting in its own right.

What if the sound of recording technology could be eliminated completely? Would it then be possible to produce a record that was not merely faithful but absolutely true to the original—that would provide "a clear glimpse into past musical events"? Those were Stockham's questions. To answer them, he devised Soundstream, which was at once a technological apparatus and an approach to recording. Instead of working with a physical record of sound waves—a grooved disc, a spool of magnetized tape with silver particles stuck to it—Soundstream worked with a mathematical one. A Soundstream recording console used magnetic tape; but instead of gathering clusters of silver oxide particles, it recorded endless sequences of zeroes and ones. It cost $50,000 to build and three times as much to own and operate. Crystal Clear Records used to make a Soundstream recording of a Virgil Fox organ recital in 1977, in conjunction with the process called direct-to-disc recording: the first of two LPs featured versions of Bach's Toccata and Fugue in D Minor and Toccata, Adagio, and Fugue that were as heavy as they were clear.

In April 1978, Telarc, a company in Cleveland whose founders were equally keen on classical music and high fidelity, booked a session for what they saw as the first commercial release in the new format. It would be a set rendered by the conductor Frederick Fennel and the Cleveland Symphonic Winds: Holst, Handel, and Bach's *Fantasie in G*. One of the founders, eyeballing the new wristwatch he was wearing, dubbed the process "digital" recording.

Many thousands of digital recordings later, Fennel's Bach *Fantasie* sounds ordinary. There is clarity, yes. It is apt that this first digital recording should be exaggeratedly mechanical, its sounds of music produced by brass valves and slides and polished nickel levers rather than by wood and horsehair. The most striking thing about this format-pioneering recording, in fact, is the format of the ensemble, which was made up of woodwinds, brass, and percussion, but no strings. The velvety side of transcription—trademark L. Stokowski, A Long Time Ago—has been shaved off, making Bach the distant ancestor of a pompish military band.

While Telarc issued a series of Soundstream releases on LP, engineers with the Sony Corporation in Tokyo were developing two new products that pointed in the same direction in different ways. One was a digital recorder, an audio offshoot of the Betamax videotape recorder. Digital was an idée fixe at Sony; one engineer said making recordings digitally, after decades of taping, was like removing a heavy winter coat.

The other product was a truly portable audiocassette player. At first it was an in-house project, created so that one of Sony's founding executives could listen to opera while traveling on business. After devising light, compact headphones, the company took the player to market in Japan in 1979. In the space-starved country, demand was great, and the next year, Sony introduced the portable audio player in multiple markets, giving it a different name in each: the Walkman in Japan, the Freestyle in Scandinavia, the Stowaway in the United Kingdom, and the Sound-About in North America.

Now it was possible to listen to recordings anywhere. As the phonograph had taken music out of the concert hall and into the home, the portable audio player—globally renamed the Walkman—took recorded music out of the home and into the street; now city life was an esplanade, the intersecting movements of bodies in space and time, point and counterpoint.

>>07>> Glenn Gould was sitting at the piano in a darkened room in Toronto, pondering his prospects.

His affair with Cornelia Foss had ended badly. She had sold the house and resumed family life in Buffalo, telling him he needed medical help: he was mentally ill, she thought. He phoned her for nearly a year, steadily but irregularly; in the end, she hung up on him as if he were a crank caller.

About the prospects of recording he had been right. Fifteen years after he stopped playing for live audiences, the recital was not dead, but the virtuoso's nightly wire-walk before a hushed crowd was no longer the center of classical music life. The recital was just one of the diverse ways in which the music could be encountered, and scholarship was making clear that that had always been the case—that the recital was the exception, not the rule.

Nowhere was it so clear as with Bach. The music of Bach was in play in a thousand places. There were events like the *Goldberg*s premiere in Berkeley, less a recital than a presentation of findings. There was *Gödel, Escher, Bach*, which had been awarded a Pulitzer Prize and made the *New York Times* best-seller list. A digital recording such as Fennel's *Fantasie* delivered the affectless clarity Gould strove for, and producers were finding that digital recording enabled them to correct, rearrange, and reprocess music at will—enabled "dial-twiddling" on a vast scale. And the Walkman enabled the listener to take the music of Bach anywhere.

As classical music moved centrifugally away from the recital and the symphonic concert, Bach took up the center, as if for the first time.

Gould had been right. So what to do about it? There in a small room in Toronto he came to a decision that would surprise everyone. He would make a new recording of the *Goldberg Variations*.

There was a simple reason: Columbia Records was ceasing its operations at 30th Street Studio; the technologically altered church would be sold to a real-estate developer, which would raze it and put up a giant apartment building in its place. Gould was attached to certain rooms no less than certain pianos, and he leapt at the chance to go to 30th Street one last time. But there were other reasons. Digital sound offered him a chance to replace the 1955 recording, whose mono sound he had considered antiquated ever since "somebody had the nerve to invent something called stereo." Bruno Monsaingeon, who had filmed several episodes of a series called *Gould Plays Bach* for the CBC, was eager to film Gould playing the *Goldberg*s. Columbia Masterworks had cobbled together an "Anniversary Album" to mark Gould's first twenty-five years with the label; Masterworks never saw a milestone it didn't like, and a big one was approaching: Gould's fiftieth birthday.

A new *Goldberg Variations* would be a last tango in the big room where Gould had consummated the act of recording.

Outside the studio, Gould had been going over his early work for years—at once sinking into self-absorption and seizing the chance to shape the interpretation of his work. For *High Fidelity* in 1974 he put together a "self-interview": *glenn gould* posing the questions to *Glenn Gould*. In an essay, "Music and Technology," he told of the primal scene of his encounters with the recording studio, the microphone, and dial-twiddling. In a piece about outtakes, he contrived a poll (and a windy analysis) to support his conviction that great recordings were improved by tape splices and that most people didn't even notice them. For a CBC documentary, "Glenn Gould's Toronto," he delivered a script of 45,000 words, ten times the length called for. When the psychologist Peter Ostwald, who knew Gould, paid him a visit with two colleagues, Gould kept them up till three in the morning playing records, tapes, and videos he insisted they hear, including *The Idea of North* at full length: "It would have been helpful if Glenn served us some refreshments, or even a glass of water, but that always was the furthest thing from his mind." When a young scholar published his dissertation on Gould's ideas, Gould reviewed the book himself for *The Globe and Mail*, praising it for complicating "the conventional image of Gould as an eccentric and erratic artist-pundit."

Musically, Gould's attention to the creative process remained a source of invention, and if there were any doubts, they were dispelled by his recordings of Bach's English suites, completed in 1976 and released the next year: a series of rushes at the music bent on making it new, fidelity be damned.

In his life, though, he was nearly overtaken by self-scrutiny. For a man who didn't bathe regularly, change his clothes, wash his hair, or eat square meals, he was strangely obsessed with his body. He saw legions of doctors. He took his pulse and blood pressure many times each day and recorded the results in a notebook, along with the effects of the many prescription drugs he was taking (one effect, a weight gain of about thirty pounds, escaped his documentation). A filmed recording session of Alfredo Casella's *Ricercari on the Name B-A-C-H* went awry when he became convinced that his hands would not obey him. "During next two weeks . . . problems increased," he recorded. "It was no longer possible to play even Bach chorale securely—Parts were unbalanced, progression from note to note insecure." When the problem persisted, making it hard for him to play fast or without pain, he conducted a "practice experiment" on himself, using oft-played Bach transcriptions as the "controls." He considered every explanation but the obvious one: that his hands and arms were strained because his battered folding chair could no longer support him.

In middle age, his body was getting in the way of the technical transcendence he sought. For him, music, especially recorded music, was a way of transcending space and time and the body. In his outtakes piece he had given a cold and beautiful definition of this kind of transcendence as the way of the artist. Writing against the idea that art should be the result of a momentary "ecstatic high," he asked puzzledly why people "could not conceive that the function of the artist could also entail the ability to summon, on command, the emotional tenor of any moment, in any score, at any time—that one should be free to 'shoot' a Beethoven sonata or a Bach fugue in or out of sequence, intercut almost without restriction, apply postproduction techniques as required, and that the composer, the performer, and above all the listener will be better served thereby." The pianist, in this scheme of things, was a music-making machine, an embodiment of human technology. Now Gould's machine was breaking down.

At the piano one night in 1979, his hand problems suddenly went away, an experience he described in the language of revelation: "For one brief moment, and only in right hand, I *had* it: that gleaming, lustrous sound was back and I realized, more than ever, that *that* was the sound of control."

"That gleaming, lustrous sound" was the sound he had first attained at 30th Street Studio in the summer of 1955. Now he had a chance to go after that sound again in a new recording of the *Goldberg Variations*, with cameras rolling. The imminent demise of 30th Street Studio, the promptings of Bruno Monsaingeon, the aural prospects offered by digital recording technology, the thick history of the *Goldbergs* that musicologists had brought to light: all these were compelling reasons to do so. But there was a reason over and above them. The *Goldberg Variations* was not only the best-known of Gould's Bach recordings. The *Goldbergs* were the Bach pieces he knew best. They were still the royal way to transcendence: recording them, he could reinvent himself, and get that gleaming, lustrous sound back.

>>08>> John Lennon was dead, shot point-blank by a fan. Bob Marley was dead of cancer. Miles Davis had taken to playing with his back to the audience; Public Image Ltd, the Sex Pistol John Lydon's new band, enraged the crowd at the Ritz in New York by playing behind a giant video screen that at once hid them from view and showed them playing. Viacom was preparing the Music Television channel. REM played regularly at the 40-Watt Club in Athens, Georgia, having made their first recordings at the Drive-In Studio in

Winston-Salem. Bruce Springsteen and the E Street Band were playing four-hour shows in Europe in support of *The River*. U2 was wide awake in America, playing a different club each night: the university rathskeller in Gainesville, the End Zone in Tampa, Ol' Man River in New Orleans, J. B. Scott's in Albany. Lou Reed had married Sylvia Morales and was living in New Jersey; in Los Angeles, Ringo Starr was set to marry his co-star in *Caveman*, Barbara Bach. The progressive rock group Sky, featuring John Williams on guitar, was suddenly, unexpectedly popular: their ear-pummeling amplified version of Bach's Toccata and Fugue in D Minor had hit the U.K. Top 5. As if in reply, a group of comedians dreamed up Spinal Tap, a heavy metal band whose Nigel Tufnel would compose a piece in D minor "influenced by Mozart and Bach . . . Really, it's like a Mach piece."

Glenn Gould was bent over the piano, bearing down on the *Goldberg Variations*.

The Sony System, the company's answer to the digital rigs developed by Philips and Soundstream, had been trucked in. An analog tape deck was running as a backup. The piano, a new Yamaha, had been tuned and tightened and relieved of its fallboard; made in Japan, it sounded, to Gould's ears, like a harpsichord made in Leipzig circa 1725. Cameras were rolling: after two documentaries that mingled music and commentary after the fact, this was Bruno Monsaingeon's first attempt to catch his subject in the act of making a new recording.

Gould bent over the instrument in the darkened studio, clutching and clawing at Bach.

Even with the sleeve photographs, the interviews, the films, most people didn't know what he looked like, and his appearance in the footage is a shock. He is wearing blue slacks and an electric blue shirt, open at collar and sleeves; he is thick, slumped, unshapely, like a blow-up doll with air leaking out of it. His head is round and jowled. His skin suggests a powdered doughnut. His hair is real but so resistant to styling that it could be a toupee. He is wearing glasses—big rectangular frames, lenses like dirty windows. His long fingers extend outward, untrimmed nails sharp as talons.

In the footage, the studio is nowhere in sight: no high ceiling, no rafters, no wooden flooring; no baffles, glass booth, mixing board, or playback speakers—nothing but a pair of microphones mounted above the piano. Strangely, the musician most devoted to the recording studio allowed the director to conceal all the trappings of the recording studio.

This studio is not a sacred space, a safe haven, or a sonically hospitable environment; it is more like a studio apartment. As in the *Art of the Fugue*, the lack of specificity is suggestive. This is the extruded inner space of Giacometti's night palace. This is the sickroom in *The Cabinet of Dr. Caligari* where the patient plays an imaginary piano. This is a cell where a prisoner in work blues does exercises, marking time through minor variations.

He was a man in a room, alone in the dark, around midnight, bent double over Bach, playing for the camera and the digital recording machine.

The sessions were held from 4:00 p.m. till midnight, three nights in April and three in May. But the footage was edited to suggest a single continuous performance, without the breaks or joshing asides heard on the outtakes. It is strange that the musician bent on doing away with the folkways of classical music—the bravura performance, the single take—took part in a film that perpetuated the very misconceptions he strove mightily to reject.

If proof were ever needed that Gould was better off offstage, this footage is it. He approved the filming of the session, and he was fully aware of the cameras. His writhings at the keyboard were themselves part of the performance. Still, looking at this footage is a kind of voyeurism. This man in electric blue all atwist at the piano is not a man rising to a historic occasion. He is a lost soul, a man on a park bench being interrogated by the police.

This footage, then, demonstrates the distinct power of audio recordings. Through the microphone and the 78, through the LP and magnetic tape, through multitrack recording and stereo, audio recordings had annexed ever vaster territories of sound with ever greater fidelity. It is easy to forget that they did so through brazen omission. The visual aspect was left to the imagination or just left out; the music was reduced to sound. To see this footage—Gould jabbing apishly at the keys—is to realize that this sensory limitation was a strength, the means to the end of technical transcendence. Unable to see, you listen; listening, you hear the music.

>>09>> At the Plaza Hotel—same city, same month—the chairmen of Sony and Philips told members of the press about a new audio format.

It was a plastic disc, twelve centimeters in diameter, coated with a microscopically thin layer of aluminum, that could contain as much music as a double LP and spin at several hundred rpm. The two companies had worked together clandestinely on the new format for five years or longer. Philips developed a laser disc cutter that encoded sequences of many thousands of zeroes and ones as "bits" on the disc, and a laser that "read" the bits back again. Sony attended to the audio side, developing the digital technology that could make those bits represent music accurately. The new format was called the compact disc. The promise was "perfect sound forever": because the laser, unlike a phonograph needle, read the data on the disc without ever touching it, the disc would not wear down over time the way an LP did. Though the compact disc (and the sophisticated equipment needed to produce it) represented a huge investment, the major record companies, after initial resistance, embraced it as the future of the record business. Herbert von Karajan sang the praises of the new disc in a press event at the Salzburg Festival: "All else is gaslight," he said.

"Perfect sound forever" was only one of the record companies' objectives. Their immediate goal was to combat the practice of home taping. Cassette decks made it possible to duplicate LPs from a turntable or FM radio with a tolerable loss of sound quality, and many thousands of people did this—so many that the record companies branded them "pirates" and blamed them for stunting the growth of the industry. The compact-disc player would deliver sound so good that cassette tape could not match it; and unlike the cassette, the CD would work in only one direction: the listener could not make CDs at home, only buy them prerecorded for personal use.

The real benefit to the business was left unstated, if record-company executives grasped it at all. The compact disc would invite listeners to replace their whole collections of LPs with compact discs—the same music, the same recordings, but encoded digitally rather than electrically or magnetically. The promise of "perfect sound forever" would make people buy all their records all over again.

The compact disc would not last forever. Compact discs scratched and smudged; their glassy surfaces cracked triangularly like windows with rocks thrown at them, and whereas a worn LP, scratchy and skipping, could still be played, a scratched CD was ruined, and gave off a jolt of sonic antimatter that cleared the room. But the compact disc would have a long run—a quarter century, as long as the long player—and it would be made to interact, in strange ways, with new developments in music on the one hand and with digital computer technology on the other.

There was no more apt candidate for Sony's first commercially available compact disc than Gould's new digital *Goldberg Variations*. It made perfect sense. Gould had all but inaugurated the LP format with his 1955 *Goldbergs*. With Stokowski's passing, Gould more than any other living classical musician had given sustained thought to the recording process, and he could be counted on to sing the song of new technology in interviews. What was more, the new format, in effect, was inviting people to revisit their record collections the way Gould, with the new *Goldberg*s, had revisited his own first record.

CBS and Sony had a different idea. The first commercial CD release (available initially in Japan) would be a record by another CBS pianist: *52nd Street* by Billy Joel, the street of its title inadvertently symbolizing the change from one era to another—from a narrow strip of late-night jazz clubs to a street flanked and darkened by corporate office towers, among them CBS headquarters, Black Rock, at Fifty-second and Sixth.

>>10>> "It was rather a spooky experience," Gould said. ". . . I found that I recognized at all points the fingerprints of the party responsible . . . From a tactile standpoint, from a purely mechanical standpoint, my approach to playing the piano really hasn't changed all that much over the years. It's remained quite stable, I think—'static,' some people prefer to say. So I recognize the fingerprints, yes, but then—and it is a very big *but*—I could not recognize or identify with the spirit of the person who made that recording . . . It really seemed that some *other* spirit had been involved, and as a consequence I was very glad to be doing it again."

Gould spoke about the *Goldberg Variations* to Tim Page, a critic for *Newsday*. He wasn't willing to do interviews in the usual gang-bang style. Instead, he identified Page as a critic who would be willing to follow his script in sympathetic counterpoint, and invited him to come to Toronto. Page later recounted the experience: a reckless drive around Toronto, a flawless interview, and then, in the middle of the night, an impromptu recital, with Gould playing Strauss transcriptions. *"Glenn Gould was playing the piano for me!* And the Yamaha became a six-foot-square orchestra; dense contrapuntal lines, translucently clear and perfectly contoured, echoed through the empty room. After lengthy fragments of *Elektra* and *Capriccio*, Glenn started to play part of the *Goldberg Variations*, but interrupted himself after a few bars, saying he could not play Baroque music without his beloved, battered folding chair that followed him everywhere."

The new *Goldberg*s set would not be released until more than a year after it was recorded—the following September, in time for Gould's fiftieth birthday, and for Christmas. In Toronto, Gould edited the analog backup tapes on his own equipment, the way he knew how; then technicians in New York retraced his steps, incorporating his edits into the digital master.

He sat for a sleeve portrait by Don Hunstein: thinning hair combed over, jaw set, large hands prominent, black clothing concealing the weight he had put on. He made recordings of some piano pieces (Bach, Brahms, Beethoven) and led a Toronto string ensemble in a reduction of Wagner's "Siegfried Idyll." It was his first recording as a conductor, thirty years after he had served as the music director for the Stratford Festival in Ontario.

On lined pads, he recorded his aches and pains, his bodily functions, and his sleeping habits, mixed in with weather reports from across Canada, which he heard on the radio.

3 a.m. Temp –7
HI Vancouver 7
LO Timmins   30
Sleep 4½ (interr. hammering) & 2½ est. intermittent . . .

>>1 1>> CBS Masterworks issued the *Goldberg Variations* in September 1982 on LP and audiocassette, each with a diagonal band in the upper right indicating that it was a digital recording.

Glenn Gould turned fifty on September 25. The next day—Sunday, September 26, 1982—*The New York Times* ran a long piece (more than 2,000 words) about the new *Goldberg*s, comparing it favorably with the 1955 recording. Gould was exultant about the piece. He called Jessie Grieg, a cousin he had known since his boyhood, and read the entire piece into the telephone. He called a number of friends and did the same thing. He called the reviewer and thanked him. "The early performance is rambunctious, exuberant, relishing its power and freedom," the reviewer, Edward Rothstein, had written. "This record is less viscerally intoxicating, but more affecting, more serious, more seductive in its depth. There are moments of too much insistence and there are seemingly inconsistent repeats, but the performance is bound tightly together. The contemplative meditation of the Aria, the splendid varieties of attack in the 15th variation, the detached and crystalline character of the epic 25th, the almost frightening clarity in the virtuosic parts—all create a 'Goldberg' that gives both a sense of ecstasy and of quiet repose.

"This will not be a performance to everyone's taste, but Mr. Gould's playing is still of crucial importance to the very music world he rejects."

And then he was dead. The next day he had a stroke in his apartment; he resisted going to the hospital, then struggled to get there; spoke with a doctor and a few visitors, grew less and less coherent, then lost consciousness; went into a coma, with brain damage indicated, and was put on life support, which was removed four days later at his father's request. The *Times* ran an obituary under the headline GLENN GOULD, PIANIST, IS DEAD; SAW RECORDINGS AS AN ART FORM.

In Austria, a writer started into a strange tribute to "our friend and the most important piano virtuoso of the century." This was Thomas Bernhard, experimental novelist. As a young man Bernhard had studied piano at the Musik-Akademie in Vienna and the Mozarteum in Salzburg. Now, just past fifty, he worked at *The Loser*, a piece of writing that was and was not a novel, about a pianist who was and was not Glenn Gould. When Gould caught the flu in Salzburg in 1958, he took a month off to recuperate—a month he spent living "the most idyllic and isolated existence" in a house in the Alps. From this scrap of biography Bernhard composed a tombeau in never-ending prose, making Gould a double of himself the way Glenn made himself a double in his self-interview and his "contrapuntal radio" programs. This Glenn Gould has just died of a stroke at the piano partway through the *Goldberg Variations*, and a lapsed pianist who knew him once in Salzburg has just heard the news. This Glenn Gould didn't really die of a stroke, or, the friend insists, of the chronic "lung disease" that Bernhard had assigned to him. His death was existential: "He was killed by the impasse he had *played* himself into for almost forty years."

There came a flood of more conventional reminiscences and appreciations. The commentators saw Gould's career as framed by his two *Goldbergs*, a beginning and an ending, debut and epitaph. But in the way of art and commerce, the new recording, Gould's fiftieth birthday, and his sudden death all together attracted listeners to the new recording who had no experience of the old one, and who, through the new record, heard Glenn Gould, the *Goldberg Variations*, and the music of Bach for the first time.

They heard a piece of music sufficient unto itself, strong and clean, spiritual in character, lit from within with patterned beauty—a piece that raised high the roofbeams, opened the windows, lit up the room, and dispelled a continent-size idea of what classical music is.

That is what I heard, at any rate. Home from college for Christmas, I was driving in the mountains, the cassette of the *Goldberg Variations* spooling in the dash. The road was a coiled spring gradually going upward, and so was the music, growing tenser and more involved, not less so. The air was chill and clear and so was the piano, the playing so precise and percussive that the pianist might have had mallets mounted on his fingers. The "runaway truck ramps," gravel slopes slanted off the roadside in the downhill stretches to slow down trucks whose brakes had failed, lent an air of peril to the journey and to the ivory-shattering runs of the faster variations. The car was a small and enveloping place, angular, metallic, electronically outfitted, and this, too, was true of the music: it was a bright, hard, functional structure midway between inside and outside, between solitude and the thoroughfare of common life.

At the top of the mountain there was a lookout, a few parking spots with a log rail running across them. I parked and looked out. What I remember is not the view of the hills but the sound of the music, or, to be more precise, the physical fact of the music, as elemental as earth and air. The cassette deck had gone off with the engine, which was now ticking and clacking under the hood. But the music was still going, rattling in the impressionable place behind the eyebrows, extending itself out of the car, out of the recording, over the guardrail, and into the world beyond Bach.

From there the drive was mostly downhill, a swift, open run to flatlands and college town, and as the driving became easier and the car gained momentum, the music, to that point an absolute correlative to the drive, became music again. Now I could hear the piano as the same instrument found in school auditoriums and hotel lobbies. Now I recognized the pattern of sound, the counterpoint, the harmony, the varieties of tempo and emotion, as a cultural pattern, at once arduous and reassuring, that I would later know as the pattern of the Baroque. Now I could hear the distance between the music and the man playing it—could hear, even though I had heard the *Goldberg Variations* only a few times and only on this cassette tape, the personality of Glenn Gould pressed up against Bach like a face against the sheet glass of the music. Now I could hear the character of the recording, intensely clear and bright, an extreme close-up.

I wish I could say that a profound insight accompanied the experience. The composer John Adams, who had an epiphany as he listened to Wagner while driving Route 1 on the California coast, came away thinking "he cares"—came away recognizing, in the music, the composer's unstinting confidence in the power of music to dramatize experience at its fullest and most complicated. But there was no special insight that day. In truth, the experience was resistant to insight, even insight-annihilating. I had read the notes to the recording that came folded like a warranty inside the clear plastic cassette box, with a picture of Glenn Gould's piano and chair and the producer's account of the recording as the last one made at 30th Street Studio. I had that sheet of notes (I still have it) in my coat pocket as I drove, program notes for the ride. But my memory of that day doesn't have to do with Gould and his story. What I felt was the sheer, fierce recognition that this music was right. I knew hardly anything about classical music, but already I knew what I liked. This—Bach—was what I liked.

>>12>> The September 1982 *High Fidelity* featured an article about Bach that was specialized even by the standards of a magazine for audiophiles.

The author was Joshua Rifkin, director of the Bach Ensemble. After Nonesuch and *The Baroque Beatles Book*, Rifkin had done graduate work in musicology at Princeton; following the success of his Scott Joplin record—which sparked a Joplin revival from Missouri to Hollywood—Rifkin had founded his own Baroque orchestra and chorus and recorded some Bach cantatas for Nonesuch. Now, under the headline BACH'S CHORUSES: LESS THAN THEY SEEM?, he made an argument about how Bach's written-out parts were used by singers in Bach's time.

He set out what he saw as the facts of how Bach had run his operation at the Thomasschule. Each singer had held in hand his own part. For most pieces there were four or five parts, not more. Parts for additional singers (called *ripienists*) were clearly marked as such. For Bach this was standard procedure: in the early cantata "Gott ist mein König," for the *St. John* and *St. Matthew Passions*, in the parts of the Mass in B Minor. Yes, he maintained a chorus of a dozen singers or more—but he did so to account for illness, absenteeism, and incompetence, not out of a wish to have his choral music sung by a dozen voices. Rifkin's conclusion: "Unless, contrary to all appearances, Bach deviated from standard practice and had more than one singer read from a part, the 'chorus' with which he presented his vocal music—sacred or secular, whenever or wherever composed—must normally have consisted of no more than four singers in all."

Already Rifkin's argument had caused controversy at a meeting of the American Musicological Society; already it had called forth a rebuttal by the Baroque scholar Robert L. Marshall for the next *High Fidelity*.

At issue was the matter of fidelity to Bach. To that point, the emphases given to the music—tempi, phrasing, articulation, even the choice of piano or harpischord—had generally been treated as matters of intepretation for individual musicians to decide, and period performance as an alternative taste.

Rifkin's argument was different. It went to the heart of Bach's vocal music—
the structure of the vocal ensemble—and made the case that Bach had a very
clear idea of what he wanted. If true, it would establish a new standard for fidelity to Bach, and call for a radical change in the way Bach's music should be
played and the way it ought to sound. It would reduce the size of certain choirs
by two thirds and would make the grand productions of the Passions and
Mass at Carnegie Hall seem circuses of gaudy excess, like Fifth Avenue at
Christmastime. It would uproot Bach's vocal music and relocate it in the pre-
classical era of troubadours and monody rather than that of the "Ode to Joy"
and *Die Meistersinger*. It would render *all* the extant recordings of Bach's vocal
music—fifty years' of recordings—unfaithful to Bach.

Rifkin developed his sense of Bach's choral ideal further through lively
scrutiny of Bach's writings: in one passage, he explained Bach's double sense of
the word *chorus* through reference to the Boston Red Sox, distinguishing between the "lineup" of singers used in particular pieces and the larger "roster"
of singers who were members of the chorus all through the year. But he made
his best argument through recordings. Made savvy by his adventures in pop
music and Hollywood, Rifkin shrewdly timed his article to coincide with a
new record. In December 1981, while Bach was playing on the radio (WKCR-
FM's holiday Bachfest) and at Lincoln Center (the Chamber Music Society's
seasonal run-through of the Brandenburg concertos), the Bach Ensemble had
gone into a Presbyterian church hidden midblock on Broadway on the Upper
West Side and recorded Bach's Mass in B Minor using just one singer per vocal
part.

The "B Minor Madrigal," they called it. Released by Nonesuch in the fall
of 1982, it exemplified new standards in the area of music-making coming to
be known as "early music" or "performance practice" or "period instrument"
or "period music" or "historically informed performance." The sleeve carried a
logo for the new Nonesuch Digital line in the upper left. It featured a blowup
of Bach's own signature rather than a dubious portrait of him by someone else.
It identified Rifkin as director, not conductor—conductor not being an established role in Bach's day. A thick booklet explained everything from the source
of that signature to the makers of the players' instruments (one violone was
made by "Harry Rhodes Brown, Washington, D.C., 1964; after Giovanni Paolo
Maggine, Brescia, ca. 1610"). Rifkin's notes on the Mass and this performance
of it ran several thousand words and set out the evidence for the emerging
scholarly argument that the Mass was made up of music written earlier: the
predominance of "the handsome calligraphic appearance of [Bach's] copying

hand rather than the hastier script that usually accompanied the act of composing," and the use of family members to copy some of the parts, suggesting that several Bachs together copied it on the road before a performance.

In a kind of coda, Rifkin, taking up a line of thought Glenn Gould had laid out fifteen years earlier, argued that a scholarly quandary about the Mass—was it meant as a whole, or a set of parts?—was rendered moot by "the medium of recording," which allowed for it to be heard track by track. He explained: "like the autograph manuscript score—but unlike a concert performance—the recording leaves the ultimate disposition of its contents open. The decision of whether the four parts of the B-minor Mass should stand alone or together lies with the individual listener—whose path through the music thus becomes as private as the music itself."

Rifkin's Mass in B Minor is aurally arresting the first time you hear it. It doesn't sound like a Mass; that is, it doesn't have the elements we expect in a Mass: the churchy uplift, the insistent loudness, the invitation to join in. And though it is all about performance—the word appears a dozen times in the notes—it doesn't sound like a performance, either. There are no chorus lines of sound (as in, say, Karajan's Mass in B Minor), no sense that the singers are set up before the listener like bricks in a wall. It sounds as if they are—the five of them—gathered around a single spot. In the opening Kyrie (in B minor, naturally) they sing the "Kyrie eleison" over and over in a way that suggests mourners at graveside, gathered together around the deceased one last time to ask for the Lord's mercy. Then in the "Christi eleison," a pair of sopranos swing up into D major and sing close harmony; they might be doo-wop singers under a West Side streetlight, or Baroque ancestors of the Philadelphians singing around a fire in a barrel in *Rocky*. They don't sound like a chorus; they sound like some people singing—some people singing the music of Bach.

The sound of the recording is singular, too. Although it was made in a church, it doesn't have an architectural spaciousness. Nor does it have the marks of a high-fidelity studio production: the velvety strings, the smoothing off of the top edges of the mix. The recording doesn't have a distinct character of its own. It sounds like the folk-pop records made by the Roches or the McGarrigles—sounds like a record made by Judith Nelson, Julianne Baird, Jeffrey Dooley, Frank Hoffmeister, and Jan Opalach, the singers in the Bach Ensemble.

The early-music movement came about in opposition to grand opera and its floating holiday parade of vocal talent. But Rifkin's Mass in B Minor frankly resembles opera in the way it foregrounds individual voices. Take the opening of the Gloria. Suddenly trumpets join in with the strings. The trumpets, built to period specifications, sound muddy and out of tune, and against them the five concerted voices are full of throaty glory, a reminder that while instrument-building practices vary from age to age, the human voice is created perfect in certain people in every generation.

With the Laudamus te, the instruments predominate: the violins skipping rope, the organ pursuing a sprightly line of continuo. The Bach Ensemble was said to be as compact and fleet of foot as Duke Ellington's orchestra, and the likeness fits: here, as in a cantata Rifkin and the group recorded later, number 78, "Jesu, der du meine Seele" (whose second movement goes, in English, "We hasten with faint but eager steps"), the continuo is a full-on walking bass, with the soprano voice wandering freely above it. Once heard, it seems elementary: the smaller the choir, the easier it is to hear the instruments, and vice versa.

The vigor of the orchestra calls our attention back to the quality of the voices. We praise thee, we bless thee, we worship thee, we glorify thee: in a Mass, the sentiments (those of Laudamus te) are doctrinal reminders ("We ought to bless thee"), but here they seem to characterize human nature. Here is a woman, clear and strong of voice, giving praise.

The total effect comes clear at the end of the Gloria, where the sound of a full chorus is at last attained. Rifkin earns this moment; he builds to it, withholding his reduced musical forces and then releasing them at a moment of maximum impact. It really does sound glorious.

The tension between the personal emphasis in the voices and the uninflected recording is what gives Rifkin's Mass in B Minor its sound. That tension, it turned out, would characterize digital recording and the compact disc. Digital technology rendered the music precisely, as Thomas Stockham had promised. It delivered perfect clarity, making good on the claims of Philips and Sony. But right away some people insisted that other qualities had been lost—spaciousness, depth, and the slight aural exaggerations that gave recorded music character and warmth, and that had come to be identified with the soul of a recording.

Rifkin's Mass in B Minor was made available on compact disc in 1982. By then Philips had initiated a program of CD releases: dozens each month, most of them classical recordings. From the beginning there was a debate over the two formats: analog vs. digital, the vinyl LP vs. the compact disc, $6.99 vs. $12.99. But the record companies acted aggressively to retire the LP, and by 1985 the CD had taken hold. Then a funny thing happened. Where in popular

music the CD prompted the labels to remaster their perennial bestsellers—
Bringing It All Back Home, Abbey Road, Dark Side of the Moon, Tapestry—in
classical music the CD had a generative effect. It prompted record companies
large and small to order up new digital recordings of the entire Western canon
of classical music, the way they had done when the long-playing record replaced the 78 in the fifties. These were opportunities for period musicians to
introduce their approach: their selection of instruments; their brisk tempi;
their clear, spare, attenuated sonic aesthetic; and their selection of works—
Monteverdi along with Verdi, Pergolesi as well as Vivaldi, Schütz before
Bach.

Thus the compact disc and historically informed performance were put in
paradoxic counterpoint. Through the demand for new recordings, especially
those done in an adjectivally suggestive new way—"first release"; "authentic";
"world premiere recording"; "on original instruments"—the CD enabled the
period-music forces to claim one piece of territory after another. In this way
the period-music sound, so congenial to digital recording and the CD, became
the new format for classical music.

There came a counterreformation. John Eliot Gardiner, Roger Nor-
rington, Christopher Hogwood, Nikolaus Harnoncourt: even among classical-
music devotees these figures and the ensembles they led (the Monteverdi Choir,
the English Concert, the Academy of Ancient Music, the Concertus Musicus
Wien) were unknowns compared with maestros such as Karajan and Bernstein or virtuosi such as Perlman and Previn (and Glenn Gould). In the wider
world they were scarcely known. Yet in the small, resource-poor land of classical music they wielded power that struck those with different ideas as ill-
gotten and oppressive—and gave performances that their detractors found
musically bloodless and historically wobbly.

Against his wishes, Richard Taruskin, a professor of music at Columbia
who led a Renaissance choral ensemble, became the period-music movement's
most incisive critic. At the 1981 conference in Boston where Joshua Rifkin
made his case for one-voice-on-a-part, Taruskin was called on to address the
relationship of "the musicologist and the performer," and in the years to follow
he took up the role of the musicologist warning the performer about "the limits of authenticity."

His brief was straightforward. The movement took an arbitrary approach
to the musical past. It claimed to establish past "performance practices," but
wound up reflecting the practices of the present more than those of the
past—a point that its leaders, so aware of the influence of social conditions on

music-making, should have understood. Out of fidelity to the musical text (and especially to the earliest version of the text) it left out all the aspects of the music that had not been notated; in its regard for the composer's intentions (and the belief that these could be found in the text), it reduced the performer to a mere executant in ways that violated well-established truths about how actual musicians in the past had actually performed. Having done away with the musician as interpreter, it seized on interpretive cues in the text and historical data from the period when the music was composed; but whatever the composer, the work, the country, or the period, it wound up stressing certain traits: clarity, lightness, speed, regularity, impersonality, and indifference to the audience. "What we had been accustomed to regard as historically authentic performances," Taruskin later explained, "I began to see . . . embodied a whole wish list of modern[ist] values, validated in the academy and the marketplace alike by an eclectic, opportunistic reading of historical evidence."

"We impose our esthetic on Bach no less than did Liszt, Busoni, or even Stokowski," Taruskin observed. "Authentic" performances, that is, were stamped with the spirit of the age: the present age, the late twentieth century.

Naturally, the controversy would come to bear on Bach. The range and quality of Bach's music-making, the abundance of his surviving texts, and the firm grasp of his music among working musicians made his music a lodestone for the period-music movement. At the same time, a half-century of revivals had made Bach popular, and this enabled period-music experts to refashion Bach esoterically and still hope to reach a good-size audience. On top of it all, an anniversary was approaching: the three-hundredth anniversary of the birth of Bach in 1685. Two complete sets of the cantatas—a historically cognizant set, conducted by Nikolaus Harnoncourt, and a conventional cycle, conducted by Helmuth Rilling—were in progress. So were new recordings of the Passions, the B-minor Mass, the keyboard works, the Brandenburgs . . . of virtually all of the works of Bach. So the music of Bach was made the subject of digital revival.

Taruskin made clear that there were period-music Bach recordings he actually liked. His essay "The Pastness of the Present and the Presence of the Past" featured a survey of seven different prehistorical recordings of the fifth Brandenburg concerto. He tracked the acceleration in tempo from Furtwängler (72 beats per minute) to Andrew Parrott (96) and Christopher Hogwood (98, performing from variant texts); and as the tempo changed, he heard the concerto change from a "vast, great, rugged" work of "imposing gravity" and "importance" to a jeu d'esprit—a musical jest. And yet he concluded the exercise by praising Gustav Leonhardt's fifth Brandenburg (96 beats per minute) for its energy, its artful good taste, and its distinction between the music's beat and its meter.

Made in a church in Haarlem in 1976, it is an extraordinary recording, from its opening, a bright D-major chord arpeggiated upward by the whole group together. There is plenty else to hear as the group sound takes root: the blunt downstrokes of the violins, like axes swung at birches on a fall afternoon; the squared-off, latticed character of the piece, even as it trundles kinetically along; the contours of the recording, airy and pocketed, so that you can practically see the musicians leaning into their stands to pump the music into the old church. This orchestra is one big wooden instrument, a vessel bearing a cargo of sound. The string instruments of the period were akin to the sailing ships of the period: wood warmed and bent around the struts of a frame, with other pieces of wood sticking out and lines strung between them to make them work together. Yes, this orchestra is a wooden ship, a small craft held together by fit, not force, and propelled by an unseen force managed through the push-pull synchrony of the crew.

The woody quality of the music is the effect of the period instruments. "For some listeners the tone of these instruments may still sound strange," Leonhardt allowed. "However, many will admit, after closer, more 'synchronized' listening, that the balance between the various instruments is achieved much more naturally, that the variety of timbres and the subtleties of intonation of the woodwinds constitute a tremendous wealth of color compared with the smoothed-out tone of later instruments . . ." By the sixth concerto, the sounds of the orchestra have blended together in a pattern of inadvertent intricacy. But the real surprise is the brisk tempo, which suggests that the past, though made of wood, was faster than the present.

Taruskin, no fundamentalist, thrilled to all this. The instruments were original, the structure "geometrical," and the tempo brisk, all hallmarks of the performance-practice approach. "But the larger metrical units and the broader pulses lend a hint of iconicity to the performance—a sense of human gait." Where others applied a rocking beat, unwittingly applying the present to the past, Leonhardt made Bach's music walking music.

>>13>> As the Bach bicentenary of 1985 approached, the Bach canon was shifting. Musicologists were making ever greater use of two techniques

of classical philology to scrutinize manuscripts and place them in a chronology. One was handwriting analysis: by identifying characteristics in the written texts of Bach's pieces—say, a certain way of writing the G clef—they could distinguish between texts written by Bach and those produced by his copyists, or "scribes"; then, by identifying particular scribes—sons, students, junior members of the music faculty at the Thomasschule—and figuring out when they had been members of Bach's circle, the scholars could place a work chronologically. The other was paper analysis: by examining the sheets of rag-based paper on which Bach's works were written, and finding the watermarks, they could further situate a work in the chronology, by establishing that it was written on paper Bach had ordered in a batch from, say, a stationer's in Köthen in 1720.

These techniques had been in use in connection with Bach's music since work on the New Bach Edition commenced in the 1950s, but with the sudden swift development of computers in the 1980s they became at once more widespread and more precise. With computers, scholars could store entire handwriting sets of Bach's scribes and call them up at will for comparison, seeking perfect matches; with computers, they could make high-resolution photographs of Bach's manuscripts and scrutinize them without subjecting the originals to wear and tear. The same technology that was bringing Bach's music into the digital present through the compact disc was rooting the music more and more deeply in the everyday life of eighteenth-century Thuringia and Saxony.

At the same time, the canon was being revised through traditional scholarly practices. In 1982, scholars cataloging the contents of a manuscript collection in the Herric Music Library at Yale were amazed to discover a cache of previously unknown works of Bach. LM4708, or the Neumeister Collection, as it came to be known, contained eighty-two chorale preludes. Christoph Wolff, now of Harvard, and Hans-Joachim Schulze, a researcher on staff at the Bach-Archiv in Leipzig, used musical and philological analysis to identify thirty-eight of them with confidence as works Bach had written in his first years as an organist in Arnstadt; and by comparing them with the adjacent pieces, identified as works of his father-in-law, Johann Michael, and Johann Michael's brother Johann Christoph, they gave a fresh view of the musical debt Bach owed to his predecessors.

What scholarship gave, scholarship took away. In the journal *Early Music* the previous year, the organist and musicologist Peter Williams had argued that Bach's single most famous organ work wasn't actually the music of Bach: BWV 565, the Toccata and Fugue in D Minor.

For Williams the work was suspect precisely because it was extraordinary. In their wish to emphasize historical practice rather than the practices of individual composers, period-music scholars had brought fresh attention to dozens of little-known Baroque composers (such as Johann Christoph and Johann Michael Bach). Those composers had been neglected because their music was considered second-rate, derivative, dull. Now they were promoted as composers whose works, in their very ordinariness, carried vital information about the way music had been made in ordinary circumstances in the past. The date of the Toccata and Fugue in D Minor had always been suspect, because the piece existed not in an "autograph" manuscript by Bach himself but in a later copy. Williams compared the piece with the organ works of Bach and other composers of the early eighteenth century, and showed that it relied on technical effects found nowhere else. It was exceptional, one of a kind. This, in his account, was why it was found only in a later copy: it was a work written by another, later composer.

The argument was not airtight: Williams could not identify the later composer, and there were plausible reasons why Bach had used effects found nowhere else in his work—parallel octaves, for example, to make up for the limitations of the organ at Arnstadt. Possibly the piece was a one-off, a work of a young genius. But a reasonable doubt had been established. Henceforth the Toccata and Fugue in D Minor would be a masterpiece with an asterisk.

>>14>>   Yo-Yo Ma was sitting in a chair onstage, quite upright. His torso was encased in a plaster cast, which kept his back straight and made his shoulders look broad, a look he had come to like. His arms had been left free so that he could hold a cello, on which he played a suite by Bach.

Nearly two decades after his audience with Pablo Casals, Yo-Yo Ma was on the verge of fulfilling the expectations that others had held for him all his life—in Paris and New York, at Marlboro and Juilliard, at Trinity and Columbia and Harvard, and now for CBS Masterworks.

He was twenty-five years old. He had had surgery to correct a curve in his spine. After a six-month convalescence—out of the public eye, save that one recital—he emerged a full-on performer for the first time; that year he played 125 concerts, 60 of them as a solo cellist with orchestra.

He had already made half a dozen records for CBS: cello concertos by Saint-Saëns and Lalo, plus the cello bits from Saint-Saëns's *Carnival of the Animals*; Haydn's cello concertos; Beethoven sonatas for cello and piano; ebul-

lient string pieces by Kreisler, Paganini, and Dvořák. Those records had
been soft openings, final expressions of the LP era.* Now he would begin a
recording career in earnest. The proof of his majority would be a new digital
recording of the Bach cello suites for release on three LPs and two compact
discs.

So he went a few months later to Vanguard Studios on West Twenty-third
Street in Manhattan. Over the years, Vanguard, originally a base for the label
of that name, had been used for a wide spread of artists, from P. D. Q. Bach
to Country Joe and the Fish to Kiss. It was one of the first studios to be
equipped with a Neve 16-track mixing desk. With 30th Street Studio closed,
CBS was using Vanguard for some classical sessions. The Soundstream console was trucked in. Yo-Yo Ma arrived with a cello nearly as old as the music of
Bach; and in five sessions he recorded the cello suites, which he had played in-
cessantly since his childhood.

Many years later, the record still sounds the way it did when it came out.
It is the sound of the vital center, the royal road rising above the trails cut and
cleared and trodden by others. It is Bach for all seasons: for richer and for
poorer, in sickness and in health. With a bowstroke it boldfaces the classic in
classical music and gives the term a fresh charge.

The center of the record, the source of its vitality, is the sound of the cello
itself. Possibly it is a 1712 Stradivarius; possibly it is a Matteo Goffriller made in
Venice ten years later. Whatever it is, in Ma's hands it is as progressively aged
as a giant redwood. Its sound is ongoing, a signal or broadcast, and the artistry
consists in how the sound is guided by the cellist. The sound pours out. It has
heft without effort. It has headroom up to thirty thousand feet; it has room
below, full fathom five. It is woody, but where other cellists carve the old
wood, this one polishes it with oil and chamois.

Obviously, the sound of the record owes something to the quality of the
recording. But in this case the thing to say about the recording is nothing at all.
The sound of the record is the sound of the cello, full stop. A hundred years
after the advent of recording, transparency has been achieved.

The record is transparent in another way. It sounds absent of autobiography. Ma's life was bound up with the suites, but the recording, though rich in
inwardness, does not tell a personal story; though made a few streets from the
apartment where he grew up, it faces forward and outward.

---

*The CD booklet for the Kreisler-Paganini record carried a band of info about the compact disc format,
boasting "Now Made In The U.S.A."—but not a word about the performing artist.

His story was just beginning to circulate outside the world of virtuosi—the story of a person who was raised for music, whose early life was a point of convergence for a vast field of forces: China, France, and North America; the cello, the music of Bach, and classical music generally. In the early tellings—whether a *New Yorker* profile or a memoir written by his mother for the Anglophone Chinese market—the hand of destiny is omnipresent. A gifted being is born to parents who recognize in him one greater than themselves. He is raised to assume great responsibilities. He accedes. He thrives. He rebels. He is allowed to go his own way, which, after a few twists, turns out to be something like the way others envisioned for him in the first place. Like the story of the Dalai Lama, the story confounds Western ideas of nature and nurture; coming-of-age is given a time-out, and things happen the way they are meant to happen. And yet for Yo-Yo Ma, as for the Dalai Lama, the surprise in the story—the guarantor of its truth—is that he turned out to be brilliantly suited for the role he was made to play.

There is another way of telling the story: as the story of a musician, devoted to Bach, who fully grasped the inner life of Bach's music and brought it to bear on his son, who made it his own.

In New York in 1962, H. T. Ma had settled the family in a one-room apartment on Madison Avenue in the Twenties. He had moved from China to Paris twenty-seven years earlier, and this time he established himself expertly. In a few months he founded a children's orchestra and gained a position as music director at a francophone school on the Upper East Side. For Yo-Yo he engaged a cello tutor, Janos Scholz, on Isaac Stern's recommendation.

"I was born when he was forty-nine, so he was an older parent, very old-world," Yo-Yo later recalled. He "was the pedagogue of the family, very strict," and for the next ten years he schooled Yo-Yo and his sister, Yeou-Cheng, as definitely as any tutor. Outside the apartment they gave recitals and met master musicians, following on their appearance with Leonard Bernstein on the *Tonight Show* in 1961. Inside, they followed a curriculum of their father's devising: practice, Chinese calligraphy, history, Bible study, French, music memorization. Each was forbidden to speak, hum, sing, or interrupt while the other was practicing. They listened to records: one favorite was an LP of Schubert trios played by Pablo Casals and friends. They sat all together for supper, Chinese-style. At the end of the day, Yo-Yo would play a Bach suite, or several. As Bach was a blessing on Casals's house every morning, Bach was a valediction on the Ma's apartment, an evening prayer.

It was a regimen, but one designed to keep the burden light. The key to

H. T. Ma's approach to music education was that children should learn music by segments. Instead of practicing exercises for many hours, they should learn a few measures until they could play them perfectly; then learn the next few, and so on. Yo-Yo learned to play Bach that way. "I learned two measures of a Bach suite every day. No more. No less," he later recalled. "I got them right. I got to recognize all the patterns in the music. I developed my memory. It also made me think about what I was doing.

"By practicing only half an hour a day, I learned three Bach suites by heart by the time I was seven. Every night, I'd play through what I knew just to refresh my memory."

The anecdote suggests the other way of telling Yo-Yo Ma's story, one in which the term *destiny* makes a kind of sense. H. T. Ma, grasping the inner life of Bach's music, had focused on its cellular structure, its basis as a sequence of inventions awaiting development. He had made this underlying pattern of invention the basis of his pedagogy. He had applied it to his children from an early age, and for Yo-Yo Ma it became a pattern for musical and personal development. Two and a half centuries earlier, Bach had offered the invention as a pattern for coming-of-age with the gift of the *Clavier-büchlein*—which included a group of inventions—to his growing son Wilhelm Friedemann Bach. In this sense, Yo-Yo Ma was his father's invention, a child raised according to a pattern that would be developed and brought to fulfillment with others.

Meanwhile, he was also being raised as a cello prodigy, Manhattan-style. He went to the Trinity School on the Upper West Side, crossing the park from the Upper East Side, where the family now lived. A new tutor, Leonard Rose, brought out points of interpretation using the local argot: "Sock it to me, baby," he'd say, or "Give it to me the way my wife gave it to me last night." Yo-Yo was entreated to take part in competitions: sacred rites for the classical-music cult centered on the Juilliard School and Lincoln Center. When Rose's managers got requests for Yo-Yo to give recitals, they went ahead and booked the dates. What was the problem? What was there not to like? But Ma's parents would not allow it, and they bowed out on his behalf. The competition circuit was too ruthless, the "recital racket" too narrow. These led young musicians to focus on music only, at the expense of the whole person.

It was a life of strenuous isolation, in which Yo-Yo Ma was recognized as a standout by other young musicians even as he stood apart from them. He sought to join them. At Juilliard, where he enrolled in a precollege program on Saturdays, he skipped classes in ear training and the like in order to sit in the cafeteria and listen to other students talk. "I *loved* going there," he recalled.

"I'd cut classes just to *be* with other people." Away from his family for a few hours, he roamed the Upper West Side and Times Square, where he saw movies, played pinball, and took in the human comedy that was in full bloom there in 1968 and 1969.

At fifteen, he had a crisis. He cut classes. He cursed at his teachers. Away at music camp, he ran wild and left his cello outdoors overnight. He dressed down and let his hair grow: one photograph shows him erect at the music stand, dressed like a Mormon in starched white shirt, tie, and black-framed glasses; the next shows him playing, loose-limbed, khakied and wire-rimmed like a freedom fighter. One time, he drank six gin and tonics before giving a recital. Another time, he was found unconscious in a Juilliard practice room and taken to Roosevelt Hospital, on suspicion of a drug overdose. He had passed out after drinking a fifth of scotch.

As the story is told, the reasons for his misbehavior are clear. He was in the throes of adolescent rebellion. He was rejecting the strictures of his plainly patriarchal family. He was asserting American-style freedom against Chinese restraint and self-subordination. He was chafing under the burden of his talent, shaking off great expectations. There is something to all that. But his rebellion is less revealing than the moments of sweet liberty that preceded it. Hearing him play the cello, Pablo Casals had told his parents to make sure he had time to play in the street with his friends. They hadn't. But he found a way. Riding his bike in Central Park, roaming the Upper West Side, making the pinball machine blink and ring—these were the first steps in a journey toward normality. He would be a well-tempered prodigy.

Those steps also suggested the path that his talent would take, with Bach in particular. The music of Bach was out in the street now, put there by technology. Somehow, Yo-Yo Ma grasped this. Strolling on the avenues, working the flippers, flying on two wheels through the park, he was not escaping the career that awaited him. He was surveying its territory.

>>15>> Harvard was the way out of Yo-Yo Ma's quandary. Leonard Bernstein had gone there; Yeou-Cheng Ma was a student there; Yo-Yo's Juilliard classmates Richard Kogan and Lynn Chang had enrolled. Presented in the stories as a surprising, daring choice for a music prodigy, Harvard could hardly have been more obvious.

And yet Yo-Yo Ma was altered profoundly by the place. Far from cloistral, it was thrillingly worldly. His studies were broad, even by the standards of the liberal arts: anthropology, the renowned "Rice Paddies" course in East Asian civilizations, Dostoyevsky and German literature in translation, as well as music and performance. He played a limited schedule of public concerts, about one a month; meanwhile, he played with the college chamber orchestra and Bach society, in a trio with Chang and Kogan, and in the pit orchestra for a Gilbert and Sullivan operetta. "No one ever knew when he practiced; he was always available," Kogan recalled. He played informally for the university community. One concert—at the Busch-Reisinger Museum, where E. Power Biggs still held forth on the pipe organ—was attended by his anthropology professor, Irven Devore, who had heard Pablo Casals play in San Juan; the next morning the professor crowed to the class that the shy boy in the back of the lecture hall was greater than Casals. Another filled up so quickly that Ma went outside to play a concert before the concert. "Even back then, the word was out about this phenomenon, and there were never enough seats," Kogan recalled. "One of my enduring images is Yo-Yo inviting a crush of people, who couldn't get tickets, into the transept of Memorial Hall at about 7:30 and playing Bach suites for them, right up to the moment he had to go on stage."

He studied with Leon Kirchner, pianist and Schoenbergian composer, who told him that he hadn't found the true center of his tone yet. He took part in a master class with Mstislav Rostropovich, who told him the same thing, then invited him to take part in a recital in Washington, D.C. But first the elder cellist and the younger one played for a dozen people in a Harvard common room. "You could see that Yo-Yo was showing off for the older man, and that Rostropovich was watching him, seeing what he could do," Sarah Crichton, a classmate whom Yo-Yo invited to watch, later recalled. "But what passed between them was tender—and was *fun* at the same time. There they were, there we were, having fun."

Two years and two hundred miles from Roosevelt Hospital, Yo-Yo Ma struck others as serene and well-adjusted. "Even at Harvard, that lobster tank of snappish egos, Yo-Yo had an air of benign hypernormalcy," his classmate Evan Eisenberg recalled. "You wavered between thinking him a reborn Taoist sage and your typical Paris-born Asian all-American boy. He would take his seat onstage as calmly as if on a bus, though you felt that if it were a bus, he would have offered his seat to an elderly lady.

"When he began to play, of course, things changed . . ."

He graduated in 1977, age twenty-one. Soon afterward he made two long-term commitments: he got married, and he signed a record contract.

The marriage was to Jill Hornor, a student from Mount Holyoke College whom he had met at Marlboro. There, she was a staff member, having played violin in youth orchestras in Boston; at Mount Holyoke, she was preparing for a career as a scholar of German literature. His parents were upset at first that he had decided to marry a woman who was not of Chinese heritage. The marriage was not an act of defiance; but it was an act of independence. As Ma put it, Hornor was the first person who asked him what *he* thought and what *he* meant.

The recording contract was with Columbia. Goddard Lieberson had left the label, and Masterworks was being revamped along more commercial lines. Like Wynton Marsalis, a trumpeter from New Orleans whose lineage, ambition, and cultivated normality would make him Yo-Yo Ma's jazz counterpart, Ma represented a new approach to the quandary of the big record companies, where classical and jazz claimed ever smaller parts of a robust market. How to cross over? How to play for both sides? Typically, the crossover record was a virtuoso take on standards, pop, and novelty songs, like John Coltrane's "My Favorite Things," or a popified classic, like "A Fifth of Beethoven." *Switched-on Bach* had done it both ways. Now Marsalis and Ma would switch it back. They would be crossover artists of a different kind. They would invite celebrity, court the establishment, cultivate the large audience, but they would leave the music out of it. The music itself needed no simplifying or improving. They would play it straight—play it purer and straighter than their ancestors.

Strong sales of Glenn Gould's new *Goldberg Variations* made clear that the public craved new instances of the classical ideal. With his recording of the Bach cello suites, Yo-Yo Ma delivered one. "This music has accompanied me for twenty-nine years," he said a few years later, "and will continue to do so for as long as I can play. It grows with you and constantly enriches you; you can never do it full justice. Each suite has its own distinctive character. The First is the simplest of the set, the most open, the most innocent. I feel that I'm out in nature; the prelude evolves like light becoming stronger. If the First Suite is sunrise, the Second, in D minor, is somber—defiant. The Third Suite is noble and exuberant; it's so human and accessible that is has become the most popular of all." That explanation—a clear, succinct statement of universals—is characteristic of his approach to the suites. It is personal, but not autobiographical. It is virtuosic, but not showy. There is darkness to it, but darkness without a moral aspect; there is drama, but the drama of the order of things, of day and night, the four seasons, youth and age.

It is also a counterpoint to Pablo Casals. Inevitably, this recording of the Bach suites called to mind comparisons with the Casals recording: Old World vs. New World, Latin vs. Asian, romantic vs. analytic, hot vs. cold. Undoubtedly, Yo-Yo Ma, who knew the Casals recording by heart, had it in mind when he made his own recordings. There are real differences. Sometimes Casals puts a little more mustard on the bow; sometimes Ma is sleeker, probably taking advantage of a second take. Ma takes a lower road to grandeur. His recording is not a personal story. It is testimony, perhaps, to the spirit of Bach himself—but not the spirit, on reflection, so much as the worldliness of Bach, who had the power to make works not frankly worldly that bear on the world profoundly even so.

That said, the obvious difference between the two sets of suites is in the recording. The difference of forty years is the difference between a living room and an operating room, between a fixed lens and a zoom lens. Casals is playing, say, twenty feet away, and the recording is pitched high and narrow, the better to capture the cello as a voice, not an instrument vibrating in space. Ma, too, is playing twenty feet away, but the recording moves right in on him: he is right here, or rather, we are right there. With his recording Casals and his cello came into the listener's living room. Yo-Yo Ma's recording brings the listener to the sonic place where his cello is.

We know the Casals sound, but we will never fully know what the music of Bach coming from Casals's cello sounded like. The technology, even at Abbey Road, was too rudimentary. Possibly a future listener will find Yo-Yo Ma's Vanguard Studios recording primitive. Possibly one does already. But its decline is not as likely. With digital recording, a corner was turned; with it (as Glenn Gould foresaw) the sound of a recording passed from text to context, from the player to the listener.

A comparison of Gould and Ma is revealing. In Ma, CBS had found the anti-Gould. He was unlike Gould in that he was not shy about performing or fussy about recording. More than that, he was unlike Gould in that he was a musician of unusual upbringing who yearned to be, and be seen to be, a normal person—not ordinary, certainly, but normal. He performed normality as virtuosically as he performed Bach. And yet in many ways he was akin to Gould and would carry on Gould's investigations into "the prospects of recording." He was like Gould in his attention to possibilities rather than a settled repertory. He was like Gould in his reluctance to repeat himself or to let himself be ensnared by routine. He was like Gould in his interest in other media and the vast popular culture in which classical music more than ever was just one choice among many.

Don Hunstein took a sleeve photograph: the cellist in concert dress, thick

black hair combed back away from big gold wire-rim glasses, right hand bearing a wedding ring, hands and eyes intent on a cello ten times his age, the
wood worn and mottled to a texture of inimitable complexity.

Yo-Yo Ma had grasped the insights of the great Bach pioneers who went
before him. Now he would make them his own. At the moment when the different approaches to recorded music began to augment rather than replace one
another, he was there to consolidate them. Like Albert Schweitzer, he was a
man of mixed background (China, France, America) whose identity was a
three-part invention. As a cellist, he would embrace what Pablo Casals had
renounced: he would be a man out in the world, not a man in a room. Out in
the world, he would take the notion of musicians playing together to places
even Leopold Stokowski had not envisioned. He would take Glenn Gould's
yearning for technical transcendence out of the studio and into the street
through the devices that would make recorded music portable. He would play
both sides, a popular artist but not a popularizer.

>>16>>   The fugue was where Bach had begun composing music. As a
young man he had sat at the pipe organs in Arnstadt and Mühlhausen and
coupled fugues with fantasias, toccatas, and chorale preludes, devising a melody and then imitating it—multiplying it, subdividing it, varying it again
and again.

Fuguelike, this development of his work was resolving to its theme. When
he first arrived at the Thomaskirche, he had returned to the cantata. Now,
twenty years later, he returned to the fugue, making it the shape of the sound
of his seniority. He assembled a second book of the *Well-Tempered Clavier*:
twenty-four preludes and fugues, a pair in each major and minor key, writing
the prelude on one side of a sheet of paper and then flipping it over and writing
the fugue on the back. He corrected the published text of the *Aria with diverse
variations*, and composed fourteen more canons derived from the aria, relishing the correspondence of the number with the sum, two plus one plus three
plus eight, of his enumerated surname. And he conceived a new work that
would sit in counterpoint to the *Aria with diverse variations*. It would consist of
a theme with diverse fugues, akin to a work Buxtehude had written around
the time Bach visited him in Lübeck. Where in the *Aria with diverse variations*
Bach had worked variations on a theme by venturing extravagantly afar from
the aria, this time he would stick closely to the theme, and would create variety
by putting it in play in fugues of all kinds: simple fugues, double fugues, triple

fugues, inverted fugues, mirror fugues, canons simplex, duplex, and triplex. Like his other keyboard works of those years it would be a piece of pedagogy: each *contrapunctus* would demonstrate a kind of counterpoint, and together they would illustrate the art of the fugue.

Fugue means "flight," and the sequence would begin as an exercise in subtraction, an effort to make a fugue as weightless as possible. He had a theme, twelve notes carved into a scrimshaw figure of melody:

He set out the theme in the alto voice and developed it through counterpoint. He set out the theme in the bass and developed it, or countered it, a different way. He inverted the theme and set it out in the tenor voice, surrounding it with counterpoint; he inverted it and set it out for development in the soprano voice. The work took flight, one fugue following another. The theme tailed itself; it met itself coming and going, in ongoing encounter, a series of openings. A fugue countering the theme with the theme, but inverted. A fugue in which the theme was countered by the theme inverted and diminished, or one in which the theme was inverted, then diminished and augmented at the same time. Through *stretto*, or close imitation, the work took on texture, like the textures he knew from the forests of Thuringia or the streets of Leipzig—bark and root, hoof and hide; through *stretto*, it became lifelike, then wholly, stubbornly, artfully alive, a created thing in its own right.

In London, Samuel Johnson had made a plan for his *Dictionary* and John Wesley was brooding over his failure as an evangelist. Jean-Pierre de Caussade, French Jesuit, was practicing spiritual direction focused on the "sacrament of the present moment." In the colonies, John Woolman, Quaker tailor, was speaking out against slavery, and Jonathan Edwards was delivering sermons that would spark an extraordinary religious revival or awakening. And in the composing room in Leipzig, Johann Sebastian Bach was fuguing: with the sounds of music students thrumming in the hallways, the calling and haggling of the Markt coming through the window, the rough-and-ready harmony of singing voices in the church, he was writing music in flagrant counterpoint. The city was occupied by Prussian troops at war with Saxony—the "Prussian Invasion," Bach called it. In the circumstances, he scaffolded a tower in thin air, drew the bars of his own cell. Structurally, the fugues all together suggest variety, a melody treated every which way; but experientially, for the listener, following by ear not eye, the effect is that of a strong brew intensified. The plot thickens; the theme is concentrated from regular to espresso; like an alloy, the sound is lighter and stronger than the base material, the way light seen through stained glass instead of in the clear blue sky is both less bright and more striking.

He assembled a single manuscript, twelve fugues and two canons, and marked some changes and corrections in the margins. There would be four-teen fugues in all. He was almost finished. All that was left to do was revise one fugue, perfect a couple of pieces, and write the concluding fugue, which he could see and hear already as if it were done and whole.

Then the world sought him out with a trio of invitations, like the trumpet figures his father had played from the town hall tower in Eisenach during his childhood, a fugue in three voices calling him back to the world.

The church of St. Wenceslas in Naumburg invited him to inspect a new pipe organ. The organ had been built by Zacharias Hildebrandt, and probably Bach had a hand in its design. Hildebrandt had been an apprentice to Gott-fried Silbermann, the designer of pipe organs from Saxony to Strasbourg. Sil-bermann, two years older than Bach, was going to inspect the Naumburg organ too.

They all met in the Wenzelskirche on September 27, 1746. Possibly Bach played one of his new *contrapuncti* on the new organ, a three-manual instru-ment with fifty-three stops. But the record of the inspection of the organ says nothing about the music made on it that day. It declares that "every part speci-fied and promised by the contract—namely, manuals, bellows, wind chests, channels, pedal and manual action, with the various parts, registers, and stops pertaining thereto, both open and stopped, as well as reed—is really there," and urges Hildebrandt to check the organ again "from stop to stop." It is signed by Bach, Court Composer, and Silbermann, Court Official Organ Builder. It is boilerplate—but the encounter was for all time, two inventors as-sessing the latest version of the instrument they had spent their lives developing.

The Society of Musical Science invited Bach to become a member. Peter

Williams in his biography tells the story: Some years earlier, J. A. Scheibe, an organist and a rival, had published a stinging critique of Bach's music in a journal in Hamburg. The thrust of it was that the music was just too complicated. Bach wrote music that other people could not play or sing. In a choir, he made all the voices equal rather than making one stand out. He obscured his melodies with "embellishment" and "turgid" accompaniment. He was guilty of "obscuring beauty with too much art." After the journal came out, other musicians rallied around Bach. One was Lorenz Mizler, once a student of Bach's, then a scholar of music at the university in Leipzig (thesis topic: "whether the art of music is part of philosophic wisdom"). In 1738, Mizler founded the Society of Musical Science, a "correspondence society": a dozen or so composers exchanging ideals by mail and newsletter, with each composing a piece of "theoretical speculation" annually. Telemann was a member. So was Handel. It is not clear why Bach was not a member from the beginning. Possibly he was absorbed in writing sacred music; possibly he was wary of "philosophic wisdom."

In 1746 Mizler published an account of Scheibe's quarrel with Bach in the society's journal, emphatically taking Bach's side. Now Bach signed on with the society, becoming its fourteenth member. Two pieces of Bachiana mark his entry. One is the piece of "theoretical speculation" he offered as the obligation of membership. It is a set of five variations on "Von Himmel hoch," a hymn written by Luther for Christmas Day. The Prussian invasion of Leipzig was over, and it may be that Bach played the hymn at a service of thanksgiving for the new peace at the Nikolaikirche on Christmas Day 1745. He sketched a theme and three variations a few months later, making a canon of each, and it says something about Bach and Luther alike that the variations, highly abstract in construction, sound like Christmas music nevertheless: in the exuberantly downward-running theme, you can all but hear the angel coming down from highest heaven.

The other is a portrait of Bach painted by Elias Gottlob Haussmann, an artist in Leipzig. It is the only portrait that can be said for sure to be of Bach. He stands in darkness, in a black coat over a ruffled shirt, stout, white-wigged, keen-eyed, thick of cheek and chin. How different he looks from his father, a swarthy horn player in a coarse shirt with an open neck. Leipzig's town councillors had sat for portraits by Haussmann, and Bach, buttoned up, upstanding, might be one of them.

Might be, except for the sheet of paper he proffers with a fleshy right hand. It is a sheet of music. It is turned outward to face us, as his offering to the

Society of Musical Science. At the top is the title *Canon Triplex a 6 voci*. It is one of the canons he had written out on the back of the published text of the *Aria with diverse variations*. The whole thing is there on a single page, notated in the painter's close imitation of the composer's handwriting, so clearly that you could prop the portrait on a music stand and play the piece from it. It makes the portrait itself, already artful, a piece of music; it makes us members of the society, receiving Bach's music through correspondence with him.

>>17>> The court of the king of Prussia invited Bach to visit. No one knows for sure how the invitation came about. Possibly it came from Bach's son Carl Philipp Emanuel, a chamber musician at the king's court, in Potsdam, near Berlin. Or it came from Bach's advocate Count Keyserlingk, who was serving as Russia's ambassador to the court. Or it came at the prompting of the king, Frederick II, who played flute with the chamber ensemble in the evenings. Or it was arranged by C.P.E. Bach at the prompting of Bach himself, who was determined to play for the king.

In May 1747, Bach set out from Leipzig for Potsdam. His son Wilhelm Friedemann, thirty-six, was with him. They traveled by coach three hundred and some miles north. Arriving in Potsdam, they entered the Old City Palace; Frederick was erecting a new palace, but it was unfinished.

Arriving in Potsdam, Bach stepped into the political conflicts of the era. C.P.E. Bach had married in 1744 and his wife had given birth to a son the next year, but the Prussian war on Saxony kept Bach from going to see them, walling him off from his new family. Now that Prussia and Saxony had made peace, he was free to visit, and to see Frederick—the most prominent music-lover in Germany at the time—as something other than an invading enemy.

He also entered into the chronicles of the period. His everyday activities are amply documented, but they took place outside of the ambit of history in the broad sense; were it not for his music, written down and passed down through time, the world beyond eastern Germany would have no evidence of his existence. No evidence, that is, except for his encounter with Frederick the Great. Because the king was the king, Bach's visit to the king's court was entered into the record right away: it was reported in the newspapers. It was entered into the record again when the two younger Bachs told a biographer what had happened during the visit.

A news report and a double batch of eyewitness testimony: by itself, either one would be as detailed an account as exists of any episode from Bach's career. Together, they are superabundantly, contrapuntally rich.

The newspaper story (based on a palace press release) has Bach going to the palace to hear the king's nightly session of chamber music, not to play in it, and is flattering to the king. Bach was waiting in an anteroom outside the royal apartments when word reached Frederick that he was there.

> His August self immediately gave orders that Bach be admitted, and went, at his entrance, to the so-called *Forte et Piano*, condescending to play, in his Most August Person and without any preparation, a theme for the Capellmeister Bach, which he should execute in a fugue. This was done so happily by the aforementioned Capellmeister that not only His Majesty was pleased to show his satisfaction thereat, but also all those present were seized with astonishment.

The other account (based on the two sons' recollections) is flattering to Bach. Bach is invited to the palace at Frederick's behest, and the king drops everything when he hears that Bach is in the house:

> . . . just as he was getting his flute ready and his musicians were assembled, an officer brought him a written list of the strangers who had arrived. With his flute in his hand, he ran over the list, but immediately turned to the assembled musicians and said, with a kind of agitation: "Gentlemen, old Bach is come." The flute was now laid aside, and old Bach, who had alighted at his son's lodgings, was immediately summoned to the palace.

Frederick called off the chamber music: he had something better in mind. He was avid for the fortepiano, an instrument that Gottfried Silbermann had adapted from an Italian design. Here was a keyboard whose strings were struck by felt hammers rather than plucked, allowing the player to produce sounds louder and softer than on the harpsichord. There were fortepianos scattered through the palace. With "old Bach" in the house, Frederick could hear what the fortepiano was capable of—could hear it played as it had never been played before.

> The musicians went with him from room to room, and Bach was invited to try the instruments and to play unpremeditated compositions. After he had gone on for some time, he asked the king to give him a subject for a fugue in order to execute it immediately without any preparation. The king admired the learned manner in which his

subject was thus executed extempore; and, probably to see how far it could be carried, expressed a wish also to hear a fugue with six obbligato parts. But as not every subject is fit for such full harmony, Bach chose one himself and immediately executed it to the astonishment of all present in the same magnificent and learned manner as he had done that of the king.

The next day, Bach was taken to see the organs at churches in Potsdam. His visit to the grandest of them, the Heileggeistkirche, had the character of a recital, and is described in the newspaper story:

On Monday, the famous man let himself be heard on the organ in the church of the Holy Spirit at Potsdam and earned general acclaim from the listeners attending in great number.

The newspaper story also has him back at the palace for a command performance, confabulating a six-part fugue on the spot:

In the evening, His Majesty charged him again with the execution of a fugue, in six parts, which he accomplished just as skillfully as on the previous occasion, to the pleasure of His Majesty and to the general admiration.

He went on to Berlin, where a friend of his, a doctor, lived on Unter der Linden, the center of the city. A new opera house had been built four years earlier, and Carl Philipp Emanuel Bach, who was with him, took him there. As Emanuel recalled, Bach was less interested in the type of music made there than in the acoustic properties of the place. He marveled at the vaulted, high-ceilinged dining hall, which reminded him (Wolff proposes) "of the mathematical art chamber, or *echonica* (echo tower), at the palace church in Weimar." To Emanuel he explained that if someone went to one corner of the oblong hall and whispered a few words very softly upward against the wall, a person standing in the corner diagonally opposite, with his face to the wall, would hear quite distinctly what was said, while between them, and in the other parts of the room, no one would hear a sound.

From Berlin, Bach returned to Leipzig and the Thomasschule. But his encounter with Frederick and the "royal theme" was just beginning. He had promised the king that he would compose a proper fugue on the royal theme and "have it engraved on copper." Now in the composing room he got down to it. As was his way, he would outdo himself. He would develop the theme in two fugues, written with the pianoforte in mind; in a set of canons; and in a trio sonata for the king's own instrument, the flute. He would have the set engraved and sent to Potsdam, continuing the encounter by correspondence. It would be enough, and more than enough; it would be a *Musical Offering*.

>>18>> In Berlin in October 1989 the Wall came down, and Bach was there.

From voluntary exile in Paris, Milan Kundera had described the Communist era as an attempt by half of the population—"the more dynamic, the more intelligent, the better half"—to create "an idyll of justice for all" in parts of Europe. "People have always aspired to an idyll," he explained offhandedly, "a garden where nightingales sing, a realm of harmony where the world does not rise up as a stranger against man nor man against other men, where the world and all its people are molded from a single stock and the fire lighting up the heavens is the fire burning in the hearts of men, where every man is a note in a magnificent Bach fugue and anyone who refuses his note is a mere black dot, useless and meaningless, easily caught and squashed between the fingers like an insect."

In the way of invention, those people sent that idea out into the world, where it took on a life of its own, and then developed grotesquely, until it "lost all resemblance to the original idea." Now they sought to stop it, "calling it back, scolding it, chasing it, hunting it down."

The peaceful revolution took flight in Warsaw, rappelled to Prague, and in September 1989 found a toehold in the Nikolaikirche in Leipzig. There, antigovernment activists held prayer services for peace, or *Friedensgebet*, at 5:00 p.m. each Monday. The meetings were themselves peaceful. The numbers of people in attendance swelled, surrounding the church, from a few hundred to a few thousand, until tens of thousands of the city's 600,000 people were assembled in the Augustusplatz, which the GDR called Karl Marx Square. The mass movement grew to 70,000, then 120,000, then 320,000. On Monday, October 9, the government sent several hundred Stasi officers to the church to suppress the crowds, but the officers, hearing the word, feeling the mood, knowing the truth, stood down. Many of them joined the protest movement that night.

Already a landmark for its association with Bach, the Nikolaikirche had become the spiritual center of the people's movement that sought to weaken

Soviet rule in Germany and then end it altogether across Europe. The interior of the church, stolid brown on the outside, had long since been renovated completely—given a whitewashed neo-Baroque interior, a too-grand nineteenth-century organ, and pillars whose capitals featured fronds like the ones on palm trees. But its place in history circa 1989 was consistent with its place in the history of Europe across a thousand years. The church at the crossroads was the site for the crisis of Europe at a crossroads. The place where Bach's *St. John Passion* had first been heard was the place where peace activists struck the first deathblows of the Cold War, the beginning of the end of the standoff between two sides. Bernd-Lutz Lange, a cabaret artist who took part in the protests, recalled: "There was no head of the revolution. The head was the Nikolaikirche and the body the center of the city. There was only one leadership: Monday, 5 p.m., St. Nicholas Church."

On November 9, after granting a series of modest concessions, a new GDR premier granted the supreme concession: he lifted travel restrictions on citizens of East Germany. The citizens had won. A hundred forty-nine kilometers north of Leipzig, their counterparts breached the Berlin Wall.

Mstislav Rostropovich, with cello, caught a flight to Berlin. He had been leading the National Symphony in Washington for a dozen years and playing recitals worldwide. He had taken part in an event at the White House with Ronald Reagan and Mikhail Gorbachev, had received a Presidential Medal of Freedom. But those were small things compared with the fall of the Wall.

He set up at Checkpoint Charlie, the crossing where tens of thousands of foreigners had had their credentials inspected over the years. A symbol in concrete, physically the Wall at that point was as crude and featureless as a parking garage. Fresh graffiti claimed the place as free territory: WILLKOMMEN IN OST-BERLIN, with the OST crossed out. There Rostropovich, just past sixty, with a shock of white hair, in a sweater vest and a blue blazer, played Bach's music for solo cello for the German people and for West German and French camera crews. A two-minute slice of footage is part of the documentary history of the period. The music is the sarabande from the third suite, in C major. Camera shutters click in counterpoint. The master's tone is quavery. Frankly, he is playing out of tune. But it is, no question, a historic performance. November 11, 1989: Bach marks the spot.

Isaac Stern caught a flight to Jerusalem on a similar mission fifteen months later. In 1960, Stern had led the effort to save Carnegie Hall from being razed for redevelopment (and he later joined Rostropovich, Yehudi Menuhin, Dietrich Fischer-Dieskau, Vladimir Horowitz, and Leonard Bernstein in singing an ad hoc version of Handel's "Hallelujah" chorus to celebrate its survival). Now he was the president of Carnegie Hall, which was marking its centenary, and he understood himself as not just a musician but "a willing and capable catalyst" in worldly affairs. Born in the Russian Ukraine, raised in San Francisco, he had made his concert debut at age sixteen with the Bach double concerto, which he had played countless times, among them in a sixtieth-birthday concert at Carnegie Hall in 1980. He refused to perform in Germany—his anger over the Holocaust was just too great—and he played in Israel at apt moments in the country's history: on Mount Scopus just after the Six-Day War, in hospitals for Israeli soldiers wounded in the Yom Kippur War in 1973, for IDF troops in the Negev.

Early in 1991, with the Bush administration rounding up coalition partners for an invasion of Iraq, which had invaded Kuwait, Stern went to Jerusalem. Experts had predicted that under threat of attack, Saddam Hussein, the Iraqi dictator, would authorize a strike on Israel with Scud missiles tipped with poison gas. Stern arranged to join the Israeli Philharmonic and its music director, Zubin Mehta, also the music director of the New York Philharmonic, in a concert at Jerusalem Hall. The audience, following a national plan of preparedness, brought gas masks. Stern was playing a Mozart concerto when an air-raid siren sounded. The audience donned their masks. Stern, Mehta, and the orchestra left the stage. Then Stern returned. "I felt some people having trouble breathing, and this sense of unease," he later said. "So I went out and shushed them down. I was so moved, looking out over that sea of masks."

Alone on stage in tuxlike concert dress, facing row after row of Israelis in gas masks, he played the sarabande from Bach's first partita for solo violin, from the fourfold opening to the long last note subsiding to nothingness four minutes later.

It was "one of the most heart-stopping moments of my life," he recalled in his autobiography. "And still I went on playing. I had picked that music because it was quiet, contemplative. A very distant explosion was heard as I played, and we learned later that the missile had fallen halfway between the concert hall and Ben-Gurion Airport. When I finished and walked offstage, I was completely overwrought, as were Zubin and the members of the orchestra. Then the alert ended, and we were informed by the military that there was no evidence of gas, and we all walked back onstage to continue the concert." The concertgoers roared and rose to their feet. Stern played the rest of the Mozart concerto, a Brahms sonata, and an encore, and then he and Mehta "drove like a low-flying missile" to the airport in order to make an engagement in Montreal. "As we flew over the Atlantic Ocean the pilot announced the beginning of the Desert Storm ground attack in Iraq."

Isaac Stern playing Bach in a gas mask: the image became an icon of the Gulf War and of the power of classical music to convey grace under pressure. But there was no photograph, because—news reports to the contrary—Stern hadn't put his mask on. "I didn't wear the mask," he said later. "I had it right offstage."

Daniel Barenboim had been appointed music director of the Chicago Symphony. In the two decades since his thrilling Bach recordings with Itzhak Perlman and Pinchas Zukerman, Barenboim had taken the conviction about classical music as a force in society as far as any living musician—in effect, accepting and reaccepting Furtwängler's invitation to make music in contested territory. In 1981 he had entered a long association with the Bayreuth festival, devoted to celebrating the immortal legacy of Richard Wagner; in 1992 he had taken a position with the Staatsoper Unter der Linden, rival of the Berlin Philharmonic. He had become an advocate not only of German-Jewish amity but of Jewish-Palestinian amity. In Barenboim's own life this impulse found fullest expression in his deep friendship with Edward Said, the Palestinian-born literary critic, at once a Columbia professor and a member of the Palestinian National Council, whom he met by chance on a hotel lift in London.

Barenboim was a pianist who was an intellectual, Said an intellectual who was a pianist. Born into a Christian family in Palestinian Jerusalem, Said had grown up in Cairo, the son of an American citizen, then was sent to boarding school in Massachusetts. All the while, he studied classical piano and followed the careers of famous pianists, Glenn Gould among them. When he and Barenboim first met he had just finished a book of "musical elaborations," featuring an essay, "Performance as an Extreme Occasion," in which he declared that Gould's writings, though awkward, were "essential as the verbal counterpoint he provided for himself as a performer." In fact, he proposed, Gould's writing was itself a performance, "an attempt to extend his ideas about performance into other realms." He saw Gould as a character out of a late tale by Henry James, a performer who, refusing to perform in public, instead changes the terms of performance altogether: "he invites friends home to perform for them."

Said and Barenboim became friends, then made their friendship a performance, beginning with a public conversation during a conference devoted to Wagner at Columbia in 1995. On the Miller Theatre stage they took up the question of Wagner's extramusical power and the relationship between his anti-Semitism and the tradition of "holy German art," the kind of art (so said Barenboim) that Wagner had at once created and warned against. But the highlight was seeing Barenboim connect the dots between Wagner and historically informed performance. Out of his own encounter with Wagner had come his idea of music as a revolt against silence, with an orchestra producing "the presence of sound in a room" night after night, at once defying silence and modeling an ideal society. For Barenboim, Wagner and his successors defied silence through epic continuity of sound—long spreads of orchestral matter, giant chords endlessly resolving. The period-practice experts sought to undo this effect through stiff rhythms, clipped articulation, and donnish attention to the past rather than to the present moment made opportune with each performance. The strange loop Albert Schweitzer had opened when he proposed Bach as the anti-Wagner had come full circle. The cult of Wagner was under siege from the cult of authenticity.

Said and Barenboim decided to make a series of it: six conversations over as many years, a suite in words about music. Though they spoke of Beethoven more than any other composer and said next to nothing about recordings, the revival of Bach through technology was never far from their musings. Barenboim's conception of music as the shaped air of a certain room on a certain night was as strong an argument as anybody's against the creeping centrality of recorded music. At the same time it made clear how wide a gap had opened up between what performers understood they were doing and the way listeners heard them doing it. Barenboim had made dozens of recordings, but still he celebrated the "unrepeatability" of each performance, the "excitement of actually being able to live a certain piece from beginning to end without any interruption, without getting out of it." Said, whose views on Glenn Gould and the problems of performance suggested he knew better, didn't challenge him. Reductively, he said: "When you think back to an important moment in your musical history or intellectual history, you don't think back to a record. You think back to an actual performance, a musical occasion."

The holy German art of Bach was central to their shared concept of what music is. For Said, as for Schweitzer, Bach is an objective religious artist, making "an attempt not so much to approach the divine but to embody the divine." To explain what he meant, Said cited the *St. Matthew Passion*: "the work always seems to be moving away from you. I think that's the fascination. Not that you say, 'Well, we're only approaching it.' You actually feel you're getting close to it, but it's always drawing away."

For Barenboim, that quality is what makes Bach more than a great German musician, an exponent of the so-called German sound. Bach is objective and universal. "The best proof of this is that you have so many great musicians from countries where this music doesn't exist," he said. "Like from India in Zubin Mehta's case, or from Japan in the case of so many wonderful musicians." Said followed up brilliantly, proposing that this was the mission of music, and of all the arts and humanities: "to maintain difference without the domination and bellicosity that normally accompany affirmations of identity."

>>19>> Strangely, Said and Barenboim passed over the drama of ancient Near Eastern strife right at the center of Bach's work: in the Passions.

Strangely, because the Holocaust, and the relationship of Christianity to anti-Semitism, was a topic under consideration throughout the West: in Steven Spielberg's film of *Schindler's List*; at a new museum of the Holocaust in Washington; in Rome, where John Paul II weighed an act of repentance for the acts and attitudes that led up to the Shoah; in unified Germany, where a public conversation about the Shoah was taking place for the first time. Several decades of biblical scholarship—source criticism, comparative linguistics, chemical analysis, the hermeneutic of suspicion—had yielded a long shelf of quasi-popular rereadings of the scriptures, books that at once emphasized the Jewishness of Jesus and traced the emergence of anti-Jewish motifs in the gospels.

Strangely, because scholars, naturally, had turned to the question of anti-Judaism in the Passions, especially the *St. John Passion*, which vividly depicts Jews taking a role in the crucifixion of Jesus. Was the *St. John Passion* anti-Semitic, and Bach an anti-Semite?

The question began with the work's repeated sung reference to *die Juden*, or "the Jews"—crude to postwar ears—and wound back to Bach's debt to Martin Luther, who did so much to reiterate and codify the notion that the Jewish people rejected Jesus and then killed him, making them murderers who themselves deserved to be done away with.

A Bach scholar named Michael Marissen sought to address the questions with a scrupulous annotation of the Passion libretto. Marissen had been raised a Calvinist in Canada and had earned degrees from Calvin College and Brandeis, mastering German old and new expressly to study Bach's vocal music. In a closely argued monograph on the *St. John Passion*, he brought the techniques of the movement for historically informed practice to bear on moral questions, so that the size of a chorus, the stress on a syllable, or the use of extrabiblical material could throw light on Bach's intentions and outlook.

He took up the problem frankly: the question wasn't whether the Passion was anti-Judaic, for there was a plainly anti-Judaic strain in John's gospel, but "whether or not Bach's music buys into the gospel's hostility to Jews" as amplified by Luther and other exegetes. He then showed the complexity of each of the would-be charges against Bach. Luther's diatribes weren't anti-Semitic per se; Luther railed against Anabaptists, Muslims, and "Papists" as well as Jews. Pilate and the Roman soldiers are also represented in the Passion as "unsavory." The references to *die Juden*—often mistaken by amateurs as "die, Jews!"— were matter-of-fact renderings of the biblical text and got no extra emphasis from Bach. The dramatic chorus, "Kreuzige," or *Crucify!*, repeated dozens of times, has its unsettling effect not because of any anti-Jewish stress, but because Bach set it so artfully—through a technique called "cross-motives," with voices crossing in imperfect harmony—that its full collective judgmental rage comes through. Anti-Jewishness in Bach was as nothing compared with that in Handel and Telemann. Above all, such blame as is pointed in the Passion toward the Jewish elders—not the Jewish people as a whole—is greatly outweighed by the chorales, which are meant to represent the inner life of the individual Christian, and whose message, relentlessly reiterated, is that each individual person, even centuries later, bears the gravest responsibility for Jesus's death, because pervasive human sinfulness brought the crucifixion on him. "I, I and my sins, / which are as [numerous as] the grains / of sand on the seashore, / they have caused you / the sorrow that strikes you / and the grievous host of pain."

It couldn't reverse the drift of expert Passion against the *St. Matthew Passion*. It wasn't meant to. Marissen welcomed the controversy over the Passion as a teachable moment, for it accomplished "a sort of redemptive work that authentically builds on the gospel and Bach's music, yet at the same time moves forward from their original sectarian and liturgical purposes." The *St. John Passion* was not the problem; it was part of the solution to the problem—for it could "provide the ethically most intelligent way for attempting to reconcile historical and modern concerns" about Christian anti-Judaism.

>>20>> In 1995, Masaaki Suzuki announced his intention to record all of Bach's surviving cantatas. The cycles by Gustav Leonhardt and Nikolaus Harnoncourt and by Helmuth Rilling were done or nearly so, and in many

ways the news of another was unremarkable. But a fresh Bach anniversary was approaching, and with it an opportunity. An organist from Tokyo, Suzuki had trained with Tom Koopman in Amsterdam before founding the Bach Collegium Japan, and he would take a modified historically informed approach, using period instruments but a medium-size choir, rather than one voice to a part. He would record the whole cycle in Japan, chiefly in the city of Kobe, in a modern chapel (completed in 1981) kitted out with a French neo-Baroque organ.

With longish hair, neat beard, and glasses, Suzuki suggested a Japanese George Harrison. It should have been no surprise that he would make a Bach cycle with one eye on Asian audiences: even before the Sony Corporation bought Columbia Records in 1988, the keenness of Asians and Asian Americans for classical music was so well developed as to be a stereotype. The surprise was in Suzuki's motive for undertaking the cycle and his testimony about "what Bach and his music mean to me."

"How is it that the Japanese, with such a different heritage, dare play the music of Bach? This is typical of the sort of question with which I was often confronted when living and performing in Holland," he recalled. Certainly there were technical difficulties. "Bach's cantatas are a true product of German culture, inextricably wedded to the German language," he explained, historically informed to the core, and Japanese musicians had to master pronunciation, phrasing and articulation, structure and counterpoint "all alien to the Japanese musical tradition."

He was hesitant, but his hesitation was overcome by an act of faith. For Suzuki was a believing Christian, and he found confidence in "my eventual complete conviction that the God in whose service Bach labored and the God I worship today are one and the same." He stressed that he did not think that you have to be a believer to perform Bach's music well or to apprehend it as a listener. But with his own faith he turned the question of cultural otherness on its head, like the theme of a fugue inverted: "Who can be said to approach more nearly the spirit of Bach: a European who does not attend church and carries his Christian cultural heritage mostly on the subconscious level, or an Asian who is active in his faith although the influence of Christianity on his national culture is small?"

In the same way, his Christian faith took the precepts of historically informed performance to a logical, paradoxical conclusion. His faith (so the implication went) was a means of fidelity to the Baroque outlook, all the more so because he was Japanese, for, as he pointed out, a German Christian and a

Japanese one were both "foreign in our parentage," gentiles rather than people of Israel. "In the sight of the God of Abraham, I believe that the two hundred years separating the time of Bach from my own day can be of little account," he declared. "This conviction has brought the great composer very much closer to me."

Suzuki had a worldly purpose, too. He commenced his Bach cycle on August 15, 1995: the fiftieth anniversary of V-J Day. Half a century after the surrender of Japan, vanquished like its German ally, this distinctly German music would resound in a Japanese hall, its destination being CD players in Asia, Europe, and the Americas. Suzuki presented the cycle as an extended gesture of supranational "inner peace," but it was no act of simple piety. He made the first cantata in the cycle "Christ lag in Todesbanden," and featured the Dutch bass soloist Peter Kooij. World War II had been hell in Japan and the whole world over. In Christ's descent to hell "in the thrall of death," told in Luther's hymn, heard in the giant terraced steps of Bach's orchestration, European and Japanese musicians went to hell and back once more even as they put hell behind them, capping each strophe with an "Alleluia!" Did it sound Japanese? Hell, no—or rather, there is no simple answer to the question. What is striking in the sound is its surpassing clarity. Through the solid-state orchestra and sixteen-channel choir, every feature is clear and sharp, images sent back from a filament camera threaded down to the underworld.

>>21>> All the while, ordinary people cherished Bach's sacred works as Christian belief clad in its worldly best.

The Cathedral of St. John the Divine played host to the *St. John Passion*. Chairs and music stands were set up in the transept at the foot of the pipe organ. Bach cassettes were placed near the cash register in the gift shop. There was a write-up in the arts section of the *Times*. This was Good Friday, New York–style: a Bach Passion done in concert dress for an audience of sophisticated ladies clutching cardstock programs that might have been printed at Tiffany's.

That is not fair to the church ladies or to the rest of us gathered together in the cathedral that night. Tourists in the city for the long weekend; wizened Upper West Siders in Reeboks for whom a concert in a church was just another night out in the neighborhood; Episcopal priests from the suburbs who would walk in procession on Easter Day: were we an audience, or a congregation, or the two in counterpoint? I was there fresh from work in midtown, a believer preoccupied with religious art, innocent of Bach's vocal music but sufficiently versed in the canon to know that a Bach Passion was a holy of holies. There in the cold stone church (the largest in the hemisphere, the program reported) the music of Bach poured forth, a giant sonic arch joining America to Europe and that cathedral to the ones I had paid a pound or a few francs to pass through the summer before. The music of Bach poured forth under the focused warmth of the spotlights trained on the musicians. I fell asleep partway through, with my coat on; but like the apostles in the Passion, I was edified anyhow. Those churches in Europe were monuments; this church, in its gritty Upper West Side way, was a living place, vitalized by Bach.

A few blocks away, the Columbia University radio station carried on the practice of playing the music of Bach at Christmastime. I tuned in for jazz and there was Bach, morning, noon, and night, straight through from Christmas Eve morning to New Year's Day or beyond. I listened and listened and felt my life changing. I was always listening to music, but music had never sounded so good as the music of Bach coming out of a boombox tuned to 89.9. Another year and I was versed in the rite of the WKCR Bachfest as if I had observed it all my life: the abrupt midmorning changeover from Charlie Parker on alto saxophone to Ralph Kirkpatrick on harpsichord; afternoons devoted to different versions of the *Well-Tempered Clavier*, or the solo violin works, or Bach's music played on microtonal instruments; the Glenn Gould festival-within-a-festival; commentary by Columbia professors or jazz superstars such as Keith Jarrett; the evening "cantata request" hours, emceed by students who sounded hardly old enough on mike to know their way around the BWV catalog and yet knew to suspend the "ch" in Bach in the back of the mouth; the red-eye broadcasts of the works for organ, the dry metallic sound pulsing off the antenna atop the Empire State Building and out and out in concentric circles to the multitude of radios, mine among them, that were kept on faithfully through the night.

Described that way, Bachfest sounds like a marathon, but in those years of first encounter especially it felt like the opposite: a prayer flag or giant quilt of music gifted to the city, a catered spread of Bach's plenty. The station had a tradition of birthday broadcasts (a day and night of Thelonious Monk every October 10) and memorial broadcasts (three days each for Fela Anikulapo Kuti and Nusrat Fateh Ali Khan, Afrobeat maestro and *qawwali* master-singer, after they died two weeks apart in August 1997). Those broadcasts are extraordinary, but Bachfest is more so. It delivers a superabundance distinctive to its namesake. The power of Bach's music derives, in large part, from the quality of superabundance: it is enough, and more than enough. The music itself is superabundant, made so as Bach's genius is doubled through counterpoint and multiplied through the pattern of invention. There is more of the music than even Bach himself could know well, and just about all of it is outstanding. In our time, the superabundance has been compounded by recordings. There are now hundreds of recorded versions of the Mass in B Minor, and each offers the experience of superabundance specific to recordings: the chance to play it over and over again. While Bach never heard the Mass in B Minor in its entirety, not once, even a casual admirer of Bach in our time can have heard it—"played" it—dozens of times.

The superabundance of Bach is found in Bachfest as nowhere else. Suddenly you are surrounded by Bach, in the midst of Bach, moving from chamber to chamber of a space that his music fills as one of the noble gases would. You go to sleep and there is Bach; you wake up and there is Bach; you go to work, go to lunch, go home, and there is Bach. It feels like a holiday in the old, holy sense of the word—feels the way the passage from Christmas to Epiphany must have felt to believers when belief was most believable, as a fruitful immersion, a plunge into the depths, a time of rest that is charged with purpose. For a graduate student without much money—by then I was one—the superabundance was literal, too. Here was a cache of music I couldn't possibly have bought; here were a poor scholar's riches, the very graduate education I sought.

I went Christmas shopping to Bachfest, hearing the violin partitas set against the incorporated jingles of Fifth Avenue. I went ice skating in Central Park and listened to the Glenn Gould festival-within-a-festival on headphones tucked under a knit cap; the icy circularity of Gould's playing (mashed up with the hip-hop playing over the PA) fit the ice of the rink like a skate blade. I went into a coffee shop on Broadway and heard the end of the cello suite I had stepped out on two minutes earlier. Bachfest is portable, personal, but not private: it is a live broadcast, cast broadly over the airwaves to the public. Requests phoned in for the "cantata request hour" make clear how many people are listening and from where. Edward Said was probably listening in his apartment on Riverside Drive, Isaac Stern on West Eighty-ninth Street, Teri Noel Towe on the Upper East Side, Louise Basbas in Morningside Heights, Rosalyn Tureck in Connecticut, Simone Dinnerstein in a practice room at Juilliard. The people of the metropolitan area were orienting their holiday around the music of Bach, as the people of the Leipzig metropolitan area had oriented their holiday around it. This was a feast of recordings, yes—but if this wasn't "live" music, the music of Bach making its way in the world in real time, what was?

From the Bachfest I was brought closer to Bach—converted to Bach—in two directions. I sought out performances, and I bought recordings.

"Christmas music of Bach and Handel, with carols following." So said *Time Out*. So I set out for a church near Blackfriars Bridge, London, having spied the listing over a pint at a pub. It was the shortest day of the year, chill and dark at five o'clock, and I don't remember the way there or the specifics of the concert. What I remember is that the old church, itself chill and dark, with huge plastered-over cracks in the walls, like palm lines, was filled with the music of Bach, and then was lit up from the inside as we held lighted tapers and sung carols, and that the little flames seemed to illuminate what I had heard and felt, the voices and orchestra swelling the church with a sound that encompassed all one could hope to feel during the run-up to Christmas, and then some. I saw a plaque noting that the church had been bombed nearly to bits in the Blitz. Those cracks are what I remember: I felt them inside, the cracks of a created thing at once broken and fixed, made whole by Bach on a blackout-dark night.

I went to St. Paul's Chapel in downtown Manhattan to hear the *St. Matthew Passion*. Holy Week that year fell at the end of a long winter; I was out in the cold in more than one respect. To go to hear Bach by myself for half a Sunday was to break a spell. The chapel (I had never been there) was an Episcopal church near City Hall, plaster and fieldstone, with a little graveyard, the whole overshadowed by the two towers of the World Trade Center. A generation after Bach, George Washington had worshipped there, another great man in a white wig. I found a place in a pew in a balcony and opened a program as big as a menu at a Greek diner. It must have given a translation of the German text, for I could follow the Passion closely enough to grasp the genius of it—to be grasped and held and transfixed by it. Here were the two choirs, one in that balcony and one in this one, calling out factionally to each other; there down below were Jesus, Peter, Pilate, the Evangelist, a quartet for all time; there behind the altar rail was the orchestra, lofting the music up into the church, the scent of sacred drama. T. S. Eliot said that hearing *Tristan und Isolde* in his early twenties was one of the great experiences of his life. So hearing this *St. Matthew Passion* was for me. This was not a version of the Passion narrative. This was the thing itself. There was an intermission. I went outside. Night was falling over the skyscrapers. I stood at the graveyard, a patch of grass studded with stone markers, each the size of an LP box set, set over the bodies of long-dead colonists, and knew—over that long winter I had forgotten—what it was to be fully alive.

I took a train from New York down south. Fifteen years into the CD era, plenty of us still didn't own CD players, and to be a late adopter, in classical music, was to stand outside the tent at the revival. As more and more new recordings were released on CD, fewer and fewer of them were released on cassette. Bach on cassette was the Brandenburgs, the Mass in B Minor, the violin stuff, the *Christmas Oratorio*, a shrunken canon for car or classroom or nursing home. It was not enough. I bought a Discman; and the night before the train ride I bought a triple-CD set of the *St. Matthew Passion* and also B.B. King's *Live at the Regal* at HMV on Seventy-second and Broadway. The trip, from New York to Durham, North Carolina, would take twelve hours; this was *viaticum*, food for the journey.

I was overwhelmed by Bach on that train like Jonah swallowed by the whale. The train pounded down the corridor to Washington, taking on bureaucrats. The Passion sounded out in the foam-tipped headphones. The orchestra rose to the Passion and then subsided to recitative, like an invading army scaling the walls of the castle and then sliding back down to peasant life. The CD booklet spelled out the parts: *Double Chorus. Dramatic Recitative. Chorus I. Recitative—Alto. Jesus. Evangelist. Jesus. Chorus.* The conductor called out the stops: Wilmington, Baltimore, New Carrollton, BWI, Union Station. Paper cups of coffee were borne aloft in cardboard trays. And the band played on; the disciples mounted the castle rock once more, up, up, up. There in a train moving at a hundred miles an hour I understood that the Passion is a story. The action moves toward the end inexorably, Jesus drawn deathward by force. It is there in the gospels, there in Bach's orchestration of the Passion, but I hadn't heard it, and no wonder: usually musicians and audience are confined in a room together, as at St. John the Divine and St. Paul's Chapel. Now, in a moving train, I could hear that the Passion moves, goes somewhere. Christian belief sees existence as teleological, aimed at a final end. That is college theology, but I had never truly felt it. Now, here, it was made plain by Bach. The music pulled the action forward, music powerful enough to pull the train across the Mason-Dixon line. That is what it felt like. But the truth of it—the jolt of insight—was that the action was pulling the music forward, that the Christian drive toward ultimate purpose gave Bach's music its astonishing drive, grasped in faith and patterned into art. On the train, that drive was wholly audible, and visible through the window of the Discman, the disc itself spinning faster than the eye could see, and visible out the windows of the train, too. Past Washington, the stops spread out and civilization fell away from the trackbed, until in southern Virginia the stations gave way to sheds or paved islands moated by gravel. Bach was taking us to another country; we were there, and almost there.

When it ended, I put on the B.B. King disc, then took it off. The music of Bach was resounding. I rode the rest of the way idly, not reading, not listening, just sitting in the presence of a sound that would not subside.

>>22>> After making a billion dollars in Hollywood through the adventures of Luke Skywalker and Indiana Jones, George Lucas returned to Northern California, where he had grown up. On four thousand acres in Marin County he built Industrial Light and Magic, a special-effects company, and Skywalker Ranch, "a full-service state-of-the-art production facility where his friends could come and work on their films in an idyllic, Northern California setting far from the fleshpots of tinsel town," as Peter Biskind described it. "Skywalker included a library, a lake, a baseball diamond, stables, and a vineyard. No building was visible from any other building. The three-acre lake was stocked with trout."

Lorraine Hunt was also from Northern California, a daughter of music teachers in San Francisco, and she set out to follow a career as a violist in the Bay Area. John Adams recalled her from a performance of his piece *Shaker Loops* in Berkeley in 1979. "Rehearsals were at ten on Sunday mornings, and she would arrive sleepy and sexy, hastily dressed, barely awake, totally alluring. She was a good instrumentalist, but there was nothing that might hint at what she would become over the following twenty years." She moved to Boston in her late twenties and fell in with musicians who were playing Bach cantatas on Sunday mornings at a Lutheran church in Back Bay, and there her career took a strange loop. She became a singer, and a remarkable one, attracting notice in the Bach cantatas and then as the soprano in Handel vocal works with Peter Sellars, the maverick director, and Nicholas McGegan, an Oxbridge-trained conductor based in San Francisco. She returned to Northern California; and one day in the compact disc's second decade she went with McGegan and a cellist to Marin County to make a recording at Skywalker Ranch. A pair of harpsichords (Berkeley replicas of Baroque originals) were uncrated and tuned at Skywalker Sound, a recording studio as technically advanced as any in the known world, and there, in the House That Obi-Wan Kenobi Built, the three musicians did some of the pieces from the *Notebook for Anna Magdalena*

Bach. There was nothing strange about this close encounter of Bach and technology: it was McGegan's shrewd use of Skywalker Sound's downtime. Its special effect involved the encounter of the harpsichord with the human voice. The record begins with Bach's first French suite, played by McGegan, cloistrally. What follows is something else: a clear, airy mezzo-soprano voice—Lorraine Hunt's voice—singing the Baroque aria "Bist du be mir" ("If Thou art near, I go rejoicing") with such lissome authority that the harpsichord is left clacking its heels behind. It is a deathbed song (translated, it goes on: "I go rejoicing / to peace and rest above the skies"), but it could burn through the fog over the Golden Gate Bridge with its body heat. So could any of the songs Hunt sang that day. All but one anticipate death (Bach, having lost one wife, hoped not to lose another), but even "Ich habe genug," his profoundest song of parting, is sung as a perfectly balanced piece of Baroque art, with regret and fear and hope and yearning all given voice at the same time.

If Hunt was Princess Leia, falling halfway accidentally into the Baroque vocal revival, Yo-Yo Ma was Luke Skywalker, emboldened by the teachings of his father and the force of his precursor to reckon with the death star of popular culture. As he approached forty, a master, a celebrity, a treasure, Ma was in a paradoxical position. He had done most of the things an onlooker would have envisaged for him. He had made several dozen records: Schubert and Haydn and Dvořák, standards, new works commissioned expressly for him. He had appeared with cello and unforced smile in venues ranging from the Reagan White House to *The Muppet Show*. He had won a fistful of Grammy Awards; he had gotten an honorary doctorate from Harvard to go with his bachelor of arts. For all that, at nearly forty he was still a young man: twenty-eight years younger than Rostropovich, twenty years younger than Casals had been when he went to Abbey Road. His crossover projects had covered the waterfront: an American music album, a Cole Porter album, a New York album, an album with the boundary-breaking vocalist Bobby McFerrin, who himself had grown up in New York in the sixties with an exacting musical father (Robert McFerrin, a baritone with the Metropolitan Opera). These were not typical crossovers, because the material on them was not much more popular in the United States than Bach was. They were close encounters with musicians outside Ma's usual ambit. They took him into new areas, or they inverted the process by bringing musicians from other traditions to his neighborhood: Stéphane Grappelli, Wynton Marsalis, et al.

On *Hush*, Ma and McFerrin duetted on the Bach "Ave Maria" and the "Air on the G String." The "Ave Maria" is all for show: journalists had dubbed Ma "the Michael Jordan of the cello," and he and McFerrin rejigged the down-the-aisle standby dazzlingly for cello and vocalese, grown-up hotshots making baskets one-handed and blindfolded from half-court. But the "Air on the G String" is the real thing, Bach reinvented. Sung by McFerrin, the long round E that opens the piece is literally an air, made of a string of breath from his embouchure; and when Ma joins him, he is barely there. The piece hadn't sounded so good since Casals played it into a big brass horn seven decades years earlier.

In the spring of 1998, Ma announced that he was retiring from the cello in order to play the bandoneón. It was a joke: the announcement came on April 1, when his record *Soul of the Tango*—adaptations of songs associated with the Argentine bandoneón master Astor Piazzolla—was riding the Billboard chart. In truth, he had just redoubled his commitment to the cello and to the cornerstone of the cello repertory with a project that suggested the direction his career would take in the years to follow.

This was *Inspired by Bach*, a six-part suite of hourlong programs for public television. Ma explained: "In 1991, Judge Mark Wolf of Boston invited me to participate in an interdisciplinary symposium on Albert Schweitzer, the musician, theologian, and physician who was also an eminent Bach scholar. Schweitzer described Bach as a 'painterly' or 'pictorial' composer" (and so "the direct antipodes of Richard Wagner"). The idea was retrograde: period-music scholars promoted the idea of Bach as producing variations on musical forms deeply embedded in Baroque society; scholars of absolute music still saw him as a pattern maker, an architect or mathematician of sound. Ma was undeterred. Inspired by Schweitzer, he jumped on the idea: "His articulation of the visual quality of Bach's music gave me the courage to begin an unusual project . . ." devoted to what Schweitzer had called "the coöperation of the arts."

For *Inspired by Bach*, Ma cooperated on the Bach cello suites with artists near and far, from the choreographer Mark Morris to the ice dancers Jane Torville and Christopher Dean and the landscape architect Julie Moir Messervy. It was a stretch, and that was the point: "Each of the artists with whom I worked has stretched the limit of their art forms, just as Bach stretched traditional limits when he wrote polyphonic music for what is essentially a single-line instrument," he explained.

Ma sought to stretch his own boundaries through a new Bach recording, inspired by the project, because "each collaborator has transformed my understanding of the suite and how to play it." Forty years earlier, Leonard Bernstein had made television an extension of the conductor's baton; now Ma sought to use TV as an instrument for audiovisual counterpoint.

Inspired by Bach was original, passionate, historically apt, and hard for the public-television crowd to grasp. Ma's new recording of the cello suites sounded genuinely fresh: swifter, more chiseled and etched, with space between and around notes once fluidly joined. The promotional materials linked Ma not to Bernstein but to Stokowski, a musician wholly recognizable in silhouette. Here was the pattern of invention exquisitely expressed, the cello suites conceived not as a foundation or ideal but as a set of inventions inviting further development. But the programs were uneven and at points only tenuously related to the cello suites. Ma's Harvard teacher Leon Kirchner—whom he had acknowledged by recording a piece of his for the *American Album* the year before—dismissed the series as "baloney, unworthy of a supreme musician like Yo-Yo." Christoph Wolff said he found parts of it "rather embarrassing." And yet Wolff understood: "Perhaps he is trying to turn the cello suites into world music, something never before attempted."

The series could have begun where it ended: with Bach in Times Square. Episode six opened *Koyaanisqatsi*-style, with a surging crowd at rush hour, and there in the sea of faces was Yo-Yo Ma, in silk shirt and dark glasses, toting his cello in a soft-sided case. He set up in an intersection, unfolding a chair and placing a hand-lettered sign (THANK YOU) in the open case. With the city behind him and the cello on its end pin, he busked with Bach's sixth suite. The scene caught the worldly qualities of the cello suites more dramatically than any harmonic garden or Renaissance drawing. And the episode as a whole introduced Bach neatly: Torville and Dean gliding across the screen, silhouetted in bodysuits or long black cloaks, at the peak of their post-Olympics fame; an English actor acting out the role of Bach in Köthen, lean and brown-haired, frankly pious but obviously an artist. This was event television devoted to wordless Baroque music and a composer whom many viewers knew as a forbidding figure, if they knew him at all.

Inspired by Bach pointed in two directions: back to Bach, and farther out into the world. Ma took both of them.

With the Silk Road Project, he traced the trade route through the Middle East and Asia, following both his own family heritage and that of strung-and-bowed instruments such as the cello.

With *Simply Baroque* he finally engaged with the movement for historically informed performance, whose coming-of-age had coincided with his own. This record began with an invitation for him to come to the Concertgebouw in

Amsterdam and play whatever he wanted. Ma said he wanted to play a period cello with a period ensemble—Tom Koopman and the Amsterdam Baroque Orchestra, as it turned out. Rather than switching instruments, he put one of his Stradivarius cellos under the knife to make it more like the cello Antonio Stradivari originally made: the bridge was replaced with a flatter and wider one, the end pin removed, the steel strings swapped out for gut ones. The performances came off, and five years later he returned to Holland to make a recording.

In *Simply Baroque*, as at Skywalker Sound, advanced technology and the ardent pursuit of the old ways inadvertently met. The photograph on the CD booklet showed Ma holding the altered cello on one knee for all the world to see that it lacked an end pin; the photograph was taken by Annie Leibowitz, celebrity portraitist par excellence. The notes made two points:

> Mr. Ma is playing a 1712 Davidoff Stradivarius prepared for Baroque performance practice by Etienne Vatelot & Jean-Jacques Rampal, Paris, and John & Arthur Beare, London, makers of fine string instruments . . .
>
> For this recording, 24-bit technology was used to maximize sound quality.

Title, setting, and retrofitted cello aside, this was a set of cello pieces done romantic-virtuoso style, like the 78-rpm "sides" Pablo Casals made in the teens and twenties. Half the record is the cello concertos of Luigi Boccherini, who composed in the era just after Bach; the other half is short Bach pieces—organ pieces, a wrenching aria from the *St. Matthew Passion*, and "Wachet Auf" ("Sleepers, Wake"), as well as the "Air on the G String" and "Jesu, Joy of Man's Desiring," all arranged for Baroque orchestra by Tom Koopman. It is a good record in spite of itself and its claim to the Baroque. In the end, a Stradivarius is a Stradivarius, and Yo-Yo Ma is Yo-Yo Ma; on gut strings as on steel strings, his burnished, peat-smoke tone is front and center, utterly recognizable: a personal voice, not a period sound.

Ma was working the culture tirelessly on behalf of the cello, classical music, and music generally, but his most effective ventures were the ones that seemed most easily done. Take the Christmas episode of *The West Wing* that featured him playing for President Bartlet. "We have polling that indicates that if Johann Sebastian Bach were alive today, he would have voted for me," the president began, then introduced Ma, in evening dress, Stradivarius in tow—an image as iconic as Stokowski's podium profile half a century earlier. The surprise was that a command performance in a fictional White House suited Ma as well as one in an actual White House, or Carnegie, or the Concertgebouw. It wasn't a diminished thing; it was the thing itself—Yo-Yo Ma playing Bach. And Ma found a way to use the guest spot to make people already familiar with Bach hear the music in a new way. The script called for the deputy communications director, Josh Lyman, to go into a "fugue state" as Ma played, with the music prompting him to relive an assassination attempt on the president in which he had been shot. Set in a White House hall all decked out for Christmas, the scene cut contrapuntally back and forth between Ma bowing frenetically at the first suite and Lyman smashing a whiskey glass and a window—in such a way as to bring out, in the serene first suite, a scarcely controlled fury.

Ma could take Bach anywhere. He allowed his recording of the Bach suites to swell with the sea in *Master and Commander*, lent his voice to an animated cartoon version of himself on *The Simpsons*. He joined Daniel Barenboim and Edward Said in the convening of the West-Eastern Divan Orchestra, an ensemble made up of young Israeli and Palestinian musicians. It took place not in Jerusalem or the West Bank but in Weimar. This was the town nearest Buchenwald, where a Nazi death camp had been; the town made renowned by Goethe, from whose sequence of poems on Islam the ensemble took its name; and of Bach, who had made music in the midst of a power struggle between rival dukes. "It doesn't pretend to be building bridges and all that hokey stuff," Said said, disingenuously. "But there it is: a paradigm of coherent and intelligent living together"—and playing together. What was Ma doing there? His participation made clear that it was larger than Jews and Arabs: it was about music as cross-cultural understanding. "There was a very tentative atmosphere in the beginning," Said recalled. "However, ten days later, the same kid who had claimed that only Arabs can play Arab music was teaching Yo-Yo Ma how to tune his cello for the Arabic scale."

The role of Ma's life, as things turned out, would involve a scene in a West Side story. He hailed a taxi on Central Park West one morning and was taken to a hotel in midtown. He paid the driver, doubtless flashing his unforced smile; he got out and went to the hotel. There he did a double-stop. His cello: Where was it? He had put it in the trunk of the cab: his other Stradivarius, from 1733, valued at $2.5 million but plainly priceless. By midday half the city was on the trail of it: hotel security, a precinct captain, two cops in a squad car, a taxi dispatcher, and the driver, Dishashi Lukumwena, who dropped off the

cab at a depot in Queens after his shift ended at four o'clock with no idea what
was in the trunk or that news radio had covered the mystery of the missing
cello all day long. All at once Yo-Yo Ma was a New York character, the absentminded prodigy. But not utterly absentminded: he was able to track down the
missing cello because he had gotten a receipt from the driver, a record of the
ride.

As with many New Yorkers, it was through a story in the *Times* that I
learned of the cello lost and found. Lenora and I read the story together, newly-
weds lingering over the Sunday paper. It was strange to think of that cello
stowed with the spare tire in the trunk of a yellow cab, because we had heard it
move the night air in the Berkshires the summer before. Yo-Yo Ma played the
Bach suites over two nights at Tanglewood, consecrating the open-backed
Ozawa Hall. The verdict was in: the hall was a masterpiece in wood cut and
joined, but we were on the outside looking in. We sat on the grassy hill at the
back of the hall, in a thicket of ergonomic folding chairs and titanium wine-
chilling tubes, as Ma played the poised fourth suite and the grave fifth one.
Meanwhile storm clouds rolled in, their menace all too well suited to the fifth
suite's dark passages. When the suite was over, a third of the people on the
lawn rose to go, the better to gain position on the narrow two-lane road away
from Tanglewood. We stayed; and just as Ma struck the first notes of the sixth
suite, the rain caved in on us. Back and forth across the neck of the instrument
went the bow, growing in intensity if not getting faster, as if the cellist were
taking the steps of a tall staircase two at a time. The rain poured down, pud-
dling in the lawn and soaking us. We moved into a patch of sodden grass where
a tartan blanket had been; and we danced, spinning and whirling along with
the music as it raced out headlong, outdoing itself. Culturally, it was a rich
moment—a work of German music played by a Chinese-Franco-American
cellist in a New England concert hall named for a Japanese conductor and
modeled after a Shaker barn. But for us it was not a cultural moment; it was
a physical one. This cello piece was a dance, and we were dancing—dancing
to Bach.

>>23>> Bach was going blind; and with the loss of sight came a stifling
silence. He could still make music. The pipe organ he could play in a pitch-
black church; the clavier was an extension of his fingertips. Pen and ink was
his main instrument, though, and it was faltering; tens of thousands of pages
of music had come from his right hand, written as quickly as they formed in

his mind, but by 1749 the dimming of his vision made it harder and harder for him to write.

Working day and night, raising a houseful of children, bearing the deaths of a dozen infants, he had been sick hardly a day in his life. Now the sickness seemed to spread from his eyes to the rest of his body The town councillors were treating him as dead already. The prince in Dresden proposed that the organist there should succeed Bach at the Thomasschule, and the Leipzig town councillors went along with it—and went around Bach, reserving a hall in mid-week so that the man could give "a trial performance for the future appointment as Cantor of St. Thomas's, in case the Capellmeister and Cantor Herr Sebast: Bach should die."

He was not dead; he was alive, inventive, inspired.

He led the Thomasschule choir and orchestra in the *St. John Passion* in the Good Friday half-light, crossing the brook Kedron to the garden with the disciples one more time. *"Rut wohl, ihr heiligen Gebeine . . ."* the choir sang at the end of it, the orchestra tolling three-note minor figures—shovel strokes behind the voices. "Rest in peace, you holy bones / which I will now no longer mourn / and take me, too, to rest"—for the grave set aside for Jesus, destined for him, was a stopper to grief, a portal to heaven.

He composed a secular cantata for the town councillors on their feast day. Then he aimed a riposte at them, arranging a fresh performance of a satiric cantata on the contest between Phoebus and Pan—recasting the last line so as to set Phoebus's lyric art against the pompous officials "raging against it."

He had composed most of the Mass in B Minor, and now he drew the parts together, combining and copying them into a single manuscript. He took parts from cantatas and other vocal works. There was only one piece missing: the *Et incarnatus est*, the part of the credo describing the birth of Jesus. Husbanding his sight, he wrote it in bursts, calling on others, his thirteen-year-old son, Johann Christian, among them, to fill out musical figures he had started. The pattern of invention, followed over a lifetime, now enabled him to surpass himself and beat back blindness.

Et incarnatus est de Spirito Sancto ex Maria virgine et homo factus est. And was incarnated by the Holy Ghost of the Virgin Mary, and was made man—made carnal, enfleshed, embodied. Bach composed a five-part figure for the five syllables (*incarnatus est*) that open this formula of faith professed, the Christian story reduced to its simplest form. As his body began to fail him he wrote this piece on the conviction that God came and dwelt among us, a human person with a human body.

An oculist performed an operation on his eyes. Afterward he could see clearly again. Then as swiftly as it had come the clear brightness subsided. He saw other people as trees but walking, vague shapes that he yearned to render in contrapuntal lines.

He could still play, and he played: clavier, cembalo, organ. Half blind, he was still unrivalled as an organist. To the "late works"—the *Art of the Fugue*, the canonic variations, the Mass in B Minor—must be added the music that he played extempore once his eyesight was too poor for him to read music. This was music past the pull of documentation: the thing itself, happening once and for all, unrecorded.

>>24>>   TRANSPORTATION TO HEAVEN, the ad in the Daily Arts section of the *Times* announced in Roman capitals on a black background.

SIR JOHN ELIOT GARDINER, THE MONTEVERDI CHOIR AND
ENGLISH BAROQUE SOLOISTS PERFORM BACH'S SACRED CANTATAS
AT ST BARTHOLOMEW'S CHURCH, 25 DECEMBER 5 PM,
27 & 31 DECEMBER 7 PM.
BOOK EARLY TO AVOID DISAPPOINTMENT

This was the Bach Cantata Pilgrimage, a great conductor's audacious attempt to mark the new millennium with a traveling roadshow of Bach's sacred music. Beginning on Christmas Day 1999 and proceeding through 2000, Gardiner and his ensemble had traveled to several dozen churches throughout Europe and performed a hundred-and-some Bach cantatas on the Sundays and feast days for which Bach had written them. Now the Bach Cantata Pilgrimage would be coming to an end in midtown Manhattan, in the Episcopal parish where Leopold Stokowski—Gardiner's most obvious precursor as a public-minded dramatist in Bach—had served as organist most of a century earlier.

The Cantata Pilgrimage represented a culmination of Bach for Gardiner personally. Amazingly, in his first years in Dorset, the portrait of Bach by Gottlob Haussman hung in his family's house, kept there by his parents, musicians who had been asked to store it there for safekeeping during World War II. As early as 1968 (at age twenty-five) he founded the Monteverdi Choir and Orchestra, whose name suggested the commitment to the "precanonical" music of the Renaissance and early Baroque. Ten years later he and the orchestra took the leap to original instruments, and took a new name: the English Baroque

Soloists. All the while, as he made standout recordings of Italian music, and English music, too—Purcell's *Funeral Music for Queen Mary*, Handel's *Music for the Royal Fireworks*—he was tending toward Bach. All this activity meant he was primed for the compact disc, and as Deutsche Grammophon ordered up new recordings of the swiftly changing repertory for the Bach bicentenary, he was in a position to make definitive "authentic instruments" versions of Bach choral music. He conducted the *St. Matthew Passion* in Communist East Berlin in 1985—having fearfully kept his distance from it. He led the Monteverdi choir in motets at the Thomaskirche in Leipzig. He conducted the B-minor Mass in Japan. He made several discs' worth of cantata recordings for DG's Archiv label, and the combination of his energy and charm and the momentum of the period-instrument movement made them something like the new standard versions.

Period performance practice was spreading outward in ever larger circles right into the nineteenth century of Schubert and Beethoven—and Gardiner founded a new group, the Orchestre Révolutionnaire et Romantique, to take a lead role. Meanwhile, he was recording a disc of Bach cantatas with the Monteverdi Choir and English Baroque soloists every year or so. In the latter 1990s he read in a magazine that he was recording a complete cycle of Bach's church cantatas. It wasn't true: but instead of sending a correction to the editor, he let an idea develop. "Why not concentrate performances of all two hundred cantatas within a single year—in the year 2000, which coincides with the two hundred and fiftieth anniversary of his death?" he asked himself. "In the year 2000 we would be celebrating the birth of the founder of one of the world's great religions. What more appropriate way to do so than via the music of its greatest musical advocate?" As he later put it: "By an odd quirk of history, the 250th anniversary of Bach's death falls exactly at the beginning of a new millennium—and as a musician, you ask yourself: well, what do I do to mark that event?"

It was easier thought up than carried out. Gardiner's ensemble typically undertook half a dozen programs a year; this would involve something like sixty fresh programs of three or four cantatas each. But Gardiner, strong-jawed and towheaded in his middle fifties, brought it off. Foundations offered funding. Well-connected friends such as Prince Charles vouched for the worthiness of the project. Deutsche Grammophon committed to release recordings of the sacred concerts on compact disc. Even if it was not (as one English eminence hyperbolically styled it) the most ambitious project in the history of musical performance, it was one sufficiently outsize to rival Bach's effort in writing three full cantata cycles in his first years in Leipzig.

The *Christmas Oratorio* in Weimar on Christmas Day and in the

Nikolaikirche on Epiphany; a cantata in Hamburg, with the *Tannenbaum* still
up in the back of the Jakobikirche; "Christ lag in Todesbanden" on Easter
Sunday in the Georgenkirche in Eisenach, in sight of the stone font where
Bach had been baptized: there in the first months of the millennial year Bach's
sacred music rang out. For every cantata on a grand human theme ("Burst out,
ye songs, sound out, ye strings! O most blessed times"—BWV 172) there was
one pietistic in its devotion ("All according to God's will, in happiness and sad-
ness . . . This shall be my watchword"—BWV 72). The pilgrimage ranged
across Europe: to San Marco in Milan and San Nicolo in Merano; St. David's
Cathedral in Wales and the Christchurch and Priory Church in Gardiner's native Dorset. At one point the ensemble was stuck overnight in an airport in
Scotland en route to the tiny St. Magnus Cathedral in Orkney, a place of un-
matched intimacy—"a church that hasn't been polluted by overuse as a heritage site," as Gardiner put it, "so we feel as the pilgrims must have felt on
pilgrimage to Rome, to Compostela, to the holy places" of Bach's time.

He was speaking to the camera: the pilgrimage was being recorded in video
as well as audio for a BBC documentary. Cameras were dollied up church
aisles during performances; the audio signal was tracked in a mobile studio
parked outside, as one had been parked outside All Hallows in London in 1935.
Betweentimes, cameras captured Gardiner burning the candle at both ends, as
Albert Schweitzer had put it, and looking progressively wearier, ruddier, more
rumpled—looking more and more like a pilgrim.

In what way was the Bach Cantata Pilgrimage a pilgrimage? What purpose did it serve, other than to mark the millennium, make the cantatas more
prominent, and produce a hundred hours of recorded music? Gardiner and
his musicians sought to answer the question for the camera. "We've taken as
our motto this year Bach's own beliefs," Gardiner explained, particularly the
belief in grace as a source of transformation—and he acknowledged that this
is hard to define. Among his own "spiritual high points" he cited a concert in
Iona that became an experience of transhistorical intimacy. There on the wave-
battered island, in a stark stone monastery church, "you were stripped bare
of any prop, any artifact, and were just there with the music . . ." he recalled.
"St. Columba had come there in the middle of the sixth century to proselytize
the Scots to Christianity, and there we were fifteen hundred years later with the
music of Bach, which seemed to fit between those four walls so perfectly."
The musicians were less precise about the meaning of it all. One youngish
singer cited the notion that the pilgrimage from one place to another found its
parallel in "a movement inside you," and quoted the Buddha to the effect that

you can't know the journey until you are the journey. Another singer was even more taciturn: "I think God puts on his best show in Bach. I don't think there is an alternative inspiration [for Bach] other than Christianity—that would be the ultimate key to it. It's a shame I don't believe it quite myself."

Gardiner is no strict practitioner of historically informed performance, which (he told the camera) "ends up in self-ridicule sometimes, it really does." And yet his Bach Cantata Pilgrimage, like Suzuki's cantata cycle, developed period performance practices to a paradoxical extreme, whether he meant it or not. In its scope, its sizable forces (four or more singers on a part), and its claim to millennial significance, his band on the run owed less to period ensembles and musicologists than to Stokowski's Philadelphians barnstorming across America. And yet the Cantata Pilgrimage frankly reliteralized the music, suggesting that, seventy-five years of sonic adventure aside, the very best way to hear Bach's sacred music is in a very old church.

>>25>> Enter Peter Sellars, agent provocateur of dramatic counterpoint. Sellars was no stranger to the big show, the lavish production, the attention-getting spectacle. He had done *King Lear* with a Rolls-Royce on stage and *Don Giovanni* as a mob opera; he and John Adams had sent Nixon to China and put terrorists on a cruise ship, making the front page of *The New York Times* and shifting the city's musical energy from Carnegie Hall and Lincoln Center to Brooklyn for the first time in a hundred years. Sellars and Adams had devised their own millennial work: *El Niño*, "an oratorio about birth in general and about the Nativity in specific"—a work, that, with its texts in English and Spanish, its echoes of medieval mystery plays, its children's choir, and its silent film of teenage Los Angeleno gang members running in the background, made the Bach Cantata Pilgrimage look straight and narrow. But even Sellars was brought low to something like reverence by Bach; and in that millennial year, with bombast abounding, he devised an excruciatingly intimate rendering of a pair of Bach cantatas, an advanced conceptual artist finally sketching from life—from Lorraine Hunt's life.

Hunt was dying: dying slowly, after the remission of cancer, but dying. Her life had taken a strange loop. She met the composer Peter Lieberson—son of Goddard Lieberson, who had run Columbia Masterworks—and he determined to compose a song cycle for her. They fell in love. He left his wife and three children to marry her. She was singing better than ever—in recitals, in a Metropolitan Opera adaptation of *The Great Gatsby*, in John Adams's opera

Doctor Atomic, in the home she and Lieberson made in New Mexico, where he set love poems by Pablo Neruda as songs for her.

All the while, she was in and out of the hospital, and for Sellars, that was enough. He devised a setting of two Bach cantatas, number 199 and number 82. For the one, she would wear a kimono. For the other—"Ich habe genug"— she would wear a hospital gown, tied loosely around her.

The work had a Lincoln Center premiere in 2000. It brought together the two opposed approaches to the performance of Bach: the historically informed approach of the Emmanuel Orchestra, practiced in performing the cantatas as part of a liturgy in a working church on Sundays; and the strong and strange misreadings of Peter Sellars, which thrived on his defiance of the music's original context. Joining them was the voice of Lorraine Hunt Lieberson, who was mortally ill.

In this "Ich habe genug" the promise of period music was fulfilled. The movement's fondness for clear, uninflected, almost dainty singing and playing ripens into vocal art with the strong emotions and dramatic power usually associated with opera, without losing its lightness, balance, and objectivity, the foregrounding of the song, not the singer.

And yet the singer was extraordinary. In his recording of the cantata from the late sixties, Dietrich Fischer-Dieskau seemed to be standing on the shore, ready to step off but unable to do so. Singing the same cantata, Hunt Lieberson seemed already to have left this world, like Virginia Woolf wading into the River Ouse. In the hospital gown she moved from side to side onstage, which in some respects resembled a hospital (no windows, lots of curtains); she clung to a steel IV pole, the bag of clear drip medication hanging from it; she trailed the pole behind her by the long plastic tube bandaged to her arm. She pulled the tube out of her arm and let it dangle. "*Ich habe genug*," she sang, over and over, and the two renderings of the German refrain—the older "It is enough" and the newer "I have enough"—capture what she was expressing. Her joy is complete; her pain is complete; she has seen her salvation, and has known enough in this world, loved enough, to let it go.

>>26>> The oculist scrubbed the surface of his eyes with a brush and drained all the blood from one, then the other. The pain was indescribable. They waited together: nothing. Bach was blind for good this time. Possibly he had been blinded by the so-called eye doctor.

The rest of him was little better: the sickness—diabetes—had spread throughout his body. It was a strange war, when Life and Death fought:

now this war, which he had dramatized in "Christ lag in Todesbanden" as a young man, was being fought in his body in the darkened apartment in the Thomasschule.

A man of faith, he prepared for death so as to welcome it when it came. A musician, he prepared musically. He had a student brought in to take directives from him. He arranged for the *Et incarnatus est* to be added to the Mass in B Minor, "cleanly written on a leaf inserted into the autograph." He made a few revisions to the sonatas for violin and harpsichord. To a motet written by Johann Christian he added an instrumental setting. With the end of his life near, the pattern of invention was reversed: for this motet, which, he hoped, would be heard at his funeral, Bach developed a musical figure that his youngest son had invented.

He died on July 28, 1750, and was buried from the Thomaskirche three days later. The oak coffin was carried out of the church and taken in procession to the graveyard of the Johanneskirche just outside the city. Seven of Bach's children with Anna Magdalena were buried there. He joined them.

Strangely, he had left no will. His possessions were divided: cash, silverware, an eighty-volume theological library, and (Malcolm Boyd reports) nineteen musical instruments—"five harpsichords . . . two lute-harpsichords, three violins (one of them a Stainer, another a *violino piccolo*), three violas, a lute, and a spinet." His son Carl Philipp Emanuel Bach ruefully remarked that Bach had never had "a really large and really beautiful organ at his constant disposal. This fact has robbed us of many beautiful and unknown inventions in organ playing that he would otherwise have written down and displayed in the form in which he had them in his head."

The music he had written down was divided: many of the cantatas stayed at the Thomasschule, and Carl Philipp Emanuel Bach and Wilhelm Friedemann Bach split up the rest, in such a way that the puzzle created by the division would take several hundred years to put together.

>>27>>   In the new century the music of Bach was benchmark and bulwark, as if it had been from the beginning. Without a Broadway show to lionize him, without an equivalent of "A Fifth of Beethoven," a Sistine Chapel or *Mona Lisa*, a *Christmas Carol* or *West Side Story* or Shakespeare in the Park, a cut-off ear or a feat of childhood precocity—not through these, but through the music itself, accompanied by technology, Bach had become the composer at the center, the name and voice for civilization.

So it was that when the era the Cantata Pilgrimage had announced was blasted open by terrorists, Bach was brought in. For ten days after the deadly attacks on the World Trade Center the three public radio stations in New York City held to an all-news format, providing exhaustive coverage of the aftermath. Then, on September 23, WNYC-FM reverted to its everyday format, classical music. It did so with a program called "Bach: Solace and Inspiration," which the host, David Garland, described as "a program to reassure and renew the spirit." John Eliot Gardiner was a guest, introducing recordings from the Cantata Pilgrimage. So was Rick Ericson, cantor of Holy Trinity, a Lutheran church on Central Park West with a decades-long practice of presenting Bach cantatas during services. So was Arthur Haas, a harpsichordist. Garland mixed in "absolute" instrumental works and expressly inspirational vocal ones: the motet "O Jesus Christ, meins Lebens Licht" and *contrapuncti* from the *Art of the Fugue*, an orchestral transcription from the *Goldberg Variations* and "Sleepers, Wake," and the violin chaconne—Bach's tombeau for Maria Barbara—in versions for violin, piano, and orchestra. He closed the program with "Sheep May Safely Graze" in Stokowski's transcription; and while the other music seemed apposite to the occasion, this piece, with the civic sweep of its strings, seemed more than adequate—seemed to add something to it.

So it was that when several million people went on pilgrimage to Rome, Bach awaited them there. Pope John Paul II died on the afternoon of Saturday, April 4, 2005. In the next seventy-two hours Rome swelled with pilgrims, who filled St. Peter's Square and the warren of streets surrounding it, waiting a day or more to pass through the basilica and view the body of the dead pope. Many were Poles, and during the open-air funeral Mass on Wednesday morning the banner SANTO SUBITO competed with red-and-white Polish flags flapping in rhythm to the pipe organ, which was amplified loud enough for it to be heard in Kraków. I was there that morning. That evening, I went to a Bach concert— the Orchestre Barocca Italiana performing cantatas in the period-correct Palazzo della Cancelleria—and the music of Bach, forest-grown, gut-strung, minimally processed, seemed the antithesis of the funeral's Slavo-Latinate Catholic pomp. Two weekends later we were back; there was a new pope, the square was dotted with gold flags, and at the end of the grand Mass of investiture, as Benedict XVI, the former Joseph Ratzinger, was conveyed through the crowd in a Mercedes-Benz, the Toccata and Fugue in D Minor, Protestant prelude and fugue to beat all, rang out loud enough to be heard in the Thuringian Forest.

>>28>> The war on terror was on, and a brave American pianist started playing Bach as "anti-terror" music, counterpoint to the drums of war at the White House and the terror-inducing experiences of his life in music.

This was Leon Fleisher, playing a transcription of "Sheep May Safely Graze."

Fleisher was a contemporary of Glenn Gould's: born in San Francisco in 1928, raised a prodigy, a soloist with the New York Philharmonic at age sixteen, one of the virtuosi who thrived on the "recital racket" Gould detested. Then in 1965, a few months after Gould stopped performing for live audiences, Fleisher stopped performing. In his case the stoppage was involuntary. "When I was thirty-six years old," he explained, "I mysteriously lost the use of two fingers on my right hand. The fourth and fifth finger started cramping, curling up, until they were firmly lodged against my palm." There was no pain, which made the affliction all the stranger. "Was it in my head? Was it some bigger malady? No one was able to tell me what was wrong." The virtuoso was handicapped, a curiosity: the one-handed pianist. A long night—thirty years long—followed, as Fleisher sought alternately to reverse his condition and to adapt to it. He thought of committing suicide. He tried remedies "from A to Z—from aromatherapy to Zen Buddhism." He rode a Vespa and grew his hair and beard long, acting out his vitality. He divorced and remarried, then divorced and remarried again. He conducted; he taught, masterfully, at the Peabody Conservatory in Baltimore, using verbal dexterity to describe effects he could not demonstrate. He became a potentate at Tanglewood. He kept playing the piano, mastering the tiny repertory written for the left hand only. Several composers had written works for Paul Wittgenstein, a brother of Ludwig, who had lost his right arm in the Great War. Dinu Lipatti had written a left-hand work when he was short of paper. Leon Kirchner, Lukas Foss, and others wrote left-hand works for Fleisher. But in Fleisher's view "probably the single greatest work for solo left hand" was a work of Bach: the violin chaconne as transcribed by Brahms for Clara Schumann to play during a bout of right-hand tendinitis. "Writing for only one hand," as Fleisher saw it, "allowed Brahms to echo both the limitations of the solo instrument and the way that Bach miraculously transcends them." This version is antihistrionic, without the violin's stress and strain; given that Bach probably worked out the chaconne at the keyboard and then adapted it for the violin, it brings the piece close to its origin, the composer working out the fingerings with his left hand and notating with his right.

Strangely, Fleisher apparently did not avail himself of the obvious way of transcending his limitation: multitrack recording. Why didn't he play the left-hand part of a piece for the microphone, then use the left hand to overdub the right-hand part rejigged for the left hand?

He had surgery for carpal tunnel syndrome, and the hand curled a little less. He played some pieces for two hands: "a bit of Beethoven here, a touch of Brahms, or, like healing medicine, the clear runs of Bach. As my fingers moved over those lines of music, I felt something lightening inside me." At Massachusetts General for a checkup, he led the doctors to the chapel, sat at a piano, and gave a recital with two hands. "It was like water after years in the desert. 'Jesu, Joy of Man's Desiring' never sounded so good."

Still his right hand wasn't right. In 1991 a neurologist in Baltimore—an amateur musician he had known for twenty years—diagnosed "focal hand dystonia." His condition was neither wholly physical nor psychosomatic. It was neurological, the result of scrambled signals between the brain and the hand. Back in 1965 the brain had received rapid repeated signals from the hand—say, during a fleet right-hand passage played over and over—and processed them as one signal. Cognitive dissonance followed. The brain stopped sending signals to the hand. The hand stiffened and curled up.

The neurologist recommended experimental treatments involving the injection of trace amounts of botulism, the most toxic of poisons. If the hand relaxed, fresh signals from the brain might get through. Fleisher took a couple of shots, then stopped. But some of the control over his right hand had returned—returned enough for him to play a piece for two hands when a dramatic occasion called for it. A musician he loved had died, and Fleisher wanted to "make a special gesture" at the memorial service:

"I played Bach's 'Jesu, Joy of Man's Desiring' . . . It's special music, mantra music, music that sounds as if it had the power to wash away all of the dirt and evils and complications of the world. It's very good for the mental health. It took me a long time to grow into Bach and to reach an understanding of the music and a feeling that I could play with what I felt it required. 'Jesu, Joy of Man's Desiring' is particularly healing. It requires an almost childlike simplicity, but it takes a lifetime's experience, I feel, to express it.

"It's also a piece for two hands."

He underwent Rolfing treatment, an intense physical therapy. Word of the Bach performance spread. Friends urged him to play "Jesu" at Tanglewood. He worked up a Mozart concerto instead, and then began to give recitals mixing pieces for one hand and for two hands. "I would open with 'Jesu, Joy of Man's Desiring,' because I thought that everybody should be able to hear that music at least once a day . . ." he recalled.

By then the botulism treatment—branded as Botox—was commonplace, a toxin made medicinal by technology. Fleisher tried it again, and this time Botox released his hand from its bondage. "I got a Botox shot, and I was cured. That's pretty much what happened. The main thing was that I got to play again, which is a miraculous gift."

He made a record: *Two Hands*. It opens with "Jesu, Joy of Man's Desiring" and "Sheep May Safely Graze," a matched pair. The text of the one is distinctly Christian, the other pastoral-universal in its imagery of sheep and shepherd: one is about the human regard for God, the other about God's solicitude for humanity. "Jesu" opens with a strong note in the left hand; then the melody begins in the right hand, which moves freely but deliberately, in a well-regulated way. The familiar countermelody, rising in the left hand, is sufficient unto itself, as if to say that the left hand alone would be enough, and the ornamentation added in the right hand is superabundance. In "Sheep May Safely Graze" the two hands move together, advancing in fours: the left hand chiming, the right hand chiseling the melody until it stands apart and upright; now the right hand is enough, and can make music independently.

Through Bach, Leon Fleisher was back; in those pieces the restorative power of the music is palpable. Heard by the listener who knows what the performer lost and found, those clear runs of Bach are transparent: the two hands with their ten digits glide across the staves, invisibly.

Postlude: Late Adopters

>>1>> "My patience is now at its end," Bach, late in life, told a fellow Leipziger, one Johann Georg Martius, in a note sent from the Thomaskirche. "How long do you think I must wait for the harpsichord? Two months have passed, and nothing has changed. I regret to write thus to you, but I cannot do otherwise. You must bring it in good order, and within five days, else we shall never be friends."

In that note, more than in any memo or dedication, Bach can be heard in full voice: the old master weary of human dealings, the genius tactfully but forcefully asserting his rights. Martius was an innkeeper; Bach had rented or loaned a harpsichord to him, for a wedding reception, perhaps, and was asking for it to be returned.

The episode is a kind of parable about the music of Bach. The music, like an instrument lent to a neighbor, has had its life to the degree that it has been made available to others; distinctly his, it thrives as shareware, music on permanent loan to us all.

Certainly Bach envisioned that his music would be made by musicians other than the pupils and workaday professionals of Leipzig. Surely he envisioned that his music would be taken up for other instruments, some known to him and others freshly invented, and that its aptness for transcription and transposition would be a means of survival through adaptation. But did he envision that his music, in time, would be "played" by people who could not sing or play a musical instrument, would be ripped and remixed and mashed up, and would withstand the process, even thrive through it? Could he have envisioned the digital present?

He could, and he did. A traditionalist in many ways, even so he composed for the future. His sense of the prospects of his music was crucial to his creative life—to the "patterns of invention" Laurence Dreyfus has explained so persuasively—and he envisioned his music being put to diverse purposes.

At his desk in the *Komponirstube* he had musicians of later generations in mind.

For him an invention was a musical figure articulated to the point where it could sustain further development. In a sense, every new rendering of a Bach work is a further development of the music. Some are better than others—more beautiful, more faithful, more expressive, more imaginative; about the boldest of them, the ones whose patterns meet Bach's most persuasively, we can say that through them Bach is reinvented.

The recordings of Bach's music represent a development of a very distinct kind. In a recording, a particular rendering of the music is made stable by technology. The paradox is that the music, thus stabilized, is rendered fluid in all sorts of other ways. It can be duplicated, packaged, and distributed far and wide; it can be "played" once or a thousand and one times.

Digital technology is a further development. Once digitized, the music stabilized through the recording process is made fluid again. It can be cut and pasted with ease; it can be sampled, treated, and Auto-Tuned; it can be combined with something else.

Who can count the ways Bach has been digitally remade? A composer at the University of California, Santa Cruz, used a computer and a Disklavier ("a digitally controlled acoustic grand piano") to generate five neo-Bach inventions derived from the originals—and that was twenty years ago. In my apartment in the early aughts, a plastic transmitter clipped to our infant sons' crib cycled through chippy electronic extracts from "Für Elise," "Eine Kleine Nachtmusik," and the first few bars of the first prelude from the *Well-Tempered Clavier*. T-Mobile offered a Toccata and Fugue ringtone for its mobile phones long before there were apps for you to create such things yourself. A graphic designer created a visual representation of the first cello suite in circles and lines, a fantasia for Bach and iPad.

Vasari concluded his *Lives of the Artists* with the certainty that the "noble" visual arts in Italy—painting, sculpture, architecture—had been given final form by Michelangelo. Five hundred years later, Arthur C. Danto, philosopher of the end of art, took pleasure in pointing out the limits of such a claim: art had ended in 1564, but the next century "saw Caravaggio and Rubens, Velazquez and Rembrandt, Poussin and El Greco, in all of whom painting attained heights that must be reckoned sublime."

Danto explained that Vasari meant an art of a certain kind had attained its true nature, and what followed was art of another kind. This was Danto's own claim about modern art—that it was what it was from the Impressionists and Cézanne, through Picasso and Matisse, on to Pollock and up to Warhol, who turned it into art-as-philosophy.

A similar claim, I think, can be made about audio recordings. From Schweitzer's wax cylinders of the Toccata and Fugue in D Minor up through the many CDs of the Bach Cantata Pilgrimage, recordings were a relatively stable entity—made, produced, distributed, bought, played, enjoyed, recommended to others. In the digital present they are something else. Digital is not a format (a material form for the immaterial) so much as a pattern friendly to formats—a pattern of invention, one might say. Digital takes over other formats and converts them into zeroes and ones, and they then can be put into new forms. In the digital present, music is not released so much as circulated—sent out so that it can go into new forms with little restraint. The formatting of recorded music has passed from producer to listener; we are all dial-twiddlers now.

The most profound aspect of recorded music in the digital present is also the most obvious. Digital means shareable. Once you have the music in digital form you can copy it, burn it, send it, upload it, pass it on.

Digitally, I was a late adopter. My wife's best friend, in New York from California, stayed with us over Christmas. This meant that she had no choice but to hear ten days of Bach pumped out of a world-band radio set on the sill of an open window. Did I know Pablo Casals's version of the cello suites? she asked, and was astonished when I told her that I did not.

The CDs came blister-packed in a manila envelope from Los Angeles, each marked in block letters with a Sharpie:

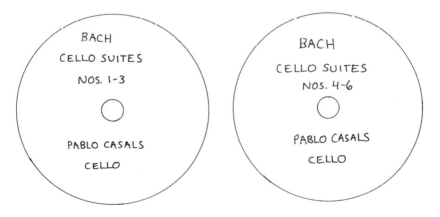

Already it is hard to remember how *samizdat*-seeming home-burned discs were in those days. Most personal computers didn't have disc-writing drives; a

CD-R was something the office manager used when he was backing up system files.

I put the CD in a boombox and no sound came out. (The machine was pre-CD-R.) I tried my computer, a Gateway with perforated sound-holes left and right. All at once there it was: those suites, that cellist, that sound. The home-burned CDs carried no explanatory notes, just a few words in indelible ink. I had to know more.

>>2>> The Internet then seemed a new way to augment or expand the worldly territory of classical music culture, which, called anemic at the time, looks robust in retrospect. To go into the vast classical room of the Tower Records near Lincoln Center at ten o'clock on a Friday night was to feel the spillover of concerted energy from Avery Fisher Hall and the Metropolitan Opera, from Tully and Juilliard—rumpled men in tweed jackets and khaki ball caps, ladies in pearls, Asian kids with soft-sided violin cases slung over their shoulders, would-be ballerinas floating down the aisles with toes pointed outward. Browsing in the Bach section was an extreme sport, choice-ridden and anxiety-inducing because the selection was so large. The row of discs for the Mass in B Minor was an arm and a leg long. Bach's sons were represented far out of proportion to their talents. There were three sets of the solo violin works by Arthur Grumiaux, with nothing to indicate why one cost $50, another $34.99, and a third the two-for-one price of $15. If you didn't see what you were looking for, in the cupboards below the racks there were cardboard boxes marked *Bach misc. clavier, Harp and other weird Bach stuff*, and so on.

Many of the discs were reissues, as record companies scooped into their vaults and put out old classical recordings for all points of the market, from *Twenty Bach Favorites* on up. The German-run, Hong Kong–based company Naxos took advantage of lapsing copyrights to reissue huge tracts of the classical past: in Bach, sets of Edwin Fischer, Wanda Landowska, Yehudi Menuhin, and a five-disc set of Pablo Casals's recordings from the teens and twenties. Other reissue series (Pearl, Biddulph, Gala) were driven by the yearning of collectors to make their long-held treasures available to other devotees. To go into Academy Records on Eighteenth Street in Manhattan was to see this part of the classical music demographic sliced to rueful perfection: white men thirty-five and older, cultivated men with twelve-dollar haircuts and suit jackets shiny at the cuffs, squinting at the racks through *Dragnet*-era spectacles, eyes on the prize of a hard-to-find recording.

Andante.com, which went up on the Web in 2001, was the Internet equivalent of Tower Records: amply funded, comprehensive, pricey, dynastic. It had a "radio" channel, a classical newswire, streaming concerts, and the Andante Boutique, which sold sumptuous CD sets of rare recordings. The set for Herbert von Karajan's *St. Matthew Passion* from the Bach bicentenary festival in Vienna came bound like a hardback book, with black tagboard sleeves like the albums of old 78s; printed texts in English, French, and German; extensive notes, and a solemn statement of purpose: "Andante is to restore recordings to their status as works of art, thereby renewing that original spirit of celebration."

It couldn't last. Andante.com attracted upward of fifty thousand unique monthly visitors, but memberships lagged, especially after the dot-com bust later in 2001. It was sold, streamlined, and then shut down, and its sets showed up at Academy: a set of recordings of Bach orchestral music by Stokowski, Busch, Furtwängler, and others, and a set of Stokowski's recordings from Bach to Tchaikovsky.

Andante's regard for Stokowski showed how specialized an enterprise it was. The nickname suggests familiarity, but Stoki is now as little known as Schoenberg and the other "difficult" composers he championed. Albert Schweitzer and Pablo Casals are still known popularly as humanitarians: a Schweitzer Foundation brings development-minded students to Gabon, and a plaque marking Casals's last house greets cruise-ship passengers disembarked for a duty-free morning in San Juan. Stokowski, a musician first and last, lives only in recordings.

In one sense, Stokowski is a victim of his own hard work. His recorded output is scattered across a dozen companies; his willingness to record certain pieces over and over again means that no one recording of a piece can be called definitive. In another sense, he is a victim of the sonic innovations he did so much to promote. Recorded sound has progressed far since the late fifties, when Stokowski was captured on tape at the far shore of his prime. The Stokowski sound, notoriously large, especially in Bach, now sounds small.

Fantasia is no longer the rite of passage for children that it once was. It is reissued periodically, but it has been supplanted by *Fantasia 2000*, a recording synched to the film by another conductor. Stoki will shake hands with Mickey in perpetuity, but the mouse has outlasted the maestro.

>>3>> There is another reason for Stokowski's demise: the demise of Big Bach. The movement toward small forces led by Joshua Rifkin advanced from the B-minor Mass and some cantatas toward the most monumental of Bach's vocal works, the *St. Matthew Passion*. In April 2002, Paul McCreesh and the Gabrieli Consort and Players recorded the *St. Matthew Passion* at a church in Denmark with one voice on a part—nine singers in all. The recording was for Archiv, DG's period-instrument arm; the CD booklet, thick as a Gideon Bible, indicated that the organ used was a neo-Baroque instrument from the year 2000, with hand-beaten lead pipes, playable in either standard or Baroque tuning.

It was a measure of the early-music movement's success that the *Passion* thus rendered sounds perfectly ordinary. Here are voices of people angry, aggrieved, distressed, accusatory, alarmed, defensive, grief-stricken. When Peter denies Jesus, he is pointed out as a man who knows Jesus by a maidservant, then a second one, and then by some bystanders, whom Bach represented with one of the two choirs. In this *Passion*, there are four singers in that chair, not sixteen or forty-eight, and their identification of Peter in ten seconds of tight choral writing (in English, "Surely you too are one of them, for your accent betrays you") is a plausible piece of realism: they really do sound like bystanders who had heard the man speak.

The sonic austerity of McCreesh's Passion was matched by the visual austerity of Jonathan Miller's semistaged *St. Matthew Passion*, presented at the Brooklyn Academy of Music and elsewhere. On stage was a plank table with some bread and wine on it; seated at it, chin in hands, was a man in street clothes and two days' growth of beard; he looked up, pivoted to the people, several dozen of them, seated in a circle around him—the disciples; the citizens of Jerusalem; the body of believing Christians; people of goodwill over the centuries, all represented in the persons of the musicians—and began to tell a story. "When Jesus had finished speaking, he said to his disciples . . ."

This Passion was sung in English, and the effect, for the native English speaker, was an aural clarity akin to the visual clarity of the staging. There, in a flagrantly ahistorical interpretation, was access to the experience of Lutherans hearing the *Passion* in church in Leipzig in 1727, who, after all, heard a story they knew sung in a language they knew, but with a beauty far out of the ordinary.

>>4>> "I don't follow instructions very well. I can't turn things on. I can't find the buttons. I like to get in, and do things, and see what happens— and I like to noodle with things. My iMac G4 allows that to happen."

Well into the new millennium, Yo-Yo Ma didn't habitually use a computer. He read his e-mail on sheets of paper printed out for him by an assistant. He was permanently attached to his cell phone, but not, alas, to its charger.

For all that, Ma was friendly with Steve Jobs, the co-founder of Apple, whom he had met shortly after recording Bach's cello suites in 1981. That he was so late an adopter made him an ideal participant in the Apple ad campaign aimed at Mac-wary people. So there he was in Friday casuals, smiling against a white background while some bluegrassy music played.

"It's beautiful. Sleek. I wanted to touch it," he said sheepishly. "For some one that is that technically challenged, I think that was my way in. Macs . . . are friendly to people like me." The Apple logo flashed onscreen. Then he was back: "I'm Yo-Yo Ma, and I play the cello."

Apple's association with classical music was as old as the Macintosh. One of the first videogames designed for the Mac, Dark Castle, booted up to a gray-scale image of a castle ("a woodcut made by binary fairies," the game enthusiast Whitney Pastorek later called it) and the transistorized sound of the Toccata and Fugue in D Minor. Later, to introduce the NeXT computer—the Mac's successor—Jobs arranged for the NeXT to "accompany" a violinist in a Bach concerto onstage at a press event in California.

Apple's "Switch" advertising campaign coincided with a comprehensive effort whereby the company would make use of musicians to entice people to switch from PCs to the Mac. Apple had developed a portable music player and, to support it, had launched a music service offering digital access to music for a simple price, typically 99 cents a song.

For Steve Jobs (acid-tripping conductor of Bach in a wheat field) music had always been a stimulant to the imagination. For Jobs (Dylan freak) music was where art and commerce met. Now music—recorded music—was becoming the key to his company's business model. If it caught on, iPod + iTunes would prompt a profound switch in the listening experience: from the album to the song, from the home stereo to the personal computer.

Several million young people had switched already. While the record companies, in casual collusion, pursued a go-slow digital strategy, Napster, Gnutella, et al., hijacked their distribution with a college-geek feat of programming called peer-to-peer file sharing. Young people suddenly disdained paying for music the way their parents had disdained fighting a war in Vietnam.

In-store sales of new music plummeted. Independent record shops closed. The need to frame a legal strategy made the record companies jittery and defensive.

Most classical music people were oblivious to these developments. And yet file sharing was already affecting classical music profoundly. For years pop music profits had carried money-losing classical music divisions. Now pop divisions were losing money.

EMI was in particular trouble. The view on the street was that the only value left in the legendary company was in "catalog": in the Beatles and the Rolling Stones, in Frank Sinatra and Queen and Pink Floyd, and in the company's vast tracts of classical recordings, such as Albert Schweitzer's Bach organ recordings from All Hallows and Pablo Casals's recordings of the Bach cello suites.

Tower Records filed for bankruptcy in 2004 and closed its stores two years later. In 2006, HMV (owned by EMI) closed all its stores in North America, and the next year Virgin Megastores did likewise. EMI was bought in 2007 by a private equity group, which sold it to Citigroup, which sold it to Universal and Sony. As the company was deboned, Abbey Road Studio was put up for sale. It was suggested that Sir Paul McCartney should buy Abbey Road and present it as a gift to the British people; like Stonehenge and Big Ben, the first purpose-built recording studio was a national treasure.

For Apple, iPod + iTunes was successful beyond any reckoning. The company reported that the iTunes Store sold a billion tracks in its first five years of operation. Twelve percent of those were tracks from classical recordings. When Deutsche Grammophon released a new *Art of the Fugue* by Pierre-Laurent Aimard, a French exponent of contemporary music making his first Bach recording, it went straight to number one—number one on the iTunes classical chart. Classical music people took notice. Naxos expanded its online offerings until they were a quarter of the company's business. A nineteen-year-old composition student at the New England Conservatory of Music, Edward W. Guo, founded the International Music Score Library Project to make scores available for free over the Internet. In *The New Yorker*, Alex Ross at once called for and celebrated a marriage between the classical culture and the online culture of downloads, streams, blogs, study aids, and digitized ephemera—an ideal he dubbed "The Well-Tempered Web."

One brick-and-mortar music retailer was still robust: Starbucks. For several years beginning in 2005 the company—following Apple to the place where art and commerce met—commissioned a series of "Artist's Choice" CD compilations to sell in its cafés. Yo-Yo Ma was an early participant. His disc began with the sarabande from Bach's fifth cello suite, played by Pablo Casals: "In an interview I heard when Casals was in his nineties," Ma recalled in the notes, "he was asked to choose the one piece he would want to play for the whole world. He selected the Sarabande from Bach's Fifth Suite. So this is a self-chosen piece by Casals of the very music he had championed throughout his life." The disc ended with the aria from the 1955 *Goldberg Variations*. "Bach is almost the only composer who is both totally objective and totally compassionate," Ma explained. "Glenn Gould found a way, through the power of his unique young mind, to abstract all of life, even though he had experienced so little of life, into his interpretation of this piece."

>>5>> Glenn Gould would have loved the Internet. A constructed space making use of electronic gadgetry in the service of self-presentation, allowing intense personal interaction without any physical contact, and making no distinction between night and day: the Web is very much like the creative space he constructed for himself.

It is no surprise, then, that Gould has thrived in the digital present. What is surprising is that now more than ever he is a visual presence. The never-ending rereleases of his records are just the beginning of the long tail of his legacy. Heard more than seen while he was alive, he now exists on video to an extent inconceivable to listeners in the United States in his lifetime: in documentaries, film festivals, box sets, and the half-lit, grainy, small-screen semi-darkness of YouTube.

What is surprising, in all this, is that there is very little "if only"—if only he could have played with Yo-Yo Ma; made a golden jubilee recording; used ProTools; played the Bachhaus in Leipzig. Nobody wishes that Gould were not dead. And what is even more surprising is that the vast evidence of the range of his musical interests—from serial music to Streisand—hasn't loosened the identification of Gould with Bach, which is complete and permanent.

In *On Late Style*, published in 2006, Edward Said characterized "lateness" as an artistic attribute running across the arts in our time. Said scarcely mentioned recordings, but his analysis of Gould's posthumous life had everything to do with Gould's approach to recordings. In Said's account, Gould intuited the situation of the near future, in which (due to recordings) many music lovers would not have a player's knowledge of music. And he recognized that, with virtuoso performances a dime a dozen (due to recordings), the ones that matter are those that seem at once to play the music and comment on it. Somehow

Gould figured this out early, and so developed an approach to Bach's work that involved "a protracted and sustained contrapuntal invention, disclosed, argued, and elaborated rather than simply presented, through performance." And Gould pursued efforts in various media that testified to "how well he understood the deep structure of Bach's creativity" and his own vocation "to carry on that kind of work in performances of Bach and other composers who were, in a sense, invented by Bach."

Said himself died of cancer in 2003; *On Late Style* was itself a posthumous production, an unfinished fugue on the theme of belatedness.

Lorraine Hunt Lieberson died of cancer a few weeks after the book's release. As with Gould, her posthumous life was assured, but for a different reason. She sang Bach in a late style consisting of singular feeling rather than contrapuntal self-scrutiny. With the death another few weeks later of Craig Smith, the music director who had led the Emmanuel Church choir and orchestra in the Sunday-morning cantata performances where Hunt had found her voice, an era ended, with Hunt as its tragic heroine.

I listened to their version of "Ich habe genug" while walking across Manhattan on a gray summer morning. Was it the music of a woman who was dying—who had faced down death once and soon would face it again? Did her death, and my knowledge of it, make the music sound different?

The recording doesn't sound more death-haunted than it did when she was still alive. But the knowledge that Hunt is dead makes certain aspects of the performance, and the cantata itself, more apparent: her vocal, for example, is full of subtle touches that make it sound like a variation on a melody she had already sung straight—makes it sound like a last verse, a recapitulation. It is so-called early music sung in a late style, that is; and it may be that Hunt's anticipation of death enabled her to bring this off. "Ich habe genug" is a cantata that begins at the end—begins with the singer's declaration, or recognition, that she has seen (in the newborn Messiah) the fullness of life, as much of life as she is likely to see. The music underscores this sentiment. The high pitch of the drama; the counterpoint already fully elaborated, the phrases fully developed; the concentrated intensity of Hunt's voice, so different from the ebullient openness of, say, the opening phrases of her takes on Handel arias—all suggest from the outset that, in this piece of music, an outer limit has been reached.

In Hunt Lieberson's "Ich habe genug" the early-music movement grew up for good. The movement so concerned with beginnings yielded a music of endings, a postmodern postlude.

>>6>> A friend in the music business told me that Simone Dinnerstein was going to be the next big thing in classical music in America, if only she could get a record contract. Dinnerstein was a New York painter's daughter who had studied with Peter Serkin at Juilliard. She had played at Tanglewood. She had won a national competition for artists judged on the threshold of significant careers. She had mastered the *Goldberg Variations* while she was pregnant with her first child. And yet she hadn't managed to interest a commercial record company in her plan to make her American debut with a fresh recording of the *Goldberg*s. Finally she decided to record the *Goldberg*s anyway. She raised the money through donations, rented the venerable recital hall at the American Academy of Arts and Letters in upper Manhattan, wheeled in her piano of choice—a restored century-old Steinway—and made the recording over three days in 2005.

My friend sent me a "private pressing" of Dinnerstein's *Goldberg Variations* CD, with headshots of the recording artist front and back. For some reason I wound up setting it aside without listening to it. We'd seen this before, hadn't we? Fifty years after Glenn Gould's *Goldberg Variations*, record-company people considered the music of Bach ideal for a debut. Young female musicians especially used Bach to go public. Lara St. John's *Bach: Works for Violin Solo* had sold 25,000 copies, a big number for classical music—and the sales had something to do with the fact that on the cover she stood unclothed in a half-shuttered room, holding the violin against her bare chest like a bustier. *Hilary Hahn Plays Bach*, with the comely seventeen-year-old virtuoso in black velvet gazing out from behind violin and upthrust bow in a soft-focus cover shot, had matched Yo-Yo Ma's *Inspired by Bach* in sales and buzz when Sony Classical promoted the two releases at the same time. Press attention focused not on the quality of the records (very, very good) so much as on the seeming paradox of sex being used to sell classical music, but the question of why Bach figured into the debutante equation never arose. St. John herself came closest to explaining it: the bare-but-for-violin shot, she said, was meant to represent a violinist's encounter with the solo works, which leaves her totally exposed.

Certainly Bach's combination of difficulty and familiarity makes every Bach debut auspicious. Certainly the artists' own tastes figure into such a decision, and the revival of Bach's music means more artists are being raised on Bach than ever before. More than that, I think, the otherworldly qualities of the music and Bach's irreducible religiosity make his work something like virginal, and so seemingly apt for a young musician's first encounter with the public. There is probably a simple commercial calculation being made, too. Sex sells, a wise man once said, and classical music people had come up with a corollary—Bach sells—for the digital present.

In the case of Simone Dinnerstein I understood the record companies' resistance. Glenn Gould had made the *Goldbergs* debut recording of all time. Why try to rival it?

Not so long afterward the record, out from Telarc with a photograph of a grown-up Dinnerstein on the cover, was the biggest-selling classical debut since 1956, some said. Suddenly Dinnerstein was everywhere: at Weill Recital Hall, on public radio, in *The New Yorker*, where she was called "the pianists' pianist of Generation X"—and at the microphone for a session of the WKCR Bachfest, delivering an extraordinary DJ mix of her favorite Bach recordings, from Kathleen Ferrier's Agnus dei (from the 1950 Vienna B-minor Mass) to a French jazz trio's Brandenburgs, from Bach done *Cubanismo*-style to microtonal variations on the *Goldberg Variations*.

Now I fished out that self-financed *Goldberg Variations* and listened to it—with self-correcting surprise. This was no debut demonstration of mastery or dexterity. It was the great work in wide angle—played in moderate tempos, with all the repeats taken, and with a sturdy confidence often called maturity. Dinnerstein had been right to take charge of her own debut. In the digital present, she is dauntlessly pursuing a fairly traditional career—recordings and recitals; solo work alternating with work for orchestra, Bach with other composers—and an audience fluent in digital media has found her.

Her record *Bach: A Strange Beauty* suggests why Bach figures into debuts so prominently. The title comes from a remark by Sir Francis Bacon: "There is no excellent beauty that hath not some strangeness in the proportion." But her playing hath much more beauty than strangeness: it is at once robust and controlled in the left hand, strictly contrapuntal and yet as casually expressive at points as Marsalis-era jazz. In fact, what makes it strange is the frank emphasis given to beauty. After a century of Bach interpreters who have stressed his music's formal qualities—canonic rigor; pedagogical utility; symbolic richness— here is a pianist grounding a career in the proposition that the music of Bach is beautiful music. And this, I think, is why Bach figures into so many debuts: because to play it well is to play it beautifully, and for Bach, that is enough.

Dinnerstein's career demonstrates the limits of recordings like Glenn Gould's—namely, that the musician who made them is now dead. Her success with Bach shows that recordings will never be enough—shows that every age needs its own Bach interpreters, who play Bach in certain rooms on certain nights, and who alone know how they will play it.

>>7>>   The violinist began with the Bach chaconne—a hard piece in any circumstances, especially in the rush hour in Washington. He had set up outside the L'Enfant Plaza Metro station, in jeans and T-shirt and baseball cap, a regular guy except for the violin, the case of which was open at his feet. He played a transcription of Schubert's "Ave Maria," romantic pieces by Estrellita and Massenet, and the gavotte from Bach's third partita, then started in on the Bach chaconne again. A thousand people walked past, heading up and out to work at the Department of Energy, the Department of Housing and Urban Development, the General Services Administration. A couple of dozen dropped money in his case. Half a dozen paused to listen and watch. He cleared thirty-two dollars.

The violinist was Joshua Bell: Sony Classical recording artist, standing-room-only draw at Carnegie Hall and the Kennedy Center. His violin was a Stradivarius from 1713. The performance—a "stunt," Bell called it—was arranged by a feature writer for *The Washington Post*. In an article, the writer, Gene Weingarten, presented the stunt as an exhibit in office workers' indifference to classical music no matter the quality; as a demonstration of the aural oblivion created by the iPod and other portable music players; as proof of the philistinism of Washington, twenty-first-century company town.

On top of all that, it represented a worldly turn for classical virtuosi. Truly, the music of Bach is indigenous to city streets: I think of the day I stopped in the subway below Penn Station to listen to two Asian violinists pass the bowed lines of the double concerto back and forth between the uptown and downtown platforms as a slanted speaker pumped out accompaniment, or the day when I arrived in Rome by tram from the airport and followed the sound of a Bach piece for solo violin through the twisty streets near the Campo dei' Fiori, or the day when, already late to teach a class, I stopped at a sidewalk bookseller's table on Broadway and wound up buying forty CDs of the Bach-Edition for a dollar apiece. Bach was already at home on the street; but Bach-on-the-street was the bailiwick of so-called working musicians. Then Yo-Yo Ma challenged the preconception with *Inspired by Bach*, and other virtuosi followed him out of the concert hall with aplomb.

The Paul Winter Consort marked the summer solstice at the Cathedral of St. John the Divine with "Bach2Brasil," filling that urban Christian canyon with a Bachian ambiance rippling off Winter's electro-treated saxophone.

Matt Haimovitz played Bach cello suites at CBGB, the epitome of the dank punk club. Haimovitz, born in 1970, had studied with Ma, then dropped out of Harvard and the recital circuit alike. CBGB was just one gig in a tour of nightclubs, cafés, and restaurants in support of a self-financed CD release of the cello suites, recorded in a church in the Berkshires. He played three Bach suites, a new piece by a living composer, and a four-string reduction of Jimi Hendrix's version of "The Star-Spangled Banner." *The Wall Street Journal's* critic griped that he couldn't hear the cello over the clinking bottles and conversations. As a gesture, though, it worked: Haimovitz wound up on *Nightline* and in classical music lore as the cellist who played Bach at CBGB.

Savion Glover tap-danced to Bach. Glover had made his name in a series of Broadway musicals culminating in *Bring in 'da Noise, Bring in 'da Funk*. In his late twenties, like Yo-Yo Ma with the cello at the same age, Glover sought at once to take tap back to its roots (in African rhythms and culture) and bring it into new contexts. *Classical Savion* featured Bach, Vivaldi, Mozart, and Mendelssohn; Glover entered wearing a tuxedo and stripped down from there. He brought heavy steps to the third Brandenburg concerto, then quieted down for the "Air on the G String"—a tribute in tap to his mentor, Gregory Hines, who had died of cancer. Thus the "Air" was made a requiem in rhythm.

In one sense, performances like those put Bach into the mix the Web and the iPod made possible. In another, they were versions of Bach of a kind that had existed all along but which technology brought to attention. A Cuban conga version of a C-minor fugue from the *Well-Tempered Clavier*; an "Ave Maria" for triply overdubbed Brazilian guitar; the agile upright bassist Edgar Meyer's run through the cello suites; a café blend of Bach and Coltrane; an hourlong recording of Bach played on the koto: they claimed equal space on the Web and iTunes, one screen away from a traditional Mass in B Minor.

Peter Blanchette plays Bach on the archguitar, a cross between a guitar and a lute: eleven strings mounted on a wide neck attached to a small peanut-shaped body. He devised the instrument with his teacher, the luthier Walter Stamel, after graduating from conservatory in 1982, and spent the next few years playing in squares and piazzas across Europe—a time "filled with sunshine, Bach, pencils, manuscript paper, language books, great food, and dozens of good friends." His *Archguitar Bach* recording is at once self-sufficient and generous, austere yet not antiquarian. For years Blanchette supported himself by selling cassettes and CDs wherever he performed. The Web now allows listeners to find him from wherever they are.

The New Century Saxophone Quartet was urged to play Bach by Joel Krosnick, cellist of the Juilliard String Quartet. Notes to the group's *Art of the*

Fugue CD point out that the four saxophones—soprano, alto, tenor, and baritone, all designed by the nineteenth-century Belgian inventor Adolphe Sax— are "a pure consort . . . more consistent in tone color from top to bottom than the brass or woodwind quartet, or even the string quartet." Such consistency suits the *Art of the Fugue* altogether. So does the saxophone itself: its timbral blend of wood and brass warms up Bach, and Bach returns the instrument indigenous to its European roots. In the first contrapunctus the four players breathe as one, each threading a sound through his horn until it vaporizes into nonsound. When the second contrapunctus begins, the chugging baritone is joined by the tenor, then the alto and soprano—large to small, low to high— but much of the sonic variety comes from the four horns' associative overtones: here are Gerry Mulligan, Sonny Rollins, Paul Desmond, and John Coltrane, playing Bach together.

>>8>> "All Bach," the scholar said matter-of-factly, tucking his iPod into a breast pocket. "Three times over. For every piece, there's a classic performance, a historically informed performance, and a personal favorite."

The huge storage capacity of the new digital players was obviously a benefit to classical-music listeners. But that scholar's all-of-Bach was an effort he'd had to undertake himself on his own time. Through the history of recordings, each new format from the 78 to the compact disc was promoted to the classical market first. Classical people spent money on audio equipment; they were sticklers for high fidelity and kept abreast of new developments in technology. Things were different in the digital present. Bach enthusiast though Steve Jobs was, Apple had taken the iPod + iTunes model to the pop-music culture first. Classical could wait. Classical-music people were late adopters.

When Jobs died in October 2011 there was a private memorial service, then a memorial service open to Apple employees. Yo-Yo Ma played the cello. Not long after they met, Jobs had asked him to play at his wedding, but Ma could not. After Jobs was diagnosed with cancer, Ma was a guest at his house in California; while Jobs's daughter Erin toyed with Ma's cello, a more perfect piece of technology than any her father had designed, Jobs asked Ma to play at his memorial when the time came.

There Ma was in Cupertino. Twenty years earlier he had played the sarabande from the fifth suite at his father's deathbed. Four weeks earlier, at the 9/11 memorial in Lower Manhattan, he had taken part in the public events

marking the tenth anniversary of the terrorist attacks, playing from the Bach
cello suites as the names of victims were read into the microphone. Now he
played part of a Bach cello suite as a tombeau for the man most aptly characterized as an inventor for his time. "Your playing is the best argument I've ever
heard for the existence of God," Jobs had told him once, "because I don't really
believe a human alone can do this."

Jobs's monument to his career was the iPad, a gray slab like none before.
He had demonstrated a prototype of the iPad to his biographer, Walter Isaacson, by calling up some Bach recordings on it: the second Brandenburg concerto, a fugue from the *Well-Tempered Clavier*, and Glenn Gould's two
Goldberg Variations. He liked both Gould *Goldberg*s—the first for its youthful
brilliance, the second for its stark soulfulness; like the iPad, he might have explained, that one was a late expression of a genius who would die relatively
young.

Musicians adopted the iPad immediately; set on a music stand or a piano's
music rack, it effortlessly displayed a digital score. Out went the brass lamps;
now and forevermore, when the lights go down all eyes will go to the rectangular glow.

>>9>>   A long row of raised wooden blocks runs like a model railroad
through a forest to a valley where a stream of clear water flows. A wooden
ball rolls down the track, descending step by step, tracked by the camera, and
with each step the ball plinks against wood, several hundred plinks in all.
Together in succession the plinks make a melody: "Jesu, Joy of Man's Desiring," played by wooden ball and purpose-built giant cypress xylophone.

The xylophone and the piece were commissioned by NTT Docomo, a
Japanese telecom company. When the ball reaches the end of the track—and
the melody—it comes to rest next to a mobile phone shaped like a kidney bean
and encased in cypress. The piece is a commercial for NTT's Touch-Wood
phone.

The commercial went viral, as a video posted on YouTube and elsewhere
was forwarded around the world. The question arose: Was it real, or technologically enhanced—a camera trick, a splice job? A video on the company's
website explained how the xylophone had been built and the commercial
made: the video was a single take, with only the sound mix altered so as to put
woody melody, wind, and water in the right balance.

Spectacularly inventive in itself, the commercial suggests the double way in which Bach's music is being developed in the digital present. Obviously, the Web is now the default means of distribution for inventive Bach. Just as it is possible to call up a video of Ornette Coleman playing the first cello suite "harmolodically" with his quartet, or the Romanian pianist Eugene Cicero interpolating "Sweet Georgia Brown" into a steady-rolling transcription of the badinerie from the second orchestral suite, or Bobby McFerrin singing the "Air on the G String" at an open-air 24 Hours Bach festival in Leipzig, or a three-part invention played by the bow-tied twelve-year-old Chinese-Canadian prodigy Tony Yike Yang, or a century-old player-piano rendition of the Toccata and Fugue in D Minor, it is possible for several million people worldwide to see a Japanese cell-phone commercial—a commercial that, wordless and set to globally well-known music, is meant, in its way, for each of them, even if they are outside the NTT Docomo market.

It also suggests how Bach is being reinvented in the digital present. Xylophone and cell phone, wood and silicon, "Jesu" and Kyushu: it works through the aggressive combination of unlike elements—the mash-up, that is. Like the stalks of wheat Steve Jobs saw moving to the music in his acid trip, the Bach mash-ups are expressions of the music at once unbidden and apt, and prone to multiply without ceasing.

Artists have always put seeming opposites together; Aristotle defined the perception of likeness in difference as the basis of all art. Digital technology just makes it especially easy to do. Even that player-piano Toccata and Fugue is a digital production, made possible by MIDI, the set of protocols that allows musical instruments to interact digitally with computers and one another. And most mash-ups are expressly, emphatically digital. A few years ago Vanessa-Mae, violinist and rebel prodigy, was featured in an over-the-top video of her version of the Toccata and Fugue in D Minor: playing on mountaintops, at cliff's edge, and in swirling sea foam; playing electric violin in hot pants, giving the camera a crotch shot. It was current, with-it, envelope-pushing, raw, and it helped make Vanessa-Mae one of the wealthiest young musicians in England; but it has become as dated-looking as the *Switched-on Bach* sleeve, because the effects were done with cameras and old-school postproduction, not with digital editing software.

DJs From Mars's Bach mash-up is different. The Turin-based electro-house duo first gained notoriety for mashing up two current pop songs, or a new song and an old one. After the hip-hop stars Jay-Z, Kanye West, and Rihanna joined together in 2009 to make a single and elaborate video for "Run This Town," DJs From Mars released "Run This Town and Fugue in D Minor," announced as such in Gothic titles in the video's opening sequence, as Rihanna removes a bandana from her face like a Muslim woman removing her veil. After a quick cut of the first figure from the toccata, the sound track goes to the steely and insistent opening bars of the fugue, which mash up effortlessly with the song's martial descent from D to C and B-flat—and even better with the imagery of a crowd turning into a torch-toting mob that moves on Rihanna as she vows that she's going to run this town. You don't have to love Bach to think that the mash-up improves on the hip-hop original—that it adds a riff of old-world menace the song called for all along.

A few clicks away, an animated caterpillar slithers through the prelude to the first cello suite, up and down a row of colored circles of different sizes—part Mondrian, part Coney Island Cyclone—which scroll past so that the caterpillar seems both to move through the music and to be kept aloft by it. This visualization of Bach is the work of Stephen Malinowski, a composer and software designer in the Bay Area. In the late seventies, as a composition student, he sought to represent music on a roll of teletype paper with a felt-tip pen. Ever since, he has pursued the goal of representing music visually through new technology, beginning with the personal computer and the MIDI interface and following through to Magnatune (an early all-you-can-eat music download service) and the iPad. The killer app was YouTube, which enabled him to distribute his work widely; when Björk, the form-breaking Icelandic musician, engaged him to create graphics for her multimedia music-app project, Biophilia, she had come to know his work through YouTube.

Malinowski's Bach visualizations look like child's play, but rely on the mathematical relationships between musical notes to establish kindred visual relationships, which often suggest Western notation digitally enhanced. A version of the cello prelude uses white bars to represent the cellist's bowing action. A visual of the prelude from the third partita for solo violin (in Lara St. John's recording) is a kind of digital crochet: a string or line executes a series of loop-the-loops, with the length of the loop, the size and color of the pegs on each end, and the thickness of the string all changing constantly to suggest the variety within a piece that moves with perfect tactile and subtactile regularity—in steady 4/4 time, that is.

Alexander Chen, a generation younger than Malinowski, created a visual of Bach's first cello suite based on eight straight lines whose lengths vary from moment to moment according to the Pythagorean formulae used as the basis for Western stringed instruments. Instead of moving left to right, the lines expand and contract in place, and so step away from Western notation. Chen was already celebrated among the digerati for rendering the New York subway map as a musical instrument; as the cello visual made the rounds, Malinowski introduced himself to Chen in the comments string. The music of Bach had made them visual comrades.

>>10>> "Time: 1976" is a poem in three eight-line verses:

> *Time for my break; I'm walking from my study down the long hallway*
>   *towards the living room.*
> *Catherine is there, on the couch, reading to Jed, the phonograph is*
>   *playing Bach's* Offering.
> *I can just hear Catherine's voice as she shows Jed the pictures:* Voilà le
>   château, voilà Babar,
> *and with no warning I'm taken with a feeling that against all logic I*
>   *recognize to be regret, as violent and rending a regret as anything*
>   *I've ever felt . . .*

The poet is C. K. Williams, and what he feels is not the familiar regret involving a past time remembered in the present and felt as past and so as lost. No, what he feels—hearing a Bach record playing, hearing the voice of his wife reading a book aloud to their son—is his mind rushing forward twenty years into a moment, same apartment, same music, in which he regrets the loss of the moment he is in here and now. What is missing from that anticipated future moment, he asks himself, that makes him feel the loss of it so strongly? Is it that his wife and son are no longer there, and he is alone with memory? Could be, but it can't be: one of them must be there, he thinks, because one of them must have put on the record, because he is sure, in that moment, that the music is not in his memory, thinks that "it must be the music— / the Bach surely is real, I can *hear* it—that drives me so poignantly, expectantly back / to remember again that morning of innocent peace a lifetime ago when I came towards them."

When I read the poem twenty years ago, I had never heard the *Musical Offering*. The poem lodged in my mind; the *Musical Offering* grew in stature until I was loath to just buy the CD and play it. Something grander, more liturgical, was called for. Then, as I heard more and more Bach, I held off; there was comfort in the thought that there was a major Bach work out there that I had never heard.

One morning conditions were ideal: a quiet apartment, a free hour, the sounds of a children's French lesson lingering. The compact disc, checked out of the library, was in a green envelope from Teldec's Bach 2000 set, carrying only a credit to Nikolaus Harnoncourt and the Concertus Musicus Wien. I put it in. After twenty years—after 265 years—here I was with the *Musical Offering*.

Where I had expected a chamber group there was a harpsichord setting down a line, plucky and austere, then a second and a third, like a grounds-keeper chalking a diamond. This was the *Ricercar a 3*, a fugue in three parts. More harpsichord followed—the same piece, or a different one? I could have looked it up, but I decided simply to listen.

Aha: there were the other instruments, flute, violin, and cello leavening the harpsichord's severity—a relief, because while the *Offering* is celebrated as an example of Bach's ability to vary a theme, the strongest impression to my ear was of the music's sameness. A canon is made of the same melody repeated in different ways, and the *Offering* is a set of canons on the "royal theme"; for all they vary, they are set predominantly in minor keys, and they all move with the same solemn gait, not the brisk walk of the cantatas or the pilgrim stride of the Passions. They are fugues without preludes, without the grand entrance of a toccata or passacaglia, without the ascending keys or major-minor play of the *Well-Tempered Clavier*, without the sparks the *Goldberg Variations* shoot off between the columnar structure of canons. In the *Offering*, canon follows canon follows canon.

From its dedication, where Bach declared that he would "consecrate an offering," the *Musical Offering* has a religious aspect. It is thought to be the kind of music that, as Frederick the Great would have reckoned it, "smells of the church." Certainly it is not like the music played in any church I know. It is chamber music for the First Church of Speculation, a string ensemble for round about midnight.

The cable box recorded 12:01, digital noonday. I got up, checked e-mail, sliced cold chicken. The light in the apartment had changed a little. The *Offering* proceeded sequentially, flaring up into the major key.

How I would listen to this piece, and what would I hear in it, if I knew, as some of the listeners at the court of the king of Prussia did, that they were probably hearing it for the first and last time?

The question was speculative. The disc was due back at the library, but the music was now in my iTunes library. Some pacifists I once met were study-ing the Lord's Prayer at the rate of a line a month. That, I expect, is how I will come to know the *Offering*: according to the pattern of the work itself, through repetition made progressively more intense as it is extended into time.

For the second time that day, I did something for the first time. With a computer open, into the search engine I typed "sheet music musical offering." Free-scores.com was offering the *Musical Offering* as a PDF file. Ten seconds later there it was, the *Ricercar a 3*. I clicked into the digital present and read the music as I listened to it.

>>11>> The "Gilded Goldbergs" is a full-length work for two pianos derived from the *Goldberg Variations*—is a work whose promise of familiarity and oddness drew me out of my rooms on a Tuesday evening and toward Carnegie Hall. I was full up with recordings; it was time to hear Bach played live.

When I got there—Weill Recital Hall, on the third floor adjacent to Carnegie Hall proper—the recital had started. Latecomers would be seated at the discretion of the usher in the red coat. So I waited in an anteroom, watching a video feed of the two pianists working the aria, wrapped female and suited-up male, their grand pianos set up side-to-side like snuggling rhinoceri. Then I was in—at the back, in latecomer's steerage. The pianists, too, were in: past the aria, past the thunderous first variation ("Expanding the theme") and the galloping second ("Simple tonal cubism"). I had not had time to read the program, only to take note of the composer (Robin Holloway, b. 1943) and the assertion *New York premiere*. It was amazing to think that in this city, site of such comprehensively intense music-making, this piece of music—that four-handed double fold of melody, that filling in of a familiar Bach riff with the wide-band harmony of Wagner—was being made here for the first time.

All the better reason to give it full attention. But the rest of life kept crowding in: an Amtrak reservation I'd forgotten to make, a brilliant piece from that week's *New Yorker* by a pianist who lamented that people who listen mainly to recorded music are blind to the human costs that went into making it. That insight in turn urged attentiveness. But I was musing: When was the last time I'd actually listened to music without doing something else—reading, writing, cooking, walking? The printed program furnished a tagline for each variation: "Simply through some keys." "Vivace à la Scarlatti." "Gigue in antiphony." Because I had arrived late, I couldn't just count along; I tried to match the music to the tag. Was this variation "Stately but energetic," or was it "Robust and a bit gormless," or was it a "Homage to Grainger"? This was like a survey class in program music all over again. When was the last time I'd listened to the music of Bach without knowing it well or educating myself while it played?

And yet I did know this music. It was, at bottom, the *Goldberg Variations*. With each variation, the arrangement went farther afield, but not around the bend. In fact, part of the pleasure in the piece was in hearing the pianists lariat a prodigal piece of experiment and bring it back home. A mashing of keys at the end of another variation brought laughter. A "brief history of Austro-German music in triple time" was just that: you could hear the pianists cycling away from Bach through Mozart, Haydn, and Schubert, right up to a treacly wedding waltz. By the thirtieth variation, in which the two pianists played a repeated figure in different keys, you could hear the "Gilded Goldbergs" as a serial account of the composer's encounter with a masterpiece shattered and reconstituted.

There is a tradition of such treatments of Bach, beginning with Max Reger's *Variations and Fugue on a Theme of J. S. Bach* of 1904. The Hungarian composer György Kurtág's *Játékok* ("Games") CD sets Bach pieces transcribed for four hands against short, ingeniously discordant works that Kurtág and his wife "play" at the piano: one hand will play only white keys and the other only black keys, and then they switch, and so on. The pianist Lara Downes performs *13 Ways of Looking at Goldberg*, in which the celebrated aria brackets works by contemporary composers who distill the piece's motifs to the point of evaporation or else vary them only slightly.

Holloway's aims, when he set out, were straightforward. The notes (I read them on the subway home) explained that he began to transcribe some of the variations for two pianos so as to play them with friends, but " 'interference' crackled the transmission," as if a Bach broadcast were scrambled with that of another composer. He decided to follow it, devising Bachian homages to Brahms, Schubert, and others. Yet even as the variations on Bach's variations grew more complicated, they remained works for Holloway and his friends to play in a pinch on the "two pianos always at the ready in my rooms at Cambridge." This clangorous reconfigured Bach had been written as *Hausmusik*, that is.

The notion of *Hausmusik* seemed at odds with the recital I'd just attended—the fabled space, the video feed, the restricted entry, the audience's ritual rising to its feet. And yet there was a vital connection. The recital was a New York premiere. Two pianists were in a room. So were a few dozen of us others. They made music, and we heard it. Who knew whether it would be heard here again?

>>12>>   The little book is brought out only a couple of times a year, and this was one of those times.

The *Clavier-büchlein vor Wilhelm Friedemann Bach* is in the rare-music section of the Yale library. For a New Yorker, it is astonishing that this work, Bach's handwritten gift to his eldest son, is just a short drive up I-95; like Bach's three-volume Bible—found in an attic in Michigan by a pastor in 1938 and now in St. Louis—it is physical evidence of Bach in our midst.

It was slipped from its pressboard case, inspected for wear, and placed on a pair of foam wedges set point to point on a wooden table. Then I took a seat as if for a test, a man in a small room—a glassed-in, underlit, climate-regulated room in the Yale library—faced with a stacked inch of thick paper, bound in golden brown sheepskin, the binding split at the left, with a few threads protruding like branches of a family tree striving for individuation.

The *Clavier-büchlein* is where the *Inventions* were invented—where Bach set out his notion of invention as a pattern at once artful and pedagogical, and where he used it extramusically to suggest a life taking shape.

Like a live performance, this hour was unrepeatable. I would never get to see the little book this way again. I paused interiorly, a mental quarter-rest. The right-hand page was smudged at the upper right—smudged with fingerprints beginning with those, I figured, of Bach himself. This was something like a firsthand encounter. Gingerly I turned the page.

The *Clavier-büchlein* begins with a two-page exhibit of musical science: a chart of keys and scales, the notes dotted in with black ink in rows ascending and descending, the names given underneath, and trills and other ornaments explained alongside. Several dozen pieces for keyboard follow: preludia, preambula, minuets, allemandes, fantasias, chorales. I turned pages, pulled between following the feeling and making it last. I recognized some of the pieces from printed editions and a Bismarck-era text saved as a PDF file on my hard drive. I tried to focus on the notation by Bach himself: the notes deep black, the stems and joinery at once precise and lavishly expressive, the titles indicated in script elegant enough for an offering to a king.

Most of the pieces are written so that they begin and end on a single page—Bach's way of adapting his music to the reproductive technology of the time. But here and there Bach, artist of superabundance, or more than enough, worked out a few more measures in the margin, a caboose to the piece.

The little book was in front of me, radiating significance. In its presence, I felt like an amateur. And yet—it occurred to me there—this book had been written for an amateur, a musician still in development.

"All art constantly aspires towards the condition of music," Walter Pater declared, and so it was here. The little book was as compact an example of Bach's music as exists. But it was not itself musical. It could not produce sound, could shape no air. It notated sounds to be produced by other means. It aspired to the condition of music.

>>13>> Glenn Gould scoffed at the idea of following the trail of Bach, as if to wall off the actual eastern Germany where the music was first made from the small rooms where he was making recordings of it. But with the Wall down, the border open, the interpenetration of Bach and world complete and thrilling, a pilgrimage to Thuringia and Saxony was in order.

That it was autumn made that corner of Germany the country of lateness, a place where every leaf and branch is in vivid decline. Erfurt, the spiffy university town where I set out, seems wholly of another time. To see the perfectly kempt Baroque houses, the wattle-and-daub taverns, the streetcar dawdling across the Domplatz—to see all this is to feel the past as a form of insulation; the town seems to close its shutters at nightfall against the prospect of history breaking out.

And yet history happened here as nowhere else. Six million Jews were murdered in these parts. To stroll through such a German town in the early evening, with the tables set in the restaurants and the faux-gaslights coming on amid the ivy, is to be spooked by the brutal fact that such benign-looking order once incubated raw evil—is to hear the glass shattering and the fists hammering on doors all over again.

Something else happened here. The Bach family, defying death, increased and multiplied. Here half a dozen male Bachs led lives in music, as organist, piper, violinist, town musician, and director of the ensemble, and to stroll across the shop-lined bridge is to hear them play and sing. Here Bach came to mean "musician," and the rest is history.

Eisenach is Erfurt's opposite, a modest town sited on the edge of a vast forest of history. The singing contest, saintly Elisabeth's almshouse, the school where Luther was educated, the castle hideaway where he rendered the Gospels in plain German: all these signs of events of great consequence were there when Bach was a child. To them, of course, his own exploits have been added, so that Eisenach is the birthplace of Bach.

He was baptized in the Georgenkirche in the center of town. Architecturally, it is one more European church (pink stone outside, three whitewashed galleries within), but a singular act with great consequences took place in the stone font up front. Alex Ross, listening to the Bach cantatas John Eliot Gardiner recorded at the church, wrote: "I pictured Bach's parents looking on at the baptism of the infant and wondering whether he would live. They had no idea." No idea that he would survive; no idea how fully and profoundly he would live—and no idea, it is safe to say, that the baptism, and the religious experience that followed on it, would matter so much. Flannery O'Connor liked to say that when she wrote a story involving a baptism she had to bend everything about it into strange forms so as to convince the reader that "something is going on here that counts." Truly, that was a baptism that counted.

The Bachhaus is a long low house with a gabled roof, a house bombed by Allied warplanes during World War II. It is not the actual house where Bach lived, but one like it; that it is a Bachhaus only approximately is all right, though, because its exhibit treats Bach's life in music, which took place mainly after he left town. Would a person knowing nothing of Bach care to see portraits of his ancestors and patrons, or the thousand-page hymnbook used in the Georgenkirche when he was a boy, or the bronze bust made from his skull? Possibly not. But a re-creation of Bach's composing room—desk, chair, table, stocks of paper, and desktop clavichord with a single manual— puts him there before us, a knowledge worker in his cubicle. And the demonstration of period instruments fills the *Haus* with music, every hour on the hour.

Past the house proper (where the bombs fell, I imagined) a new wing is given over to exhibits on Bach's music. Manuscripts in glass cases; pipe-mounted iPads preloaded with slide shows on prelude and fugue, temperament, parody, and the like; big dangling pods with cushioned insides, inviting you to climb in and sit and swing and listen to snippets of recordings: such is the twenty-first-century-museum-as-multimedia-experience. And yet the place was quiet: the music of Bach was piping through several dozen individual sets of headphones, an orchestral suite of sonic miniatures.

The city of Leipzig, too, was bombed during World War II, then rebuilt aggressively by the GDR. What this means is that the Leipzig of Bach's time is overlaid with a steel-and-glass modern city. Walk ten minutes from the Hauptbahnhof and you hit the Nikolaikirche among the shoe shops and kebab counters; walk another couple of minutes along a pedestrian mall—luggage, chocolate, silk scarves—and you see the Thomaskirche tower and the blocky

Thomasschule behind. You've just arrived, but you've already seen the places in Leipzig most powerfully associated with Bach.

Inside the Nikolaikirche is a series of plaques telling the story of the Monday prayers for peace and the eventual overthrow of the Communist government. The plaques in the Thomaskirche chronicle the life of Bach, a story told in full digital glory in the freshly renovated Bach-Museum in an apartment house opposite. Saturday afternoons a *Benefizkonzert* is given by the church's standing ensemble and choir, mainly for tourists brought by diesel bus.

I saw those things, did those things. I ate a bratwurst at the Thüringer Hof, where Bach may have eaten once upon a time; I sat among claques of German retirees in the Motel One, looking out at the grimy Nikolaikirche, and marveled at the strangeness of a modern budget hotel located across the street from one of the most significant churches in Europe.

Mostly, I walked in the pedestrian mall. Bach's fixity has been overstated: although he did not get to Paris, Rome, or London, his work took him all over Saxony and Thuringia. That said, the quarter mile between the two churches was his main journey for a quarter of a century. He walked it thousands of times—and on the walk from the Nikolaikirche to the Thomaskirche, from the Thomaskirche to the Nikolaikirche, he worked out a pattern encompassing the world from his place in it. Inside the churches—for the Benefizkonzert at the one, for an actual benefit for women's rights at the other—I sat in astonishment at the fact that I was in Bach's airspace, that these buildings had once been filled with music by Bach himself. But it was out walking that I felt fully in his presence. The two churches, the quarter mile between them, the paving stones, the autumn air and autumn light: all the proportions were right. Richard Taruskin, in an article about Steve Reich, explained that most music has "what musicologists call a 'subtactile pulse': a strongly articulated, rock-steady rhythmic unit that lies just beneath the level of the 'felt beat,' or tactus, the beat that conductors show or that we normally walk or waltz or exercise to." This subtactile pulse enabled Reich, as a student in 1950, to recognize the common motion of Bach's fifth Brandenburg concerto, bebop, and the "Danse Sacrale" from Stravinsky's *Rite of Spring* when he played records of them close together, and subtactile pulse became the basis of Reich's own music.

The subtactile pulse of Bach's music is what makes Bach's music sound contemporary—what makes it apt for our time, that is. The subtactile pulse, too, I would propose, is what makes Bach's music urban music—music to move about a city with, in little journeys often repeated. The subtactile pulse of Bach is what kept me outside those historic churches, walking the stretch of earth between them over and over again. There was plenty of Bach on my mobile phone, but I wasn't listening to it. I had heard enough of the music to feel it subsonically in the streets of Leipzig, where Bach had walked, and I was walking.

>>14>> And then it was Christmas, and Bachfest was on. On the car radio, on the computer via Internet stream, on a radio in the kitchen while the pope mumbled through a televised Mass from St. Peter's. Out in the street that morning, out of reach, I had searched for a WKCR phone app but (a late adopter) couldn't find one.

That year, even more than usual, the spirit of the Bachfest was general in New York City. The Chamber Music Society programmed the Brandenburg concertos, and Bargemusic featured the *Goldberg Variations* at its floating recital hall near the Brooklyn Bridge. Gidon Kremer played the second partita for solo violin during Lincoln Center's White Light Festival, "an annual exploration of the transcendent power of music and art"—making Bach's stony monument for Maria Barbara into a beam of light. Matt Haimovitz paired the first Bach cello suite and the Hendrix "Star-Spangled Banner" at Zuccotti Park for Occupy Wall Street. A raffish chamber group called the Knights choreographed a performance of Bach cello music in the subway, stationing cellists on the platforms at stops on the F line so that a southbound rider would hear snatches of the first prelude as the doors opened each time. Near City Hall, J&R Music World screened the promotional DVD for Yo-Yo Ma's *Songs of Joy and Peace*—and during a break in the recording of the "Wassail Song" the camera caught Yo-Yo riffing on Bach.

The Bach event that drew me was a lunchtime poetry reading punctuated with organ music by Bach and other composers in a church on lower Broadway: St. Paul's Chapel, site of my life-extending encounter with the *St. Matthew Passion*. I would go downtown on the lunch hour, measure my experience of Bach across twenty years, and be back at the office by two thirty.

On the subway that day I clicked into the *Well-Tempered Clavier*, Keith Jarrett's recording for ECM, the first one I really knew, and the one I like best: even in an age of all-but-unlimited choice, first love lasts. I had grown up thinking of Jarrett as a jazz musician of the freest kind—sideman with Miles Davis in his sketchiest years, bent-backed revenant of improvisation—so was surprised to hear him on the Bachfest one year speaking about the Bach keyboard works in terms of bracing severity. "This music doesn't need my help,"

Jarrett said. Other musicians could go ahead and work their personal variations on Bach, but not him. The music was sufficient unto itself.

Now, on the downtown train, preludes and fugues flying past, I felt care-
less and irreverent, listening to the *Well-Tempered Clavier* straight through. I
could hardly hear the pieces individually, such was their richness. It was mid-
December and I made a resolution: Come the new year, I would go through a
prelude each morning, Pablo Casals–style, letting Bach and the iPhone loop
me over the Manhattan Bridge and into the workday.

Physically St. Paul's Chapel was the same as ever: walls of pink, ceiling in
baby blue, flags of the thirteen colonies, Great Britain, Ireland, and France.
But the chapel, itself historic, had been struck by history. When the World
Trade Center was destroyed, people in flight sought refuge there. Then rescue
workers slept there. Then, with disaster subsiding, with two buildings forever
gone, pilgrims sought an encounter with one that was still standing, and fes-
tooned it with relics of the days after.

The place was full; I took the last thatched seat. This was my first Bach
outing since Leipzig, and I could see the chapel as akin to the Nikolaikirche, a
historic church reinvented for a new historical moment.

The poet—Lawrence Joseph—stepped to the microphone and started to
read. There came imagery from life at the tip of the island: "What time is it?
There's a taxi on the way downtown. Sulphurous yellow's hot sheet rose, furious counterpoint . . ." The organist played: Couperin. The poet read. The organist played: Buxtehude. The poet read, an account of sunset in latter-day
Mannahatta. "Now evening comes fast from the sea," he said; and now the music of Bach came fast from the organ, two lines of melody slowly ascending and
sharpening while the pedal maintained a medium-grade, uninflected F. It was
a *pastorelle*: BWV 590, an early work, "pre-Weimar" in *The New Grove*. It is
the sort of work often called "celestial": a bright and migratory line in the right
hand set against a smooth and methodical one in the left, all undergirded by
that pedaled low F. "Now evening comes fast from the sea . . ." I thought of
Albert Schweitzer's appraisal of Bach's music as pictorial, an insight crucial to
Yo-Yo Ma in his encounter with Bach. I could see evening coming in fast from
the sea. Could I hear it? I couldn't say. I could feel it coming, I felt it welling up
in my eyes: a wave of gratitude—gratitude for the music of Bach, and surprise
that I had come to the far side of an encounter with it.

Gratitude because the encounter was unbidden and unexpected, a gift
outright. What could be better, with children safely to sleep and spouse a whis-
per away, than to spend a thousand and one nights with Bach in the middle of

one's life? How better than to spend a thousand and one nights than with these musicians, and all the others—Harry Christophers and the Sixteen, Philipp Herreweghe and the Collegium Vocale Gent; Bob van Asperen and his trunk organ, Jean-Guihen Queyras and his gut-string cello; Murray Perahia and András Schiff at their modern pianos; Emma Kirkby and Deborah York and their perfect human voices?

Surprise because it wasn't supposed to happen. For one thing, this is the kind of encounter that allegedly doesn't occur in the digital present. The old standards and practices are no more; wax cylinders and brass-horn phonographs, animated movies made from hand-drawn "cels," shellac 78s and vinyl LPs smelling of cardboard, the walnut hi-fi rig and the rubberized yellow Walkman you could take underwater—all have been displaced by digital technology. Yet digital technology, omnivorous and agnostic, has brought the old ways along, albeit at one remove.

For another, this is the kind of encounter that supposedly no longer happens with classical music. The revival of Bach, the surge in attention paid to his music, the summary recognition of his eminence, the spread of the Bach diaspora like the ever-widening circles of a 50,000-watt radio broadcast—all this has taken place in an era in which the conventional wisdom says classical music is in sharp decline. This encounter has taken place late in the day, off the grid, outside the standard deviation, statistically unrecorded.

One night not long ago, with a text open on the computer and the music of Bach playing—some cantatas from the Bach Cantata Pilgrimage, which iTunes groups all together so that they seem to be episodes in one long story— I felt a sudden freedom in the thought that my own long story in Bach would soon be over. At the same time, I knew that I could happily spend another thousand and one nights with Bach; I felt that I could devote the rest of my life to his music.

For the here and now, this book is my offering. The hope is that it is in accord with the patterns of invention practiced by Bach and his electric interpreters. It is a piece with many parts, some developed more elaborately than others. Possibly it smells of the church. Probably it is more Anglophone than its subject. Certainly it is a product of technology. I am composing it on a keyboard fully enabled for music, and music-making: iTunes, Garageband, a WQXR bookmark, headphones cabled into an eighth-inch jack, a last vestige of the transistor radio. There are guitars and a piano in the other room, but this keyboard is my instrument. I am touching the keys again and again with the ten digits of my two hands, putting one word after another in the hope that a couple hundred thousand of them, mastered and sequenced, will amount to a kind of music.

"If I were called in / to construct a religion / I should make use of water." So Philip Larkin's poem "Water" begins; the assignment thus given, the poem spells out the symbols and rites of a watery faith.

I would not be so bold as to construct a religion around the music of Bach. The religion out of which Bach constructed his music is religion enough, and it is hard to imagine the music as any more religious than it is. And yet I have sought something religious in the recordings of Bach's music—have tried to proceed from Glenn Gould's notion of "technical transcendence" toward the patterns of transcendence that precede it. The music of Bach is manifestly a source of transcendence. The best reinventions of Bach in our time have been, in their different ways, transcendent; and they have been, in their ways, faithful to Bach, fugues developed from his prelude. Their transcendence is a key to his, and vice versa; and the story of how the music of Bach has been reinvented in our time can suggest what in our time transcendence is—the forms it takes, the realms it seeks. There is transcendence in these recordings; we can reverse-engineer a spirituality of technology from the life encoded in them.

Et incarnatus est, from the Mass in B Minor, is a very late expression of Bach's life in music: the sentence in the Nicene Creed which declares that divinity itself was given physical form, embodied in space and time.

For most of their history, recordings have been seen as music in disembodied form—music alienated from the social, physical, contingent acts that went into its making. There is something to this. All of us have had encounters with live music that recordings cannot rival. And yet our collective experience of music—developed across several generations schooled in the experience of recordings—has opened another side of recorded experience. If you were a musician today and wanted to set yourself in counterpoint to the age the way Glenn Gould did, you would make music only in singular performances; you would refuse to be recorded. Now it is music played live that seems insubstantial and elusive, made somewhere once for a little while and then allowed to go away. Now it is recorded music whose place in our lives is so robust and reliable as to seem a physical force, a record not just of the sounds made by some people in a prior time but of the lives we live in the present in its presence.

Ours is a city of sonic ruins, a Rome of aural superabundance. The works of our precursors surround us, irregularly preserved but thick on the ground, and we move through our days in the patterns they imply. We could no more do without them than we could raze our houses and dwell in the raw elements. It may be that there is nothing spiritual in all this; it may be that our every response, even our every response to the music of Bach, has a material basis. Even if it were so, though, our experience of recordings, as the recorded life of Bach reveals, has made us fluent in the practices that traditions of the spirit prize: scrutiny of the past, open communication across the ages, a reluctance to judge by appearances, and the recognition that the dead continue to speak and that the sounds they make, amplified right, are a kind of music.

Notes

Acknowledgments

Index

Notes

PRELUDE

There is a Bachhaus in Eisenach, a Bach-Museum near the Thomaskirche in Leipzig. Lonely Planet's *Germany* touts the Musikinstrumenten-Museum-Berlin on p. 123, in a section devoted to the sights of the Kulturforum; the museum is at Tiergartenstrasse 1.

The Obituary, written by Bach's son Carl Philipp Emanuel and his student Johann Friedrich Agricola, was published in 1754; it is in *The New Bach Reader*. It indicates that Bach left three harpsichords to his son Johann Christian. The one at the museum came to be known as "the Bach cembalo" in the nineteenth century. The museum's audio guide reveals that the EMS instruments on display are not the very ones used on *Wish You Were Here* but ones identical to them.

Leonard Bernstein opened an episode of his TV series *The Joy of Music* (telecast March 31, 1957) by suggesting that the viewer probably thought Bach's music dull, and went on: "Maybe the trouble is that you don't get a chance to know it; you don't hear much Bach. After all, to hear Bach you have to go to certain churches faithfully, or to certain very special little concerts." The script was published in *The Joy of Music* (Simon & Schuster, 1959).

The pianist and writer Jeremy Denk spelled out the role of the *Goldberg Variations* in *The Silence of the Lambs* (1991) on npr.org in March 2012; the *Goldbergs* figure into the 1988 Thomas Harris novel, too. In the film *The English Patient* (1996), set in Italy during World War II, a nurse is playing the *Goldberg Variations* on an all-but-ruined piano in a bomb-shattered monastery when a soldier expert in defusing bombs comes upon her; the suggestion in the scene that follows is that Bach makes the place bombproof. In an episode of *The Sopranos*, Carmela Soprano, hoping to improve her daughter's chances of admission to Columbia, goes to lunch with an admissions officer, and as they enter the restaurant the *Goldberg Variations* is playing in the background. Yo-Yo Ma played the sarabande from the fifth suite at the World Trade Center site on September 11, 2002; Steve Jobs played the second Brandenburg concerto and a fugue from the *Well-Tempered Clavier* on his iPad2 when he demonstrated the device to Walter Isaacson, who recalled the encounter in *Steve Jobs* (Simon & Schuster, 2011); Jobs also compared Glenn Gould's two recordings of the *Goldberg Variations*.

The question of the Bach revival is taken up at length in *The New Grove Bach Family*, ed. Christoph Wolff (Norton, 1983); in the *Oxford Composer Companions: J. S. Bach*, ed. Malcolm Boyd, consultant editor John Butt (Oxford, 1999); and by individual biographers. The nature of revival is considered in *Reformations: A Radical Interpretation of Christianity and the World 1500–2000*, by Felipe Fernández-Armesto and Derek Wilson (Scribner, 1997). Albert

Schweitzer's *J. S. Bach*, written in German and published in 1908 as an expansion of a 1905 French edition, was published in London by Breitkopf and Härtel in 1911; the Dover paperback (1966), widely available in the United States, reproduces the 1911 edition. The revival chapter—which serves as a bridge between the biographical text and the critical-interpretive one—is called "Death and Resurrection." Christoph Wolff gave his biography of Bach (Norton, 2000) the subtitle "The Learned Musician." The Baroque understanding of *inventio* and Bach's own conception of it are developed thrillingly by Laurence Dreyfus in *Bach and the Patterns of Invention* (Harvard, 1996); Edward W. Said discusses the book at length in his essay on Glenn Gould, "The Virtuoso as Intellectual," in *On Late Style: Music and Literature Against the Grain* (Pantheon, 2006).

Bach's use of transcription and parody figure into every biography; parody is explained especially cogently by Malcolm Boyd in *Bach* (Oxford, 2000) in the chapter "Parodies and Publications." The introduction of the Soundabout is recalled in *Playback*, by Mark Coleman (Da Capo, 2003). Coleman, p. 155, paraphrases an article from *Billboard*, the music industry trade magazine (December 8, 1979): "Described as 'Sony's Tiny Stereo Player,' the Soundabout was a handheld, 14-ounce playback-only machine that used headphones and standard-size cassettes. Retail price: $199.99."

The entry under Bach for the *Well-Tempered Clavier* in *The Rough Guide to Classical Music on CD* (Rough Guides, 1994) mentions the inclusion of the first prelude on the *Voyager*s "in order that any alien civilization intercepting the machine would gain some idea of the capabilities of the human species." A Wikipedia entry for *Voyager* describing what was called *The Golden Record: Music from Earth* declares that the prelude was number one from book two, not book one; the *Golden Record* also included the first movement of the second Brandenburg concerto in a recording by Karl Richter and the Munich Bach Orchestra, and the gavotte from the third partita for solo violin in a recording by Arthur Grumiaux. Glenn Gould, in the notes to the 1956 Columbia LP of the *Goldberg Variations*, proposed that the evident but not fully explicable relationship between the aria and the variations leaves listeners "forced to revise our criteria, which were scarcely designed to arbitrate that union of music and metaphysics—the realm of technical transcendence." The notes are reprinted in *The Glenn Gould Reader*, ed. Tim Page (Vintage, 1990).

The subtitle of Joseph Horowitz's book *Classical Music in America: A History of Its Rise and Fall* (Norton, 2005), and to a lesser degree the book itself, suggests how twinned the notions of establishment and decline are in this art form's American story. Joseph Cornell's imagined courtship of long-dead ballerinas is made extraordinarily vivid in *Utopia Parkway: A Life of Joseph Cornell*, by Deborah Solomon (Farrar, Straus and Giroux, 1997). The aura of the Holy Trinity string trio has been captured especially well by Teri Noel Towe on his Thursday morning radio broadcasts on WPRB-FM.

Of the many books that draw parallels between the life cycles of different art forms, and their relationship to physical and social conditions, Lewis Hyde's books *The Gift* (Random House, 1980) and *Common as Air* (Farrar, Straus and Giroux, 2010) are especially eloquent; each meets Hyde's own double definition (stated in the preface and afterword to a 2007 Vintage reissue of *The Gift*) of "an economy of the creative spirit" and a "prophetic essay."

The young woman learning to play the piano in the Rockies is Thea Kronberg, heroine of Willa Cather's 1925 novel *The Song of the Lark*; the dangling man is me, inwardly singing a song I'd written, called "Experience," on the streets of Manhattan and the Bronx in the summer of 1985.

PART I: REVIVAL

1

Albert Schweitzer's recordings at All Hallows by the Tower are included on two compact discs: *Bach Organ Works: Albert Schweitzer* (EMI Classics, 1993) and *Albert Schweitzer Plays Bach, Volume 1* (Pearl/Pavilion, 1993).

2

The EMI disc gives December 18, 1935, as the recording date; the Pearl disc includes six works recorded in London and three recorded in Strasbourg the next year, and describes all six works from the All Hallows session as recorded December 16–18, 1935. *Volume 2* includes fourteen more recordings from the Strasbourg sessions, made at the church of Sainte-Aurélie in October 1936. The Pearl discs were assembled by an all-star team of Bach collectors and archivists: Teri Noel Towe loaned the recordings; Seth B. Winner did the transfers; Allan Evans wrote the notes. The notes for *Volume 1* feature Prof. Archibald T. Davidson's description of Schweitzer playing a Silbermann organ in Strasbourg in 1921; *Volume 2* features the journalist Louis-Edouard Schaeffer's account of the sessions at Sainte-Aurélie. I have drawn freely on both descriptions, transposing details to All Hallows as appropriate.

Schweitzer described his life up to 1932 in *Out of My Life and Thought: An Autobiography* (trans. C. T. Campion; Holt, Rinehart and Winston, 1949). An earlier book, *Memoirs of Childhood and Youth*, was more detailed about his childhood, but I have followed the later book, together with James Brabazon's biography (Syracuse, 2000). He warned that "civilization is melting away in our hands" in *Out of My Life and Thought*. He set out the occasion of his vow in the chapter of his autobiography called "I Resolve to Become a Jungle Doctor," stated his wish to do "something small in the spirit of Jesus" in a letter to a friend shortly before his thirtieth birthday, reprinted in *Albert Schweitzer: Essential Writings* (ed. Brabazon; Orbis, 2005), and characterized himself as "an old cart horse" in a letter to Hewlett Johnson, dean of Canterbury Cathedral, whom he saw on the 1935 trip, paraphrased in the epilogue to the autobiography. The background of the recording sessions is set out by Brabazon, pp. 384–85, who quotes a Schweitzer *Bulletin* sent out to Schweitzer's supporters that at the time the organ set was— another superlative—the "largest plan of consecutive gramophone record making ever undertaken by any artist." There is a brief history of the HMV mobile unit in *EMI: The First Hundred Years*, by Peter Martland (Ruth Edge, consultant editor; Amadeus, 1997). The toccata runs 2:24, the fugue 6:33 in the Pearl set.

3

Life, October 6, 1940, published a profile of Schweitzer under the headline THE GREATEST MAN IN THE WORLD. Schweitzer's passage about every artist as an "instrument maker" is in *J. S. Bach*, volume 1, p. 204. T. S. Eliot's activities in 1935 are set out in *Eliot's New Life*, by Lyndall Gordon (Farrar, Straus and Giroux, 1989). The first quartet is "Burnt Norton." Schweitzer spoke of "religious elevation" in music in *J. S. Bach*, volume 1, p. 18.

4

Martin Luther celebrated music as "one of the best arts" in *The Table-Talk of Martin Luther* (trans. William Hazlitt; Lutheran Publication Society, 1997). The place of music in Luther's Christianity, and its relation to the word, is set out in *The Reformation: A History*, by Diarmaid

MacCulloch (Penguin, 2004), especially the section "Telling Out the Word," where the Jesuit Adam Cotzen's remark about the killing power of Luther's hymns is quoted. My discussion of ear and eye also draws on Eamon Duffy's review of *The Reformation of the Image*, by Joseph Koerner, in the *London Review of Books*, August 19, 2004. "This Will Kill That" is part two of book five of *Nôtre-Dame de Paris*, a gloss on the Archdeacon's remark that "the book will kill the building!" This translation is by John Sturrock (Penguin, 1978). *The Reformation: A History*, by Patrick Collinson (Modern Library, 2004), includes the chapter "Words, Language, and Books," which informs this section, as does Felipe Fernández-Armesto and Derek Wilson's *Reformations*.

5

The family history features in all the English-language Bach biographies. Bach himself told the story of Veit Bach in the Genealogy, printed in *The New Bach Reader*, pp. 283ff; he wrote of Veit Bach's cittern, "which he took with him even into the mill and played upon while the grinding was going on. (How pretty it must have sounded together!) Yet in this way he had a chance to have time drilled into him." The etymological link of Bach to *bachen* (an old German term for "baker") is suggested by Geck; another tradition (one followed by Beethoven, among others) emphasizes that Bach is the old German word for "brook."

Lonely Planet's *Rough Guide: Germany*, p. 280, describes Eisenach as "a small town on the edge of the Thuringian Forest whose modest appearance belies its association with two German heavyweights: Johann Sebastian Bach and Martin Luther." The "famous Tourney of Song" of 1207 (as Wolff calls it) forms the basis for a plot of Wagner's *Tannhauser*. Elisabeth's life is summarized in *The Oxford Dictionary of Saints*, ed. David Hugh Farmer (Oxford, 1992). Simon Winder's *Germania* (Farrar, Straus and Giroux, 2010) is a beguiling guide to the German history and lore of the period.

Boyd tells of Ambrosius Bach ascending the Rathaus twice a day; the porticoes can still be seen on the Eisenach town hall. A portrait of Ambrosius hangs in the Bachhaus in Eisenach, with a note explaining that an open collar indicated a horn player; the portrait is reproduced in several biographies.

6

The stone font still exists at the Georgenkirche. In an essay about John Eliot Gardiner and Masaaki Suzuki in *The New Yorker* (April 11, 2011), Alex Ross put it this way: "Listening to 'Christ lag' [in a recording of a performance led by Gardiner at the Georgenkirche], I pictured Bach's parents looking on at the baptism of the infant and wondering whether he would live. They had no idea."

The story of Bach's career as the fulfillment of destiny is found in different degrees in Schweitzer, Wolff, and Geck. Bach characterized the family's "musical inclination" at the beginning of the Genealogy he compiled in 1735.

Christoph Wolff in his biography of Bach emphasizes Bach's striving for independence. The hand-drawn family tree is reproduced in *The New Bach Reader* and made gridlike there and in Boyd; tables of "The 'Weimar Bach' Pedigree" and "Maria Elisabeth and Johann Ambrosius Bach's Children" are in Wolff; Williams sees the Genealogy as setting out "an (as it were) apostolic succession." To my knowledge, no recent biographer asks the question directly: Why should Johann Sebastian be the genius and not one of his brothers or sisters? Of the family's musicality, Geck asks: "Does it result from a particular genetic predisposition, or is it the music-saturated air that causes little Johann Sebastian Bach to feel from the first moment that in this world he will thrive only as a musician?"

7

Bach is characterized as "a pure and strong fuguist" in the Obituary in *The New Bach Reader*. The role of the *exempla classica* is spelled out by Wolff, p. 48, and elsewhere. The moonlight story, told in the Obituary, is featured in all the biographies, with skepticism in different degrees. Bach's sense of how musicians learn is given in the third person in the Obituary, p. 300.

8

Wolff expounds on Bach's courage and independence at the beginning of his chapter "Bypassing a Musical Apprenticeship: From Lüneberg to Weimar." The quoted passages are from the previous chapter, "Sebastian's Musical Beginnings," p. 42.

9

This history of the organ is drawn from Schweitzer's *J. S. Bach*, from MacCulloch's *The Reformation*, and also from *All the Stops*, by Craig R. Whitney (Public Affairs, 2003). Wolff, p. 30, characterizes the Baroque pipe organ as "a large-scale mechanical instrument whose complexity was unsurpassed by any other machine in the seventeenth century." Others say there was one more complex: the sailing ship.

Johann Christoph Bach is called "a real wonder" in the Genealogy; his complaint about the poor quality of the Ohrdruf organ is found in *The New Bach Reader*. The Lüneberg music library is especially well characterized by Boyd, p. 13, who reports that the library "was unfortunately destroyed by fire in about 1800." Wolff sets out Bach's curiosity about the organs of North Germany, pp. 52ff.

The solitary character of the organ is explored in *The True Life of J. S. Bach*, by Klaus Eidam (trans. Hoyt Rogers; Basic, 2001), p. 19: "two bellows-pumpers sufficed to place a whole world of sound at his disposal, dependent on his will and skill alone."

10

Bach's religious education is set out with authority in *Bach Among the Theologians*, by Jaroslav Pelikan (Fortress, 1986), who effortlessly makes the case for Bach as a "fifth evangelist" and for the sacred music, written for the liturgical calendar, as representing "the four seasons of J. S. Bach."

11

Lutheran services for Holy Week are set out in several biographies, and the theological significance of Easter probed in depth in *Bach Among the Theologians*. Bach's departure from Lüneberg, treated in all the biographies, gets close attention from Boyd, pp. 15–16, who ruefully declares, "Bach's movements in the months that followed [his departure from Sangerhausen] cannot now be traced . . ."

12

Bach's time at Arnstadt is surveyed precisely in the *Oxford Composer Companion* entry for the town; the details of his rented room and horse and carriage, found in *The New Bach Reader*,

p. 40, are cited by Williams, *A Life In Music* (Cambridge, 2007), p. 37; the description of the organ there is cited here. Wolff (whose book includes a photograph of the organ) says that it had twenty-one stops, not twenty-three. An exhibit at the Bachhaus in Eisenach features a video of an organist playing the instrument, renovated again in recent times, and surrounded by a scraped and gut-renovated ceiling. A photograph of a plain-looking organist's console from Arnstadt is in *Bach*, by Peter Washington (Everyman's Library, 1997), p. 32. Bach's manner of testing an organ is described by Johann Nikolaus Forkel (b. 1749), who had Bach's sons Wilhelm Friedemann Bach and Carl Philipp Emanuel Bach as sources for his biography, *Johann Sebastian Bach: His Life, Art, and Work*, published in 1802; the English translation by Charles Sanford Terry was published in 1920 (Vienna House, 1974). Forkel, p. 69, concludes: "When the examination was over, especially if the instrument pleased him, Bach liked to exhibit his splendid talent, both for his own pleasure and the gratification of those who were present."

The contract for Bach's service at Arnstadt is in *The New Bach Reader*, p. 41.

13

Wolff, p. 92, remarks that at Arnstadt Bach "experienced circumstances that bordered on the ideal." The Arnstadt chorale preludes are included in the batch of Bach manuscripts known as the Neumeister Collection, at Yale; the organist Werner Jacob recorded them for EMI (2 CDs, 1987); notes for the EMI release are by Wolff.

Bach's visit to Buxtehude is treated in all the biographies. Boyd and Geck, in *Johann Sebastian Bach: Life and Work* (trans. John Hargraves; Harcourt, 2006), give the dates and name the Buxtehude works performed on the occasion; Geck follows immediately with a discussion of the Toccata and Fugue in D Minor (BWV565), p. 56, and the questions surrounding the work's composition and dating. Eidam describes the effect of broken chords in a lengthy discussion of BWV565, pp. 43–47. Wolff in a section about Bach's compositions at Weimar, p. 169, characterizes the work as revealing of Bach's "self-taught" qualities as a composer: "as refreshingly imaginative, varied and ebullient as it is structurally undisciplined and unmastered."

14

Albert Schweitzer treated the organ works in volume 1, chapter XIII of *J. S. Bach*; even as he characterized a group of early works, he made clear that "we can only surmise in what order the works came," p. 269. His argument for Bach as "a terminal point" appears at the beginning of volume 1, in the chapter on "Subjective and Objective"; his argument for Bach as expression of a lost spiritual unity is at the very end of volume 2.

15

Graham Robb portrayed France outside Paris in *The Discovery of France: A Historical Geography from the Revolution to the First World War* (Norton, 2007). Charles-Marie Widor told the story of his first encounter with Schweitzer in a preface to the 1908 German edition of Schweitzer's *J. S. Bach*, reprinted in the Dover edition. A Schweitzer polemic against modern organs was published as a pamphlet in Paris in 1906; Whitney quotes Schweitzer in *All the Stops*, p. 89. The nickname "Bach born in Alsace" is given in the notes to the EMI CD of Schweitzer's organ recordings. Widor's praise of Bach as "the greatest of preachers" is from the 1908 preface.

The Search for the Historical Jesus is a common source of material for anthologies of Schweitzer's writings, such as *The Spiritual Life* (Ecco, 1999) and Orbis's *Albert Schweitzer: Essential Writings*.

16

Widor told the story of the origins of Schweitzer's Bach book in the 1908 preface, and Schweitzer picked up the story in *Out of My Life and Thought*. The history of the Paris Bach Society is told in the *Oxford Composer Companion* and elsewhere. Schweitzer made his remark about Bach's music as "the nature and the unfolding of German art" in an early chapter of *J. S. Bach* on "The Roots of Bach's Art."

17

Schweitzer recounted the revision of the Bach book in *Out of My Life and Thought*, and told the story of Bach's supposed decline in the "Death and Resurrection" chapter of *J. S. Bach*, volume 1; "His Greatness Not Recognized" is the title of a section of the chapter. The stories of Bach's music as lost treasure and as knowledge passed from one musician to another are mingled inchoately in the book; I have told them separately for clarity and contrapuntal effect.

18

Schweitzer sets out the relationship of Wagner to Bach in a section of the "Death and Resurrection" chapter called "Liszt and Wagner"—and quotes Wagner's essay "What Is German?": "If we would comprehend the wonderful originality, strength and significance of the German mind in one incomparably eloquent image, we must look keenly and discerningly at the appearance, otherwise almost inexplicably mysterious, of the musical marvel Sebastian Bach." Schweitzer, having told the story of Bach's "resurrection" up to "Bach and the Present Day," then remarks: "All this, however, constitutes only the external history of Bach's victory"; in effect arguing against himself and the story of Bach's unity under threat, he declares that the true evidence of Bach's victory can be seen throughout the music of the nineteenth century: "Since Mendelssohn, every composer of any significance has been to school with Bach, not as a pedantic teacher, but to one who impels them to strive after the truest and clearest expression, and to achieve impressiveness not by the wealth of the means they employ but by the pregnancy of their themes." That is, he sees them solving, after the example of Bach, what he, in volume 2, p. 5, calls "the basic problem of all music,—the question of the nature of thematic invention."

   Schweitzer declares that "the hearer became exigent" in "Liszt and Wagner," p. 258. He observed of Bach that "his immense strength functioned without self-consciousness" in *J. S. Bach*, volume 1, p. 166.

19

Schweitzer's long epistolary friendship with Hélène Bresslau—eventually a mutual courtship which led to marriage—is treated thoroughly by James Brabazon, who points out that Bresslau is mentioned only once in *Out of My Life and Thought*, and their daughter, Rhena, not at all. The relationship is also gone over by Harold Fickett in an unpublished biography.

   Schweitzer described the gift of a zinc-lined piano with organ pedals in the chapter of his autobiography called "First Activities in Africa 1913–1917"; he took up playing the instrument shortly before the Great War broke out. He remarked on "experience of the world" in volume 2 of *Philosophy of Civilization*, on Bach's concern for "graphic characterisation and realism" in "Bach and Aesthetics," the chapter that opens volume 2 of *J. S. Bach*, and on the Brandenburg concertos in volume 1, pp. 406–407.

20

This history of early audio recording is informed by a number of books: *Playback*, by Mark Coleman; *The Ambient Century*, by Mark Prendergast (Bloomsbury, 2003); *Good Vibrations*, by Mark Cunningham (Sanctuary, 1998); *Selling Sounds: The Commercial Revolution in American Music*, by David Suisman (Harvard, 2009); *Capturing Sound: How Technology Has Changed Music*, by Mark Katz (University of California Press, 2004); and *EMI: The First Hundred Years*. *Listen to This*, by Alex Ross (Farrar, Straus and Giroux, 2010), includes the essay "Infernal Machines: How Recordings Changed Music." Roland Gelatt's *The Fabulous Phonograph* (Collier, 1977) is dated but still straightforwardly authoritative. David Bodanis's *Electric Universe* (Crown, 2005) is a vivid telling of what is called "The Shocking True Story of Electricity." Evan Eisenberg's *The Recording Angel* (McGraw-Hill, 1987; 2nd ed., Yale, 2005) broke open the discussion of recordings as an aural phenomenon unto themselves; the book is, as John Rockwell remarked in *The New York Times*, "One of the most original series of insights into music, recorded music, and the recording process to have come along since the invention of recording itself, more than a century ago."

21

The story of the HMV mobile unit in *EMI: The First Hundred Years* includes, on p. 80, a photograph of the truck taken outside Hereford Cathedral, 1927. It was rumored that the fourteen-year-old singer of "Hear My Prayer" had dropped dead as he attained the last note. The book includes a photograph of the orchestra and giant chorus at the Crystal Palace, p. 125, and posters for the Bayreuth Wagner Festival, pp. 129 and 130.

22

Albert Schweitzer describe his Abrahamic "sacrifice" in *Out of My Life and Thought*, chapter 18, and there characterizes his return to organ recitals as a form of fund-raising: "And if for a time I did lose my financial independence, I was now able to win it again by means of organ and pen."

The electric-powered organ revival is chronicled expertly in *All the Stops*, where Craig Whitney makes especially clear how the electric-powered pipe organ made it possible for American musicians and impresarios to reinvent the European organ tradition for forward-looking, commercially minded North America.

Bela Lugosi performs Bach in *Dracula* (1931); Boris Karloff in *Black Cat* (1934).

23

James Brabazon gives the circumstances leading up to Schweitzer's recordings for Columbia. Allan Evans's notes to *Albert Schweitzer Plays Bach, Volume I* draw on a Strasbourg newspaper's report that Schweitzer made some recordings in 1928 using "an organ decided on by his record company (the organ at Queen's Small Hall, London) but the recordings "did not turn out to his satisfaction—the organ was too harsh. He sought an appropriate instrument in London, and played next on the organ of All Hallows by the Tower, Barking." The reporter's article ran in the *Neueste Nachrichten*, November 11, 1936. A display at the church of All Hallows reports that the organ was built in 1909.

Events surrounding Schweitzer's sixtieth birthday are recounted in the postscript to *Out of My Life and Thought* and in Brabazon's biography. Schweitzer remarked on German surrender of the individual will in *Out of My Life and Thought* and the acts of "brutalized humanity" in an address, quoted there, that he gave to mark the hundredth anniversary of Goethe's death, Frankfurt, March 22, 1932. The exchange of letters with Goebbels is also recounted by Brabazon, who notes that a friend of Schweitzer's had warned him to beware of "National Socialist Bach worship." Schweitzer's remark about Bach and religious humanity is from *J. S. Bach*, volume 1, p. 264.

24

Benjamin's essays were published in English in two volumes: *Illuminations* (ed. Hannah Arendt, trans. Harry Zohn; Harcourt, Brace, and World, 1953; Schocken, 1969) and *Reflections* (ed. Peter Demetz, trans. Edward Jephcott; Harcourt Brace Jovanovich, 1978; Schocken, 1986). *Illuminations* includes Benjamin's essays "The Work of Art in the Age of Mechanical Reproduction" and "The Story-Teller." Hannah Arendt sketched Benjamin's life in her introduction; Susan Sontag chooses the best, the most telling details in her portrait of Benjamin, the title essay of *Under the Sign of Saturn* (Farrar, Straus and Giroux, 1980). Benjamin himself quoted Valéry in the essay about art and mechanical reproduction, which in a more recent translation carries the more literal title "The Work of Art in the Age of Its Mechanical Reproducibility."

25

I gathered details of All Hallows' history and physical appearance during a 2007 visit, from a flier given out there, and from the church's website. Compact discs of Schweitzer's recordings are sold in a kiosk at the rear of the church.

Schweitzer's remark about burning the candle at both ends is from the "Postscript" to *Out of My Life and Thought*, as is his peroration about religion as a force, drawn from the Hibbert Lectures, given at Manchester College, Oxford, and printed in the *Christian Century*, November 21 and 28, 1934. A book of his was published under the title *At the Edge of the Primeval Forest*. The image of Schweitzer at the organ is drawn from the 1936 report of the Strasbourg session quoted in the notes for *Albert Schweitzer Plays Bach, Volume II*; I have transposed it to London.

PART II: A MAN IN A ROOM

1

Pablo Casals produced two memoirs. *Conversations with Casals*, by José María Corredor, was published in French in 1954; an English edition, translated by André Mangeot, was published by E. P. Dutton in 1956. *Joys and Sorrows: Pablo Casals, His Own Story*, as told to Albert E. Kahn, was published in English in 1970; Eel Pie Publishing, London, published a paperback edition in 1981. These books are the basis for many books in English, among them two biographies: *Pablo Casals: A Biography*, by H. L. Kirk (Holt, Rinehart, and Winston, 1974), and *Pablo Casals*, by Robert Baldock (Victor Gollancz, 1992). In general, this account is drawn from the two memoirs as directly as possible, with the biographies consulted for details and context.

Casals described his practice of playing Bach every morning in the first chapter of *Joys and Sorrows*. About this "benediction," he went on: "But that is not its only meaning for me. It is a rediscovery of the world of which I have the joy of being a part. It fills me with awareness of the wonder of life, with a feeling of the incredible marvel of being a human being. The music is never the same for me, never. Each day it is something new, fantastic and unbelievable. That is Bach, like nature, a miracle!"

His efforts with the Orquestra Pau Casals are recounted in both memoirs and both biographies. Casals called those years "the most fruitful of my life" in the "Music in Barcelona" chapter of *Joys and Sorrows*; he recalled the celebratory performance of Beethoven's Ninth, and then the one interrupted by a fascist coup, and the republic "drowned in blood" in the chapter "Triumph and Tragedy."

George Orwell wrote about the Spanish Civil War in *Homage to Catalonia* (1938), Ernest Hemingway in *For Whom the Bell Tolls* (1940).

Casals's remark about the cello and baton as weapons is cited in *Joys and Sorrows*, p. 224. Robert Baldock describes Casals's "concentrated burst" of recordings at the end of his chapter "Casals and the Spanish Republic," and my point about his strategic use of the recording studio is developed from Baldock's gloss on Casals's remark, p. 157: "If he could not use them on the concert platform to the extent he wished, Casals would do so by means of the gramophone."

The legend of Casals's "discovery" of the cello suites, presented in both memoirs (with some variations), is gone over in both biographies. Baldock calls the Abbey Road session Casals's "first serious recording of the Bach Unaccompanied Suites"; in Kirk's biography, the recordings are referenced only in the discography, by Teri Noel Towe.

Alberto Giacometti's combine-sculpture *The Palace at 4 a.m.* is in the Museum of Modern Art, New York.

Casals stated his aim of playing a work fresh each time in *Conversations with Casals*, at the end of the chapter "On Interpretation," which is full of similar insights, about the interpretation of Bach's music in particular.

2

Bach's remark about a singing style in playing is found on the title page of the *Inventions and Sinfonias* of 1723, reproduced with translation in *The New Bach Reader*, pp. 97–98.

The invention of the dynamic microphone is explained by Roland Gelatt in *The Fabulous Phonograph*, by Mark Coleman in *Playback*, and elsewhere. The roots of the cello suites in court dances—a staple of liner notes—is set out in the entry for the cello suites in the *Oxford Composer Companion*, written by John A. Butt.

3

Casals set out his "attitude to life" and bemoaned contemporary music's "lack of humanity" in *Joys and Sorrows*, p. 51.

4

The story of Bach's dalliance with a "stranger maiden" is told in high style in the biographies. Boyd proposes that the word usually rendered as "stranger"—*frembde*—should be rendered "unauthorized," and suggests that "as someone scarcely out of his teens, [Bach] must have appeared intolerably arrogant and self-willed." The suggestion that he was "ashamed" of the choir is found in the rebuke of November 11, 1706, printed in *The New Bach Reader*. All the biographers go over the notorious episode in which Bach, on a street in Arnstadt, called a student bassoonist, three years older than he, a "nanny-goat," prompting the bassoonist to draw his sword—but it seems to me that they overplay the significance of the episode out of a wish to add color and drama to their texts, so I have left it out here.

Wolff, p. 106, details Bach's request for a wagon to transport his possessions to Mühlhausen, and, pp. 108–109, describes the condition of the Blasiuskirche organ, said elsewhere (on tags in the Bach-Museum in Leipzig, for example) to have been small, with only a single manual. Bach's request for dismissal, June 25, 1708, is in *The New Bach Reader*.

Washington describes the conflict between the two dukes in Saxe-Weimar and reproduces a period illustration of the Himmelsburg chapel. The engraving showing the two dukes is on display in the Bachhaus in Eisenach. Geck, p. 79, describes Bach's circumstances on the market square, the growth of his family there, and the music-making in the Bach household. Forkel, p. 57, tells a story that suggests the place of music in the household: ". . . he once boasted to a friend at Weimar that he could play at sight and without a mistake anything put before him. But he was mistaken, as his friend convinced him before the week was out. Having invited Bach to breakfast one morning, he placed on the Clavier, among other music, a piece which, at a first glance, seemed perfectly easy. On his arrival, Bach, as was his custom, sat down at the Clavier to play or look through the music. Meanwhile his friend was in the next room preparing breakfast. In a short time Bach took up the piece of music destined to change his opinion and began to play it. He had not proceeded far before he came to a passage at which he stopped. After a look at it he began again, only to stop at the same place. 'No,' he called out to his friend, who was laughing heartily in the next room, 'the man does not exist who can play everything at sight. It can't be done.' With that he got up from the Clavier in some annoyance."

5

Wolff, Geck, and Williams (progressively more tentatively) introduce the idea that "Christ lag in Todesbanden" was written as an audition piece; Wolff, p. 103, places Bach's audition on Easter Sunday, and the Oxford entry for this cantata, by David Schulenberg, remarks that "it has been suggested that . . . it is his earliest surviving sacred vocal work." The idea that Bach used it to audition the Mühlhausen musicians is my own, as is the graphic representation of the structure of the cantata. The English translation here is from the Archiv Produktion CD (*Kantaten BWV 56, 4, 82*), featuring Dietrich Fischer-Dieskau and the Münchener Bach Chor, conducted by Karl Richter. Set against the view that it is "astonishing" is Geck's account, pp. 280–85: "[His admirers] should not succumb to the temptation to make him into an artist who towered above his age in every way. In fact, the cantata 'Christ lag in Todesbanden' makes it clear that Bach came only gradually to full mastery of his craft, regardless of any flashes of genius. By basing his cantata's large-scale form on the choral transcription pattern 'per omnes versus' (a pattern familiar to every organist), he was on solid compositional ground."

The careers of the mapmaker Gerardus Mercator (1512–94), the clock maker and color theorist Robert Hooke (1635–1703), and the lens maker Antoni van Leewenhoek (1632–1723) are sketched in *The Discoverers*, by Daniel J. Boorstin (Vintage, 1985).

The translation of *Wass mir behagt, ist nur die muntre Jagd* is given in the *Oxford Composer Companion*, which cites a 1992 article by Michael Marissen on the link between the F-major Sinfonia (that of the first Brandenburg concerto) and this cantata, a link maintained by Boyd, Geck, and others. Wolff, p. 135, proposes that it may be Bach's first secular cantata and discusses the source-text; Geck, p. 416, calls it "one of Bach's earliest efforts at Italian cantata style and da capo aria"; Williams, p. 108, declares: "It is a pathbreaking work, the first of its kind for Bach . . ." I know the cantata from a 1992 recording by the Falloni Chamber Orchestra and the Hungarian Radio Chorus, conducted by Mátyás Antál (Naxos CD).

6

The remark about the organ work in the Obituary, printed in *The New Bach Reader*, is quoted in *Bach*, by Peter Williams, himself an organist. A perusal of *The New Grove Bach Family* suggests that Bach wrote about half his organ works at Weimar. The box set characterized here is *Bach: Complete Organ Works*, by Walter Kraft (Vox, 12 CDs, 2006), recorded on period-appropriate organs in Europe, 1961–67, for release on LP. The *Orgel-büchlein* is characterized especially well by Boyd, p. 52ff., who reminds his readers that its title page was written later, to make it one of a set with the *Inventions* and other "didactic" works. A thick hymnal like the one Bach used in his boyhood is on display at the Bachhaus in Eisenach.

7

The parallel between Venice and Amsterdam is my own, based on evocations of the two cities in many books, and also on insights about Catholic and Protestant cities in *Reformations*.

Washington gives a vivid account of the rivalry between Wilhelm Ernst and Ernst August, with Johann Ernst figuring in. Vivaldi's life is sketched in the *Rough Guide*, Bach's encounter with his music in Boyd's chapter "Orchestral, Instrumental, and Keyboard Music." "Heated harmonies" is a loose translation of *L'estro armonico*, as explained in the notes, by Charlotte Nediger, to the 2004 recording by the Tafelmusik Baroque Orchestra, conducted by Jeanne Lamon (Analekta CD/DVD). Boyd, in his section on Bach's organ works, p. 48, stresses Bach's encounter with Bonporti's *Invenzioni da camera*. Dreyfus's insights about invention run through *Bach and the Patterns of Invention*, beginning with the opening pages; he characterizes Bach as a "discoverer and tinkerer" on p. 32. Bach gave his sense of the invention on the title pages of the *Inventions*, reproduced in *The New Bach Reader*, p. 98; Dreyfus's adapted translation is quoted here. Schweitzer, in a passage called "His Method of Working" (volume 1, chapter XI), remarked contrarily: "One would have expected that this richly inventive genius would have been so overwhelmed by the weight of ideas that thronged within him that he could not have kept to one theme alone, but would necessarily have given voice to them all. It was not so. Everything points to the fact that Bach did not invent easily, but slowly and with difficulty."

Wolff, p. 167, makes the astonishing point that only 15 to 20 percent of the music Bach composed at Weimar is now known to us. He describes Bach's efforts in chamber music at Weimar; following Forkel, he emphasizes Bach's debt to classical rhetoric of order, coherence, and proportion. *Oxford*'s entry on the cello suites, by John A. Butt, suggests that "some of them might date from Weimar." *The New Grove Bach Family* indicates that the lute suite in E minor is from Weimar "or earlier," and places the others in Köthen or Leipzig. The arrival in Weimar of a *Lautenwerck* sent by Johann Nikolaus Bach, "its inventor and maker," is recounted by Wolff, p. 176, who adds, "it is hard to imagine that Johann Sebastian did not have a leading hand in this musical business transaction with his cousin in nearby Jena." A 1980 reconstruction of a *Lautenwerck* (c. 1718) is pictured in the *Oxford Composer Companion*, p. 275; the title page of the suite *aufs Lautenwerck* is pictured in the booklet packaged with *Works for Lute, BWV 995–997*, CD 121 in Teldec's 153-disc Bach 2000 edition, where that suite is played by Michele Barchi.

8

Casals described his early years in both memoirs, with slight variations from one account to the other. The account of his discovery of the cello comes mainly from *Joys and Sorrows*, pp. 30–34. In *Conversations*, p. 17, he points out that the organ in El Vendrell "was an old instrument, made at the same period as the one Bach played when in Leipzig."

Robert Hughes characterized bourgeois Catalonia and Catalan *modernisme* in *Barcelona* (Knopf, 1992).

The account of the Café Tost comes from *Conversations*, p. 25; that of Albeniz's invitation from *Joys and Sorrows*, pp. 47–48. His memory of his "discovery" of the Bach cello suites is from *Joys and Sorrows*, p. 46, his recognition of their "exceptional importance" from *Conversations*,

p. 27; his sense of their "glittering kind of poetry" is from *Conversations*, his sense of their "full architecture and artistrya" from *Joys and Sorrows*. As the story is told in *Conversations*, his father had already bought him a full-size cello. His memory of the "musty shop" is from *Joys and Sorrows*, his account of the "gradations of musical allusion" in Bach from *Conversations*, p. 114—where Casals contrasted this worldly side of Bach to the "exclusively religious side," which he felt had been overemphasized.

9

Casals's account of his twelve years' study of the cello suites is drawn from *Joys and Sorrows*, p. 47. Though he gives no religious motive for his devotion, his first years with the suites were also "a period of religious mysticism" (*Conversations*, p. 29), and although it did not recur, he said that "I think that I possess an essentially religious mind."

He described his duty to find his own way and a "state of mind" at the very beginning of the chapter of *Conversations* (pp. 182ff.) called "On Interpretation." The account of his feeling "at loggerheads" with the world is from *Conversations*, pp. 28–29, that of his shadowy prayer life from *Joys and Sorrows*, pp. 51–52.

Madrid gets a whole chapter in *Joys and Sorrows*, and Casals's remarks about his subsequent life as an incidental musician in Paris are from pp. 70–71. He described the "new world" of the cello suites in *Conversations*, p. 27.

The coming of age of audio recordings is recounted, with different emphases, in *Playback*, *The Ambient Century*, *Good Vibrations*, *Selling Sounds*, *The Fabulous Phonograph*, *EMI: The First 100 Years*, and *The Recording Angel*. "Gramo-fright," described by Fred Gaisberg in *The Music Goes Round* (Macmillan, 1942), is cited by Mark Coleman in *Playback*, p. 18. Paul Auster's 1982 memoir is called *The Invention of Solitude*.

Casals explained Bach's foresight into the development of the cello as a solo instrument in the first "Music of Yesterday and Today" chapter of *Conversations*, p. 138.

10

The early history of mobile recording is given in *EMI: The First 100 Years*.

Fritz Kreisler's recordings of the Prelude in E and the "Air on the G String" are included in *The Kreisler Collection: The Complete Acoustic HMV Recordings* (Biddulph, 2CDs, 1989); the notes say they were made in Berlin "a year later" than Joachim and Sarasate's first recordings, made in 1903. The double concerto is from *The Kreisler Collection: The Early Victor Recordings (Vol. II)* (Biddulph, CD, 1990); the booklet, which includes a photograph of the two violinists, gives the recording date; the quote is from the notes, by Wayne Kiley. The recording details for the early Bach orchestral recordings are drawn from *Johann Sebastian Bach: Orchestral Music* (Andante, 3 CDs, 2001).

The account of the Gramophone Company, touched on in all the histories, is drawn mainly from *EMI: The First 100 Years*; the history of EMI Studios at Abbey Road is based on that book and two others: the EMI-authorized *Abbey Road*, by Brian Southall (Patrick Stephens, 2001), and Mark Cunningham's *Good Vibrations*. Pathé's newsreel of the opening ceremony featuring Sir Edward Elgar can be seen on YouTube.

11

Pablo Casals recalled making a recording in Paris in 1903 and recording a duet with the violinist Eugène Ysaÿe the next year. In *Joys and Sorrows*, p. 116, he recalled that the recording "of the Schubert trio in B Flat . . . was to remain in demand for many years." But the archivist Tully Potter is skeptical, for "no trace of those recordings has ever been found." Potter adds: "It almost beggars belief that the man who, from at least 1905, was regarded as the finest cellist in the world . . . did not set foot inside a recording studio until 1915, when he was 38." Potter's insights are found in the notes to volume 3 of the Naxos set of Casals's *Encores and Transcriptions* (5 individual CDs, 2003–2007). The set includes ninety-nine short pieces that Casals recorded in the acoustic era and the early electric era. It is not for sale in the United States for copyright reasons; Academy Records in Manhattan made it available to me in a situation that itself beggars belief.

The two English biographies of Casals become crucial sources once Casals's career takes shape and a precise dating of events becomes important. Kirk's, the more thorough at nearly seven hundred pages, suffers from the author's indifference to recordings; Baldock's, which tracks Kirk's book closely in places, is enlivened by choice quotations.

Casals described his relentless touring in the United States in *Joys and Sorrows*, pp. 100–109, and gave a vivid account of the dice game gone awry in *Conversations*, pp. 50–51.

"The precise moment when Casals first played a cello suite in public is a conspicuously missing piece of information in an otherwise highly documented public career," Eric Siblin observes in *The Cello Suites* (Grove Atlantic, 2009). Inspecting press clippings in the Catalan National Archives, Siblin found a review of a recital in Barcelona, October 17, 1901, citing Casals's performance of "the 'Suite' of Bach," and one from Madrid ten days later, which earned Casals "a prolonged standing ovation." In the next three years, Siblin declares, Casals played full cello suites in "London, Paris, Rotterdam, Utrecht, New York, Montevideo, and Rio de Janeiro."

Baldock, p. 65, tells of Casals playing the Bach C-major suite at Mendelssohn Hall in New York, March 8, 1904.

Casals in *Joys and Sorrows*, p. 126, told the story of the promoter who insisted he play the scheduled Bach suite at a public rehearsal before the concert, because the people there expected it—even if he had no need to rehearse a Bach suite. The concert promoter finally offered to pay him double—for the rehearsal and the concert; Casals gave the second payment to the orchestra's musicians fund.

Kirk, p. 283, tells the story of a Muriel Draper dinner party with the Holy Trinity and Henry James as guests. In her memoirs, *Music at Midnight*, Draper recalled the Brahms piano trio in B minor: "As the music progressed and the incomparable tone of Casals' cello was heard in the short solo passage of the first movement, [James'] solemnly searching eyes fastened on Casals' face, and he seemed to listen by seeing. When Thibaud began the brilliant passage for violin in the second movement, his eyes left Casals, as if he had drunk him in through all his organs of sight—music, hands, bowing and all—and centred on Thibaud . . ."

Kirk, p. 196, describes Casals playing "some of the quiet sections of the Bach cello suites" at the bedside of the painter Eugène Carrière, who had suffered a stroke; on p. 247, he tells of Casals playing a Bach suite for Edvard Grieg, who said: "This man does not perform; he *resurrects!*"

The Princeton story is from Kirk, p. 353, who recounts that Casals "went through a complete Bach sonata" for the student "while Bauer dressed for the recital"; it seems likely that he was referring to a suite for solo cello.

Casals's relationships with Guilhermina Suggia and Susan Scott Metcalfe are presented more candidly in the biographies than in the memoirs. As Baldock puts it: "Guilhermina Suggia is an absence in the autobiographical literature on Casals. In *Conversations with Casals* . . .

she is mentioned only once, not by Casals but by his interlocutor. In *Joys and Sorrows . . .* she appears not at all." Metcalfe fares better, but the memoirs give no sense of why Casals married her in the first place or precisely what broke the marriage apart.

Casals and Suggia's conjugal division of the Bach suites is described by Baldock, p. 86.

Naxos's *Encores and Transcriptions 3: The Complete Acoustic Recordings* gives the recording date for each of the seventeen pieces. Tully Potter's notes indicate that the recordings were made for Columbia. It is possible that there were nine sessions, rather than eight.

Casals remarked on the limits of the gramophone in *Joys and Sorrows*, p. 116, and went on: "As a matter of fact, even to this day I find phonograph recordings far from fully satisfying."

Casals's early electrical recordings are found in the Naxos set, which gives the recording locations and dates: the Musette, January 31, 1928; the Adagio, February 28, 1927. The set also includes the "Air on the G String," in two versions recorded by Columbia, May 5, 1916, and April 29, 1920; the Adagio, recorded by Columbia, February 21, 1925; and the Air, recorded by HMV at Queen's Small Hall, March 5, 1930.

12

Casals's early electrical recordings are also included on *Pablo Casals Plays Brahms* (Pearl CD), which includes a recording of excerpts from Boccherini's sixth sonata made in Barcelona. The Holy Trinity's classic recordings of Beethoven's *Archduke* trio and Schubert's first piano trio are on a disc in EMI's Great Recordings of the Century series, with notes by Lionel Salter, which include the recording details: the Schubert at Kingsway, July 5 and 6, 1926; the Beethoven at Queen's Small Hall, November 18 and 19, 1928.

Pablo Casals Plays Brahms, with notes by Charles Haynes, indicates that the Double Concerto was recorded in Barcelona in 1929, with Alfred Cortot conducting. "Komm, süsser Tod," recorded in Barcelona, June 16, 1929, is on Naxos's *Encores and Transcriptions 2*, with notes by Tully Potter, as is a transcription of the Andante from Bach's second violin sonata (June 19), the Boccherini, and works by Tartini, Cassadó, Vivaldi, Mendelssohn, Rimsky-Korsakov, Laserna, and Haydn, all from Barcelona.

Casals described the effect of "Komm, süsser Tod" in *Conversations*, p. 114 (adding: "One cannot describe the serene expectation of death in a more perfect way") and his premonition of his father's death in *Conversations*, p. 77.

Casals told the story of his encounter with Schweitzer in Edinburgh in both memoirs. The long quotation here is drawn from *Joys and Sorrows*, pp. 215–16; in *Conversations with Casals*, Casals remarked that Schweitzer's Bach book (called *Bach: Le Musicièn-Poète* in France) had led him to see "how our two poetical visions were alike on this rare subject," p. 10; that he played concerts and recitals in Edinburgh, "and Schweitzer showed great enthusiasm for my playing of Bach."

Segovia's Bach recordings are available in EMI's Great Recordings of the Century series, as is Landowska's 1933 recording of the *Goldberg Variations*. Edwin Fischer's *Well-Tempered Clavier* is on CDs from Pearl and Naxos, Menuhin's 1930s recordings of the violin concerti on a Naxos CD. In *Conversations with Menuhin*, by Robin Daniels (Futura, 1980), Menuhin called Lindbergh "my boyhood hero," p. 33, and described the "massive structure" of the D-minor partita. Casals in *Conversations*, p. 189, recalled hearing Menuhin play a Bach partita in Paris: he thought his gifts were great and his technique perfect, but remarked on "what to my mind was missing in his performance of the *Partita*, namely, that it was not fully alive." When Casals mentioned this to Georges Enesco, Menuhin's model, Enesco said the reason was that Menuhin had not used bowing effects that weren't used in Bach's time. "I was sorry to find him tied up to this idea, which I considered a traditionalist prejudice"—the idea of fidelity to past practice that would become central to the movement for historically informed performance.

Roland Gelatt in *The Fabulous Phonograph*, p. 261, gives a partial roster of the Society program: "Before World War II brought the Society program to a halt, the recorded literature had been expanded by it to include Albert Schweitzer performances of Bach's organ music, the *Forty-Eight Preludes and Fugues* performed on the piano by Edwin Fischer, Bach's unaccompanied cello suites in the seminal interpretations of Pablo Casals," et cetera.

The photograph of Schweitzer, Casals, and Tovey in academic garb is reproduced in the photo section of Baldock's biography. The story of Casals's departure from Edinburgh is drawn from *Joys and Sorrows*. In the telling of the story found in *Conversations*, Schweitzer says to the parting Casals: " 'Listen, since *thou* must go, thou must at least say *thou* to me before we part.' Of course I said a few things to him, after which we embraced each other, overcome by emotion."

13

Orwell's description of war-torn Barcelona is from *Homage to Catalonia*, p. 5. Auden considered the civil war on the "arid square" of Iberia in the poem "Spain" (1937). Casals recalled the Spanish Civil War at length in both memoirs; the remarks here are from *Joys and Sorrows*, pp. 218ff. His remark about the relative worth of his recitals is from *Conversations*, p. 213.

Both biographies go over Casals's departure from Barcelona; Baldock is somewhat more precise with dates. For recording session dates, I have considered the two biographies, the discography Teri Noel Towe provided for Kirk's biography, and booklet notes for many reissue CDs. Fred Gaisberg recalled his work with Casals in *The Music Goes Round*, which is drawn on amply in the biographies, in *EMI: The First 100 Years*, and in CD notes. Eric Siblin gives further background in *The Cello Suites*. Casals's statement of independence is a headnote to the chapter "On Interpretation" in *Conversations*, p. 182. The photo spread from the *Illustrated London News* can be seen and read on the Web.

14

EMI's studio complex at Abbey Road is described in *EMI: The First Hundred Years*; in Southall's *Abbey Road* and in *Good Vibrations*. The question "Are we all ready?" and some of the visual details are drawn from the Pathé newsreel of the studio's opening eight years earlier. Southall mentions the smell of smoke at Abbey Road.

The notion of the cello suites as a *Gradus ad Parnassam* is in Geck's biography, p. 603. Casals in *Conversations*, p. 108, described the maid at his estate in San Salvador humming Bach as evidence of Bach's greatness: "This man, who knows everything and feels everything, cannot write one note, however unimportant it may appear, which is anything but transcendent. He has reached the heart of every noble thought, and has done it in the most perfect way."

The appealing circularity of the cello suite in C major was pointed out to me by Michael Marissen. Karol Berger explains the circularity of Bach's music in *Bach's Cycle, Mozart's Arrow: A Essay on the Origins of Musical Modernity* (University of California Press, 2007).

15

The schedule of recordings at Abbey Road is given by Southall, p. 32, who describes Winston Churchill's reaction on visiting the studios: "My God, I thought I'd come to the wrong place. It looks like a hospital."

Casals described the challenge of creating "live shapes" in the "On Interpretation" chapter of *Conversations*, p. 184, and the relationship of discipline and spontaneity p. 204.

The notes to EMI's Great Recordings of the Century CD of the cello suites give the recording date for the second suite as November 25, 1936; the two biographies' discographies and the Naxos reissue all give the date as November 23, 1936, the same date as for the third suite.

The story of Robert Johnson, and of his first recording session in San Antonio, is told in *Mystery Train*, by Greil Marcus (Dutton, 1975); in *Deep Blues*, by Robert Palmer (Penguin, 1982); in *Searching for Robert Johnson*, by Peter Guralnick (Dutton, 1989); in the liner notes for *Robert Johnson: The Complete Recordings* (Columbia/Legacy, 1990); and in *Escaping the Delta: Robert Johnson and the Invention of the Blues*, by Elijah Wald (HarperCollins, 2004). *A Day That Changed Music History*, a radio documentary about the two recordings, produced by Joe Richman for Radio Diaries at my prompting, aired on NPR on the seventy-fifth anniversary of that day, November 23, 2011.

18

Casals's first encounters with Prades are described in the "Before and During Exile" chapter of *Conversations*, in the "Exile" chapter of *Joys and Sorrows*, and in the two biographies.

Casals said he spent a year preparing to record the cello suites in *Conversations*, p. 209, near the end of the chapter "On Interpretation"; in the same breath, he stated his conviction that music loses its vitality when passed through a machine. About the act of making a recording he expounded at length, pp. 190–91, saying that it led the performer to strive too hard for perfection: "Making a disc, where at least an external perfection is required, is conducive to mechanical performance. At a concert performance a slight hesitation or mistake may pass unnoticed, or in any case the general musicality of the performer can make up for it   but the fact is that when making a gramophone record where every little detail is registered, the imposition on the artist is a real servitude and, what is worse, a dangerous servitude in regard to his inspiration or his musical feeling. We are now surrounded by mechanism everywhere."

Fred Gaisberg in his memoirs gave an account of the Prague session that produced Casals's great recording of the Dvořák concerto; it is quoted by Baldock, who chronicles Casals's subsequent travels. The photograph of a gladiatorial Casals appears on the front of the CD. Casals's recollections are in *Joys and Sorrows*, his remark about "the leaves of the trees" from the "On Interpretation" chapter of *Conversations*, his insight about Bach's grasp of the cello as a solo instrument in *Conversations*, p. 138.

Bach's composition of the sixth cello suite is set out by Boyd, who, in a note, p. 95, gives the reference from Spitta's biography describing the suite as written for the *viola pomposa*, adding that Bach's *viole pompose* were made in Leipzig, "which suggests that if Bach did invent the instrument it was after he wrote the cello suites." The *Oxford Composer Companion* entry on the cello suites, by John A. Butt, declares that the suite was written "for a five-string instrument (perhaps a violoncello piccolo)." Entries for the two instruments in *Oxford* stress that the violoncello (played on the leg) is not the same as the viola pomposa (played on the arm). Michael Marissen and other scholars doubt not only that Bach wrote the suite for the *viola pomposa*, but that Bach invented the instrument at all. For his part, Casals was abreast of the scholarship of his time when he remarked, in *Conversations*, p. 120, on Bach's wish to transcend "technical limitations" by inventing the *viola pomposa*.

17

Casals's declaration of conscience is in *Conversations*, his recollection of dark days in Paris in *Joys and Sorrows*. The arias for soprano and harpsichord, of course, are those in the *Notebook for Anna Magdalena Bach*, some of them composed by Bach himself and some by other composers. *Scordatura* is explained in the *Oxford Composer Companion*. Casals's widely quoted remark that "the only weapons I have ever had are my cello and my conductor's baton," which varies from one text to another, is given that way in *Joys and Sorrows*, p. 224.

Siblin in *The Cello Suites*, p. 115, quotes two letters, in the archive of the EMI Group Trust in London, that Casals wrote to the Gramophone Company in connection with the recording of the fourth and fifth suites. "Two Bach suites are for me the most terrible things to record," he wrote on June 5, 1939, and on July 5 he wrote that the strain of doing so "has cost me, besides several months' work and the exhausting effort of the recordings, a full week in bed as always."

PART III: PLAYING TOGETHER

1

Accounts of Bach's imprisonment vary: Williams, p. 122, says distinctly that "Bach was in prison in Weimar, held in the 'district judge's chamber or cell,'" but goes on to speculate, p. 125, that this was "something more like a room in a debtor's prison than a prison cell of popular imagination." Boyd, p. 42, says Wilhelm "had him placed under arrest and held him prisoner." Geck, p. 96, suggests that Bach may have been punished physically. Wolff, p. 183, suggests that "he made some demand—for an earlier dismissal, perhaps, or something else related to his imminent departure—that embroiled him in a situation where he lost his temper." The quote from Ernst Ludwig Gerber's *Historisch-biographisches Lexikon der Tonkünstler* is quoted by Wolff and, in a different translation, by Geck, who makes clear just how renowned Bach was locally when he took the job in Köthen. Washington suggests that incarceration was commonplace for musicians. The wedding of Ernst August and Eleonore Wilhelmine is described by Wolff, p. 177, who describes Bach's hastening to Köthen as "questionable," p. 184, and yet notes that Bach inspected an organ in "nearby Leipzig" only six days later.

2

Leopold's wont to show off his orchestra is described by Wolff, p. 210; Bach's travels, especially to Berlin, are detailed in Wolff's chapter "Travels and Trials." Paul Badura-Skoda characterized the *Clavier-büchlein* as a precious gift in *Interpreting Bach at the Keyboard* (Oxford, 1995).

3

Wolff characterizes Carlsbad, pp. 101–102; Bach's son Carl Philipp Emanuel called his parents' marriage "blissful" in the Obituary, which is also the source of the passage recounting Maria Barbara's death and Bach's arrival home.

The sources for the superlatives applied to the solo violin works are the notes for the Philips/Decca 2-CD set of recording by Arthur Grumiaux; the entry for the solo violin works in the *Oxford Composer Companion*; the Bach entry in *The Rough Guide to Classical Music on CD*; and *Bach: A Life in Music*, where Williams contends that they are not unaccompanied.

Helga Thoene's argument for the chaconne as a musical headstone is found in the booklet for *Morimur*, by the Hilliard Ensemble, Christoph Poppen, violin (ECM, 2001); Geck judges the argument "speculative at best" in his chapter "The Cöthen Demonstration Cycles"; Michael Marissen thinks the argument fundamentally unsound, pointing out that Lutherans of Bach's time and place considered *gematria* something like an occult practice and therefore regarded it as sinful.

Many biographers place the composition of the Brandenburg concertos, and their dedication in March 1721, prior to Bach's encounter with Anna Magdalena Wülcken, but there is no rock-solid reason to do so. Boyd, p. 74, soberly observes of Bach that "there is nothing to link his name with Anna Magdalena's before 25 September 1721, when they both acted as godparents to the son of Prince Leopold's butler . . ." Williams, p. 153, straightforwardly remarks of Anna Magdalena that "she could well have come in contact with him before he was a widower" or on one of the "professional visits" to neighboring courts "that both of them, as fee-paid musicians, are known to have made over the period 1720–1." Wolff, p. 216, though focusing on ways they may have met in 1721, allows that "we don't know how Bach knew her, where he heard her for the first time, nor where and when he hired her." Awkwardly, he treats the career of the singer Anna Magdalena Bach (as she is called) before treating the death of Maria Barbara Bach.

Wolff, p. 218, gives the date of the wedding, places it "at home, by command of the Prince," and makes the vivid point that the wedding was held midweek so that church musicians could get back home in time to play at Sunday services in the churches where they were employed. Wolff and other biographers point out that Bach, anticipating the wedding, ordered plenty of wine, at the cost of nearly more than two months' salary.

4

Leopold Stokowski recalled the role of music in his childhood in *Music for All of Us* (Simon & Schuster, 1943), p. 69. His preference for children over adults as an audience is reported in *Classical Music in America*, p. 294, where Horowitz gives a vivid account of a Philadelphia Orchestra performance of Saint-Saëns's *Carnival of the Animals*.

The most extensive biography of Stokowski is *Stokowski: A Counterpoint of View*, by Oliver Daniel (Dodd, Mead, 1982); Abram Chasins's *Leopold Stokowski: A Profile* (Hawthorn, 1979) is lively, patchy, and subjective; its title and jacket pun on Stoki's celebrated podium profile. Stokowski's supper with Walt Disney is described in both biographies, and also in *Walt Disney: The Triumph of the American Imagination* by Neil Gabler (Random House, 2006) and in *Walt Disney's Fantasia*, by John Culhane (Harry N. Abrams, 1983). Chasins proposes that his friend Stokowski went big right away; Stokowski's own recollections are given in Daniel's biography. Gabler reports that Disney and Stokowski had met and corresponded and that Disney had taken Stoki on a studio tour. "Why don't we sit together?" is Stokowski himself, quoted by Culhane, p. 15.

Disney's work on *Snow White* and his side enthusiasm for "The Sorcerer's Apprentice" are described by Gabler.

The account of Stokowski's career draws on the two biographies, on Horowitz's masterful portrait in *Classical Music in America* (the hardcover first edition reproduced a "cel" of Stoki from *Fantasia* on the dust jacket), and on *Perfecting Sound Forever*, by Greg Milner (Faber and Faber, 2009), whose "aural history of recorded music" is enriched at many points by his telling of Stokowski's story.

The account of transcription draws on the *Oxford Composer Companion* and the *Harvard Brief Dictionary of Music*.

5

Horowitz gives a history of classical music's emergence in *Classical Music in America*; John Rockwell stresses the German emphasis in the chapter on Ernst Krenek in his breakthrough book *All American Music* (rev. ed., Da Capo, 1997); Horowitz's later book *Artists in Exile* (HarperCollins, 2007) has a very strong chapter, "The German Colonization of American Classical Music." Alfred Kazin portrayed Willa Cather masterfully in *On Native Grounds* (Harcourt Brace, 1942); the Cather section may be the strongest single section of that extraordinary book. The contributions of MacDowell and Ives are set out in *Classical Music in America* and also in *America's Musical Life*, by Richard Crawford (Norton, 2002), p. 378.

Alex Ross in *The Rest Is Noise: Listening to the Twentieth Century* (Farrar, Straus and Giroux, 2007) offers a further insight about how classical music changed in America: by the twenties, he explains, p. 150, "a gap had opened up between the ideal of modernism as the antithesis of mass culture and the reality of America as a marketplace in which absolutely anything could be bought and sold." Two other recent books give emphasis to the effects of the record business on music: *Selling Sounds*, by David Suisman, and *How the Beatles Destroyed Rock 'n' Roll*, by Elijah Wald (Oxford, 2011)—the latter in many ways a sequel to Wald's book *Escaping the Delta*. But to my mind none of these books captures just how great a change was the sudden ubiquity of records and radio as the Depression flattened out.

John Cage's exploits are recounted in *The Rest Is Noise* (quoted here); in *Minimalism*, by K. Robert Schwarz (Phaidon, 1996); in *All American Music*, where he is given a whole chapter; and in Mark Katz's *Capturing Sound*. Schoenberg's characterization of him as "an inventor—of genius" is from *Conversing with Cage*, by Richard Kostelanetz (Psychology Press, 2003), p. 6.

6

Stokowski envisioned "entirely new means of tone production" in 1929. Chasins described him as a man of three centuries in his prologue, p. xiii. Stokowski called the microphone "the electric ear" in an article for *The Atlantic Monthly*, "New Vistas in Radio" (January 1935), long available on the magazine's website (www.theatlantic.com) and quoted in *Perfecting Sound Forever*, p. 66.

Both biographers remark on the blend of fact, exaggeration, legend, and untruth in the story of Stokowski's origins; so does Joseph Horowitz in *Classical Music in America*.

The organ at St. Bart's is described vividly by Craig R. Whitney in *All the Stops*, which includes an expert account of Stokowski's time there; so does *Stokowski and the Organ*. Daniel gives the specifics of Lucy Hickenlooper's courtship of the young Stokowski; Chasins, p. 15, quotes her friend Marie Dehon, a parishioner at St. Bart's, as saying that "he looks like a poetic Viking." Stokowski's swift rise to conductorial eminence features in all the books; the Cincinnati musicians' praise for Stokowski was in an open letter to the Cincinnati *Times-Star*, December 4, 1911, printed in *A Counterpoint of View*, p. 90, and quoted in *Classical Music in America*, p. 180.

Stokowski's reaction to Mahler's *Symphony of a Thousand* is given in *Classical Music in America*, p. 183. His distaste for acoustic recordings and his efforts in his first electrical sessions are recounted by Greg Milner, who writes that Stoki "crossed the river" to record *Danse macabre*. Many of those early recordings, long available for listening through the Stokowski portal at www.classical.net., can be heard at www.stokowski.org, which concentrates on his work with

the Philadelphia Orchestra. Many significant Stokowski recordings, from the thirties espe-
cially, are available in the set *Leopold Stokowski: Maestro Célèbre* (Trumpets of Joy, 5 CDs, n.d.).
Pablo Casals's Abbey Road recording of the *New World Symphony* is on *Pablo Casals Plays
Dvořák*, which gives the recording date as October 30, 1937.

"Another musician" who pondered the mystery of Stokowski's recorded sound was Glenn
Gould, in "Stokowski in Six Scenes," in *The Glenn Gould Reader*. Horowitz calls Stokowski
"the ultimate sonic sybarite" in *Classical Music in America*, p. 289.

7

Stokowski's account of his swift progress in Bach, "my favorite composer always," is given in
Leopold Stokowski: A Profile, which lacks documentation. Stoki also recalled, "As a boy I was
soaked in Palestrina and Bach and Beethoven and their contemporaries . . ."—a remark
quoted in *A Counterpoint of View*, p. 64.

The Bach-expert organist at the Royal College of Music was Walford Davies; the St. James
parishioner Hilda Galloway, in a letter given in Daniels, p. 23, recalled being "entranced" by a
Stokowski performance of the Toccata and Fugue in D Minor; that piece was described as a
"sensation" at St. Bart's in the notes to *Stokowski Legend*. Stoki's first and last programs at
St. Bart's are given in *Stokowski and the Organ*.

Smith in *Stokowski and the Organ* tells the story of the organ roll Stoki presented in a rosewood box, reports that Bach himself had transcribed "Wachet auf" for organ, p. 153, and af-
firms that Stokowski was faithful to the organ texts in his transcriptions. Ivan March (see
below) reports that Stokowski led early performances of the *St. Matthew Passion* at St. Bart's;
Oliver Daniel reports that Stokowski led the first Philadelphia Orchestra performances of
"Wachet auf" and the *Christmas Oratorio*. Stoki's programs from Cincinnati through 1940 are
given by the Leopold Stokowski Club at classical.net. Wanda Landowska was a featured soloist with the Philadelphians on May 16 and 17, 1923, playing a program that included Bach's
Italian Concerto; the notes at classical.net, which indicate that she played both harpsichord and
piano in those programs, don't say which instrument she used for the Bach. Chasins, p. 117,
reports of Stokowski that Landowska was one of the "handful of solo artists whose performances he found memorable."

Stokowski's transcriptions of "Wachet auf" and the Passacaglia and Fugue in C Minor can
be found in much later recordings (1957–58) on *Stokowski Legend: Famous Bach Transcriptions*
(EMI CD/DVD, 2004). The notes, by Ivan March, give the early history of his transcriptions,
calling the Toccata and Fugue in D Minor a "sensation" at St. James's. Smith in *Stokowski and
the Organ* reports that Bach had transcribed the work in the other direction, setting it for organ. A recording of the Passacaglia from November 16, 1936, is included in the Andante set
Leopold Stokowski: Conductor (4 CDs, 2001).

Stoki's adventures in the early thirties are chronicled in both biographies; his abandonment
of the baton in favor of the spotlight is made vivid by Chasins, who describes the hand-injuring
incident, quotes the remark about "handmade music," and quotes the program note explaining
the new lighting given out at the beginning of the 1926 season, p. 104.

Stokowski's characterization of the Toccata and Fugue in D Minor is given in the New
York Philharmonic's program notes at www.nyphil.org. The recording of that work from
April 6, 1927, is included in the *Leopold Stokowski: Conductor* set; the 1927 recording of the
New World Symphony is at www.stokowski.org. Roland Gelatt in *The Fabulous Phonograph* char-
acterized Stoki's Toccata and Fugue as one of "a half dozen [Victor] issues that set a world

standard for reproduced sound; the Brahms First, Beethoven Seventh, and Franck D minor symphonies, Rimsky-Korsakov's *Scheherazade*, Stravinsky's *Firebird* Suite, and—most arresting of all—the Stokowski transcription of Bach's Toccata and Fugue in D minor. This was electrical recording at its most powerful, luminous, and enveloping."

8

This account of the history of radio is drawn from Greg Milner's *Perfecting Sound Forever*, from Tom Lewis's *Empire of the Air: The Men Who Made Radio* (HarperCollins, 1991), from *The Ambient Century*, and from *The Label: The Story of Columbia Records*, by Gary Marmorstein (Thunder's Mouth, 2007). Stokowski's broadcast of October 6, 1929, is described in *A Counterpoint of View*, pp. 306–307, and his activities in the Depression in *Classical Music in America*, pp. 288–96, where Horowitz, who has heard the Bell Labs recordings, cites Rachmaninov's praise of the Philadelphians as the greatest orchestra ever.

Stokowski's concert for unemployed musicians is recalled by Chasins (who was there), p. 142; the program of a later benefit concert for unemployed musicians is given in the Stokowski section of www.classical.net. A recording of "Christ lag in Todesbanden" made in 1931 is in the *Maestro Célèbre* set. *Time* featured Stokowski on its cover, April 28, 1930; his conflicts with Arthur Judson are described in both biographies and in *Artists in Exile*, where Horowitz describes the gathering of European moderns in California; there is a vivid portrait of that whole world in *The Rest Is Noise*.

9

The account of Disney's early years and rise in Hollywood is rooted in the account given in Neil Gabler's biography. The animator Frank Thomas's comparison of Disney to "an organist playing all the stops" is quoted by Gabler, p. 221. *The Three Little Pigs* can be viewed on YouTube. Will Hays, president of the Motion Picture Producers and Distributors of America, was the movie figure who credited the film with ending the Depression, p. 186.

10

Stokowski's remark about the receding limitations of music is quoted by Evan Eisenberg in *The Recording Angel*, p. 124; Eisenberg's portrait of Stokowski is more insightful and forward-looking than any other. The full remarks are found in the Lewiston (Maine) *Daily Sun*, December 15, 1931, found through Google; possibly the article was a syndicated one, written and published elsewhere. Stokowski's experiments with recording technology and telephones lines are described in *Perfecting Sound Forever*, pp. 64–73, where Milner gives an expert synopsis of Stokowski's approach and outlook.

The Youth Concerts are treated in a whole chapter of *A Counterpoint of View*, which takes in the objections to the "Marseillaise" and the "Internationale." In the same chapter, p. 333, the pianist Eugene List describes calling on Stokowski at his apartment: "I went up and there was this hushed atmosphere. Whoever let me in said, 'Quiet.' He was poring over the Bach B minor Mass because he was going to do it shortly . . ." Stokowski's letter of resignation is given in the next chapter, p. 335. The admirer who considered the loss of Stokowski "unthinkable" was the mother of the orchestra's board president, Curtis Bok. Horowitz makes his true and unorthodox point about Stoki and Philly in *Classical Music in America*, p. 294. The Christmastide performances of the Mass in B Minor are documented in the list of Stokowski's programs at www.classical.net.

11

The Disneys' European tour is described in *Walt Disney: The Triumph of the American Imagination*; the photo of animators studying a live deer is in the photo insert.

Disney dismissed the furor over Nazism as an overreaction in the *Los Angeles Times*, August 12, 1935. The composer Paul Hindemith, as Horowitz tells the story, visited the Disney studios as an admirer of *Snow White* and found the artists (as he wrote to his wife) "so tightly regulated that it makes you ill . . . They draw only Mickey Mouse and Donald Duck." Of "the great music god Stokowski," Hindemith went on: "When I saw what kind of trash he was making and that he was wearing an ultramarine blue silk shirt and a lemon-yellow cravat with his albino-like face I really could not muster up the proper feeling of awe . . ." *Artists in Exile*, p. 115.

12

The conversion of the Pan Pacific Auditorium from skating rink to concert hall is described by Daniel, p. 347. Vintage photographs of the auditorium are on Wikipedia. Stokowski's valedictory remarks to the orchestra, quoted by Chasins, p. 147, were made at the final rehearsal. The program included Brahms as well as Bach and Wagner.

The Big Broadcast of 1937 was released in 1936, *100 Men and a Girl* in 1937. A film featuring Stokowski as Bach evidently was proposed before these films, but Chasins, p. 168, says that "fortunately" it never materialized.

13

Disney's fascination with "The Sorcerer's Apprentice" is recounted by Neil Gabler, who passes over Disney's interest in Arturo Toscanini's version, mentioned in John Culhane's *Walt Disney's Fantasia*. Disney's letter to his New York agent Hal Horne, cited in brief by Gabler, is quoted more fully by Culhane, p. 81, and by James A. Pegolotti in *Deems Taylor: A Biography* (Northeastern University Press, 2003), p. 235. His memos to the staff are quoted in *Walt Disney's Fantasia*, where Culhane gives the rough description of the dream sequence involving Mickey Mouse, p. 96. The letter of an "enthused" Disney is cited most fully by Chasins, p. 171; Stokowski's reply is given by Culhane, p. 81, and Stoki's suggestion that Mickey Mouse be dropped, pp. 96–100.

Gabler gives the details of the *Snow White* premiere, Daniel the details of Stokowski's "final" concerts, December 13 and 14, 1937. Stokowski's transcription of Bach's Prelude and Fugue in E Minor, recorded December 12, can be heard at archive.org. The others are included in the *Maestro Célèbre* and *Leopold Stokowski: Conductor* CD sets.

The photograph of Stokowski and Greta Garbo in Rome, hiding their faces from paparazzi, is in *A Counterpoint of View*. Chasins gives a vivid account of the January 1938 filming sessions; the music actually used in the film was recorded in Philadelphia more than a year later. Because Stokowski didn't propose including the Toccata and Fugue in D Minor until that November, the Bach sequence that opens the movie may not date from the January 1938 all-night sessions, noirishly appealing as it is to think of the silhouetted musicians walking after midnight, wired on coffee.

14

The account of a fantasia is drawn from Williams's and Boyd's biographies of Bach and especially from the *Oxford Composer Companion*. Boyd quotes Reinken, p. 73; Mattheson's retrospective account of the audition, printed in the Cöthen section of *The New Bach Reader*, p. 91, does not include the term *stylus fantasticus*, which he applied to Bach in 1739. *Walt Disney's Fantasia* makes clear, pp. 32–39, that Stokowski urged Bach on Disney. The title of the film was a hanging question right up to the end; having introduced the term to Disney, Stokowski was nervous about it, especially about Americans' insistence on saying it with a long *a* in the middle. A title contest was held at the Disney studio, Gabler recounts, p. 316, and drew nearly eighteen hundred suggestions. One was *Highbrowski by Stokowski*.

15

Stokowski's exchange with Disney in story meetings about the nature of the Toccata and Fugue in D Minor is given by Culthane in *Walt Disney's Fantasia*, pp. 39–41. It is given in quotation marks there, in the form of a script here. Culhane and Gabler both described Disney's working methods, the role of Oskar Fischinger, and the process of story meetings, which were presented by Paul Hollister in "Genius at Work: Walt Disney," *The Atlantic*, December 1940. Chasins, a musician, was put off by the need for explanations; as he saw it, p. 174, "Walt was scared to death by the very name of Bach, so that Stoki was in the double role of teacher and salesman. He was not talking to musicians—he had to explain the work to people who really couldn't understand." Disney's hope to change motion pictures with the "Concert Feature" is recounted by Gabler, p. 306. His characterization of himself as a person who would walk out on the Toccata and Fugue in D Minor—from a story meeting—is quoted by Gabler, p. 301.

16

Fantasia has been rereleased many times in many formats. This account is based on a "Special 60th Anniversary Edition" featuring "Walt Disney's Original Uncut Version." Disney's stress on a single image was recalled by the continuity man Mike Pike, quoted by Culhane, p. 42: "And the theme! Oh, my God! Don't forget the theme! It repeats seven times throughout the *Fugue*!"

17

Disney's flip comment about the war is quoted by Gabler, p. 348.

Schweitzer's activities during the run-up to the war are set out in Everett Skilling's "Postscript 1932–49" to *Out of My Life and Thought* and in Brabazon's biography. Pablo Casals describes his attempt to gain passage in both memoirs. Stoki's efforts with a new orchestra are set out in *A Counterpoint of View*, in a chapter called "The All American Youth Orchestra." In the chapter "Bach-Stokowski," p. 444, the violinist David Madison recalled Stokowski's copyist, Lucien Cailliet, transcribing the third partita aboard ship more or less as the orchestra played it: "He had a music score in front of him and as we went along he filled it in. He had it ready the next day for copying. We all got together and copied out all the parts. We rehearsed it and when we got to South America we played it . . ." A Gala CD collects the orchestra's 1941 recordings of those Bach "symphonic transcriptions."

A history of the London lunchtime concerts initiated by Myra Hess is given on the National Gallery website, www.nationalgallery.org.uk. The first concert was given on Tuesday, October 10, 1939. "Jesu, Joy of Man's Desiring" is a transcribed chorale from cantata 174; various Hess performances of her transcriptions can be heard on YouTube. Nearly seventeen hundred concerts were given at the National Gallery during the war; one series presented all forty-eight preludes and fugues from the *Well-Tempered Clavier*, another the complete *Art of the Fugue*.

18

Gabler sets out the events surrounding the release of *Fantasia*, including the *New York Times* review of *Pinocchio*. He quotes the *Times* review of the *Fantasia* premiere and reports that it rained in New York that evening. Janet Flanner's evocation of wartime Paris is from a "Letter from Paris" (signed Genêt), *The New Yorker*, December 7, 1940, p. 52. *The Atlantic* ran its profile of Disney in the December 1940 issue; Stokowski was featured on the cover of *Time*, November 18, 1940. Disney commented on the reception of the film in a letter to Stokowski, quoted by Daniel, p. 39. Stokowski's recording session the day after the premiere is on the Gala CD, which gives the recording dates. His insight about music and "the brotherhood of man" is from *Music for All of Us*.

The account of Bach in the Blitz is drawn from *Blitz*, by Margaret Gaskin (Harcourt, 2005), p. 118; Ernie Pyle's description of the Alert is on p. 206; the schedule for the Sunday Home Service of December 29, 1940, is on p. 272; parts three and four of the *Christmas Oratorio* were scheduled for 9:25 p.m. Gaskin describes the destruction of All Hallows in detail, pp. 258–59; she describes the organ melting inside a neighboring church, St. Lawrence Jewry, p. 250.

19

Schweitzer described civilization "in darkness" in a summary of his thought for the *Christian Century*, November 21/28, 1934, quoted in *Out of My Life and Thought*. His wartime activities are described by Everett Skillings in the book's postscript: a 1946 letter by Emma Haussknecht, a nurse at the clinic, is excerpted there, p. 207. Skillings describes the origins of the Fellowship; Schweitzer mentioned his hope of taking a vacation in a letter to the Fellowship on the occasion of his seventieth birthday in January 1945, excerpted in the postscript, pp. 209–10.

Brabazon, who chronicles the war years in detail, tells of Schweitzer hearing one of his own recordings on the BBC, p. 394.

20

Casals's life during wartime, amply recounted in the memoirs, is fleshed out in the two biographies. Casals recalled nights of music-making in Paris in *Joys and Sorrows*, p. 243, and spoke of the photo of Ysaÿe in *Conversations*, p. 85, explaining that it was given to him in 1939 by the English musician Philip Newman, who had gotten it from Elisabeth, who took the photograph. Casals told the story of the SS's visit to his villa in both memoirs; this passage combines an excerpt from *Joys and Sorrows*, pp. 240–41 (where he mentions listening to BBC broadcasts during the war), with one from *Conversations*, p. 217.

The dates of EMI's releases of the cello suites are set out in Siblin's *The Cello Suites*; on p. 115, there is a footnote about their initial release: "The 12-inch 78 rpm records were released on the Victor label in three installments, beginning with suites two and three in 1940, one and six the following year, and four and five in 1950." A note to the footnote, p. 281, indicates that "the discs were released in England earlier than in North America, with the first two installments appearing in 1938 and the third one in 1948."

Casals expressed his wish that the recordings "could be sped up slightly" to Lev Ginsberg; it is quoted in Baldock, p. 156. He developed the same idea in *Conversations*, p. 209: "I should like to hear what has been done with the recordings of the Bach suites I made in 1937 and 1939, which have been adapted for long-playing records. It took me over a year to prepare these. I should be interested to see if the slow movements are not spoiled by mechanical factors, and if the personality of the performer comes through. As a rule, I prefer to hear the records I have made played faster. In the case of my records of the Bach Suites I like to hear them a tone, even a tone and a half, sharper. The difference of keys does not worry me at all."

PART IV: TECHNICAL TRANSCENDENCE

1

James Watson told the story of the discovery of the structure of DNA in *The Double Helix* (1968; Touchstone, 2001); the quoted passage is on p. 171. Richard Powers elegantly combined the discovery of DNA and Bach's *Goldberg Variations* in a novel, *The Gold Bug Variations* (William Morrow, 1991), treated in the notes to part six here.

This account of the postwar outlook is grounded in *Postwar*, by Tony Judt (Penguin Press, 2005), and *The Age of Extremes*, by Eric Hobsbawm (Vintage, 1996). Greil Marcus evokes "the old, weird America" in a book by that title, originally published as *Invisible Republic* (Holt, 1997). Albert Einstein's love of music is treated in *Einstein: His Life and Universe*, by Walter Isaacson (Simon & Schuster, 2008). The *Life* photograph can be seen on the Web. Einstein's remark about "the clear contructions of Bach" is widely quoted, especially in anthologies of his remarks; the others are from a photocopied sheet given to me by John McPhee.

Donald Tovey's distinction between "architectural" music and "dramatic" music is set out in *The Art of Fugue*, by Joseph Kerman (University of California Press, 2008).

The history of Steinway is the subject of much journalism and the book *Piano*, by James Barron (Times Books, 2007), and figures into *Romance on Three Legs: Glenn Gould's Obsessive Quest for the Perfect Piano*, by Katie Hafner (Bloomsbury, 2008).

2

Rosalyn Tureck's story is told in the notes to various CDs: EMI's reissue of her 1957 *Goldberg Variations*, in the Great Recordings of the Century series; VAI Audio's CD of a 1948 Town Hall recital, called *The Young Visionary*; Deutsche Grammophon's two double-CD sets of the *Well-Tempered Clavier*; and the double-CD set of the Bach partitas in Philips / EMI Classics' Great Pianists of the 20th Century series. It was rounded out in obituaries for her published in *The New York Times* (by Allan Kozinn; July 19, 2003) and on the *Guardian* website, www .guardian.co.uk (July 19, 2003). She described her "sudden blinding insight" about Bach numerous times, using slightly different language each time, this account is taken from the *Great Recordings of the Century* booklet. A *New York Times* review (December 29, 1937) of an all-Bach Town Hall Recital makes reference to an earlier recital featuring the complete *Goldberg Variations*. The *Times* ran a review of a 1944 recital featuring the *Goldberg Variations* (February 6, 1944). The paper also reviewed her *Goldberg*s recitals in 1946 (October 2, 1946) and 1947 (October 23, 1947). From the 1947 review: "The work takes an hour and fourteen minutes to play. At the conclusion, in response to applause that brought her back to the stage four times, Miss Tureck rightly explained that she couldn't play anything else after such a master work. But she could repeat some of the variations if the audience would request them. It was a tribute to the clarity and distinctness with which she set forth each of the thirty variations that members of the audience had no difficulty in recalling them individually by number. They called out at least a dozen"—which suggests, too, that the *Goldberg*s, in part through Tureck's efforts, were by then much better known, especially to pianists, than is usually acknowledged. The photograph of Tureck at the piano is reproduced in the *Great Recordings of the Century* booklet.

There is plenty of other evidence that the *Goldberg Variations* were already prominent as concert pieces. In a conversation with Pablo Casals that took place prior to 1954, José María Corredor remarked that Donald Tovey had played them in Berlin in 1901, and, according to a biographer, "this interpretation of the work made a sensation in the German capital, where the audience seemed to be hearing it for the first time," Corredor said, adding, "however incredible this may appear." Casals replied: "It is not so surprising. Something of the same kind happened to me with the Bach Suites. It was necessary to show the Germans how mistaken they were in their conception of how to play Bach. The *Goldberg Variations* played by Tovey sounded like a new work . . ." Wanda Landowska played the *Goldberg Variations* at Town Hall in February 1942, and, according to her companion, Denise Restout, in "Landowska the Writer," published in *Landowska on Music* (Stein and Day, 1964), "the endless ovation she received from both the audience and the press after her stunning performance will remain engraved forever in the annals of music in New York." As early as 1933 (the year of her first electric recording of the *Goldberg Variations*), Landowska had written a long, learned note about the *Goldbergs*, marveling at how the work had "remained forgotten for so long." Also in early 1942, Claudio Arrau made a recording of the *Goldbergs* for RCA Victor in New York, having played the work during a twelve-recital series of Bach's complete keyboard works in Berlin in 1935 and 1936. His recording (Tom Deacon explains in notes to a 2003 Philips CD reissue) was set aside and forgotten after Landowska, who was older and better known, made a plan to record the *Goldbergs* for the same company.

An Introduction to the Performance of Bach: A Progressive Anthology of Keyboard Music Edited, with Introductory Essays, by Rosalyn Tureck was published in three slim volumes (Oxford, 1960). Tureck stated her view of the need to adhere to the "frame and idiom" of the work itself in the preface, where she also seemed to rebut the early *Times* review that characterized her as a child of the "mechanical age." She stressed that music is an art and not a "mechanical reproduction," and declared: "I do not wish to prescribe a precise and unalterable formula in this edition, to be carried out by every individual with the repetitiveness of a duplicating machine."

3

Tureck founded a research organization called Composers of Today in 1949. George Orwell's transposition of the 4 and the 8 in 1948 was explained to me by Robert Giroux, editor in chief at *1984*'s American publisher, Harcourt Brace. The early history of television is set out in *The Master Switch*, by Tim Wu (Knopf, 2010); the history of Fender electric guitars in *Fender: The Golden Age 1946–1970*, by Martin Kelly, Terry Foster, and Paul Kelly (Cassell, 2010). The development of the long-playing record is treated in *Playback*, in *The Ambient Century*, in *EMI: The First 100 Years*, and in *The Fabulous Phonograph*, where Roland Gelatt remarked on Stokowski on p. 279.

Gelatt also dramatized the postwar recording boom, singling out Landowska's 1946 recording of the *Goldberg Variations*. Landowska's American years are chronicled in "Landowska the Writer." The history of magnetic tape is treated in the several histories of audio recordings cited here; the first reel-to-reel tape recorder used at Abbey Road is shown in *EMI: The First 100 Years*, p. 152. The summer-solstice press conference is described in *The Label*, p. 163.

4

Elizabeth Bishop's letter to Robert Lowell is in *Words in Air: The Complete Correspondence Between Elizabeth Bishop and Robert Lowell*, ed. Thomas Travisano with Saskia Hamilton

(Farrar, Straus and Giroux, 2008). During the WKCR Bachfest one year, Teri Noel Towe conducted an interview with Rosalyn Tureck devoted to her Town Hall recital of November 17, 1948; together, they listened to the recording piece by piece, swapping insights about it. I sought a recording of the interview from both Towe and WKCR, but neither the collector-scholar nor the station would provide one; I hope to draw on it in a later edition.

Tureck's recital at the Technical Hall in Ottawa was reviewed in the *Ottawa Citizen*. Her program at the Eaton Auditorium was confirmed for me by telephone and e-mail by an archivist of the Women's Musical Society of Toronto, sponsor of the recital.

5

Glenn Gould is the subject of many books, among them three biographies: *A Life and Variations*, by Otto Friedrich (Random House, 1989); *Glenn Gould: The Ecstasy and Tragedy of Genius*, by Peter F. Ostwald (Norton, 1997); and *Wondrous Strange: The Life and Art of Glenn Gould*, by Kevin Bazzana (Oxford, 2004). The two later biographies are indebted to *Glenn Gould: Music & Mind*, by Geoffrey Payzant, written as a Ph.D. thesis and then published by Key Porter Books in Toronto, and reviewed in *The Globe and Mail* by Gould himself. Gould's remarks about Tureck are taken from *Conversations with Glenn Gould*, by Jonathan Cott (Sarah Lazin Books/Little, Brown, 1984), pp. 62–64.

The Glenn Gould Reader, edited and with an introduction by Tim Page (Vintage, 1990), brings together Gould's writings, sensibly and persuasively organized; this book is the case for Gould in all the roles that have been claimed for him other than pianist: cultural critic, visionary, sage, technological adept. The extracted prose pieces here are drawn from essays in that book, and from interviews: "homophonically inclined" from a 1970 interview quoted by Bazzana, p. 63, "the Philharmonic broadcasts" from the CBC film *Glenn Gould on Record* (1960), Hofmann's recital in Toronto from the Radio Canada broadcast *At Home with Glenn Gould* (1959), *Fantasia* from "Stokowski in Six Scenes," Gould's debut with orchestra from "A Desert Island Discography," and the vacuum-cleaner moment from "Advice to a Graduation." Payzant's chronology "Glenn Gould from Ten to Twenty" is an appendix to *Glenn Gould: Music & Mind*. A subsequent, more detailed chronology by Kevin Bazzana is featured on www.glenngould .com. Gould described "indulging in experiments at home with primitive tape recorders" from "Music and Technology," and the relative roles of foreground and background from "Advice to a Graduation."

Gould executed a faithful imitation of a Schnabel recording during his debut with orchestra, recalled in "A Desert Island Discography." Payzant's "Glenn Gould from Ten to Twenty: A Chronology" is appendix I to *Glenn Gould: Music & Mind*.

6

The translation of the Magnificat (Luke 1:46–56) is taken from the notes to the recording by the Academy of St.-Martin-in-the-Fields, Neville Marriner, conductor (EMI CD, 1991).

Bach's dispute at Köthen after the prince married an *amusa* is set out in the recent English-language biographies. The term *amusa* is Bach's own; he recalled his time at Köthen in a letter of 1730, in *The New Bach Reader*. Washington, p. 75, stresses the limits of non-Calvinist education there.

The description of Leipzig is based especially on Wolff's biography, chapter eight, and on materials I observed in Leipzig's churches and other sites during a 2011 visit. Pelikan characterized the church year as the "framework" of Bach's genius in his chapter "The Four Seasons of J. S. Bach," p. 10. Wolff's account of Bach's application to the liturgical year in chapter eight is extensive, with tables and other apparatus. Wolff hails the Magnificat on p. 289.

7

The report of Bach's arrival in Leipzig, from the Hamburg *Staats- und Gelehrte Zeitung*, May 29, 1723, is in *The New Bach Reader*; Wolff uses it at the head of his eighth chapter. The selection process is set out in detail by Wolff and Williams (who provides a chronology), drawing on materials in the *Reader*. The description of Leipzig and its churches is based on my 2011 visit. Pelikan, wholly enthusiastic about sacred music, even so declares, p. 9, that "the nonfestive cycle of the church year could become quite dreary and didactic" and that "this presented a genuine challenge for the church musician, as Bach discovered when he moved to Leipzig . . ." Pelikan quotes Philipp Spitta, whose *Bach* (2 vols., 1873, 1880) is the basis for much subsequent biographical writing about Bach: "Remarkable as was the activity displayed by him as a church composer during this period, yet he had no opportunity of showing himself in his full greatness until the beginning of the ecclesiastical year 1723–1724."

A Table of the "First Annual Cantata Cycle" is in Wolff, pp. 270–71. The two cantatas singled out for discussion here are "Die Elenden sollen essen" (BWV 75) and "Die Himmel erzahlen die Ehre Gottes" (BWV 76). The *Oxford Composer Companion*, in an entry by Daniel R. Melamed, takes up the notion that the celebrated motet "Jesu, meine Freude" was composed at the time, concluding that "there is no evidence to support the much discussed hypothesis that it was composed for a 1723 memorial service." Bach's first months in Leipzig and his responsibilities there are treated brilliantly in Williams's sections "New Life in Leipzig" and "The Place of Cantatas."

8

Pablo Casals described receiving the *Bach-Gesellschaft* in *Joys and Sorrows*, p. 261. Alexander Schneider's effort to fund it is described by Baldock, pp. 186–87, and in Martin Leigh's notes to *Bach Festival Prades 1950* (Pearl, 2 CDs). Casals called Prades a "Pyrennean retreat" in a 1945 address to the people of England, reprinted in *Conversations with Casals*, p. 221. His postwar engagements are set out by Baldock, his vow explained in *Joys and Sorrows*, p. 257: "I would not play again in public until the democracies changed their attitude toward Spain." He described "renewing contact with Bach's immortal message" each morning in his introduction to *Conversations*. In a note he prepared for the 1950 Prades festival, quoted in *Conversations*, p. 109, he put it this way: "The miracle of Bach has not appeared in any other art. To strip human nature until its divine attributes are made clear, to inform ordinary activities with spiritual fervour, to give wings of eternity to that which is most ephemeral; to make divine things human and human things divine; such is Bach, the greatest and purest moment in music of all time."

José María Corredor recalled his visits to the Master in *Conversations*, Bernard Greenhouse his lessons in a 1992 interview with Robert Baldock, which features in Baldock's biography, pp. 177–80. The visit of the young American woman who would go next to see Schweitzer is in *Conversations with Casals*, p. 230. The invitations to Casals are in Baldock, p. 184–85. Baldock characterized the festival and detailed Columbia's involvement in his chapter "Resurrection: The Bach Festival." Much of the local detail is drawn from Flanner's "Letter from Prades" (signed "Genêt"), *The New Yorker*, June 17, 1950. *Life* ran its photograph on May 15, 1950.

9

The description of occupied Vienna is taken from Gottfried Kraus's notes to Andante's 3-CD set of the 1950 *St. Matthew Passion* (2003), with the Vienna Symphony and Choir led by Herbert von Karajan; Menuhin's performances are remarked on in those notes, too. "Gunther Ramin, choirmaster of Leipzig's St. Thomas Choir, played the D minor Toccata and Fugue to open the first concert . . ." Kraus notes. Dinn Lipatti's story is told in the notes to EMI's Great Recordings of the Century CD of Lipatti's recordings of Bach, Scarlatti, and Schubert. The story of the Bachhaus renovation is told at the Bachhaus, the story of the *Neue-Bach-Gesellschaft* in the *Oxford Composer Companion*.

Theodor Adorno's "Bach Defended Against His Devotees" is in *Essays on Music*, ed. Richard Leppart (University of California Press, 2002). The different stages of Adorno's life are recounted in different ways in *Artists in Exile*, *Postwar*, *The Rest Is Noise*, and *The Bach Reader*.

Baldock's richly detailed account of the 1950 Bach Festival in Prades is the most vivid section of his biography of Casals. *Life*'s second story about the festival ran June 26, 1950. Casals's letter to President Truman is given in Kirk, pp. 464–65. Lipatti's last concert is described in the EMI liner notes, which do not identify the Bach chorale he played.

10

Glenn Gould gave an exuberant description of his CBC radio debut as the opening of "Music and Technology," in *The Glenn Gould Reader*. He described his determination to "set out on my own snowshoes" in Joseph Roddy's *New Yorker* profile "Apollonian," included in *Variations*. The cottage is pictured in the photo insert of *Wondrous Strange*. Bert Gould's remark about his son's preparations is quoted by Friedrich, p. 40. Gould called the tape recorder "the greatest of all teachers" in a conversation with a friend, quoted by Ostwald, p. 89. The photograph of him working a tape recorder is in Ostwald's biography, p. 91.

Gould declared that he learned the *Goldberg Variations* "entirely on my own" in a 1959 interview excerpted in a footnote by Bazzana, p. 113; his insights about the work are from the liner notes to the so-called 1955 recording, printed in *The Glenn Gould Reader*.

11

Life ran a photo essay under the headline THE GREATEST MAN IN THE WORLD—THAT IS WHAT SOME PEOPLE CALL ALBERT SCHWEITZER, JUNGLE PHILOSOPHER, October 6, 1947; Brabazon uses this as a subtitle to his chapter about Schweitzer's U.S. visit, where he describes the time Schweitzer was mistaken for Einstein on the Zephyr, the two polls, the Nobel Peace Prize, and the petitions to which he was signatory. The *Time* cover and article were dated July 11, 1949. Schweitzer's epilogue to a scholar's study of his philosophy is in the postscript to *Out of My Life and Thought*.

The account of Schweitzer's time in Europe after the war is my own; the view of the camp, registered by the English reporter James Cameron for the *News Chronicle*, is reported by Brabazon, pp. 431ff.; Brabazon reproduces Schweitzer's correspondence with Einstein about the *Philosophy of Civilization* and other matters, pp. 401–403. Dr. Charles R. Joy and Melvin Arnold, two American donors to the hospital, recorded their impressions of a visit to Lambaréné in an article for the *Christian Register*, September 1947, quoted by Brabazon, p. 403.

Albert Schweitzer, released in 1957, was released on DVD by Roan in 2005; the bonus features include Thurston Moore, of the band Sonic Youth, speaking on the play "The Words of Schweitzer and the Music of Bach." Brabazon, p. 454, points out that Schweitzer did not see the film until 1959. The sleeve of the Columbia Masterworks LP *Albert Schweitzer: Bach*, designed by Ben Shahn, can be seen on the Web; the recording process dubbed the "Schweitzer Technique" is explained in the Schweitzer entry on Wikipedia. Brabazon, p. 428, mentions the record player given to Schweitzer for his eightieth birthday in 1955.

12

The Prades box set was on view for a time in the window of Academy Records in Manhattan. Pearl's 2-CD set contains the Brandenburg concertos and the *Musical Offering*. *Billboard* reported their staying power in its distinctive argot, February 3, 1951.

Robert Snyder's documentary of Pablo Casals can be seen in segments on YouTube; an obituary in the *Los Angeles Times*, March 22, 2004, gave particulars of Snyder's career. Casals's post-Perpignan travels are described by Baldock. The photograph of Schweitzer and Casals is in Kirk, p. 468; Casals said "Schweitzer was kind enough to come and see me in Zurich" in *Conversations*, p. 101, and recalled their conversation, p. 231, prompted by Corredor, who asked him about the photograph.

Yousuf Karsh's project In Search of Greatness is described in the book by that title (Knopf, 1962); many of his photographs can be seen on the Web. W. Eugene Smith's journey is a topic in the biography of him by Sam Stephenson (Farrar, Straus and Giroux, forthcoming); Smith's later photographs of Glenn Gould are featured in the "tray card" of *A State of Wonder*. The photograph of Casals and Schweitzer striding through Gunsbach, trailed by Marta Montañez, is in the photo section of Baldock's biography.

13

Music Quickens Time, by Daniel Barenboim (Verso, 2008), includes the essay "I Was Raised on Bach." Barenboim recalled his command performance for Wilhelm Furtwängler in a public conversation with Edward W. Said, March 8, 2000, published in *Parallels and Paradoxes: Explorations in Music and Society* (ed. Ara Guzelimian; Vintage, 2004). Barenboim made his remark about music as a "no-man's-land" later in the conversation.

14

Bert Gould's account of how he invented the adjustable folding chair is quoted by Friedrich, p. 49. Glenn Gould's CBC performances were issued on two separate CDs in 1993 and 1995. The first disc features Partita No. 5, the Sinfonias, the *Italian Concerto*, and the *Concerto in D Minor*; the second disc, the *Goldberg Variations* and four sets of preludes and fugues from the *Well-Tempered Clavier*. The recordings are made from CBC airchecks (archival recordings made by the company during the broadcast) and acetates such as those given to the artists. Gould in "Music and Technology" explained the pleasure the acetates gave him: "I was presented with a soft-cut 'acetate,' a disc which dimly reproduced the felicities of the broadcast in question and which, even today, a quarter-century after the fact, I still take down from the shelf on occasion . . ." The notes to the 1995 disc report: "In the case of the *Goldberg Variations* Gould's own disc is the only known copy of this performance"—an amazing instance of a recording artist acting as his own archivist.

To review these recordings, I put them in chronological sequence on an iTunes playlist—using recording dates given in the notes—and compared the sequence with the table of Gould's radio performances included as an appendix to Friedrich's biography.

Kevin Bazzana's incisive characterization of Gould's view of Bach is on p. 92 of his biography. The circumstances of Gould's *Goldberg Variations* broadcast on the summer solstice are given in the notes to the CBC CD.

Gustav Leonhardt's recording of the *Goldberg Variations*, played on harpsichord in Vienna, June 1953, was reissued on a Vanguard Classics CD in 2005. Gould quoted Ralph Kirkpatrick in his notes to the 1955 *Goldberg Variations*, printed in *The Glenn Gould Reader*.

Gould's efforts to assemble an all-Bach concert, and the circumstances of the concert itself, are described in detail by Bazzana, p. 113, whose book is strong on the distinctly Canadian aspects of Gould's story. How the critic Harvey Olnick came to attend the concert, and how he reacted to Gould's playing, is in Ostwald, p. 108.

15

Gould's U.S. debut is treated in all three biographies, and in the notes to *A State of Wonder*, by Tim Page; Page must know as much about Gould as anyone alive, but the notes state in apparent error that Gould played the *Goldberg Variations* at the Washington recital, and made them its "centerpiece." Friedrich gives the New York program, p. 41, and declares, p. 45, that "taking no chances before this important audience, Gould played the same pieces he had played so successfully in Washington." The triumph of New York over Boston as a classical music center is dramatized in Horowitz's *Classical Music in America*. The program is given in the biographies, all of which draw on Paul Hume's review in *The Washington Post* ("Masterly Recital Played by Pianist Glenn Gould," January 3, 1955). Gould told Joseph Roddy, who attended the recording session for the fifth partita in reporting the *New Yorker* profile, that in 1957 he had played the piece more than five hundred times since first playing it at age eighteen. Bazzana, p. 147, gives a list of great musicians who played at Town Hall in January 1955; I have chiseled it down to musicians especially devoted to Bach.

Otto Friedrich, who interviewed David Oppenheim, tells the story of the tip Schneider gave Oppenheim, p. 44, and tells of a hundred people going to see Gould backstage at Town Hall. The *Times* review by "J.B." (John Briggs) ran January 12, 1955.

16

J. M. Coetzee's "What Is a Classic?," which originated as a lecture given in Graz, Austria, in 1991, is in *Stranger Shores: Literary Essays 1986–1999* (Penguin, 2002). The state of play of Bach recordings circa 1955 is assembled from the notes to the named recordings and from the Recordings entry of the *Oxford Composer Companion*; the state of play of popular music is assembled from *The Rolling Stone Illustrated History of Rock & Roll*, ed. Jim Miller (Random House/Rolling Stone Press, 1980), and *Last Train to Memphis: The Rise of Elvis Presley*, by Peter Guralnick (Little, Brown, 1994). The link of Bach to Bill Haley through the Pythian Temple is my own, derived from a close reading of the notes to the recordings.

The history of 30th Street Studio is given at www.gothamist.com, which features photographs of the exterior.

17

Gould's CBC performances of the Sinfonias (March 15, 1955) and the Concerto in D Minor (March 29, 1955) are on the CBC CD. The crush of admirers after a Winnipeg concert is recalled in "Reminiscences," by John Roberts, in *Variations*. Ostwald in his chapter "First Contact with Psychiatry" argues that Gould's mental ailments were aggravated by his success, and reports Gould's emergency room visit, p. 121. Gould spoke of his fear of dealing with people in conversation with the photographer Jock Carroll for *Weekend*, quoted in Ostwald, p. 122.

The dates of Gould's sessions at 30th Street Studio are given in the notes to various *Goldberg Variations* CDs. Gould's behavior in the studio was described in the press release Columbia put out about the sessions, quoted by Payzant, pp. 15–16, and then ad infinitum, especially about Gould's predilection for "arrowroot biscuits." Photographs of Gould's gloved hands, stockinged feet, and chair are in *Variations*, pp. 36–37. The Columbia staff photographer Dan Weiner took photographs of the sessions. Martin Mayer, interviewed by Friedrich, pp. 50–51, recounted accompanying Gould to his hotel near Central Park: "Was that the St Moritz?" Gould's choice of Steinway 174 is set out in *Romance on Three Legs*, pp. 174–75. Gould can be heard jousting with a technician in the outtakes from the sessions included in *A State of Wonder*; the 1955 recordings of three Sinfonias are included in Sony's reissue of the *Goldberg Variations*; in the reissue of the *Two and Three Part Inventions*, there is both a complete take and an "outtake" for Sinfonias 8, 15, and 9. Bazzana in a footnote, p. 242, reports that "Gould noted in 1966 that he had previously attempted integral recordings of the *Inventions* in 1955 and 1963, 'and on both occasions had rejected the results out of hand.'" The recording date for the Sinfonias is given in the notes to the CD of the *Inventions*. The passages about the nature of invention are from Laurence Dreyfus's *Bach and the Patterns of Invention*. Gould's and Scott's patter can be heard in the outtakes.

Saul Bellow's remark is from a letter of June 14, 1955, in *Letters* (Viking, 2010). Flannery O'Connor described her New York trip in letters published in *The Habit of Being* (Farrar, Straus and Giroux, 1979); the trip is dramatized in my book *The Life You Save May Be Your Own* (Farrar, Straus and Giroux, 2003), as is Dorothy Day's preparations for a demonstration at City Hall. Alberto Giacometti's exhibitions feature in *Giacometti*, by James Lord (Farrar, Straus and Giroux, 1986). The Viking editor Evelyn Levine's remarks on the manuscript of *On the Road* are in *The Beats: A Literary Reference*, ed. Matt Theado (Carroll & Graf, 2001), p. 159, as is the photograph of Allen Ginsberg's apartment on Montgomery Street, p. 235; the Vienna Philharmonic *Mass in B Minor* LP was identified with a magnifying glass and a Google search. The passage about the apartment is from a note Ginsberg wrote about the photograph, also on p. 235; the passage about "angelheaded hipsters who . . . build harpsichords in their lofts" is quoted at considerable expense from *Howl* (1956).

18

The dates of Gould's *Goldberg Variations* sessions are given in the notes to *A State of Wonder* and elsewhere. Gould's essay "The Prospects of Recording" (1966) is in *The Glenn Gould Reader*. The philosophical aspects of Gould's approach to recording were first explored by Geoffrey Payzant in *Music & Mind*; I have sought to develop them—to amplify them—here. Gould's evocation of the postwar Bach as an "artisan" is in "Stokowski in Six Scenes," in *The Glenn Gould Reader*. His practice of learning pieces—entering them into memory—away from the piano is discussed in Bazzana, p. 326, and elsewhere.

19

Columbia's press release, by Debbie Ishton, is cited by Otto Friedrich and others. Dan Weiner's photographs of the 1955 sessions are on the sleeve or booklet of many editions of Gould's 1955 *Goldberg Variations*. The outtakes are included in *A State of Wonder*. Gould's account of how he recorded the aria last, in twenty-one takes, from a 1967 CBC radio broadcast, is quoted in Payzant, p. 37.

20

Gould spoke about "solitude" apropos of Schoenberg in his television documentary *The Age of Ecstasy, 1900–1910*, which aired on the CBC in 1974. He characterized "a state of wonder" in his 1962 essay "Let's Ban Applause," reprinted in *The Glenn Gould Reader*. He commented on the *Goldberg Variations* in his notes to the Columbia LP, also in the *Reader*.

21

Gould's activities in the second half of 1955 are reported in Bazzana's biography, and in his chronology for www.glenngould.com; the formal studio photograph of Gould, by Donald McKague, is in Ostwald, p. 118. Gould's boyhood friend John Beckwith recalled him dating a CBC staff member and showing her the *Goldberg Variations* sleeve in "Shattering a Few Myths," included in *Variations*. Friedrich, p. 286, gives her name: Elizabeth Fox.

22

The catalog listing of the *Goldberg Variations* LP is given in Bazzana, p. 153. André Malraux's *The Voices of Silence*, published in its definitive English form by the Bollingen Press in 1953, has as its part I "Museum Without Walls." Gould cited the book in "The Prospects of Recording" in 1966 and referred to "this Malrauvian museum" in "Should We Dig Up the Rare Romantics?" in 1969. His insight about "that replenishment of invention" is from "Advice to a Graduation," given in 1964. All three essays are in *The Glenn Gould Reader*.

23

Gould's remark that he didn't enjoy being a "concert performer" is quoted by Bazzana, p. 181. He was characterized in *Maclean's*, April 28, 1956; *Time*, February 6, 1956; and *Harper's Magazine*, March 1956. Gould called 1956 "the most difficult year I have ever faced" in an interview quoted by Friedrich, p. 55. He recharacterized Bach in the sleeve notes for his recording *Beethoven's Last Three Piano Sonatas*, released in September 1956, and remarked on Albert Schweitzer in "The Dodecacophonist's Dilemma," a 1956 essay reprinted (as are the sleeve notes) in *The Glenn Gould Reader*.

Glamour is quoted in Friedrich, p. 53; *Glamour, Vogue*, and *Life* in Bazzana, p. 156. Gould's confession of his maladies to Jock Carroll is quoted in Bazzana, p. 358. Gelatt's suspicion of "Columbia's selling campaign" is in Bazzana, p. 255. Gould's recital schedule is given, with some variations, as an appendix to Friedrich's biography and on www.glenngould.com. Audience and press reactions are given in all three biographies. Gould spoke at length about his stage manner to journalist Bernard Asbell in 1962, quoted in Friedrich, p. 60.

Leonard Bernstein described his encounter with the *Goldberg Variations* in "The Truth About a Legend," in *Variations*; he dates it as the summer of 1955, and says the record (which was released in early 1956) "had just come out." The timeline at www.leonardbernstein.com gives the birthdate of Alexander Serge Leonard Bernstein as July 7, 1955. Possibly Bernstein was given an advance pressing of the Gould sessions from mid-June, though such a pressing would had to have been made virtually overnight.

The *Times* ran Harold C. Schonberg's catty review of Bernstein's performance with Gould April 7, 1962.

Bernstein recalled Gould's visit to his apartment in "The Truth About a Legend" and more effusively in an interview with Friedrich, p. 71, which is quoted here. Friedrich gives details of their recording session, pp. 71–72. Ostwald's chapter "Telephone Calls" brings together many accounts of the Gould-Bernstein collaboration, including Bernstein's sexual remark, recalled by Anton Kuerti, p. 145; Ostwald in a note comments: "It isn't clear whether Lenny's remark was made directly to Glenn or to a group of guests within his hearing."

24

James Brabazon's *Albert Schweitzer: A Biography* is especially strong on Schweitzer's role as a voice of peace in the nuclear age, particularly in the chapter "The Nobel Peace Prize and the Bomb." Schweitzer's letter to Dwight Eisenhower is in Brabazon, pp. 457–58. Pablo Casals's courtship of Marta Montañez and his relocation to Puerto Rico is described in both biographies. Baldock's chapter "Epiphany: The Discovery of Puerto Rico" is very pointed both on Casals's motives for the move to Puerto Rico and on his alliance with Schweitzer. "During April 1958," Baldock observes, p. 234, "Casals was strongly affected by three radio appeals broadcast by Schweitzer . . ."

25

"Battleship grey and midnight blue are at the top of my personal color chart," Glenn Gould declared in "Stokowski in Six Scenes," explaining his dislike for *Fantasia*. "The north has fascinated me since childhood," he announced in the prologue to his CBC radio documentary *The Idea of North*. He described his visit to the USSR in "Music in the Soviet Union." All are in *The Glenn Gould Reader*. The programs are given in Friedrich and on www.glenngould.com; the photograph of Gould in silhouette is in *Variations*, p. 94, with the caption "Concertizing in Moscow." Bazzana, p. 171, stresses the effect of Gould's Bach in Russia: "Regarded as an ecclesiastical composer, Bach was frowned on by many musicians in the officially atheistic Soviet Union. Gould's Bach arrived with the force of a revelation. As more than one Russian musician would say, even decades later, they played and thought about Bach one way before Gould, another way after . . . Most of the critics focused on Gould's Bach almost to the exclusion of everything else. The consensus was that he had revealed not only the intellect and structures of Bach, but the passion and lyricism and humanity, too." Gould's letter to his parents of June 3, 1957, from *Glenn Gould: Selected Letters* (eds. John P. L. Roberts and Ghyslaine Guertin, Oxford, 1992), is quoted in Ostwald, p. 157. Gould called Bach "out of touch with his time" in "Music in the Soviet Union," and disdained pilgrimages in search of Bach in his sleeve notes to Beethoven's last three piano sonatas; both pieces are in the *Reader*.

"Stokowski in Six Scenes," commissioned by *The New York Times Magazine*, was published in *Piano Quarterly* in 1978, and in *The Glenn Gould Reader*. Stokowski's activities in the late 1950s are chronicled in Chasins's *Leopold Stokowski: A Profile* and Daniel's *A Counterpoint of View*; Daniel, who arranged the 30th Street Studio session for his friend Henry Cowell, quotes the composer William Bergsma, who was in the control room, about Stokowski's approach, p. 666, and reports, p. 660, that Stokowski made his first recording for Capitol—of Holst's *The Planets*—in the summer of 1956. Earlier that summer, Stokowski had been strongly urged by producers of a concert in Zurich not to open with an American composition or one by Bach. Stokowski was "irate," Daniels says, and wrote: "What is wrong with his music? The three compositions I suggested are beautiful as music, with deep mystical qualities. They are seldom heard in the concert hall. Sometimes they are played in Churches, but not all organists can play this profound music with understanding; and even when it is well played, not everyone goes to Church.

"If the objection to Bach is on the question of principle that Bach's music should not be played, except in its original form, is it not being overlooked that of all the musicians in the whole of history, Bach is the one that made the most transcriptions? Bach would certainly not agree with the prejudice against transcriptions."

Gould's remarks about touring are from a 1968 CBC television profile, quoted in Bazzana, pp. 175–76. Gould's bout with the flu is detailed on pp. 184–85.

26

Virgil Thomson's denunciation of the "Music Appreciation Racket" is quoted by Joseph Horowitz in *Classical Music in America*, p. 439. The script for Leonard Bernstein's *Omnibus* program about Bach, telecast March 31, 1957, is in *The Joy of Music*.

James Friskin's 1956 recording of the *Goldberg Variations*, made at the Brooklyn Masonic Temple, was released as a Vanguard Classics CD. Rosalyn Tureck's 1957 *Goldbergs* is in EMI's Great Recordings of the Twentieth Century series, which gives the dates of the sessions. Her remark about a "valid" performance is from the preface to her *An Introduction to the Performance of Bach*; with it the onetime prodigy seems to knock the prodigy with the cudgel of "experience." Grete Sultan's non-take-two recording of the *Goldbergs* was released on CD by Concord, with notes that mention the comparison with the *Well-Tempered Clavier*. Mstislav Rostropovich's 1956 recording of the second and fifth cello suites was reissued on CD by Vanguard Classics. Jascha Heifetz's 1952 recording of the sonatas and partitas for solo violin was rereleased on CD by RCA as two discs in the Jascha Heifetz Collection; the use of the "direct-to-disk" process in the recording is described on www.jsbach.org. A Columbia CD collects E. Power Biggs's *Bach Organ Favorites* from the fifties and sixties; his story is told by Craig R. Whitney in *All the Stops*.

Gould's late-fifties Bach recordings are cataloged in an appendix to Friedrich's biography and on www.glenngould.com. Friedrich mentions Gould's royalties and his yen for the stock market, p. 292; Bazzana discusses Gould's income in detail, pp. 239–40; Ostwald mentions Gould's second thoughts about Walter Homburger's management, p. 192. Katie Hafner in *Romance on Three Legs* tells the story of Gould's romance with Steinway CD 318. Bazzana mentions Gould's plan to set a Donne sonnet; Ostwald follows Gould's effort to write a string quartet, and features a photograph of him working on it.

"Bodky on Bach" is in *The Glenn Gould Reader*, as are most of Gould's essays, lectures, reviews, and other journalism. Ostwald tells the story of his developing friendship with Gould, whom he calls a "superhypochondriac" on p. 188. Gould's fling with a harpsipiano is set out in Friedrich, p. 92, and his epiphany in South Bend on p. 93.

Ostwald, p. 178, tells that he mentioned *Conversations with Casals* to Gould in a letter, February 23, 1959, and goes on: "He liked it . . ."—which suggests that Gould in reply said that he had read it and liked it. Gould's devotion to Thomas Mann is set out in all the biographies; Bazzana makes the most of it, pp. 133–34, pointing out that Gould took part in a CBC memorial broadcast after Mann's death in 1955 and later planned to make a documentary about him. Mann's letter about Casals, sent from Erlenbach-Zürich, March 1954, is printed in full in the front matter of *Conversations with Casals*.

Gould's thirtieth birthday is a milestone touched on by Friedrich, p. 98. Gould's eventual Columbia producer Andrew Kazdin, in his memoir *Creative Lying: At Work with Glenn Gould*

(Dutton, 1989), explained the company's practice of mapping out Gould's plans for recording with him several seasons in advance, always encouraging him to record the music of Bach as often as possible.

Gould remarked on the "harmonic architecture" of Bach's music in "Bodky on Bach"; he called it the "harmonic landscape" in "Art of the Fugue" and the "harmonic environment" and "the adventurous and subjective harmonic traffic of Baroque art" in "So You Want to Write a Fugue?"—all in *The Glenn Gould Reader*. His account of the "aura of withdrawal" in the *Art of the Fugue*, and its promise of "uncompromised invention," is in "Art of the Fugue."

PART V: BOTH SIDES NOW

1

Pablo Casals's new life in Puerto Rico is documented in the two biographies; Baldock is particularly perceptive on the different aspects of the island's symbolism for Casals. Baldock discusses the changes in Casals's vow, along with Alexander Schneider's strenuous objections, on pp. 232–33. Casals's explanation of his "duty to do something" through music, given in 1962, is quoted in Kirk, pp. 530–31. The UN concert is a set piece in both biographies; a photograph of Casals and Horszowski rehearsing in the General Assembly hall is in Kirk, p. 509. Casals's statement, with its tip of the hat to Albert Schweitzer, is quoted at length by Kirk, pp. 506–10. He is called a "geriatric superstar" in Baldock, p. 235. Baldock, p. 228, mentions that one pianist proposed to Casals for the music festival in Puerto Rico was Glenn Gould, "who, he observed to Schneider, 'has not aroused enthusiasm.'"

"The Music Mountain," by Alex Ross, published in *The New Yorker*, June 29, 2009, is in his collection *Listen to This*. Casals's master class at Berkeley can be seen on YouTube.

2

Albert Schweitzer's renunciation of the organ is recounted in Brabazon's biography, pp. 499ff. John Donne wrote of renouncing "the mistress of my youth, Poetry, for the wife of mine age, Divinity" in a 1623 letter to the Marquis of Buckingham. Schweitzer's decision to speak out after Dag Hammarskjöld's death is in Brabazon, pp. 481–82.

The story of the Kennedy White House's courtship of Casals is found in both biographies; Baldock tells it with relish. The observation that Casals's decision to go followed on the raising of the Berlin Wall is my own; Casals spoke of a time to take a side in *Conversations*, p. 212.

Stokowski's letter to Casals is reproduced in *Joys and Sorrows*, p. 285. Hiao-Tsiun Ma's letter to Casals (saying that Yo-Yo Ma "thinks of you almost every day") is given by Baldock, p. 229, who remarks on H. T. Ma's "direct approach." Possibly the letter followed on the White House performance and broadcast. Helen Epstein in "Yo-Yo Ma," published in *Esquire* (1981) and then in her book *Music Talks* (Penguin, 1988), tells of Ma playing for Isaac Stern, Alexander Schneider, Pablo Casals, and Leonard Rose. The story of Yo-Yo Ma's encounter with Casals is told in *My Son, Yo-Yo*, by Marina Ma, as told to John A. Rallo (Chinese University Press, 1995). In the story, Casals had just received an invitation to perform at a benefit for a national cultural center—the National Pageant for the Arts—and decided to put forward Yo-Yo Ma as a performer. In a profile in *The New Yorker*, by David Blum (May 1, 1989), Ma recalled: "At home, I was to submerge my identity. You can't talk back to your parents—period . . . I became aware that if I was to be a cellist playing concertos I would have to have ideas of my own; that's one of the great things about being a musician. My conflict was apparent to Pablo Casals, to whom I was presented when I was seven. I don't remember what he said about my cello playing, but he did suggest that I should be given more time to go out and play in the street." Ma turned seven on October 7, 1955, seven weeks before the pageant, held on November 29, 1962.

Ma's mother, Marina Ma, in *My Son, Yo-Yo*, adds that Schneider told them that their apartment was in the same building where Casals had kept an apartment for many years. And she recalls noticing the marks made on the floor of Casals's apartment by his cello's end pin, suggesting that it was a place where he had spent considerable time, although he lived mainly in Puerto Rico in those years.

3

Stokowski's travails are gone over in the two biographies, in Daniel's at great length; the *Look* remark about Gloria Vanderbilt is quoted by Chasins, p. 212. His full schedule of conducting and recording is set out in Daniel, in the chapters "'Hooston,'" "The Summer of 1956," "The 1956–57 Season," "At Seventy-five," and "Season 1958–59," and the details of his recording contracts in "Capitol—United Artists—Everest." His transformation of the London Symphony Orchestra was praised in the London *Times*, quoted on p. 669; his taking advantage of "the art of recording" by Alfred Frankenstein in *High Fidelity*, quoted on p. 719. Mid-fifties recording innovations are described in *Good Vibrations*, *Perfecting Sound Forever*, and *The Ambient Century*; stereo is explained especially well in *The Fabulous Phonograph* chapter "The Sound of Stereo," as is the record-company practice of releasing both mono and stereo recordings, the complex production of stereo LPs, and the bonanza of the 1958 Christmas season. The development of stereo headphones, introduced in 1958, is recalled by John Koss in a video on www.koss.com. AKG, based in Vienna, produced mono headphones beginning in 1949, according to a brief history on www.akg.com. That classical-music devotees were early adopters of new technology is a running theme of the books on the history of recordings, so taken for granted that it is scarcely remarked on.

Stokowski's quarrel with Capitol Records is set out in Daniel's chapter "Capitol—United Artists—Everest"; his memo about 1958 recordings made with the French National Radio Orchestra—of works by Ibert, Ravel, and Debussy—is quoted on p. 680. Colin Wilson remarked in the *Record Review* that the orchestra's sound had been "polished till it glitters," and Alfred Kaine that it "sounds as if it had been recorded in a subway" in the *American Record Guide*, quoted on p. 682.

Stokowski's recordings of Bach transcriptions, made for Angel/EMI at the Manhattan Center (now called City Center) in February and August 1957 and February 1958, are on the EMI CD *Legend: Stokowski/Bach*.

Marshall McLuhan's key texts are in *Understanding Media: The Extensions of Man* (McGraw-Hill, 1965); his remark about exaggeration is from a letter to Robert J. Leuver quoted in *Marshall McLuhan: Escape into Understanding* (Basic, 1997), itself quoted in *Subversive Orthodoxy*, by Robert Inchausti (Brazos, 2005), p. 133.

4

Good Friday practices at the Thomaskirche, Leipzig, are described in the chapter "The 'Great Passion' and Its Context," in Wolff's biography. The insight about the resemblances among the "twin" Thomas, the structure of the Thomaskirche, the structure of the *St. Matthew Passion*, and its character as a "fraternal twin" of the *St. John Passion* is my own; Geck, p. 402, declares:

"Bach's passions are unequal sisters." Boyd, p. 156, makes the point that they share the same first chorale; Wolff especially emphasizes that the text of the *St. Matthew Passion* is purpose-built, not patched together like that of the *St. John Passion*. Christian Friedrich Henrici's role and past history with Passion oratorio is in the Picander entry of the *Oxford Composer Companion*; Geck, p. 151, points out that Henrici worked as a tax collector. All the biographers give the date of the first performance and remark that Bach himself was at the organ. The view of the interior of the church circa 1727 is based on an engraving reproduced in *J. S. Bach: Life, Times, Influence*, ed. Barbara Schwendowius and Wolfgang Dömling (Yale, 1984), and captioned: "This view shows the interior of the Thomaskirche as Bach would have known it," and on personal observation of the church itself and an exhibit about its architecture during a visit to Leipzig.

Klaus Eidam, pp. 208–9, remarks that "much ink has flowed about the *St. Matthew Passion*." Boyd's insight about the four levels of action is on p. 155 of his biography, and a discussion of its "monumental" quality on p. 157; Wolff's insight about its unity, p. 297, is developed thoroughly in the pages that follow; Geck's about his classicism is on p. 402. Karol Berger in *Bach's Cycle, Mozart's Arrow* develops the sense of time in the Passion in extraordinary fashion; he sees a further layer of time—that between the biblical events and the Evangelist's narration of them. The English translation of the gospel text is developed from a literal translation by Michael Marissen. The "satisfaction" theme is the subject of an entire chapter of Pelikan's *Bach Among the Theologians*.

Boyd's insight about the "two distinct timescales" of the *St. Matthew Passion* is on pp. 157–59. Bach's subsequent revisions to the *Passion* are set out in prose and tables in Wolff's biography.

5

Stokowski's encounters with the *St. Matthew Passion* are scattered through Daniel's biography: singing it in Temple Church, p. 439; leading an early American performance, p. 44; with the Philadelphians in 1917, p. 300; as a benefit for war resisters, p. 439 and note 9 to that chapter. Daniels also notes a 1963 performance with Beverly Sills as soprano soloist, and there were doubtless other performances, too. Stoki's deprecating remarks about the Collegiate Chorale are in Daniel's chapter "Bach—Stokowski," pp. 439–40.

The account of Ralph Vaughan Williams's recovery of traditional music is drawn especially from *Electric Eden*, by Rob Young (Faber and Faber, 2011), and from *The Rough Guide to Classical Music on CD*. The *Oxford Composer Companion* entry on reception and revival crisply observes: "Meanwhile at the Leith Hill Festival, founded in 1905, the composer Vaughan Williams (1872–1958) continued to conduct works by Bach, notably the *St Matthew Passion*, in performances which showed little or no regard for 'authenticity' in the interpretation of Baroque music." The same book's entry for recordings observes: "Ralph Vaughan Williams (1872–1958) once remarked in a BBC broadcast (c.1950) that the 'average English parlour contained *The Soul Awakening* framed on the wall, *The Way of the Eagle* on the bookshelf, and the *St Matthew Passion* on the pianoforte.'" The circumstances of Williams's final performance of the *Passion*, gone over in the notes to the Pearl CD subtitled "the Leith Hill Festival Performance of 1958," have been filled in through reference to annotated correspondence about the festival on exploringsurreyspast.org, in which the date is given as March 5, 1957, rather than 1958. Percy Grainger's exploits are set out in *Electric Eden* and in the notes to the Biddulph CD *Grainger Plays Bach and Chopin*. Williams's death is chronicled on www.rvwsociety.com.

Dietrich Fischer-Dieskau recalled his *St. Matthew Passion* sessions with Karl Richter in *Reverberations* (trans. Ruth Hein; Fromm, 1990). This sketch of Otto Klemperer's career is drawn from Joseph Horowitz's books *Classical Music in America* and *Artists in Exile*, Alex Ross's book *The Rest Is Noise, EMI: The First 100 Years*, and the *Rough Guide*, as well as the notes to the EMI CD issue of the *St. Matthew Passion*. His remark about his fees is quoted in the EMI book, p. 200. The history of Kingsway Hall is set out in the EMI book; I have rounded it out with details from the Web. The seating chart is given in the CD booklet; the photograph of Klemperer with pipe is printed in the *Rough Guide*. "Slow to the point of stateliness" is from the *Rough Guide*, Fischer-Dieskau's remark about "ritardando" from *Reverberations*, pp. 153–54. Rev. Richard John Neuhaus considered the crucifixion in *Death on a Friday Afternoon* (Basic, 2001). Klemperer's recording of Brahms's *A German Requiem* is on CD in EMI's Great Recordings of the Century series, and in the iTunes Store.

6

The title page of the *Clavier-Übung*, with its translation, is reproduced in *The New Bach Reader*, pp. 129–30, along with the poem Bach sent to Köthen. His letters of recommendation, in the *Reader*, are on behalf of Jacob Ernst Hübner, p. 126, and Christoph Gottlob Wecker, p. 132. The story of the "puzzle" canon was told by Bach's critic Johann Mattheson in 1739, quoted in the *Reader*, pp. 329–30.

Bach's dispute with the university music director over music for Christiane Eberhardine, documented in texts in the *Reader*, is described vividly by Boyd. This account of the "Trauer-Ode" is based on the Archiv recording by John Eliot Gardiner, and on the notes. The report on Christiane Eberhardine's funeral is in the *Reader*.

Bach's efforts at Prince Leopold's funeral are described in Wolff and elsewhere; the second is described by Geck, who sees it as a culmination or capstone of Bach's efforts in sacred music; cantata BWV 174, "Ich liebe den Höchsten von ganzem Gemüte," is discussed in the *Oxford Composer Companion* entries for the cantata itself and for the Brandenburg concertos.

Bach's "Short But Most Necessary Draft for a Well-Appointed Church Music, with Certain Modest Reflections on the Decline of the Same," dated August 23, 1730, is in the *Reader*, with one page reproduced, p. 148; it figures in all the biographies, and is a central text in the ongoing consideration of the appropriate size of the instrumental and vocal ensembles in the performances of Bach's music. Wilhelm Friedemann's trip to Halle on his father's behalf is summarized by Boyd, p. 72. Bach's visit to Kassel (also spelled Cassel) to inspect an organ—on which he played BWV 538, the "Dorian" Toccata and Fugue in D Minor—is documented in two local newspaper reports in the *Reader*, pp. 155–56; Boyd, p. 63, indicates that Bach played BWV 538. I know the work especially from the *Complete Organ Works* set by Walter Kraft.

7

The sleeve photograph of Glenn Gould at the organ of All Saints' Anglican Church in Toronto appears on a Sony 70th Anniversary Edition CD of Gould's recording of parts of the *Art of the Fugue*. Gould wrote about his native city in the essay "Toronto," collected in *Variations*, and his relationship with Toronto is a main theme of Bazzana's biography. Kazdin and Hafner especially also treat Gould's practice of commuting between Toronto and New York. Ostwald discusses his apartment in the Inn on the Park. Gould said he had set up the organ registrations "only at the last minute" in the CBC interview of April 30, 1967, quoted in Payzant, p. 46; he called it "up for grabs registrationally" in "Korngold and the Piano Sonata," liner notes to another pianist's 1974 LP, reprinted in *The Glenn Gould Reader*, p. 201. Gould's declaration to a

BBC producer that "I shall give no more public concerts," in a letter of April 1962, is quoted by Friedrich, p. 98. Roberts remembers the *Goldbergs* coming on during dinner with Gould at a Chinese restaurant in "Reminiscence," in *Variations*. p. 231. Gould's resistance to Columbia's warnings about quitting is in the same essay, same page.

Gould's activities in the early sixties are set out by Bazzana; his recording schedule is given in an appendix to Friedrich's biography and in the timeline on www.glenngould.com, assembled by Bazzana. In his biography Bazzana, p. 241, quotes Gould: "My idea of happiness is 250 days a year in a recording studio." The television programs from those years, many of them posted in bits and pieces on YouTube, exist all together (nineteen hours in all) on ten DVDs in *Glenn Gould on Television: The Complete CBC Broadcasts, 1954–1977* (Sony Classics, 2011). Gould's early history with the *contrapuncti* is given by Friedrich, pp. 60–63, who quotes Gould late in life calling them "my favorite Bach work," p. 312. Gould characterized their "intense, self-entrenched concentration" and Bach's "magnificent indifference to specific sonority" in "Art of the Fugue," in the *Reader*.

Walter Kraft's *Complete Organ Works* exists in a 12-CD set, Lionel Rogg's in individual CDs. Rogg's, recorded by a Swiss label left unnamed even on the British LPs, were pressed and distributed by Oryx Recordings, Burton-on-Thames, and distributed by Keith Prowse Wholesale, 117 Fulham Road, Chelsea, London. I own volume eight, which is disc two of the *Clavier-Übung III*. Gould's cultivation of the "dry" sound of the All Saints organ is explained in Bazzana, pp. 260ff.

Terry Riley's encounter with LaMonte Young in New York is dramatized in *Minimalism*, by K. Robert Schwarz, and his career sketched vividly in *The Rest Is Noise*, by Alex Ross; Gould derided his approach in a late-1960s CBC radio piece about *In C*, in the *Reader*.

8

Andrew Kazdin explained Gould's process of recording the *Two and Three Part Inventions* in *Creative Lying*, expanding on Gould's own account in his sleeve notes for the recording, reproduced on the Sony CD reissue. Gould's history with the Steinway grand piano CD 318, which figures into all the biographies, is central to Katie Hafner's *Romance on Three Legs*, which gives Gould's history with a series of pianos. "Arnold Schoenberg" and "Strauss and the Electronic Future" are in *The Glenn Gould Reader*. Vladimir Horowitz's return to concert performance is described in the notes to the Masterworks CD set *Horowitz Live and Unedited: The Historic 1965 Carnegie Hall Return Concert*. Gould's recording process is recounted in *Creative Lying*. The programs for his recitals in Chicago and Los Angeles are given in Friedrich's biography. His encounter with the Fosses, and their subsequent dealings with one another, are set out copiously in *The Secret Life of Glenn Gould: A Genius in Love*, by Michael Clarkson (ECW, 2010), and in *Genius Within: The Inner Life of Glenn Gould*, a documentary film by Michèle Hozer and Peter Raymont (2010). His 1964 CBC recording of Jan Pieterszoon Sweelinck's *Fantasia in D* was added to his 1971 *Consort of Musicke* LP for the 1993 CD release; of it, the www.amazon.com customer reviewer Kevin Orth observed: "The 'bonus' Sweelinck piece is further evidence of Gould's genius, but the sound quality is absolutely atrocious—taken from Canadian television in 1964 it sounds like something from a basement behind the Iron Curtain in the darkest, most technologically challenged days of Stalin's Cold War." The video—with Gould playing on a stage decorated with Stonehenge-style columns of ersatz marble—can be seen on YouTube. Otto Friedrich noted in his biography, pp. 60–61, that Gould played from the *Inventions* and the *Art of the Fugue* in recitals in New York in 1956 and Moscow in 1957.

9

Yo-Yo Ma recalled his father's purchase of a cassette recorder in 1964 in "A Virtuoso and His Technology," by Seth Schliesel, *The New York Times*, September 30, 2004.

10

Ringo Starr's appraisal of Beethoven is quoted in *The Beatles Forever*, by Nicholas Schaffner (Cameron House, 1977), still the best book about the Beatles and the background to the treatment of the Beatles in this section. Cassius Clay's spoken-word album for Columbia figures in *The Label*, pp. 294–95, in which Gary Marmorstein has plenty to say about Bob Dylan and Barbra Streisand. EMI's run of number one singles is reported in *Abbey Road*, p. 84. The London *Times* appraisal of Lennon and McCartney as songwriters is quoted in Schaffner, p. 23, who gives the set lists for the concerts in Washington and New York. The photograph of the Beatles making a recording in Abbey Road Studio Two is in *EMI: The First 100 Years*, p. 249; the one of John and Ringo opposite a two-manual organ is in *Abbey Road*, p. 95. George Martin's insight about Abbey Road as a "refuge" is quoted on p. 91.

Glenn Gould disparaged the Beatles in his essay "The Search for Petula Clark," published in *High Fidelity* in November 1967 (just following the highbrow mania for *Sgt. Pepper*) and reprinted in *The Glenn Gould Reader*. Federico Fellini's *La Dolce Vita* (1960) is available as a Criterion Collection DVD; Richard Locke, professor of writing in the School of the Arts at Columbia University, called my attention to the way the music of Bach figures into the film. Nicholas Schaffner in *The Beatles Forever* reported that twice as many guitars were sold in 1964 as the year before. The Byrds' lyric in "So You Want to Be a Rock 'n' Roll Star" runs: "Just get an electric guitar / and take some time, and learn how to play." George Harrison's praise for Andrés Segovia is quoted in *Beatles Gear*, by Andy Babuik (Backbeat, 2nd rev. ed., 2002), p. 119. John Williams's debut release is mentioned in *The Label*, p. 361; his background is given on Wikipedia, as is Julian Bream's, and the sleeves of their LPs can be seen and compared on the Web. There is a perceptive comparison of different guitar approaches to Bach in *Practicing: A Musician's Return to Music*, by Glenn Kurtz (Vintage, 2008). The scene on Page Street in Haight-Ashbury is drawn from *Summer of Love: The Inside Story of LSD, Rock & Roll, Free Love and High Times in the Wild West*, by Joel Selvin (Plume, 1995), pp. 8–10.

The Beatles' increasingly diverse selection of instruments is set out with great precision in *Beatles Gear*. Their way of working up a "head arrangement" is described in *Abbey Road*. That book gives John Lennon's remark about "In My Life" and Bach, p. 91, citing John Lennon, interviewed by Jann Wenner for *Rolling Stone* in 1971; Wenner's famous "Lennon Remembers" interviews took place in 1970 and were published in book form in 1971. Martin's explanation of how he executed the solo is given in *Beatles Gear*, pp. 169–70. In "Infernal Machines," his essay about music and recording technology in *Listen to This*, Alex Ross remarks: ". . . even Glenn Gould would have had trouble executing the mechanically accelerated keyboard solo in 'In My Life.'"

11

Albert Schweitzer's last days are recounted in Brabazon's biography. An obituary was published in *The New York Times*, September 6, 1965; *Time* ran an obituary for Schweitzer in the issue dated September 17, 1965, and praised Schweitzer as "an anachronism," June 21, 1963. Schweitzer described his "sympathy full of regret [for] . . . the whole creation" in *Out of My Life and Thought*. p. 186. The link of "reverence for life" with Lutheran notions of "satisfaction" is my own. His observation about Bach's "nostalgia for death" is in *Albert Schweitzer: Essential*

Writings, p. 69. The Vox Continental is described in detail in the 1965 chapter of *Beatles Gear*.

In the front matter to *A Sense of an Ending* (Oxford, 1967), Frank Kermode explains that the book originated in a series of lectures given at Bryn Mawr College in the fall of 1965. Wanda Landowska's remark is a characterization of *Landowska on Music*. Myra Hess's stroke and subsequent attempt to record a Haydn sonata are described in the notes to a BBC Legends CD featuring solo performances of Bach, Haydn, and Schumann. Pablo Casals's mid-sixties activities are set out in the two biographies; his remark about living "a thousand years" is in Kirk, p. 524, where Kirk makes mention of Casals leading a performance of the *St. Matthew Passion* at Carnegie Hall in 1963; the performance was scheduled from 5:00 to 11:00 p.m., with a break for dinner in the middle. Daniels in his biography of Stokowski, p. 787, reports that Stoki led a *St. Matthew Passion* the same year, with Beverly Sills as the soprano soloist.

Glenn Gould's review of Stokowski's world premiere, "The Ives Fourth," in *Musical America*, July 1965, is in *The Glenn Gould Reader*. Stokowski's letter to Gould in response is noted in Kirk, p. 802.

12

Gould, in "Stokowski in Six Scenes," also in the *Reader*, explains that "I was working for *High Fidelity* magazine on an essay called 'The Prospects of Recording,' and, as a counterpoint to my text, the margins were to be given over to corroborative or contradictory testimony from a variety of expert musical witnesses. Everyone agreed that Stokowski's comments were a 'must.' " The essay features the scene of his arrival, with Leonard Marcus, at Stokowski's apartment.

Gould delivered "Advice to a Graduation" on November 11, 1964; the CBC broadcast "Dialogues on the Prospects of Recording" on January 10, 1965. He made a record of Beethoven sonatas in April, one of Schoenberg songs in June. All dates are from Kevin Bazzana's timeline on www.glenngould.com.

"Advice to a Graduation" is in the *Reader*. Ostwald, pp. 217–19, asserts, without supplying evidence, that Gould began to work up the "Prospects" script at the cottage on Lake Simcoe after his "retirement" in 1964. John Roberts's efforts are detailed in his essay "Reminiscences," in *Variations*, and filled out in Bazzana's biography. The CBC program can be heard on a website with the name Ubuweb: Sound, at www.akatoo.com; the transcription of Gould's remarks is my own. Gould's recollections of his first interview with Stokowski are in "Stokowski in Six Scenes," in the *Reader*, as are his recollections of their recording session together. Abram Chasins, in *Stokowski: A Profile*, p. 244, quotes a conversation he and Stokowski had about the recording. "I finally said, 'It seems obvious that everyone was doing everything except rehearsing enough to get the soloist, the conductor, and the orchestra into musical alliance.' 'Correct,' he said . . .'"

Dates of Gould's 1966 recordings are given in the appendix to Friedrich's biography. The four-part CBC series *Conversations with Glenn Gould* focused one episode each on Bach, Beethoven, Strauss, and Schoenberg; the timeline on www.glenngould.com gives the broadcast dates: March 15 and 22, April 5 and 19, 1966. *Duo* aired May 18, 1966. All the programs are included in *Glenn Gould on Television*. Gould's essay "Yehudi Menuhin," with its reference to Albert Schweitzer, published in *Musical America*, December 1966, is in the *Reader*, as is "The Prospects of Recording," from *High Fidelity*, April 1966. The image of a structure "not terminal but radial" is from Gould's sleeve notes to the 1955 *Goldberg Variations*, also in the *Reader*. Gould recorded preludes and fugues nos. 1–8 from book 2 of the *Well-Tempered Clavier* at 30th Street Studio on August 1966, according to Friedrich's appendix, making additional recordings in early 1967.

13

The description of Zimmermann's coffeehouse is based on a 1712 engraving reproduced in Wolff's biography, p. 359. The coffeehouse figures into all the biographies; *The New Grove Bach Family* gives the performance schedule and other particulars; Geck argues eloquently for the music made there as "a wonderful example of cultivation of music by the middle class," p. 191, and for the Collegium Musicum as "not the first but certainly the most important institution of its kind in Germany, a forerunner of the Leipzig Gewandhaus concerts, [which are] the epitome of this specifically bourgeois cultural form," p. 198. The comparison of Bach with Orpheus is quoted in Wolff, p. 367.

Wolff, pp. 360ff., gives a table of the music Bach composed for the elector of Saxony. Title pages and dedications are in *The New Bach Reader*. The notice about the resumption of performances at the coffeehouse is in the *Reader*, p. 156. Wolff, pp. 367 ff., gives a detailed account of the developing B-minor Mass, emphasizing that it was completed "by July 1733 at the latest." The description of the nighttime procession to the elector's palace in Leipzig is in the *Reader*, p. 164. The transformation of the processional into the opening of the *Christmas Oratorio* is set out in Boyd's chapter "Parodies and Publications." The insight about Bach's use of the sacred calendar to give his music a sense of permanent occasion is indebted to Jaroslav Pelikan's chapter "The Four Seasons of J. S. Bach" in *Bach Among the Theologians*.

The title page of part three of the *Clavier-Übung* is reproduced in the *Reader*, p. 203. About the debt to Handel in Bach's *Goldberg Variations*, set out as early as the *Obituary*, Wolff, pp. 377–78, is especially emphatic: "The variations are based on a thirty-two-measure theme, exposed in the ostinato bass line of an aria and in its first eight measures identical with the theme of Handel's *Chaconne avec 62 variations*, HWV 442, a work dating from 1703–1706 that was published later in his 1733 *Suites de Pièces pour le clavecin*. The chaconne had already been printed separately around 1732 by Witvogel in Amsterdam, a publisher known to have used Bach as a distributor . . ." Michael Marissen, in correspondence, suggested that the melody is a familiar one in Baroque music and that it is thus unlikely that Bach took it over directly from Handel.

14

Joshua Rifkin recalled the making of *The Baroque Beatles Book* in the notes to a 2009 Nonesuch CD reissue; the notes are on www.richieunterberger.com. Judy Collins's career is outlined in *The Faber Companion to 20th Century Popular Music*. In the *Baroque Beatles Book* reissue notes, Rifkin explains the link between Bach and Collins: "It was doing *The Baroque Beatles* that got me hooked up with Judy. She came around to some of the editing sessions; the whole Elektra gang showed up at one time or another, and she was close to Mark [Abramson, producer of the Beatles record] in those days. Everyone seemed to like what I could do with an orchestra, both writing and directing, and by the time we did the concert in the spring of '66, *In My Life* was already in the works. I was able to take my kind of classical and heavily baroque-influenced sensibility, and turn it loose on Judy's folk and pop material." Collins describes the record and the session in her autobiography, *Sweet Judy Blues Eyes: My Life in Music* (Crown, 2011).

Paul McCartney's night at home watching a BBC broadcast of the English Chamber Orchestra is described in *Good Vibrations*, pp. 148–49; the trumpeter Pete Mason's recollections are given there. The telecast of "All You Need Is Love," recounted by Nicholas Schaffner in *The Beatles Forever*, is included in the 5-DVD set *The Beatles Anthology* (1995). Many people have pointed out that "Blackbird" resembles the bourée in Bach's first lute suite in E minor; the music writer David Hajdu pointed it out to me. The detail about Bach and the Stooges is from

Rip It Up and Start Again, by Simon Reynolds (Penguin, 2006); about Bach and Led Zeppelin from *Electric Eden*, by Rob Young. The sarabande of Bach's first violin partita, in B minor, arranged for handbells and amplified guitar, can be heard in the recording of Pentangle's concert at the Berkeley Community Theatre, May, 29, 1970, on www.wolfgangsvault.com; the Move's "Cherry Blossom Clinic" is on their 1968 LP, *Move*; "Cherry Blossom Clinic Revisited," from their 1970 album, *Shazam*, is played at the beginning of Terre T's Saturday-afternoon radio show on WFMU-FM in New Jersey.

The first recital of P. D. Q. Bach's music at Town Hall was reviewed in *The New York Times* April 26, 1965; the live recording was released by Vanguard as *Peter Schickele Presents An Evening with P.D.Q. Bach* later in the year. Schickele told his predecessor's story in *The Definitive Biography of P.D.Q. Bach* (Random House, 1976).

Robert Moog's history is given, by himself and others, in the notes to the *Switched-on Boxed Set*. The story of the record's history with Columbia is told in *The Label*, pp. 407–408. The text of Glenn Gould's radio commentary on Terry Riley—spoken over Riley's *In C*—is in *The Glenn Gould Reader*, with the notation "From a CBC broadcast, late 1960s." Gould's essay "The Record of the Decade," in *Saturday Night*, December 1968, is in the *Reader*.

15

Il vangelo secondo Matteo was released in 1964, *Chronik der Anna Magdalena Bach* in 1968. The 1969 poster for *Fantasia* is reproduced in *Walt Disney's Fantasia*, p. 5. Virgil Fox's *Heavy Organ* show is described in the notes to the DVD *Virgil Fox: The Bach Gamut* (Circles International, 2004). Dietrich Fischer-Dieskau's history with Bach is given in his autobiography, *Reverberations*. Europe 1968 is evoked in Tony Judt's *Postwar*. The dates of Fischer-Dieskau's recordings of the Bach cantatas are given in the notes to the Arkiv CD, as is the translation followed here. Roland Barthes remarked on Fischer-Dieskau in "The Grain of the Voice," in *Image-Music-Text* (trans. Stephen Heath; Hill and Wang, 1978). The Velvet Underground's "It's Just Too Much" is on *1969 Live*, recorded in Dallas and San Francisco in October and November.

Arvo Pärt's career is recounted in "The Sound of Spirit," by Arthur Lubow, *The New York Times Magazine*, October 15, 2010. A remarkable 2005 performance of *Credo* by Tõnu Kaljuste and the Estonian Philharmonic Chamber Choir is on YouTube.

The photograph of Perlman, Zukerman, and Barenboim appears on the EMI CD reissue. *EMI: The First 100 Years*, p. 298, states of Perlman: "His first recording for EMI in July 1971 was an album of Bach violin concertos with the English Chamber Orchestra conducted by Daniel Barenboim . . ." The description of the music given in the Bach section of the *Rough Guide*— "This recording dates from the late 1960s, when Perlman, Zukerman and Barenboim frequently played together"—led me to see a resemblance to the Beatles. There are brief biographies of Perlman in *EMI: The First 100 Years*; Casals's benediction on Zukerman is described by Baldock, p. 252. The film version of *Fiddler on the Roof*, featuring Isaac Stern's violin, was released in 1971. Yaron Ezrahi explained the role of the violin in post-1948 Israel in conversation; Ezrahi is partnered with Ruth HaCohen, a prominent Bach scholar. Studio One is characterized in *Abbey Road* as the location for orchestra recordings, and notes on the recording at www.arkivmusic.com say it was made there. Barenboim's essay "I Was Reared on Bach," with von Bülow's characterization of the *Well-Tempered Clavier* as the "Old Testament," is in *Music Quickens Time*; his insight about orchestral accompaniment as subversive is in the section of that book called "The Orchestra," made in response to a remark of Edward W. Said's, paraphrased by Barenboim, that "music is a little bit subversive."

Perlman, Zukerman, Barenboim, and the English Chamber Orchestra recorded the Bach concerto for two violins in July 1974, as reported on www.arkivmusic.com. Barenboim's remark about counterpoint is in "The Orchestra," in *Music Quickens Time*.

16

Glenn Gould quoted Leopold Stokowski on war, and recalled their December 1969 interview, in "Stokowski in Six Scenes," in *The Glenn Gould Reader*. The photograph of the two of them bent over a desk is in the photo insert of *A Life and Variations*; others are in *Variations*. Gould's radio activities, which figure into all the biographies, are treated in detail in *Music & Mind* and *Wondrous Strange*. The end of Gould's affair with Foss is detailed in *The Secret Life of Glenn Gould: A Genius in Love*; Leonard Bernstein's remark about Lukas Foss and Bach is on p. 162.

Columbia's commitment to Gould's Bach recordings is set out in *Creative Lying*, by Andrew Kazdin, who describes Gould's Toronto recording operation in invaluable detail. The dates of the sessions for book two of the *Well-Tempered Clavier* and the *Overture in the French Style* are given in Friedrich's appendix, as are the recording and broadcast dates for his renditions of works by Orlando Gibbons. The notes to the CD rerelease of Gould's *Consort of Musicke* are by Michael Stegemann, a late master of booklet and program notes. The story of the destruction of Steinway CD 318 is told in greatest detail in *Romance on Three Legs*. Gould's visit to the Marlboro Music Festival is recounted parenthetically in *Wondrous Strange*, p. 311, and Yo-Yo Ma's in "Yo-Yo Ma," by Helen Epstein, published in *Esquire* (1981) and then in *Music Talks* (Penguin, 1988). Baldock's biography of Casals, p. 255, places Yo-Yo Ma at Marlboro in the summer of 1972. Gould remarked on Casals and the zeitgeist in "Glenn Gould Interviews Glenn Gould about Glenn Gould," in the *Reader*; he characterized Casals's Romantic-cum-Baroque approach in *Conversations with Glenn Gould*—the same passage, pp. 63–64, where he explained what Rosalyn Tureck's playing meant to him. He went on: "Casals has a moment in a documentary I've been working on—it's a line that he always uses, and he used it again with me—in which he talks about the fact that his playing of the Bach Suites for unaccompanied cello was only regarded as revolutionary because, as he put it, the Germans didn't understand him and didn't understand Bach—they didn't understand that Bach was a human being. But I don't agree with him, because—well, I don't know how you feel, but to me the most interesting Bach orchestral performances that I know of have come out of Germany— notably Karl Richter's." *Casals: A Portrait for Radio* can be heard at www.akatoo.com.

17

Casals recalled his premonition of his father's death in *Conversations*, p. 77. His remark that the cello is "my oldest friend" is quoted widely. He made his last Bach recordings in 1966; the background is in Baldock, p. 250. Fischer-Dieskau's recollection of Casals is in *Reverberations*, p. 332. Casals's death and the memorial arrangements are described in the two biographies; Bazzana, p. 312, reports that *Casals: A Portrait for Radio*, unfinished when Casals died, was broadcast on January 15, 1974.

Stokowski's repatriation to England is set out in *A Counterpoint of View*, where Daniels describes his last Columbia contract, p. 909; his late recording of the Toccata and Fugue in D Minor, p. 899; and the performances of the "Air" and the "Little" Fugue, p. 907. A 1974 recording of the Toccata and Fugue in D Minor is in the Special Collections of the University of Pennsylvania, and can be heard through the university library's website. His efforts with a chamber orchestra in Rouen are on YouTube, as is a rehearsal for what was to be his final concert.

His golden-anniversary Grammy Award for the 1927 recording of the Toccata and Fugue in D Minor is described in Chasins, p. 255. His death and memorial arrangements are set out in Daniel, pp. 915–24. Gould's celebration of Stokowski's embrace of the "higher calling" of technology is in "Stokowski in Six Scenes," in the *Reader*.

Virgil Fox's recital at St. Mary's Cathedral in September 1976 is featured on *The Bach Gamut*. The Band's New Year's Eve performance of "Chest Fever," with Garth Hudson's riff in reference to the Toccata and Fugue in D Minor, is on *Rock of Ages*. Joan Acocella, in *Mark Morris* (Farrar, Straus and Giroux, 1994), pp. 35–36, tells of Morris and his friend Page Smith, a cellist, learning to whistle Bach's *Two-Part Inventions* together. It had an effect: Morris's dances set to the music of Bach are spectacularly inventive. Joshua Rifkin's *Scott Joplin: Piano Rags* was released by Nonesuch in 1973. Mikal Gilmore described the Van Halen brothers' musical upbringing, and quoted producer Ted Templeman, in "The Endless Party," *Rolling Stone*, September 3, 1980. The expression "transcription travesties" is Glenn Gould's, used ironically in "Stokowski in Six Scenes."

PART VI: STRANGE LOOPS

01

The *Oxford Composer Companion* entry for the *Goldberg Variations* reports that Bach visited Count Keyserlingk in Dresden in November 1741, probably taking the *Goldbergs* with him for presentation; this entry also characterizes the *Goldbergs* as Bach's most "demanding" work for keyboard. Peter Williams declares that it "is now supposed" the *Goldberg Variations* were printed "just before" the Dresden visit, and goes on to say that "copies were doubtless in Bach's baggage." He describes the work's symmetry, p. 236 (my description tracks his closely), points out that J. G. Goldberg, keyboardist to Kayserlingk, was only twelve or thirteen when Bach composed the variations, and floats the conjecture that the variations were composed for Wilhelm Friedemann, Bach's son and Goldberg's teacher, who was organist at the Frauenkirche in Dresden.

02

The American premiere of the fourteen canons derived from the *Goldbergs* aria was reported in the Musical Events section of *The New Yorker*, by Andrew Porter, June 7, 1976, and reprinted in *Music of Three Seasons* (Farrar, Straus and Giroux, 1978). The teacher was Alan Curtis, a professor of music at the university; the student was Bruce Alan Brown, an undergraduate. The history of the *Handexemplar* is given there, and also in the essay "Fourteen Canons (BWV 1087): Foundation or Culmination? A Re-evaluation of Their Position Among Bach's Late Works," by Elise Crean, available through the Young Scholars' Forum on www.bachnetwork .co.uk. The *Handexemplar* itself is available online as a PDF file. Wolff's essay "The Handexemplar of the Goldberg Variations" is in *Johann Sebastian Bach: Essays on His Life and Music* (Harvard, 1991). Boyd, pp. 213–14, introduces the standard reasoning that the fourteen canons must have been composed before 1746, when the thirteenth of them was depicted in Haussmann's portrait of Bach at the time of his entry into the Mizler Society, and goes on: "It has been suggested that all fourteen canons may have been planned expressly for presentation to the society." The suggestion was made by Nicholas Kenyon in an article about the *Handexemplar* in the *Musical Times* (1976). Wolff, in his essay on the *Handexemplar*, introduces the fact that, according to traditional numeration, the sum of the letters BACH (2+1+3+8) equals 14, the number of canons Bach added to the *Handexemplar* of the *Goldberg Variations*.

The argument for the 1740s as a time when Bach worked the frontiers of sacred music follows on Wolff's argument in his biography, p. 438, that the B-minor Mass "reflects a long-term engagement and . . . a comparable [to the *Art of the Fugue*] systematic musical exploration that Bach defined for himself."

03

Steve Jobs's acid trip involving Bach and a wheat field is recounted in chapter three of *Steve Jobs*, by Walter Isaacson (Simon & Schuster, 2011). The photograph of Jobs in his Los Gatos living room, 1982, was taken by the White House photographer Diana Walker, and can be seen on the Web. About it Jobs said: "This was a very typical time. All you needed was a cup of tea, a light, and your stereo, you know, and that's what I had."

04

Douglas R. Hofstadter tells the story of the conception of *Gödel, Escher, Bach* in the preface to the twentieth-anniversary edition (Basic, 1999). Steven Spielberg's film *Close Encounters of the Third Kind*, set in Muncie, Indiana, not in California, was released in 1977. Harold Bloom's short book *The Anxiety of Influence* was published in 1973; a successor volume, *A Map of Misreading*, was published in 1975. The quoted dialogue is from Hofstadter, p. 279.

Hofstadter's theme, thus loosed in literature, would be developed by a writer situated all but doctorally on the research prairie of Champaign-Urbana, Illinois. This was Richard Powers, dubbed a "systems novelist." Powers would take the four-by-four bass pattern of the *Goldberg Variations*, pair it to the four-stranded pattern of DNA, and produce a fourfold prose work peopled with odd figures from Big Science, one of them an aging prodigy alone in a dark lab ("tipped forward in a tilt-and-swivel chair behind a desk littered with electronic instruments") listening day and night to an LP of the *Goldberg Variations* "ground from a cheap stereo that hid its low tech in the corner." The goal was a novel in which (as a prefatory quatrain put it)

> Two men, two women, their requisite friends,
> acquaintances, strangers and impediments,
> two couples at an arm's length of thirty years bend
> in ascending spiral dance around each other.

Deflating its own pretensions, the novel (published by William Morrow in 1991) would be called *The Gold Bug Variations*—and the looping intelligence of *Gödel, Escher, Bach* would find a base, if not a home base, in precision-engineered fiction.

05

Paul Taylor's dance *Esplanade* was taped in Nashville in 1979 for PBS's *American Masters*; a different performance is included in the documentary *Dancemaker*, by Matthew Diamond (Docurama, 1998). Taylor set the dance *Junction* to Bach cello suites in 1961, and commented on it at several points in his autobiography, *Private Domain* (Knopf, 1987).

06

Thomas Stockham's story is told in *Perfecting Sound Forever* and in his obituary in *The New York Times*, January 31, 2004. Virgil Fox's direct-to-disc recordings of the two toccata pieces can be heard at www.amazon.com, as can Fennel's Soundstream-recorded *Fantasia*. The history of the Sony Walkman was given in *Time*, August 5, 1999.

07

The aftermath of Glenn Gould's affair with Cornelia Foss is told in *The Secret Life of Glenn Gould*. The late history of 30th Street Studio is given at www.kindofbluegallery.com, the website for a New York photography gallery that in 2008 mounted an exhibit of photographs taken at the studio over the years. Gould's decision to rerecord the *Goldberg Variations*—one of the most profound decisions of his life—gets relatively scant attention in the biographies. Friedrich attributes it to Gould's experience of listening to the 1955 recording again, which Gould described to Tim Page in the interview included as disc 3 of *A State of Wonder*. Ostwald, p. 316, asserts that the *Goldberg Variations* "had long been planned as the third installment of Bruno Monsaingeon's *Glenn Gould Plays Bach* series," and quotes Gould, from the film, giving the invention of stereo as the reason to rerecord the *Goldbergs*. Bazzana, p. 451, describes a trip Gould took to New York in June 1980: a visit to 30th Street Studio "reminded him of what a 'terrific hall' it was, with its 'rare mix of clarity and fidelity with qualities of warmth and spaciousness.'" The story of Columbia Records' *The Glenn Gould Silver Jubilee Album* is told by Kazdin, p. 158: the album was Gould's idea.

Gould's "self-interview," "Glenn Gould Interviews Glenn Gould About Glenn Gould" (from *High Fidelity*, February 1974), "Music and Technology" (*Piano Quarterly*, Winter 1974–75), "The Grass Is Always Greener in the Outtakes: An Experiment in Listening" (*High Fidelity*, August 1975), and an adaptation of his script for "'Toronto'" are in *The Glenn Gould Reader*. Ostwald mentions the length of the script, p. 309, and tells the story of his May 1977 visit to Gould's apartment during a meeting of the American Psychiatric Association, pp. 296–98. Gould's review of *Glenn Gould: Music & Mind*, by Geoffrey Payzant (Van Nostrand Reinhold, 1978), published in *Piano Quarterly*, Fall 1978, is in the *Reader*. The English suites were recorded in sessions from 1973 to 1976, as indicated by Friedrich's appendix, and were released in 1977.

Ostwald describes Gould's personal habits and medical preoccupations in detail in his chapter "Approaching Middle Age"; his diary entries about his hand problem, from June 1977 onward, are excerpted and analyzed on pp. 298–302. His definition of "the function of the artist" is in "The Grass Is Always Greener in the Outtakes," in the *Reader*; it runs against Gould's several earlier definitions of the artist's goal as "a state of wonder" or "ecstasy," which have been repeated endlessly and uncritically in Columbia and Sony press materials and then by other writers. Gould's April 1978 diary entry about "that gleaming, lustrous sound" is quoted by Ostwald, p. 307.

08

John Lennon was murdered on December 8, 1980; Bob Marley died on May 11, 1981; Miles Davis played with his back to the audience on the tour for *The Man with the Horn* (1981). Simon Reynolds in *Rip It Up and Start Again* describes Public Image Ltd's "live video" show at the Ritz, May 15, 1981, p. 222. The history of Music Television Networks is told in *I Want My MTV*, by Craig Marks and Rob Tannenbaum (Dutton, 2011). There is a day-by-day chronology of REM's career at www.remtimeline.com, Bruce Springsteen and the E Street Band's at www.songkick.com, and U2's at www.U2tours.com. Michael Hill's notes to the CD reissue of Lou Reed's album *The Blue Mask*, released in February 1982, describe Reed as "a changed man—married again, clean and sober, living part-time in a rural New Jersey retreat"; the cover design is by Sylvia Reed. The entry for Ringo Starr in *The Faber Companion to 20th Century Popular Music* makes mention of Starr's 1981 marriage to Barbara Bach. Sky's electrified version of the Toccata and Fugue in D Minor is on *Sky 2*, released in 1980; there is a striking live video on YouTube. *This Is Spinal Tap* was released in 1984; in an article on www.guardian.co.uk, September 21, 2000, Michael McKean, who played the guitarist David St. Hubbins, recalled that beginning in early 1980 he, Rob Reiner, Christopher Guest, and Harry Shearer "began meeting daily to furnish Spinal Tap with a believeable past."

Gould's choice of piano, detailed in Ostwald and by Katie Hafner in *Romance on Three Legs*, is remarked on by Bazzana, p. 446–48, who quotes Gould: "Think harpsichord—I want a harpsichord." Tim Page's notes to *A State of Wonder* (which features the analog recording from 1981 rather than the digital one) explain that in the digital recording process "as a precaution, most records were recorded simultaneously onto high-output analog tape." Another reason was Gould's long practice of editing his records on eight-track reel tape in Toronto, described by Kazdin in *Creative Lying*, pp. 141ff. Friedrich, the least technologically minded of Gould's biographers, gives a detailed account of the sessions, based on interviews with Monsaingeon and the record's producer, Samuel Carter. Monsaingeon's film of Gould recording the *Goldberg Variations* was produced from a shooting script; Gould made a chart showing the relationships between the "pulses" of the variations, reproduced in Bazzana, p. 454.

The film is available in several DVD editions and can be seen in segments on YouTube. The silent film *The Cabinet of Dr. Caligari* is from 1919.

09

The Sony-Philips press conference at the Plaza Hotel—May 27, 1981—is described by Greg Milner in *Perfecting Sound Forever*, pp. 211–12; the physical properties of the compact disc are explained on pp. 191–94. Karajan's declaration "All else is gaslight" is quoted in *The Ambient Century*, p. 89. Billy Joel's *52nd Street* is described as "the world's first commercial CD release" by Milner, p. 215.

10

Gould recalled the "rather spooky experience" of listening to his 1955 *Goldberg Variations* again in an interview with Tim Page, quoted by Friedrich, pp. 302–303, included as disc 3 of *A State of Wonder*. Friedrich explains that the interview was largely scripted in advance by Gould. Page's recollections are in the notes to *A State of Wonder*. Don Hunstein's photograph of Gould appeared on the 1982 LP release and on later cassette and CD editions. Gould's work on Wagner's "Siegfried Idyll" with an ensemble of Toronto chamber musicians at St. Lawrence Hall, July 27–29, 1982, is recounted in Bazzana, pp. 479–80, and Ostwald, pp. 322–23; Gould dubbed the group the Academy of St. Lawrence in the Market. His other sessions are detailed in Friedrich's appendix. Friedrich, p. 315, indicates that Gould hoped to make a fresh digital recording of the *Two- and Three-Part Inventions* and possibly the Italian Concerto. Gould's diary entry, with notes on the nighttime temperatures across Canada, is in Friedrich, p. 318.

11

The *New York Times* review article about the *Goldberg Variations*, by Edward M. Rothstein, ran on Sunday, September 26, 1982, under the headline GLENN GOULD REVISITS A BACH MASTERWORK.

Gould's stroke and subsequent death are recounted with heavy foreshadowing in the biographies: Friedrich's last chapter is called "The End," Ostwald's last two chapters "The Last Years" and "A Fatal Stroke." Bazzana's ends elegantly, noting that the shock of Gould's death prompted fresh interest in his music: "The extraordinary posthumous life of Glenn Gould had begun."

Thomas Bernhard's *The Loser* (translated by Jack Dawson; Vintage, 1993) was published in German by Suhrkamp in 1983. In an afterword to the Vintage edition, Mark M. Anderson gives the context. For the novel to have been published in 1983, Bernhard must have started writing it soon after Gould's death.

Gould's 1981 *Goldberg Variations* was the first version I heard, on a cassette ordered through the Columbia Record Club. John Adams described having "a revelation while driving along a ridge in the Sierra foothills—not Saul on the road to Damascus, but Dognam on the road to Downieville," in *Hallelujah Junction: Composing an American Life* (Farrar, Straus and Giroux, 2008), pp. 100–102. It was the spring of 1976; he was driving a Karmann Ghia and listening to Wagner's *Götterdämmerung* on "a bulky portable Sony cassette deck, a TC-158, about the size of a small satchel, with a built-in speaker and a carrying strap. With the portable Walkman still years away, I had to laboriously make cassette tapes off my LP collection so that I could take them anywhere I went."

12

Joshua Rifkin's article in *High Fidelity* was a distillation of a longer essay, "Bach's Chorus: A Preliminary Report," in *Musical Times*, vol. 123 (1982), which was itself an expansion of a paper given at a meeting of the American Musicological Society in Boston in 1981, together with a performance of the so-called B-Minor Madrigal. Richard Taruskin in the introduction to *Text and Act* (Oxford, 1995) recalls: "the conductor's face-off with Professor Robert Marshall was mobbed and memorable—but it was an indubitable benchmark." Rifkin's ideas about Bach's chorus are developed further in the notes to *Mass in B Minor* (Nonesuch, 1982) and in *Bach's Choral Ideal* (Klangfarben Musikverlag, 2002). Robert Marshall's "Bach's Choruses Reconstituted" ran in *High Fidelity* in October 1982; his "Bach's Choruses: A Reply to Rifkin" was published in *Musical Times*, vol. 124 (January 1983). There were further exchanges up to 1995 and later; the controversy is summarized in the notes to the chapter "Triple Counterpoint" in *Inside Early Music*, by Bernard D. Sherman (Oxford, 1997). The Bach Ensemble's recording of Cantata BWV 78 is on an Editions de l'Oiseau-Lyre disc with BWV 140 and BWV 51. The aptness of the walking bass line to the lyric "We hasten with faint but eager steps" was pointed out to me by Michael Marissen. Philips's CD reissue series is set out in *Perfecting Sound Forever*, pp. 213–28.

Richard Taruskin gives an account of his 1981 talk "The Musicologist and the Performer" in the introduction to *Text and Act*. He led the choir Cappella Nova. The second essay in the book, developed from a 1984 talk, is called "The Limits of Authenticity: A Contribution." His position is set out in "On Letting the Music Speak for Itself," derived from his 1981 talk, and in the introduction, which is called "Last Thoughts First: Wherein the Author Gently Replies to a Few of His Critics and Takes Tender Leave of the Topic." Nikolaus Harnoncourt's complete cantata set was issued by Teldec, Helmuth Rilling's by Hänssler. Taruskin's essay "The Pastness of the Present and the Presence of the Past," developed from a 1988 paper, is in *Text and Act*. The 1976 recording of the Brandenburg concertos by a nameless ensemble led by "Gustav Leonhardt, Harpsichordist and Conductor," is on two separate CDs in Sony's Essential Classics series. Leonhardt's remark about "'synchronized' listening" is extracted from an essay in the CD booklet.

13

The Bach-Museum in Leipzig has illuminating (and illuminated) presentations on the transformation of Bach scholarship by technology, the personal computer and laser technology in particular. Wolff and Schultz's identification of previously unidentified works of Bach in the Neumeister Collection at Yale is set out in the *Oxford Composer Companion* (which reports that it was announced in December 1984 by Wolff and Harold E. Samuel—a Yale librarian), and in the notes to EMI's 2-CD set *The Arnstadt Chorale Preludes*, played by Werner Jacob, which includes an explanation from Wolff. I have also drawn on a 2002 doctoral dissertation by Sara Ann Jones, "The 'Neumeister Collection of Chorale Preludes of the Bach Circle': An Examination of the Chorale Preludes of J. S. Bach and Their Usage as Service Music and Pedagogical Works." The argument of Peter Williams's 1981 article "BWV 565: A Toccata in D Minor for Organ by J. S. Bach?" is taken up by Geck, p. 56, and by Wolff at several points—notably pp. 72 and 169—which add up to a vigorous if indirect argument in favor of maintaining the presumption of the work's authenticity. The argument on pp. 169–70 is characteristic: Wolff cites the pieces as a possible example of the free compositional style that led Forkel to characterize young Bach as a "finger composer," and goes on: "Perhaps the most prominent surviving example of this course, which Bach 'did not follow long,' is the organ Toccata in D minor, BWV 565, as refreshing, imaginative, varied, and ebullient as it is structurally undisciplined and unmastered; and we can understand only too well why the self-critical Bach did not use this *coup de main* later on for teaching purposes (which also explains its oddly peripheral transmission)."

14

This portrait of Yo-Yo Ma draws on "Yo-Yo Ma," by Helen Epstein, a profile published in *Esquire* in 1981 and in *Music Talks: Conversations with Musicians* (Penguin, 1988); "A Process Larger Than Oneself," by David Blum, a profile of Ma published in *The New Yorker*, May 1, 1989; *My Son, Yo-Yo*, by Marina Ma, as told to John A. Rallo (Chinese University Press, 1995); two *New York Times* pieces by Ma's fellow Harvard undergraduate (and *Recording Angel* author) Evan Eisenberg, "Through College and Life, in Harmony" (July 15, 2001) and "For Yo-Yo Ma, All the World's a Band" (April 28, 2002); and "Yo-Yo Ma's Journeys," by Janet Tassel, a profile in *Harvard Magazine* (May 2003), among other books and articles. Blum describes the operation and its aftermath, with doctors arranging for an upper-body cast cut away so that Ma could practice; he quotes Ma joking that the cast gave him "broad shoulders, a fabulous physique" and that "I didn't play concerts. That's not quite true: I did play one concert, of Bach suites." Epstein reports that he played 125 concerts in 1981. Ma's discography is on www.yo-yoma .com. The notes for the 2009 CD reissue of Ma's cello suites give the dates of the recordings at Vanguard Studios—February 23, April 19–20, and May 11–12, 1982, and indicate that Soundstream was used and that Don Hunstein took the sleeve photograph. A brief history of Vanguard Studios is in the Wikipedia entry for Vanguard Records. At the time of the *Esquire* profile, Ma was playing a Gottfriller cello made in 1722; the Hunstein photograph shows his cello's aging.

Various biographies and profiles suggest that Yo-Yo Ma and his older sister, Yeou-Cheng, appeared on *The Tonight Show* in the late fall of 1963. Blum mentions the LP of Schubert trios featuring Pablo Casals as a Ma favorite. Ma described his father's teaching method in the *Esquire* profile, his experience with Leonard Rose in the *New Yorker* profile. The photographs of him in a white shirt and then in a khaki one are in *My Son, Yo-Yo*, pp. 94 and 98. For the *New Yorker* profile Ma told Blum about the encounter with Casals: "I don't remember what he said about my cello playing, but he did suggest that I should be given more time to go out and play in the street."

15

Leonard Bernstein graduated from Harvard in 1939. Evan Eisenberg tells of a string trio made up of Ma, Kogan, and Chang. The *Harvard Magazine* profile sets out his course of study, gives Kogan's recollections, tells the story of Professor Devore's shout-out to Ma in class the morning after a recital, and reports Kirchner's comment about Ma's tone. Sarah Crichton recalled the Ma-Rostropovich common-room recital in conversation at the offices of Farrar, Straus and Giroux, where she is the publisher of Sarah Crichton Books. His parents' initial unease with a mixed marriage is described in the *New Yorker* profile, Ma's delight that Jill Hornor wanted to know what he thought in the *Harvard* profile. The revamping of Masterworks is summarized in *The Label*, p. 323; the comparison of Ma and Marsalis, and their approach to crossing over, is my own.

Ma's remarks about Bach's cello suites are in the *New Yorker* profile. The comparisons of Yo-Yo Ma to Pablo Casals, Glenn Gould, and Albert Schweitzer are my own.

16

The *Oxford Composer Companion* entry for the *Well-Tempered Clavier* indicates that "Bach finished compiling Part 2 about 1742," that "a revised version was finished by 1744," and that he "continued to make minor improvements to the work after 1744." The history of the *Handexemplar* is told in the text and notes to part V, "Both Sides Now." Recent scholarship — drawn on by Boyd, Wolff, and Williams—indicates that Bach turned to the *Art of the Fugue* around the time he completed the *Goldberg Variations* and book two of the *Well-Tempered Clavier*. Here is Williams, p. 249: "A positive, musical inspiration for this scheme must also have been the current and recent work on WTC2, whose huge variety of style, theme-type and of course key could alone have led to the idea of a different kind of variety, i.e. one with a single master-theme and a single key, both to be explored to hugely different ends." Boyd, pp. 220–27, is especially strong on the nature of the different *contrapuncti*.

Bach recalled the "Prussian invasion" in a letter of October 6, 1948, in *The New Bach Reader*, p. 234, and quoted by Wolff, p. 426. He inspected an organ in Naumburg with Gottfried Silbermann, September 27, 1746; their report is in the *Reader*, pp. 221–22. The invitation from the Society of Musical Science is treated in all the biographies; Williams's account, based on one in the Obituary, is given out of chronology in a section called "'Theoretical Speculations,'" pp. 328ff. An entry in the *Oxford Composer Companion* treats the *Variations on "Von Himmel Hoch"* in detail. The Haussmann portrait of Bach—in Haussmann's own 1748 copy, now in a private collection in Princeton, New Jersey—is the frontispiece to Wolff's biography; a detail is on the dust jacket of his biography and Boyd's biography. Wolff, opening a chapter on Bach's domestic and professional life, p. 391, introduces the point that Haussmann painted typological portraits of the Leipzig town councillors, and observes that Bach, portrayed holding a piece of music, rather than at a keyboard, is thus portrayed as a composer rather than as a cantor and music director.

17

The *Oxford Composer Companion* entry for the *Musical Offering*, by Michael Marissen, calls Bach's visit to Potsdam "the most fully documented event in his otherwise unglamorous career"; the visit is a set piece in all the biographies, and also the subject of *Evening in the Palace of Reason*, by James R. Gaines (Fourth Estate, 2005). Their story is told here through six excerpts from the documents. The newspaper story, from the *Spenersche Zeitung*, Berlin, May 11, 1747, is in *The New Bach Reader*. The account based on Wilhelm Friedemann Bach's and Carl Philipp Emanuel Bach's recollections is in Forkel's biography, pp. 15–17. The fortepiano is explained by Boyd, p. 202, and more fully by Wolff, p. 413, who quotes Bach's contemporary Johann Friedrich Agricola on Bach's evaluation of Silbermann's fortepiano: at first he found it "too weak in the high register and too hard to play"; Silbermann bristled at the criticism, but took it to heart, and after many years produced a fortepiano that met with Bach's "complete approval." The account of Bach's execution of a fugue with six obbligato parts is Forkel's; the account of his recital at the church of the Holy Spirit in Potsdam is from the *Spenersche Zeitung*, as is the account of his second six-part fugue. The account of his visit to the new Berlin opera house is from a letter from Carl Philipp Emanuel to Forkel, quoted by Wolff, p. 428. Bach's determination to write out the fugue, have it engraved, and send it for presentation to the king is from Forkel's biography; the detail about the copper engraving is from the *Spenersche Zeitung*.

18

Milan Kundera likened state communism to a Bach fugue in *The Book of Laughter and Forgetting* (1978; trans. Michael Henry Heim; Penguin, 1981), pp. 8–9; a little later in the novel, a female character tries to striptease to a Bach suite. The Monday meetings at the Nikolaikirche in Leipzig are set out in the brochure given out at the church and in the Wikipedia entry for the church; the opening generally is recounted in Tony Judt's *Postwar*, pp. 610–16.

Rostropovich's performance at the Berlin Wall can be seen on YouTube; Stuart Proffitt, publisher of the Penguin Press in London, recalled it for me as "a lament for all those whose lives had been ruined by the Wall, and those who had actually died trying to cross it. There was a reprise ten years later, with Timothy Garton Ash and, as a surprise guest, Rostropovich; never have I seen so many stolid German men in grey suits so visibly moved."

In 1991, Rostropovich recorded all six suites for EMI, which made a commemorative video (excerpted in the notes) in which he recalled meeting Pablo Casals in Paris apropos of the Casals Competition for cellists, and hearing him play Bach: "It was a rhapsodic interpretation of Bach, I'd say, like a dialogue, keenly aware phrase-by-phrase of the listener's reaction."

Isaac Stern's efforts to save Carnegie Hall from demolition are described in *The Vintage Guide to Classical Music* (Vintage, 1992) which shows him and the others singing "Hallelujah"; on www.carnegiehall.org; and in his autobiography, *Isaac Stern: My First 79 Years* (Knopf, 1999), a chronicle of his career. The story of his playing an unaccompanied Bach suite early in the first Gulf War is on pp. 284ff.

Daniel Barenboim tells his own story, sideways, in *Music Quickens Time*; other details are given in Ara Guzelimian's preface to *Parallels and Paradoxes: Explorations in Music and Society* (Vintage, 2004), which sets out particulars of Edward Said's life, too. Said's book *Musical Elaborations*, comprising lectures Said gave at the University of California, Irvine, in 1989, was published by Columbia in 1991. Said and Barenboim's conversation about Wagner took place on October 7, 1995. It and their subsequent conversations at Carnegie Hall are reproduced in *Parallels and Paradoxes*.

19

Steven Spielberg's film *Schindler's List* was released in 1993, and the United States Holocaust Memorial Museum opened the same year. The prospect of a Vatican apology for the Holocaust was set out in my article "John Paul's Jewish Dilemma," *The New York Times Magazine*, April 26, 1998. The opening to a discussion of the Holocaust in Germany is explored in *The Wages of Guilt*, by Ian Buruma (Farrar, Straus and Giroux, 1994). The new, technical biblical scholarship was synopsized artfully in "Who Do Men Say That I Am," by Cullen Murphy, *The Atlantic*, December 1986.

Michael Marissen's *Lutheranism, Anti-Judaism, and Bach's "St. John Passion"* (Oxford, 1998) includes an annotated literal translation of the libretto.

20

Masaaki Suzuki's text "On Starting the Complete Recordings of J. S. Bach's Cantatas"—with the colophon "The 50th Anniversary of VJ-Day (15th August 1995)" is in the booklet to volume 1 of the series (BIS CD, 1995–98), which opens with BWV 4, "Christ lag in Todesbanden." Sony's purchase of Columbia Records is described in *The Label*, pp. 535–36.

21

The church in London where I heard "music of Bach and Handel, with carols following" was probably St. Anne and St. Agnes, Gresham Street. The *St. Matthew Passion* that took me to North Carolina is a 3-CD set on Vanguard Classics, recorded July 28–August 8, 1977: the English Chamber Orchestra and the Ambrosian Singers, conducted by Johannes Somary, with Ernst Haefliger as the Evangelist and Barry McDaniel as Jesus.

22

The history of Skywalker Ranch and Lucasfilm is told in *Easy Riders, Raging Bulls*, by Peter Biskind (Simon & Schuster, 1998), pp. 380–81.

Lorraine Hunt's story is told in John Adams's *Hallelujah Junction*; in the *New York Times* obituary, "Lorraine Hunt Lieberson, Luminous Mezzo, Dies at 52," by Anthony Tommasini, July 5, 2006; and in Alex's Ross's memorial piece, "Fervor," in *The New Yorker*, September 25, 2006. Nicholas McGegan explained his approach to recording in an interview in *Inside Early Music*. *Clavierbüchlein für Anna Magdalena Bach (a selection)* was recorded at Skywalker Sound, September and November 1990, and released by Harmonia Mundi USA in 1991; the cellist was David Bowles, playing a Baroque cello made by Barak Norman in 1708.

Yo-Yo Ma performed at the Reagan White House on October 6, 1987; did a guest spot on *The Muppet Show* during the show's initial five-year run, 1976–81; and was awarded an honorary doctor of music at Harvard in 1991. *Hush* was released in 1992; the story of Ma's April Fools' Day 1998 statement of his plan to quit the cello was recounted in the *Harvard Crimson*, June 5, 2001. *Inspired by Bach* aired on PBS in 1997. Kirchner's and Wolff's criticisms of it are in the *Harvard Magazine* profile, as are Ma's insights about the Silk Road as "the Internet of antiquity" and the cello as "a remarkable mix of art and technology." The *Silk Road Project* was released by Sony in 1998; an accompanying set of music from along the Silk Road (*The Silk Road: A Musical Caravan*) was released by Smithsonian Folkways in 2002. *Simply Baroque* was released in 1999. The Christmas episode of *The West Wing*, "Noël," aired December 20, 2000. *Master and Commander* was released in 2003; a Yo-Yo Ma character figured into *The Simpsons*, February 20, 2000. Ma joined Daniel Barenboim and Edward Said at Buchenwald in Weimar in August 1999, as Said recounted in a conversation of March 8, 2000, in *Parallels and*

Paradoxes. The story of Ma's lost Stradivarius was reported in "In Concert, Searchers Retrieve Yo-Yo Ma's Lost Stradivarius," by Katherine Finkelstein, *The New York Times*, October 17, 1999. Ma played all six Bach cello suites at Ozawa Hall over two nights in August 1998.

23

Wolff, p. 442, remarks that "as far as we know, Bach suffered no serious illness at any point of his life, with the striking exception of the final year." Analysis of Bach's handwriting suggests that his eyesight deteriorated early in 1749. The low dealings of the Leipzig town councillors are considered in all the biographies. The performance of the *St. John Passion*, April 4, 1749, is listed in the table of Chronologies in the *Oxford Composer Companion* and elsewhere. The performances of BWV 29, "Wir danken dir, Gott, wir danken dir" (for the town councillors) and BWV 201, "Geschwinde, geschwinde, ihr wirbelnden Winde (The Contest between Phoebus and Pan)" are set out by Wolff, pp. 444–46. Wolff especially stresses the attention Bach gave to completing the Mass in B Minor, pp. 438–42, declaring that "we know of no occasion for which Bach could have written the *B-minor Mass*, nor any patron who might have commissioned it, nor any performance of the complete work before 1750," and goes on to propose it as "the vocal counterpart to *The Art of Fugue*" as a "mighty setting [that] preserved the musical and artistic creed of its creator for posterity." Boyd, pp. 189–90, allows that it may have been written for a particular occasion, and remarks that "one of the more convincing arguments . . . is that put forward by the German scholar Wolfgang Osthoff, who suggested that it may have been intended for the consecration of a new Dresden Hofkirche in 1751." Boyd goes on to call it "just as likely" that Bach wrote it "not with any idea of performance in mind, but as a kind of monument or summation of his life's work." There is another possibility: that Bach wrote it without performance in mind, but as a work sufficient and expressive in its own right, and not as a summary or compendium of techniques developed elsewhere; that is, Bach may have drawn on the full range of his techniques in order to develop the material at hand—the full Mass—rather than as a development of the material of his career.

Wolff, p. 447, matter-of-factly declares that "Apart from inserted canonic sections of the Agnus Dei, the 'Et incarnatus est' movement of the *B-minor Mass* is the last newly composed vocal setting by Bach," that the last new instrumental setting is the "the unfinished quadruple fugue from *The Art of Fugue*," and that both "were written no later than the first weeks of 1750." The oculist John Taylor performed cataract surgery on Bach twice in 1750; Williams, p. 264, deftly sorts fact from hearsay in the accounts of the operations and their consequences. The biographies, which lay great stress on Bach's blindness, leave unstated the fact that Bach's abilities as a keyboardist did not depend on eyesight, so I have emphasized that fact; it is worth pondering whether and how Bach's progressive loss of sight led him to play the organ or clavier differently than formerly—because of the encroaching darkness, or because of the diminishing prospects that the music he played would eventually be written down.

24

The ad for John Eliot Gardiner's Bach Cantata Pilgrimage ran as the back page to a section of *The New York Times* in fall 2000; I folded and saved it. Gardiner's story, and the story of the Pilgrimage, are told on the BBC DVD *Bach Cantatas*, recorded during the journey, as well as in the liner notes for individual DVDs, which give months and sites of the recordings; in "Distant Musical Pilgrimages, Recorded on the Run," by James R. Oestreich, *The New York Times*, May 8, 2005, and in "The Book of Bach," by Alex Ross, *The New Yorker*, April 11, 2011.

25

Peter Sellars's staging of Bach cantatas 199 and 182, featuring Lorraine Hunt, was produced at Lincoln Center early in 2001, and at other venues thereafter. Alex Ross described a March performance at John Jay College in "Concert Rage," *The New Yorker*, March 28, 2001; an audience member rose and began yelling at the stage partway through "Ich habe genug." Remarkably, there seems to be no full-length professional video of these signal works by the most video-cognizant of directors.

26

The particulars of John Taylor's eye operations are set out in Wolff, p. 448; Williams, p. 264, introduces the possibility that postoperative infection was the cause of Bach's death, and also conjectures that the eye ailments were brought on by untreated diabetes, and that this was the eventual cause of death. Rifkin in the notes to his *Mass in B Minor* recording remarks that the Et incarnatus est was "cleanly written on a leaf inserted into the autograph," and goes on to suggest that Bach borrowed the piece from another composer. Williams reports his last revisions to sonatas and his instrumental setting for a motet by J. C. Bach, p. 265, and, p. 268, gives the details of his funeral and burial in the Johanneskirche churchyard, "out through the Grimma Gate," among them the fact that "no less than seven of his children had already been buried there . . ." The disposition of Bach's music and effects is set out by Boyd, pp. 208–209.

27

A distillation of "Bach: Solace and Celebration" can be heard on www.whyc.org. My article about the death of John Paul II and the election of Benedict XVI, "The Year of Two Popes," was published in *The Atlantic*, January 2006.

28

Leon Fleisher tells his story in the notes for *Two Hands* and in *My Nine Lives*, with Anne Midgette (Anchor, 2011).

POSTLUDE: LATE ADOPTERS

1

Bach's dunning letter to Johann Georg Martius is in *The New Bach Reader*, pp. 233–34; Wolff, p. 411, characterizes the arrangement as a rental, not a loan.

Glenn Gould referred to Bach's "magnificent indifference to specific sonority" in *Art of the Fugue*, in *The Glenn Gould Reader*.

Bach by Design: Computer Composed Music, by David Cope, was issued as a Centaur CD; Cope's software program is called Experiments in Musical Intelligence, or EMI. Alexander Chen's visualization of the prelude of the first cello suites, described later in the Postlude, can be viewed at www.baroque.me and elsewhere.

Arthur C. Danto's argument about the end of art, developed throughout his body of work, is set out especially cogently in *Encounters and Reflections: Art in the Historical Present* (Farrar, Straus and Giroux, 1990).

2

The history of Andante.com is told in an article—an obituary of sorts—by its former managing editor, Ben Mattison, in *Playbill*, February 1, 2006. The Albert Schweitzer Fellowship sends medical students to Gabon; an Albert Schweitzer Foundation for Our Contemporaries works against cruelty to animals. Megan Hustad described the plaque on Pablo Casals's house in San Juan to me. *Fantasia 2000* (1999) featured sound track music performed by James Levine and the Chicago Symphony Orchestra; Peter Schickele took part in the orchestral transcriptions.

3

The *St. Matthew Passion* by the Gabrieli Players, led by Paul McCreesh, was recorded at Roskilde Cathedral, Denmark, in April 2002, and released on CD by Archiv Produktion in 2003. Jonathan Miller's *St. Matthew Passion* was presented at the Brooklyn Academy of Music in 1997, 2001, and 2009; excerpts from a performance in the Netherlands can be seen on YouTube.

4

Yo-Yo Ma's commercial for the Apple's "Switch" ad campaign of 2002–2003 can be seen on YouTube. His relationship to technology was set out in "Extending Technology's Reach," by Seth Schiesel, *The New York Times*, September 30, 2004. His friendship with Steve Jobs is set out by Walter Isaacson in *Steve Jobs*. Whitney Pastorek recalled Dark Castle, and her passion for it, in the essay "I Am Telling You This Because I Trust You Not to Use It Against Me," published in *Gamers*, ed. Shanna Compton (Soft Skull, 2004).

The decline of EMI was chronicled in *The New York Times* in many articles, particularly "EMI"s New Boss Sees Cracks in Music World," by Tim Arango, June 1, 2008. The proposed sale of Abbey Road was reported on www.guardian.co.uk, February 17, 2010. The success of Piere-Laurent Aimard's *Art of the Fugue* was reported to me by Richard Locke of Columbia University. Edward W. Guo's digital sheet music enterprise was reported in *The New York Times*, February 22, 2011. "The Well-Tempered Web," by Alex Ross, ran in *The New Yorker*, October 22, 2007. The text of Yo-Yo Ma's "Artist's Choice" CD was kindly provided to me by Shaunna Harrington and Greg Papastoitsis, friends in Watertown, Massachusetts.

5

Edward W. Said, in *On Late Style* (Pantheon, 2006), pp. 116–17, declared: "It is worth our while, I think, to explore Gould's connection with Bach, and to try to understand how his lifelong association with the great contrapuntal genius establishes a unique and interestingly plastic aesthetic space essentially created by Gould himself as an intellectual and a virtuoso." The Lincoln Center film festival Glenn Gould Unveiled, curated by Evan Eisenberg, took place in fall 2006. *Glenn Gould on Television* was released on ten DVDs in 2011.

Lorraine Hunt was memorialized in "Lorraint Hunt Lieberson, Luminous Mezzo, Dies at 52," by Anthony Tommasini, *The New York Times*, July 5, 2006, and in "Fervor," by Alex Ross, *The New Yorker*, September 25, 2006. The *Times* ran an obituary for Craig Smith on November 19, 2007; Smith's life and work were then celebrated in an Internet radio program by his friend Christopher Lydon. *Lorraine at Emmanuel*, a CD featuring Hunt singing Bach and Handel with the church ensemble, was released by Avie in 2008.

6

The private pressing of Simone Dinnerstein's *Goldberg Variations* CD was given to me by Martha Bonta, then with IMG Artists, now with WQXR, along with a profile of the then little-known pianist in *The Philadelphia Inquirer,* April 6, 2005. The recording was released commercially by Telarc in 2007. Telarc released Dinnerstein's *The Berlin Concert* in 2008, Sony her *Bach: A Strange Beauty* in 2011. Dinnerstein did guest-DJ sets during the WKCR Bachfest in 2010 and 2011.

Lara St. John's *Bach: Works for Solo Violin* was issued by Well-Tempered Productions in 1996, *Hilary Hahn Plays Bach* by Sony in 1997.

7

"Pearls Before Breakfast," by Gene Weingarten, ran in *The Washington Post,* April 8, 2007. The Paul Winter Consort performed "Bach2Brasil" June 18–19, 2004. Matt Haimovitz's CBGB gig was reviewed in *The Wall Street Journal,* October 16, 2002. The *Nightline* segment about Haimovitz can be seen on YouTube. Savion Glover's "Classical Savion" was described in separate pieces by Deborah Jowitt and Elizabeth Zimmer in *The Village Voice,* January 12–18, 2005. His interpretation of the "Air on the G String" can been on YouTube.

Tiempo Libre's *Bach in Havana* and Paulinho Nogueira's *Bachianinha* are available in the iTunes Store. *Bach / Coltrane* (Zig Zag CD, 2008) is a production of the Raphael Imbert Project, led by a French reed player. *Koto Sebastian Bach 2000,* by Mieko Miyazai with Edison and Company, was issued on CD by 32 Records in 2006; Alan Williams, longtime publisher of the Viking Press, first urged me to look into Koto renditions of Bach. The New Saxophone Quartet's interpretation of the *Art of Fugue* (Channel Classics, 2004) was given to me by the quartet's baritone saxophonist, Brad Hubbard; the CD notes describe the background.

8

A bare-bones report about the memorial for Steve Jobs, and Yo-Yo Ma's role in it, ran on www .wsj.com, October 17, 2011. Ma's visit to Jobs's house is recounted in Isaacson's *Steve Jobs,* as are Jobs's demonstration of Bach on the iPad and his remark about Ma's playing as akin to a proof of the existence of God. That Ma played the sarabande at his father's deathbed—his father's last request—is reported in the *Harvard Magazine* profile of Ma.

9

NTT Docomo's commercial for the Touch-Wood phone can be seen on YouTube, as can Ornette Coleman's quartet performance of the prelude from Bach's first cello suite; "Swinging Bach," by Eugene Cicero, videotaped in concert in Köln in 1997; and Bobby McFerrin's "Air on the 'G' String" at the 24 Hour Bach festival, held in Leipzig in 2000. There are many Tony Yike Yang videos on YouTube. The player-piano rendition of the Toccata and Fugue in D Minor is on an antique instrument adapted for MIDI by Ragtime West, which posted a video on YouTube. Vanessa-Mae's video, also seen on YouTube, was released by Angel/EMI in 1994, when she was fifteen. *The Sunday Times* of London identified her as the wealthiest young musician in the UK in 2006, as reported on Wikipedia.

DJ From Mars's "Run This Town and Fugue in D Minor" is on YouTube; their website is www.djsfrommars.com. Stephen Malinowski's visuals can be seen on www.musanim.com, which also incorporates a bio, press, and an elaborate timeline illustrating his progressive adoption of new technology. Alexander Chen's visual of the prelude to the first cello suite is at www .baroque.me.

10

"Time: 1976" is in C. K. Williams's *The Vigil* (Farrar, Straus and Giroux, 1997). The *Oxford Composer Companion* includes a detailed entry on the *Musical Offering*.

11

"Refracted Bach," a festival organized by the Dessoff Choirs, took place in winter 2012; the pianists Stephen Ryan and Catherine Venable played Robin Holloway's "Gilded Goldbergs" at Weill Recital Hall at 7:30 on February 7. Max Reger's *Variations and Fugue on a Theme of J. S. Bach*, played on piano by Rudolf Serkin, is on a Sony Classical CD; Kurtag's *Games* is on an ECM CD. Lara Downes's *13 Ways of Looking at the Goldbergs* was released by Tritone Music. "Flight of the Concord," by the pianist Jeremy Denk, about his effort to record Ives's "Concord" Sonata, appeared in *The New Yorker*, February 6, 2012.

12

The *Clavier-büchlein vor Wilhelm Friedemann Bach* is in the Herric Music Library at Yale; the story of its acquisition is told on the portal for Friends of Music at Yale on www.yale.edu. Bach's Calov Bible is in the library of Corcordia Seminary in St. Louis; the story of its acquisition is told on the library's website, www.library.csl.edu.

13

Alex Ross envisioned the baptism of Bach in "The Book of Bach," in *The New Yorker*, April 11, 2011. Flannery O'Connor explained how she sought to render a baptism in fiction in "Novelist and Believer," in *Mystery and Manners* (Farrar, Straus and Giroux, 1969). Richard Taruskin explained "subtactile pulse" in "A Sturdy Musical Bridge to the 21st Century," in *The New York Times*, August 24, 1997.

14

Lincoln Center's *White Light* festival is described at www.whitelightfestival.org. A video of Matt Haimovitz's performance of part of Bach's first cello suite at Zuccotti Park is on YouTube. Zachary Woolfe reviewed "Thru-Line," the Knights' rendering of the first cello suite along the MTA's R line, in *The New York Times*, December 22, 2011. *Songs of Joy and Peace* was released in fall 2011 in an edition with an accompanying DVD, produced by David Lai.

Keith Jarrett's Bachfest remark about Bach's keyboard works—"This music doesn't need my help"—shows up also in "Is Jazz Dead?" by Geoff Dyer, in *Otherwise Known as the Human Condition: Selected Essays and Reviews* (Graywolf, 2011). Lawrence Joseph's reading at St. Paul's Chapel was part of Trinity Church's Bach at One series, which was scaled back severely shortly afterward, then reinstated. Joseph's poems, among them "Now Evening Comes East from the Sea," are in *Codes, Precepts, Biases, and Taboos: Poems 1973–1993* (Farrar, Straus and Giroux, 2005). Philip Larkin's "Water" is in *The Complete Poems* (Farrar, Straus and Giroux, 2012).

Acknowledgments

A book is a work of many hands; a nonfiction book can be a symphony of a thousand. To all who lent a hand (or two) with this one, my deepest thanks:

At Farrar, Straus and Giroux: Jonathan Galassi; Eric Chinski, Andrew Mandel, and Sarah Crichton; Debra Helfand, Chris Peterson, John McGhee, Tricia Wygal, and Christopher Caines; Miranda Popkey, Karen Maine, Jesse Coleman, Kevin Doughten, Cara Spitalewitz, and Georgia Cool; Jeff Seroy, Katie Freeman, Sarita Varma, and Laurel Cook; Devon Mazzone, Marion Duvert, and Amanda Schoonmaker; Spenser Lee, Adam Hocker, Ryan Chapman, and Nicholas Courage; Rodrigo Corral, Jonathan Lippincott, and Peter Richardson.

At Georgetown: Thomas Banchoff, John J. DeGioia, Howard Gray, Erik Smulson, Jose Casanova, Katherine Marshall, and Melody Fox Ahmed; at Columbia, Richard Locke and Phillip Lopate; at Fordham, James VanOosting; at Yale, Suzanne Lovejoy, Emily Ferrigno, and Miroslav Volk.

Lydia Wills, John McPhee, Pankaj Mishra, Mitchell Duneier, Thomas Cahill, Mario Marazziti, Timothy Shriver, and Lawrence Joseph.

Michael Marissen and Lauren Belfer; Joe Richman and Sue Jaye Johnson; Martha Bonta and Mark Rotella; Philip and Carol Zaleski; Yaron Ezrahi and Ruth HaCohen.

Bettina Schrewe, Stuart Proffitt, Isobel Dixon, and Lisa Baker; Alexandria Giardino, Robin Creswell, Blake Eskin, Megan Hustad, and Jay Weissman; Ben Ratliff, David Friend, David Hajdu, and Evan Eisenberg; Abigail Rasminsky, Sarah Ramey, and Joseph Shapiro.

Scott Stossel at *The Atlantic*, Scott Adkins at Room 58, and Charles Hutchinson at Academy Records.

Elaine Jordan and the late David Jordan; Michael and Donna Todaro; Leonardo, Pietro, and Milo Elie, who grew along with the book; and especially Lenora Todaro, who let the music of Bach fill our lives for a thousand and one nights.

Index

F

G